Retain 2006

CONTRIBUTIONS OF
BLACK WOMEN TO AMERICA

Volume I

THE ARTS
MEDIA
BUSINESS
LAW
SPORTS

Edited By

Marianna W. Davis

1982

Kenday Press, Inc.

Published 1982 by Kenday Press, Inc.

Post Office Box 3097
Columbia, South Carolina 29230

Copyright, 1981 by Marianna W. Davis, Editor

Library of Congress Cataloging-in Publication Data
Main entry under title:

Contributions of black women to America.

    Includes bibliographies and indexes.
    Contents: v. 1. The arts, media, business, law, sports — v. 2. [without special title]
    1. Afro-American women. 2. Afro-American women—
Biography. I. Davis, Marianna W.
E185.86.C585   973'.0496073   82-80761
                                                          AACR2
Library of Congress catalogue number: 82-80761

* * * * *

This volume was prepared pursuant to Grant No. G007801169. The activity which is the subject of this presentation was supported in whole or in part by the U. S. Department of Education under the Women's Educational Equity Act Program. However, the opinions expressed herein do not necessarily reflect the position or policy of the U. S. Department of Education, and no official endorsement by the U. S. Department of Education should be inferred.

This volume is dedicated to my —

Mother - Mrs. Laura Bowman White Frederick
Maternal Grandmother - Mrs. Mariah Lyons Bowman
Maternal Great Grandmother - Mrs. Sallie Sweetenberg Bowman
Maternal Great Great Grandmother - Mrs. Nancy Shell Bowman
Paternal Grandmother - Mrs. Annie M. White

* * * * *

CONTRIBUTIONS OF BLACK WOMEN TO AMERICA: A NATIONAL RESEARCH PROJECT

ADVISORY BOARD

The research, writing, and editing for this volume were supported and financed in part by The Women's Educational Equity Act Program of the U. S. Department of Education and by The Ford Foundation.

CONTRIBUTIONS OF BLACK WOMEN TO AMERICA
VOLUME ONE

Contents

Each Part contains a table of contents, an introductory essay, notes following each chapter, a bibliography, and an index.

PREFACE

All achieving, notable Black women in Arts, Media, Business and Commerce, Law, and Sports, representing 200 years of American history, could not be written about in this one volume. Two years of research and writing simply is not sufficient time to cover adequately the contributions made by American Black women to the making of America. Without a doubt, Black women were and still are the "builders" in these United States of America. They stand as survivors at the socio-political, educational, cultural, economic, and religious crossroads of the American scene. They yet suffer the pangs of racism and sexism.

But, if I had decided to spend ten or twenty years on the research and writing of the contributions of Black women, thousands of Black girls and young women would be denied access to the kind of motivational material this book represents. The statistics clearly show that Black girls who make career choices do so in traditional fields. Many simply fail to look across the horizon to rewarding careers in other fields. This book is written mainly to "save" Black females as well as any other females who need to anchor their lives, to be inspired toward meaningful career patterns. This books is also written for those, males included, who want to see and understand the historical connections of Black women to the American scene.

If readers want to receive a brief education on the historical contributions of Black women in America, I suggest that they read this book along with Volume II, published as a result of the research conducted. Volume II covers Civil Rights, Education, Medicine and Health, Politics and Government, and Sciences.

The original intent of the project that produced this book was to research, develop, and disseminate through book form information on the significant contributions of Black women over a 200-year period, 1776 to 1977, covering 50 states. To accomplish this, a field researcher per state, with ten regional supervisors to assist in the critiquing of data, was planned. Further, the intention was to rely heavily upon primary sources, including interviews, family papers, and church records. Additionally, the project established a set of criteria for each of the ten research topics, and these criteria were validated *before* the field research began on outstanding Black women.

What eventually happened, however, is familiar to anyone who has done research. The design had to be altered from time to time. To begin, funds were not sufficient to hire a researcher per state and the District of Columbia; therefore, several states had to be combined under one researcher. In those combined states, as in all states, volunteer resource persons proved to be extremely important to the research efforts. Secondly, I believed that primary sources would be easy to find; that people would readily share valuable information about notable Black women; that, following the advent of Black studies and women's studies, libraries and research centers would have a substantial collection of primary sources on Black women. My belief did not meet with reality. Therefore, the writers of the ten manuscripts had to rely on many more secondary sources than I had anticipated. Yet, the primary sources that we did find added substance to the materials. Finally, the criteria as originally established had to be altered somewhat by me. Our materials did not allow us to begin with the year 1776 in each of the ten subject areas. Since the data from the field was submitted on established reporting forms, these forms had to be reviewed first by the research assistant and then by me. In certain cases where the woman did not meet the criteria, I made the decision to include her if her life and work stood out as a clear example of achieving against great odds or if she were a pioneer in a particular field. For example, in business, many Black women could not profit a million dollars within a year's time, but their businesses were profitable and they set the pace for others to follow. I included several of these women in the section on business and commerce. But, even with this effort, I realized that many other notable Black women were not included in the research from the field. With only two years to complete the project, the local staff and I reached out across the country to get important information on certain Black women or to fill in certain gaps in the research. So, I continue to say here, our work is but a scratch on the surface. There is still much more to be done by others who are interested in continuing this valuable research on Black women.

How does one conduct research, write, and edit ten manuscripts in two years? Only by working with a sense of commitment and dedication to a cause closely related to the civil rights efforts of the 1960's and to the women's movement of the 1970's can one accomplish such a feat, I think. Many of the persons associated with this research project did just this. It all started, however, when I thought about my great-grandmother, my mother, some former students, and others.

The story goes that my maternal great-grandmother was fiercely proud and openly aggressive in community, church, and educational affairs. Family history tells that she would dress in her finest, walk with parasol in hand up Pine Street from the family home to the Office of the President of Allen University in Columbia, South Carolina, and sit with the President to discuss the direction the college ought to go in the

1920's. Merely being a homemaker was not the challenge she sought.

As a high school student in the 1940's, I saw my mother stand up to white men who came to our house demanding the NAACP (National Association for the Advancement of Colored People) membership list. She was the secretary of the Orangeburg, South Carolina Branch and an elementary school teacher. My mother held her own—refusing to give up the list, because many Black teachers would have lost their jobs for holding NAACP membership. I never forgot my mother's expression nor her words. From this encounter, I later found myself sitting in jail with my students when teaching at my alma mater, South Carolina State College. In fact, I followed them to jail, disguising myself as a nurse in order to pass by the racist jailer. Again, I saw Black females, packed into tiny, cold, damp cells, refusing to give up their dignity. They stood there, wet from the dousing of firemen's water hoses, singing and clapping. What audacity! What spirits! What courage! Their tears christened me. From that moment on, I became compassionately and aggressively involved in the cause of Black women. Their struggle became my commitment.

Then in the early 1970's, I began turning toward the issues and concerns of all women. Working locally and nationally, I came full circle in 1978 to the moment at 3 o'clock one morning when I jumped out of bed from a command hitting my conscience: write ten books on the contributions of Black women to this country.

I wrote a proposal to the Women's Educational Equity Act Program at the U.S. Department of Health, Education, and Welfare. With funding, I started on a two-year exciting and fulfilling mission that ended with the publication of two volumes, including this one.

To be Black and female is to be emotionally involved with this project. Finding it difficult to reach an objective opinion through a single reading, I read and edited each manuscript three or four times in an effort to present to our readers a significant document, with special meaning for young readers, especially Black females.

The purpose of this volume, therefore, is multi-faceted: it serves the young Black female who needs inspiring; it serves the student who needs an accurate account of American history; it serves educational equity, for it shows that these women have been omitted from school curricular materials; it serves the cause of civil rights, for it pays tribute to the Black woman who is the object of double jeopardy—racism and sexism.

While this volume does not include hundreds of other achieving Black women in the research areas represented here, it does point the way to further research and publication. I consider this continued work on the contributions of Black women to America a mandate for scholars, especially those Black and female.

With the Black woman at the bottom of the economic ladder, she needs books that not only highlight her historical contributions, but those that also motivate and encourage her and her "sisters" to reach for and climb to the rung nearer to the top of that ladder.

Perhaps this volume will help.

Marianna W. Davis, Editor
Benedict College
Columbia, South Carolina

ACKNOWLEDGEMENT

Two Black women, one young, one old, sustained me during the long hours needed to move this project to fruition. Mrs. Elizabeth Alsop, a 92 year-old native of Virginia, now living in Philadelphia, is a descendant of General George Washington, according to historical documents. When she heard about this project on the contributions of Black women to America, she invited me to spend several days reading selections from her collection of letters stored in a trunk in the attic of her son's home in the Germantown section of Philadelphia. I found the collection invaluable! The mother of nine sons and daughters and now a great-grandmother, Mrs. Aslop said to me: "Now you have to write for all of us colored women—dead and alive; don't stop. Finish this and start again." Dr. Cecelia Nails Palmer of Oklahoma served as one of the project's field supervisors. She died an untimely death in 1980 before this volume was finished. From her hospital bed, she urged me to complete this "tribute to Black women."

All Black women achievers across 200 years, worthy of inclusion in this volume, simply could not be named. As editor, I am responsible for any shortcomings in the content of this book. As director of the two-year project under which this volume was developed, I am also responsible for the manner in which the research was conducted and subsequent data compiled.

I am indebted to many, many people who contributed to the development of this volume. From the beginning of the project, words of encouragement came from friends and scholars across the United States. Some, like the two above, inspired me; others advised me on a regular basis; still others recommended highly qualified persons to work with the project. I value their words of encouragement and their deeds of kindness. Among them are Dr. Benjamin F. Payton, formerly of the Ford Foundation, now President of Tuskegee Institute; Charles Harris of the Howard University Press; and Dr. Daniel Collins of Harcourt Brace Jovanovich in San Francisco. Of course, persons eventually associated with the project became staunch supporters; in fact, they became public relations specialists for CONTRIBUTIONS. I thank these women and men for giving the project national visibility and for giving me their warm support.

The librarians at Benedict College gave this project high priority on their daily agenda. I thank Mrs. Gretchel Frierson, Ms. Mary Hendrix, Mrs. Mimia Paschal, Charles Dunn, and Dr. Vernon Gettone for their constant assistance to the research efforts.

Among other librarians, I owe special thanks to Mrs. Emma Davis of the Research Libraries in Chicago, Mrs. Janet Simms of the Moorland-Spingard Research Library at Howard University, Mrs. Montez Byers of the Thomas F. Holgate Library at Bennett College, Mrs. Annie G. King of the Hollis Burke Frissell Library at Tuskegee Institute in Alabama, William R. Lewis of the Social Sciences Division of the Boston Public Library, Dr. Sylvia Render of the Library of Congress, and the staff of the Black Women's Oral History Project at the Schlesinger Library at Radcliffe College.

Many organizations volunteered their services, materials, and special reports to our project. Among these groups are the Black Archives, History, and Research Foundation of South Florida, Inc. and the Black Women's Club of Omaha, Nebraska.

Of special significance is the financial contribution to this project from the Ford Foundation. In the final editing stages of the books, Dr. Mariam Chamberlain, Program Officer at the foundation, supported our research by approving my request for editing funds. And at EBONY magazine, Ms. Beverly Coppage and Basil Phillips were especially helpful to us as we sought pictures of women to be included in the two volumes. Mrs. Deborah Willis-Thomas, photographic specialist at the Schomburg Center for Research in Black Culture of the New York City Public Library, was of tremendous help in identifying and obtaining many pictures for the volumes.

A special thanks is due Ms. Rossie Colter who spent months working as a volunteer for the project. She conducted interviews, wrote reports, and documented various sources. Spending her own money to travel to various locations in order to read personal letters, to document dates in family papers, to interview people, especially elderly persons, Ms. Colter deserves this special note of gratitude for her own sense of commitment to this history of Black women.

Dr. Augustus Rodgers, a social scientist, insisted that I use both primary and secondary sources. We did this, mainly because of his assistance in helping us locate many of these sources. I also thank Dr. Phyllis Klotman, Judge Russell DeBow, Mrs. Elva Peguese DeJarmon, Dr. Carolyn McIver, Mrs. Bessie Pearson Jenkins, Mrs. Mabel Ashe, Mrs. Faye Chestnut, Mrs. Ermanese Bolton, Mrs. Carol Cooper, and Ms. Dixie Lee Baker for their kind assistance.

While many of my professional colleagues at Benedict College assisted me in many ways, five of them stand out among the group: Dr. Addessa Lewis, Dr. Ruby W. Watts, Zack Weston, Dr. LaMyra Davis, and Dr. Louis Bone who cajoled, urged, and insisted upon a scholarly approach to the writing and editing of this volume. Beyond this stance, they also found time to read through a page here and there, suggesting changes. I am especially grateful to these five professionals for their encouragement, their positive attitude, their sincerity, and their help. I also thank Dr. Robert Scott, Dr. Collidge Johnson, and Dr. Henry Ponder, President of Benedict College, for their support.

Nine Benedict College students served the project well. I thank Rochelle Jones; Gloria Middleton; Sandra Reeves; Stephanie Shell; Curt Jackson; Charles Thomas, Jr.; Hattie M. Lee; James Wardell Brown; and Angel Ashford.

At the Women's Educational Equity Act Program office in Washington, D.C., Mrs. Carolyn Joyner, program officer, and William "Bill" Hopkins, grants officer, showed great patience and understanding as I struggled to interpret all of the federal and program regulations. I was indeed fortunate to have had these specialists to call upon, and I am grateful to them.

Several of the local staff persons were more than employees. They were dedicated and committed individuals who became excited (and nervous) with each passing day abouth the finished product—the books. I am appreciative to Bernard Hazzard, graphic artist; Dr. Patricia Bell, evaluator; Tom Love, bibliographer; Dorothy Grant, typist. The project simply would have "suffered" if it were not for two other staffers: Mrs. Blondell Jennings Capell, researcher, and Gerard P. Terio, IBM specialist in word processing. They gave unselfishly of their time and energy to see the work completed. I am especially indebted to them.

But the most important persons to this volume are Ms. Paula Giddings, Ms. Janell Walden, Dr. Alba M. Lewis, Attorney Dewaren Johnson, the writers of the original manuscripts. Their dedication carried them beyond the regular work, making this volume a reality.

In the final stages of the development of the manuscripts, two longtime colleagues and personal friends assisted me with editing details—Carl Senna, a professional editor, who lives and works in Boston, and Dr. James Lee Hill, professor of English and founder of two college journals, who works at Albany State College in Georgia where he is Chairman of the English Department. I am indebted to them.

The publication of this volume was realized because of the assistance of the Columbia Urban League, Inc. and of Bankers Trust of South Carolina. Therefore, I am especially indebted to James T. McLawhorn,

Jr., President of CUL, and to Julian Turner, President of Bankers Trust.

The three sisters who taught me how to walk - Mrs. Laura Bowman Frederick, Mrs. Mattie Bowman McIver, and Mrs. Ermanese Bowman Bolton - also taught me how to be compassionate and caring. Three retired school teachers, they spent hours and hours of volunteer time filing papers and cards, addressing envelopes, and running errands for me. The first of the three is my mother; the other two my aunts. My father, Hiram E. Frederick, Jr., never allowed me to falter in completing this task begun July 1978. I love him for being such an excellent cheerleader for me. Finally, one who understood my urgency to do this research on Black women and who understands my drive is my son, Kenneth R. Davis. I am especially grateful to him for helping me to be both a good mother and a dedicated, professional Black woman.

Marianna W. Davis, Editor

PART I.

THE CONTRIBUTIONS OF BLACK WOMEN TO AMERICA:
THE ARTS

Manuscript Writer
Paula Giddings

Consultant
Sandra E. Gibbs, Ph.D.

Evaluators
Margaret Walker Alexander, Ph.D.
Poet and Novelist
Jackson, Mississippi

Phyl Garland
Columbia University
New York, New York

Richard Long, Ph.D.
Director
Department of Afro-American Studies
Atlanta University
Atlanta, Georgia

Joe Nash
Director
Black and Multi-Ethnic Christian Education
Resources Center
New York, New York

Leo Twiggs, Ph.D.
Professor of Art and
    Director of Museums
South Carolina State College
Orangeburg, South Carolina

Editor
Marianna W. Davis, Ed.D.

THE ARTS
Table of Contents

INTRODUCTORY ESSAY

BLACK WOMEN IN THE ARTS

In this volume, the author and editor have registered the achievements in America of Black women in the arts. The time period is that beginnig in slavery and ending somewhat beyond the third quarter of the 20th century. The categories include both the "high" and "popular" arts. Thus, at one and the same time, the achievements have been a dramatic, ironic juxtaposition of confident and competent strides up the steep inclines of a long trail a-winding.

Increasing the drama is the fact that the strides were taking place amidst both general American and special racial doubts, whether or not specific individuals always allowed such doubts to reach the foreground of their consciousness. America doubted itself only somewhat less than it doubted Blacks. America suffered an inferiority complex, pretensions of Neo-classicism, and ached for European acceptance instead of asserting its uniqueness and aesthetic as well as political and economic independence. The famous novelist Henry James has testimony on the subject.

Henry James, in his biography of the 19th century novelist Nathaniel Hawthorne (1879), argued that America provided a culture which was too thin for artists, and thus caused them to labor without the possibility of the very great achievements possible within the rich European traditions. In *American Scenes* (1907), he spoke of the great amount of history needed to create traditions. Obviously, Blacks, looked upon then as people without a history, would seem to other Americans to be without the basics necessary for art. The general idea was the Blacks suffered from "nothingness."

W.E.B. DuBois, in *The Souls of Black Folk* (1903), described the way in which the Black self-conscious artist was open to internalizing America's low opinion of Black creativity. "The innate love of harmony and beauty that set the ruder souls of his people a-dancing and a–singing raised but confusion and doubt in the soul of the Black artist; for the beauty revealed to him was the soul beauty of a race which his larger audience despised, and he could not articulate the message of another people." Thus, this "larger audience" would enjoy Blacks' popular songs during the plantation period as something humorous or exotic. But, as Alain Locke stated in *The Negro and His Music* (1936), American appreciation and imitation of the popular music would become general only after it was adapted for minstrels. (The same principle is applicable to the dance.) Black artists would have to enter minstrel tradition and convey the feeling of their own native creations through white conventions. James Weldon Johnson in *Black Manhattan* (1930) gives a progress report which reveals certain triumphs but also the tremendous struggle of artists and producers. Slowly, the genuine folk materials were breaking through. In the 19th century, the Fisk Jubilee Singers had led the way to securing acceptance of the spirituals, although some white responses to the singers still evoked them as children of nature. Blacks gained pride in spirituals as a Black creation of America's only native music. But James Trotter in *Music and Some Highly Musical People* (1881), though unstinting in his praise, registered also overtones of double-conscious-ness—the division within the self, as DuBois described it, between one's American status and internalizations and one's appreciation of Blackness: "The songs they [Fisk Singers] sang were for the present, forming a delightful novelty, and serving a noble purpose. Still it must be sadly remembered that these Jubilee songs sprang from a former life of enforced degradation; and that, notwithstanding their great beauty of melody, and occasional words of elevated religious character, there was often in both melody and words what forcibly reminded the hearer of the unfortunate state just mentioned; and to the cultured, sensitive members of the race represented, these reminders were always of the most painful nature." Trotter looked forward to "the model of slave 'spirituals'" giving way to "such music as befits the new order of things."

Monroe Majors also reflects the 19th century Blacks' concern with art as evidence both of talent and attainment of civilization in his valuable book, *Noted Negro Women*, (1893), although he is concerned with the spread of Black women's achievements and does not confine himself to music. Perhaps he also reflects more closely the 19th century attitude regarding the ennobling role, through its inscriptions: 'A race, no less than a nation, is prosperous in proportion to the intelligence of its women.' "The criterion for Negro civilization is the intelligence, purity and high motives of its women." "The highest mark of our prosperity and the strongest proofs of Negro capacity to master the sciences and fine arts, are evinced by the advanced position to which Negro women have attained." And so on. The text contains similar language.

There can be no doubt that women brought to the context of the struggle in the arts not merely the two-ness described by DuBois as comprising the Blacks' double-consciousness (Black *and* American) but also a three-ness; Black, American, and Woman. Jane Showalter in *A Literature of Their Own* (1977), though a discussion of British women novelists, has a formulation which contributes to our sense of the context if we are not overly rigid in applying it. She first describes the struggles of literary subcultures (Black, Jewish, Canadian, Anglo-Indian, or "even American"): First, "prolonged imitation of the prevailing modes of the dominant tradition" and internalization of its "standards of art and its view on social roles"; second, "protest against these standards and values, and *advocacy* of minority rights and values, including a demand for autonomy"; third, "self-discovery, a turning inward freed from some of the dependency of opposition, a search for identity." The corresponding categories for the three struggles when involving women are listed as "feminine," "feminist," and "female."

There may be a number of things qualifying Black women's relationships to the categories without destroying their pertinency, and these qualifying elements may need to be considered if we are to get the full meaning and picture of their struggles in the arts. The first consideration is that Black women and men were early cast into the same boat, though they may be said to occupy different parts of the boat. As Alain Locke saw the situation, Black artists, on one wave length, tended to share a common condition. In the matter of a tradition (which theoretically could have reduced the impact of the majority cultural), there was the elaborate African achievement in the arts, to which he pointed in *Negro Art Past and Present* and in "The Legacy of the Ancestral Arts," *The New Negro* (1925). There was not a ready road to a re-absorption of the African tradition, he seemed to think, but possibly an ability to gain more from it than whites, who were benefitting from it, were able to seize. Presumably, some spiritual kinship still existed between American Blacks and their African ancestors. Second, for many of the arts, there was a folk tradition—always under threat of debasement by the "larger audience," but one which, if properly used by Blacks, could create genuine definitions of existence not entirely included in the premises of the majority culture. Thus, in terms of pragmatic conditions, there were resources for Blacks, male and female, which could oppose the majority culture more effectively than could white women—who had no other culture than that which obviously oppressed them.

A second consideration is that, for the arts, Black women seem to have shared, during the 19th century, a common pursuit of mastery with other artists without the kind of separate consciousness which we have been made accustomed to since the Harlem Renaissance of the 1920's. I say this tentatively. In autobiographies of 19th century women preachers, on the other hand, there seems to be a forced sense of separateness. In Dorothy Porter's *Early Negro Writing*, (1971), for example, Jarena Lee in her autobiographical statement "The Life of Jarena Lee" obviously encounters the necessity to battle the male definition of preacher as male only. Maria Stewart, an obvious intellectual, also included in *Early Negro Writing*, may have overtones of a separate sentiment but explicitly her statement is a passionate advocacy of religion, a passionate attack upon racism, and an implicit identification with the revolutionary feeling of the dead David Walker of *David Walker's Appeal* (1829-1830). Yet, one is aware, that in several works women are intensely aware of their existence as women whether or not they generally tend to think of themselves in an identical way of that of the majority culture.

A third consideration is that Black women artists found themselves making complicated relationships with the white and Black groups. The first woman poet to follow Ann Bradstreet as a woman poet was Phillis Wheatley, whose first book publicaton was in 1773. Wheatley was thus in a position of artistic leadership for women, for Blacks, and for Americans in general. Bradstreet had faced sexist deprecation. According to Ann Stanford in *The Women Poets in English* (1972), Ann Bradstreet, though protected by her husband's status and the uneasy tradition of the "writing" gentlewoman, was aware of carping criticism and critics who felt that she should exchange the pen for the needle and acknowledge the inferiority of female wits and their accomplishments as either stolen or occurring by chance. Admired by Blacks and paternalistic whites, Phillis Wheatley would evoke from the white liberal Thomas Jefferson the dictum that, "Religion, indeed, has produced a Phillis Whately [sic]; but it could not produce a poet." Perhaps a still more complicated leadership position during the 19th century was that of the sculptor, Edmonia Lewis. Elsa Honig Fine in *The Afro-American Artist* (1973) points out that the chronicler of 19th century artists Henry Tuckerman "urged Americans to abandon their Neoclassical pretensions and work in the more natural style of Edmonia Lewis." One is provoked into speculations regarding what it must have meant to be aware of two minority cultures as sources (Black and Indian) and two majority cultures as demanding judges and afforders of resources of "high culture." "However," continues Fine, "by this time Lewis herself was engulfed in the sentimental Neoclassicism sanctioned by the academicians."

The 20th century also feeds in pressures which complicate the simple outlines of categories. Helen A. Johnson's interesting picture history *Black America on Stage* (1978) reveals women playing a very strong role in recapturing the arts of the theatre in both the "musicals" and the "serious" drama. Perhaps as a concession to conditions of the majority *and* the minority audiences most of the talented women are light-skinned. Sisseretta Jones, Johnson points out, played a role in the transition between minstrel comedy and the musicals by interrupting her concert tour as one of the great sopranos and forming "her own company, Black Patti's Troubadours." In the production, according to Alain Locke in *The Negro and His Music* (1936), she "sang her operatic and concert repertory, with ensemble numbers with what was one of the first really good stage choruses." Women had written also for the minstrel stage and acted for it, but, Johnson states, they gained stature with the development of operettas. Among the husband and wife teams portrayed in *Black America on Stage*, Ada Overton Walker, the wife of George Walker, revealed a talent "that matched his," a fact easily obscured by the tendency of the audience to emphasize the talented male. And one could go on mentioning the complications which suggest the nuances affecting all categories. But perhaps the foregoing will suffice to make the turning to categories useful and to throw light upon the winding trail and steep inclines they include. Now to some general use of the categories. They, of course, overlap, and actually older attitudes frequently recrudesce; thus, often, a new spirit is sufficiently at the foreground of consciousness to create a vanguard representing it while older attitudes and spirit survive. So our chronology retains tentativeness.

First, "prolonged imitation of the prevailing modes of the dominent tradition" characterizing the *feminist* category needs to be discussed. In this category, Black men and women share the same broad objectives. It will be useful to consider this period as extending from the beginnings of women's appearances to about 1920, the time during which the Harlem or Negro Renaissance surfaced. The Black motif, shared by men and women, other than standard artistic aspirations, is that of proving the capacity of Blacks for the highest artistic achievement. Thus the participants must impress an America with inferiority feelings and anxious for European approval, a fact which means that gaining both American and European exposure and training is important for the Black artist representing "high" culture (concert stage, painting, sculpture, etc.). It is clear, I think, that the legacy for the 20th century Blacks would be, for the most part, the tasks of uniting American, European, and patterns representing native Blackness (African heritage, history of Blacks in America, and folk creativity) artistic achievements. In terms of social class, the note struck is that of the rising Black middle class. Indeed, both women and men emphasized the presence of a Black middle class which promised quick assimilation of Euro–American traditions. I have already referred to Edmonia Lewis in sculpture. In painting, a cryptic paragraph in Porter's *Ten Afro-American Artists of the Nineteenth Century* refers to Annie E. Walker, painter, and gives illustrations: "Born Alabama. Graduated Cooper Union for the Advancement of Science and Art, 1895. Later studied at Academic Julien, Paris. Exhibited Paris Salon, 1896." The two illustrations are devoted to either very light–skinned or white women.

But the real drama of this first period seemed to have been provided by the women singers, who, before the end of slavery, were active upon the concert stage. They were there challenging both American and European white singers. Black commentators report their achievement with the greatest of excitment and provide elaborate press notices regarding their reception. On the folk level, I have already referred to the Fisk Jubilee Singers. Monroe Majors of *Noted Negro Women* celebrated particularly "Jennie Jackson DeHart, the famous soprano of the original Fisk Jubilee Singers." The elaborate celebration of Majors and Trotter suggests the middle class bias of the upward strivings of the Black middle class. The singers were proof of both the Blacks' capacity to achieve the status and standards of the great arts and of the warmth and illumination provided by artistic striving. In this period the direct protest occurs in poetry and novels, the literary arts, which also help to register the presence of a Black middle class. Thus we have spilled over, in literature, into the second period.

Secondly, "protest agaist these standards and values, including a demand for autonomy and advocacy of minority rights and values," prevails. This effort is also largely a joint effort with men. However, there is a growing woman's self-consciousness. Nella Larsen, Zora Neale Hurston, and later, Gwendolyn Brooks are precursors of the seeing of woman on her own terms which a vanguard is concerned with in the 1970's. Obviously this period goes up through the 1960's and includes general contributions and those on which the concern with Blackness will also build. Mamie Smith, Bessie Smith, and others broke through in the establishment of the Blues. Katherine Dunham and Pearl Primus dealt firmly with folk traditions, our African heritage, and the general principles of art in the dance, and others have built upon their achievements. Mahalia Jackson almost singlehandedly established the power and art of Gospel music. Mary Lou Williams, Ella Fitzgerald, and others emerged as important innovators and pioneers in jazz music and song, with Williams' contributions being primarily that of the composer and pianist. Forecasting the 1970's concerns with the Black woman on her own terms are such voices as those of Nikki Giovanni, Sonia Sanchez, Mari Evans, Carole Rogers, and Jewel

Lattimore. One, of course, could name others, but the foregoing names will carry the communication. By the 1960's there was an attempt to submerge individual and sex concerns within a unity of Black voices, but the breakaway voice of Nikki Giovanni rose above the chorus of consensus.

The major problem Black women artists confronted within their own group was the impact of machismo. The 1960's Black Art Movement tended to insist upon a subordinate position for women, as bearers of warriors, as inspirers, and as keepers of the home. This posture was probably most unrealistic regarding the educational attainments of women. Thus, it was only predictable that a revolt would occur, and a third stage would be introduced.

Finally, in the Showalter category, this third stage is "self-discovery, a turning from inward freed from some of the dependency of opposition, a search to identify." Thus we have a recognizable vanguard in all fields. In literature, the situation is represented by such persons as Toni Morrison, Alice Walker, Gayl Jones, and Ntozake Shange. A recent polemic is by Michele Wallace — *Black Macho and the Myth of the Superwoman.* Yet the new period, involving all the arts, contains so much more. I have suggested earlier that old myths and old persuasions do not really die out, but that a vanguard for the entrance of new tensions and persuasions makes itself felt. In the newest artists of whatever category of the arts, there can be simply a reveling in modernist freedom and the opportunity fully to confront the range of modernist resources in the arts. There can be a freedom in the expression of Blackness. There can be a commitment to militancy and Blackness. And there can be a commitment to an American priority.

In the pages of this book revealing the energy, resourcefulness, and success of Black women, you will find that on the way to artistic excellence all persuasions are represented.

George E. Kent, Ph.D.
Department of English
University of Chicago

PROLOGUE

Brought to the New World in an involuntary servitude, Africans could transport only parts of their traditional cultures.[1] As captives of a massive, trans-Atlantic migration which lasted over three hundred years, the Africans were important to the New World for the labor they provided a burgeoning capitalist plantation economy, not for their artistic creativity. Despite attempts to suppress and even destroy the reservoir of human creativity exhibited by the newly transplanted Africans, the fragmented customs, mores, and expressive components of their traditional cultures coalesced to provide the springs of their creative genius.[2] In the arts, expecially the expressive arts, the transplanted African has given America a distinctive artistic legacy from his homeland. Wherever he was forced to settle, or has subsequently gone on his own, the confluent interactions of his and other cultures have produced cultural traditions in which the African presence is undeniable.

Unrecognized, underrepresented, but not uninfluential, the African–American woman's artistic contributions to America have been too long ignored. A blend of African and Western influences, her artistic contributions have been made inspite of the existing myriad of contributions about who she is; and most often, she has been burdened by a quadruple consciousness forced upon her. She has had to see herself as an American, Black, American woman, and Black American woman.[3] Out of this multiple artistic legacy which is important to her development, important to the Black community, and important to America, the Black woman has assured her place in the artistic archives of America; we have only to recognize it.

CHAPTER I

THE DANCE

Out of Africa

With the millions of Black immigrants who were deposited in the New World came their particular world view —one in which culture was not separate from one's daily life but an integral part of it. African folktales, poetry, sculpture and music were inextricably a part of their daily life, but perhaps most essential to African cultural/life expression was the dance. Dance not only provided the primary entertainment in the African's life; it was a celebration of life. It was an important means of communication, the means by which the rituals and drama of life were played out.

Before the first Blacks were brought to North America in 1619, they populated the islands of the Caribbean and South and Central America. It was in these parts of the New World where Westerners first saw and recorded the African dance. From their descriptions, it is evident that the dances, contrary to the stereotypes, were highly structured, with room for individual expression within the structure. Three primary African dances, the Calenda, the Chica, and the Juba, seemed to form the basis for most dances the Africans performed in the New World. In these dances, Black women had a specific role. Although cast in the role of a coquette, they could challenge their male counterparts in dance.

These dances were performed by Blacks on traditional holidays and at weddings, social get-togethers and work feasts, like the end of the harvest. Another important occasion for dance was the funeral rite, which utilized the oldest form of African dance—the ring or circle dances. African religious ceremonies were accompanied by still another important dance ritual known variously as Vodun, Shango, Obeah and Myalism, Nanigo and the Shuters.

Into America: The Transformation of the Dance

When large numbers of African slaves began coming to America in the 18th century, they brought with them the music and dance that were witnessed in the Caribbean. However, in the United States the dominant Protestant culture, combined with the colonists' fears of rebellion, restricted the traditional forms of expression—particularly in the South. The restrictions the colonists placed on the Africans did not stop the dance, but transformed it, the result being that the use of bones, hand-clapping and virtuoso footwork took the place of instruments. This development hastened the evolvement of such Afro-American dances as the Buck and Wing, the Pigeon-Wing, the Jig, and the Cake-Walk. In these dances emphasis was more on the foot than the body. Since the dances were often performed on the plantation in front of whites, their entertainment rather than ritual value was more important, and much of the sexual connotation was taken out of the dances, particularly on the part of the female.

Black dance was also seen on "the legitimate stage" in New York. Beginning in 1821, Blacks had their own African Grove Theater, which offered Shakespearean plays and singing. Women, too, took part in the productions. On one occasion two solo dances were performed, including a hornpipe danced by a woman who played Desdemona in *Othello*.

"What Did They Do To My Dance?"

Although white impersonations of Black dances have been documented at least as early as the Revolutionary War period, with the appearance of Jim Rice's character, "Jim Crow," in 1828, whites imitation of Black dancing became a national phenomenon. Rice is said to have seen a lame Black groom singing and dancing one day and copied his movements for his act of "Jump Jim Crow," which he performed in blackface. Of course, Rice's dance was a grotesque caricature of forms of Black dance which evolved from Africa, but for his efforts, he became known as the "Father of blackface minstrelsy."

By the 1840's, a group called the Virginia Minstrels, composed of four white men, became the first formal minstrel group to perform on the stage. They performed in blackface, as did the troupes that followed them, according to a standard formula. Part One of the Minstrel show began with an overture that was followed by a comic question and answer period and song. The entertainers were seated in a semi-circle flanked by the endmen, "Mr. Tambo and Mr. Bones." Part One ended with a Walk-Around. Performer Tom Fletcher attributes the structure of Part One as the innovation of a well-known Black family troupe performing in the 1840's—John Luca and his troupe. The second part of the Minstrel was called the Olio, and it consisted of singing, dancing, and other acts. The final part, or the Afterpiece, was an extravaganza which involved the entire cast. It was usually a burlesque of a serious drama which was popular at the time.

Although the forms of African dance were corrupted by white imitators entrenching a number of Black stereotypes, Black influence in American entertainment was seen clearly for the first time. Critic Arthur Todd noted roots of the Minstrel show:

These shows were basically a development of the primitive tradition of circle and hand clapping dances. For theatrical purposes, the entertainers were seated in a semi-circular line of chairs on the stage. Here the ringleader of the dance became, in transition, the "interlocutor" or master of ceremonies. Those who sang the melody for the dance were transposed into the Chorus, some becoming "end" men, one at either "end" or side of the circle. The rest of the chorus performed the same functions as did the line in Africa—they clapped their hands or shook tambourines. Every man in the chorus had the opportunity for a solo bit of some sort, just as had the Negro in many of the primitive African ceremonies.[4]

More importantly, the development of minstrelsy opened the door for Black performing troupes—at first using the same format, including the blackface, but later evolving into a more creative and exciting form.

Reauthenticating the Dance

By 1890, some revolutionary changes were occurring in Black minstrel shows. In that year, a Black production organized by Sam T. Jack became one of the first troupes to omit blackface make-up, but even more significantly, it was the first troupe to introduce women into the cast. Jack's *The Creole Show* used sixteen talented and beautiful women to make up the traditional minstrel semi-circle. Florence Hines, called the "American Vesta Tilley," was a fantastic male impersonator who performed as the interlocutor between male end-men. Dora Dean, who was also in the show along with her partner and husband Charles Johnson, would later help to make the "Cake-Walk" the rage of Europe. From that decade on, almost every show had Black women performing in them, a development which helped lead Black performance away from the minstrel tradition to the popularity of couples performing. Dean and Johnson, for example, became a popular Vaudeville act which lasted through the 1930's. Dean, who was a beauty, was the first Black performer to wear thousand dollar costumes.[5]

In 1895, John Isham's *The Octoroons* made an even further departure from the minstrel tradition. Like *The Creole Show*, it also used glamorous women, but this time not only as chorus members but principals. A year later the same producer's *Oriental America* abandoned the cake-walk walkaround finale for one of operatic medleys. Three years later came the first Black show to be organized, produced and managed by Blacks and the first to make a complete break from the Minstrel pattern. Bob Cole's *A Trip to Coontown* (1898) was the first Black musical comedy, according to James Weldon Johson, and the first show to have a continuous story line and cast of characters.

During the summer of the same year, *Clorindy—The Origin of the Cakewalk*, with music by Will Marion Cook and lyrics by Paul Laurence Dunbar, used the basic steps of the plantation dance, infused with the pizzazz of high fashion and class, made the new rage. "The Calkwalk", said Langston Hughes, "was performed by handsome couples, the women gorgeously gowned and nobody in blackface. . . . the dance was a joy." The principals of the show were Ernest Hogan and Belle Davis. The original cakewalk was performed with a kind of shuffling movement; but in *Clorindy* it was made a smooth walking step with the body held erect, observed Emery. The result was, as Cook himself noted, Negroes that cakewalked like "angels . . . Black angels."

The next Black musicals which gained unprecedented popularity were those starring Bert Williams and George Walker. At the turn of the century, they were in a string of hits including *The Sons Ham, In Dahomey, In Abyssinia* and *Bandana Land*. Although Williams and Walker dominated the musical comedies written by Cook, Black women performers such as Lura Bowman, Hattie McIntosh, Madah Hyers, and Lottie Williams were also prominent. Perhaps the most important female attraction, however, was Ada Overton (Walker). She "was beyond comparison the brightest star among women on the Negro stage in the period," and not "many degrees less than the two principals,"[6] observed Johnson. Whether doing the buck-and-wing, the cake-walk or even some form of "grotesque" dancing, "she lent the performance a neat gracefulness of movement which was unsurpassed by anyone" observed Tom Fletcher. "Those of us who actually remember her, are pretty well agreed that she was Florence Mills and Josephine Baker rolled into one." Fletcher reports Overton was Mills' idol and tried to follow in her footsteps. It was Overton who taught Mills the song "Miss Hannah from Savannah," which had started the young Mills on the road to stardom.

Overton reached the peak of her career when producer William Hammerstein (father of Oscar Hammerstein) chose her to do a serious dance interpretation of *Salome* at the famous Hammerstein Theater. More than a superb talent, Overton became an example of the new female talent which was emerging in the period. The development of the theater gave a new status to the actress during a period when performers were exhibiting greater talent and women other than "high yellow" were being accepted by the audiences. Overton was also expressive of the new race-pride. She subscribed to the philosophy that "by carefully studying our own graces, we [Blacks] learn to appreciate the noble and beautiful within us." Without learning to appreciate ourselves, she warned, "we will spend our lives imitating other people and depreciating ourselves."[7]

Between the closing of *In Dahomey* and the opening of *Abysinnia* in 1906, George Walker, with the help of Hattie McIntosh, formed a group of women dancers known as *The Abysinnians*. A featured performer in the group was Elida Webb, who was destined to become the first known Black female choreographer on Broadway.[8] Succeeding the Williams and Overton era, J. Rosamund Johnson and Bob Cole teamed up to write *The Shoofly Regiment* (1906), and *The Red Moon* (1908), musical comedies with an emphasis more on dancing than singing. James Weldon Johnson observed that the plays had "a sprightlier, and prettier chorus, and which, though it could not sing so powerfully, could out-dance the heavier chorus of the other companies by a wide margin."[9]

A few years earlier, however, another dancer had come into the spotlight when the jazz band, The Memphis Players, played theater engagements. The start-studded cast at the Proctor's Theater included Ida Forsyne, who was the dancer in the show. The Players were soon booked for an international tour, and during their tour, Forsyne left the group, choosing to stay in Russia for almost a decade. She became the "cakewalking toast of Russia" in the early 1900's and upon her return years later, she aided Jerome Robbins in choreographing his "Cakewalk" for the New York City Ballet.[10]

Despite the many notable gains that Blacks had made in Broadway theater around the turn of the century, their progress was rudely interrupted by a new wave of racial antipathy sweeping the country. By 1910 Blacks had been completely excluded from the "Great White Way"—an exclusion that would last for seven years. Consequently, Blacks in New York had to do what Blacks in many other parts of the country had already done: establish their own theaters. One of the most prominent of these was the Lafayette Theater in Harlem. There were many important theater presentations there, but it was in 1913, when a musical called *Darktown Follies* played there, that the theater attracted the attention of whites. The "carriage trade," including such personage as Florenz Ziegfeld, trekked uptown for the first time to see the theater's introduction of another Black dance which would soon take the country by a storm. The dance called "Ballin' the Jack" appeared in the finale of the first act. Emery described the dance as a "serpentine, circular, shuffling dance that resembled the Ring-Shout and the Snake-Hip in its undulating motion." Other dances featured included the Cakewalk and the Texas Tommy. Ethel Williams, a star of the show, described the latter as similar to the Lindy but with two basic steps, and a kick and a hop three times on each foot followed by an extemporaneous step such as sliding, turning or pulling."

In the meantime, Black dance was developing new forms in the South, outside of the commercial glare of the northern cities. Banned by the churches, Southern dance found its spawning ground in the dance halls and Jooks—bawdy houses—where Blacks congregated to dance, drink, and gamble. It was especially in such places that many notable dance steps were conceived before they circulated throughout the country. For example, Zora Neale Hurston, the writer and anthropologist, attributes the origins of the Black Bottom, the Big Apple, the Charleston, Ballin' the Jack, the Shimmy, and the Mooche to the South.

The dances transported from the South and new ones were performed nightly in such Harlem dance halls as the Savoy, the Renaissance, and the Alhambra. Such dance crazes as the Lindy Hop, the Shag, the Suzi Q, and the Camel Walk took turns. Harlem nightclubs, such as the Cotton Club and Small's Paradise, added popularity to the dances by having the entertainers perform them. For example, the Cotton Club's Cora La Redd's act did much to popularize the dance, Truckin'. Whites, intrigued by these Harlem happenings, picked up dances too, but by the time they learned one dance, Blacks had long gone on to another.

The opening of *Shuffle Along* in 1921 catapulted the popularity of Black dance and music to unprecedented heights. The show "was the clarion call for every Black artist in America," noted renown dance historian Joe Nash, and certainly many of them answered it. Danceable tunes by Flournoy Miller, Aubrey Lyles, Noble Sissle, and Eubie Blake became enduring hits, with the likes of Caterina Jarboro, Trixie Smith, Adelaide Hall, Lottie Gee, and Gertrude Saunders making up the cast. Josephine Baker, the star to be, was in the chorus line.

Shuffle Along, beyond its inherent charm, was significant in many ways. It became a success largely on its own terms and marked the beginning of national interest in the Charleston and Black Bottom. It was revolutionary in that it was the first production to "bring authentic ragtime and jazz dancing to Broadway, [radically] altering the future direction of musical comedy".[11] Additionally, it became the vehicle for unprecedented stardom for several in the cast, and among those, the performer, who rode it to its most dizzying heights, was a petite little woman named Florence Mills.

Born in 1895, Mills had given her first performance at the age of four and made her professional debut in Williams' and Walker's *Sons of Ham*, where she became famous singing "Hannah from Savannah." By the time she was eight, Mills was an accomplished dancer and singer. Seven years later, she was playing in vaudeville with her sisters in the Mills Trio and later starred with Cora Green and Ada "Bricktop" Smith in the Panama Trio.

It was, *Shuffle*, however, that catapulted her into the national spotlight. The impact of Mills, who had replaced the ailing Gertrude Saunders in the show, was immediate. Claude McKay described her performance as "mimicking and kicking her marvelous way over the heads of all the cast." A *New York World* critic was fascinated that the petite, feminine, and graceful form of Mills could be suddenly transformed: "She becomes all mouth in a moment. She makes faces. Her hands become crazy pointers. Her body struts and stalks and makes golliwoggles. She flings herself into hilarious postures and all as spontaneously as a blackbird flitting his feathers while he whistles at the sun."[12] After leaving *Shuffle*, Mills became the star of Lew Leslie's *Plantation Revue* (which also played in London), *Dixie to Broadway*, and *BLACKBIRDS* (1926). She was scheduled a repeat performance in *THE BLACKBIRDS* of 1928, but before the show opened, Florence Mills, at the age of 32, was dead.

Florence Mills, star of the theatre
(photo courtesy Schomburg Center
New York Public Library)

Her particular mode of dancing was, as one paper cited, "the outstanding contribution to terpsichore for many a long day." But perhaps her greatest legacy was expressed by a critic from the *London Telegraph* after her death. "Behind the high energy of her comic performances was a serious woman who was concerned about the status of her race," the writer said. And at the base of her dancing and singing, "Somewhere one sensed the sad dignity of a race which the world had treated unjustly—a kind of sensibility which made all our memories of nigger-minstrel buffoonery seem shabby and dull . . . . "[13]

After *Shuffle*, a slew of similar shows were produced, one of the most important being *Runnin' Wild* in 1923. It was this show which featured the hit song and the hit dance by the same name: The Charleston. This dance probably had its origins in the traditional Juba dance. Katherine Dunham has noted, for example, that she saw Charleston steps in a Haitian dance called La Martinique, and Melville Herskovits recognized Charleston steps in the ancestral rites for the chief of the Ashanti tribe in Africa. In America, however, the choreographer honed the ancient dance into a classy, upbeat one and made it a national phenomenom. That choreographer was Elida Webb, who had been a member of the Abyssinians. Webb, the first known Black female choreographer on Broadway, also put her considerable talents at work in *Ziegfeld Follies* and *Showboat*, as well as in the Cotton Club and the Alhambra.

In 1924, *Chocolate Dandies* hit the stage and with it emerged another of the most important Black female stars in theatrical history: Josephine Baker. Baker first got noticed for her antics on the chorus line. During this period, Helen A. Johnson reminds us, "the chorus girl was all the rage." Excited reviewers constantly talked of the "yellow and seal skin browns" that made them up. After all, "they were the ones who forced the white girls to change from prancers to dancers, the Black men and women having taught them."[14] Baker's antics, however, were not the only evidence of her creativity. Eubie Blake has remarked that when she was in the chorus of *Shuffle*, she would routinely forget the designated steps only to make up new ones that were more spectacular.

But it was in *La Revue Negre* in 1925 in Paris that Josephine Baker would gain her first real acclaim. She became the personification of *Le Jazz Hot*, catching fire in earnest, when she appeared on stage at the Folies Bergere wearing nothing but a girdle of bananas. Critic Andre Levinson described the performance as "one of a sinuous idol that enslaves and incites mankind. . . . It was she who led the spellbound drummer and the fascinated saxophonist in the harsh rhythm of the

Blues. It was as though the jazz, catching on the wing the vibrations of this mad body, were interpreting, word by word, its fantastic monologue. The music is born from the dance and what a dance!"[15]

Like Mills, Baker had not found success overnight. She, too, started at an early age, making her first nightclub appearance at eight years old; and by the time she reached the age of 15, she left her St. Louis, Missouri home to join a Bessie Smith show. From there, she found Paris at her feet. She introduced the Black Bottom and Charleston to European audiences and created the "continued vogue for jazz music in France," according to Langston Hughes.

Josephine Baker - star of stage and screen, singing in Paris, France
(photo courtesy of EBONY)

Ironically, the bejeweled, Patou-gowned and French singing girl from St. Louis was not received warmly when she returned to the United States in 1936 and appeared in the *Ziegfield Follies*. Perhaps she was not understood; nonetheless, it would be fifteen years before she appeared again in America, breaking all box office records at the Strand Theater. In 1951, *Ebony* Magazine noted: "The legend named Josephine Baker has come home again to her native land to score an artistic triumph that show-business historians will probably call the most remarkable of our times . . . at the age of 44 [she] achieved the one great success that ironically eluded her in the 26 years of her remarkable career: a smash hit in her own U.S.A."

As remarkable as her career was, Josephine Baker, beyond the stage was a story that was as much a part of her legend as her performances. During World War II, Baker was a spy for the French Resistance Movement, from which she earned the Legion of Honor and Rosette of the Resistance medals. When she returned to the States in the Fifties, she refused to play any nightclub that did not allow Blacks in the audience. As a result, the Copa City Club in Miami reversed its discriminatory policy, paving the way for the lifting of the color bar in Miami. And as evidence of her commitment to a world without race hatred. Baker and her husband adopted fourteen children of various nationalities and colors, which she called her "rainbow family."

Black Concert Dance

Perhaps because of the popularity and success of Black dances in America, it was assumed by many whites that these dances were the only form of the art to which Blacks should or could aspire. The first crack in the dyke of this conventional wisdom came with the performances of the Creative Dance Troupe of Hampton Institute in Virigina. Under the direction of Charles Williams and Charlotte Kennedy, the troupe first presented its repertoire of modern, folk, and African dances outside of its campus in 1925. The most significant contribution was the dance spirituals, performed for the first time. Hampton had done for the dance what Fisk's Jubilee Singers had done for the spirituals over a half-century earlier. Although the Hampton dancers were amateurs, their influence as performers, and even more so as teachers of the dance, was significant, observes Nash. They were pioneers. Nash also notes that Charlotte Kennedy choreographed the Company's outstanding "Middle Passage."

Seven years later, a Black dancer, Hemsley Winfield, organized the Negro Art Theater Dance Group. On April 29, 1931 the troupe of 18 dancers performed what was billed as the "First Negro Dance Concert" in America. Among the group's soloists was Edna Guy, who performed "A Figure From Angkor Vat" and choreographed movement for the spirituals "Weeping Mary" and "Git on Board Little Children." Their performance was called "the outstanding novelty of the dance season," and the "beginning of a Negro school of dancing," by a critic of the *New York Times.*

This important recital was followed by the 1934 all-Black production of the Gertrude Stein, Virgil Thompson opera, "Four Saints in Three Acts," with six dancers, including Mabel Hart. In 1934, Asadata Darora premiered his African dance drama *Kykunkor,* featuring Frances Atkins and Alma Sutton. Its impact was great: "It undoubtedly opened the door for the African American in the field of concert dance," noted

Emery. *Kykunkor* also proved that "Black dancers, working with material from their own heritage, could be successful on the American concert stage," and it demonstrated that dances done by Blacks could be seriously considered as an art form.[16]

The debut of the American Negro Ballet in 1937, under the direction of Eugene Von Grona, was another attempt to establish a major Black dance company to perform modern dance works or neoclassic dance compositions. Lavinia Williams and Mabel Hart were members of the troupe. Organized in 1934 by the German modern dancer, Von Grona, his ballet company used compositions by Duke Ellington, W.C. Handy, Stravinsky, and Bach, among others. Of the dance group, James Weldon Johnson noted that Von Grona was "defying the traditions that would limit the Negro's art to native or instinctive art, and this performance marks an epoch in the life of the American colored people and the dance." The group later appeared as a "Swing Ballet" in Lew Leslie's "Blackbirds of 1939" starring Lena Horne. But this dance troupe was before its time. Von Grona, unable to get bookings or find sponsorship, was forced to disband the company.

Because of her influence as a teacher as well as a dancer, the next three decades can be properly characterized as the Dunham Years.*

Dunham had just returned from the Caribbean where she had studied dance on a Rosenwald Fellowship. At the University of Chicago, she had established her own school of dance and studied under the anthropologist Melville Herskovits, who had influenced her decision to study dance in the Caribbean. It was during her study, cites Emery, that Dunham laid the foundations for the choreography that would elevate the status of the Black dance to a new level. It was Dunham who "opened the West Indies as an area for source material and was the leader in developing entertaining productions from the authentic ethnic material."

Katherine Dunham became the director for the Negro Unit of the Chicago branch of the Federal Theater Project in the latter thirties. She staged and choreographed its productions of *Emperor Jones* and *Run L'il Children*. She also presented her own dance entitled "l 'Ag' Ya," called by critic Hallie Flanagan a dance which "dealt with folk material from Martinique, shaping with authority the native grace of our Negro Dancers."[17]

---

*Two other dancers of primary importance beginning in the Forties were Belle Rosette and Pearl Primus, who also made similar contributions in terms of the African dance and dances which protested discrimination against Blacks. Because they were born outside of the United States, they do not fall under the purview of this study which is limited to American-born Black women.

In 1939 Dunham became dance director of the New York Labor Stage, where she choreographed the dances for the musical, *Pins and Needles*. With the money she earned, the choreographer supported her own troupe of nine dancers and managed to stage her own concert, *Tropics and Le Jazz Hot* in 1940 at the Windsor Theatre, New York City. The concert, subtitled *From Haiti to Harlem* was composed of dances characterized by critic John Martin as "beautifully racial" and "the nearest thing that has yet been shown hereabouts . . . of a true Negro dance art." *Tropics* established Katherine Dunham as an internationally known dancer.

Katherine Dunham - dancer
(photo courtesy of EBONY)

A year later she and her company appeared in the musical *Cabin in the Sky,* and subsequently, a number of foreign and Hollywood films of which *Stormy Weather* is the best known. In 1943, she and her company opened at the Martin Beck Theater in a production called

Tropical Revue, which received good critical notices. Comprising the troupe was a number of excellent dancers who would establish reputations in their right: Lavinia Williams, Lucille Ellis, and Sylvilla Fort. An interesting note regarding the *Revue* is that one of its numbers entitled "Rites of Passage," which was a religious ceremonial dance, was considered a bit too uninhibited for some of the critics, and was actually banned in Boston.

The Dunham company's next musical in 1945, *Carib Song*, was less successful, but one of Dunham's dances, "Shango," was considered one of her best choreographic efforts. In the same year, she opened the Dunham School of Dance in New York, its purpose being to encourage Black students and "to take our dance out of the burlesque—to make it a more dignified art." Sylvilla Fort became its supervising director, stressing what became known as the Dunham technique—" a combination of classical ballet with Central European, Caribbean and African elements."[18] Later Fort established her own school and taught at New York's Clark Center of the Performing Arts and at Teacher's College. Choreographing Langston Hughes' *Prodigal Son*, Fort developed her own technique which synthesized folklore and dance from Africa, the Caribbean and American Jazz.

Bal Negre staged in 1946 and including Lucille Ellis and Eartha Kitt in the performance, was regarded by many critics as Dunham's best revue to date, having "a new dignity . . . a new taste." Following the revue, the Dunham group went to Europe for two years. They returned to New York in 1950 after their triumphant seasons abroad. Dunham, living in Haiti for several years afterward, presented a new dance revue, *Bambouche*, which included dancers from Africa, among them the Royal Dancers of the Court of the King of Morocco, in 1962. A year later, she became the first choreographer to work at the Metropolitan Opera where she choreographed *Aida* for the 1963-64 season. In 1968, rather belatedly it seemed to many, she received the coveted *Dance Magazine* Award.

The contribution of Katherine Dunham to the dance is almost inestimable. Arthur Todd noted that she "put Negro dancing on the map once and for all" (at least in terms of its *white* acceptance). Harriet Jacobs observed that her choreography and costuming paved the way "for the acceptance of the Negro dancer as artist," while critic John Martin noted that Dunham unfolded "the true premises of the American Negro dance." Unquestionably one of Dunham's greatest contributions to the art was the number of performers that were influenced and/or taught by her. They include: Lucille Ellis, Eartha Kitt, Vanoye Aikens, Marlon Brando, Jean-Leon Destine, Sylvilla Fort,

Pearl Reynolds, Peter Gennaro, Talley Beatty, and Ruth Beckford.

One of the most prominent dancers of the group influenced by Dunham, and who went on to establish her own niche in the dance world, was Lavinia Williams (Yarborough). Williams was a dancer with the American Negro Ballet and appeared in the DeMille ballet "Obeah" with the American Ballet Theater before joining Dunham's company. Subsequently, she taught at the Dunham school and appeared in the musical *Show Boat*. Afterwards, Williams was invited by the Haitian Government to teach and develop their National Folklore Group. She became the director of Haiti's Theatre de Verdure and founded the Haitian Academy of Classic and Folklore Dance in 1954. Never returning to America to live, she continues her important contribution of shaping Haitian folk forms into theatrical entertainment without sacrificing the authenticity of their traditional dance culture.

The collective talent and determination of these Black women dancers broke down many barriers which circumscribed the potential of the performer on the concert stage; but up until the Fifties, it was felt by most of the dance establishment that Blacks were both tempermentally and physiologically incapable of the more "refined" modern dance and the ballet.

By 1951, however, two Black women would explode the remaining racist myths as they became the first soloists to dance in the major opera houses in New York. Janet Collins and Mary Hinkson opened the gates for the extraordinary dancers to come in both modern and ballet dance forms.

Collins, who received most of her training on the West Coast from Carmalita Maracci, Adolph Bolm, and Lester Horton, first received critical attention when she made her New York debut at the YMYWCA in 1949. There she performed two of her own compositions, a Mozart "Rondo" and two Black spirituals. Of her performance John Martin wrote that she displayed "a rich talent and a striking theatrical personality." The same year, Collins was named Debutante of the Year by *Dance* Magazine, which described her as "an extraordinary wisp of a woman who can move as though blown by the wind, who can range from the sensuously animal to the austere, from prankish humor to indefinable pathos." When she appeared in Cole Porter's *Out of This World* two years later, Arthur Pollack observed that she "dances with something of the speed of light, seeming to touch the floor only occasionally with affectionate feet . . . . That she could leave it and never touch it again seems easily possible. What she does with it and in the air immediately above it, is breathtaking."

Despite these acclamations, when Collins attempted to join the Ballet Russe, she was rejected on account of her color. However, the Metropolitan Opera Ballet Company found special parts for her to perform. She was the Ethiopian in *Aida*, danced the part of the gypsy in *Carmen*, led the Bacchanale in *Samson and Delilah* and was the leading dancer in *La Gioconda*. She became the first Black ballerina in the United States. Choreographing and touring with the Met, she had become its premiere danseuse by 1951—a position she would hold for four years. During the year Janet Collins was named Dance Debutant #1 in New York in 1949, the Joseph Richard's First Negro Classic Ballet, with ballerinas Bernice Harrison and Yvonne Miller, made an impressive debut in Hollywood, California.

Another renowned dancer, Mary Hinkson, was a student of Martha Graham and Louis Horst. She became a member of the Graham company in 1951, making it the first major company to accept Black dancers. Hinkson danced many of the Graham company's featured roles, including creations in *Canticle for Innocent Comedians, Seraphic Dialogue, Acrobats of God* and others. She took over Martha Graham's role as "The Awakener" in *Samson Agonistes* and created the title role for New York and London premieres of *Circe* in 1963. Her dancing, as described by Ernestine Stodell, is essentially lyrical and excelling in "roles which demand fluidity of motion and tensile strength such as *Circe* . . . which Miss Graham choreographed especially for her."

Other notable performances throughout Hinkson's career, included her creation of the only woman's role in Donald McKayle's *Rainbow 'Round My Shoulder* (1959) and the featured role in Balachine's *Figure in the Carpet* at the New York City Ballet (1960). She also danced with Alvin Ailey in Belafonte's *Sing, Man, Sing*. Like so many of the Black dancers before her, Hinkson's contributions as a teacher loom as great as those she made as a performer. She taught with the Graham company, the Juilliard School of Music, the School of the Performing Arts, and the Arthur Mitchell Dance Theater of Harlem. Making dance history with Hinkson was Matt Turney, a formidable Black woman, who also helped to set the standards in the Graham Company.

Following the trailblazing of Collins, Hinkson, and Turney, a number of dancers of significance emerged during the Fifties into the Sixties. The most prominent, listed by Joe Nash, included: Raven Wilkinson (who danced with the Ballets Russe), Yvonne McDowell, Delores Brown, Thelma Hill, Barbara Wright, and Helen Taitte. Yet it was Carmen DeLavllade, who, according to Nash, was "perhaps the most sought after dancer in history." Following Hinkson's tenure at the Met,

Carmen DeLavllade danced there during the 1955-56 season, when her greatest role was in *Aida*. She had received her early training with Lester Horton and became the leading soloist of the company. After Horton's death in 1953, she moved from Los Angeles to New York where her first important engagement was in the musical *House of Flowers* which played on Broadway in 1954. Subsequently she danced with the Capitol Ballet, and the companies of Goeffrey Holder and John Butler. (Later DeLavllade married Holder). In 1962, she joined Alvin Ailey's company as a featured dancer. It was also billed as the DeLavllade-Ailey American Dance Company. She danced concurrently with the New York City Opera Ballet (1962-65), where she created one of the few leading roles in Butler's *Carmina Burana*. She also performed with the Donald McKayle Dance company, creating the girl in *Reflections in the Park*. A guest artist with the Boston Ballet and the American Ballet Theater in 1965, she created the principal roles in the *Four Mary's* and the *Wife in Frail Quarry*.

DeLavllade is well known for her ability to be simultaneously, "sinuous and soft, all the while with great reserves of technical fire," notes Emery. "There are few such extraordinary dancers in any generation." Walter Terry observed that watching her move" ... with flowing gestures of arms and fingers or taking an arabesque-like stance in lyrical slow motion or cutting the air with eager leaps ... [she] seems to transcend mere form as she gives us the very radiance, subdued or brightly shining, of dance itself."

In 1966, Carmen DeLavllade received the *Dance* Magazine Award with the citation: "Beauteous symbol of today's total dancer, she conveys the sensuous pleasure of movement with simplicity, elegance and superb control."

Among DeLavllade's major contributions to dance was her encouragement and commitment toward a young, talented dancer who, after being "discovered" by Agnes DeMille in Philadelphia, made her New York debut in the American Ballet Theater's *Four Mary's* where DeLavllade was the principal. That dancer was Judith Jamison, destined to become one of the most extraordinary dancers in the history of the art.

It did not look that way for awhile, Jamison did not continue with the Ballet Theater. She became hopelessly depressed when she unsuccessfully auditioned for Donald McKayle, who was putting together a television special; however, an artist who had recently formed his own company, was watching Jamison's audition from the wings—on the advice of DeLavllade. Soon afterwards, the man, Alvin Ailey, asked Jamison to join his company. With Ailey, she performed in

Revelations, Phoebe Snow, and several other shows with the other dancers such as Lucinda Ransom, Loretta Abbott, and Takako Asakawa. When Ailey ran out of money, Jamison did a short stint with the Harkness Ballet, returning to Ailey once the disbanded company was reassembled. Soon afterwards, Ailey would create the vehicle for Jamison's meteoric rise in the dance world: "Cry" which was dedicated "For all Black women everywhere, especially our mothers."

"Cry," to be performed as a solo, was created with Jamison in mind. As Olga Maynard observed, "it was to Jamison what 'The Dying Swan' was to Pavlova." Of her performance, Maynard concluded that "Jamison is an intuitive dancer, generating agony and pity . . . . Even in a spontaneous gesture, she seems ritualistic because of her strangely heretical beauty. It is this spiritual element, more than her physical being that imports a mythic quality to her dancing. Of all living dancers, she may be the least in need of a partner, so profoundly is she Woman incarnate".[19] Besides other stunning roles with Ailey's company, including the "Parasol" part in the classic *Revelations,* Jamison has performed in a variety of dance forms. She danced in Bernstein's *Mass,* performed at the Met and even appeared in such obscure works as the "Legend of Joseph."

The latter ballet was conceived by Richard Strauss, and after its first appearance in 1914, was considered a White Elephant, eluding any success in its staging; that is, until Jamison and Kevin Haigen took on the leading role of the ballet at the Vienna State Opera. The two principals, observed critic D.M. Horst Koegler, decided the ballet's sensational success. Of Jamison's performance he noted: "Judith Jamison is like a Nubian Princess . . . . The aristocracy of her bearing is matched only by her passion. It's as if she were Othello's sister. She uses her endless arms and legs like a spider to ensnare Joseph. Later in the ballet, her newly found faith and self-confidence lend her a dignity which surrounds her like a halo."[20]

In 1972, Judith Jamison became the third Black woman to receive the *Dance* Magazine Award. Appropriately, it was presented to her by Katherine Dunham, who called her the Goddess and Priestess of dance and "one who embodies the oldest and most profound concept of Woman."

The Sixties and Seventies provided a rush of new Black dance talent in the form of companies and choreographers, as well as dancers. Perhaps the most important addition to contemporary dance was the formation of Arthur Mitchell's Dance Theater of Harlem in 1968, which not only permanently dispelled the lingering myth that Blacks could not successfully perform ballet, but debunked the myth that great dancers of the genre were limited to those who were trained at an early age. Important dancers that emerged out of Mitchell's company included the lyrical Lydia Abarca and the fiery grand Virginia Johnson, Laura Brown, Gayle McKinney, and Melva Murray White.

Other dance companies have been created and/or directed by Black women. Thelma Hill was instrumental in forming Ballet Americana, featuring the gifted Delores Brown from Philadelphia. The company appeared in Scotland and London as The New York Negro Ballet. It disbanded by 1959. The Philadelphia Dance Company (Philadanco), directed by Joan Meyers, featured such outstanding dancers as the lyrical and passionate Debora Chase. The Capitol Ballet Company, a regional company in Washington, D.C., opened its doors in 1961 under the direction of Claire Haywood and Doris Jones. Sandra Fortune was one of the company's most outstanding dancers. Another group, the Joan Miller Dance Players, also made its appearance during this period, as did the Sounds in Motion Company created by an emerging choreographer, Diane McIntyre. Glory Van Scott, whose *Sojourner Truth Suite* received critical acclaim, and Blondell Cummings are two more choreographers of note.

Of importance to dance history is Raven Wilkinson, who ranks with Dunham, Primus, and Collins. Wilkinson encountered many problems with the Ballets Russe de Monte Carlo, especially during tours in the South. She was the first Black ever to dance the purely classic roles in an international company. Also of importance is Jamie Bauer, a former Humphrey-Weidman trained dancer, who became a soloist with the Roland Petit Les Ballets De Paris in 1955. She represents the second Black modern dancer dancing on pointe in repertoire. Other dancers noted for high performance qualities include Carole Johnson (editor of the first Black dance newsletter *The Feet*), Diana Ramos (Her-Pomare Company), Carolyn Adams, distinguished soloist with the Paul Taylor Company. All these women contributed immensely to the Black dance aesthetic, and they maintained the standards of technique and performance established by the pioneers of the 1940's and 1950's.

One of the most significant dancers to emerge after Jamison is Sarah Yarborough (daughter of Lavinia Williams) who, in the late Sixties and Seventies, performed with the San Francisco Ballet, the Harkness Ballet, and the companies of Alvin Ailey and Donald McKayle. Her formidable technique brought a new dimension to Ailey's modern/jazz dance repertoire. Other upcoming dancers include Donna Wood, who is emerging as the major star of Ailey's group and has been performing "Cry"; Dyane Harvey and Anna Benna Sims.

Sarah Yarborough, dancer
with the Alvin Ailey Dance Theatre
(photo courtesy Johan Elbers)

As late as 1966, Mary Hinkson was quoted in *Dance* Magazine as saying " . . . . in one way the label 'Negro Dancer' is realistic. Society hasn't completely eliminated racial considerations. We will have to speak of the 'Negro Dancer' until people are finally considered only on the grounds of their talent and merit."[21] In this society people will probably always speak of the "Negro" or Black dancer. The hope is, of course, that the apellation will denote all of the rich traditions and heritage that Black dancers bring to the stage—like, for example, their Russian counterparts—without the term signifying preconceived limitations. But if, on the one hand, there will always be "the Black dancer," on the other hand, it cannot be denied that performers of Afro-American descent have proven themselves in so many different forms of dance, and so elevated the significance of Black dance that the form is rapidly being assimilated into the mainstream American experience. By the late Seventies, for example, a dance critic observed: "Just what is Black dance anyway? It is something all-Black companies do, but also something done by integrated companies. It is neo–classical ballet, disco, Cunningham variations, Afro-Caribbean rituals, pointedly political, pointedly abstract, and just plain entertainment."[22]

NOTES

[1] Houston Baker, Jr., *The Journey Back* (Chicago: University of Chicago Press, 1980), p. 2.

[2] Baker, p. 2.

[3] Ora Williams, *American BlackWomen* (Metuchen, New Jersey: Scarecrow Press, Inc., 1973), p. xvi.

[4] Lynne Fauley Emery, *Black Dance in the United States From 1619 to 1970* (Palo Alto: National Press Books, 1972), p. 191.

[5] Emery, p. 208.

[6] James Weldon Johnson, *Black Manhattan* (New York: Alfred A. Knopf, 1930), p. 107.

[7] Helen Armstead-Johnson, "Some Late Information on Some Early People," *Encore American and Worldwise News*, 23 June 1975, 4, 12, p. 52.

[8] Armstead-Johnson, p. 53.

[9] J. Johnson, p. 109.

[10] Langston Hughes and Milton Meltzer, *Black Magic* (New York: Bonanza Books, 1967), p. 92.

[11] Joseph Nash, "Dancing Many Drums," *National Scence Magazine*, SeptemberOctober, 1976, IV, p. 8.

[12] Jeanne Noble, *Beautiful Also Are the Souls of My Black Sisters* (New Jersey: Prentice-Hall, 1978), p. 238.

[13] Noble, p. 238.

[14] Armstead-Johnson, p. 53.

[15] Emery, p. 230.

[16] Emery, p. 251.

[17] Emery, p. 254.

[18] Emery, p. 258.

[19] Olga Maynard, "Judith Jamison," *Dance* Magazine, Vol. XIVI, No. 11, November 1972, p. 24.

[20] D.M. Horst Koegler, "John Neumeier's New Tour de Force: 'Legend of Joseph'," *Dance* Magazine, Vol. LI, No. 6, June 1977), p. 89.

[21] Harriet Jackson, "American Dancer, Negro," *Dance* Magazine, Vol. XXXX, No. 9, September 1966, p. 30.

[22] Linda Small, *"Black Dancers, Black Travelers,"* Dance Magazine, Vol. LIII, No. 10, October 1979, p. 78.

CHAPTER II
THEATER

The Pioneer Period: The African Grove

Although comedies and musicals dominated the productions of early Black theater, it should be remembered that the first Black dramatic company on record was The African Company, which specialized in Shakespearean plays and other classics. The African Company was located in a building called the African Grove at the corner of Bleeker and Mercer Streets in Greenwich Village, New York. Founded in 1821, the African Grove Theater highlighted Black minstrel entertainment that was popular as early as the mid-eighteenth century.

James Hewlett, the principal actor of the theater, starred in the company's production of *Othello, Richard the Third* and other classics, and Ira Aldridge, who later joined the troupe, was first inspired to act by seeing the productions at the Grove. Eventually, of course, he became the first internationally known Black tragedian when he played Othello opposite Edmund Kean's Iago in Europe.

Although it is not as well known, Black women too, were part of the casts at the Grove. On one of the old playbills, for example, a Miss Welsh is listed as playing the female parts in *Richard the Third*. On another occasion a Black woman played Desdemona in the Shakespearean play and performed two solo dances. Additionally, the Grove had an ensemble that performed some operatic and folk songs, as well as ballet dance programs.

During the Grove's heyday, New York City was already the theatrical capitol of the country, supporting four theaters, including the African Grove. The audience for the African company was primarily Black, reflecting the relative progressiveness of New York's Black community. Many had attended the African Free School, the city's first public education facility, which started in 1787.

The early decades of the 19th century was also a time when many whites, desirous of a theater to express their own folk values, openly showed their disdain for more sophisticated fare. Pretentious actors, in some cases, were physically removed from the stage and riots broke out. One can imagine, then, the problems a Black theater group doing the classics might have. During one of Aldridge's performances, for example, whites attending the African Grove's production of *Hamlet* interrupted a soliloquy of Aldridge to demand that he sing "Possum Up a Gum Tree." It was incidents like this one which forced the African Grove, as reported in the *National Advocate*, to have " . . . graciously made a partition at the back of the house for the accomodation of whites."

Eventually, the theater was forced to close because of the "inroad of whites coming for a lark and bringing disorder and wanton mischief . . . ." The Grove closed during the same time that the "Father of blackfaced minstrelsy," Jim Rice, became famous with his "Jump Jim Crow." Another seventy years (by 1898) would elapse before Blacks appeared on stage in New York City in a show produced, directed, and performed by themselves.

Background

Before and after the tenure of the African Theater, the Black character on the stage—whether actually played by a Black actor or not—was often stereotyped and ridiculed. As early as 1769 the play, *The Padlock*, caricatured a West Indian slave named Mungo. Other plays with Black characters attempted to justify slavery by showing the slave's capacity for violence, as in *The Fall of British Tyranny* (1776) which showed Black slaves agreeing to kill their masters after being freed; by stereotyping them as shuffling, cackling Negro servants as in *Triumphant Love* (1795); or as loyal slaves refusing freedom, as in the play *Guerilla* (1863).

Even abolitionist plays with good intentions stereotyped Black characters, including Black women. Particularly evident was the image of the "tragic mulatto." *Uncle Tom's Cabin* (1853), *The Octoroon* (1895), and New Yorker's *Strategem* (1792) all fall into this category. The first extant play by an Afro-American, *The Escape* or *A Leap for Freedom* (1858) by William Wells Brown, depicting the life of a fugitive slave, and J.C. Swayze's *Ossawatomie Brown* (1859), revealing Black characters involved in John Brown's raid, were notable exceptions.

After the Civil War the stereotypical images of Blacks in theater altered little. An early exception was *Fool's Errand* (1881) by Albion Tourgee, which sympathized with the newly emancipated slave. One of the more notable productions of the period occurred in 1877 when Emma Louise Hyers and her sister Anna Madah Hyers, famous concert singers, organized a company which produced a play called *Out of Bondage*, a four-act musical. In 1901 Black novelist Pauline Hopkins wrote of the production: "The introduction of this drama in which for the first time all characters were represented by colored people, marks an era of progress of the race. Never, until undertaken by these ladies, was it thought possible for Negroes to appear in legitimate drama." With the exception of the performances in the African Grove Theater, the 1877 revival of *Uncle Tom's Cabin* first seen in 1853, and the Hyers sisters subsequent productions of *The Underground Railroad* and *Princess Orelia of Madagascar*, Hopkins was accurate. Not until after the turn of the century would Blacks be seen *playing themselves* in legitimate theater.

Beginning in 1890, a number of Black musicals departed from the minstrel tradition, introduced authentic Black dance and music, and featured Black women on the "legitimate" stage for the first time. They were *The Creole Show* (1890), *The Octoroons* (1895), *Oriental America* (1896), *Clorindy—The Origin of the Cakewalk* (1898), *The Gold Bug* (1896), *The Sons of Ham* (1900), *In Dahomey* (1903), *In Abysinnia* (1906) and *Bandana Land* (1907). The shows introduced such Black female performers as Stella Wiley, Ada Overton Walker, Maggie Scott, Inez Clough, and Abbie Mitchell.

The Harlem Theater Movement

The first theater to produce plays in Harlem was the Crescent Theater located at 135th Street. Another theater in Harlem, the Lincoln Theater, produced one of the early Harlem plays, *The Odd Man's Boy* (1914), by Henry Cramer. The Lincoln also featured lowcost movies, which presented too much competition for the Crescent; therefore, managers of the Crescent leased the Lafayette Theater on 132nd Street and Seventh Avenue and hired two Black producers, Lester Walton and Eddie Hunter. In 1915 Walton and Hunter brought over a stock company from the Lincoln Theater to perform in the Lafayette. Under their aegis, Anita Bush, who was among the group, formed the Lafayette Players in 1915. Known as the "Little Mother of Black Theater," Bush had always dreamed of an opportunity to show that Blacks could be successful in straight drama. The players performed original dramas as well as their own versions of downtown hits. Such shows as *Madame X, On Trial, Dr. Jekyll and Perlmutter* were box office hits. The casts of these shows became just as famous to Harlemites as their white counterparts were downtown. Black female performers in the casts included Inez Clough, Ida Anderson, Evelyn Ellis, Lottie Grady, Laura Bowman, Susie Sutton, Cleo Desmond, Edna Thomas, Hilda Ottley, Evelyn Preer, and Abbie Mitchell. Although other stock companies were found in Dallas, Kansas City, Washington and Chicago, the Lafayette remained the most famous. It operated successfully for 17 years, producing 250 dramas, and introducing legitimate drama in 25 cities.[1]

Although any Black theater success should be noted that the Lafayette Theater's production of J. Leubrie Hill's *Darktown Follies* marked the beginning of the end of a very important era: a Black theater for Black audiences. Black actors and actresses, unlimited by familiar taboos, had experienced a new sense of freedom in the Lafayette Theater productions. In the *Follies*, for example, romantic scenes between Blacks were introduced, and Black actresses in particular were able to find a new sense of identity. As actress Ruby Dee noted of the performers in the all-Black troupe: "They had a chance to more fully express the depths of their talent."[2] *Follies* also began the white trek uptown which lasted for many years to come. The result was that Black performers began staging plays that could be successful downtown instead of continuing to play to all-Black audiences.

Debut Into the Dramatic Mainstream

In 1917, an important event occurred in Black theater history. James Weldon Johnson called it the most important in that it marked the beginning of a new era. In that year, three dramatic plays by Ridgely Torrence were performed by the Colored Players at the Garden Theater in Madison Square Garden. It was the first time, noted Johnson, that "Black actors in the dramatic theater [commanded] the serious attention of the critics and of the general press and public." The three plays were *The Rider of Dreams*, a comedy about Black rural life; *Granny Maumee*, a tragedy of the color-line, which contained a striking Vodun scene, and *Simon Cyrenian*, the story of the Black man, Simon, who was Jesus' cross-bearer. The women in the casts included Blanche Deas, Marie Jackson Stuart, Fannie Tarkington, Inez Clough, Lottie Grady, and Muriel Smith. A leading critic of the time, George Jean Nathan, cited Clough as giving a performance among the top ten of the year. In the midst of the Player's continued successful performances, however, the United States declared war on Germany, suspending theater activity.

During the aftermath of the War, came the flowering of Harlem Renaissance, a period when Blacks became more aware of their racial heritage. It was also a period when whites challenged European aesthetic values and expressed a new sense of American nationalism in their work. Included in this new focus on American life was the focus on Black life. Black folk material gave new life to American theater.

Alain Locke, author of the *New Negro* agreed with many theater devotees of the day that an integrated theater, using Black thematic material, would improve the quality of American theater. "The dramatic endowment of the race has not been completely stifled," he noted; the Black temperament "still moves natively and spontaneously in the world of make-believe with the primitive power of imaginative abandon and emotional conviction."[3] Although the "integrated" plays of the Renaissance period were only partially successful, the plays written by white authors, while not effectively utilizing the stuff of authentic Black culture, did at least provide the opportunities for talented Black actors and actresses to get experience in other than musical or comic roles. The independent Black efforts toward theater were not wholly successful either. The vital missing component in most instances was Black playwrights of high quality, who had had the opportunities to improve and learn their craft. Indeed, the opportunities had been few. Women of the period were active in all of the Black theater productions and were instrumental in maintaining Black theater groups. The groups, however, for the most part, usually disbanded either because of lack of resources, dissension within the group-or both.

Mainstream Theater

In 1919, Eugene O'Neill's *The Dreamy Kid* and Butler Davenport's Bramwell Players' *Justice* were produced at the Provincetown Playhouse and the East Twenty-Seventh Street Theater, respectively. The latter contained an important part played by Rose McClendon, one of the most important actresses of the period. A year later, O'Neill produced *The Emperor Jones*, starring Charles Gilpin. Though Gilpin received national notoriety for the part, neither this play nor the others were enthusiastically received by the Black community. It should be noted, however, that these plays were among the relative few that offered Black roles which were not comic figures. In 1921 *Shuffle Along* exploded on the scene, followed by a spate of musicals which introduced authentic dance and music for the first time since *Follies*.

In 1923, Evelyn Preer had a leading role in Oscar Wilde's *Salome*; and in the same year *Chip Woman's Fortune*, by Willis Richardson, was called the first serious play by a Black playwright. Preer as Salome received good press reviews as did others in the cast, including Laura Bowman. Richardson's play was so successful that it eventually went to Broadway. Both plays, plus an original interpretation of Shakespeare's *The Comedy of Errors*, were put on by the Ethiopian Art Players, organized by Raymond O'Neill and Mrs. Sherwood Anderson. In June of that year, the plays were staged at the Lafayette Theater.

Also in 1923, *Taboo*, a white-authored play about African Vodun, introduced Paul Robeson to the professional stage. Other plays, including *Roseanne* (1924), which featured Gilpin and McClendon, and *All God's Chillun Got Wings* by O'Neill, were less-than-successful attempts to depict Black life. The latter play was unmistakenly the most controversial in this genre. Starring Paul Robeson, it was about a Black intellectual who falls in love and marries a white woman "beneath his station." Although the press predicted a race riot on its opening night, it was produced without violence.

In 1925, the play *Appearance* was performed by a mixed cast. Authored by a Black playwright, Garland Anderson, it concerned the doctrines of Christian Science, and was produced at New York's Frolic Theater. Other "integrated" plays of the period included *Lulu Belle* (1926), produced at the Belasco Theater with a majority Black cast that included Black actresses Evelyn Preer and Edna Thomas; *Black Boy* (1937), based on the Richard Wright novel, in which Fredi Washington had a prominent part; *Deep River* (1926), which included the contralto Charlotte Murray and Rose McClendon. Ethel Barrymore remarked of McClendon's performance that it was "one of the most memorable, immortal moments in the theater." In 1926, *Abraham's Bosom* featured McClendon and Abbie Mitchell in important parts.

Black Community Theater

One of the primary goals of Blacks during the Renaissance period was the development of independent Black dramatic theater. Consequently, a number of theater groups and playwrights—a number of them women—emerged in the period. In 1920, the National Association for the Advancement of Colored People's drama committee presented Angelina Weld Grimke's three-act play, entitled *Rachel*. The play is of significance, Jean-Marie Miller, "as an early full-length Black authored protest piece."[4] It is also one of the earliest American plays to refute the negative Black image, using characters from the Black middle-class to protest vigorously against racism. Critic Arthur P. Davis called *Rachel* "the first successful stage drama written by a Negro."[5] Grimke is also the author of another full-length play, *Mara*, which concerns the plight of the southern Black woman and her powerlessness to shield herself from the sexual exploitation of white men.

In the latter part of the 1920's, W.E.B. DuBois organized the Krigwa Players via the NAACP and *Crisis* Magazine. Concerned that the folk play not be lost to total obscurity, he supported plays written and produced by Blacks. Two of the mainstays of this "Little Theater Movement" were Georgia Douglas Johnson and Eulalie Spence. The repertoire of the Krigwa players included Willis Richardson's *Compromise*, Georgia Douglass Johnson's *Broken Banjo and Blue Blood*, and Eulalie Spence's *Brothers and Sisters of the Church Council*. Another theatrical innovation during the period was the Harlem Experimental Theater, founded in 1928 by Regina Andrews, Gladys Reid, Inez Wilson, Jessie Fawcett, Dorothy Williams, Benjamin

Locke, and Harold Jackman. Its repertorie included *Plumes, No Count Boy, Prodigal Son,* and *Climbing Jacob's Ladder.*

By 1929 Adam Clayton Powell had become the driving force behind the Negro Art Theater, which included Laura Bowman in its production of *Wade in the Water.* Also in 1929, there were two other important theater events: the Dunbar Players offered Alice Brown's *Joint Owners of Spain* at St. Mark's Church, with Eulalie Spence as the director and Wallace Thurman's *Harlem* opened, featuring Isabell Washington and Inez Clough.

In the 1930's, the differences between Black and white theater became more pronounced. Whites, intentionally or not, reverted to Black caricature in such plays as *Green Pastures, Mighty Wind a Blowin',* and *Scarlet Sister Mary,* featuring Ethel Barrymore in blackface. At the same time, there was a renewed effort to provide major Black theater. This provision was personified by Rose McClendon and Dick Campbell, who formed the beginnings of the Negro People's Theater. McClendon, who was starring in Langston Hughes' controversial play *Mulatto* at the time, had been a significant force in theater for some time. The first production of the People's Theater was their version of Clifford Odet's *Waiting For Lefty* which played to a full house at the Rockland Palace in New York. Unfortunately, this was the last production of the group, for McClendon died soon after. Many of the players in the group subsequently joined the Negro unit of the Federal Theater.

Other local groups of the period offered productions at the Young Men's Christian Association, Saint Martin's Episcopal Church, and Saint Mark's Church. Richard Huey and actress-director Venezuela Jones had groups of their own. A stock company, the Harlem Players, reopened the doors of the Lafayette and presented two productions, *Sailor, Beware* and *Front Page.*

The Works Progress Administration

With the establishment of the Works Progress Administration's Federal Theater, Blacks were better able to participate fully in the theater process. Federal funds provided for Black involvement in many of the aspects of stage production, including writing, directing, producing and the more technical aspects. In New York, the Harlem Unit of the Works Progress Administration (WPA) produced such productions as Frank Wilson's *Walk Together Children,* and a Black version of *Macbeth* at the Lafayette Theater under the aegis of Orson Welles and John Houseman. Thomas had previously starred in the 1926 play, *Lula Belle,* and in the 1933 production, *Run, Little Children.*

Macbeth opened on April 14, 1936, and drew 59,271 patrons who saw it. Another group, Langston Hughes' Suitcase Theater, was also in full swing, producing the rousing experimental play, *Don't You Want to Be Free?*, with performers like Emma Jones, Mary Savage, and Gilbert Price.

During the latter part of the Thirties, Dick Campbell and Muriel Rahn organized one of the most ambitious Black theater groups to date: the Rose McClendon Players. Its purpose was to develop community theater aimed at creating a solid foundation for actors, playwrights, directors, and technicians. Profits from the productions, notes Loften Mitchell, paid for the teaching services of Theodore Komisarjevsky of the Moscow Art Theater. Librarians Jean Blackwell (Huston) and Carolyn G. Thorpe invited Campbell to use the basement of the Schomburg Collection in Harlem as an actor's workshop. The McClendon Players officially began in 1939 and presented plays by Sheldon Hale Bishop and Alain Locke. Other productions included *A Right Angle Triangle*, with Carol Wilson and Marjorie Strickland Greene, *Joy Exceeding Glory*, *On Striver's Row*, and *Booker T. Washington*. The Rose McClendon Players disbanded at the beginning of World War II, but its troupe included a number of performers who would later gain national reputations: Ruby Dee, Ossie Davis, Helen Martin, Frederick O'Neal and Jane White.

During the late Thirties, a number of Black women gave extraordinary performances in *Mamba's Daughters*, which played on Broadway. In the cast were Georgette Harvey, Fredi Washington, and Anne Wiggins Brown. The most important contribution of the play to the history of theater, however, was that it introduced Ethel Waters— who was already a successful singer and nightclub performer—to the theater stage.

One of the most exciting developments of the Forties was the establishment of the American Negro Theater (ANT). Formed in 1940, with Abram Hill as its playwright-director, its players included Ruby Dee, Harry Belafonte, Sidney Poitier, and a number of the former Rose McClendon players. Sheltered in the basement of the 135th Street Library in Harlem, the theater produced plays by Hill, Theodore Brown, and Owen Dodson, among others.

One of the Black theater's earliest female pioneers, Osceola Adams (Archer), was also involved with the ANT. In 1913, she had made her debut on the Howard Theater stage in Bulwer-Lytton's *Our Lady of Lyons*. At the American Negro Theater, Archer served as its acting coach and director. In 1946, she directed a touring company which presented the comedy *On Striver's Row*. Included in the cast were

Norma Wallen, Geneva Fitch, Doris Allen, and Leticia Toole. Archer was also a founder and actress of the Harlem Actors School, which was supported by WPA funds.

The American Negro Theater's most successful production was not one about Black life, but a comedy about a Polish family. *Anna Lucasta*, written by Philip Yordan and adopted for Black actors, Hilda Simms as Anna and also included actresses Alice Childress and Ruby Dee. It was such a hit in Harlem that it was taken to Broadway in 1944 and had a run of three years and 957 performances. Later it was made into a film starring Eartha Kitt. Unfortunately, the very success of the play contributed to the downfall of the American Negro Theater, according to Langston Hughes: "The group consciously began to aim its uptown productions at downtown consumption," he observed, "thereby losing its ethnic touch as well as its community audience."[6] The group soon disbanded. Since their appearance, Hughes further concluded, "there has been nothing like it in Harlem for the development of either actors or playwrights."

Other notable shows in the Forties included *Cabin in the Sky*, starring Ethel Waters, and *Carmen Jones*, with Muriel Smith and Muriel Rahn alternating in the leading roles. Of Rahn's performance, the *New York Times* observed that "She brings a personal dignity and sincerity to the part, and her singing is not only accurate and full-bodied, but charged with dramatic cogency. Miss Rahn's Cora is the core of the piece, its fire and conscience." In 1945, Lillian Smith's *Strange Fruit* introduced Jane White to the theater public, and Countee Cullen and Arna Bontemp's *St. Louis Woman* featured an award-winning performance by Pearl Bailey. Deloris Martin in *Finian's Rainbow*, Annabelle Hill in *Kiss Me Kate*, and Juanita Hall's award-winning performance as Bloody Mary in *South Pacific* were highlights of the period. The Forties was also the decade when concert dance came into fullswing. Katherine Dunham's *Bal Negre* and *Carib Song* were presented on Broadway as was *Showboat*. In 1948, the American Negro Theater presented *Sojourner Truth* by May Miller. Other actress of note during this period included Eulabelle Moore in *Male Animal*, Evelyn Davis in *Southern Exposure*, and Rosetta LeNoire in *Four Twelves are Forty-Eight*.

On Broadway, Estelle Hemsley played a leading role in the critically acclaimed *Take A Giant Step* in 1953 and Jane White in Caribbean writer Edgar Mittelholzer's *Shadows Move Among Them*. Ellen Holly played the "colored girl" in Alan Paton's *Too Late the Phalarope*, a drama about apartheid in South Africa. Beah Richards added an important dimension as the grandmother in the revival of *Take A Giant*

Step; and a new trend was begun in the theater at the Greenwich Mews when Hilda Haynes was cast as a Jewish mother in *Monday's Heroes*. Also in 1953, Ruby Dee appeared in the hit play *The World of Sholom Aleichem*, a story about the noted Jewish writer, and Vinie Burrows was seen in Joshua Logan's *The Wisteria Trees*. In 1957 Loften Mitchell's *A Land Beyond the River* featured Diana Sands and Helen Martin, and in the following year, Lena Horne's career was resuscitated by her performance in *Jamaica*, for which she won the Drama Critics Poll.

Two of the most important theater events of the Fifties were the Ethel Waters performance in *Member of the Wedding* by Carson McCullers and the emergence of the first significant Black female playwright—Alice Childress. *Member of the Wedding* was the season's winner of the Drama Critics Circle Award for the Best Play-of-the-Year. In it, Ethel Waters got star-billing over Julie Harris and Brandon deWilde. In her role of Bernice, observed Langston Hughes, Ethel Waters brought "a surprising new power to the dramatic stage. She gave an additional human dimension to the conventional 'Mammy' of old—one of both dignity and gentleness—that endeared her to theatergoers without the use on stage of the handkerchief head dialect and broad humor of former days. In her portrayals of illiterate Negro mothers of the South," Hughes continued, "Ethel Waters was a mistress of the 'laughter through tears technique' which she brought to perfection as Bernice."[7]

The Fifties also brought about the birth of The Council of the Harlem Theater. It consisted of four Black drama groups, and it was formed to support other local groups, to prevent scheduling conflicts of the production of plays, and to agitate for those plays which were an accurate reflection of Black life. Among the productions that benefitted from the Council was a play entitled *Just a Little Simple*, Alice Childress' adaptation of Langston Hughes' *Simple Speaks His Mind*.

The Trailblazers

Until the 1950's, with some exceptions in the smaller community theaters, Black women had yet to break into any other aspect of the theater than acting. Even in that milieu there were few roles that were authentic enough or had the potential for the kind of pathos that can catapult an actress to acclaim-especially from her own community. One major reason for this, of course, was that there were reams of good plays written by Black women which had never been produced. However, with the advent of Alice Childress as the first Black female playwright of national significance, things began to change for the better. Childress was followed by Lorraine Hansberry—who was followed by a new Black theater movement which created a number of Black plays, Black women playwrights and even a few directors as well.

Throughout this period, musicals continued ad infinitum, some would say ad nauseum, but they, too, expanded the roles of women, providing them effective vehicles for careers in other fields as well. Primarily known as an actress at the time, Childress' adaptation of Hughes *Simple* was a successful one. "In a highly skillful manner she used Jess Simple as the master-of-ceremonies in a Harlem variety show,"[8] observed Loften Mitchell. The same evening that Alice Childress presented her adaptation of Langston Hughes' play, she included her own one-act theater piece entitled *Florence*, a play about a mother who, on her way to New York to "save" her daughter from a theater career, is confronted with a hypocritical white actress and decides to stay home and encourage her daughter to persevere.

Two years later Childress wrote *Gold Thru the Trees*, a musical revue which paralleled the struggle of American Blacks to those in South Africa. In 1955, she produced her *Trouble in Mind* which deals with a Black actress who refuses to play the stereotypical role in a play dealing with a Black lynching in the South. *Trouble* won an Obie Award for the best off-Broadway production of the 1955-56 season. The play, first seen at the Greenwich Mews Theater, was the first major work by Childress produced outside of Harlem and the first work by a Black woman playwright produced off-Broadway. Childress had already earned a great deal of respect for her acting in *Anna Lucasta*, *The Candy Story* and the *Emperer's Clothes*; but now, "the professional theater saw her outside her native Harlem, writing with swift stabs of humor, her perception and her consummate dramatic gifts," noted Mitchell.[9] Yet, Childress represents a major dramatic figure rarely produced. "There is a tragedy involved here, commented Ruby Dee, that can't be underestimated. Alice Childress is a splendid playwright, a veteran, indeed a pioneer. She has won awards, acclaim, and everything but consistent productions."

Dee's observations were never more true than with Childress' prize-winning play, *The Wedding Band*, which was produced first in 1966 at the University of Michigan and featured Dee, Abbey Lincoln, and Clarice Taylor. The play takes place in South Carolina in 1918 against the backdrop of the First World War. Its central focus is a domestic conflict about an interracial love affair between a white man and a Black woman. *Wedding Band* was not produced in New York, however, until 1972, despite its good reviews when it first appeared. Two years later, it was nationally televised. "It is difficult to think of a play by a Black writer earning the reviews that *Wedding Band* earned in 1967 and then having to wait until 1973 to reach the New York stage," concluded Dee.

Alice Childress - playwright
(photo courtesy of Afro-American Studies
Dartmouth College)

Born in Charleston, South Carolina, Alice Childress was a member of the American Negro Theater of Harlem for ten years. From 1956–58 she was a weekly columnist for the Afro-American newspapers. Her other works include *The World on a Hill*, a white woman's view of West Indian life (1968); *Wine in the Wilderness* (televised) in which a snobbish artist discovers that an "uncultured" Black woman is the true wine in the wilderness for the revolution (1969); *String*, in which the credibility of an aging man is questioned when he is accused of stealing (1969); *The Freedom Drum*, a story about the Montgomery Bus strike (1970); *Mojo*, reminiscences of a Black couple about the past (1970); *When the Rattlesnake Sounds*, a play about Harriet Tubman (1975);

and *A Hero Ain't Nothin' But Sandwich*, a story about a young drug addict (1977).

Ruby Dee, who played the lead in *Wedding Band* and received the Drama Desk Award for her performance, is herself a trailblazer. She served her apprenticeship with the American Negro Theater, and received some recognition for her Broadway role in *Anna Lucasta* and in the 1953 hit play *The World of Sholom Aleichem*. Dee also appeared in several films, including the *Jackie Robinson Story*. Subsequently she was a collaborator with Julian Mayfield in his film, *Uptight*.

In 1971 Dee had another award-winning performance as the lead in *Boesman and Lena*, a compelling play by Anthol Fugard about apartheid in South Africa. In the same year she was acclaimed for her performance in the Harry Belafonte production of *Buck and the Preacher*. She and her husband, Ossie Davis, are well-known for their reading appearances and national radio show. Unmistakenly the turning point in her career—as it was for a number of Black performers—was her role in the Black play that made theater history: *A Raisin in the Sun*.

The production of *A Raisin in the Sun* in 1959 was perhaps the most important event in the history of modern Black theater. Its lists of "firsts" alone are significant: it was the first play written by a Black woman to be produced on Broadway; it was the first Broadway play to be directed by an Afro-American (Lloyd Richards) in over half a century; it was the first Black play to receive the coveted New York Drama Critics Award—which it won over entries by Tennessee Williams, Eugene O'Neil, and Archibald MacLeish.

The significance of the play transcends these "firsts," however. The success of *A Raisin in the Sun* reflected the deep changes that were occurring in the society. "Whereas it had taken perhaps 150 years to get society where O'Neill could make his protagonist Black, and a further 30 years to crack the separate but equal hypocrisy, now, within months and often from day-to-day, the pattern visibly changed. Audiences stood ready to welcome and understand 'inside' problems, characters, little people, performing in a world of other little people...."[10] This new "readiness" on the part of the audience was justified for the characters within the play—Beneatha, Walter Lee, Lena, and Ruth Younger—provided them with authentic, intimate portraits, and though some are more important to the play than others, all are drawn carefully and are substantial entities of and by themselves.

A Raisin in the Sun is still the seminal play of this generation. It contains humor and the essential American themes of upward mobility and a young girl's search for identity. More importantly, it has yet to be surpassed in its characterization of the Black mother who symbolizes the family strength, tradition, and discipline that transcend generations. Played effectively by Claudia McNeil, the portrait struck the death knell of the "Mammy" stereotype and made those images heralded earlier seem hollow and anachronistic. Finally, the play is important because it anticipated the themes that would be so prevalent in the coming generation. For the first time in a mainstream production since the Harlem Renaissance, the Black American links with Africa, and the strength of the Black family and racial pride are explored.

Lorraine Hansberry - playwright
(photo courtesy of EBONY)

Hansberry's second Broadway play, *The Sign in Sidney Brustein's Window*, was dismissed by many Black, and white critics alike. Most of the characters are white, and totally unlike her first play, this play depends on the philosophical dialogue for its substance. Although it was ahead of its time it is an important expression of Hansberry's deepest personal philosophy, for the point of the play is her persistent belief in the worth of the human spirit and thus the affirmation of the meaningfulness of life despite the prevailing existential concepts of absurdity, "nothingness," and fatalism. The play received mixed reviews, condemning it to an early death on Broadway. And, Hansberry herself was dying of cancer. In a spontaneous gesture the actors and other distinguished members of the literary and theatrical world fought to keep it open. They did until January 12, 1965, when Lorraine Hansberry died at the age of 34. Martin Luther King, Jr. said of Hansberry: "Her commitment and spirit . . . her creative literary ability and her profound grasp of the deep social issues confronting the world today . . . will remain an inspiration to generations yet unborn."[11] Testaments to his words are found in Hansberry's posthumus publications: *To Be Young, Gifted and Black*, a compilation of her writings; *Les Blancs*, about revolution in Africa; and *The Drinking Gourd*, a drama about slavery.

The brilliant characterizations of *Raisin in the Sun* also provided important vehicles for some of the most important performers in Black theater and film history. Sidney Poitier played the role of Walter Lee, making his theater debut, but the play also catapulted into the public eye one of the most important Black female stars, Diana Sands. Diana Sands had first come to the attention of the critics in her role in George Bernard Shaw's Off-Broadway *Major Barbara* in 1954. Her performance as Beneatha in Hansberry's play thrust her into the spotlight and won her the Outer Circle Award for the best supporting actress. In the same year, 1959, she was selected by the critics of *Variety* as Broadway's most promising actress.

Perhaps her most outstanding scene in *Raisin in the Sun* is the one in which Beneatha (Sands) is slapped by Mama for denying the existence of God. When Sands screamed out "in comic-pathetic rage that there was no God," observed critic Donald Bogle, "she revealed herself as a magnetic compelling actress."

But her significance goes beyond these accolades as Bogle also notes. Diana Sands offered an entirely new theater persona for the Black woman on the stage, and was an important pioneer. She "ushered in the contemporary, untyped intelligent Black woman. She was neither mammy nor mulatto."[12]

Sands continued this new image through her perfection of her craft, a penchant for which she was well known. Following her appearance in Hansberry's play, she returned to Broadway in *Tiger, Tiger, Burning Bright* in 1962 and also had leading roles in James Baldwin's *Blues for*

Mr. Charlie (1964) and *The Owl and the Pussycat.* Sands also paved the way for Black actresses to appear in the "classics" in the modern era. She played the leading roles in *Macbeth, Caesar and Cleopatra, Phaedra, Antony and Cleopatra* and *Saint Joan.* Subsequently she played leading roles in the films, *The Landlord,* and *Georgia, Georgia* based on a work by Maya Angelou.

But at the height of her career, Diana Sands too was smitten with terminal cancer. She died on September 21, 1973.

The next important Black female playwright to appear on the theater scene was Adrienne Kennedy whose play, *Funnyhouse of the Negro* (1963), featuring actress Ellen Holly, won the Obie Award for the season. No play could be more different from *Raisin in the Sun* than this one; however, Kennedy has found herself largely ignored and victimized by the same syndrome that Hansberry suffered as a playwright. Aishah Rahman observed that both were punished for refusing to stay in their "dramatic place." She further notes that despite Kennedy's Obie, she "remains largely unrecognized—one suspects because she dared to venture into formal realms where only white male playwrights are really welcome. Critics who otherwise worship Pinter and Ionesco have labelled Kennedy's work 'too personalized or too abstract'."[13] Kennedy's other plays include: *A Beast Story* (1969); *Evening With Dead Essex* (1973); *Lesson in a Dead Language* (1968); *The Owl Answers* (1969); *A Rat's Mass* (1971); and *Sun* (1969).

An important recent trailblazer is one of the first successful Black female theater directors Vinette Carroll, who despite her parents wishes that she find more "legitimate" work, chose theater. Although she was a Ph.D. psychology candidate at Columbia University, the "siren-call" of the theater was too attractive. Her first professional debut as an actress was in *Caesar and Cleopatra* in 1956, followed by *Tambourines to Glory, Prodigal Son* and others. She directed Hughes' *Black Nativity,* the Spoleto Festival of Two Worlds in 1963, Loften Mitchell's *Harlem Homecoming, The Flies* in 1966, and *Desire Under the Elms* in 1974. Always known in theater circles, she became especially popular when she was the director of the Unit Actors Studio and the associate director of the Inner City Repertory Theater. Her greatest successes as a director came when she became head of the Urban Arts Corps, a funded inner-city theater program. From this program came such plays as *Don't Bother Me I Can't Cope* and *Your Arms Too Short To Box With God.* Founded by Carroll in 1967 and sponsored by the New York State Council of the Arts, it serves as a showcase for minority performers. Additionally, Carroll has won an Emmy and an Obie Award, and most recently her production of *When*

Hell Freezes Over I'll Skate was produced as a National Education Television Great Performance.

Overview of Modern Black Theater

The Black theater movement which began in the Sixties ushered in a new era of theater for and by Afro-Americans. A number of the plays produced in this period—particularly those of Imamu Baraka and Sonya Sanchez—was highly political. The most frequent theme in the plays was the exposure of Black urban street life. Perhaps understandably, Black theater, having the first opportunity to do so, appeared very much to revert to the naturalistic realism of the Richard Wright era.

This new Black theater movement hastened significant developments. There were more grass roots participation and a proliferation of regional theaters and workshops throughout the country. Notable examples include the Washington, D.C. Repertory Theater, the Free Southern Theater, and Val Gray Ward's Kuumba Workshop in Chicago. In addition, several traditional theater institutions were revitalized such as the Karamu Theater in Cleveland—which has a long history of Black theater, and New York's Henry Street Settlement theater, directed by Woodie King.

New major theaters which showcased Black plays also appeared in the sixties, among them the Negro Ensemble Company and the New Lafayette Theater. New organizations also sprang to life like the Black Theater Alliance (BTA), which sought to coordinate activities of Black theater life. The director of the BTA was Joan Sandler. A number of Black women also formed their own companies. Barbara Ann Teer created the National Black Theater; Hazel Bryant, the Afro-American Total Theater; Ellen Stewart, La Mama; Yvonne Madison, the Brownsville Laboratory Theater; and Muriel Cherry, the Soul and Latin Theater.

The sixties and seventies also introduced a number of new Black women playwrights, including J.E. Franklin, Barbara Molette, Marti Evans Charles, and Ntozake Shange. In addition, more women became known for their performances behind the curtain. Among them, Shaneuille Perry, who directed many of the plays for the Negro Ensemble Company, has become one of the most important persons in the theater today. Novella Nelson also made her directing debut and was a producer at Joseph Papp's Public Theater in New York, as was Glenda Dickerson at the National Washington Theater. In the technical end of the theater, Sandra Ross and Shirley Pendergast made their specialty lighting; and Edna Watson and Judy Dearing Parks, costuming. Ross received the Audelco Award for costume and general excellence in 1971. On the managerial side, in addition to Joan Sandler, Horacena Taylor and Helaine Head are noted theater managers.

The Black theater movement also had an impact in mainstream theater. However, Jean Genet's *The Blacks*, in 1960, pre-dated the movement as such. It boasted of a long list of notable stars, among them Maya Angelou, Abbey Lincoln, and Cicely Tyson. In the 1960's and 1970's Black actresses also had greater opportunities to perform in non-Black plays and in musicals which featured Black music and dance, and Blacks formed their own organizations to promote interest in the theater. One of the most significant was the creation of the Audelco Awards, founded by Vivian Robinson, Renee Chenoweth, and Doris Smith.

Also during the Sixties and Seventies, Black women performed on stage "outside of" the Black theatre movement. Diahann Carroll led the period's bonanza of award-winning performances of women when she received the Tony Award for her role in the Broadway musical, *No Strings*.

Black theatre musicals garnered awards for Black women including Melba Moore, who won the Drama Desk Award for Ossie Davis' *Purlie* (1960-70) and Leslie Uggams who received the Tony Award for *Hallelujah Baby!* (1967-68). Three years later, Linda Hopkins in *Inner City* and Jonelle Allen in *Two Gentleman of Verona* received the Drama Desk Award. Virginia Capers and Ernestine Jackson won the Perry and Theater World Awards in 1971 and 1973, respectively, for their performances in *Raisin*, a musical version of Hansberry's play.

The early seventies was also the period when the talented composer and lyricist Micki Grant won the Drama Desk Award for her compositions in Vinnette Carroll's *Don't Bother Me I Can't Cope*. She also was the collaborator of J.E. Franklin's 1974 musical *Prodigal Daughter*. In that same season, Lola Falana received the Theater World Award for *Dr. Jazz;* and Dee Dee Bridgwater, the Tony, for her performance in *The Wiz*. Although Stephanie Mills did not win an award for her performance in *The Wiz*, she deserves full recognition in this volume because of her artistic talents and accomplishments. Born in 1959 in Brooklyn, New York, she was a child star, singing and acting since she was 10 years old. Mills, a recording artist for the Motown label, is the winner of seven Tony awards for her stage appearances. Delores Hall, for her performance in *Your Arms Too Short To Box With God*, won the Tony Award in the following season. And in the 1975-76 season, Vivian Reed won the Drama Desk Award for *Bubbling Brown Sugar*, a musical which had a successful run of Broadway.

Stephanie Mills - recording artist and popular singer
(photo courtesy of EBONY)

The sixties and seventies were also years for non-traditional
"musicials." One of these was Melvin Van Peebles' *Ain't Supposed to
Die A Natural Death*, whose scene of action was the urban ghetto.
Actress Beatrice Winde received the Theater World Award for her
performance in the play. On the other end of the musical scale, two
Black women led theater grops which utilized music as the basic means
of theatrical expression. Barbara Ann Teer's National Black Theater
used African drums, dance, skits, and chants in its 1972 production of
A Revival: Change! Love! Organiza! Also, Hazel Bryant's Afro–
American Total Theater produced *Makin' It, Attica, Trick or Truth,*
and *Black Circles,* among others.

Other highlights of the period in non-traditional theater were Vinie
Burrows one-woman shows, including *Walk Together Children* (1968),
using African folktales, myths, and legends. In a similar vein, Linda
Goss is currently one of the leading griots, dramatizing authentic Afro-
American and African folktales.

A number of Black dramatic actresses also received a number of
awards in this era, affirming their reputations as talented performers. In
the 1960-61 season, Vinnette Carroll received an Obie for her
performance in *Moon on a Rainbow Shaw!* One of the most heralded
actresses in the decade was Gloria Foster, who received the Obie
Award for her roles in *In White America* (1963-64 season) and *Medea*

Vinie Burrows - Broadway actress and feminist,
speaking at Women's International Conference
in Copenhagen, Denmark in 1980

Vinie Burrows - actress and advocate of women's
rights, at the University of Amager
in Copenhagen, Denmark

(1965-66). For her latter performance, *The New York Times* observed, "*Medea* springs to passionate stage life because of the soaring performance of Gloria Foster." The talented actress was also highly acclaimed for her appearance in the productions, *The Cherry Orchard* and *Sister Sonjie.*

The following season saw the extraordinary performance of Beah Richards in James Baldwin's *Amen Corner*, for which she received a Theater World Award. She also had memorable performances in several films, including *Hurry Sundown*. Seret Scott and Barbara Montgomery won the Drama Desk Award for *My Sister My Sister* (1973-74) and Loretta Greene (*The Sirens*, 1973-74), Marlene Warfield (*The Great White Hope*, 1968-69), were acclaimed with Obie's for their performances.

One of the leading female playwrights of the period was J.E. Franklin, who received the Drama Desk Award for her play *Black Girl* (also made into a film) in the 1971-72 season. The director for the theater production was Shaneuille Perry, one of the leading Black female directors in the theater. Perry received the Audelco Award in 1976, and has also directed a number of other Black plays, including *Jamima* by Black playwright Marti Evans Charles, and the Negro Ensemble's award-winning production of *Sty of the Blind Pig*. Another Black woman who emerged as a director during the period was Glenda Dickerson, who is also a playwright. Her *Jesus Christ—Lawd Today* premiered at the Black American Theater Company in Washington, D.C. in 1971.

Other playwrights who made their debut in the period include Barbara Molette (*Rosalee Pritchett*); Sonia Sanchez (*The Bronx is Next*), Pearl Lomax (*We Don't Need No Music*), and Carol Freeman (*The Suicide*).

This era of the Black woman in the theater ended with a dramatic note: the award-winning production of *For Colored Girls Who Have Considered Suicide When the Rainbow is Not Enough* by Ntozake Shange. The controversial play laid bare the inner turmoil of modern Black women in an age when their relationships with their men are being reexamined. It is a feminist play, performed as a choreopoem and often devastating in its impact. The work was sometimes haunting, sometimes tragic, often humorous, and perhaps the most talked about theater event since *Raisin in the Sun*. Critics called the Broadway production a "compelling" city of "pain, anger, defiance, scorn, and finally anguish," a "howling protest" that "fills a vacuum until now undescribed in literature" and "a gripping celebration of the pain, dignity, and the triumph of Black women in their quest for identity."

The significance of Shange's work was that it introduced a new persona of the Black woman on the stage. Although other character types of Black women were introduced in this period, few transcended the "new" images, which resembled Carmen Jones with a gun in her hand. But *Colored Girls* is not just a play about Black women; it is a play from a Black woman's perspective. It was the first play that reflected the new Black woman's sensibility prevalent in the novels of Toni Morrison and Alice Walker. It broke away from the standard fare of the matriarchal image, or the subordinate-to-your-man image and thus will assuredly affect Black plays which come after it.

NOTES

[1] Francesca Thompson, "Final Curtain for Anita Bush," *Black World,* Vol. XXIII, No. 9, July 1974, p. 60.

[2] Lindsay Patterson, ed., *Anthology of the American Negro in the Theater* (New York: Publishers Company, Incorporated, 1970), p. 134.

[3] Arthur P. Davis, *From the Dark Tower* (Washington: Howard University Press, 1974), p. 58.

[4] Jean-Marie Miller, "Angelina Weld Grimke: Playwright and Poet," *CLA Journal,* Vol. XXI, No. 4, June 1978, p. 514.

[5] Davis, p. 58.

[6] Langston Hughes and Milton Meltzer, *Black Magic* (New York: Bonanza Books, 1967), p. 125.

[7] Hughes and Meltzer, p. 198.

[8] Loften Mitchell, *Black Drama* (New York: Hawthorn Books, Inc., 1967), p. 146.

[9] Mitchell, p. 169.

[10] C.W.E. Bigsby, ed., *The Black American Writer*, Vol. II: *Poetry Drama*, (Florida: Everett Edwards, Incorporated, 1969), p. 158.

[11] Davis, p. 203.

[12] Donald Bogle, *Toms, Coons, Mulattoes, Mammies, and Bucks* (New York: Viking Press, 1973), p. 198.

[13] Aishah Rahman, "To be Black, Female, and a Playwright," *Freedomways*, Vol. 19, No. 4, 1979, p. 257.

CHAPTER III
MUSIC

Roots: First Musicians

The Africans who were brought to America, beginning in the 17th century, came primarily from the West Coast of Africa. They came from such countries now known as Senegal, Guinea, Gambia, Sierra Leone, Ivory Coast, Ghana, Togo, Benin, Nigeria, Cameroon, Gabon and parts of the Congo. Although the culture in these countries were not monolithic, they did share an important element in common: the significance of music in their culture.

The African influence on American culture, therefore, is most perceptible in the realm of music. It is the synthesis of the African and European musical styles that created the most distinct American art form. Black women played an important role in the shaping of music in America, both in the popular and traditional modes which used African music as its base and in European music. In every category Blacks, especially Black women, brought their own history and ancestral memories to bear on the euphony of America.

At the beginning of their sojourn here, the Africans unfamiliar with the English custom or language while at the same time confronted with the shock of slavery, expressed themselves most prevalently through the language of music. One of the most poignant documents of early resistance on the part of slaves was recorded in Boston in 1639. In that year, a visitor of a slaveholder recounted the protest of a Black woman slave who had been a queen in her own country and now found herself being forced to cohabitate with another Black to breed slaves. Wrote the observer:

> The second of October, (1639) about 9 of the clock in the morning Mr. Maverick's Negro woman came to my chamber window, and in her own Country language and tune sang her very loud and shrill, going out to her, she used a great deal of respect towards me, and willingly would have expressed her grief in English . . . .

America: Of Drums, Hymns, and Syncopation

In the early colonial period the rich musical culture of the Africans was circumscribed and reshaped to become a part of that of the early white pioneers, who had little more than their psalm books. Most of the music in the early colonial society was vocal and sung in the meeting-house, the church or the home. Even in the church, the first permanent organ was not brought to the New England colonies until 1714. Blacks attended churches with the whites, though they were confined to segregated pews. They sang the slow-moving psalms of worship along with the colonists, and often shared in the singing of church-related events like weddings.

Another kind of prominent music in the early colonies was that used for the social dances that took place there. Blacks were often called upon to play for these events, the most common instrument used for them being the fiddle. Very early in the history of the country therefore, there was a tradition of Black musicians playing for social dances of whites; and there are numerous accounts of Blacks who were known as good "fiddlers." A rich source of those accounts is the occasional newspaper advertisements of runaways identified by their proficiency for playing the fiddle and other instruments.

Black musicians were also utilized for playing the martial music in the colonies. During the Revolutionary War, for example, the Virginia Act of 1776 stated that Blacks "shall be employed as drummers, fifes or pioneers." In the North, Blacks also had the opportunity to play their music for their own celebrations. In the New England colonies for example, an important holiday was Election Day, where Blacks elected their own "Governors" who were, in many cases, proxies for white authority. Election Day was celebrated with parades in which slaves marched in their finest apparel to the music of fifes, fiddles, "clarinets" and drums. These Election Day celebrations began in Connecticut in 1750 and continued through the late 1850's.

As early as 1821, Blacks in New York established the African Grove Theater which put on Shakespearean plays and offered musical and dance selections. A playbill from the theater showed that it offered operas, overtures by three-piece ensembles, sentimental ballads, folk and comic songs. Black women were also included in many of its productions.

The most prominent—and traditional—celebration of Northern slaves was the Pinkster Day celebrations which took place on Pentecost Sunday. Pinkster day originated with the Dutch of New Netherlands and was later adopted in parts of Pennsylvania and Maryland. The celebration sometimes lasted as long as a week after Pentecost and was taken over by the Blacks completely, who aggregated on the appointed day and danced and sang in the African tradition. The event became quite a spectacle, characterized by James Fenimore Cooper as "the great Saturnalia of New York Blacks." The center of the Pinster ritual was the African dance, and "the principal music a drum made from a wooden eel-pot with a cleanly dressed sheepskin drawn tightly over its wide end." Vocal sounds and handclapping for the dances were provided by the women who were not taking part in the dances. This and other minor slave festivals, as

well as the storytelling and singing of Black women helped keep
*African culture alive in America.

Another music tradition developed in the Black church. In 1787, two
Methodist ministers, Richard Allen and Absalom Jones of Philadelphia,
broke away from the white Methodist Church because of its
discriminatory practices. Allen ceased all affiliation with the white
church structure, formed the African Free Society in that year, and in
1974, opened the doors of the Mother Bethel African Methodist
Episcopal Church. One of the most important of Allen's innovations
was the substitution of his own hymnal for the standard Methodist text.
The new hymnal was tailored to his all-Black congregation and included
several of the Isaac Watts hymns, which were favorites of Blacks, a
number of folk songs and even some of Allen's own hymns. The hymnal
contained church songs which were lively and texts particularly
meaningful to Blacks.

The evolvement of African-American music in the South was shaped
by the very different circumstances of Blacks living there. There was
little emphasis on Christianizing the slave, who was often isolated on
the plantations and beyond the reach of missionaries. With the larger
number of slaves in the South consigned to harsh labor and treatment,
there was fear that conversion of the slaves would lead to further
obstinence on their part. "As for baptising the Indians and Negroes,"
wrote the Reverend Hugh Jones in his book on Virginia, Maryland, and
North Carolina, "several of the people disapprove of it; because they
say it often makes them proud and not as good servants." Whites
"disapproved" the practice of Christianity by Blacks to the point of
barring free Black ministers from preaching to them. Of course, these
prohibitions did not stop Christian worship by the southern slaves, but
it did result in their creation of rituals to maintain many of their original
Africanisms, as reflected in their music which engendered antiphonal
singing, spirituals, and African rhythms that inspired "possession."

In the more formal religious services of the slaves, they followed the
traditional agenda of having the designated slave preacher read psalms
followed by congregational singing.* The preacher was often the song
leader in these services. Long-meter and common-meter hymns were
common, notes music historian Elieen Southern, and sometimes the
leader was an older woman. Such a woman would have the traditional

---

*African culture was also very much alive because of the music, singing, and dancing in
Congo Square, New Orleans.

---

*The practice of "lining out" is a feature of hymn singing in Black churches.

role of caring for the children during the hours the parents worked and teaching them the prayers and hymns. Following the standard service there was often the "Ring Shout," African in its origin, in which men and women clapped their hands, sang in loud monotonous tones, and engaged in the traditional ring-circle dance, trying to induce possession. Religious dances that sought to induce possession differed from the more social forms of dance.

Most of the music played by the slaves was done so for festive occasions under the watchful eyes of the planters. On the larger plantations, these occasions included weddings, pre-Lenten and Christmas celebrations and social dances. Again, slave musicians used fiddles and the percussion was rendered by clapping, stamping, and using instruments such as jaw-bones. Fiddlers were especially in great demand and were often hired out to other plantations or dances in the towns. The other dominant form of music on the plantations was the work songs.

Each plantation had its own repertory of work songs which were special to each kind of work. One example was the corn song which was sung at corn shucking time. On many plantations, observed Southern, there was one slave or more whose responsibility was to supply songs for the annual jubilees. On the Hungerford plantation, this designee was a young girl by the name of Clotilda who provided the "jingling rhymes" as well as the melodies for the songs. The association of music with work was a tradition as old as Africa. Out of it came the field hollers which were derived from the West African whoop, shout, or cry. What distinguished it from other sounds was the "blue note" produced by a "twisting of the voice with an abrupt breaking off at a higher pitch."[2] It would be later transcribed into Blues and Jazz.

Outside of the Southern plantations the greatest opportunities for Black musicians in the region were the cities of Charleston and New Orleans. In the first half of the 18th century, Charleston, a port of entry for many of the Europeans—including musicians—was "the musical center of the Eastern seaboard," according to Southern. The first performance of an opera there took place in 1735. There was a number of Black musicians in Charleston employed to play at the dances and even the overtures in the theaters. It was New Orleans, however, that became the epitome of musical expression by the 19th century.

New Orleans boasted as many as three opera companies playing at the same time. There were concerts, brass band parades, the Mardi Gras, and especially Congo Square. Although African dancing was confined to the daylight hours on Sundays, New Orleans was one of the few places in the South where such activities took place after the Stono Rebellion. Each group of Blacks who took part in the Congo festivities had its own orchestra, consisting of drums, banjoes (made from gourds), jawbones, and rattles. The women, as was traditional, took part in the singing and dancing, which continued throughout the day, and at times reached such a crescendo that the dancers would fall, fainting to the ground. When the dances were finally banned in the 19th century, the Congo musicians, along with others, went "underground," to the clubs and taverns. In the New Orleans taverns, musicians danced to and played their fiddles, flutes, clarinets, triangles, tambourines, and drums to the nascent music which would be identified in later years as Jazz—the only classical music indigenous to America.

Unusual in New Orleans, too, were the slave orchestras which were made up of small ensembles playing for the parties in town and on the nearby plantations. Out of the unique Creole culture emerged the elegant Quadroon Balls —attended by free Creole women and well-to-do white men. Ironically, the orchestras which played for the quadrilles and other similar dances were composed of Creole men, and many of the musicians who played for the dance orchestras at night could be seen parading the streets during the day. These Black musicians had a special penchant for brass bands and took their music seriously. They were known to study music with the players associated with the French opera house and city orchestras. Some even studied in Paris.

Vocal music was also an important part of Black life. There was a separate section reserved for free Negroes and slaves in the opera houses. Many visitors to New Orleans, according to Southern, were shocked to hear slaves singing operatic arias in the streets. Blacks also participated in the concert music of the city. As early as the 1830's they formed the Negro Philharmonic Society, which had over a hundred members and presented concerts and visiting artists in performance.

The Trailblazers

By the 19th century the northern city of Philadelphia was also providing opportunities ofr Black musicians, especially among the relatively high number of well-to-do Blacks. In 1841 an anonymous monograph entitled *Sketches of the Higher Classes of Colored Society in Philadelphia* noted the pursuit of knowledge by the Black middle class and the establishment of the Philadelphia Library of Colored Persons in 1833. The library was the first of its kind. It served as a book repository and sponsored concerts, lectures and debates. The author also noted that music was a prominent part of Black Philadelphians' amusement and that the young women were expected to be able to exhibit some musical skill as a sign of their upbringing. It is little wonder then, that the first Black woman musician to gain national and international recognition would have emerged in Philadelphia.

Elizabeth Greenfield was born a slave in Natchez, Mississippi in 1809 but was adopted by a Quaker who brought her to Philadelphia as a child. Despite the Quaker religion's prohibitions against music, Greenfield's considerable talents, which also included her ability to play the harp and guitar were encouraged. After the death of her adopted mother, she decided to travel to Buffalo to seek her fortunes there. While she was on board the ship heading for her destination, a wealthy white woman heard her sing and was so impressed that she became her patron. Upon reaching Buffalo, Greenfield was invited to give a series of concerts by the Buffalo Musical Association, launching her career. The *Buffalo Express* called her the "African Nightingale" and favorably compared her to Jenny Lind. A newspaper in New York commented on her appearance and forebearance: "She is a person of ladylike manners, elegant form and not unpleasing though decidedly African features and her marvelous powers, she owes none to any tincture of European blood." On another occasion in 1852, a notice from the *Toronto Globel* described her vocal powers: " . . . The amazing power of the voice, the flexibility and the ease of the execution took the hearers by surprise . . . . The higher passages of the air were given with clearness and fullness, indicating a soprano voice of great power . . . . It is said that she can strike thirty-one full, clear notes; and we could readily believe it."

Greenfield, who also played the piano, was talented enough to be invited to Europe. After a benefit concert in Buffalo and in New York before an audience of 4,000, Greenfield toured England in 1853. There she met Stow, who introduced her to the Duchesses of Sutherland and Argyle, and they in turn sponsored several of her appearances there; but the highlight of her career was a command performance before Queen Victoria at Buckingham Palace in 1854. A year later, she gave a benefit concert for Mary Ann Shadd, a Black abolitionist. Eventually, she retired to Philadelphia and opened a voice studio where she worked until her death in 1876.

Elizabeth Greenfield, known as the "Black Swan," was not the only one to make a musical contribution to the antislavery struggle. In fact, music was a significant part of the Black quest for freedom. After the 1830's, abolitionist societies grew more militant, became more interracial, and later both men and women worked together within them. A typical antislavery meeting during this period included songs that inspired and underlined the common determination of the freedom fighters. Sojourner Truth, for example, was well known for her speaking ability, as well as the original songs which she sang at the meetings. William Wells Brown collected the most popular songs in a book entitled *The Anti-Slavery Harp*. Other singers who performed for the abolitionist cause was the well-known Luca family, a troupe which consisted of the father, mother and two sons. They were especially popular in New England, and conducted successful tours throughout the North. In 1853, the Luca's performed at a meeting of the Anti-Slavery Society of New York. In the mid-1850's, they teamed up with the Hutchinson family, who were popular white antislavery singers.

Despite the abolitionist effort, a number of laws in the 1850's entrenched slavery rather than mitigated it. The Fugitive Slave Law, the repeal of the Missouri Compromise, and the Dred Scott decision, reaffirmed the abolitionists' resolve to aid runaway slaves. They had aided fugitives for a very long time. Now they would organize the northbound routes and provide pre-determined stations along the way. The system was called the Underground Railroad, and through it hundreds upon hundreds of slaves followed the North Star to freedom. Slaves preparing for escape often sang songs with a *double entendre* as a means of communication and inspiration. Frederick Douglass, for example, remembers singing "I am Bound for Canaan" while plotting his escape. To the unknowing, Canaan was Heaven, but to the slaves it had another meaning as well: "The North was our Canaan," observed Douglass.

The great heroine of the Underground Railroad was Harriet Tubman who made numerous trips across the Mason Dixon line and personally escorted hundreds of slaves to freedom. The signal for Tubman's presence was a song:

Dark and thorny is de pathway Where de Pilgrim makes his ways; But beyond dis vale of sorrow Lie de fields of endless days.[3]

When the slaves heard this song, Southern notes, whether they actually saw Tubman or not, they made preparations to head toward "Canaan." Other spirituals with a double meaning also served this purpose, including *Bound to Go, Steal Away to Jesus,* and *Swing Low, Sweet Chariot.*

Despite the efforts of the slaves and abolitionists, it took the Civil War to loosen their chains. Blacks participated in the war in every capacity, including providing much of the martial music and the singing in the contraband camps. After the Emancipation Proclamation, a number of spirituals like *No More Auction Block for Me, Babylon is Fallen* and *Before I'd be a Slave* became popular. Other new songs reflected the lives of Blacks during Reconstruction, a period of violence, unemployment and new restrictions on their freedom. Additionally, the prison song was born in this era, and there were new songs about work on the levees and the railroad.

After the Civil War, the new sense of freedom that Blacks shared engendered a number of musical developments. In the South, itinerant musicians played music with a new syncopated rhythm in the honky–tonks that mushroomed. The music was called rag-time, but it would not be until near the turn of the century when white pianists copied it and Black musicians reauthenticated it, that it would become popular throughout the country. Another important development of the period was the renaissance of the spiritual. Of course, this form of music, cited by Alain Locke as "the most characteristic product of the race genius," was not new.

After the War

During the post-Civil War period, there developed an interest in the Negro Spiritual as never before. In 1867, the first collection of Negro Spirituals was published, *Slave Songs of the United States* by William Allen, Charles Ware and Lucy McKim Garrison, but it would take some young Black college students to present the profound beauty of the spirituals to the world. They attended Fisk University, which was established a year before the publication of the first collection of spirituals. Fisk's musical director, George White, encouraged the choir to sing spirituals as well as other songs. His desire to have the students sing outside of the campus and the need for the school to raise funds, resulted in the decision for the students to sing spirituals, first in nearby towns, and eventually throughout the country. In those days, observes Eileen Southern, "This was not a decision lightly made; the students were not minstrel singers, their program included no jokes, no dances, no catchy tunes. The American public had not yet heard the religious music of the slaves and had given no indication that it was ready to hear it."[4] Still, White set out on October 6, 1871, with eleven singers, "a skillful young Negro pianist" named Ella Shephard, and a teacher–chaperon, Miss Wells. They called themselves the Jubilee Singers.

The event that catapulted them to fame was the World Peace Jubilee in 1872. The Fisk Jubilee singers were to sing the refrain of the "Battle Hymn of the Republic," while the verses were sung by a local Black singing group. When the orchestra began the song on too high a pitch level, the opening lines were disastrous, but the Jubilee Singers took this cue to sing out strongly and, with their well-trained voices, easily reached the high notes. Marsh gives an account of the episode in his book, *The Story of the Jubilee Singers* (1880): "Every word . . . rang through the great Coliseum as if sounded out of a trumpet. The great audience was carried away with a whirlwind of delight . . . . Men threw their hats in the air and the coliseum rang with cheers and shouts of 'The Jubilees! The Jubilees Forever' . . ."[5]

The Jubilee Singers took Black folk music to places where it had not been heard before. They were invited to sing before the crowned heads of Europe, and audiences in Germany, Switzerland, and Great Britian. Within seven years, the singers raised $150,000, much of which was used to erect a new building named Jubilee Hall. In 1872, the Hampton Singers of Virginia embarked on a similar program.

Only one of the original group of Jubilee Singers as far as is known, reached the concert stage. She was Patti Malone, who was selected by Frederick Loudin when he formed his group that traveled throughout the world in concert for eighteen years. After the group disbanded, Patti Malone remained in Europe, changing her name to Desire Plato, and continued to sing on the concert stage.

While the Jubilee Singers were popularizing the traditional music of the Afro-American, a duet called the Hyers Sisters was demonstrating the Blacks' interpretations of European music. The two sisters, Anna Madah Hyers and Emma Louise Hyers, first won critical acclaim at their debut in Sacramento, California in 1867. Over 800 people heard the striking soprano and contralto voices of these young girls. Two years later, a Boston critic wrote of their performance.

> They are aged sixteen and fourteen years, and, after a casual inspection, may be called musical prodigies. They are, without a doubt, destined to occupy a high position in the musical world.
>
> Anna sings not only alto, but tenor, and both with great excellence. They sang "Ah fors' e lui" from *Traviata*, "M'appari" from *Martha*, and the "Miserere" from *Trovatore*, each with remarkable clearness and accuracy, and surprised all with the general skill they displayed. Anna also has the faculty of reaching E-flat above the staff. Judging from the present data, they are on a par vocally with our better concert singers; and a further hearing may place them in rank with more pretentious vocalists.[6]

The Hyers sisters made history again in 1877 when they organized a company which produced a musical called *Out of Bondage*, a four-act musical comedy written for them by Joseph Bradford of Boston, one of the first Black efforts of legitimate theater. Later the sisters sang at the Salt Lake City Theater in 1871, toured the East with concerts in New York and Boston and had a successful Western tour in 1877-78. At a Peace Jubilee Concert, they received 13 encores after a program. At the end of their career, M.A. Majors in *Noted Negro Women* remarked that they "have traveled around the world, sang before the crowned heads of Europe and become a household word in the musical circles of the United States."

Although it was still premature for the acceptance of bonafide Black opera singers, Blacks' interest in this field was steadily growing. As early as 1872 the Colored American Opera Company was established in Washington, D.C. The three women in the nine-person troupe, often singled out in the press for their performances, were Agnes Gray Smallwood, soprano, and Lena Miller and Mary Cookley, contraltoes. Black musical societies were also established in Cincinnati, San Francisco, Boston, and New York, among other cities.

Probably the most talented concert artist emerging during this period was Marie Selika, called by James Weldon Johnson "the first colored singer with both the natural voice and the necessary training and cultivation . . . ."[7] Madame Selika (in private life, Mrs. Sampson Williams) toured the United States and abroad during the 1880's, winning the praise of the critics for the "surprising sweetness and extraordinary compass" of her coloratura soprano voice. When she sang in Paris, the critic of Le Figaro wrote:

> Madame Selika sang in great style. She has a very strong voice, of depth and compass, rising with perfect ease from C to C, and she trills like a feathered songster. Her range is marvelous and her execution and style of rendition show perfect cultivation. Her Echo Song cannot be surpassed. It was beyond any criticism. It was an artistic triumph.[8]

Proficient in German, French, and Italian, she took her stage name from the heroine of Meyerbeer's opera, L'Africaine. She visited Europe with her husband who was an aspiring baritone singer, known as Viloski. Madame Selika managed to have an extraordinary career as noted by Majors:

> Madame Selika has been on the stage 17 years, during which time she has travelled five years in Europe, has sung before the Czar of Russia, an her many triumphs abroad have won for her such fame as no other Negro woman of her time can boast. By special invitation she has sung for President Hayes, and on more than a dozen occasions where thronged by thousands of the lovers of her sweet intonation, she has been universally pronounced "the greatest colored singer of the globe." . . . Her rightful position as an accomplished singer is by the side of Jenny Lind, Parodi, Nilsson, Patti and Elizabeth Greenfield.[9]

Flora Batson, born in Washington, D.C., was also popular. Brought to Providence, Rhode Island at the age of nine, she became a member of the then famous Bethel Church Choir of that city. There she attracted hundreds of people to the church to hear her sing. During her successful career, she appeared at Steinway Hall, New York; the Academy of Music, Philadelphia; and the largest music halls of the Eastern cities. Batson was called by the New York World, "the colored Jenny Lind."

On the basis of Flora Batson's press reviews, one can understand

Majors' comment that "probably no American singer has been more strongly endorsed by the press." The *Portland Oregonian* for example, commented that "The press of the country, from the Atlantic to the Pacific, unite in crowning her the greatest singer of her race, and worthy to rank among the great singers of the world." Another comment in the *Boston Transcript* underscores one of the several motivations Blacks had in entering the entertainment field: "Flora Batson, with her wonderful voice, has a divine mission to aid in breaking down the stubborn walls of prejudice, which must sooner or later give way in our Nation's progress toward a higher civilization."[10] Batson toured throughout the United States, Europe, Africa, Australia, and New Zealand.

During this era, there was also a number of Black female pianists who gained reputations. Rachel Washington, a pianist/organist from New England, was the first Black to receive a diploma from the New England Conservatory in Boston.[11] She was active as a music teacher and choir director and occasionally performed in recitals. Fannie Howard, born 1885 and the wife of Joseph Douglass, son of Frederick Douglass, was a pianist who studied at the Oberlin Conservatory and occasionally accompanied her husband on his concert tours. The era also witnessed the emergence of accomplished singers. Among them were Anita Patti Brown, a gifted soprano, who had concert engagements in the United States, the Caribbean, South America and England; and Rachel Washington, who sang at Hammerstein's Theater in New York City and subsequently went to Europe where she won the notice of Madame Marchesi, the famous voice teacher. While abroad, Washington sang in command performances for the Queen of Spain, the Duchess of Albany, and the Princess of Saxe-Coburg.

Black Music Comes of Age

On the other end of the musical spectrum, there were exciting innovations occurring in the theater. The old minstrel form, with its plantation stereotypes and Stephen Foster imitations of Black music, was quickly fading by the end of the 19th century. Two important developments would come to the theater as a result: authentic Black music, assimilating all of its various forms, would be heard on the stage; and Black women, previously barred from the theater stage, would have another avenue other than the vaudeville to exhibit their musical potential. Sixteen such well-costumed and attractive women appeared for the first time in Sam T. Jack's *Creole Show* in 1890.

Five years later, women appeared not only in the chorus but as principals in John W. Isham's *The Octoroons*. In 1896 the same producer departed further from the minstrel tradition by substituting a finale of arias for the traditional chorus march. Maggie Scott and Inez Clough sang solo choruses from *Faust*, *Martha*, *Rigolette*, and *Carmen*. *Oriental America* was the first Black show to be presented on Broadway proper and the first to make a definitive break from the burlesque, according to James Weldon Johnson.

Sissieretta Joyner Jones,
International opera star of the 1800's
(photo courtesy Schomburg Center,
New York Public Library)

The innovations in Black musical theater created a vehicle for one of the most remarkable singers of the era, Sissieretta (Joyner) Jones. A trained singer who had studied at the New England Conservatory of Music, Jones quickly acquired a reputation for her performances. In 1888, she made her public debut in New York City, and in July of that year, toured the Caribbean where she was showered with gifts and rave reviews. She made concert appearances, singing sentimental ballads and operatic pieces in the United States, Europe and Canada—including a command performance for the Prince of Wales. In 1892, she was summoned by President Harrison to sing at the White House; and in the same year, her appearance at Madison Square Garden's "Grand African Jubilee", was such a spectacular success that she was seriously considered by the managers of the Metropolitan Opera House to play in its productions of *Aida* and *L'Africaine*. That however never materialized—it was still early for a Black prima donna. Still, the critics raved over her. The January 8, 1883 issue of the *Chicago Tribune* said of her singing: the "tones in the lower and middle registers [are] of surpassing beauty, and those of the upper are remarkable for their clear, bell-like quality." The review continued, noting that whether she sang arias, ballads—comic or sentimental—there was a plaintiveness in her voice, "that no amount of schooling or training could eradicate...." Not that she wanted it eradicated, for that plaintiveness was a reflection of "the blues note" passed from generation to generation of Black musicians. In addition to her singing ability, Johnson observed, she also had "the physical figure, the grand air, and the engaging personality" required of a star.

American critics soon dubbed Jones "Black Patti," after the Italian prima donna Adelina Patti; however, Jones disclaimed any comparison to the Italian, feeling that the name carried with it a sense of condescension. In 1896, the year of *Oriental America*, brilliant songwriter Bob Cole was engaged to compose the music for a travelling show called "Black Patti and the Troubadors." It was an eclectic program, including acrobats, dancers, singers, vaudeville and minstrelsy, with Jones as the main drawing card. She made no other concessions, however, to vaudeville, for as Margaret Just Butcher observed, she disassociated herself from the rest of the show. For her part, she sang operatic arias which were eventually a separate entity of the show called "the operatic kaleidescope." In this part of the show, the scenery, costumes and action centered around such operas as *Lucia, Il Trovatore, Martha*, and *El Capitain*. The Troubadours played for seventeen years, traveling to Mexico, Cuba, the West Indies and South America. Additionally, as Johnson notes, it was one of the few big Black shows to play successfully in the South.

Around the turn of the century there occurred a significant new trend that had a great impact on the Black musician. Led by musicians such as Antonin Dvorak, director of the National Conservatory in New York, there developed a new emphasis on the native forms of American music. Dvorak used Black musical elements, including the spiritual, in his work, spearheading the emergence of a school of "nationalistic composers," among them Harry Burleigh, Clarence Cameron White, Nathaniel Dett, John Wesley Work, Sr., and Will

Marion Cook. The brilliant possibilities of orchestrating Black music found their way into the theater primarily through Cook. These possibilities were further explored with Black female performers expressing their potential as dancers and as singers on the theater stage. In 1898, Cook's *A Trip to Coontown*, with its distinct plot and consistent story line was the first show to break completely from the minstrel pattern. Not uncoincidently it was also the first show to be organized, produced and managed entirely by Blacks. In the same year Cook's music in *Clorindy: The Origin of the Cakewalk* was the first demonstration of the possibility of Black syncopated music. As such, the musical was ahead of its time, observed Butcher, and "hinted at the symphonic development of Negro syncopation and harmony which was not to be achieved fully for another ten or fifteen years."

Subsequently, Cook created the less successful *Jes Lak White Folks*, whose chief claim to fame was the introduction of Abbie Mitchell, who would later become famous both in the theater and as a singer. This production was followed by the *Sons of Ham*, the *Gold Bug*, *In Dahomey* and *In Abyssinia*, starring Bert Williams and George Walker. Equally engaging was the female star of these shows, Ada Overton (Walker). She represented the best of Black female performers of the time. Overton had great dancing ability, style and a deep sense of racial pride. She was also an excellent singer who, according to Tom Fletcher, could sing ragtime as well as ballads with equal effectiveness. Cook later teamed up with J. Rosamund Johnson (co-writer with J. W. Johnson of "Lift Every Voice and Sing") to do such musicals as *The Shoofly Regiment* and *The Red Moon*, which were true operettas according to James Weldon Johnson.

About the same time in 1905, the first modern jazz band made its debut in New York. Described by Johnson as a "playing-singing-dancing orchestra," the group called themselves the Memphis Players and eventually toured throughout the United States and Europe. The "singing" parts were performed by Abbie Mitchell, making her one of the first modern jazz singers. Ida Forsyne was the dancing part. At their debut, the wondrous sounds of the harmony of the different streams of Black music were heard. The orchestra was dominated by banjos, mandolins, guitars, saxophones, and drums in combination. There was also a violin, a couple of brass instruments and a double bass, which established the first time that musicians *played* one part like the melody, while *singing* another, such as the alto. The Players introduced "the dancing conductor," and the "trick trap drummer." Seven years later, James Europe's Clef-Club musicians staged a concert in which 125 instrumentalists played cellos, double-basses, cornets, saxophones, clarinets, trombones, drums, banjos and mandolins against a background of 10 upright pianos. In 1913, the Lafayette production of *Darktown Follies* incorporated the syncopation beat into the theater, and its hit song "Rock Me in the Cradle of Love", sung lovingly by the tenor to the play's soubrette introduced explicit romance on the Black stage.

The musical theater would not truly light up again until *Shuffle Along* in 1921, which was the first show to introduce authentic ragtime and jazz dancing on Broadway. Not only did it produce enduring hits like "I'm Just Wild About Harry" and "Love Will Find a Way"—it produced brilliant stars like Florence Mills, whose style was described by the *New York World* as going ". . . from molten notes . . . into jazz slides and minors that somehow make music."

The Blues

There was another side to the gay, rhythmic music that drove dancing feet and shaking bodies to stardom. It was a music, born in the South, which made its way steadily up the Mississippi River to New York and other cities north of the great divide. It was melancholy but not passive. It was the expression of the side of Black life that whites never saw or cared about. It expressed the feelings of the people crowded in the tenements of despair. It was the despair of northern promises unkept, of the uncomprehending forces that drive lovers apart; it was the plaintive race memory that had been passed in the blood from the days of the Middle Passage. It was the blues.

No one knows when the musical form of the blues really started. The earliest notation of the blues, as a state of mind, was recorded in Charlotte Forten's journal, written in 1862, when she was on Edisto Island in South Carolina. The free-born aristocrat had come there to teach the first group of freedmen after the outbreak of the Civil War. After a particularly bad evening there, she wrote that "I came home with the blues." LeRoi Jones (Imamu Baraka), on the other hand, theorizes that the blues as a musical form was born when Blacks lost the hope of ever returning to their country and began to try and reconcile their stolen lives with America—in other words when Africans became Afro-Americans. This realization, according to Jones, shaped the 12-bar phrases and three-line stanzas, expressed in AAB form, and using the "blue note"—a flattening of the third and seventh notes of the scale in any key.

W.C. Handy, a popularizer of this musical form, heard the blues as early as the late 1800's. His "Memphis Blues" and "St. Louis Blues", written in 1912, were instrumental in popularizing the form.

Before then, Gertrude Pridgett (Ma) Rainey was singing the Blues in a tent show called the "Bunch of Blackberries" at the Opera House in her hometown of Columbus, Georgia. Rainey, who said she first heard the blues sung by a young girl in Missouri, incorporated the music in her own shows and claims to have given it its name.

One of the most celebrated vehicles for Blues singers was the Rabbit Food Minstrels, organized by F.S. Woolcott, who hailed from Mississippi. The stage of the traveling "Foots" usually consisted of boards on a folding frame with gasoline mantle lamps as footlights. There were no microphones, and those whose voices were not strong enough used megaphones. Most of the "Classic" blues singers of note served their apprenticeship in these tent shows which traveled, as Oliver notes, from Florida to Fort Worth, from North Carolina to New Orleans and from Missouri to Mexico.

Among the first prominent and best known singers on the circuit was Ida Cox, "with her hard and nasal voice" that sang in one key. She was greatly admired throughout the South and eventually formed her own traveling show, called "Raisin' Cane", which continued for many years.

But it was Rainey with her superior voice who was considered the Mother of the Blues. Born in 1886, she also toured with the Rabbit Foot Minstrels. She met her husband, John Rainey, when he came to town in a traveling show and married him when she was eighteen. They worked some years together under the name of "The Assassinators of the Blues." Ma was as colorful as her lyrics, with her gold-toothed grin, flashy clothes, headband, and her necklace of twenty-dollar gold pieces. Paul Oliver described Ma Rainey's voice as a deep contralto and her singing as that with great power and feeling, "in broad impressive sweeps of sound." Even her most boistrous songs, he noted, had a melancholic tincture to them and her low-downess had no rival on the tent shows.[12] She used the jug bands, kazoos and barrelhouse pianists, and wrote most of the songs herself. They were songs described by Oliver as boistrous but with a melancholy mood underlying them, lowdown and meaningful. Among her repertoire of songs were "Bo–Weavil Blues" and "Counting the Blues."

Ma Rainey, who also sang with the C.W. Parks' and Al Gaines' Minstrels before she formed her own troupe, became well-known throughout the South, however, she did not record her first record until 1923, and cut her last recording in 1928. By 1934 she had retired from the road and bought two theaters as an investment. She died quietly in her home five years later.

Rainey had a tremendous impact on the development of the blues.

She provided the link to the urban blues which swept over the North beginning in 1920, although she disdained the latter's sophistry, instrumentation or audience. Many tried to imitate her, but she had no rivals—with the exception of Bessie Smith. It is said that of the two, Rainey was the greater mistress of an audience, that no one could "work" her audience like she did, but Smith was the better singer. Rainey credited herself with influencing Bessie Smith after hearing Smith sing in Chattanooga and taking the younger singer into the Rainey show. Smith always denied the story, saying instead that her main influence was a little known singer, Cora Fisher. In any case, if Rainey was the Mother of the Blues, Smith soon became its Empress.

Born in 1898, in Chattanooga, Tennessee, Smith was orphaned at a young age in that city's poverty-torn tenements, and left home to join her brother who was performing in a minstrel show. She made her first appearance at the age of nine at the Ivory Theater. The next decade she spent with the Rabbit Foot Minstrels and the Florida Cotton Blossoms and in dives and tent shows along the Gulf Coast. It was in Selma, Alabama in 1917, where Frank Walker of Columbia Records "discovered" her working in a gin mill, and Smith subsequently came to New York to record her first record in 1923.

Bessie Smith was not the first classic blues singer to record her song. That distinction belongs to another Smith—Mamie—in 1920, when the director of Okeh records was convinced to record her in the place of the ailing Sophie Tucker. Mamie Smith's "Crazy Blues" sold 75,000 records a month, with record producers discovering for the first time the rich vein of the "race record" market. In quick succession Lucille Hegamin, Lillyn Brown, Edith Wilson and Alberta Hunter cut records for different companies, but it was not until Bessie Smith recorded a composition of Alberta Hunter's, one of the few women blues composers at the time—named "Down-Hearted Blues" in February of 1923 that the great potential of the race market was revealed. In six months, Smith's recording sold over 780,000 copies. At the height of the blues era, the classic women singers were selling 5 million records a year. The figure is even more extraordinary in view of the fact that the records were purchased, for the most part, by poor Blacks and cost $.75 a piece—an inflated figure for those days.

That the blues was first developed in a segregated milieu and later recorded for a segregated market helped to maintain the musical form's authenticity. For this, Smith also deserves credit. She was a perfectionist when it came to her own recordings and maintained their absolute integrity. It was as if she knew, observed historian Sharon Harley, that she was leaving them for posterity. At the height of her career, Smith was the highest paid Black entertainer in history. From her first earnings of $125 for each side of her first disc, she earned as much as $2,000 a week.* Smith kept up a grueling schedule on the TOBA circuit,** often doing ten shows a day, seven times a week, and traveling from Jacksonville to Little Rock, from Kansas City to Birmingham.

Bessie Smith - popular singer of the blues
(photo courtesy of EBONY)

---

*It has been estimated that Columbia Records made $8 to $10 million on her.

**The Theater Owner's Booking Agency (TOBA) circuit was the main vehicle by which Black performers played in the forty or so major theaters throughout the country that Blacks patronized. The low pay and often inadequate accommodations of the circuit made some of the performers quip that the initials really stood for "Tough on Black Artists," or after a really bad night—"Tough on Black Asses." Nevertheless the TOBA Circuit gave employment to hundreds of Black Artists.

Smith's popularity was not only because of her great voice, technique and showmanship. There was something more, observed Chris Albertson in his book, *Bessie*. Her "magic ingredient was her ability to get an audience to identify with her songs; while the pop singers of the day were busy building a 'Stairway to Paradise' or making love 'Neath the South Seas Moon', Bessie sang of mean mistreaters and two-timing husbands with tragicomic optimism, offering advice to the dejected, and made it quite clear that she herself was not immune to such problems."

The "tragicomedy" that Smith exploited so effectively was the essential element of the blues mode. The attraction of the blues and of Smith was that "they at once express the agony of life and the possibility of conquering it through sheer toughness of spirit," observed Ralph Ellison.

By 1933, the year of Smith's last four recordings and four years after the crash of the stock market, her commercial viability had declined with that of the rest of the country. After a brief comeback in 1936, she died in a fatal car crash a year later. Accurately called "the world's greatest blues singer," she is accredited with urbanizing the blues sound. Though like Rainey, she preferred the southern audiences; unlike "Ma" she was attracted by the kind of "silky" orchestration that Fletcher Henderson's band provided. Smith had a tremendous influence on such performers as Mahalia Jackson, Sidney Bechet, Billie Holiday, and Ethel Waters. In fact it was the latter, with her own even more refined style, that began to create a new vogue in blues singing and popularized the form with white audiences.

Late in Smith's career, Ethel Waters was booked at a vaudeville show in Atlanta. Smith protested, telling the management that she would not tolerate another singer on the show, but Waters was not just *any* singer. She had a reputation for singing a new kind of "sweet" blues that was sung low and soft. The crowd demanded that Waters perform, too, and she did, singing *St. Louis Blues*. The crowd went wild and Smith sensed that this was the beginning of the end. "Come here, long goody," Smith said to Waters, "you ain't so bad. It's only I never dreamed that anyone would be able to do this in my own territory and with my own people."[13]

When Waters recorded "Down Home Blues" and "O Daddy" for the Black Swan Recording Company,* these became its first hits. Waters,

---

*The company was one of the first to be owned by Blacks. It was formed in 1921. W.E.B. DuBois was on the board; Fletcher Henderson was the recording manager, and William Grant Still its musical director.

known as "Sweet Mama Stringbeans," first became famous in the Plantation Revue after Florence Mills left the show. Josephine Baker was then in the revue's chorus, and when a producer came down to the show, she asked Waters to star in another revue that was going to be put on in Paris. Waters asked for too much money, however, and the producer asked Baker to go in her stead.

In 1927, Waters was the star in the musical, *Africana*. She dominated that show as Mills had in *Shuffle Along*. Her style was as important as her voice, which was not nearly the quality of Smith's, but was more appealing to a certain kind of audience. In many instances, as in Chicago when both the singers were engaged at the same time, Smith would sing to the audiences in the Black Southside, while Waters was packing them in at the white spots in "the loop."

Ethel Waters, movie actress and recording artist
(photo courtesy Schomburg Center
New York Public Library)

James Weldon Johnson captured the famous style of "Sweet Mama Stringbeans" when he wrote:

Miss Waters gets her audiences through an innate poise that she possesses;
through the quiet and subtlety of her personality. She never "works hard" on the
stage. Her bodily movements, when she makes them, are almost languorous.
Indeed she is at her best when she is standing perfectly still, singing quietly. Her
singing corresponds to her bodily movements; she never overexerts her voice;
she always creates a reserved power and compels the listener...Miss Waters also
has a disarming quality which enables her to sing some songs that many singers
would not be able to get away with on stage. Those who have heard her sing
"Shake That Thing" will understand.[14]

Waters also appeared in *Blackbirds of 1930, Rhapsody in Black* (1931), *As Thousands Cheer* (1933), and *At Home Abroad* (1935). After success as a blues singer, supper club entertainer and Broadway star, Waters would subsequently become a star of the stage and screen.

Other blues singers of the era are also worth noting. Clara Smith, also with Columbia records, was billed as the Queen of the Moaners. She had a style reminiscent of Bessie Smith and was the only singer to ever record with Bessie Smith. Bertha "Chippie" Hill of Pratt City, Alabama sang in clubs in Harlem before moving to Chicago to sing with King Oliver. Later she joined Ma Rainey but retired at the age of twenty-four to raise a family. Sippie Wallace sang in the Smith style. She sang in New York in 1923, in Detroit and with the TOBA Circuit. Additionally, she showcased with Louis Armstrong and his wife Lil Hardin.

"Memphis" Minnie McCoy was born in Algiers, Louisiana and had a hard-driving style reminiscent of blues men like Bill Broonzy. In fact, she once competed against Broonzy to see who possessed the most prowess with a guitar. Despite Broonzy's attempts to get her drunk before the contest, she was more than his match. "Memphis Minnie can make a guitar cry, moan, talk and whistle the blues," declared Broonzy. Other singers included Mary Johnson (Signifyin' Mary), Victoria Spivey, Lottie Beaman, Daisy Martin, and Edith Johnson, and a contingent of New Orleans singers who were able to sing regularly with jazz bands; Esther Bigeau, Edna Hicks, Lizzie Miles, and Ann Cook. By the end of the twenties, however, interest waned in the classic blues singers, who actually recorded for little more than a decade but were popular as singers for the next 30 years.

Along with the blues, jazz music emerged in more definite forms during this period. In 1923 in Chicago, Joseph "King" Oliver and his Creole Jazz Band cut a phonograph record of the jazz in Chicago. In his group, which had come from New Orleans to the Windy City, was Lil Hardin on piano, as well as sidemen Johnny Dodd, Jimmie Noone, Honore Dutrey, Bill Johnson, and Warren "Baby" Dodds. In 1924, Oliver coaxed his young protege still in New Orleans to join him—Louis

Armstrong. Subsequently, Armstrong formed his own group, which included Lil Hardin (whom he later married), his pianist. She became the first well-known female jazz instrumentalist in an area where women were traditionally inhibited from participating.

Of Concerts, Choirs, and Composers

Black women were also a part of other forms of music outside of the glitter of Broadway, the grit of the TOBA circuit and the grist of the jazz halls in the period. They were making concert appearances here and abroad, developing the growing musical departments within Black schools, training choirs and organizing choral societies.

Hazel Harrison was among the noted pianists of the period. Born in LaPorte, Indiana, she studied uner Victor Heinze and later with Ferrucio Busoni and Egon Petri in Germany. While in Berlin during the years 1903-1906, she played with the Berlin Philharmonic Orchestra. Her concert tours, which did not begin until the 1920's, took her throughout the United States and included appearances with the Chicago, Minneapolis and Los Angeles Symphonies. Press notices referred to her piano talent as one exhibiting "sweeping barvara passages" "brilliantly crisp tone, with sonority" and "wholly matured art conception and universally smooth flowing technic." In later years, Harrison combined a teaching career at Howard University with her concertizing. From a frank review by Henrietta Weber, musical director of the Chicago *Herald Examiner*, one can glean the problems that Black concert musicians still faced. After commenting that Harrison had "a real gift," Weber said that "it seems too bad that the fact that she is a Negress may limit her future plans." The critic recommended that her press agent "put her forward under a name with Spanish flair" and then "a big future would be open before her."

Also successful in concert music was Anita Patti Brown. Two other Black musicians, Estella Pinckney Clough and Emma Azaila Hackley, were cited by Maud Cuney-Hare as being among the prominent musicians who "labored conscientiously to increase the appreciation for good music by Negro audiences and to win recognition for colored interpreters of classical music."[15] The former was one of the stalwarts of the Samuel Coleridge-Taylor Society in Massachusetts, named after the Black classical musician. The organization was prominent enough for Coleridge-Taylor to accept an invitation while in Europe to attend the Society's presentations of one of his compositions, *Hiawatha*. At the concert, Clough performed as the soprano soloist.

Emma A. Hackley's contribution to Black music was even more significant. Inspired to pursue a musical career after hearing Sisseretta sing in Detroit, she became a noted singer and violinist in her own right. After moving to Denver, Colorado, she became the assistant director of the largest white choral group there, drawing the praise of the *Denver Times*, which commented that she was a "talented and well-educated musician who brought the Monday Musical Club to its present high standard." Hackley's real dedication, however, was to the Blacks in the city. The *Denver Post* pointed out that she was not only one of the best violinists in the city, but that under her direction, "Denver is doing more musical work among the coloured people than any other city in the West."

The efforts of dedicated Black musicians like Hackley did not prevail without meeting some resistance. Many Black performers of the times had begun spurning the use of spirituals in their repertoire. This was also a period when Blacks were suffering from musical stereotypes; as noted previously, many whites felt that Blacks should not endeavor to perform in classical music, but use their natural gifts, which needed no training, to sing black music. On the other end of the spectrum, particularly, Black students in the universities became intrigued with the new wave of jazz music that was beginning to sweep the country. They felt that the spirituals were "a reminder of the misfortunes of the race," noted Cuney, and resented the insistence of white audiences that they sing spirituals to the exclusion of other music. Howard University's choir, for example, went on strike in 1909, refusing to sing spirituals.

After moving back East just before World War I, Hackley found her real niche in the musical world. Hackley became a musical missionary traveling throughout the country to perserve the popularity of the spirituals, stimulate a greater interest in the work of Black composers, many of whom were rearranging the traditional songs and encourage Black youth with talent to get training and pursue a career in music. Towards these ends, she established the Normal Vocal Institute in Chicago in 1912; became famous for organizing numerous folk song festivals at Black universities like Tuskegee, Morgan, and Howard; established a scholarship for promising students (one of the first winners was Clarence Cameron White, who went on to become one of the nation's leading violinists and composers); and used her influence to place the right musicians in the right places. An example of the latter was her use of her influence to get her own candidate, R. Nathaniel Dett, appointed as Musical Director of Hampton Institute over the choice of the President of the institution.

One of Hackley's crowning achievements was her becoming the director of the "People's Choir" of the large Chruch of the Crucifixion in Philadelphia. Her work with the choir, 100 voices strong, made them among the leading spiritual groups in the country. Always high on Hackley's agenda was to single out those who she felt had particular talent and personally encourage them. In her choir during the period was a young, twelve-year-old singer whom she paid special attention to. Her name was Marian Anderson.

Marian Anderson - world renown contralto
(photo courtesy of EBONY)

The Lady From Philadelphia

Internationally famous Roland Hayes took an interest in Marian Anderson's career and appeared with her in cantatas and oratorias. In fact, from the beginning, Marian Anderson received much support from the Black community, especially from her music teacher, Mary Patterson, who had always refused payment from Anderson's widowed mother who was a domestic. Anderson was always encouraged to sing in the churches, schools and places like the Young Women's Christian

Association. Recognizing her talent, the young prodigy's church set up a trust fund so that she could study under the great teacher, Giuseppe Boghetti. In 1924, Anderson won first prize in a field of 200 contestants in a competition sponsored by the New York Philharmonic Symphony at Lewisohn Stadium in New York. Soon afterwards she went to Europe. In 1929, she received a Rosenwald Fellowship and four years later made her debut recital in Berlin, followed by two years of successful concertizing. It was not until her 1935 concert in Salzburg, a full eleven years after her success at Lewisohn stadium, however, that Anderson received real critical acclaim.

In Berlin, she sang her usual repertoire of Bach, Beethoven, and the Spirituals, but it must have been an extraordinary event. Seated in the audience was the maestro, Arturo Toscanini, who said after her performance, "A voice such as this comes once in a hundred years." Vincent Sheean, author of *Between the Thunder and the Sun*, described Anderson's forte—the spirituals:

> At the end of the [last] spiritual, there was no applause at all—a silence instinctive, natural and intense, so that you were afraid to breathe. What Anderson had done was something outside limits of classical or romantic music: she frightened us with the conception, in musical terms, of course, but outside the normal limits, of a mighty suffering.[16]

By 1938, under the management of impresario Sol Hurok, Anderson had one of the most grueling schedules on the concert circuit, singing in 92 recitals in seventy cities. She had become one of the most popular and well paid singers on the circuit.

Despite Anderson's success, her career was not without its humiliations and controversy. She was often barred from first-class accommodations. The epitome of such insults came in 1939 when the Daughters of the American Revolution refused to grant the internationally known singer permission to sing in Washington, D.C.'s Constitution Hall. The action of the DAR caused a national furor, with First Lady, Eleanor Roosevelt, promptly resigning from the organization. Anderson was subsequently offered the use of the Lincoln Memorial for an outdoor recital on Easter Sunday, and on that day 75,000 people showed up to hear her sing, including members of the Supreme Court, Congress, and the Cabinet.

With all her triumphs, one had yet eluded her, and in fact, all Black artists until then; but in 1955, one year after the Supreme Court school desegregation decision, she was to also accomplish it; to be the first Black to appear on the stage of the Metropolitan Opera House. On January 17th, she made her debut there in Verdi's *Un Ballo* in *Maschera*. Ten years later, Marian Anderson gave her farewell recital at Carnegie Hall, ending her career as the world's leading concert contralto of the 20th century and the best-known Black singer in the history of music.[17] The key to her extraordinary presentation was that Anderson actually had two voices. "The upper half . . . brilliant and flexible and heady, a soprano for all technical and interpretive purposes," observed Marcia Davenport, "the lower half . . . that hair-rising deep voice, the like of which I have never heard and which, I suspect, has never been heard before."[18] Although Anderson's interpretation and execution of European music was superb, there were many who felt that the real depth of her talent was heard in the spirituals. When she sang the latter, as Virgil Thompson wrote, "she leaves off being a lovely icicle and becomes a flame."

One of the songs in the great contralto's repertoire was "Songs to the Dark Virgin." When Anderson introduced it, the critic Eugene Stintson called it "one of the greatest immediate successes ever won by an American song." The composer of that piece of music was Florence Price, the first Black woman to be recognized as a significant composer. A graduate of the New England Conservatory of Music, Price studied there with Chadwick and Converse. She wrote a wide range of musical compositions, including concertos, chamber music, solo pieces for violin and piano, and spirituals. Her most famous piece is her classic "My Soul's Been Anchored in the Lord." In 1925, she received the prestigious Wanamaker Award for her "Symphony in E Minor," which the *Chicago Daily News* called " . . . a faultless work, a work that speaks its own message with restraint and yet with passion . . . . (it) is worthy of a place in the regular symphonic repertory."[19] Among Price's other works are "Symphonic Tone Poem," "Concert Overture of Negro Spirituals," and "Little Negro Dances" for chorus and orchestra. Price also played her works with leading symphonies, performing one of them with the Chicago Symphony Orchestra in 1932.

Two years later, pianist Margaret Bonds played Price's "Concerto in F Minor" with the Women's Symphony in Chicago to critical acclaim. Inspired by Price's work, Bonds decided to concentrate on composing as well. She had a master's degree from Northwestern University and later studied at Julliard. Her awards and fellowships included a Rosenwald and Roy Harris and Wanamaker Award. One of Margaret Bonds' earliest works to attract attention was a setting for the classic Langston Hughes' poem "The Negro Speaks of Rivers," a song which has been in the repertory of such singers as Etta Moton and Lawrence Winters. Subsequently, Bonds collaborated with Hughes on one of her most popular works, "The Ballad of the Brown King," a cantata for solo voices, chorus and orchestra. "Three Dream Portraits," again with words by Hughes, is considered her finest piece of writing for voices and piano.[20] Bonds' larger works include "Mass in D Minor" for chorus and orchestra and music for "Shakespeare in Harlem," and adaptation of another Hughes work. In addition, the great diva Leontyne Price later utilized a number of her settings of spirituals for concerts.

Another composer of distinction is Undine Moore. Born in 1905 in Jarrett, Virginia, she has written such compositions as "Weary Blues" and "Mother to Son," both inspired by Langston Hughes' poems. Moore received a scholarship to go to the Juilliard School of Music and earned a master's degree from Columbia University. Subsequently, she taught at Viriginia State College. Her compositions are a blend of several streams of Black music: ragtime, gospel, jazz, and the spirituals, but she is a woman who always thought of herself as a teacher who composes rather than who teaches. And well she might, for as a professor she can boast among her students the likes of Billy Taylor, composer Phil Medley, and the great opera star Camilla Williams. Leon Thompson, conductor and educational director of the New York Philharmonic Orchestra, also studied under her tutelege. From 1970 to 1972, she was a co-director of the Black Music Center at Virginia State, which sought to promote the appreciation of Black music.

By the time Dorothy Maynor made her debut on the Town Hall stage in 1939, there had been ever so narrow a path already cleared by the careers of Roland Hayes, Paul Robeson and particularly Marian Anderson.

Born in Norfolk, Virginia in 1910, she was first encouraged by Nathaniel Dett at Hampton Institute. She received her first critical attention when she auditioned in 1939 for Serge Koussevitzky at Tanglewood. He is said to have exclaimed, "The whole world must hear her!" Critic Noel Strauss immediately began publicizing her name. News of these events, of course, preceded her Town Hall debut, and the sense of expectation in the air was evident before she came out on stage. When she did, she sang a repertoire of Bach, Handel, Schubert, Wolf, Strauss, and Black spirituals. The moment had been seized with great success, the New York Times reported: "Miss Maynor's voice is phenomenal for its range, character, and varied expressive resources. It is equally adapted to music of a lyric or dramatic character. The voice has power as well as rich color."

The soprano was immediately engaged for recitals and solo appearances throughout the country. She made records for RCA Victor in between her tours, which took her also to Europe, Canada, and Latin America. In 1941, Maynor made her debut at Carnegie Hall.

Koussevitzky, who was the conductor of the Boston Symphony, characterized Maynor "as the greatest singer of the century." Such a declaration made the years after her debut even the more tragic, for by 1942, Maynor had begun to lose her voice. In that year Virgil Thompson sadly observed in the *Herald Tribune*, "There can be no further question, I think, that her vocal technique is woefully inadequate and that her voice itself is in danger." Fortunately, her recordings preserved her voice at its height. According to Abdul, "No one has sung on records a more exquisite performance of "Depuis le Jour' from *Louise*. And her singing of Schubert's 'Der Hirt auf dem Felsen' is unsurpassed." Maynor, forced to retire from the stage, established a school in Harlem to inspire and train other young artists.

The Twenties and Thirties was an era when a number of white artists used Black folk material in their own work—particularly on the stage. Most of them retained the same stereotypes that were prevalent in earlier times (and remain even today), but at least the portrayals became more sympathetic as the years passed and provided an opportunity for some Blacks in the arts field, who seized the opportunities as stepping stones in their own careers.

Perhaps the most prominent musical of the period to fit this category was George Gershwin's *Porgy and Bess*, produced in 1935. One of its stars was Anne Brown who had studied at Juilliard. It is said that after Gershwin heard her sing, he created the title role with her in mind. After leaving the stage in 1942, Brown, in order to establish a successful concert career, had to go abroad to do so, settling in Sweden.

Porgy was also important in the career of one of the country's most important musicians, Eva Jessye. Jessye was a choral director for the first production of Gershwin's show. It was because of her that Black music, particularly the spirituals used in some of the most successful productions of the period, remained authentic.

Before her assignment to *Porgy*, Jessye studied under Will Marion Cook, and by 1926, she was appearing nightly on the radio with her choir on the "Major Bowles Family Hour." Her reputation as an organizer of ensembles and quartets grew and she was soon asked to direct warmups in Broadway theaters. Her Dixie Jubilee Singers became well known, and in 1929, King Vidor asked her to come to Hollywood to train a choir for his film *Hallelujah!*.

Jessye's work was praised by critics for "the high quality of musicianship, painstaking discipline and showmanship."[21] In her shows she also made a special point to use some of her favorite composers, including Cook, J. Rosamund Johnson, and John Work. Jessye's published collections include "My Spirituals" (1927), "The Life of Christ in Negro Spirituals" (1931), "Paradise Lost and Regained" (1934) and the "Chronicle of Job" (1936), a folk drama. Along with Hall Johnson, she became the foremost preserver of the spiritual in the modern period, continuing the legacy of Emma Azalia Hackley.

Black musicians' efforts to maintain the authenticity in the Twenties and Thirties probably influenced the development of a related form of music, gospel, then in its formative years. By the 1930's Mahalia Jackson and Thomas Dorsey had become a team, and together they forged the path for gospel to transcend its narrow confines in the Holiness churches to become a popular music from throughout the country and the world. The roots of gospel extend from the year 1895 when the Bishop Charles Henry Mason withdrew from the Baptist church to sing more "spirited" songs and formed the Church of God in Christ.[22]

The "father of gospel music" is the Reverend Charles Albert Tindley who established a church in Philadelphia after migrating from the South, and in 1905, published the gospel favorites "Stand By Me" and "We'll Understand It By and By." In the same year, Lucie Campbell of Memphis, Tennessee, composed and published "Something Within Me." Six years later, the "father of modern gospel" composed his first song in Atlanta, Georgia at the age of eleven. After a sting as a blues singer and a piano accompanist to Ma Rainey, Thomas Dorsey pursued a musical career in gospel. In 1927, he started publishing songs (he would compose over 400 in all) and teamed up with the singer Rebecca Tolbert in Chicago, traveling from church to church performing his music.

It should be noted that these songs were not received without controversy. Many believed that gospel songs were outside of the perimeters of sacred music, but Dorsey persisted, and in 1929, met a young woman who had come to Chicago from New Orleans, where she had heard the likes of Jelly Roll Morton, King Oliver, and Louis Armstrong. She had also heard Ma Rainey and Bessie Smith. But Mahalia Jackson's orientation was not toward the Blues—it was best revealed in "spreading the good news."

In 1932 Dorsey opened the first Black publishing house for Gospel music, and employed Roberta Martin, then a teenager, as the pianist for his choir. In 1935, he wrote "Precious Lord, Take My Hand" and met the Ward sisters in Philadelphia and urged them to become gospel singers. Two years later he became the official pianist for Mahalia Jackson, who had been singing in the first gospel group in Chicago, the Johnson Singers.

It was actually Sister Rosetta Tharpe, however, who became the first widely known individual gospel singer to attain national prominence. Accompanying herself on the guitar, she traveled widely, and attracted large crowds. In the late Forties, her biggest hits were "Strange Things Happening Everyday" and "Three Little Fishes and Five Loaves of Bread." Later, the Angelic Gospel Singers introduced the first "group" concept in gospel singing. Their most popular record was "Touch Me, Lord Jesus." By 1950, however, it was the Clara Ward Singers who were the most famous. They became known for their "show-business" presentation, complete with their lavish robes and wigs, along with such songs as "Surely, God is Able," "Move On Up a Little Higher," and "Just Over the Hill." Clara Ward, the leader and pianist of the group, has over 200 composed songs to her credit. The group was also the first to appear in Las Vegas (1962).

But it was Mahalia Jackson with her concert at Carnegie Hall in 1950 who really gave gospel music wide appeal. Her appearance was followed by more at the Newport Jazz Festival, concert halls and stadiums, here and abroad. In the Fifties, Jackson became the leading gospel singer in the country, a mantle she never relinquished. Other important gospel singers subsequent to Jackson were the group, Dorothy Love and the Original Gospel Harmonettes, Shirley Caesar, Dorothy Norwood, and Beverly Glen. Toward the end of the Sixties, a new school of gospel called the California School made the cool renditions of gospel music more popular. Led by Doris Akers, this new phase of gospel music is melodically more sophisticated, harmonically more complex, more in the style of the popular song and rendered by a large singing group. The Edwin Hawkins Singers with their "O, Happy Day," is perhaps the most prominent example of the new mode of gospel.

The influence of gospel on other music and even other arts is inestimable. It has become a part of the Black theatre; for example, *Black Nativity* and *Prodigal Son* written by Langston Hughes and *Trumpets of the Lord* by Vinnette Carroll, were vital byproducts of gospel. Alvin Ailey used gospel in his classic dance piece, *Revelations*. By the Fifties, gospel had incorporated a mixture that included blues and jazz, that was made up of the rhythm and blues music of such singers as Willie Mae Thornton and La Vern Baker. In addition, prominent folk singers, such as Elizabeth Cotton, would integrate gospel in their music.

R & B and Rock-n-Roll

In the year 1955 *Billboard Magazine* proclaimed that Rhythm and Blues had taken over the Pop field. In that year R & B sales increased

200 percent over that of the previous one. What had happened was that whites were now buying "race" records as a result of the music being pushed on the independent radio stations, which proliferated after the decline of network radio.

With whites involved in the market, R & B was renamed Rock-n-Roll. The sound was a combination of gospel, blues and jazz and was characterized by "driving rhythms, slurred lyrics and open sexuality."[23] The music, as it developed over the years, represented a distillation of the big-band jazz sound super-imposed over blues and the boogie structure.

Not only did white audiences get involved with this formerly all-Black music, white performers did too. Most notable was Elvis Presley who, among other white performers, imitated the style of the R & B'ers. The leading Black female R & B singers of the period included Etta James, Big Mama Thornton, Ruth Brown, LaVerne Baker, and Erma Franklin. All of their hits were reissued by white artists who made considerably more from the record than the singers. The most dramatic example was that of Big Mama Thornton who was the first to record "Hound Dog"." It sold 2 million copies. Three years later, Elvis Presley recorded the tune. The rest is history. Thornton only received $500 in royalties, but Presley used the song as a launching pad to become one of the wealthiest entertainers in the history of the business.

Though not receiving the money nor the acclaim that they deserved, the R & B forerunners left an important legacy for those singers both Black and white who would follow them.

Opera: First Forays

Despite the success of earlier Black singers in concert, still elusive was the Black singer successful in the field of opera. This began to change with the first Black singers who, though excluded from American operatic circles, gained respect for their talents in Europe. One of the pioneers in this was Madame Lillian Evanti who made her operatic debut in the title role of Delibes' "Lakme" with the French Nice Opera Company in 1925, becoming one of the first Blacks to sing operatic roles in Europe. After her debut she sang coloratura soprano opera roles in France and Italy until the mid-Thirties, including *La Traviata, LeCoq d'Or, Romeo and Juliet* and *Lucia di Lammermoor.* Still, America showed it was unready to accept a Black singer in its major opera houses. Although Evanti had a repertoire of 24 operas by 1932 and was invited to audition for the Met in New York by its general manager, Giulio Gatti-Casazza, who had heard her sing in Italy, the Met board vetoed the idea on the basis of her being Black.

Upon her return to the United States, Evanti made appearances with the Negro Opera Company as the principal aide to its founder, Mary Caldwell Dawson. Dawson, for two decades, beginning in 1941, had "carried forward almost singlehandedly the banner of Black opera."[24] Madame Evanti played Violette in the company's *La Traviata*, which was presented at Watergate in Washington, D.C., with over 15,000 attending the performance. Later, Evanti was invited to the White House to sing for Presidents Roosevelt, Eisenhower and Truman. She also wrote compositions herself. For Ghana's independence celebration in 1957, she wrote a "Salute to Ghana." She was also the composer of "My Little Prayer," "Speak to Him Thou" and "The Mighty Rapture", which were published by W.C. Handy. Evanti, though unsuccessful in her quest to be recognized on the American opera stage, helped blaze the trail for others to do so, the first of whom was Caterina Jarboro.

In 1930, Jarboro made her debut* as Aida at the Puccini Opera House in Milan, Italy. She performed in Europe for three years in such operas as "The Queen of Sheba" and "L'Africaine", in which she appeared at the Paris Opera. Upon her return to America she became the first Black singer to sing with a major opera company in the United States. The year was 1933, and Jarboro, who years earlier could be seen on the chorus line of "Shuffle Along", sang the role of Aida with Alfred Salmaggi's Chicago Opera Company at the Hippodrome in New York City, winning critical praise for her performance.[25] The *New York Times* called her "Italian diction remarkably pure and distinct, a musicianly feeling for phrase and line, and a voice whose characteristically racial timbre, husky and darkly rich, endowed the music with an individual effectiveness." Despite her success, she suffered the fate of so many Black leading ladies in all the fields of the arts: there was just no place for her to go. Eventually she returned to Europe, never to perform with an American company again. It would not be until 1945 when another Black would appear with a major American company.

Another great singer who made a Town Hall debut—this one in 1942—was the soprano Ellabelle Davis. She was also successful and enjoyed high critical acclaim. "Her voice is of extraordinary persuasive texture," the *Herald Tribune* said, "gleaming limpidity through its wide range. She has an innate musicality and sense of style found only in the true artist." She, too, sang recitals throughout the United States, Latin

---

*Though Jarboro was the first Black to sing with a major company, she was not the first to sing the role of Aida. This distinction belongs to Florence Cole-Talbert who sang it at the Treatro Communale in Cosonza, Italy with success.

America, and Europe. In Mexico and Chile, Davis sang the title role in
Aida. One of the important moments in her career, says Adbul, came
when the League of Composers commissioned a work for her from
Lukas Foss, entitled *The Song of Songs*. She sang its premiere with the
Boston Symphony under Koussevitzky in 1947, after which she sang it
often with other orchestras.

A year before Davis' Town House debut in 1945, contralto Carol
Brice became the first Black to win the coveted Naumburg Award.
Throughout her concert tours of the Fifties and Sixties, she was
accompanied by her brother —pianist Jonathan Brice. During the
Sixties she made appearances with the New York City Opera. Her
recording of *El Amor Brujo*, observes Abdul, with Fritz Reiner
conducting the Pittsburgh Symphony, "exploits her ravishing chest
tones." Born in 1922 in Indianapolis, Brice attended Talladega College
and the Juilliard School of Music. Other orchestras she appeared with
were the Kansas City Symphony, the Pittsburgh and Boston
Symphonies, and the San Francisco Symphony, among others.

Jazz Into Song

The first part of this chapter has documented that the Black women
helped establish, enrich, and preserve the integrity and energy of every
kind of music. The women who followed took the torch from them,
refined, broadened, and added new colors and shapes to that legacy. In
jazz, after the decline of its "King" Melvin James "Sy" Oliver, others
continued to take up where he left off. Oliver had declined to play at the
Cotton Club, and in his stead, a young man by the name of Edward
Kennedy "Duke" Ellington was asked to perform there.

Several Black female singers became well-known by singing in the
Duke's band. One was Adelaide Hall, who had been in some of the
earlier musicals. In 1926, she was the soprano on the two sides, "The
Blues I Love to Sing" and "Creole Love Call." Critic Barry Ulanov
notes that Hall's lovely soprano on the latter, which was a wordless
vocal, was almost an *obbligato* in itself. She went on to record two
other sides with Ellington from the *Blackbirds Revue* in 1933.

Ivy Anderson joined Duke's band in 1931, after a stint with Anson
Week's band at the Grand Terrace in Chicago. Joining Ellington, she
had "the fortune to have a voice and personality that fitted an orchestra
and an era so tightly that she was and will be remembered as long as the
music and the time are remembered," observes Ulanov, and "she was
as sophisticated a singer that jazz has produced."[26] What was
interesting about her style and presentation was the contrast of her
exquisite and well-coiffed manner and her "improper" rough voice, and

frequent sardonic smile. Anderson remained with Ellington for eleven years, until she had to retire on account of worsening asthma. Some of her most remembered hits were "My Old Flame," "I Got It Bad and That Ain't Good," "Stormy Weather," "Rocks in My Bed," and "It Was a Sad Night in Harlem." Ivy Anderson also recorded a song that ushered in a new era: it was called "It Don't Mean a Thing If It Ain't Got That Swing."

The Swing era ushered in by Duke Ellington was a new and exciting sound that swept the nation still on its emotional as well as financial knees during the latter years of the Depression. Actually the music was not that much different from the jazz of the Twenties and early Thirties. Why it became an era unto itself seems to be reflection in the new spirit, the new feeling, that musicians brought to it rather than any aural difference in the music itself.

Another important band leader of the period was Chick Webb. In 1934 he found his band in need of a good vocalist, so he decided to go to one of the infamous amateur nights at the Apollo Theater in Harlem. After he heard a number of average singers and musicians, the introduction of a young, innocent looking girl made him sit up and take notice. She was "nervous but personable" and sang a popular tune of the time, "Judy." The extraordinary quality of her voice made him decide that he would hire her for his band immediately. Her name was Ella Fitzgerald.

Born in 1918, she was only a teenager at the time. Originally from Newport News, Virginia, she had lost her parents as a young child and was educated in an orphanage in Yonkers, New York, Not only did Webb give her a job but he took her into his home with him and his wife. Fitzgerald was one of those intuitive singers, "one with an extraordinary feeling for singing the way a good jazzman plays, improvising, first rhythmically, in later years, melodically. She had a little girl's natural stage presence and great communicable warmth. Ella Fitzgerald gave the final push needed to make the band the real success it soon became."

By 1938 she had become famous by recording, "A Tisket-a-Tasket." Upon Webb's death, Fitzgerald his logical successor, inherited the band. She led what was now billed "Ella Fitzgerald and Her Famous Orchestra" until 1942. Subsequently, she collaborated with Louis Armstrong, the Delta Rhythm Boys, Eddie Heywood, and the Inkspots. One of Fitzgerald's greatest marks of distinction, was her "scatting" vocabulary, a term she practically invented. Versatile, she was also capable of imitating Louis Armstrong's gutteral style, which she did in "Basin St. Blues." When she performed duets with the trumpeter/singer, observed Ulanov, she demonstrated the catholicity of tastes that has been her hallmark.

Fitzgerald also wrote several songs, including "You Showed Me The Way," "Oh, But I Do," "Robins Nest," and "It's Up To Me And You", after the death of Martin Luther King. Never the focus of much publicity, Fitzgerald is considered the ultimate musician's musician. Few would disagree with the assessment of Bing Crosby: "Man, woman or child, the greatest singer of them all is Ella Fitzgerald."

A singer who did get a lot of publicity, much of it bad, was Billie Holiday. She was perhaps the most influential Black female singer in history. Born Eleanora Fagan Gough in 1915, she had her first professional audition just fifteen years later. It was at a small club in Harlem called Jerry Preston's. There was an old man playing in the corner of the club, and Preston told' her to sing. She began singing "Travelin' All Alone". Before she had finished, the story goes, the customers had stopped drinking, turned around, and were openly weeping.

Holiday had a haunting voice, one which carried the blues beneath any song that she sang. Though she was influenced by Bessie Smith and came at a time when all young singers were trying to imitate Ethel Waters, she created her own individual style from the beginning. It was a style, as Ulanov described it, which was "big, brash, subtle, super-sensitive, a sour-sweet sound, the shape of which she manipulates so that it comes out flat, round, harsh *pianissimo*—one of the most beautiful vocal sounds in jazz . . . " She was another natural singer whose motion underlined every song. "You just feel it," she said, "and when you sing it other people can feel something too . . . There are a few songs I feel so much I can't stand to sing them . . . " Holiday cut her first record in 1933, the first of 350 she would make throughout her career. She toured with Count Basie, Artie Shaw, and Teddy Wilson. She endured the rather curious twists that discrimination can bring when she would have to make herself darker with the Black bands so she would not be mistaken for white, but had to be concerned about the darkness of her complexion when she was with white bands.

During this period in the late thirties, Billie Holiday opened at the Cafe Society Downtown in New York City, one of the most prestigious clubs extant at the time. Though she sang to the carriage crowd there, her big song of the time was the haunting, protest number, "Strange Fruit" (1939), called by Brendt "the most emphatic, passionate musical testimony against racism before Abby Lincoln's 'Freedom Suite'."[27] "Like very few singers in our time, like no other uncompromising jazz singer in our time, Billie was a big box-office attraction," observes

Ulanov. She and Teddy Wilson were the only Black entertainers on 52nd Street when jazz moved to "Swing Street." Going against the grain in associating with whites, she was once fined for sitting at a table with a white musician.

Billie Holiday, recording artist and stage performer
(photo courtesy Schomburg Center
New York Public Library

The Nineteen-Forties were both summits and nadirs for Holiday. She sang and acted in a film, *New Orleans*, with Louis Armstrong. In 1946, she also had her first solo concert which *Down Beat* reported was "an event to go down in history. [She was] unsurpassed in her own field as a great and individual song stylist . . ." These were the years she recorded *God Bless the Child*. Then, in May of 1947, she was arraigned for the violation of drug laws. She volunteered to go to the government drug rehabilitation center in Anderson, West Virginia, where she remained for a year and a day. Ten days after she got out, she gave a concert at Carnegie Hall to a packed house. Still, there were many who were wary of associating with an ex-dope addict, and many of her "friends" shunned her. Others who were supportive, like John Simmons, convinced her to go see Lena Horne perform at the Strand one evening. When Horne was told that Holiday was in the audience, she came down from the stage, walked up the aisle to where Lady Day was sitting and hugged her.[28]

In the late Forties and Fifties, she had her own show on Broadway, and made successful tours in Europe. In 1956, her album *Music for Touching* was considered by Nat Hentoff as one of the most penetrating of any jazz musician or singer. She was particularly known for her blues notes, which could "begin slightly under pitch, absolutely without vibrato, and gradually be forced up to dead center from where the vibrato shakes free, or it may trail off mournfully; or at final cadences, the note is a whole step above the written one and must be pressed slowly down to where it belongs."[29] Holiday was also noted for her phrasing, juxtaposing and transposing, in the alteration of harmonies. It is no wonder that Frank Sinatra would say of her, "It was Billie Holiday . . . who was and still remains the greatest single influence on me . . . with few exceptions, every popular singer in the United States during her generation has been touched in some way by her genius." But the monkey on Billie Holiday's back would not desist. She died, in the midst of withdrawal, in 1959.

New York City was the foremost hot spot for the jazz during this era, but Kansas City, Missouri was developing its own style and big names. One musician who found herself in this vibrant center was Mary Elfrieda Winn. In 1929, she joined the Andy Kirk Orchestra in Kansas City. It was here that Winn, who later became known as Mary Lou Williams, made her musical mark. She was in that mid-western city where Count Basie was then serving his apprenticeship and Charlie Parker was a local high school student, observed Phyl Garland. Williams' heroine was Lovie Austin, a pianist who had once accompanied Bessie Smith and Alberta Hunter.

Lovie Austin, born in Chattanooga, Tennessee, in 1887, had toured with Irving Miller's "Blue Babies", and subsequently played the TOBA Circuit with the "Sunflower Girls" and led her own "Blues Serenaders." She eventually settled in Chicago, and for 20 years, was musical director for the Monogram Theater and later directed the Gem and Joyland theaters. Mary Lou Williams describes her first seeing "this Black woman, sitting in the orchestra pit in a theatre in Pittsburgh with her legs crossed at the piano. She had a cigarette dangling from her mouth. She was playing the piano with her left hand, conducting the band with her head, and writing music for the next act with her right hand."[30]

Williams worked both as an arranger and composer for Kirk, and later for Benny Goodman and Duke Ellington. After performing with her second husband, Shorty Baker, she set off on her own. When in New York, she performed at the Cafe Society Downtown, owned by Barney Josephson, one of the few club owners who ran an integrated club in the Forties. In 1946, she became one of the first jazz musicians to perform with a symphony orchestra when she played her own composition, "Zodiac Suite," with the New York Philharmonic. In 1952, she left for Europe and spent two years playing in London and Paris. One day, as Garland describes it, she walked off the stage in Paris and virtually dropped out of sight for several years.

Mary Lou Williams · pianist and arranger
(photo courtesy of EBONY)

When she reemerged she was a converted Catholic and incorporated her religious passion into her music. The fusion of religious music and jazz emerged in her cantata, "St. Martin de Porres: Black Christ of the Andes," which she wrote in 1964, a year before Duke Ellington presented the first sacred concert in San Francisco. When she returned to New York in the late Sixties, Garland reports, Williams was so disheartened by the state of jazz that she asked her old friend Josephson, now the proprietor of a restaurant in Greenwich

Village called the Cookery, if she could play there. In 1970, she did just that and helped to create a resurgence of jazz in the city.

In 1971, choreographer Alvin Ailey created one of William's three settings for the Catholic Mass for his American Dance Theater. Four years later, some 3,000 people packed St. Patrick's Cathedral to hear her afternoon mass, Dances of Praise, celebrated. Williams was the first jazz musician to perform there. She also comes under the category of a musician's musician, the fate which often leaves such a person in relative obscurity from the public. Yet, concluded Garland, "She has been the foremost woman instrumentalist, though her stature is not confined by sex."[31]

After the Second World War, jazz entered a new phase. The big-band sound was declining and Black musicians, in a new mood and unhappy about the number of whites who became known as the standard-bearers of Swing, and in one instance even named the "King" of it, embarked upon a new form. It was something no one had ever heard before. Its intuitiveness was such an integral part of it that it would be difficult for those outside of the Black cultural context to imitate. Williams was fascinated by it, and during the Forties associated with its progenitors: Charlie (Bird) Parker, Thelonious Monk, Bud Powell, and Dizzy Gillespie, among others. The new innovation was described as a form of jazz that "escaped from the two-bar statement and swinging void," the "lengthening of melodic lines which weakened the grip of the two and four-bar riff." The music was simply called Bop, and it was mainly women who translated it into song.

In scat-singing songs like "Flying Home" and "Lady Be Good," Ella Fitzgerald sang the bebop phrases, finding the verbal equivalents, commented Ulanov, for the trumpet, trombone and saxophone sounds. In 1939, in her recording of "Tain't What You Do It's The Way You Do It," she ended one of her scat phrases with the word "rebop", which was "undoubtedly the first appearance of the first accredited name . . . for the music."[32]

Another voice that carried the message of bebop came from a young woman who wanted to be a concert pianist, but whose family could not afford the training. Instead Sarah Vaughan became one of the great vocal virtuosos of the era. Like Fitzgerald before her, Vaughan was first noticed at the Apollo, where she won an amateur night contest in 1942. In fact the headliner for the show was Fitzgerald, and like her predecessor, Vaughan too was heard by a musician who would have a major impact on her musical future. In Vaughan's case, that musician was Billy Eskstine, who was then singing with the Earl "Fatha" Hines' band, which included important musicians like Madelaine Green.

After a year, Vaughan eventually left the group, had a lean year in 1944, and then joined Eskstine's band which he had formed after leaving Hines. Still, things were not really happening for Vaughan. She left the Eckstine band after about six months and began singing at the Copacabana Lounge, followed by another six months at the Cafe Society Downtown. Vaughan then made a recording with Teddy Wilson, the pianist, who had been instrumental in Holiday's success at Musicraft.

The story of her first 1946 recording session is a telling one. On hand in the studio was one of the vice-presidents of the music company. Upon hearing Vaughan sing, he exclaimed "Good, God, she can't do that. Tell her to sing it straight. That stuff will never get anywhere. We'll lose our shirt." He was right; the company did eventually "lose its shirt", not because of but in spite of Vaughan's singing. For her, the vicissitudes of the business were finally going her way. She went to the heart of jazzdom in New York's 52nd Street, where she sang at the Onyx and Downbeat Clubs.

Sarah Vaughan - recording star of stage and screen
(photo courtesy of EBONY Magazine)

The year of her debut on The Street, she was making $75 a week; a year later $900. A year after that there was no small club which could pay the money she was now worth. By 1949, she had sung in clubs from coast to coast, in the $3,250 a week class and still soaring. In that same year she moved to Columbia Records and recorded Todd Dameron's "If You Could See Me Now," which finally began to reveal her musical heights. Subsequent recordings of songs like "Body and Soul," "Don't Blame Me," "Tenderly," and "I Cover the Water-front" established her as one of the most important singers of the scene. Her style of "filling intervals, breaking half-notes into eights, of quarters into sixteenths, and careening melodic variations,"[33] has been widely imitated by almost every singer who has succeeded her. She is one of the giant influences on the scene. Along with Billie Holiday, Ulanov notes, she has "broken every commercial tradition, every bigoted bar," and has made "America accept musicianship . . . and a governing jazz sound that springs from bop and courses beyond."

Sarah Vaughan was not the only important singer who made her debut in 1942. In the same year, the extraordinary Lena Horne appeared at Benny Goodman's Carnegie Hall concert. Immediately, this young woman, who began in the chorus line at the Cotton Club in its early days, surged into the consciousness of the nation. Subsequently, Horne appeared at the Cafe Society Downtown, and was then swept up by the movies to be a motion picture singer for the next five years. The significance of Horne did not lie in any musical innovation, as she would be the first to admit. She was not the intuitive singer others before her had been, but she did have a "fine husky voice," as Ulanov notes, and most importantly she worked diligently to make it express her own individual identity.

The extraordinary beauty of Lena Horne, combined with her classy and sensuous manner, would have been enough to make her a star, but she was never satisfied with that as her career in films, on the stage, and particularly as a singer. She refused to imitate the Florence Mills style, as Noble Sissle and later Lew Leslie wanted her to do, observed Jeanne Noble.[34] She searched for something else, and there were those willing to help. Foremost, there was Lennie Hayton, the arranger and musical director for MGM (whom she eventually married) who taught her the considerable amount of music that he knew. As a result, "her musical tastes did not merely advance; she became a part of the vital vanguard, those hardy souls who have clearly formulated ideas in the generally abstruse field of music, who can articulate their ideas and do."[35] Under the guidance of Billy Strayhorn, Lena Horne began to understand "the dissonances" of Stravinsky; under Hayton she studied Hindemith. "She began to approach modern music in general with urgency and expectancy," Ulanov observed.

Other important jazz singers who emerged in the Fifties were Carmen McCrae, "who had the sober musicianship, stylistic assurance, and taste of Sarah Vaughan and Ella Fitzgerald," and Abbey Lincoln, whose songs of protest, many written in collaboration with her husband Max Roach, were sung with strong expressivesness and commitment and were the best vocal interpretations of Roach's music. Also during the Fifties and into the early Sixties, the concept of "modern blues" emerged. The most successful of the singers in this genre was Dinah Washington, called "The Queen of the Blues," who sang with Lionel Hampton and his orchestra early in her career. Washington, the bridge between R&B music and jazz, influenced Aretha Franklin. Washington's successor was Esther Phillips, called "Little Esther," who while still a teenager, had a hit record "Double Crossing Blues" which sold a million copies. Other notable singers in this era were Ruth Brown, LaVerne Baker, Betty Carter, Etta James, and Gloria Lynne.

Opera—The Millenium

The decade of the Forties was also significant for Black women in the classical music field. Although many Black singers had penetrated the walls of segregation—if not discrimination—in the jazz field, success in the opera world remained elusive. Because of the peculiar nature of the world of opera, there is perhaps no more poignant story in music than that of the Black woman, often poor and reared in a segregated community, rising to the heights of the operatic stage. The classical singer faced a different kind of discrimination and hardship than the Blues and popular singers, Jeanne Noble points out. The classical music business was run by rich, aristocratic intellectuals. Its cultural foundations were foreign to most people who lived simply. Black women not only had to traverse those gaps of experience, as Noble notes, but their first audiences would be a community of Black people who felt, for the most part, that classical music was less than an essential part of their lives. For many of these singers, however, the Black audiences endured. "They patiently suffered through classical programs knowing they would be rewarded in the end with a few spirituals."[36] Many members of the audiences, on the other hand, did not come just to be entertained; they believed in the artists and were anxious to provide them support. Leontype Price, Marian Anderson, and Grace Bumbry, for example were all supported by Black colleges and sororities at the beginning of their dramatic ascent to international fame.

In the field of opera, Blacks did not really begin to make their mark until the 1950's, but once they did, they provided some of the most exciting opera in its history. The concert singers, too, continued to uphold the tradition that Elizabeth Greenfield started in the nineteenth century. But beginning in the forties, the most successful concert artists were also those singers and instrumentalists who were in some way associated with opera companies.

As mentioned earlier, the National Negro Opera Company, organized by Mary Caldwell Dawson, presented Verdi's *Aida* at the Chicago Opera House in 1942, and also Verdi's *La Traviata* in Madison Square Garden two years later. The leading roles were sung by Madame Evanti. Then in 1946, all of the pounding on the doors of major opera companies down through the years finally became too loud to be ignored. In that year, the New York City Opera employed Black singers as principals—among them Camilla Williams. A recipient of the Marian Anderson Award just three years before, Williams sang the leading role in Puccini's *Madame Butterfly* at the opera house. Her debut was a success. "She produced some full and brilliant notes in the first act of the love duet, which brought down the house, and there was another ovation for her beautifully voiced 'One Fine Day," noted Robert Hague in *P.M.* She subsequently played leading roles in *Pagliacci, La Boheme, Aida* and *Faust*; but still the time had not come when an opera star would make an indeliable impression on the major stage. Black singers continued to achieve outside of operatic music. In 1949 for example, Zelma George gained national attention in the Karamu Theater's production of Gian Carlo Menotti's opera *The Medium*. She sang the role of Madame Flora and was asked to perform at the Arena Theater in New York the following year. Her debut was received with a standing ovation.

In the Fifties, the National Negro Opera Company's production of *The Ordering of Moses* and *Ouanga*, written by Black composers R. Nathaniel Dett and Clarence Cameron White, respectively, provided Black singers and instrumentalists valuable experience. In addition, the interminable productions of *Porgy and Bess* and *Four Saints in Three Acts* provided Black musicians with opportunities to manifest their talents. *Carmen Jones, My Darlin' Aida*, and *Ballad for Bimshire* by Black composer Irving Burgie, also served that purpose.

In 1955, a significant operatic achievement was realized when Addele Addison sang the title role of *La Boheme* at the New York City Opera. Three years before, her debut at Town Hall "set critical minds on a search for new adjectives to describe her artistry," noted Abdul. Another critic observed that she had a truly "beautiful voice of pearly lustre and clarity, a generous share of warmth and feeling." She also possessed an "intelligence to make the singing artistically effective." After her debut, she concertized in the Soviet Union, Canada and throughout the United States, singing with the symphonies of the New York Philharmonic, Boston, and Cleveland.

Then, in 1956, the Metropolitan opened its doors for the first time to a Black leading soprano, Mattiwilda Dobbs. A graduate of Spelman College in Atlanta, Dobbs had made successful operatic appearances in Europe before coming to the Met. She had seasoned her performances in the major houses in Europe, including Milan's La Scala and London's Covent Garden, where she sang leading roles in *The Nightingale, LeCog d' Or, Rigoletto,* and *Siegfried.* After returning to the States in 1954, she appeared at Town Hall, singing the role of Zebinetta in Strauss' *Adriadne auf Naxos.* Hailed by critics as "a singer of exceptional virtuosity," she set out on a 1955 around-the-world tour and later that year recorded the complete performance of *The Pearl Fishers* and *Zaide.*

Mattiwilda Dobbs · soprano
(photo courtesy of EBONY)

In Dobbs' debut at the Met, she sang the role of Gilda in *Rigoletto*, a role she had previously sung only in English. "By any standards," commented the *New York World Telegram and Sun*, "Miss Dobbs is a remarkable artist, very much in tradition of great coloraturas, in that her phrasing and shading are fully as fascinating as her breathtaking agility in live and perform in Sweden.

The Prima Donna Absoluta

It would be a Black woman from a working class family in Laurel, Mississippi, however, who would earn the greatest accolades from the opera world. Leontyne Price, the Mississippi native, is the *prima donna* of the era. Her achievements stand high, not only in comparison to other Black singers but to those of the entire opera world.

Even as a young woman, Price showed the breadth of her singing talents. She early got the reputation as a particularly effective funeral singer. Noble relates the story that at one funeral she whipped the mourners into such a frenzy that the funeral director had to tell her to stop singing. That was probably the last time that such a request was ever made. Price showed such promise that Paul Robeson once gave a benefit performance for her to help raise funds for her musical training. In addition, a local white family also contributed to her support. After attending Central State University in Ohio, she received a Juilliard Scholarship. From that point on, she captured the hearts and praise of all of those in ear's reach. When Virgil Thompson heard her, he invited her to sing in his *Four Saints in Three Acts*. The same thing occurred when Gershwin heard her; he wanted the diva to sing in his *Porgy and Bess*. When Stravinsky and Samuel Barber heard her in Europe, where she had gone for a two-year tour, they also asked Price to introduce their songs.

By the time of her Town Hall Debut in 1954, there was already great interest in her career. A year later, she became the first Black star to appear in an opera on television, where she sang Puccini's *Tosca*. Following this in 1958, she made her debut in Vienna at the State Opera with the great conductor Herbert von Karajan in 1958. Two years later she made her first appearance at Milan's La Scala. When she made her debut at the Met in 1961, interest in this extraordinary singer had reached the point of frenzy, notes Abdul. Her performances of the part of Leonora in *Il Trovatore* did not disappoint her audience, for at the conclusion of the opera she received a forty-two minute ovation, one of the longest in the history of the prestigious Met.

Her Leonora, commented *Time* Magazine, "proved to be a remarkable portrayal of a woman in whom dignity struggled with desperation and in whom grief somehow shone more movingly through a profound sense of repose. The amalgam of qualities made her fourth act aria *D'amor sull'ali rosee* a dramatic as well as a technical triumph. It was perhaps the most widely applauded moment of the present Met season.[37]

Leontyne Price - opera star, enroute to Rome to sing
in the opera "Aida"
(photo courtesy of EBONY)

During that season Price also played the role of Cio-Cio-San in *Madame Butterfly*. In it, her enactment of the difficult suicide was done "with a dignity that many a famed soprano is unable to muster." But Price is most acclaimed for her portrayal of Aida. Abdul calls her the definitive Aida of our generation. It was a triumph, noted *Time*. "[Price] moving about the stage with a feline greace, passing with a kind of visceral instinct through moods that were supplicating and menacing, aggressive and sweet, she achieved one of the great Aidas in operatic history. Sustaining all of the performances was the voice, unfurling like a bright banner from the stage through the opera house."[38] "No singer," concluded the critic, " is better capable of straddling both the lyric and the dramatic moods than she is, and none possesses a voice that is more secure throughout its considerable range."[39] Her range is extraordinary. Price's voice is capable of reaching from the "G" below middle "C" to the "D" above high "C." When the famous conductor Herbert von Karajan was asked to describe her voice, the maestro mustered: "It gives me goose pimples."

During the early part of Price's career, most critics felt that only Maria Callas was comparable to her, but the difference between them, one critic observed, was that "Callas expresses the torture of her life through her voice: Price expresses her joy."[40] Price was asked by the Met to open the following season in Puccini's *Girl of the Golden West*. In 1966, when the Met first moved to Lincoln Center, she was also asked to perform in honor of the opening in Samuel Barber's *Antony and Cleopatra*, which he wrote especially for her.

There is no honor in her field that has escaped her, no milestone that has eluded her.

And yet her warmth, her down-homeness and her sense of humility is also a part of the legend of Leontyne Price. Jeanne Noble tells the classic story in her book about a reporter asking Price "if centuries from now you wanted future men to unearth a time capsule symbolizing the greatest achievements of modern life, what would you include?" The prima donna without a moment's hesitation replied, "an Aretha Franklin record."

Other prominent prima donnas also graced the stage in the wake of Leontyne Price. Harlem-born Martina Arroyo began by singing Lieder and oratorio. In 1959 she was one of the national winners in the Met's Opera auditions and thereby won a guest contract. In 1963 she debuted at the New York Philharmonic, singing the lead in Barber's *Andromache's Farewell.* And after her 1965 season at the Met, she appeared each season there-after, becoming the first soprano to sing two consecutive opening nights there in twenty years. Arroyo has sung at the Vienna State Opera, the Paris Opera and London Covent Gardens. She has performed in *Aida, Madam Butterfly, Tosca, Macbeth,* and *Don Giovanni,* among others.

Another prima donna, Grace Bumbry, was the first Black to sing a major role at the Bayreuth Festival in 1961. Born in Saint Louis in 1937, and a graduate of Boston University, she made her debut in the Paris Opera in 1960, and subsequently appeared in Europe, South America,

London, Vienna and at the La Scala in Milan. She has also sung at the White House in a command performance. In 1965, the mezzo-soprano made her Met debut as Princess Eboli in Verdi's *Don Carlo*, after which she received three solo curtain calls. This is rare, Abdul observes, at the opera house where most of the world's great singers have sung. In describing her performance, Abdul noted that it was immediately apparent that Bumbry had star quality. "She swept in on cue," he said, "and paused majestically for that extra split second that marks a star from the run of the mill debutante. The audience burst into a stormy ovation before she had sung one note." The critic continued, commenting on the star's big moment in the Third Act of the opera when she sang the famous, "O, Don Fatale." "Here she exploited her remarkable range, deep chest tones, creamy middle voice, and soaring high notes—all beautifully equalized and technically secure." Recently Bumbry has sung the soprano roles such as Tosca, Salome, and Lady Macbeth.

Grace Bumbry - soprano
(photo courtesy of Christian Steiner)

One of the most popular of the current opera singers is the beautiful and talented Shirley Verrett. Born 1933, in New Orleans, Louisiana, Verrett first became intrigued with opera when she saw Callas sing the title role in *Norma*. Afterwards, she went on to achieve one of the most successful of careers in the opera. When her family moved to California, she studied under Anna Fitziu, who lived in Hollywood. Then it was to Juilliard, and afterwards first prize for singing SaintSaens aria, "My Heart at thy Sweet Voice" on Arthur Godfrey's talent show. When she got the nod to sing the title role in *Carmen* at Italy's Spoleto Festival of Two Worlds in 1962, she could see the heights of the opera world on the horizon. In quick succession she sang the same role at Moscow's Bolshoi Opera, Delilah in Saint-Saen's *Samson and Delilah* and subsequently Princess Eboli *(Don Carlo)*.

These successors were followed by more appearances at the Vienna State Opera and Covent Gardens. After appearing in *Carmen* at the New York City Opera in 1964, she debuted at the Met in the same role four years later. She sang several more seasons at the Met before appearing in the Dallas and San Francisco Opera houses, however, it was at the Met in 1974 that Verrett "added new laurels to her already brilliant career by singing both leading roles in the house's first presentation of Berlioz's two-part opera, *Les Troyens*, a five-hour tour de force," notes Carruthers.[41] She had been scheduled for the soprano role but had to take over the mezzo role too when one of the singers became ill. "Verrett's vocal prowess in both registers and her appealing characterizations electrified the opera world. The two parts contrast vocally and dramatically," Carruthers observed, "one calls for a Cassandra who is cold and sexless, the other for an ardent, seductive Dido."

In the 1975 season, Verrett played the role of Neocle in Rossini's *Siege of Corinth*, followed a season later by that of Madame Lidoine in Poulenc's *Dialogues of the Carmelites*. Of her Norma, sung at the San Francisco opera house, *The San Francisco Chronicle* observed: "There have been vocally purer, melodically more irrestible Normas, but none more essentially dramatic, more electric in responses and emotional change, bolder in movement and gesture." Verrett has been criticized in some circles for switching from her traditional mezzo to the more spotlight-oriented soprano roles in mid-career. Her terse reaction to the criticism has been that she is "singing with the same voice that God has given me, and if a role suits my voice, and it says mezzo, or soprano or contralto, I'll sing it."

In Concert: The Sixties and Seventies

"Her voice is every bit as glorious as that of Kirsten Flagsted, only warmer, and her communication of text is remarkable. She has an excellent command of German and French and her song interpretation has style and elegance." The description is that of soprano Jessye Norman, who has become a specialist in Wagner's five Wesendon Lieder. She has recorded these songs as well as Isolde's "Liebestod" with Colin Davis and the London Symphony Orchestra. Her concert appearances, notes Abdul, all seem to point to an Isolde—the first Black one. Born in Augusta, Georgia in 1945, and a graduate of Howard University and the Peabody Conservatory of Music, Norman made her debut at the Deutsche Opera in Berlin in 1969. She has appeared in the following operas: *Idomeneo, L'Africaine,* the *Marriage of Figaro,* and *Aida.* She made her debut at La Scala in 1972, and has appeared in guest performances with the Los Angeles Philharmonic, the Boston Symphony, and the Chicago Symphony, among others. Additionally, She has toured both Europe and South America.

Several other singers made their debuts in the Seventies. Clamma Dale, with "her velvet, smooth voice," made her longawaited debut at Alice Tully Hall under the auspices of the Walter W. Naumburg Foundation in 1976. Dale, a native of Chester, Pennsylvania (1948), graduated from Juilliard, and made her debut at the New York City Opera in 1975, followed by an appearance at the Houston Opera Company in 1976. In November of 1976 Kathleen Battle and Faye Robinson assumed major roles with the New York City Opera and Barbara Hendricks made her recital debut. Battle performed the role of Susanna in *The Marriage of Figaro* of the New York City Opera, and "possesses a light, perfectly schooled voice and the stage presence of a veteran singing actress."[42] Robinson played the role of Violetta in the company's production of *La Traviata*—only the second time in history that a Black has played this role. Barbara Hendricks made her New York recital debut at Town Hall, on November 14, 1976. "Her artistry measures up to that of the best singers currently heard in the area," commented Abdul. She has a bright crystal clear voice in the Erna Berger tradition, but warmer."[43]

Instrumentalists

The last decades have also brought forth a number of important instrumentalists as well. In 1965, Phillipa Schuyler premiered her composition *Nile Fantasy* in Cairo, Egypt. Schuyler, who died tragically two years later in a helicopter crash in Vietnam, was one of the most brilliant prodigies of our times. Born in 1931 in New York, She began playing the piano at the age of four, and made her first major New York appearance at the age of fifteen. In 1946, she appeared at the Lewisohn Stadium in New York and played   Saint Saen's "Piano

Concerto in G Minor" with the New York Philharmonic before 12,000 people. The *New York Times* Observed: "She revealed herself as a pianist without regard to age, of extraordinary natural talent. Her grasp of the broad line of each of the three movements of the concert was complete and she disclosed an imagination to be found only in artists of a high level." Two years earlier, at the age of thirteen, Schuyler— daughter of the *Pittsburgh Courier* columnist George Schuyler—had already composed an orchestral piece entitled "Rumplestiltskin," which she also played at her Philharmonic Hall debut. In 1953 she made her debut at Town Hall. These early accomplishments, however, were not enough to satisfy and absorb her mind. She also became a journalist and author of international dimensions.

Phillipa Schuyler, pianist
(photo courtesy Schomburg Center
New York Public Library)

Another important instrumentalist is Natalie Hinderas. Hinderas made what was described as a sensational debut with the New York Philharmonic as a soloist in *"Ginastera's Piano Concerto"* in 1972. *The*

New York Times, describing her playing of this monumental work, said: "The solo part is a blockbuster and it was brilliantly played by the deceptively dimunitive pianist." Hinderas had just come from a triumphant playing of this work with the Philadelphia Orchestra, notes Abdul. She played that concerto with "fire and brilliance."

Hinderas has also become known as a civil rights advocate and has been instrumental in expanding opportunities for Black artists. She broke the traditional silence of many classical musicians on this subject in the press. After an interview with the *Washington Star* in 1971, for example, the paper noted: "The internationally recognized foremost Black woman pianist has come to the conclusion that although the composers of music were color blind, many impresarios, conductors, and managers in the United States are biased when it comes to hiring Black artists."

Hinderas was one of the first Black pianists to be managed by a major studio in the Fifties—Columbia Artists. She made major appearances on NBC television and concertized throughout the country. A graduate of Oberlin and Juilliard, Hinderas made her first appearance at the age of three, performed a full-length piano recital at age eight, and played with the Cleveland Woman's Symphony at the age of twelve. She made her Town Hall debut in 1954. Currently a Professor of Music at Temple University, she has recorded "Natalie Hinderas Plays Music by Black Composers."

Francis Cole is another pioneer musician. The first known Black harpsichord player, she received a standing ovation after she finished playing Bach's "English Suite No. 2 in A Minor" at the Carnegie Recital Hall in 1971. A graduate of the Cleveland Institute of Music and Columbia University, Cole began studying the piano in Cleveland at the age of three. After her New York recital, the *New York Times* noted that "She played a difficult program with fluency, flair and imagination. Cole, like most harpsichordists, is a passionate soul; unlike most she reveals it in her performances . . . she proved herself an artist to keep in mind."

Since then, Abdul observes, she has played in over 100 recitals in England, Germany and the United States. Though she was considered by the *Times* an artist to "keep in mind," no critic covered her Alice Tully Hall appearance in 1975. Another achievement to her credit is that she founded the Harpsichord Festival at Westminister Choir College.

Other Black female instrumentalists of note include Ann Hobson, a harpist with the Boston Symphony; Patricia Prattis Jennings, a former pianist with the World Symphony who joined the Pittsburgh Symphony in 1964; Elaine Jones, tympanist, who was the first Black musician to play for the New York City Opera and Ballet and the first Black to have a major position in the San Francisco Symphony; Frances Walker, concert pianist, sister of composer George Walker; flutist D. Antoinette Handy, who made solo appearances with the New Orleans Philharmonic, the Orchestra International of Paris and the Orchestra Musica Viva (Switzerland); Lucille Dixon, Bassist and Manager of the Symphony of the New World; and Bobbi Humphrey, one of the leading jazz flutists in contemporary music.

A notable first is Joyce Brown. She is the first woman to conduct and serve as musical director for a Broadway show. The production was *Purlie*. Jack Kroll of *Newsweek* observed that "Joyce Brown does the best job in the pit I have ever seen, infecting the entire show with her musicianship, vitality and upbeat emotion." Brown is the first Black Woman to open a Broadway show from the pit, even though she had conducted several as a replacement. Well-prepared for her position, she attended Columbia University's Teacher's College, the New York College of Music, and New York University. Starting out as a conductor for summer stock, night club acts, and choirs, Brown's first musical conducting job on Broadway was as a replacement conductor for "Golden Boy." She has also done musical arrangements for Las Vegas shows as well as for the Latin Quarter and the Tropicana, famous night clubs.

Another significant first is Margaret Harris, one of the first Black female conductors in the history of the United States. When Harris was able to imitate a song her mother played on the piano at the age of two and a half, her mother realized that she had a prodigy. Margaret Harris, born in Chicago, Illinois in 1943, was able to read music at the age of three—the age at which she performed her first concert. She graduated from Juilliard, where she studied piano and composition.

Harris got her "break" in conducting by accident. Asked to replace a pianist at the last minute for a European tour of a show called "Black New World," she joyfully accepted. On the plane to Europe the producer of the show, in an act of desperation, asked if she would conduct the score because the assigned conductor had been stricken ill. Without rehearsal, she made her first debut as a conductor, and it was successful. She made her United States debut with the Chicago Symphony Orchestra in 1971, followed by guest conductor appearances with the Los Angeles, St. Louis, Minneapolis, and San Diego Symphonies. She was also the musical director of the Broadway plays *Hair*, *Two Gentleman of Verona*, and *Raisin*. In 1972 and 1973, she appeared as a soloist for the Los Angeles Philharmonic, playing her original piano concerto. Some of her original compositions include "Collage One," "Dear Love," "Grievin," and "Tonite's Goodbye." "In composing music I have many elements to draw on," she commented. "There's my background in performing and conducting and also the ethnic thing. I'm close to Black musical forms while my training is in the classical tradition. I like melodic music that reaches the heart."

Soul—Where the Music Meets

On the crest of the sixties, there appeared a number of singers who defied the traditional musical classifications of the past. They brought to bear on their song a synthesis of all the musical forms that Black women had achieved before them. It was as if they distilled their entire musical history from the field hollers to the most sophisticated classical music and sang it. Phyl Garland would call it "soul." The music of these singers was more weighted on one side of the musical spectrum than the other, but they all expressed a marvelous synthesis.

One of the first singers of this modern era was the inimitable Nina Simone. Phyl Garland describes her music as "laced with classical techniques . . . with a touch of Bachian counterpoint intermingled with the improvisation of jazz and blues." Langston Hughes, upon hearing her, described her style in another way. "She is strange," he wrote in 1962, "she is far out and at the same time common . . . She is unique. You either like her or you don't. If you don't, you won't. If you do— wheeeouuueu! You do." Not surprisingly, Simone had an eclectic musical background. As a child traveling with her mother, who was a minister, she played the piano in numerous revival tents and store-front churches in North Carolina; But Simone's real desire was to be a concert pianist. She studied at Juilliard and the Curtis School of Music, however, financial necessity made her accept club dates wherein she played more popular music. At this point, notes Noble, there she was as two singers: there was her Eunice Waymon, her given name, who played "serious music"; and there was Nina Simone, her stage name, who played popular music.

In 1959 she made a hit record, "Porgy". Afterwards she attracted a kind of cult following among the hip white carriage trade and performed her "strange" style in sequined gowns, looking like a "curved G" at the piano, as Maya Angelou described it. But that was before the Sixties. It was also before the Civil Rights revolution swept the country, and it was before the little girls attending church in Birmingham were ripped asunder by a bomb; before the courageous Medgar Evers was murdered in front of his Mississippi home. These incidents in 1963, blew the lid off of an already American pressure cooker, evoking in that year a song called "Mississippi Goddam"—called by Garland "a milestone in modern protest music." Simone took off her sequined gowns and embarked on the crusade. "Music," she had come to feel, "serves no other purpose than to reflect the times." Simone, notes musicologist Lou Holloway, was "one of the first singers to use her music to assist the civil rights movement, rather than just be an entertainer in the midst of it." Only Robeson, Holiday, and Abbey Lincoln before her had combined fervent protest with music—Simone even more directly than the others.

By 1966, when she recorded the haunting "Four Women" which exposed one of the most sensitive subjects in the Black community, the intra—racial prejudice of color and miscegenation, Simone had become the leading singer of protest. "Four Women," observed Phyl Garland, was "one of the most powerful and moving social documents to come out of the Black man's heritage."[44] Two days before she was scheduled to sing a concert in 1968, Martin Luther King, Jr. was assassinated. Twenty-four hours later, Simone's bassist, Gene Taylor, composed "The King of Love is Dead." She sang it at the concert in Connecticut with all of the passion the occasion demanded. She ended her appearance with Dorsey's "Precious Lord, Take My Hand." The controversy that surrounded Simone during this period heaped continuing pressure on her as a performer. In 1974, she sang a song called "It is Finished" and dropped out of sight. Simone will, like Mary Lou Williams, had done before her, reemerge to revolutionize American musical form.

Aretha Franklin and Roberta Flack, both popular artists, reflect each side of Simone's dual musical legacy.

"There is an Aretha Franklin in every Black woman, screaming to come out." The words were expressed by Lena Horne; the sentiment shared is universal. In the same year that Simone recorded "Four Women," Franklin made her impact on the world with the album *Aretha Arrives*, featuring "I Never Loved a Man." She had indeed arrived. A year later, critic David Llorens summed up a year full of urban insurrections, the slogan of Black power, and the new leadership of the Student Nonviolent Coordinating Committee. "It was the summer of 'Retha, Rap and Revolt'," Garland quotes him as saying. It was also the year of "Respect."

Like Simone, Aretha Franklin's first notion of music was lodged in the gospels and spirituals. Her father had one of the largest churches in the Midwest, and it was there that she made her "professional debut" at the age of twelve. Later with her sister and two others, she formed a gospel singing group. She received a good musical education from a family friend, Mahalia Jackson, as well as from a boarder in the Franklin home—James Cleveland—who taught her piano. After hearing Clara Ward sing at her aunt's funeral, she decided that she definitely wanted to be a singer, and listening to Sam Cooke influenced her decision to sing popular music. Franklin recorded her first record, "Precious Lord, Take My Hand," at the age of 14; her first forays into the pop field were to follow. When the seemingly omnipresent John Hammond of Columbia Records heard a demo of her singing "Today I Sing the Blues," he offered her a contract. "She had the best voice I've heard in my twenty years," he said. In 1963 she made it at the Newport Jazz Festival, but she was still primarily on the "Chitlin Circuit."

It was not until she signed with Atlantic Records that her career soared. Her recording of "I Never Loved a Man" in 1967 put her on the map. In quick succession, she got five gold records, sang successfully at Philharmonic Hall, appeared on the Tonight Show, and went on a seven-city tour with Harry Belafonte for the benefit of the Southern Christian Leadership Conference. *Billboard, Cashbox,* and *Record World* chose her as the best vocalist of the year. She "rewrote" the National Anthem when she sang it at the Democratic National Convention in 1968. She became the youngest Black singer ever to appear on the cover of *Time.* Two other Black women singers, Marian Anderson and Leontyne Price, had previously appeared on the cover of *Time. Time* noted, "What really accounts for her impact goes beyond technique: it is her fierce, gritty conviction." It is also her style, one which synthesizes Blues, gospel, spirituals, and pop. "She is the standard bearer of the soul phenomenon," observed Phyl Garland," . . . the consolidated Bessie Smith, Billie Holiday, and Dinah Washington."

The third of this great triad of Black singers is Roberta Flack. Her music tilts furtherd to the other side of the spectrum that Simone represents. Flack, too, desired to also become a concert pianist, and was studying to do so until her father died and she had to leave school. Like Simone, too, she was forced to find work in a club, in her case, Mr. Henry's in Georgetown, Washington, D.C. She, too, had a cult following among Washington's elite, until she was heard by jazz pianist Les McCann who was a Founding Father of funky jazz. He helped get her a contract with Atlantic Records and by 1970 she was the recipient of the highest awards in the business.

Her style is a potent combination of European and Black musical overtones. It is reflected in her music which ranges from "Angelitos Negros" to "The First Time I Ever Saw Your Face" to "I Told Jesus" to "Killing Me Softly." It is the kind of style which made it possible for Flack to do a standing-room only performance at New York's

Roberta Flack
(photo courtesy of EBONY)

Philharmonic Hall, on the heels of a successful engagement at Harlem's Apollo Theater. Nestled within her lugubrious singing style is a phrasing somewhat akin to that of Billie Holiday's. Her technique is so fine that musicians of every stripe have taken notice of it. Martina Arroya suggestions, for example, when asked how a young singer should prepare for an opera career, included listening to Flack from whom "you can get some of the most beautiful phrasing in the world."

Other singers sharing this multifaceted Black musical legacy include Dionne Warwick, who began her career singing gospel, and then teamed up with songwriter Burt Bachrach to become one of the most successful popular singers; and Nancy Wilson who, according to the weekly *Time* magazine, "figures to become the greatest pretender to Ella Fitzgerald's crown for a long time to come."

Nancy Wilson
(photo courtesy of EBONY)

Further toward the pop side are such great singers as Gladys Knight, Patti Labelle, and Diana Ross. It is the latter, however, who emerged, in Garland's words, as the first truly modern pop singer—whether you like her or not. Ross was a member of the famous singing group The Supremes until 1970. In what critics call the decade of the Supremes, 1960-1970, the group sold over 25 million records and more gold records than any other group except the Beatles. The modernity of Ross, boosted by her successful movie appearances, lies in the fact that she is the first pop star to have the benefit of the most up to date public relations machinery in the business. The latter part of her career has been carefully structured, her persona contrived—in the best sense of the word. Thus present-day Diana Ross is a total performer. She appeals to the traditional pop set, as well as the supper clubs in New York, Los Angeles, and Las Vegas. In 1972, her successful career earned her the Entertainer of the Year Award from *Cue* magazine.

Black women have made their impact and their presence known in every form of music. From Elizabeth Greenfield to Diana Ross, Bessie Smith to Leontyne Price, Alberta Hunter to Florence Price and Lil Hardin to Natalie Hinderas, they have made an important contribution to the American musical form. One of the most extraordinary aspects of their collective styles, no matter how far apart, is that they all shared the common bonds of their traditional music.

One cannot imagine a world without them.

NOTES

[1] Lerone Bennett, *The Shaping of Black America* (Chicago: Johnson Publishing, 1975), p. 30.

[2] Phyl Garland, *The Sound of Soul* (Chicago: Henry Regenery Company, 1969), p. 53.

[3] Eileen Southern, *Readings in Black American Music* (New York: Norton, 1971), p. 130.

[4] Southern, p. 249.

[5] Southern, pp. 250-251.

[6] James Trotter, *Music and Some Highly Musical People* 1881; rpt. New York, NY: Johnson Reprint Publishing Corporation, 1968), pp. 174-175.

[7] James Weldon Johnson, *Black Manhattan* (New York: Alfred A. Knopf, 1930), p. 99.

[8] Monroe N. Work, *Negro Year Book* (Tuskegee, Alabama: Tuskegee Institute, 1937), p. 475.

[9] Monroe A. Majors, *Noted Negro Women* (1893; rpt. Freeport, New York: Books for Libraries Press, 1971), pp. 308-309.

[10] Majors, p. 93.

[11] Southern, p. 255.

[12] Paul Oliver, *The Story of the Blues* (New York: Chilton Book Company, 1969), p. 63.

[13] Jeanne Noble, *Beautiful Also Are The Souls of My Black Sisters* (New Jersey: Prentice-Hall, 1978), p. 226.

[14] Johnson, pp. 209-210.

[15] Maud Cuney-Hare, *Negro Musicians and Their Music*, 2nd ed. (New York: Decapo Press, 1974), p. 240.

[16] Southern, p. 423.

[17] Southern, p. 422.

[18] Raoul Abdul, *Blacks in Classical Music* (New York: Dodd, Mead & Company, 1978), p. 88.

[19] Abdul, p. 53.

[20] Abdul, p. 54.

[21] Southern, p. 434.

[22] Horace C. Boyer, "Gospel Music Comes of Age," *Black World*, Vol. XXIII, No. 1, November 1973, p. 46.

[23] Steve Chappel and Reebe Garofalo, *Rock-n-Roll is Here to Pay* (Chicago: Nelson Hall, 1977), p. 231.

[24] Abdul, p. 148.

[25] Abdul, p. 128.

[26] Barry Ulanov, *A History of Jazz in America* (New York: DeCapo Press, 1972), p. 180.

[27] Joachim Brendt, *The Jazz Book* (New York: Lawrence Hill and Co., 1975), p. 328.

[28] Nat Shapiro and Nat Hentoff, eds. *The Jazz Makers* (Westport, Connecticut: Greenwood Press, Pub., 1957), p. 291.

[29] Shapiro and Hentoff, p. 294.

[30] Phyl Garland, "The Lady Lives Jazz," *Ebony* Magazine, October 1979, p. 62.

[31] Garland, "The Lady Lives Jazz," p. 62.

[32]Ulanov, p. 252.

[33] Ulanov, p. 290.

[34] Noble, p. 251.

[35] Ulanov, p. 256.

[36] Noble, p. 272.

[37] "A Voice Like a Banner Flying," *Time* Magazine, 10 March 1961, p. 58.

[38] "A Voice Like a Banner Flying."

[39] "A Voice Like A Banner Flying."

[40] "A Voice Like A Banner Flying," p. 59.

[41] Ben Carruthers, "Shirley Verrett: I'm Singing With The Voice That God Has Given Me," *Encore American* and *World wide News,* 19 March 1979, p. 29.

[42] Abdul, p. 117.

[43] Abdul, p. 118.

[44] Garland, *The Sound of Soul,* p. 178.

CHAPTER IV

ART

Africa and the Colonial Period: Anonymous Artists

As in other forms of cultural expression, the African was richly endowed with skills in the plastic arts. Weaving, metalwork, sculpture, pottery-making, and skillful surface decoration with color were the principal arts. In fact, as Margaret Butcher notes, "everything in the category of the European fine arts except easel painting, marble sculpture, engraving and etching (and even the techniques of engraving and etching are represented in the surfacing, carving of much African art) was known to Africans."[1] While some of these skills were either lost during the Middle Passage or buried beneath the crude requirements of slave labor, others were simply forgotten in the Colonial New World that lagged far behind Europe in artistic development. Thus, the development of Black artists in America was essentially the "regaining of a kingdom", an evolvement in which "they were unconciously recapturing a lost artistic heritage."[2]

African art skills were "technical, rigid, controlled and disciplined; characteristic African art expression is, therefore, sober, heavily conventionalized, and restrained."[3] In fact, the African-American's culture is often characterized by emotion and exhuberance, and in art, the use of bright colors is one of the cultural survivals which distinguish the African experience in America. The few artistic traditions that survived in America are found in their purest form, in the isolated areas of the country where Blacks have been shielded from Western acculturation. They include the basketweaving which still exists on the Gullah islands of South Carolina; the iron ritual figures in parts of Virginia; the stoneware vessels, shaped in the forms of anguished human faces and ceramic works also found in South Carolina.

The early Black artisans, most of them are anonymous, did preserve their sense of the aesthetic as they learned the skills required of the new nation. By the 18th century, these artisans played a significant role throughout Colonial America. They designed and forged the elaborate wrought-iron grilles still found in New Orleans and Charleston. They lent the concept of the circular house with a central fireplace, built the large and glorious mansions of the Southern planters and constructed government edifices. Even in the North, the beautiful Jansen House, built in 1712 on the Hudson River with its hand-forged hinges and delicately detailed fireplace is attributed to African handiwork, states art historian James Porter. In many cities there were more Black artisans than white, and in others there were significant numbers of them engaged in these skills, including sewing, embroidering, painting, cabinet-making, printing, weaving, and blacksmithing.

In Africa, basketry, weaving, and pottery were the province of the women, and it is likely that many practiced these skills in America as well. Still, until 1885, Butcher notes, any Afro-American who had artistic rather than artisan ambitions confronted almost an impossible barrier. Of course, race was a large factor in this, but it was not the only one. In the fine arts, America still looked toward Europe. "Serious" artists were forced to study abroad.

Despite the obstacles, several Black artists did manage to penetrate these barriers. In 1862, a Black man, Edward Thomas, organized the first major exhibition of Black fine and industrial arts in the country. And in this period three significant Black artists emerged. They were the pioneers and included Robert Duncan, the first Black atelier artist; Edward Bannister, the first Black to earn recognition as an American regional painter of consequence; and Edmonia Lewis, the first Black sculptor of prominence.

The First Sculptor

After acquiring some training at Oberlin College, one of the few institutions of higher learning that admitted Blacks, Edmonia Lewis went to Boston, Massachusetts. There she met the popular sculptor, Edward Brackett, who gave her clay, modeling tools, and a "baby's foot." Three weeks later she returned to his studio with the reproduction of the foot, the artistic rendering of which brought praise from the sculptor. Subsequently, he gave her a cast of a woman's hand, and to carry out her assignment she made her own set of modeling tools from those which Brackett had first given her. Brackett was again impressed by the results. Lewis soon received a letter from the sculptor to "a lady who gave her eight dollars." With that, Lewis opened a studio of her own. Above the door, Porter notes, read a sign "Edmonia Lewis, artist."

Her first work, praised by her friends, was a medallion of the head of John Brown. The second was a bust of Colonel Robert Gould Shaw, a Civil War hero and leader of the first all-Black regiment in the Union forces. Both were works completed by 1864, and the latter was immediately purchased by the late Colonel's family and exhibited at the Boston Fair for the Soldier's Fund. One hundred copies of it were sold and with the money she earned, Lewis set out for Europe.

While in Rome she attracted the attention of Harriet Hosmer and Hiram Powers, neo-classicists who had influenced her work along those lines. In Rome, she completed a commissioned piece, a bust of Dionysus Lewis of New York and also a group of Indian pieces. She also completed a group of sculptures depicting Blacks after hearing of the Emancipation Proclamation. By 1865, "Hagar," "The Marriage of Hiawatha," "The Departure of Hiawatha and Minnehaha," the bust of Lewis, and the emancipation group were completed in clay. "Forever Free," a marble piece, was completed a year later after friends had helped her financially and sent to America for exhibition in 1868.

Lewis' first works reflected an artistic attitude of realism marked by emotionalism, observed Porter. These characteristics and the subjects of her works may have been a reflection of her background and experiences. Edmonia Lewis was born of an Indian mother and Black father. She told a reporter of the London *Art Journal*, while in Europe, that the first twelve years of her life were spent "in the wilds, fishing, hunting, swimming, and making moccasins." But she yearned to be an artist and abandoned her early life to pursue a career. "I often longed to return to the wilds," she told the reporter, "but my love of sculpture forbad it." With the help of abolitionists she managed to attend Oberlin, but was dismissed in 1862 for allegedly attempting to poison two white students. In the wake of the accusations, Lewis was beaten by a vigilante group of whites, but was eventually found innocent after being defended in a court of law by the eminent Black attorney, John Mercer Langston.

Lewis strongly identified with both her Indian and Black heritage. In a letter from Rome, for example, she mentions the fact that she did "Forever Free" without pay for William Lloyd Garrison. "Mr. Garrison has given his whole life for my father's people and I think I should give him a few months work," she wrote. Her sculpture "Forever Free" depicts a Black man and woman who are overcome with emotion on receiving the news of the Emancipation. The work exhibits an amateurish technic, yet its very crudity imparts a strength that saves it from the commonplace. It is a noteworthy attempt to express the poignant feelings that swept over the Negro on his "morning of liberty." In 1867, Lewis did a fine group sculpture entitled "Madonna and Child," which is said to have been purchased by the Marquis of Bute for an altar piece. Between 1869 and 1871, she did a portrait medallion of Wendell Phillips, a memorial monument to Harriet K. Hunt, and two small groups of children in the poses of sleeping and awaking. She returned to the United States and later executed a fine bust of Longfellow commissioned by Harvard College. In 1870, she held a brief exhibition of her works in Chicago and a year later was back in Rome.

In 1873, Lewis was commissioned to execute a marble copy of the head of Octavius-the result was one of her most famous works known as "The Young Augustus." Mrs. Elizabeth Chase purchased the piece, calling it "the best reproduction of the original then offered by any artist in Rome." By this time Lewis had acquired a national as well as international reputation, and in 1873, she returned to America with "The Marriage of Hiawatha," "Asleep," "Love in a Trap," and a bust of Abraham Lincoln. All five were exhibited at the Pine Street Exhibition Hall of the San Francisco Art Association. Two were sold in San Francisco, and the remaining three pieces were displayed at the City Market Hall in San Jose, where more than 1,600 visitors attended the exhibition. The San Jose Library Association raised funds to acquire the bust of Lincoln; Mrs. Sarah Knox, a wealthy patron of the arts, purchased "Asleep" and "Awake," both of which eventually found their way into the San Jose Library Collection as well.

Lewis returned to the States again in 1875 when receptions were held in her honor in Boston and Philadelphia. In 1876, she exhibited several of her pieces in the Philadelphia Centennial Exposition of that year. It was her "The Death of Cleopatra" which drew the most attention and won an award there. Of this work, Lorado Blondell Taft wrote the following criticism in *Artists of the Nineteenth Century:*

> This was not a beautiful work, but it was a very original and striking one, and it deserved particular comment, as its ideals were so radically different . . . . The effects of death are represented with such skill as to be absolutely repellent. Apart from matters of taste . . . it could only have been reproduced by a sculptor of very genuine endowments.[4]

It was radically different from those adopted by Story and Gould in their statues of the Egyptian queen. It was "evidence of changed outlook of artists," noted Porter.

Unfortunately, the piece has since disappeared. Henry Tuckerman, the chronicler of 19th century artists, visited her studio in Rome and later wrote: ". . . Miss Lewis is unquestionably the most interesting representative of our country in Europe. Interesting not only because she belongs to a condemned and oppressed race, which labors under the imputation of artistic capacity, but because she has already distinguished herself in sculpture, not perhaps in the highest grade, but in its naturalistic, not to say the most pleasing form . . ."[5] Tuckerman urged Americans to abandon their neoclassical pretentions for the more natural style of Edmonia Lewis; however, Lewis herself had come under the influence of the neoclassicists. Porter commented that this style was utilized to make her own crude realism conform to the discipline of that style.

After a brief period of popularity, Lewis sank into obscurity and finally died, the date of death having never been verified. In 1943, James

Porter reported that her works, "Awake," "Asleep" and the Lincoln bust were relegated to "dust-cover" oblivion at the Municipal Library in San Jose until 1968 when a frequent visitor recognized them. "Had the circumstances of her life and talent been more fortunately balanced, observed Porter, she might—with her originality of approach—have led the American school of the later Nineteenth Century in the attempt to coordinate the disparate trends in American sculpture."[6] But unfortunately, Lewis is largely forgotten.

However, the next Black female artist of note would carry on the legacy, beginning at the point of the apex of Lewis' art. She was Meta Warrick Fuller.

Meta Warrick Fuller

By the close of the century, however, the Black visual artist entered another phase. Butcher calls the years 1890-1914 the journeyman period for the Black arts. These were the years of advancement on the part of Blacks in many areas—including the strengthening of their church and businesses, the emerging of Black women's national organizations, and the recognizing of Black entertainers on the Broadway stage. Advancement for Black artists was not as promising, for the exploration of their own African heritage was not yet in vogue. In fact, it was a period when the Black was the subject of pernicious caricature at the hands of white writers and illustrators, and the ascendency of Booker T. Washington, with his emphasis on industrial education diminished the national interest in the cultural advancement of Blacks. Despite these obstacles, observed Porter, the work of a number of Black artists indicated an "upsurge toward finer and more lasting values by the Negro masses in the last quarter of the Nineteenth Century." The artists included Ella D. Spencer, a watercolorist; and Lottie Wilson Moss, reputedly a sculptor. In addition, this was a period that produced the first Black artist to successfully combine trained technic with natural genius—Henry O. Tanner.

A contemporary of Tanner's, Meta Vaux Warrick Fuller, was the "greatest vindicating example of the American Negroes' conquest of fine arts."[7] Born in Philadelphia June 9, 1877, Warrick received her early training in the Pennsylvania School of Industrial Arts to which she had won a three-year scholarship. At her graduation in 1899, she was awarded the first prize for a metal crucifix showing Christ in anguish and an honorable mention in clay modelling. Warrick had shown a remarkable understanding of anatomy, which was both a reflection of her natural ability and academic training.

In 1899 Warrick sailed for Paris to further explore artistic possibilities. There she studied under Raphael Collin, the figure painter, and M. Carles. She then went to the Academie Colarossi and lectured on anatomy at the École Des Beaux Arts under M. Injalbert. During those years, "she led a life of isolated desperation as a struggling young Black artist, her hours filled with intense work and study."[8] It was her last year in Paris before her work-filled hours paid off. She was given a letter of introduction to Auguste Rodin, the great sculptor, and visited him at his studio in Meudon, carrying some smaller pieces of her sculpture for him to criticize. His eyes were immediately drawn to one of her pieces no more than eight inches high—a plaster sketch entitled "Man Eating His Heart," sometimes called "Secret Sorrow." It is reported that the master sculptor looked at the piece for a few minutes and then said to her, "My child, you are a sculptor; you have sensed the form in your fingers."

With the praise of Rodin, her career soared. Her work was exhibited in M. Bing's celebrated salons, among others, and she sold some of her work in Paris. When her group, "The Wretched," was unveiled at the Paris Salon in 1903, a contemporary critic hailed her as a young genius, an artist of "power and originality." Warrick's return to the United States was one of a tremendous let down. There was no one here to give her the inspiration that Rodin and other artists had. When she attempted to sell her works, she was told that they were "domestic work," during a time when European art was in vogue, however, the Philadelphia School of Industrial Art did honor her with an exhibition. Her sculpture was called "interesting" and "extremely individual, showing a morbid, strong imagination and the influence of Rodin, who had great interest in her progress."

The turn of the twentieth century was a period when state fairs and expositions commissioned a number of Black artists to exhibit their work, expanding their opportunities. For example, artist Pauline Powell (1872), showed her work at the Mechanics Institutes Fair, in 1890, becoming the first Black artist to be exhibited in her home state of California. In 1907 Warrick was commissioned by the Jamestown Tercentennial Exposition to render a tableau which represented the progress of Blacks. Though several other commissions came her way after she returned, her work was never in enough demand for her to be financially independent. Therefore she had to depend on her family and impeded the progress of her career.

In 1909, Warrick married Dr. Solomon Carter Fuller of Liberia. Soon after their marriage, a fire destroyed her earlier works. Settling in Framingham, Massachusetts with her husband, "she began to be consumed by family life, and even though she continued to do some sculpture, her work turned more and more to portraiture and traditional religious themes. After the fire, commented James Porter, "there was a more sober individuality that characterized her work. Gone was the former stylfulness and impressionism of surface." An exhibit of hers in 1914, which included "Four Seasons" and "The Magi," expressed greater selfconsciousness and "check-reined technic." Porter implies that her later sculpture, embodied in pieces like the "Water Boy," described as a sentimental ethnic piece, was more in keeping with her calm and gentle manner than her earlier works. One wonders, however, about the true motivations beneath this drastic change in style. Her first original work, "Head of Medusa," marked her debut as "sculptor of horrors." In explaining the anguish of her "The Crucifix of Christ," she said, "If the Savior did not suffer, then wherein lay the sacrifice?" It was her Saturnalian conceptions which had created a sensation at the l'Art Nouveau Galleries in Paris. Her tortured forms, said Porter, showed her regard for science and design in the realization of aesthetic feeling.

Commenting on her later work, Butcher observed, "Her subjects and moods became more placid and optimistic," such as in her pieces "Mother and Child," "Life in Quest for Peace," "Watching for Dawn," and "Immigrants in America." They were "pleasant, but lacked the powerful originality of the earlier pieces," Butcher continued. One of the most significant pieces, according to the culture critic, was "Ethiopia Awakening," which blended the early seriousness with later optimism, showing a semi-Egyptian female figure emerging from a case of enveloping hands like an awakening mummy.

Meta Fuller's husband died in 1953, and in her last years of life, she was said to find solace in the church. She died in 1968 at Cushing Hospital in Framingham, Massachusetts. "Her death," says Hoover, "was much in keeping with how she had been treated in life, ignored and neglected by the art world." Several critics agree that Fuller's importance exists because of her earlier work which was "although grim and terrible, . . . are also vital and from them speaks the very tragedy of the Negro race," commented Benjamin Brawley in *Negro Genius*. One example of this expression was a sculpture she did for the 50th Anniversary of the Emancipation Proclamation. Fuller did a lifesize plaster group of a youth and a maiden, both standing under an overshadowing figure representing their servitude. Hoover described the piece in this manner:

> They have just been set free, and behind them, Humanity personified is urging them on while race hatred is holding them back. Bewildered, they stand looking to the future with nothing in their hands to help them, and with only the scantiest

clothing covering them. Humanity, while urging them forward, weeps for their discouraging state.[9]

Meta Warrick Fuller was the first Black artist to delve deeply into the emotions of anguish and pain as a part of the Black experience.

Born in the same year and in the same city, as Fuller, was artist May Howard Jackson. Unlike Fuller, however, she received all of her training in the States. Never outstanding as a thematic modeller, notes Dover, she "excelled at forthright portraits of forthright men." Examples are her busts of Kelley Miller, W. E. B. DuBois, and Francis Grimke. Other works such as the "Mulatto Mother and Her Child" and "Head of a Child" were attempts to portray, according to Butcher, "the dilemma of the halfcaste and the significance of a new, young, emerging composite humanity" respectively. This social concern was not sentimentality reflected nor over-emphasized, observed Butcher. "When a school of Negro sculpture emerges," Butcher concludes, "Mrs. Jackson's work will be seen in a new perspective as noteworthy pioneering." Jackson, Butcher also notes, "was the first Black artist to break away from the academic cosmopolitanism and turn to frank and deliberate racialism." In this way, she was a forerunner of the Harlem Renaissance point of view.

The Renaissance

At the turn of the century, the aesthetic value of African art was "discovered" by European critics and artists who had been searching for a new style and philosophy of art. European art had become sterile and listless; impressionism's possibilities had been exhausted. While Europeans discovered art, Americans discovered the Negro. Painters like Winslow Homer, Robert Henri, and George Bellows painted Blacks realistically and devoid of the stereotypical characterizations of the earlier period. As in the other arts during the Renaissance period, young Black artists of the late Twenties and Thirties "plunged into the substance of Negro life and experience and caught its characteristic idioms far more deftly than their predecessors had."[10] In addition, there was less indifference about the Black artist than ever before. As in the other art mediums, organizations like the National Association for the Advancement of Colored People and the Urban League—and their publications—encouraged the painter and sculptor with words and, also importantly, with financial support. In addition, the Harmon Foundation, established in the Twenties, also gave exhibits for Black artists as well as awards and grants for study.

Several Black women artists emerged in these two decades: Lois Jones, who still remains the most prominent female artist to date; Augusta Savage, whose influence as a teacher and fighter for Black artists' rights left an important legacy; Selma Burke, also a dedicated teacher as well as artist; Elizabeth Prophet, who is not well known but is of importance; and Laura Wheeler Waring, a portrait painter.

Laura Wheeler Waring, born in Hartford, Connecticut in 1887, studied at the Pennsylvania Academy of Fine Arts in Philadelphia between 1918 and 1924 and at the Grand Chaumiere in Paris from 1924-25. Art critic David Driskell describes her works as ones painted with a realism "revealing not only her scrupulous objectivity, but the serene affection with which she regarded her subjects." In fact, Driskell goes on to say it was the concern and sense of warmth, as well as her choice of colorful personalities to depict, that distinguished her work from that of other contemporary portraitists. Waring's paintings were not broadly brushed portraits but direct expressions. Some of her work included "Alma," a portrait of the artist Alma Thomas, which is done in dramatic dark hues rather than Waring's customary bright colors,[11] and "Little Brown Girl." Her work, observed Porter, was the sensibility mate of a Jessie Redmon Fauset and thus more appealing to the middle-class.

One of the most important figures in the history of Black art in America was Augusta Savage. Born in 1900 in Green Cole Springs, Florida, she showed her predilection for sculpture as a young child. By 1921, as a result of a recommendation from a prominent sculptor, Solon Borglum, she was admitted to tuitionfree Cooper's Union. In the school's four-year course, Savage mastered the first year's course in a week, and the second in a month; but unfortunately, when the next year rolled around, the young artist had no money. The head of the school, Mrs. Reynolds, called a board meeting: Would the board consider giving financial aid for the first time in its history to this promising student who was the first woman to study there? The board did.

When some of the members of the community heard about the talented student, they pitched in. Sadie Peterson, a librarian at the 135th Street branch of the New York City library commissioned her to do a portrait of W. E. B. DuBois. She was also commissioned to do a portrait of Marcus Garvey.

Later, Savage went to France on a summer scholarship in 1923, after making national headlines when her application was first denied because of her race. Upon her return, she showed her work at the Sesquicentennial Exposition in Philadelphia in 1926. Subsequently, W. E. B. DuBois helped her get a scholarship to the Royal Academy of Fine Arts in Rome, still Savage had to raise $1,500 in order to go. Although she was nationally known, the young artist was forced to work in factories and laundries in order to subsist. Her task was made more difficult due to her earlier protests. She had been marked as a troublemaker and was excluded from exhibits, galleries, and museums because of that reputation.

Inspired by the examples of Fuller and Tanner, however, she never gave up. One day she saw a young Harlem boy on the street and was intrigued by the reflection his life imprinted upon his face. The result was one of her most famous portraits, "Gamin." Says the authors of 6 *Black Masters*, it "caught the vitality, humanity, tenderness, and wisdom of a boy-child in the streets." Soon after it was finished, Eugene Jones of the Urban League and John Nail, a businessman and art enthusiast, saw it and were determined to help. Through their offices they were able to procure her a Rosenwald Fellowship which she received for two consecutive years. The stipends of $1500 and $1800 respectively were enough for her to go abroad to Rome. Once she got the fellowship, others in the community helped her raise money for her wardrobe and expenses.

Savage studied at the Grand Chaumiere, under the noted artist, Charles Despiau. Her works were exhibited in a number of Paris salons, and she won citations from the Salon d'Automne and the Salon Printemps de Grande-Palais. With the advent of the Depression, however, she returned to the States. Those years were particularly hard on Black artists who had a difficult time even under the best of circumstances. In Europe, even Tanner could not sell his work. After her return she did several popular pieces, "Envy," which attracted critical attention, and "A Woman of Martinique." She was the first Black elected to the National Association of Women Painters and Sculptors. Her artistic development, it seemed, was taking a new direction—a direction displeasing to some of her Black colleagues. She had "set aside her own convictions to learn techniques and to carve subjects that convey a certain joy of life—but which happen to be trivial," observed James Porter. Breaden and Henderson observed that, with the coming of the Depression, Savage felt that the opportunity to create "the kind of sculpture she had once dreamed of was gone, probably forever, for her."[12] So she rededicated her energies toward another aspect of the arts: finding and teaching young Black artists. In this her contribution was invaluable. Among her students were Norman Lewis, William Artis, and Ernest Crichlow.

As the Depression weighed heavier, Savage would pick up the threads of another role familiar to her: leader and spokesperson. At the beginning of the Works Progress Administration art project—which provided essential jobs for artists - the administrators had to be convinced that Black artists did in fact exist. By the time Savage dealt with the press, threatened politicians, led delegations of angry artists to the offices of government bureaucrats, the WPA got the message. Savage was also one of the main organizers of the Harlem Artists Guild, to which she was elected its second president. In the Thirties, the outgrowth of all of these organizational activities was her directorship of one of the largest art centers in the federal arts programs, the Harlem Community Art Center, which enrolled about 1,500 students.

Her attitude toward her work was readily revealed when she responded to the criticism that too much of her time and energy was devoted to these extra-curricular activities and not enough to her own art. "I have created nothing really beautiful, really lasting," she said. "But if I can inspire one of those youngsters to develop the talent I know they possess, then my mounument will be in their work. No one can ask more than that." Savage's last major work was a commission for the 1939-40 New York World's Fair. Inspired by James Weldon Johnson's, "Lift Every Voice," she created a harp, sixteen feet tall, whose strings tapered down from the heads of a line of singing Black girls and boys. "The base of the harp," describes Bearden and Henderson, "was formed by a mammoth forearm and hand, with the fingers curving gently upward to complete the support. Kneeling in front of this representation of the musical gifts of the Black people, a Black youth tenders this gift to mankind through outflung arms."

Augusta Savage died in New York in 1962. Five years later her work "Gamin" would draw the most attention in the largest Black show held in this century in New York. Though her individual potential was never realized, that she was to recognize it in others would be her greatest legacy.

In terms of technique, Elizabeth Prophet is considered by Porter as a "sculptor of firmer concentration and more fluent temperament" than Augusta Savage. At the time of Porter's book, she was the artist-in-residence at Atlanta University, after studying at the Rhode Island School of Design, where very early, she had attracted a great deal of attention by "her stark, aggressive portraits in wood." Subsequently, she studied in Europe at L'Ecole Nationale des Beaux Arts de Paris, afterwhich she worked eight years and received considerable acclaim throughout Europe.

She returned to Rhode Island in artistic triumph. Her wood sculpture entitled "Discontent" was awarded first prize in 1930 at the Newport Art Association competition and was later purchased for the Rhode Island School of Design Museum. Countee Cullen described it as a face "Dantesque in its tragedy, so powerful in the red polished cowl that envelopes it, that it might stand for the very spirit of revolt and rebellion."[13] Another of the award-winning sculptures was "Silence," a brilliantly executed piece which is a woman's head in marble.

Prophet used Black subjects exclusively for her models, and in them, "the pride of race that the sculptor feels resolves itself into an intimation of noble conflict marking the features of each carved head."[14] The pride was reflected in her sculpture "Laughing Man," that "while a figure in pure white marble, Cullen noted, "might be taken to exemplify the unfathomed laugh of her race at a world it does not understand and which can never understand it."[15] Her sculpture "Congolaise" was another example of this, as was "Head of a Negro." The former was purchased by the Whitney Museum in New York. Both pieces reflect the terse style of the sculptor, "which is founded in happy union of elemental mood and massive forms."[16] The gifted Elizabeth Prophet, like her predecessors, died without being dutifully recorded in the art history texts. She lived her last years as a maid.

Selma Burke, who was an art instructor at the Harlem Center, spent most of her time teaching sculpture. Trained both in the United States and Europe, she is particularly deft at sketching animal forms in clay, a technique which "served her well in evoking the images of her subjects in stone and keeping the outline fresh, until realized. There is an idealistic intent in her sculpture," observes Porter, a quality that was evoked in her pieces "Lafayette" and "Salome," which were exhibited at the McMillan Galleries in New York in 1941. Selma Burke also designed the sculpture for the Roosevelt dime. More recently, the artist founded the Selma Burke Art Center in Pittsburgh, Pennsylvania.

The Modern Period

Lois Mailou Jones began her extraordinary career by receiving four successive scholarships to the Boston Museum of Fine Arts. She left the city since the school had no faculty openings; it was suggested that she teach at a Black University. Before she dedicated a good part of her life to that, however, she continued studies at the Academie Julian and the Ecole des Beaux Arts in Paris, in Rome and at Columbia and Harvard Universities where she has subsequently taught since 1945.

Lois Jones' reputation was based on her textile designs and fashion illustrations. Later however, she became identified with the work of the French painter, Cezanne. "Thus far her painting has been in the tradition, but not in imitation of Cezanne," observed James Porter. "Miss Jones wishes to confirm Cezanne but at the same time to add an original not of her own. . . . She has a commanding brush that does not allow a nuance of the poetry to escape. Sensuous color delicately adjusted to mood indicates the artistic perceptiveness of this young woman." It was her "Still Life" that Porter singled out as proof of her artisitc abilities and which, shown at the Pennsylvania Academy of Fine Arts, was instrumental in gaining her an artistic reputation. From there her work was chosen for major exhibitions, such as the one sponsored by the Harmon Foundation in 1930-31 in New York; the Salon des Artistes Francais, Paris in 1938-39; the Corocoran Gallery of Art in Washington, D.C. in 1939, 1951, and 1968; and the Museum of Fine Arts in Boston, in 1970 and 1973, among others.

Lois Mailou Jones - artist

Her work falls into three distinct categories: "early genre realism; a reference to African symbolisms; and since 1945, a strong identification with the arts and people of Haiti, where the artist spends much of her time" and where she is married to the distinguished Haitian painter, Pierre Noel. Some of her most notable paintings are "Notre Dame de Paris" (1938), "Jennie" (1943), "Mob Victim" (1944), "Dahomey" (1971). She is the first Black woman to accumulate a large representative body of works to present.[17] Probably the most eloquent words about her career were issued by Edmund Gaither:

Lois Mailou Jones is one of the few figures in American art to achieve a long, exciting and inspiring career in which there is no room for defeat, dullness and trickery. Whether it is the Lois Jones of the early fifties and sixties watching "Peasants on Parade, Haiti," or Lois Jones of today reflecting on "Dahomey," . . . it is always the Lois Jones in full control of her design and her colors. Few could so

freshly see the world over a forty-year period. . . . [She] has long been a catalyst for
artists, particularly Black artists.[18]

"She is known throughout the world as a great art teacher and a painter
of amazing versatility," concludes artist David Driskell. Her oeuvre
includes oil paintings in the style of the late 19th century French school,
figurative subjects depicting scenes of American social injustice, and
more abstract, design-oriented pieces in acrylic.

Many Black artists born either in the 1920's or the years just before
that period felt a number of "pulls" on what direction their artistic
expression should take. As with the writers, a new sense of
universalism and the coming of the integration ideal also pervaded the
artists. In anticipation of the militant period, however, there were also
voices which forecast the nationalist Black art movement. Black
women artists represented all of these streams of thought.

Elizabeth Catlett's "Mother and Child," a sculpture that was her
master's thesis, won first place in the national Chicago American
Negro Exposition of 1940. "The simple rotund massiveness of the work
exemplifies good taste and soberly thoughtful execution," observed
James Porter. "It avoids those pitfalls of sentimentality and
over-elaboration into which have fallen so many . . . The negroid quality
in 'Mother and Child' is undeniable and the work has poise and
profound structure."[19]

Born in Washington, D.C., Catlett studied at Howard University
under Lois Jones. In the Forties, she exhibited at Atlanta Univeristy,
the Newark Museum, and the Institute of Contemporary Art, among
others. In the 1950's she went to Mexico, where she studied terra cotta
and wood carving. Catlett subsequently got a job as an assistant at the
Taller de Grafica Popular, where she met her future husband,
Francisco Mora, an artist. In 1960 and 1962, her work received a major
award at Mexico's First Annual show, and in 1961, she was invited to
give a keynote address at a gathering about artists at Howard
University. There she made her position clear as to the attitudes about
art that Black artists should have. It was no longer necessary for Black
artists to prove that they were as good as white artists, she said. "The
job is to look into our Black communities for inspiration—to work for
our Black people—and to show the link between our struggle and that
of other similarly warped and oppressed peoples." Between 1941 and
1969, Catlett won eight prizes and honors, four in the United States and
four in Mexico. In 1966 she created a bronze nine foot figure, "Olmec
Bather," for the National Polytechnic Institute of Mexico. Pieces like
"Black Unity" attest to her philosophy, as does "Malcolm X Speaks For
Us," which won the acquisition price of the National Print Salon.

Catlett has become a citizen of Mexico where she lives and works.

One of the foremost engravers/printmakers/painters is Norma Morgan, who was born in New Haven, Connecticut. She won her first award for a self-portrait from the New England Division of the National Scholastic High School Art competition. She later attended the Hans Hofman School of Fine Arts and the Arts Students League, both on scholarships. In 1954 she had her first one-woman show of oils and etchings in New York; in the following year, her "Granite Tor" won first purchase prize for engraving in the Annual Print Club show in Philadelphia and became a part of the Philadelphia Museum's permanent collection. The prize marked, for her, the first major one she had won in an open show. In the following year, the Museum of Modern Art purchased "David in the Wilderness" and "Granite Tor." Intrigued by the Scottish Moors, she often used them as a subject of her work. The American Artists Professional League awarded Morgan its gold model for graphics when she exhibited the conventional farmhouse entitled "Moor Claimed." Many one-woman exhibitions followed.

Morgan is an artist who subsequently seemed to be influenced by the New Black awareness in the arts. "As I grow older," she has said, "I am inclined to work with subject matter among my own people. We have such a great art heritage."

The Sixties and Seventies .

As in the other phases of Black life, the Sixties ushered in a new era in the plastic arts. A significant number of Black women artists emerged in this period—many more than in the past where there were relatively few who were allowed or had the opportunity to transcend obscurity. The reputations some of the new artists gained were due to the Black support systems created independently of the influence of establishment critics. A few Black art galleries opened their doors in this period, and there was a vital grass roots movement that gave birth to community art centers, workshops and museums. Groups like the Organization of Black American Culture (OBAC) in Chicago created projects like the "Wall of Respect"—a collective effort on the part of Black artists to depict Black heroes in mural fashion.

The new emphasis on Black awareness also unearthed several primitive painters, who were born in the last century but gained contemporary notoriety during our times. Later in the period, a number of feminist artists appeared on the scene. Additionally, once the Black artists search for their identity had been realized or discarded, possibilities for other than political art opened up for exploration. In the Seventies, there was also a number of abstractionists who made their recent appearance on the Black art scene.

A Black woman representative of the militant Black art that manifested in the Sixties is that of Faith Ringgold. Born in 1934, in Harlem, Ringgold used the American flag in her work for political comment. "The flag is the only truly subversive and revolutionary abstraction one can paint," she says. Her first one-woman exhibit in 1968 was boldly political, comments Fine. The painting "Die" has as its subject a bloody street riot. "The Flag is Bleeding" shows a Black woman arm-in-arm with a Black man carrying a knife, and an unarmed White man. A flag dripping with blood is the background. In her "Flag for the Moon: Die Nigger," the stripes on the flag are painted in such a way that when the painting is turned slightly to the right, the stripes spell "Nigger." Addressing both racism and sexism, Ringgold and several other Black artists organized a group called Women Students and Black Liberation, whose main purpose was campaigning for at least fifty percent female representation in all future Black art exhibits.

Faith Ringgold - painter, standing before her work, FOR THE WOMEN'S HOUSE, installed 1972 at the Women's House of Detention, Rikers Island, New York City
(photo courtesy of Rufus Hinton)

Another artist who resides in New York is Camille Billops, She specializes in ceramic sculpture. She has been exhibited at the Huntingdon Hartford Foundation, the New York Cultural Center, and in Moscow, in the Sixties and early Seventies. Billops is also an art critic whose articles have appeared in *Newsweek*, the *New York Times*, and the *Amsterdam News*. She is a co-founder of the Hatch-Billups College and is presently teaching at Rutgers University.

Harriett Kennedy, born in 1939 in Cambridge, Massachusetts, was one of two Black female artists to have her work exhibited in 1970 at the Boston Museum of Fine Arts in the Afro-American (New York-Boston) Exhibit, (the Museum's first Black exhibit). She is a recipient of the Boit Award from the Boston Museum School and the Smith-Mason Gallery Award in sculpture in 1971. Her most noted works, "Black Gothic," "The Root Man," and "The World of Dr. Buzzar" have been exhibited in various galleries, including the James A. Porter Gallery, Johnson C. Smith University, Carnegie Library, the Institute of Modern Art in Boston, and Howard University.

Harriet Forte Kennedy
sculpture and museum administrator
(photo courtesy of Linda Thomas)

Another important artist, Samella Lewis, has also made significant contributions to the arts through her writing and curatorships. Born in New Orleans in 1924, she was one of the first Black women to receive her doctorate in the arts, hers from Ohio University. With a specialty in

Asian, African, and European arts, in addition to Black American art, she has been a consultant for the National Endowment for the Arts and the Second World Black and African Festival of the Arts and Haitian Culture, in 1977. Lewis has been a guest curator for the Santa Barbara Museum: "Contemporary Black Art"; the Ankrum Gallery: "Art of African Peoples"; and the La Jolla Museum: "Dimensions in Black," 1970. Her publications have also been an asset to the much neglected field of the documentation of Black arts. They include *Black Artists on Art*, I and II; *Portfolios of Contemporary American Artists*; and *Art: African-American.*

Samella Lewis - artist and gallery owner

Lewis' artistic works are found in the permanent collections of the Baltimore Museum of Art, the Atlanta University Museum of Contemporary Art, the Oakland Museum, and numerous others.

Kay Brown is best known for her dramatic collages. She has exhibited at the Acts of Art Gallery in New York which is owned and operated by Nigel Jackson, a painter who believes in the exhibition and sale of work of Black artists independent of Establishment critics. Brown's work is often topical and almost always political. One of her works is entitled "Remember Biafra." Other pieces of her works have featured Dick Gregory, Imamu Baraka, Medgar Evers. Brown is also a contributor to the *Feminist Art Journal*. She is a member of the Black art collective, Weusi Nyum-Ba-Ya-Sanaa. Other members of the group who share a similar sensibility include Carole Byard, Valerie Maynard, Miriam Francis, Marian Straw, Charlotte Amezor, Marcia Jameson, Sheila Beckles, and Camille Billops.

Other of the new generation of young Black artists, reflective of the Black awareness movement, include Melonee Blocker, who studied at Columbia University and has exhibited at the Los Angeles County Museum; Gloria Bohanon who has her Master of Fine Arts degree from the Otis Art Institute and has exhibited at the Los Angeles Artist's Association Gallery; Mkele Egozi, with a Master of Fine Arts from Washington State University, who has shown her work at the Vincennes Art Fair in Chicago; Varnette Honeywood, a graduate of Spelman College, whose works have been presented at the Contemporary Crafts Gallery in Los Angeles; Gloria Brown Simmons, who has a Master of Fine Arts from California State College and who produced the first Black exhibit at the Smithsonian Institute, from which she received a scholarship; and Barbara Chase–Riboud. Chase–Riboud, sculptor, who holds fine arts degrees from Temple University and Yale University, has exhibited in numerous galleries, including the Museum of Modern Arts, the Salonde La Jeune, the Museum of Fine Arts in Boston, and the Bertha Schaefer Gallery in New York.

Primitive Painters

Two primitive painters who were "discovered" only relatively recently are Clementine Hunter and Minnie Evans. Hunter, born 1892 at Hidden Hill Plantation in central Louisiana, was in her sixites before she ever tried to paint. Now, nearly a hundred years old, she is one of the most popular Black artists. At the age of sixteen, Hunter picked cotton on the Melrose Plantation in Louisiana where, eventually, she became a cook and seamstress. When a guest who was a painter left behind some paints and brushes, she was tempted to "make her mark," as she puts it. Encouraged by another guest at the Melrose house who saw that she had talent, she began painting at the age of about sixty. Her work has been purchased by famous Americans, and two of her paintings were chosen to be included in the national art tour, The Black American Artist: 1750-1950. She was first exhibited at Northwestern

State University in 1950, an exhibition she was barred from attending because she was Black. Her work, full of religious themes and rural scenes, now sell for up to $900 per painting.

Minnie Evans, born 1892 in Long Creek, North Carolina, started painting seriously in 1935. She is sometimes referred to as the "innocent surrealist" because of her primitive Biblical themes" that seem to express the wish of the artist to become a medium of a greater external force," notes David Driskell. He goes on, "She is likened to Klee for her calligraphic figures; Rousseau for her visionary elements, and Black for her apocalyptic subjects". She has exhibited at the Little Gallery in Wilmington, North Carolina; The Indian Museum of Art; the Museum of Folk Art; the Museum of Modern Art in New York; the Studio Museum in Harlem; and the Whitney Museum of American Art, also in New York—all in the Sixties and Seventies.

Abstract Artists

One of the most prominent abstract artists did not take herself seriously as a painter until she was 68 years old. Soon after she did, others quickly recognized her as well, and she became one of the most highly touted Black artists of the modern period. Her name was Alma Thomas. Thomas was the vice-president of the noted Barnett-Aden Gallery when it opened in 1943. She was always interested in art, and in 1950 when she retired from the school system in Washington, D.C., she devoted her full time to painting. Her earlier paintings included "Tenement Scene, Harlem." It is characterized by "slashing, exhuberant, brush strokes . . . controlled by dark, almost gridlike lines, which begin to delineate the tenement buildings."[20]

Essentially, Thomas' work was inspired by nature. Typical is her painting "Lunar Rendevous," which contains "dabs of small colored tesserae, suggesting a mosaic like effect."[21] Judith Wilson described her work in this mode as "brilliant wheels of color and pulsating rows of paint that dance on the canvas in eloquent expression of the flowers and foliage she loved." Some of Thomas' works on the other hand, were inspired by the lunar program and include "The Launching Pad," "Blast Off," and "Sunrise Creeps on Earth." She received the acclaim of critics like Hilton Kramer of the *New York Times*, and in 1972 she had the rare opportunity to have a one-woman exhibit at the Whitney Museum in New York. Then 77 years of age, Thomas died in 1977.

Another highly praised artist is Bettye Saar, whose main artistic materials include discarded objects like shells, feathers, and bones. Saar is concerned with the "metaphysical, referential and spiritual qualities within the natural, organic and man-made objects she recycles." Her work has been characterized as "intuitive, mystical, personal, intimate, ritualistic, referential, private and collective."[22] There are three distinctive styles in her work. Her early pieces used symbols of astrology and the occult. The second is what she calls mojos, wall hangings that combine mystical symbols with natural objects such as leather, feathers, fur, and driftwood. The third style is more outrightly political. She takes derogatory images and "liberates" them an example is her famous "Liberation of Aunt Jemima," which shows the well-known figure as an aggressor, wielding a spatula. Saar also has nostalgic pieces and those emphasizing the greatness of figures in Black history, like the Queen of Sheba. Some of Saar's other noted works include "Black Girl's Window" and "Grandma's House." In 1975, Saar was one of the few Black artists to have a solo exhibit at the Whitney Museum.

The imagery in Suzanne Jackson's work "is personal to the point of being esoteric," observed Linda Bryant. "Distorted yet recognizable figural forms interact with vignettes presenting the viewer with seemingly symbolic and spiritual narratives." Jackson's work, including the pieces "Witches, Bitches and Loons" and "Splash," has received commendation from many leading Black artists, including Romare Breaden.

"Numbers of arrows provide the referential linkage between order and disorder, and content and thematic elements in the personal iconography of Hwardena Pindell," notes Bryant. Her work is characterized by concern for energy, mysticism, automatism and ritualistic process. At first expressing this attitude by the use of only dots which appeared as if they were uniformly placed and seemed to float on the canvas surface, Pindall's most recent work has also incorporated hair, board slats, and color pigment, giving it a three-dimensional appearance. Her works include "untitle #4, 1973" and "Video Drawing: Swimming Series, 1976."

Other artists in the abstract mode include Ellen Banks, who utilizes collages, water colors, diagonal, horizontal or vertical straight-edged shapes. Along with Harriett Kennedy, Banks was the other of two women who exhibited at the Afro-American Exhibit at the Boston Museum of Fine Arts in 1970. She has also been the recipient of the Prix de Paris in 1967. Elaine Crossley creates her work using the Cubist method and employs pastels, portraits, geometric design, abstracts, and mixed media. She has had a one-woman show at the College of Notre Dame in California.

Institution Builders

A number of Black women were instrumental in the founding of art centers and organizations, as well as being artists themselves. Alice Gafford, for example, had a prominent role in the development of the Los Angeles Art Association in 1937. She also inaugurated the Val Cerde Art and Hobby Show in 1946. Born in 1886 in Tecumseh, Kansas, she did not get involved in the art world until the age of seventy. Previously, she had had a distinguished nursing career, even working at one time with Daniel Hale Williams, the noted Chicago physician.

After moving to Los Angeles, Gafford enrolled in a two-year course at the Otis Art Institute. Since 1937, she has received more than 25 awards and has had her paintings displayed on three continents and at many of the major American galleries, such as the Howard University Art Gallery, the Long Beach Museum of Art, and the Charles Bowers Memorial Museum.

Georgette Powell, born 1916 in Charleston, South Carolina, was the founder-director of "Tomorrow's Art World Center" in 1966 in Washington, D.C., a community-oriented workshop in the visual arts. A graduate of Cooper-Union Art School, she designed and executed murals for the Harlem Hospital and the Queens General Hospital as an employee of the Federal Arts Project from 1936-1938. Her work is exhibited at such major galleries as the National Gallery of Art in Washington, the Smith Mason Gallery in the same city, and the Carnegie Institute in Pennsylvania.

Ionis Martin (1936, Chicago) organized the first "Through Young Eyes" art exhibit in Hartford, Connecticut in 1968. A former student of Aaron Douglass at Fisk University, she is an artist-printmaker and has won prizes in the Greater Hartford Arts Festival. In 1976, she won prizes in the Canton Gallery and the Green Open and Members' shows. Martin is a founder of the Artists Collective, head of the Fine Arts Commission for the City of Hartford and a corporator of the Redbrook School.

Perhaps the most important Black art school that has been established is the Elma Lewis School of Fine Arts. Founded in 1950 by Elma Lewis, a civic leader and dance and drama instructor, it currently has a staff of over one hundred distinguished faculty and an enrollment of 700 students. Located in Boston, Massachusetts, the school provides instruction in drawing, graphics, and ceramics, in the plastic arts and in other disciplines. The school also sponsors exhibitions in cooperation with the Boston Museum of Fine Arts. In 1968, Lewis was also the founder and director of the National Center of Afro-American artists.

The story of the Black women in the plastic arts is one of triumph in the face of the tremendous obstacles of racism, sexism, and class snobbery. They were an integral part of every major art movement, from the pioneer period to abstractionism, in the contemporary phase of art history.

It is interesting to note, that despite the expense of the process and the technical difficulty, a disproportionate number of Black artists were sculptors; and the majority of sculptors were women. No one has explored that phenomenon, but perhaps its reason is found in the unconscious memories of Africa. There, sculpture took the form of carved figures that were utilized for masks, cult objects, and ancestor representation. The sculptor was the bridge between the religious hierarchy and the rest of the community. As such, the artist was part of both the secular and the sacred. Magic powers were ascribed these creators and a special aura surrounded their role in the African society.

NOTES

[1] Margaret Just Butcher, *The Negro in American Culture* (New York: Alfred Knopf, 1972), pp. 207-208.

[2] Butcher, p. 208.

[3] Butcher, p. 208.

[4] James A. Porter, *Modern Negro Art* (New York: Dryden Press, 1943), pp. 61-62.

[5] Elsa Honig Fine, *The Afro-American Artist* (New York: Holt, Rinehart, and Winston, 1971), p. 66.

[6] Porter, p. 63.

[7] Butcher, p. 220.

[8] Velma J. Hoover, "Meta Vaux Warrick Fuller: Her Life and Art," *Negro History Bulletin*, March-April 1977, 40, 2, p. 678.

[9] Hoover, p. 678.

[10] Butcher, p. 235.

[11] David Driskell, *Two Centuries of Black American Art* (New York: Alfred A. Knopf, 1976), p. 141.

[12] Romare Bearden and Harry Henderson, *6 Black Masters of American Art* (New York: Doubleday, 1972), p. 93.

[13] Countee Cullen, "Elizabeth Prophet: Sculptress," *Opportunity*, July 1930, p. 204.

[14] Porter, p. 139.

[15] Cullen, p. 205.

[16] Porter, p. 139.

[17] Benny Andrews, "New Colors, Old Canvas," *Encore American and Worldwide News*, 23 June/4 July 1975, p. 64.

[18] Andrews, p. 64.

[19] Porter, p. 142.

[20] Fine, p. 152.

[21] Linda Goode Bryant and Marcy S. Phillips, *Contextures* (New York: Just Above Midtown, Incorporated, 1978), p. 17.

[22] Bryant and Phillips, p. 62.

CHAPTER V
THE IMAGE OF BLACK WOMEN IN FILM

Not until the era of the talkies, which began with Al Jolson's *The Jazz Singer* in 1927, did Blacks have the opportunity to play in films. However, prior to this time, Noble Sissle and Eubie Blake had made experimental sound shorts. During the pre-Civil War minstrel period, the Blacks' image in blackface had preceded the actual appearance in film.

From the beginning, the white version of the Black character was limited to five types: the Tom, the coon, the tragic mulatto, the mammy, and the Black buck, according to critic Donald Bogle.* Within this milieu, Blacks strove for artistic integrity by the only means left to them: their creative approach to a part, outright protest or by making their own films. But the capital and the potential power involved with filmmaking still made it the medium Blacks had the least control over. Their victimization in film was the consequence.

Of the character types described by Bogle, the mammy and the tragic mulatto were the particular masks that Black women wore. The tragic mulatto had one of its first appearances in the movie entitled *The Debt* (1912). *The Octoroons* and *In Slavery Days* also used the tragic mulatto character, which ran the gamut of the likable woman who would have led an ideal life if she had not that drop of you-know-what, to a basically evil and degrading creature.

"Mammy," that kindred spirit to the coon, made its appearances in films like the blackface version of *Lysistrata* and the *Coontown Suffragettes* (c 1914). The latter movie got the feminists and the Blacks in one stroke as it depicted a group of militant mammy washerwomen organizing a movement to keep "their good-for-nothing husbands" home, notes Bogle. Then there was also the Aunt Jemima, the female counterpart to Uncle Tom and a variation of the mammy. Jemima was often religious, content with her role, shares the same values as the whites and generally "sweet, jolly and good tempered—a bit more polite than mammy and certainly never as headstrong."[1] She made her appearance in 1916 with *The Wooing of Aunt Jemima*.

It would take D.W. Griffith's *Birth of a Nation* in 1915, however, to demonstrate the epitome of the negative Black image. The movie, depicting the Reconstruction period, so incensed the National Association for the Advancement of Colored People that it picketed

*Bogle's *An Interpretive History of Blacks in American Film* remains as the most incisive and comprehensive book on the subject to date. This chapter is highly indebted to it.

the New York premiere. The film also provoked riots in Boston and Chicago; it was eventually banned in five states and nineteen cities— but not before it would leave its mark. Technically, *Birth* was an extraordinary achievement, but the film enhanced its effectiveness by exploiting the worst fears in the white psyche. The film also exploited certain stereotypes of women, both Black and white, which would influence generations of movie making.

In the characterization of Lydia, who is the mistress of a white carpetbagger, Griffith explored the possibilities of the "dark, sinister, half-breed as a tragic leading lady."[2] Lydia was haughty and lusted for power. She was hostile to whites and was the only female in the film that was capable of demonstrating any sensuousness. Bogle observes that Griffith was the first major producer to divide the women's roles according to their color. Both Lydia and the mammy in the film were played by white actresses in blackface, but the latter was considerably darker, overweight, middle-aged, desexed. Despite the more positive characteristics achieved by Blacks in theater, literature, dance and the arts during the period, "Blacks were divested of any worthwhile human qualities and projected as reprehensible beings, crooning across movie screens for the sole benefit of largely illiterate and gullible white audiences."[3]

Independent Black Films

Beginning in 1914, a number of independent Black filmmakers attempted to produce their own movies about Blacks. The first film, *Darktown Jubilee*, starring the famous Bert Williams, was met in Brooklyn with not only hisses and howls but full-blown race riots. The event presaged the Black producer's problem in becoming established in the industry. Constantly, he was plagued by financial distribution and technical problems as well as physical violence. Nevertheless, more than 100 firms and corporations were founded to produce Black films. Though some of these were white, a good number was Black as well. The most prominent of the Black producers was Oscar Micheaux, who produced over 30 movies between 1918 and 1948, including the first Black talkie in 1931. Black female stars like Ethel Moses, dubbed the "Negro Harlow," emerged out of the independents. Bea Freeman, another one of Micheaux's leading ladies, was known as the "sepia Mae West."

The first Black movie star to really emerge out of the independent Black films was Edna Morton (the colored Mary Pickford), who was advertised as a "teasing brown," a torrid dancer who had the "grace and abandon of her race."

In the end, the independents just could not compete with Hollywood, though many Black actors like Lena Horne, Paul Robeson, Nina Mae McKinney, Moms Mabley and Louise Beavers got either their starts or apprenticeship experiences in independent Black films. The Black film actor and actress would have to fight for their artistic integrity through the industry's inherently racist system, and in the next decade, that fight would make banner headlines

With the advent of sound in the movies there was another significant development. Despite the success of the first talkie, it made most blackface renditions absurd. Secondly, with sound, one needed music, rhythm, dancing—life. Who could best provide it? Blacks, of course. And so the period 1927-1940 was one of the years of a major breakthrough for Black actors and actresses, for now they, rather than a blackfaced version of them, would be on the screen. This turn of events did not presage a more positive image, however, and in a way, the development was more deleterious. There has always been a negative relationship between the technological innovation in the American film and the Black character, noted Pines.[4] So with the advent of sound, the negative image became even more realistic! The stereotype could now be indelibly seared in the American psyche.

And the stereotypes flourished. In Fox's production of *Hearts in Dixie* (1929), the inevitable plantation scenes were rife with gay pickaninnies, sleepy slaves, and liver-lipped coons singing "Massa's in the cold, cold ground." The *New York Times* called it "faithful in its reflection of black men of those days down yonder in the cornfields." The real significance is that this was the beginning of another blackface tradition that would haunt Black actors and actresses for generations: their own caricature of themselves. *Hallelujah*, produced by MGM and directed by King Vidor, was the second of the major spectacles of the era. Technically superb, it is the story of a "good" Black young man who fights the temptations of the flesh, personified by the mulatto, Chick. Eventually he spurns her for his local sweetheart and enjoys the open arms of his patient Christian family at home. Not only did it become an American classic, notes Bogle, but it was the precurser of all-Negro musicals. The theme of the film would be seen in later films such as *Carmen Jones*. The blues singer Victoria Spivey appeared in that film as the "sad-eyed" sensitive girl back home, but the real star of the movie, and one who launched her career through it, was Nina Mae McKinney.

Born Nannie Mayme McKinney in Lancaster, South Carolina in 1913, McKinney and her family eventually moved to New York. There she was struck by the lights of Broadway and got a part in Lew Leslie's

"Blackbirds of 1928." Vidor spotted her in *Blackbirds* and chose her for *Hallelujah's* leading part when she was but seventeen years of age. She is called by Bogle the archetype of the sex object, one which dictated the behavior of leading ladies from Lena Horne to Lola Falana. She is a tragic mulatto, half woman, half child, torn between impulse and moral self-discipline.

Nina Mae McKinney - movie actress
(photo courtesy of Marjorie Clinton McMurray)

McKinney was the first Black actress recognized on the screen. *New York Post's* Richard Watts, Jr. called her "one of the most beautiful women of our time." Irving Thalberg said that "she was one of the greatest discoveries of the age." On the strength of her performance, MGM signed her up to a five-year contract, her dramatic success would be short-lived. There were just no roles for a Black leading lady, nor would there be for over 30 years. McKinney was the first of many leading lady types whose career would get trapped in the cul-de-sac of American racism and white perception.

Just five years after *Hallelujah,* McKinney would be forgotten. She did have some success, however, in Europe, where she was billed as the Black Garbo and sang in cafes and night clubs in Paris, London, Budapest and Dublin.[5] In 1935 she played opposite Paul Robeson in Zoltan Korda's *Sanders of the River* in England. McKinney returned to the United States and acted in some independent Black films. Her last important role was *Pinky* in 1949. Though her career was not totally successful, she did influence many of the actresses, particularly Dorothy Dandridge, who came afterward. She died in 1967, a year before her posthumous induction into the Black filmmaker's Hall of Fame.

The final Black film of the 1920's was *St. Louis Blues,* starring the incomparable Bessie Smith. She plays herself, a blues singer wronged by her man, Jimmy the Pimp. The only real distinguishing factor of the film is Bessie Smith's extraordinary ability to express Black pain,[6] and her great capacity to express a particular kind or earthy sensuousness.

The Thirties Servants Speak Their Minds

Blacks are America's metaphor, observed Richard Wright, and never was this truer than after the stock market crash of 1929. The Black servant was loyal: his master's best friend in an age where people were losing faith in everything. The servant provided comic relief and assurance in a time of tension and insecurity. The most famous Black woman servant in the film of the period was Louise Beavers. She was at one time the most important actress working in films. Beavers was the first distinctive mammy character, "the perfect foil and background for Mae West, Jean Harlow, and Claudette Colbert."

Beavers carefully groomed her persona as the mammy figure. She force-fed herself to attain the "proper girth," took lessons to learn the southern dialect, since she was a native of Cincinnati, Ohio, and made professional white chefs actually prepare the food in her films, for she hated to cook. By 1933 Louise Beavers was a veritable fixture on the screen, having done ten films in the previous years. By the end of 1933 she had added *She Done Him Wrong* (Mae West) and *Bombshell* (Jean Harlow) to her list. But, of course, it was *Imitation of Life* in 1934 for which she is best known.

The humiliation that Beavers endured is illuminating and illustrates what a lot of Black actresses were going through. Bogle reports that the young white actress who plays the daughter, Peola in *Imitation,* became visibly repelled when she learned that Beavers was to play her mother. Beavers, on the other hand, protested the word, "nigger," being used in the film, and with the aid of the National Association for the Advancement of Colored People, got it removed from the script. However, she was reportedly commanded to say the word "Negro" in the front office over and over again as a form of punishment.[7]

After her role in *Imitation*, Beavers played in a stream of mediocre movies. The only opportunity she had to escape the stereotype that she had helped to transfix on the screen was in 1950 when she played Jackie Robinson's mother in the *Jackie Robinson Story*. Her last important appearance was as a maid in the television series, *Beulah*. Beavers died in the early Sixties.

Louise Beavers was not the only actress who was catapulted by the box-office hit, *Imitation of Life*. The adult Peola was played by Fredi Washington, an actress who for a long time was considered the great Black hope.[8] She was sophisticated and talented. She had the charisma as well as the ability to be a leading lady. Born in Savannah, Georgia in 1903, Washington began her career as a nightclub and cafe entertainer. Upon coming to Harlem in the Twenties, she and her sister Isabelle Washington were among the most attractive of the social set. Fredi Washington had some success in the touring company of *Shuffle Along*, followed by her stage appearances in *Singin' the Blues* and *Porgy*. On the stage Washington often encountered the same problem that would circumscribe her entire career: she was too Black to be white and too light to play many Black roles. After all there were not many like the mulatto Peola around, but there were a few. She played a Black girl passing for white in *Black Boy*, a film in which she played opposite Paul Robeson. In 1933 she played a Harlem slut in *Emperor Jones,* again with Robeson. Bogle observes that Fredi Washington proved too sophisticated and intelligent for the role. In her other roles, including that of Peola, she showed the promise of both sensitive and provocative acting performances. In *Imitation*, her character emerged as the archetypal tragic mulatto figure.

Washington would share the fate of the other actresses of her ilk, for there was still no place for a leading Black actress in film. Eventually Fredi Washington returned to the stage, and in 1930, gave an excellent performance as Ethel Waters' rebellious child in *Mamba's Daughters*. But by 1940, her future had been spent.

Although the characterization of the tragic mulatto altered a little, that of the mammy was on its way to a transformation. Prior to the debut of Hattie McDaniel, the "mammy" image had been somewhat meek, but McDaniel emerged as the servant of the era, one who spoke her mind, became the social equal of her mistresses and the literal mother figure, Bogle observed. McDaniel arrived in Hollywood in the late 1920's. Born in Witchita, Kansas in 1898, she was the thirteenth child of a Baptist minister. She began her career by working in road companies and got a job singing on the radio at the age of seventeen with Professor George Morrison's orchestra.

The extraordinary film image of McDaniel evolved slowly. In the beginning the three-hundred pound actress played the typical submissive roles. But then in films like *Judge Priest* (1934) with Stepin Fetchit, her rebelliousness began to emerge, coming into its full expression in *Alice Adams*, starring Katherine Hepburn, the following year. In the movie Hepburn, McDaniel's mistress, puts on aristocratic airs to try to attract a beau from a higher social station than hers. McDaniel's contempt for this sham is unmistakeable. And her gum chewing, lethargic exits and entrances, and strutting about, with an unmistakable attitude of scornful reproach while pretending to be the model servant, created a new kind of mammy character, one that was very funny.

In 1936, McDaniel was in eleven films, including *Show Boat* and the *Postal Inspector*. In *Saratoga* with Clark Gable and Jean Harlow, her special role, which transcended that of the servant-master with Gable, and a mother-figure with Harlow, was again seen. It is said that when David O. Selznick tested Hattie McDaniel for the role in the epic *Gone With the Wind*, he decided immediately that only she could play the mammy part. Consequently he made script changes to accommodate the particular character that she had now made her trademark.[9] The role, which manifested no sense of inferiority on her part, permitted a kind of grandeur that got her the Academy Award for Best Supporting Actress—a *first* for Blacks.

At the other end of the spectrum of the Black mammy characterization was that of Prissy in *Gone With the Wind*, played by Butterfly McQueen. Bogle describes the characterization of McQueen as one marked by fragility, hysteria and absurdity—one that was almost other worldly. In contrast to McDaniel, he notes, McQueen could take a big scene "and condense it into the tiniest of lyrical poems," while McDaniel could make a monument of a small scene. Born in Tampa, Florida, in 1911, McQueen developed into a character that was a combination of the comic and pathetic. Her waif-like quality and "artistic mayhem" served to provide a needed relief from the building tension of certain scenes in *Gone With the Wind*, but when her character was used improperly, as it often was in subsequent movies, she appeared as an unintelligent and scatter-brained fool. She, herself, was embarrassed when she had to deliver the line, "Who dat say Who dat when you say dat?" in a film.

Following her performance in *Gone With the Wind*, she made some

15 other films. She made her Broadway debut in *Brown Sugar* in 1937, and subsequently appeared in *Brother Rat* and *What a Life*. In the Forties and Fifties McQueen's career took a disastrous turn and she had to support herself by being a sales clerk, waitress and dishwasher at various times. She was rediscovered in the Sixties when she appeared in the off-Broadway play *Curley McDimple*, and *Gone With the Wind* was reissued. She also had a part in *Purlie Victorious*. A recipient of the Black Filmmaker's Hall of Fame Award in 1975, McQueen remains active in the Harlem community where she resides. Presently, she is teaching at the Mt. Morris Marcus Garvey Recreational Center.

The Forties: Glamour Over Gloom

By the Forties, there were no more villains and jesters, notes film historian Bogle. The servants—now that the depression was over— "exchanged their mops and pails for zoot suits and sequined gowns." Even as servants, Blacks were expected to show off their ability to entertain, thus, Bill Robinson danced and Hattie McDaniel sang. Then, by the mid-Thirties, the Swing Era was reaching its peak. Filmmakers discovered the entertainment value as well as the practicality of inserting lively, swinging, musical segments in the films. These were usually specific musicial interludes that could be shot separately and easily extricated from the film sequence in case too many white viewers became offended in the sensitive markets. Again, Blacks were used to ease the tensions of what was in *this* era a sense of anxiety created by the war. The glamourous ladies, the high-stepping vivacious musicians could offer escapes into fantasy and boost morale. And so, this was the era to see a musical interlude of an orchestra of Duke Ellington or Louis Armstrong or Cab Calloway.

Two superstars of this era were Black women: Hazel Scott, an excellent pianist who consistently carried herself with a sense of pride and integrity, and the super-star of them all—Lena Horne. Lena Horne had been unwillingly pushed into show business at the age of sixteen by her stage-struck mother. Beginning as a chorus girl in the Cotton Club, she emerged as the most important figure of the period. She was already a star when she came to Hollywood in the Forties. She had successfully starred in Leslie's *Blackbirds* production of 1939, her first feature role on Broadway. She had also played prestigious night spots and had been featured in articles in *Time* and *Life* magazines. She also brought something else with her to Hollywood. Shuttled about as a child, she had been primarily raised by grandparents who were racially conscious and who had instilled some of the self-same principles in their almost too-beautiful grandchild. Walter White, head of the National

Association for the Advancement of Colored People at the time, was interested in her career. He was convinced that Horne could alter the depiction of Blacks in American movies.

Lena Horne - movie actress, singing in MGM's
"Meet Me In Las Vegas"
(photo courtesy of EBONY)

Horne refused maid parts, which had an unforeseen consequence. Many Black Hollywood people saw her as a threat to their livelihood, not to mention as a commentary on their own sense of integrity. They accused her of being a tool of the NAACP. She was not going to find much support with them, but it did not dampen her determination. Horne's first role in a film was *Panama Hattie* in 1942, with Red Skelton and Ann Southern. She made a brief appearance, but was sumptuously dressed. She made quite an impression. In the following year, Horne would perform in the first of the up-against-the-pillar routines in the first big all-star musical of the era, *Thousands Cheer*. She saw her future clearly. She would be cast as an exotic, a sex-object, but her character was so intact, as Bogle notes, she was too much of a lady to be a believable slut. Other "pillar pictures" followed and Horne was not happy about it. "They didn't make me a maid," she said, "But they didn't make me anything else either. I became a butterfly pinned to a column singing away in movieland." Then in 1943 came the huge successes *Cabin in The Sky* and *Stormy Weather.* Both featured the Katherine Dunham Dance Company, and the latter film, along with the song by the same title, established Horne's reputation in Europe. But by the Forties, however, she would run into trouble with MGM, partly because of her relationship with Lennie Hayton, and partly because of her self-directiveness. The studio, according to Bogle, started making it difficult for her to get not only movie parts, but night-club engagements as well. Two roles which should have gone to Horne—Julie in *Showboat* and another role in the *Bright Road* went to Ava Gardner and Dorothy Dandridge, respectively.

Still, things would get worse before they got better. Lena Horne was listed in the Red Channels of the McCarthy era, and was blacklisted from radio and television because of her interest in the Council of African Affairs and her friendship with Paul Robeson. It looked as if her career would end prematurely, but Lena Horne was not through yet. Her career was born again with her part in the Broadway show, *Jamaica*, with Harry Belafonte, and with subsequent film and club dates.

1950-1970: From the Shadow Into the Light

For film, the era of the Fifties could be remembered "as apathetic and sleepy-eyed, vulgar and hypocritical, grandiose, spectacular and tasteless.[10] Racially it was marked by the vicissitudes of the Black struggle in America: the "whitelisting" of the McCarthy period, the giving of the Nobel Peace Prize to Ralph Bunche, Marian Anderson breaking the racial barriers of the Met, the death of Emmett Till, the rise of Martin Luther King, Jr., federal troops into Arkansas to protect the Blacks attempting school desegregation and testing the national will of the 1954 Supreme Court Decision. It was an era when the film industry had to compete with television and provide more than the mindless entertainment of previous years. For the first time the prospective audience had to be lured away from the home, as Bogle notes, and the fantastical was replaced by the "message" movie, the stereotypical "types" replaced with personalities that people could relate to in some way.

Sidney Poitier, Ethel Waters, and Dorothy Dandridge were the leading Black stars of the decade. Of the three, it was Dorothy Dandridge who would become one of the most successful Black stars to date, certainly the most successful leading lady, says Bogle, and unfortunately, probably the most tragic. Born in Cleveland in 1924,

Dandridge was the daughter of a minister and an actress-comedienne. She began her show-business career performing in vaudeville shows with her older sister. By the time she was fifteen, she appeared with her sister and another singer as "The Dandridge Sisters," touring with the Jimmy Lunceford Band. At sixteen, like Lena Horne, whom she subsequently beat out for several seminal roles, she performed at the Cotton Club. During the Forties she appeared in nightclub acts and several films, including *Lady From Louisiana*, *Bahama Passage*, *Drums of the Congo*, *Ebony Parade*, and *The Hit Parade of 1943*. But it was not until the Fifties that she appeared in her first starring role, *Bright Road*, which also featured Harry Belafonte. In the film she revealed a "soft, radiant, melancholic quality," observed Bogle. And then in 1954, her appearance in *Carmen Jones*, established her, as the film critic noted, as the "definitive tragic mulatto."

Dorothy Dandridge, movie actress
(photo courtesy Schomburg Center
New York Public Library)

The story of her getting the part in *Carmen Jones* is an interesting one. At first, thought too sophisticated to play the role by Otto Preminger, Dandridge was said to concoct a whole new "look" and mode of behavior to get the part. She was successful and thus rode the wave that the film, which was the most publicized and successful all–Black spectacle in history, provided. Said *Newsweek* of her performance: "The range between the two parts [*Carmen Jones and Bright Road*] suggests that she is one of the outstanding dramatic actresses of the screen." Dandridge's place as a star was assured. She was the subject of cover stories from publications like *Paris Match* to *Ebony*. She was the first Black movie star to be nominated for an Oscar for the best actress. Dandridge also made history as the first Black actress to be shown in a romantic relationship with a white man on the screen. As dubious as that distinction seems to be, it is a testament of her importance as a star. The film was *Island in the Sun* (1957), and though it had predictable reactions from the Southern states particularly, it still grossed $8 million.

Despite these successes, Dandridge followed the well-worn path of other actresses of her style, like Fredi Washington and Nina Mae McKinney. There was a limitation, still, of how far a tragic mulatto type could go in America. Her next three pictures were filmed abroad, *The Decks Ran Red*, *Tamango* and *Malaga*. Dandridge had fled the country, like so many other entertainers, looking for an "opportunity to play diversified, untyped characters. But she too encountered only disillusionment and repeated compromises," according to Bogle.

Her last important American film was *Porgy and Bess*, in 1959. As Bess, she was brilliant, allowing neither Pearl Bailey, Sammy Davis, Jr., nor her co-star Sidney Poitier to upstage her. For her performance, she won the Foreign Press award as best actress in a musical. But she was to appear in only two more pictures. "Producers and directors seemed unable to think of her in any terms but that of the exotic, doomed mulatto," observed Bogle, "and already by the late 1950's and early 1960's the mulatto figure was dated." In addition, her life off the screen was an eery reflection of that on the screen. In 1965, at the age of forty-one, Dorothy Dandridge died, a tragic personification of the roles Hollywood had reserved for her.

After Dandridge, there would be more critical focus on the film itself, rather than the actress. In *The Jackie Robinson Story* (1950), no one could fail to be charmed by Ruby Dee's appearance as the dedicated wife, notes Bogle. *The Saint Louis Blues* (1958) featured Eartha Kitt, Pearl Bailey, Ruby Dee, Mahalia Jackson, and Ella Fitzgerald.

Eartha Kitt - actress and singer
(photo courtesy of EBONY)

The film adaptation of *A Raisin in the Sun* (1960) was eminently more successful than most of its cinematic predecessors. It featured a newcomer to the stage, Diana Sands, who, with her "witty and winning characterization of Beneatha, . . . revealed herself as a magnetic, compelling actress." Diana Sands, continued Bogle, "ushered in the contemporary, untyped intelligent Black woman . . . neither mammy nor mulatto." This new and more positive characterization showed the possibilities for Black women when the script was written by a Black woman. Later, Sands appeared in *An Affair of the Skin* (1963), *The Landlord* (1970), where she managed, "amid heavy dramatics, to impart a comic, light-hearted side to her character;" and *Doctor's Wives* (1971) where she proved that "talent could transcend material." In *Georgia, Georgia* (1972)—the first film with a screenplay by a woman—by Maya Angelou, Sands' leading dramatic role, though not wholly satisfying, according to Bogle, was nonetheless compelling.

Claudia McNeil also got good reviews as the strong Mama in *A*

Raisin, and she proved a powerful, if not charismatic, figure that was the nucleus of the Younger family. The one performance that retained its full intensity in the film was that of Ruby Dee. Previously seen in films like *No Way Out*, *The Jackson Robinson Story*, *Go Man Go*, *Edge of the City*, *Virgin Island*, and *Take Another Step*, Dee revealed the full potential of her acting abilities in *Raisin*. In it she "forged her inhibitions . . . and her taut ache to convey beautifully the most searing kind of Black torment. The rest of the cast exploded with obvious rage," observed Bogle, "but Ruby Dee's tension in contrast, was all the more immediate because it was so well controlled." In subsequent performances, where she could use the trembling kind of inhibitive quality that she possesses to good advantage, included *Uptight* (1969) and *Buck and the Preacher*. Her appearance in the TV drama *Roots* was also powerful.

A number of art films, which looked to more than commercial success, also revealed some interesting characterizations of Black actresses. There was Vinnette Carroll's portrayal of the hostile mother in *One Potato, Two Potato* (1964). Abbey Lincoln made her acting debut in *Nothing But a Man* (1964) and provided "one of the warmest black female characterizations of the decade, . . . with appropriate strength and passion." Gloria Foster whose acting style is described by Bogle as "the most naturalistic of any Black actress in American pictures," showed herself in this film as well as in *Cool World* (1963) as an "introspective actress of great power." Foster's subsequent films included *The Comedians* (1970), the *Angel Levine* and *Man and Boy* (1972).

It was not until Otto Preminger's *Hurry Sundown* (1967) that the "first major, big-budget, star-studded motion picture to center on the militant spirit of the mid-sixties and the Black revolt," was produced. The film, filled with racial cliches, the signature of Preminger films containing Blacks, revealed a new characterization via Diahann Carroll. In her previous roles in *Carmen Jones* and *Porgy and Bess*, she was an attractive, pert but non-exotic sensual type. Bogle describes her as "the postintegrated woman" and in *Paris Blues* (1961) she first emerged as a "middle-class Negro lady type." She came closer "in speech, dress, mannerism, looks, and lifestyle to the great white 'ideal' than any Black actress before her." Her character in *Sundown* was of an educated Northern Black woman whose indignance about discrimination came more from the head than the heart. The unfairness of prejudice is based on the fact that it prevents her from entering the mainstream society, whose value she accepts.

Beah Richards in *Sundown* came off better than any other Black actor in the film, notes Bogle. Cast in the beginning as a polite mammy character in the film, there was always the sense that beneath the gentility and unblinking courteousness, there was all of the bitterness, passion and hatred waiting to explode. The audience was not disappointed. Though the script did not provide for the proper evolution of her character when she finally screams out that she had been wrong in her mammyish attitude, and desperately entreats her son to fight, she easily emerges as the heroine of the film.

The only illuminating portrayal in the 1966 film, *A Man Called Adam*, was that of Cicely Tyson's which was called sensitive and intelligent by the film critic. The only significant thing in *The Love of Ivy* was that it showed, for the first time, the first love scene between Blacks in a popular movie. The film starred Abbey Lincoln and Sidney Poitier. In *The Slaves*, "Barbara Ann Teer provided the picture with its only genuine moments of anguish and pain."[11] In 1972, Diana Ross, made her film debut in *Lady Sings the Blues*, a film about the life of Billie Holiday. She was impressive in the performance, though it was not as reflective of the character of Billie Holiday as it was Ross' individual and personal interpretation of the character. Bogle calls her portrayal "charming, intelligent, and pervasive, her performance is solid and often invigorating."

But the most important film event of the year was *Sounder*. A warm picture, it brought to the fore the more important Black film actress to date—Cicely Tyson. It is both a commentary on the film industry and the versatility of Black women who performed in it, that all of the actresses, with the exception of Tyson, were more noted for their performances in other mediums than the film. She is the first genuine movie star since Dandridge, and she transcends all of the stereotypes to become the first genuine film actress of historical significance.

Sounder marked Tyson's exposure to a larger audience. Before 1972, she had a kind of cult following. Her appearances in *A Man Called Adam*, *The Comedians*, and the television series, "East Side, West Side" showed her to be an actress of distinction. But it took her appearance in the Martin Ritt movie to giver her larger-than-life pro-portions. As Rebecca, the sharecropper's wife, Tyson was called "the first great Black heroine on the screen," by the eminent *New Yorker* critic, Pauline Kael. She added, "Her Rebecca was worth waiting for. She is visually extraordinary. Her cry as she runs down the road toward her husband, returning from prison, is a phenomenon—something even the most fabled actress might not have dared."

"Her performance was a revelation," noted *Encore* art critic, Ivan Webster. "No one knew that a Black actress playing an ordinary woman, a sharecropper's wife in the South during the Depression could hold a national movie audience in her spell,"[12] but she did, earning the Oscar nomination for "Best Actress" and the Best Actress Award from the National Society of Film Critics. Two years later, Tyson made another dramatic breakthrough in the television movie, *The Autobiography of Jane Pittman*, where she "aged" from a young woman to that of a 110-year-old sage. "Tyson not only performed with supreme technical grace, but achieved another cultural feat: a gifted Black actress won over a national audience playing a non-heroic woman."[13] She received an Emmy for the performance.

Cicely Tyson - star actress of screen and television
(photo courtesy of EBONY)

Subsequent television appearances by Tyson included the portrayals as Wilma Rudolph's mother, as Coretta King, as Kunta Kinte's mother in *Roots*, and as Harriet Tubman in *A Woman Named Moses*. One reason why the emergence of Cicely Tyson is so important is that the beginning of her popularity began in the era of the "Blaxploitation film." Between 1970 and 1972, there were 50 such movies, including *Superfly, Shaft, Melinda,* and *Sweet Sweetback's Badaaaasss Song.* Despite what one feels may be the value of these films, there were few roles which gave vent to the dramatic possibilities of Black actresses. Tyson's appearance in *Sounder* subsequently was a breath of fresh air. In fact, it is Tyson's career which has dramatically opened up the possibilities of the Black actress who throughout the history of film has been pinned to stereotypes as surely as Lena Horne was to her pillar. Hopefully others will soon follow Cicely Tyson in realizing the dramatic possibilities inherent in both the past and future of the Black woman's experience in America.

NOTES

[1] Donald Bogle, *Toms, Coons, Mulattoes, Mammies, and Bucks: An Interpretive History of Blacks in American Film* (New York: Viking Press, 1973), p. 9.

[2] Bogle, p. 14.

[3] Jim Pines, *Blacks in Films* (London: Cassell & Collier Macmillan Publ. Ltd., 1975), p. 13.

[4] Pines, p. 14.

[5] Bogle, p. 33.

[6] Bogle, p. 34.

[7] Bogle, p. 64.

[8] Bogle, p. 60.

[9] Bogle, p. 89.

[10] Bogle, p. 159.

[11] Bogle, p. 225.

[12] Ivan Webster, "A Woman Called Tyson," *Encore American and World Wide News*, 6 November 1978, p. 24.

[13] Webster, p. 25.

CHAPTER VI

POETRY AND NOVELS

The Colonial Period and "The Mother" of Black Literature

The America to which the first generations of Africans came possessed little of the rich culture that existed in their native land. The colonists' level of music, dance, and the handicrafts, paled in comparison to those of the African continent. Although the colonists had brought with them the mind-set of their native England, they brought little of its culture. Besides, during the colonial period, the hard work required to clear the land, the poverty-stricken background of most of its inhabitants, and religious prohibitions left little time or inclination toward the arts. As late as 1762, Shakespeare's *Othello* could be presented only in Newport, Rhode Island, by advertising it as a "moral dialogue."[1] As for the written word, an observer noted, with "Shakespeare, Marvell, and their roistering successors of the Restoration within living experience [the early colonial poets] produced regional mounds of trite versification . . . "[2]

If things were wanting in the colonies in general, the cultural activities of the women were more so. They were confined for the most part to the domestic tasks of the society, and education for them was looked upon with suspicion. "The great mass of American females could boast for few accomplishments, save house-wifery," noted the 19th century writer Margaretta Matilda Odell. "They had few books besides the Bible. They were not expected to read, much less write." Until 1773 only one American woman, Anne Bradstreet, had published a volume of verse.

Against this background, it is quite extraordinary that women, Black women, or particularly Black women in bondage produced any art at all. However, in 1746, Lucy Terry, a slave in Deerfield, Massachusetts, witnessed an Indian raid there. She then wrote a poem about it. It was the first poem known written by an Afro-American, and it has been described as the best and most comprehensive account of that incident.[3]

The most remarkable Black poet of the period arrived in Boston Harbor from Senegambia in 1761. She was purchased by the Wheatley household, named Phillis, and became the "Mother of Black Literature." After 16 months in America, she was able to read English. By the age of twelve, she was studying Latin and was soon able to translate the *Ovid*. She read English literature and used Alexander Pope's work as a stylistic model. By the age of fourteen, says

Richmond, Wheatley was "a poet, as full-fledged in the art as any of her contemporaries," though she was neither male, nor white, nor free, nor in Europe.

Three years later, the reputation of Phillis Wheatley would go beyond the reaches of the Massachusetts colony. The event which would make her known throughout the colonies was the publication of an elegy dedicated to the Reverend George Whitefield, who died in 1770. The poem was published as a broadside with the legend, "By Phillis, a Servant Girl of 17 Years of Age, belonging to Mr. J. Wheatley, of Boston:—And has been but 9 Years in this Country from Africa." The poem appeared in Boston, Newport, Philadelphia, and New York in at least several editions, and in London in two.[4] Whitefield, an evangelist, had been the chaplain to Lady Huntingdon of England, the founder, spiritual leader, and financial patron of an early Methodist circle. But more than a chaplain, he had also served his English patroness as a missionary in the colonies. The poem resulted in Wheatley's being invited to London at the invitation of Lady Huntingdon.

PHILLIS WHEATLEY

Servant to Mr John Wheatley of Boston.

(photo courtesy of EBONY)

In the Spring of 1773, Wheatley, now twenty, was crossing the Atlantic again, but this time as a passenger rather than a slave. She was looking forward to meeting the Lady of Huntingdon, having her verse published in England and trying to mend her physical frailties that came as a result of the harsh New England weather. Though there is some doubt that she actually met the Countess, in all, her trip seemed successful. In a letter to the only Black friend of Wheatley's that chroniclers know about, Obour Tanner, she wrote of her warm reception and the "unmerited" civility of the English. Unfortunately, her trip was cut short, due to the illness of her mistress in the colonies. She returned to a nation on the precipice of war.

From all indications, Wheatley's *Poems on Various Subjects, Religious and Moral* sold well, and her friend Obour Tanner aided the poet in getting subscriptions for the verse. But, as Richmond observes, Wheatley's poetic career would become a victim of history. Only a month after the first shipment of 300 volumes were received into the Boston Harbor in May of 1774, the infamous dock was blockaded on orders of the British Parliament in revenge of the famous Tea Party of December 16, 1773.

Early on in the War, Wheatley continued writing poetry, most notably an ode to General George Washington in 1775. One of the more interesting footnotes of history is Washington's granting of an audience to Wheatley in his Cambridge headquarters in 1776. "I cannot refrain" said one chronicler, "from noticing the visit of one, who though a dark child from Africa and a bondwoman, received the most polite attention of the Commander-in-Chief . . . . She passed half an hour with the Commander-in-Chief, from whom and his officers, she received marked attention."[5] The timing of Washington's invitation, shortly before he reversed his policy to allow limited conscription of Black Soldiers into the Revolutionary army, led some to speculate that his "marked attention" had some political motivation.

By 1778, the father, mother and daughter of the Wheatley household were dead. The one remaining son had gone to England. Wheatley was manumitted and married a freedman, John Peters, in that year. These were difficult times in post-Revolutionary New England. There was inflation, and the society was still in disarray. It was particularly difficult for a Black poet who could do nothing else but write. But she continued at her craft.

In 1779, a notice in Boston's *Evening Post and General Advertiser* offered a volume of Wheatley's poems for sale. The ad promised a volume of 300 pages, listing the titles of 33 poems, with only the poem addressed to George Washington previously published. Also promised were 13 letters, three of them to the Lady of Huntingdon and one to Dr. Benjamin Rush. The advertisement however, seemed to elicit no responses. The reasons were probably many. Odell, Wheatley's biographer, observed that the winter of 1779 was a season of general poverty. Wheatley's friends of former days were scattered far and wide. In addition, Richmond notes, the asking price for the hardcover and "paper" editions, 12 and 9 pounds respectively, was probably too high even in those inflation-ridden times. In any case, the publication never got off the ground, but although Phillis Wheatley had little encouragement, she continued to write poems. Finally, in 1784, three poems of Wheatley's were published. By the time they appeared in print, Phillis Wheatley had been dead for several days. She was found in a "common Negro boarding house," where she was forced to "earn her own subsistence" in squalid surroundings. Her third child was lying ill by her side—dying a few hours after the mother.

The critical reception of Wheatley's verse shared the vicissitudes of her own life. One of the most unkind remarks came from Thomas Jefferson. "Religion indeed has produced a Phillis Wheatley," he said, "but it could not produce a poet." Others, however, felt differently. Henri Gregoire, the prominent abbe in the French Revolutionary era, in his treatise, *De la Litterature des Negres* (1808), castigates Jefferson for appearing "unwilling to acknowledge the talents of Negroes, even those of Phillis Wheatley. . . ." The abbe noted responses to her 1773 volume, including one from Voltaire, who, writing to the Baron Constant de Rebecq in 1774, said: "Fontenelle was wrong in saying that there were never any poets among the Negroes; there is in fact one Negress who writes very good English verse." Johann Friedrich Blumenbach, a German often referred to as the father of anthropology and an original investigator of ethnic categories, described *Poems on Various Subjects* in 1865 as "a collection which scarcely anyone who has any taste for poetry could read without pleasure."

Black critics, disappointed in Wheatley's seeming lack of racial consciousness, vapid neo-classical style, and fervent religiosity, which appeared to have made her glad to come to the land of Christianity from pagan Africa, have been particularly critical of her work.

Richard Wright explained these shortcomings away by saying that Wheatley's benevolent treatment in her household made her feel that "she was at one with the Colonial New England culture." The scholar, J. Saunders Redding, called her work "negative, bloodless and unracial." These comments, however, do not really address the question of Wheatley's lack of race consciousness in her work. Although she was no militant by any standard, it should be taken into account that her accomplishments alone undermined slavery. In 1788, the British abolitionist Thomas Clarkson noted, "if the authoress *was designed for slavery* . . . the greater part of the inhabitants of Britain should lose their freedom." Wheatley's presence alone was an indictment of the concept of the inferiority of Blacks that formed the underpinning of slavery. But beyond this, the full body of Wheatley's work (including her letters) when studied reveals that she was racially conscious and expressed it in her writing. At least two poems of Wheatley's expressly referred to Blacks: the one dedicated to the Black artist Scipio Moorhead, and one whose subject was the African writer, Terence. The poem was entitled "To S.M., A Young African Painter on Seeing His Works," written in 1773. In a letter to the Lady of Huntingdon, written in 1773, is another of several examples of her expression of concern for fellow Blacks.[6] "It gives me very great satisfaction to hear of an African so worth [sic] to be honored with your ladyship's approbation and friendship as him who you call your Brother," she wrote, probably referring to the Countess' public praise of Philip Quaque, the first African ordained priest in the Church of England. And in 1775, she responded to a naval officer's written praise of Africa in the *Royal American Magazine* by a poem of praise herself. One of the lines read:

> . . . and pleasing Gambia on my soul returns
> With native grace in 'spring's luxuriant reign
> Smiles the gay mead, and Eden blooms again.

This is the last time Africa is praised by a Black American writer until the Renaissance period in the first quarter of the twentieth century, noted Robinson.[7]

Nineteenth Century: The Black Woman's Struggle for Selfhood and Freedom

Although the next major Black woman poet did not appear until 1854, there was a number of utilitarian literary activities in the earlier part of the 19th century. By 1830, Black women had become actively involved in Northern antislavery societies and often wrote the tracts and pamphlets for the organizations. In addition, a number of slave narratives like Linda Brent's *Incidents in the Life of a Slave Girl* appeared. The racism of white women in the interracial abolitionist societies of the period inspired at least one poem by Sarah Forten, calling upon women at the First Anti-Slavery Convention of American Women in 1837 to abandon racial prejudice. Additionally, speeches were published, most notably those of the feminist abolitionist, Maria Stewart, who was the first American born woman to embark on a career of public speaking. During this period also, a number of Black women's literary societies promoted the reading of "polite" literature and original literary pieces which were criticized by the group.

By the 1850's a series of setbacks for the antislavery crusade enraged abolitionists. The Fugitive Slave Law of 1850 and the repeal of the Missouri Compromise shortly thereafter evoked a new militancy and emotional outcry. A poet named Frances E. Watkins Harper reflected the Black mood so accurately that after her 1854 publication, *Poems on Various Subjects*, "she was easily the most popular poet of the time," remarked the editors of *Negro Caravan*. Harper was also a political activist and throughout her life was involved with the abolitionist, and women's movements, including suffrage issues.

Frances E. Watkins - writer
(photo courtesy of EBONY)

Before the war, her energies were primarily devoted to the former and she read her work to packed lecture halls filled with antislavery sympathizers. These turbulent times were not ones of bellettristic letters. Harper's verse, mostly in the ballad form, appealed to passion rather than academic perfection. She sold over fifty thousand copies of her first two works of poetry, commented William Still, mostly to those who listened to her eloquent lectures. *Poems on Miscellaneous Subjects* went through twenty editions in twenty years.

Like the young poets of the civil rights period in the next century, Harper's work aimed directly at the cruelty of Black injustice. And like them, she could read her work with a "disarmingly dramatic voice and gesture and sighs and tears," noted critic William H. Robinson. When she rendered poems like the "Slave Auction" that included the lines "And mothers stood with streaming eyes / And saw their dearest children sold / Unheeded rise their bitter cries, / While tyrants bartered them for gold"—she left hardly a dry eye in the house. In another poem, "Bury Me In A Free Land," she made the emotional appeal to have herself buried where one may even "Make it among earth's humblest graves, / But not in a land where men are slaves."

After the war, Harper's poetry included themes which reflected her other interests. The woman's theme was prevalent, such as in the poem "A Double Standard" that ends with the line, "And what is wrong in woman's life / in man's cannot be right." In some of her other works she harped on the subject of suffrage in the Reconstruction period. Another issue that underlined the black support for woman's suffrage was the hope that women would not "sell" their votes or be as physically intimidated as the men were during this difficult period. One of Harper's poems, "Deliverance," from her 1872 book, *Sketches of Southern Life*, which expresses the concerns of the folk in this era, reflects this concern through the following lines:

> You'd laughed to seen Lucinda Grange
> Upon her husband's track
> When he sold his vote for rations
> She made him take 'em back.

Other volumes of Frances E.W. Harper include *Forest Leaves* (her first work which has not been located), *Moses, a Story of the Nile*, which went through three editions by 1870, and *Poems*, which was published in 1870 and had a second edition in 1900. She was also a novelist, in fact, the second Black woman to publish a novel (*Iola Leroy*, in 1892*), and she was the first Black woman to publish a short story ("The Two Officers," in 1859).[8] Although Harper's work was not brilliant according to literary standards, it achieved what it set out to do: evoke "powerful flashes of imagery and statement," as Redmond observed.

After Harper, no major woman poet emerged until the Harlem Renaissance period; however, a lesser known poet who wrote at the turn of the century was Alice Dunbar-Nelson. The wife of Paul Laurence Dunbar, she was a poet, short story writer, a journalist and an inspiration to other writers. Her volumes of verse include: *Violets and Other Tales* (1894), and *The Goodness of St. Tocque* (1899). She was also the editor of *Masterpieces of Negro Eloquence* and *The Dunbar Speaker* (1920), in which some of her poetry is represented.

*The first was Emma Dunham Kelly who published *Megda* in 1981.

The poem most often anthologized of hers is "The Sonnet," which shows her mastery of the form. Popular too is Nelson's poem, "Sit and Sew," which laments her "woman's place" during the war. Alice Dunbar-Nelson's work did not incorporate Black themes very often. The critic Kerlin has described poems like "The Lights at Carney's Point" as containing "fine symmetry, highly poetic diction and great allusive meaning."

The life and death struggle of the Reconstruction Era had left little time for literary pursuit. But by 1890, a new phenomenon had emerged. Women were asserting their rights to vote and transcending the traditional roles relegated to them in the society. Black women were a part of this national trend but had their own concerns as well. This was the era of the national Black clubwoman's movement that worked toward social improvement and political power. It was a period of great concern for the increasing violence against Blacks in the South, as evidenced by the anti-lynching campaign initiated by Ida B. Wells.

In addition, Black women were increasingly the target for character assassination. In fact, it was one such attack that precipitated the first National Convention of Colored Women in 1895. These attacks were bad enough in themselves, but they also had far-reaching effects. Prejudgement of the morality of Black women was often the rationale for refusing to employ them in other than domestic service. Although black women refuted these vicious charges, they generally believed that if they showed themselves to be the models of the Victorian code, which prevailed at the time, that much prejudice would be diminished. Other concerns were race loyalty, the connotations of miscegenation, the injustices of the Reconstruction period and the relationship of religious principles to the quest of freedom. Also of interest was the interracial debate between the Booker T. Washington and W.E.B. DuBois factions.

All of these concerns were addressed in the fiction written by Black women during the late nineteenth and early twentieth century. As in earlier periods, the exigencies of the Black situation demanded a utilitarian literature. "The value of any published work," observed the prominent clubwoman of the period, Gertrude Mossell, "especially if historical in character, must be largely inspirational." It is interesting to note however, that just about all of the protagonists in these novels were mulattoes. There may be a number of reasons for this, but certainly the character of mixed blood was a convenient vehicle for illustrating many of the racial injustices of the period. The presence of mulattoes showed the injustice of prohibiting interracial marriage yet encouraging sexual liaisons between the races. Black women alone bore the brunt of this circumstance. As Pauline Hopkins noted, "Marriage is made illegal between the races and the mulattoes increase. Thus the shadow of corruption falls on the Blacks and not on the Whites without whose aid the mulattoes would not exist." The mulatto character, particularly those who could pass for white, was also a convenient *deux ex machina* to stress race loyalty.

This was certainly true of Frances Harper's *Iola Leroy, or Shadows Uplifted* published in 1892. The mulatto heroine, Iola Leroy, is tricked into slavery, rescued by Union soldiers, and meets a white aristocratic doctor who, not knowing her race, falls in love with her. When he realizes she is Black, he still wants to marry her and take her away where she will not be known. Iola Leroy spurns the offer, however, primarily because of her concern for the children which would come out of this liaison. She decides, instead, to find her family scattered by the War.

Although there are critics who berate the novel for not containing elements of protest, the novel's concern goes beyond such a purpose. *Iola Leroy* "was not intended as a racial protest novel only," observed critic Rita B. Dandridge, "particularly when the actions of the female protagonist are considered." The novel, she continues, "should be viewed as a woman's novel presenting the difficulties of the protagonist . . . as a Black and a woman.[9] This is in keeping with the feminist concerns of the day. Another morale of the story relates to race loyalty and ethics. By denying herself marriage to the white doctor, Dandridge notes, Iola Leroy, "affirms the morality of Black motherhood and passes up the golden opportunity to overcome the stigma of her race. To Iola, being recognized as a Black mother is just as important, if not more so, as being treated justly as a Black."[10]

Tangled Threads and *Kenneth*, two other novels published as late as 1920 by Zara Wright, also reflect the theme of the mulatto spurning a life of racial anonymity to serve the race. Like other Black writers, however, Black women did write the more traditional protest novels during this period. *Contending Forces*, by Pauline Hopkins, is considered by one critic as the most forceful protest novel authored by a Black woman (until 1965), with the exception of Ann Petry's *The Street*.[11] Hopkins' novel is the story of several generations of the family of a wealthy planter, including both Black and white offspring. One hundred and fifty years of Black history are recounted in the novel, and it deftly illustrates that the motives which attend racism remained the same after the Emancipation Proclamation. The novel also calls for militant action at a time when the ideas of accommodationist Booker T. Washington were holding sway. Pauline Hopkins felt that Blacks could

best defend themselves by ". . . using the very methods of the South . . .
[by creating] sentiment *for* the race and *against* it detractors.[12]

Hopkins also commented on the anti-lynching campaign in full sway
by the date of the publication of the book. As Ida B. Wells later proved,
the notion that the motivation of murdering Black men in the South was
the raping of white women was scorned by a character in the book.
Lynching does not stop crime; it is but a subterfuge for killing men. . . .
"No; it is not rape. If the Negro votes, he is shot; if he marries a white
woman, he is shot; if he accumulates property, he is shot or lynched—
he is a pariah whom the national government cannot defend."[13] This
quote should be seen as another rationalization of the lynch law.
Novelists like Hopkins, also took the opportunity to expose the fact
that Black woman were the victims of sexual brutality perpetrated by
white men.

The other dominant theme of Black women's novels in the period
was the moral or religious principle, but these principles were not
expressed only in the name of piety. Survival of the race was a major
concern, and it was thought by many whites that Blacks would hasten
their own destruction if they succumbed to certain temptations—
especially drink. Religion, too, for Blacks was pivotal to their lives, not
only in the spiritual sense, but also in the social action sense, when
interpreted through the Black perspective. Black women, during this
period, based their arguments for social equality on Christian
principles. If Blacks held up their end of the Christian contract, then the
onus of responsibility fell on the whites. " . . . you cannot willingly
deprive the Negro of a single right as a citizen without sending
demoralization throughout your own ranks," warns a character in
Leroy. But that exhortation would only be valid if the character of
Blacks were beyond approach. This, in part, explains why just about all
of the characters in the novels of the period are models of perfection
and nobility. During this period, the novels written by Black women
were used as a vehicle to communicate the strategies for racial survival.
They also reflected their most compelling concerns of the period:
begging the question of humanity for all Blacks. The next period
reflected same social concerns, but the literature would also be shaped
by the myriad of the Renaissance.

The Harlem Renaissance: The Novelists

After the first World War, the trickle of Blacks making their way
North became a flood. Many found their way to Harlem, New York.
Between 1914 and 1920, its population grew from 50,000 to 80,000. By
1930 there were 200,000 Blacks living in Harlem.

It should be remembered that prior to this migration, the NAACP was founded by W.E.B. DuBois and others in 1909. This social action was taken as a result of the Springfield riots and other protest movements for the rights of Black Americans. The NAACP became involved in court action in its struggles for the civil rights of Blacks. On the other hand, the National Urban League, founded in 1911 as the result of the merger of three organizations, set its objectives as 1) to open new opportunities for Blacks in industry, and 2) to help Black migrants in their problems of adjustment in the cities.

The Harlem Renaissance was a separate and a cultural movement of the 1920's. And these three events—the founding of the NAACP, the Urban League, and the establishing of Harlem Renaissance—are to be seen as three different activities of the early 1900's.

Harlem became a cultural melting pot of Blacks from the South, the Caribbean, and Africa and a number of post-War forces set the cauldron boiling. A. Philip Randolph, who established the Brotherhood of Sleeping Car Porters and Maids in 1920, was flirting with socialism. Marcus Garvey captured the imagination of the masses with his "Back to Africa" scheme.

A new generation was taking control, to paraphrase Margaret Walker, and their values and lifestyles were reflected in the arts of the period. Langston Hughes, the poet, expressed the sentiment in another way: "We young Negro artists who create now intend to express our individual dark-skinned selves without fear or shame," he wrote in the *Nation* in 1926. "If white peoople are pleased we are glad. If they are not, it doesn't matter. We know we are beautiful. . . ."

Playwrights and novelists responded to this new cultural nationalism in part by exploring the folk and Black folk lifestyle in their works. Underlying this new philosophy was the belief that Blacks represented the genuine folk tradition. Consequently, Blacks exhibited a new interest in their African heritage and their "Negroness." They were also begging the question of their humanity. "How grand it was", observed Nathaniel Huggins in *The Harlem Renaissance*, "to be valued not for what one might become . . . but for what was thought to be one's essential self." The Harlem Renaissance gave birth to a plethora of new works by Blacks, including a number of Black women novelists and poets. Though they all wrote under the same "New Negro" banner, they had different interpretations on what it meant.

For Jessie Fauset, the term meant "putting one's best foot forward", much in the tradition as the novels of the previous period. She wrote four novels: *There is Confusion* (1924), *Plum Bun* (1928), *The*

Chinaberry Tree (1931), and *Comedy, American Style* (1933). In comparison to her predecessors, however, Fauset was not only more prolific, but had better control of the form. She wrote more novels between 1924 and 1933 than any other Black American woman and is considered the first to be an accomplished novelist. Fauset carried the torch of women of the previous generations who took the responsibility for expressing the racial strategies of selfhelp, racial loyalty, the Black nobleness of character and patriotism. After World War I, Watson noted, novels of Black women were even more expressly used as intraracial tools of self-examination and reflection. In the Twenties, however, Christian values were supplanted by middle-class values and race-consciousness, the latter of which came out of the new Black nationalism of the period.

Despite the evidence of a Black middle-class of significant proportions, the image of the Black was still one of the lowly down-trodden. In the introduction to *Chinaberry Tree*, Fauset addressed this issue. "It seems strange to affirm as news for many that there is in America a great group of Negroes of education and substance who are living lives of genteel interests and pursuits." Fauset was of the group of writers who believed that one of their duties was to expose such individuals. Again, one could reiterate that their motive went beyond snobbish appeal, though there was probably some of that too. There was the feeling that accomplishment was the cornerstone of respectability, and respectability could eradicate prejudice. "For Afro-Americans in the 1920's," notes Huggins, "individual achievement connotated more than personal comfort and ease. The future of the race seemed to depend on men and women making it in America." Those who did make it, it was further believed, helped lower the barriers for others. All in all, this strategy made the believers of this strategy not just bourgeois, but as Watson phrased it, militantly middle class.

Critic Stanley Braithwaite called *There Is Confusion* an "outstanding achievement in fiction." The novel deals with the success-oriented character, Joanna Marshall and her lover Peter Bye, whom she is determined to make a success as well. The confusion comes when these purposeful Negroes are still discriminated against by the larger society. The novel preaches against cynicism and the suitability as well as the desire of Blacks to be in the mainstream.

Fauset's three other novels, *Plum Bun*, *The Chinaberry Tree*, and *Comedy, American Style*, dealt with passing and race loyalty, the innerworkings of Black middle-class society and intraracial color prejudice, respectively. Jessie Fauset served other important functions as a part of the Renaissance. She was the literary editor of the *Crisis* for seven years and also worked with *The Brownies' Book* as literary and later managing editor. Two years after she joined the *Crisis* in 1919, she was a delegate to the Second Pan-African Congress, accompanying DuBois and Walter White, and wrote two articles about it in the *Crisis*. She was also a patron of the younger writers like Langston Hughes and Countee Cullen.

Nella Larsen was another important novelist of the Renaissance period. She utilized some of the same themes as Fauset but was far more intense and bitter, Arthur Davis observed.[14] She published two novels *Quicksand* (1928) and *Passing* (1929). The theme of the latter is explicit in its title and the book does not rise above other novels of this genre. But *Quicksand*, however, is one of the most interesting novels of the period. Much of what is known of Larsen's life seems to be reflected in this book about a mulatto woman who is the offspring of a Black father and Danish mother. The woman, Helga Crane, leaves her teaching position at a small Southern University which resembles Tuskegee, and visits her white uncle in Chicago. He refuses to see her but does give her money and suggests that she go visit her relatives in Denmark. Although she is seen as an exotic curio in the Scandinavian country, she is welcomed with open arms by her Danish family, and even receives a proposal of marriage from one of the country's leading artists. She yearns, however, to be among Black people, and returns to Harlem. When she is unable to get the lover she truly wants there, she ends up marrying a crude, peasant Black minister and resigns herself to a provincial life in a small Southern town.

Larsen's character, as imperfect as it is, is a self-directed and individual one. Notes Davis:

> Although Helga's mixed ancestry and the race situation in America naturally influence her, Miss Larsen seems to be saying that they are not the sole causes of Helga's tragedy. She is the victim of her own inability to make the right decisions, a hang-up which the author suggests *may* come from frustrated love, or from brooding over a father who deserted his family, or from strong unsatisfied sexual urges, or from all of these causes as well as the racial situation. Helga is a superb creation. With the probable exception of Kabnis in Toomer's *Cane*, she is the most intriguing and complex character in Renaissance fiction.[15]

Quicksand, then, represents a new departure in the novels of Black women. It is written from within, transcending the formulaic novels before it. It also reflects the "double-consciousness" that DuBois spoke about. For there was a part of Helga in every one of the cultures she found herself in: Scandinavia, Harlem, "Tuskegee" and Black rural life. Yet in the end, none, could fully satisfy her needs and she is unhappy in all of them.

The third and most important novelist of this group is Zora Neale Hurston. She is still the most prolific major Black woman writer in America, with seven full-length books, two plays, numerous essays, short stories and articles to her credit. Hurston was an excellent folklorist. A student of the eminent anthropologist, Franz Boas at Barnard, she received a Guggenheim Fellowship to study folklore in Haiti and other parts of the Caribbean and Louisiana. Her findings, underpinned by her own experiences in Eatonville, Florida—Hurston's hometown —resulted in some of the best Black folklore in print. An important aspect of her work was the recreation of the folk language and although the authors Charles Chesnutt and Paul Laurence Dunbar had written in Black dialect before her, Hurston's was the most authentic.

Two of Hurston's folkloric books are *Mules and Men* (1935) and *Tell My Horse* (1938). *Horse* is an account of the Vodun religion which Hurston studied for a time under Luke Turner, nephew of the American priestess Marie Leveau. Of the second book, critic Mary Helen Washington observed: *"Mules and Men* goes far beyond the mere reproduction of the tales; it introduces the reader to the whole world of jook joints, lying contests, and the tall-tale sessions that made up the drama of the folk-life of Black people in the South."[16]

The religion that Afro-Americans forged from their experience in this country also interested Hurston. The subject is most effectively revealed in *Moses, Man of the Mountain* (1939). The book is a fictional allegory of the Biblical story; the Israelites are the Blacks in this story. Moses, who is empowered by Hoodoo, leaves Goshen to build a nation. The theme of the work is that freedom consists of more than being given "liberty by one's enslavers. It is an internal matter and must be won as an individual.[17] American Negroes, like the Israelites, *Moses* says, must create their own nation. The abandonment of the African heritage, the internalization of the dominant group culture and beliefs would proscribe true freedom, which comes from "the indigenous intellectual, emotional, and spiritual elements in the Afro-American culture." Even with this, one had to still overcome inertia to lead a meaningful existence as a race. "It ain't just to get you all out of Egypt," says Moses, "it's to make something out of you afterwards."

Hurston's most successful books *Jonah's Gourd Vine* (1934) and *Their Eyes were Watching God* (1937) combined her knowledge and feeling for the folk with her brilliant abilities as a novelist. *Jonah's Gourd Vine,* which catapulted Hurston to national acclaim, is the only novel to examine so thoroughly the cultural meaning of the Black's acceptance of Puritanism, notes Watson. The work is about the trials and tribulations of Big John Pearson, a minister and ladies' man, as he tried to lead his flock righteously despite the "evil" temptations that bedevil him. Hurston also examines the role of the preacher in the Black community through the character of Pearson, who must constantly remind his people of his humanness, with all the imperfections of the species. The novel, then, goes much beyond the concept of Christianity as it was written about in the past.

Zora Neale Hurston, literary writer
(photo courtesy Schomburg Center
New York Public Library)

In the story of Pearson, Hurston expressed her belief that the Black church is the embodiment of Afro-American culture. As such, she saw Christianity as a thin veneer over traditional belief. Consequently, the way was paved for confrontation between the two cultures. The novel also presents one of Hurston's literary trademarks, the image of a strong self-directed woman in the character of Lucy Pearson, wife of the preacher. Lucy's personality is so forceful that her husband is even afraid to be in the same room with her when she is on her deathbed. Important to Lucy is that she pass on this sense of spirit to her daughter: "You always strain tuh be de bell-cow, never be de tail uh nothin'" she tells her.

The image of the strong Black woman is most effectively rendered in what many critics feel is Hurston's best novel, *Their Eyes Were Watching God*. Here, as Washington writes, "Hurston the creative artist and Hurston the folklorist were perfectly united.[18] The story of Janie, the protagonist, and her search for romantic fulfillment is probably the best and most convincing love story in Black fiction. Janie's odyssey is revealed through "folk language, folkways and folk stories [which] work symbolically . . . as a measure of a character's integrity and freedom."[19] As such the book represents more than a romantic escapade. "Deeper than its love story," wrote Washington, "is Janie's search for identity, an identity which finally begins to take shape as she throws off the false images which have been thrust upon her because she is both Black and a woman in a society where neither is allowed to exist naturally and freely."[20] Consequently, Washington stated, "Janie is one of the few—and certainly the earliest—heroic Black woman in the Afro-American literary tradition."

Zora Neale Hurston was the most controversial writer during the period of the Harlem Renaissance. She was as free-spirited as her characters it seemed, and had an iconoclastic lifestyle at a time when Black intellectuals were relatively doctrinaire. As a result she found herself in the middle of ideological crossfire. On one side was the genteel school of writers who sought to carry on the tradition of showing Blacks at their idealistic, middle-class best. On the other side were the militants, or the "race" people vigorously protesting racism and oppression. Hurston represented neither school of thought prevalent at the time. Not only did she not create characters out of the genteel tradition; her characters were often more victimized by Blacks than by racism. To exacerbate the situation, she also expressed these views personally. The race question, as defined in her day, left her unmoved, she once told *Time* magazine. And in *World Tomorrow* she wrote in 1928:

> There is no great sorrow damned up in my soul, nor lurking behind my eyes. I do not mind at all. I do not belong to the sobbing school of Negrohood who hold that nature somehow has given them a low-down dirty deal and whose feelings are all hurt about it. . . . No, I do not weep at the world—I am too busy sharpening my oyster knife.

Some felt that Hurston appeared a little too happy—particularly in front of white folks. She was derided for playing the role of the "Darkie" in front of them—most scathingly in Wallace Thurman's play *Harlem*, but it is interesting to note that Hurston was a lone voice criticizing the Supreme Court decision of 1954, because she felt Blacks did not need integration to live fulfilled lives. Of course, this was another opinion which drew less than praise from her colleagues. These facts are important because in the opinion of some critics, like Washington, Hurston's controversial life-style and personality negatively effected objective critical analysis of her work—then and even today.

Two other of her books, *Seraph on the Swanee* (1948) whose characters are poor Whites, and *Dust Tracks on the Road* (1942), her autobiography, were the least effective of her works. They were written near the end of a controversial career when her enthusiasm had probably understandably waned. "Bitter over the rejection of her folklore's value," wrote her biographer Robert Hemenway, "especially in the Black community, frustrated by what she felt her failure to convert the Afro-American world view into the forms of prose fiction, Hurston finally gave up." Zora Neale Hurstron died in poverty and obscurity in 1960.

The Harlem Renaissance: The Poets

The period of the Renaissance largely belonged to the poets. It was a time when a number of major anthologies were published such as *The Book of American Poetry*, edited by James Weldon Johnson (1922) and *Caroling Dusk* (1927) edited by Countee Cullen. More than any other form, the poetry of the period captured the new rhythm and the perspective of the Renaissance. The first Black woman to gain major acclaim as a poet after Frances Watkins Harper was Georgia Douglass Johnson, the most prolific of the female poets. Between 1918 and 1938 she published three volumes of poems: *Heart of a Woman* (1918), *Bronze* (1922) and *An Autumn Love Cycle* (1928). A fourth, *Share My World*, was published in 1962, four years before her death. Johnson wrote primarily in the ballad stanza form. Like her contemporaries, she wrote raceconscious lyrics, but her "intellectually-based" work deals primarily with loneliness, sorrow, seasons, and unrequited love.[21] She also spoke from a feminine perspective, particularly in her first book, *The Heart of a Woman*. In the title poem of that volume, she writes of the heart of a woman, who, like a bird, "goes forth with the dawn" but "falls back with the night."[22]

Another poet was Anne Spencer. Her poetry was concise, technically sure, and it showed a relationship to the Imagist school of poets. Sterling Brown called her the "most original of Negro women poets" and she has also been considered the "first Afro-American poet" to show such a high degree of maturity. Spencer was also included in Cullen's anthology and when asked for biographical material, she gave the following temperament-revealing contribution:

> Mother Nature, February, forty-five years ago, forced me on the stage that I, in turn, might assume the role of a lonely child, unhappy wife, perplexed mother—and so far, a twice resentful grandmother. I have no academic honors, nor lodge regalia. I am a Christian by intention, a Methodist by inheritance and a Baptist by marriage. I write about some of the things I love, but have no civilized articulation for the things I hate. I proudly love being a Negro woman—it's so involved and interesting. We are the PROBLEM—the great national game of TABOO.[23]

Her poetic forms are described by critic Gloria Hull as an eccentric mixture of free verse and rhymed iambic based lines, defying any precise categorization. Spencer also had more than a streak of feminism in some of her verse. In a "Letter to My Sister" she wrote: "It is dangerous for a woman / to defy the gods; / To taunt them with tongue's thin lip / Or strut in the weakness of mere humanity."[24] Her poetic instincts were not unerring, notes Hull, but her terse, almost elliptical style was original. Her work was replete with unconventional diction and vivid images and metaphors.

Youngest of the group is Helene Johnson. She was also the most militantly racial. Her work anticipates the use of colloquialism in the poetry of the Sixties, as well as some of its themes. Born in Boston in 1907, she went to Boston University and Columbia. Another uncollected poet, she was published in *Opportunity* and *Vanity Fair*.

Although she used the colloquial form, she was aware, as James Weldon Johnson noted, that a poem written in dialect, colloquial or street language "demands as much work and workmanship as a wellwrought sonner." Her work also revealed her personal philosophy. Only an examination of the African past and innate rhythmic richness will allow the Black man to maintain both his past glory and present sanity. Christianity is inferior to cultural worship in the spiritual wellbeing of Blacks. For Johnson, there was no internal struggle between Christian training and pagan urges like that in the heart of Countee Cullen.

Lesser known but important poets of the period include Gwendolyn Bennett and Angelina Grimke. Bennett was an artist by occupation, and her poetry was visual, recreating scenes and colors. She was on the editorial staff of *Opportunity*, in which several of her poems appeared. In the summer of 1926 she helped start a literary magazine called *Fire*. The idea of it was to force the prevailing establishment to recognize the younger artists and writers and abolish the "conventional Negro-White ideas of the past." But the *Fire* soon went out. About Bennett's best poems, stated Redmond, "one recalls the depth of Black womanhood revealed in the poetry of Frances W. Harper. One of her best poems is

"To A Dark Girl" which is "a mediation on the sisterhood that retains aspects of 'old forgotten queens'."[25]

Another important poet of the period was Angelina Grimke who was also a playwright. Redmond wrote that her poetry "more than slightly presaging Gwendolyn Brooks . . . contains some of the most distilled language in modern American poetry." "Scintillating, precise, poignant, she writes of love, seasons, darkness, and high spirits during her maturing years—the things typified in the phrase, 'the New Negro',"[26] he continued. Though Grimke had been publishing her poetry for years in periodicals, she did not become well-known until she was included in Countee Cullen's anthology, *Caroling Dusk* (1927). According to Arna Bontemps, Grimke helped to create and maintain momentum in the Renaissance for the second echelon of poets who published in the period. Lines such as "Why beautiful still finger, are you Black? / And why are you pointing upwards?" have made critics characterize her poems as ones of "quiet agony and despair."

Although these women were considered minor Harlem Renaissance poets, one should take note that one reason for this label is because only Helene Johnson's work was collected during this period. These Black women poets were comparable in quality, if not in quantity, to many of their male counterparts who were collected. In addition, a number of the women mentioned did not live within New York at the time, and therefore were outside of the mainstream of literary life in the Renaissance capital.

The Transitional Writer: Bridges to a Movement

The two decades that preceded the racial explosion of the Sixties simmered with Black optimism. Yes, discrimination continued but at the same time, there had been significant strides made under the Roosevelt administration. In addition, America was reborn as it emerged out of the depression and the Second World War. There was renewed faith in the system, hegemony on the international scene and the promise of first class citizenship at home. Certainly the dream of equality was right around the corner, but for the writer this new climate which anticipated the 1954 Supreme Court decision presented a dilemma. "One must keep in mind the paradox involved," wrote Arthur Davis. "There was no actual integration anywhere. . . . the everyday pattern of life for the overwhelming majority [of Blacks] remained unchanged. But there was—and this is of utmost importance—the spiritual commitment and climate out of which full integration could develop. The Negro literary artist recognized and acknowledged this climate."[27]

As long as there has been race consciousness, Black writers have protested in their literature. The tradition reached its peak in Wright's work of the late Thirties, but in the past World War II period, the writers played that tradition down in search of more "universal" themes. This may explain why Gwendolyn Brooks' *Annie Allen* (1949) was less racially conscious and strident than *A Street in Bronzeville* and why Ann Petry's *The Street* (1946) was followed within a year with *A Country Place*, a novel whose main characters are white. Zora Neale Hurston also abandoned the Black folk in *Sewanee*. While writers stopped writing for a time, the switch in mood could explain the hiatus between Margaret Walker's *For My People* (1942) and her next book of poetry, *Prophets for a New Day* (1970). The dreams of change, however, soon hardened into strident demands for it.

The appearance of *For My People* by Margaret Walker in 1942 was one of the most important events in Black literary history. It was the first book of poetry by a Black woman, since that of Georgia Douglass Johnson, and Walker was the first Black poet to appear in the Yale Series of Younger Poets. Most importantly, however, the volume still stands as a classic work of poetry. Walker, breaking the tradition of her female predecessors, enlarged the scope of poetic expression for Black women. Her poetry is not delicate, nor circumspect about her strong emotions. "Indeed when measured against the tradition established by most of her female predecessors, her work is startling," observed Redmond.[28]

The poems in the volume fall into three categories. The first uses the grand sweep of Black history, using universal themes. The title poem utilizes this method:

> For my people everywhere singing their slave songs repeatedly: their dirges and their ditties and their blues and jubilees, praying their prayers nightly to an unknown god, bending their knees humbly to an unseen power.[29]

Another poem in this group, "We Have Been Believers," is important because it presages the militant mood of the Sixties: "We have been believers believing in our burdens and our / demi-gods too long. Now the needy no longer weep / and pray; the long suffering arise, and our fists / bleed against the bars with a strange insistency."

One of Walker's most often used themes is her love for the South. Her words indicate more than a mere geographic preference, but the need to return to the original dwelling place of her soul. In "Southern Song" she says: "I want my body bathed again by southern suns, my soul / reclaimed again from southern lands." In "Delta," Walker writes of the South as a sense of strength: "banding the iron of our muscle with anger."

Margaret Walker Alexander - poet, teacher, writer, novelist
(photo courtesy of EBONY Magazine)

The second part of *For My People* incorporates folk material. In it we meet "Big John Henry," "Bad-Man Stagolee," and "Molly Means"— "Who was a hag and a witch; / Chile of the Devil, the dark, and sitch." These are excellent poems, drawing upon the rich Black folk-American culture, and rendered in the traditional ballad stanza. The last section of the book is comprised of sonnets which are philosophical in tone

Margaret Walker is the first Black female poet whose work stands among the best of American poets. Like the finest Black musicians, her work—particularly her free verse—carries an intuitiveness that taps the deepest sources of the Black sensibility. Black poetry, Walker feels, "comes from the deep recesses of the unconscious, the irrational, and the collective body of our ancestral memories."[30] Her work is reflective of that philosophy, making it among the most important in the literature of Afro-Americans. Twenty-eight years after *For My People*, Walker published a second volume, entitled *Prophets for a New Day* (1970). In this book, the poet uses her considerable talents to capture the mood of the early years of the civil rights movement. Poems like "Girl Held Without Bail," "Sit-Ins", and "Ballad of the Free"—drawing on the memories of Vesey, Turner, and the rest—stresses the ideals of the movement.

In these poems, Walker's ability to evoke the preacher, like Biblical rhythms in the former book, is used in full force. Throughout the work the Old-Testament characters are used as metaphors for the new Black leaders. Amos, for example, is Martin Luther King and her two verses "Amos-1963" and "Amos (Postscript-1968)" are two of the most moving poems in the book.

The tone of *Prophets* is optimistic as in the former volume. For example, although she speaks of "Jackson, Mississippi" and "Birmingham" with all of its potential for violence, she maintains the vision of ". . . light drenched streets puddled with the promise / Of a brand-new tomorrow." *Prophets* seems to answer some of the questions posed in the former volume. In *For My People*, she asks "When will I burst from my kennel an angry mongrel / Hungry and tired of my dry bones and years?" In *Prophets*, the time has come in the "Ballad of the Free": "The Serpent is loosed and the hour is come / The last shall be first and the first shall be none." *Prophets*, concludes Arthur Davis, "is the best poetical comment to the civil rights movement . . . "[31] Walker's third volume, *October Journey* (1973), continues her tradition of excellent verse.

The second seminal poet of the transition period is Gwendolyn Brooks. Like Walker, she is a bridge between the pre-Sixties period and the new Black arts movement. Most of her poems are found in *A Street in Bronzeville* (1945); *Annie Allen* (1949), which won her the Pulitzer Prize for Poetry in 1950; *The Bean Eaters* (1960); *In the Mecca* (1968); *Riot* (1969); and *Family Pictures* (1970). Gwendolyn Brooks is the most heralded Black poet in history. With too many awards to mention here, she is particularly noted for her poignant portraiture rendered through a mastery of craft that few can equal. The most prevalent setting in the poet's works are the Bronzevilles of America, drab and sometimes violent places where the human spirit manages to triumph, if only momentarily, which it is forced to dwell. In the appendix of her autobiography, *Report From Part One*, Brooks wrote:

> . . . I wish to present a large variety of personalities against a mosaic of daily affairs, recognizing that the *grimiest* of these is likely to have a streak of sun.
>
> In the Mecca were murders, loves, lonelinesses, hates jealousies. Hope occurred, and charity, sainthood, glory, shame, despair, altruism.[32]

Instead of the large subjects and the martial passions that Walker evokes, Brooks focuses in on individual characters which represent all of the qualities mentioned above. And she is capable of drawing them in free verse, Chaucerian rhyme royal or the sonnet-ballad. Brooks' poems contain some of the most memorable characters in literature. In *Bronzeville* there is DeWitt Williams on his way to Lincoln Cemetery who was "nothing but a plain black boy."[33] Davis characterizes this poem as one of Brook's finest protest poems without a word of protest in it. In the ghetto we also meet Satin Legs Smith with his scented lotion, his artificial flower, and his hysterical ties. Yet with all of his "sartorial splendor," as Davis puts it, the poet does not allow him to heroically defy his environment. He remains a personification of the sterility of the ghetto.

One of the most prevalent themes of Brooks poetry is the intraracial color prejudice among Blacks. In these poems, the "distance" that Brooks is known for is spurned. All sense of dispassion disappears in "The Ballad of Chocolate Mabbie," who experiences the heartache of color prejudice as a child; and in the "Ballad of Pearl May Lee," Brooks is not sympathetic with a Black who is lynched for neglecting his dark girl for a white woman because of "his taste for pink and white honey." In fact, there is more room in her heart for whites who are violent towards Blacks. In "Chicago Defender Sends a Man to Little Rock," the reporter concludes that people in their vicious pettiness should be pitied rather than hated for their excesses. After all, "The loviest lynchee was our Lord."

There are also themes of women in Brooks poetry. In comparing the lively life-loving "rites of Cusin Vit" with the "obituary for living lady" who is introverted and religious, Brooks notes the spectrum of lifestyles in *Bronzeville*. Her most poignant poem is perhaps "The Mother" which deals with a woman who has had a number of abortions. The mother wants to shield her unborn form their predictable futures in the inner city; however, her decision to "kill the unborn" is not made without ambivalence: "If I poisoned the beginnings of your breaths, / Believe that even in my deliberateness I was not deliberate. . . .Believe me, I loved you all."

Brooks portraits are those of individuals who make the best of their situation, and through her simple lines in the title poem of *The Bean Eaters*, one somehow senses the warmth and satisfaction of the poor elderly couple. *In the Mecca*, it too, offers striking portraits of the characters in the microcosm of the ghetto, but by 1968, Brooks also internalized the new militant Black spirit of the times. The tone found in such poems as the previous "Little Rock" has no place here.

For example, there is "Way-Out Morgan," who "listens to blackness stern and blunt and beautiful," collects guns, and "predicts the day of Debt-pay shall begin." She also inserts a young poet who influenced her work greatly during this period, Don Lee (Haki Madhubuti): "Don Lee wants / a new nation / under nothing; . . . . / wants / new art and anthem; will / want a new music screaming in the sun." In this volume, too, she writes poems for Medgar Evers, Malcolm X and the Blackstone Rangers, a gang in Chicago for whom she ran workshops.

Gwendolyn Brooks - poet
(photo courtesy of EBONY)

Another volume, *Riot*, appeared in 1969, published by Broadside Press. According to Brooks, "It rises from the disturbances in Chicago after the assassination of Martin Luther King." *Family Pictures*, another Broadside publication, was issued in 1970. Its longest poem, "The Life of Lincoln West," describes a young boy whose physical "ugliness," i.e. undiluted Blackness, makes him the victim of many slights and revulsions. But when he overhears an anthropologicallyminded white identify him as the "real thing," little

Lincoln West takes a new pride in himself. During the latter Sixties and Seventies, therefore, Brooks made a dramatic and highly touted turnaround in her point of view. She is the only Black poet to date to attempt to superimpose such precise and classical craft on Black aesthetic expression. Her journey, much of it expressed in her autobiography *Report From Part I*, is a fascinating one. The poetry of Brooks, successor to Carl Sandburg as Poet-Laureate of Illinois, is "multilayered, complex, and womanly, tragic and profound," notes Redmond.

Two other poets of note in this period are Naomi Long Madgett and Gloria Oden. Naomi Long Madgett's books include: *Songs to a Phantom Nightingale* (1941), *One in Many* (1946), *Star by Star* (1965, 1970), and *Pink Ladies in the Afternoon* (1972). One of her best poems is "Mortality." In it the poet says that of "all the deaths" one is the most sure, drawing vultures who "recognize" the "single mortal thing" that holds on to life. They wait hungrily for the time "When hope starts staggering." Madgett is presently the publisher of the Lotus Press which published *Deep Rivers: A Portfolio: 20 Contemporary Black Poets* (1974).

Gloria C. Oden won a John Hay Whitney Opportunity Fellowship just two years after Gwendolyn Brooks received the Pulitzer. The award was for *The Naked Frame: a Love Poem and Sonnets*. A part of the village poets scene in New York, Oden read poems like "Review from Staten Island" in coffeeshops. In the poem, an item in view is "spewed up from the water." "As when emotion too far exceeds its cause," the poem suggests, there is the theme of unrequited love. Retreating from heartbreak, she reminisces: "I, too, once trusted the air / that plunged me down. / Yes, I."

One of the best novels to come out of the transition period was *The Street* by Ann Petry (1946). The protagonist of the book is Lutie Johnson who is upright, honest, hardworking, and who comes to New York to make a better life for herself and her family. However, "the street" offers little solace or support for her. Because she is forced to work away from home for long periods, her husband deserts her. She and her son move into a tenement, only to be victimized by the landlord, the janitor, and even a musician who is supposed to be Lutie's friend, but whom she is finally forced to kill. The environment she finds herself within "is so demanding that even her attempt to struggle . . . gives her more stature in her failure than most people earn in victory,"[34] as one critic puts it.

Yet, Lutie's own sense of moral integrity prevents her from prostituting herself or compromising her principles. She is a compassionate and insightful woman; she is affectionate and understanding toward her son; but all of these sterling qualities can not save her. She ends up abandoning her son, the one person she loves in the world, and becoming a fugitive from the law.

Petry was a devotee of the naturalist school of protest fiction which sought to show the effects of a racist environment on its victim, no matter how strong and noble the character may be. In *The Street*, Petry's purpose was "to show how simply and easily the environment can change the course of a person's life,"[35] the author said of the work. The protest comes in the words of a critic: "Decent human beings are ruined by social forces they cannot come to terms with."[36] The book is well-written, and it received the Houghton Mifflin Literary Award. Critic Arthur Davis considers the book perhaps the best novel to come from the followers of Richard Wright.

Ann Petry - novelist
(photo courtesy of EBONY)

Petry is the author of two other adult novels, *Country Place* (1947) and *The Narrows* (1953). The former book's characters are all white, and the setting is a small New England town. The novel deals with class and religious prejudices and the disruption of relationships that result when men go off to war. *The Narrows* concerns Black life in a small New England City. Its message seems to be that Black communities in the North, without the bonds that are found in the South, are much more sterile than their Southern counterparts. The book also explores an interracial romantic relationship that ends in disaster. These two novels have little of the power that *The Street* contains; however, they all have the common theme of the effect of the environment on the individual. Petry also wrote children's books and a collection of short stories, *Miss Muriel and Other Stories* (1971).

Gwendolyn Brooks also made an appearance as a novelist in this period with her *Maud Martha* (1953). Brooks uses many of the same themes found in her verse in this poetic novel. Maud Martha lives in Bronzeville, and leads the same kind of drab life we find in the characters of Brooks' poems. Martha lives with a husband who is oblivious to her emotional needs, is drained by the efforts to take care of her child, and has the additional pressure of facing bigoted employers day after day. In this series of vignettes, we discover that Maud Martha also experiences color prejudice from her light-skinned husband. We follow Martha through the episodic structure of the book and discover through Brooks' sensitive and subtle characterization that despite the metallic grayness that permeates her life, she is intelligent, strong, and capable of enjoying fully the small pleasures that come her way.

One day, however, the quiet Maud Martha rebels against her employer and quits. Therein is revealed the integrity and self-respect of the character that has remained intact through all of her hardships. Her employer had trespassed upon the sanctity of her being, and nothing to Maud Martha was worth that. Her action was not particularly dramatic or spectacular, but done with the simple pronouncement that after all: "One was a human being. One wore clean nightgowns. One loved one's baby. One drank cocoa by the fire—or the gas range—come the evening in the wintertime." Poor, dark-skinned, unfulfilled Maud Martha rises to the occasion. For despite everything, she demanded to be treated like a human being, and despite everything, there were occasions for dignity, compassion, courage and contentment. *Maud Martha* remarks Arthur Davis, is "one of Gwendolyn Brooks' most sensitive and understanding works. The reader leaves the little volume with a deeper-than-surface insight into the lives of poor Black folk in the

Thirties and Forties."[37] The work is also one of the first major women's novels to have a dark-skinned protagonist. And its message is almost in direct contradiction to the naturalist school of writing which Petry represented.

In 1959, Paule Marshall's *Brown Girls, Brownstones* offered yet another view of Black life—this from the West Indian community in Brooklyn, New York. The story centers around Selina Boyce, who is a young woman living in a household where her father and mother have different value systems. The mother, Silla, is determined to realize the material promise of America, symbolized by her owning a brownstone. Her father, Deighton, is a more impractical dreamer and looks forward to returning to his native home in Barbados to build a "dream house" on his few acres of property there. The struggle between the parents on how to utilize their limited resources becomes vicious, and Selina, in the beginning, takes the side of her father. Eventually, their different dreams result in the separation of Selina's parents and her father's eventual suicide.

In the end, Selina finally resolves the conflict with her mother and comes to understand her. At the same time, however, she has become determined to leave the community, which unlike Bronzeville, has served as a protective enclave, sheilding her from the harshness of the "real world." At the novel's conclusion, Selina sets out to find her own values. In this novel, Marshall presages the rebellion against materialistic middle-class values that would emerge more forcefully during the Sixties. She also anticipates the conscious choice of female Black characters to determine their own lives, independent of the wishes of their men. Lastly, *Brown Girls* is a forerunner of identifying the positive aspects of the inner city.

The Sixties: "The Serpent is Loosed"

It started in 1955 when Rosa Parks refused to move to the back of the bus in Montgomery, Alabama, but five years later there would be a revolution within the revolution. It was in 1960 when young Black college students took the movement in their hands and began sit-ins throughout the South. Conventional resistance within the confines of the law had made them impatient. The only way to create change, they felt, was to disregard the laws on the books, which were stacked against them. The Black poetry movement that began to make an impact on Black literature followed much the same course. Traditional literary convention was thrown to the winds; the creation of new Black aesthetic was the order of the day. Though scholars still debate whether a new philosophy of art was actually achieved, just about all students of the new movement agree that it ushered in a new era of Black literature.

In some respects, what became known in some circles as the New Black Renaissance was similar to that which had taken place in the earlier part of the century. The two movements, Harlem Renaissance and Black Arts, shared a more concentrated focus on the African heritage, Black music, protest against the establishment (white and Black), the rediscovery of folk values and use of the Black idiom as poetic material. As in the earlier period, there was a proliferation of books written by Black authors, seminal anthologies and a wider dissemination of the work to other than the educated elite. But there were three essential differences. In the Sixties the new harvest of Black poetry was not confined primarily to one geographical location. Poets flourished throughout the United States. Secondly, although the Harlem Renaissance publications like *Opportunity* and *The Crisis* published Black works, the publishing organs and journals in the Sixties were independently owned by Blacks. Broadside Press, *Black World*, *The Journal of Black Poetry* and Third World Press are several examples.

Perhaps the most important difference was the philosophy underlying the new Black poetry movement. As Robert Hayden observed in his anthology *Kaleidescope*, the Harlem Renaissance was primarily an aesthetic and philosophical movement, whose goal, in the eyes of many, was integrationist. The Black movement of the Sixties, however, was political in its thrust. The only integration sought was that, as Don Lee puts it, of "negroes with Black people." And, as Bernard Bell points out, "art was viewed as a weapon in the Sixties." "We want poems that will kill," announced LeRoi Jones. These poets did not look toward white critics for approval; they looked toward the Black community. In 1966 at a major writer's conference at Fisk University, the novelist John Oliver Killens conducted a writer's workshop which included a number of the young poets whose strident voices would be heard later in the decade. A transitional literary figure himself, Killens had also invited some of the "old guard." For the first time, the two groups met in a literary setting. At that conference were Margaret Walker, Margaret Burroughs, and Dudley Randall, among others. Margaret Walker recalled the conference as being the first time she met Dudley Randall, who, along with Burroughs, had the idea of collecting the poems read there on Malcolm X and publishing them. The result was one of the first publications from his Broadside Press, which proved to be a seminal part of the Black Arts poetry movement.

Among the most important Black female poets who emerged in the period were Nikki Giovanni, Sonia Sanchez, Carolyn Rodgers, Lucille Clifton, and Mari Evans. Nikki Giovanni is the most prolific of the group. There are fourteen books to her credit, including *Black Feeling, Black Talk, Black Judgement* (1970), *Re-Creation* (1970), *My House* (1972), *Poetic Equation: A Conversation Between Nikki Giovanni and Margaret Walker* (1974), *The Women and the Men*, and *Cotton Candy On a Rainy Day* (1978).

In her books, there is a distinct evolvement of attitude and thought. During the early part of her career, the militancy of her work distinguished her from many of the other female poets. In the poem "Of Liberation," she warned that "Our choice now is war or death." Later, as reflected in *My House* and subsequent books, her emphasis was more introspective. In her works were themes of love, the city, childhood, the rites of woman-passage, Africa, and the Afro-American culture. A poem in an earlier book, "Nikki-Rosa," presages this new tone. A verse reads: "your biographers never understand / your father's pain as he sells his stock / and another dream goes / And though you're poor it isn't poverty that concerns you . . ."

Her latest book of poetry, *Cotton Candy* completes a cycle. In its introduction is the statement that "The militant poems are long gone, which is not to say that she no longer stands by them but that they are the truth of another time." The sassy, hand-on-the-hip love poems are also scarce. . . . *Cotton Candy* is the most introspective to date and the most plaintive. It speaks of loneliness, personal emptiness, and love which is not unrequited but, even worse, misunderstood and misbegotten." The introduction goes on to say, "The mood is not despair or self-pity. It is more the pensiveness that comes from realizing that another cycle of one's life has been completed": ". . . Now i don't fit / beneath the rose bushes / anymore," reads a line in the book. Much of Giovanni's influence stems from her popularity as a public speaker (reminiscent of Frances Harper), media personality, and as editorial consultant to a magazine. She has also experimented successfully with setting her poems to gospel music on two albums, *Truth Is on Its Way* and *Like a Ripple on a Pond.*

Sonia Sanchez is the author of *Homecoming* (1969), *We aBaddDDD People* (1970), *It's A New Day* (1971), *Love Poems* (1973), and *A Blues Book for Blue Black Women* (1974), among other books. The themes in her work include the return to Black identity *(Homecoming)*, Black manhood, love, and redefining values for children. She can be mystical, introspective, humorous, and militant. The latter is expressed in her poem "Malcolm" when she says ". . . I'll breath his breath and mourn / my gun-filled nights." In "definition for black / children" she instructs

that "a policeman / is a pig / and he shd be in / a zoo," and in matters of
love Sanchez suggests that "hurt" is not the "bag" that black women
"shd be in." Sonia Sanchez is also capable of personal emotion in her
work as when she, as a young girl, remembers the first introduction to
her step-mother. Much of her verse is also in Black dialect and shaped
for its auditory potential. She too has moved toward a more
introspective poetry in recent years.

Mari Evans, characterized by Redmond as a transitionalist, "shifted
from the civil rights period of the early phase to, finally, a more obvious
politically 'Black' stance of the later period." She "employs irony,
suspense, and rich folk idioms in free verse."[38] Evans is easily one of the
most gifted Black poets of the period. Whether she is being humorous,
as in "The Rebel," where she wonders out loud if curiosity seekers at
her funeral will think she really died or is just "causing trouble" or
philosophically—"If there be Sorrow, it should be for the things not yet
dreamed, realized or done." Her verse is effective and moving.

Mari Evans, poet

Like Brooks, Evans finds a rich subject in the unheroic, who nevertheless, hang on voraciously to their handfuls of self-pride. "I may scrub floors / but / I don't / get on my knees," says a maid in one of her poems. Perhaps Evans is best known for her classic poem, "I Am a Black Woman," which has also become the signature poem of the Black woman's awareness era. With the concluding lines, "Look at me and be renewed," the poem, characterized by Redmond as a major one, "combines the best of the modernists techniques with a quasi musical score so as to give the impression of someone singing or humming along with the reader." Love is also another major theme of the poets' work: "with your lips / withdraw the nectar from / me," she asks in the appropriately titled "Marrow of My Bone." Mari Evans' themes also include violence, loneliness, Africa, and self-pride. She has published I Am a Black Woman, J.D., I Look At Me, and Rap Stories (children's books) and Singing Black. Her poetry has appeared in over 150 textbooks and anthologies.

The literary evolvement of Carolyn Rodgers is manifested in Paper Soul (1968), Songs of a Blackbird (1969), Blues Gittin Up (1969), How I Got Ovah —which was nominated for a National Book Award in 1976—and The Heart is Ever Green (1978). The change of tone is as significant as her refinement of technique in The Heart. Rodgers has gone from a poet of despair to one who has seen "her own becoming". Her sensibility has moved from the blues to gospel—i / told Jesus / be allright / if / he / changed / my name. In How I Got Over, Rodgers began to find herself and The Heart represents her sense of resolution, making reconciliation possible.

Lucille Clifton, currently the Poet-Laureate of Maryland, is the author of Good Times (1969), Good News About the Earth (1972), and An Ordinary Woman (1974). Her children's books have included Some of the Days of Everett Anderson, The Black BC's, and Everett Anderson's Christmas Coming. Even the titles of her books suggest something about her spirit and temperament, notes Redmond. Her work is often a celebration of things: Black culture, womanliness, the hearth-like comfort, intimate friendship, and love. Her poems, short, economical, direct, center around a number of themes: sisterhood, and feminism, birth and regeneration, racial pride and Africa. She utilizes humor, irony, and folk wisdom.

A distinguishing characteristic of her work is that unlike many poets who use the symbols of the earth as similes, Clifton uses them as metaphors and they pervade her poetry: "i agree with the leaves," she says in one poem. Her frequent use of the themes of birth and regeneration are never merely a literary device but are of a personal poignancy: "may the art in the love that made you / feel your fingers, may the love in the art that made you / fill your heart," she writes in one of her more sentimental poems. Clifton writes more about women as subjects than most of the other Black female poets, for she "entered the earth in a woman jar," and, she observes "the whole world of women / seems a landscape of / red blood and things / that need healing."

Lucille Clifton - poet
(photo courtesy of EBONY)

In her simplicity, Clifton expresses a certain kind of spiritual oneness with the earth that makes you smell the wet leaves around you, the moist soil of the earth, the blood of birth. Such feelings as she evokes are similar to those of Toni Morrison's novels. Within this setting, the theme of regeneration is particularly piquant, and again it is all the more powerful because its roots are personal. In a poem addressed to her mother, who passed away at the age of forty-three, she says: "i have taken the bones you hardened / and built daughters." In another autobiographical poem, she speaks of her grandmother, her namesake, who shot a white man in Virginia, "Killing the killer of sons." Her grandmother was one of the first women hanged in the state, and the poet proclaims that Lucille "already / is an Afrikan name." In *Ordinary Woman*, Clifton is also prone to be self-deprecating, as the title of the book and the title poem suggest. At the age of thirty-eight, she is "plain as bread / round as a cake / an ordinary woman."

Other important poets of the period include June Jordan and Audre Lorde. June Jordan published *Who Look At Me* (1969), the anthology *Soulscript*, and *New Days: Poems of Exile and Return* (1974), among others Redmond characterized her work as "concise, analytical, and allusory, her poetry is in a free-verse style characteristic of practically all the recent Black poetry." Audre Lorde's books include *The First Cities* (1968), *Cables to Rage* (1970), *Head Shop and Other Poems*, and *From a Land Where Other People Live*. She is one of the more talented poets and has an increasingly feminist perspective in her work. Redmond describes her works as ones that cut "sharp paths of light across the ignorance and confusion around her." "The light that makes us fertile / shall make up sane," she predicts in one poem.

A good but often overlooked poet is May Miller, whom Gwendolyn Brooks called "excellent and long-celebrated." Daughter of heralded educator Kelly Miller, her work can be found in three volumes: *Into the Clearing* (1959), *Poems* (1962), *Lyrics of Three Women* (1964) a collection in which she is one of three poets represented. Miller has been a lecturer, teacher, and dramatist and has published her poems in a number of magazines, including *The Crisis*, *Phylon*, and *The Nation*. Like Miller, Alice Walker's verse, *Once* (1968) and *Revolutionary Petunias* (1973) shows her to be an excellent poet as well as novelist, short story writer, and essayist. Alice Walker uses the themes of her experiences in the civil rights movement and of being a Black woman: "The silence between your words / rams into me / like a sword," she writes powerfully in one poem.

Margaret Danner, described as richly sensitive, was born in Kentucky but spent most of her life in Chicago, where she was once the editor of *Poetry*. Her poems in that publication earned her the John Hay Whitney Fellowship. She has also published four volumes of poetry, *Impressions of African Art Forms in Poetry* (1962), *To Flower* (1962), *Poem Counterpoem* (with Dudley Randall, 1966), and *Iron Lace* (1968). ". . . moving towards you is like / touching leaves in autumn" reads a memorable line from a poem by Pinkie Gordon Lane. Born in Philadelphia in 1923, Lane is the author of *Wind Thoughts* and *The*

Mystic Female, and she is the editor of *Discourses on Poetry* and *Poems by Blacks III.* Though primarily a prose and script writer, Maya Angelou has also published two books of poetry: *Just Give Me a Cool Drink of Water 'Fore I Die* (1971), which was nominated for the Pulitzer Prize, and *Oh, Pray, My Wings Are Gonna Fit Me Well* (1975). But, as recognized by readers across the nation, especially college students, Angelou's autobiography, *I Know Why The Caged Bird Sings* (1970) is one of the most moving non-fictional works by a Black woman in the United States. Born 1928 in St. Louis, Missouri, Angelou, also a lecturer, played the role of Nyo Boto, the grandmother, in the highly acclaimed *Roots,* the ABC-Television series.

Maya Angelou - Poet-autobiographer
(photo courtesy of EBONY)

The Sixties and Seventies: From the Marches to Pen Power

The new Black awareness took more time, understandably, to reveal itself in the novel. The first major works of the period were more a reflection of traditional themes than the new mood generated by the Sixties and Seventies. Emphasis here, therefore, will be on those works which are representative of new subject matter, approach, or theme.

Although Margaret Walker's *Jubilee* (1966) offers a traditional historical theme, its publication at a time when the Black perspective shifted makes it significant. But *Jubilee* is also significant because, in Phyl Garland's words, "it is one of the most beautifully written novels produced by Blacks or whites, and the characterizations of the times are poignantly precise." The novel is based on the life of Walker's greatgrandmother, Margaret Duggans Ware Brown. It spans the antebellum period to the period of Reconstruction. The protagonist is Vyry, a mulatto house servant, who was persecuted by her mistress, survived to become a cook in the big house, and then meets Randall Ware, a freedman and blacksmith. They marry, but at the outbreak of the Civil War, Ware joins the Union forces. After seven years of waiting for his return, Vyry marries a hard working, if less interesting, Black man. After suffering through being exploited as sharecroppers and burned out by the KKK, they find a reasonably peaceful life when Vyry's skills as a midwife make the couple welcomed in a small community. Walker's purpose was to give an accurate delineation of the history of the period. The actions and attitudes of Vyry are not superficially contrived to be the perfect heroine in the sense of the traditional novels, nor an artificial militant to satisfy the critics of a latter day. It is simply a Black woman's quest for freedom and dignity against incredible odds. Perhaps it was not until the Sixties, that an authentic character in a novel of this type could emerge.

Similarly, Paule Marshall's *The Chosen Place, The Timeless People* (1969) avoids the stereotypes that a story about a white anthropologist and his wife coming to a small Caribbean island to improve the life of its people—who refuse to change—can elicit. The central figure of the book is Merle Kinbona, a middle-aged resident of the island who is attempting to reconstruct her life; her husband has left her, taking their child with him to Africa. Against a backdrop of the people of the island chafing under the remnants of British colonialism, and ritually keeping the money of an historic slave rebel alive, both Kinbona and Saul Amron, the anthropologist, struggle to keep their psychological lives intact until they are able to face the unresolved issues in their personal lives. Merle, does finally summon up the courage to search for her family—and herself—in Africa. Although the islanders show themselves unprepared for outright rebellion, Marshall implies that violence may be the only method to truly change the quality of their lives on the island. Merle Kinbona is one of the most fascinating characters in Black fiction, an imperfect but genuine heroine, who contains many psychological layers. Kinbona's search for her identity in Africa presages the concern for the meaning of one's African origins in later works. Without being propagandanistic, Marshall's book is one of the most political novels in the period—and one of the finest.

In 1970, several books of note surfaced: Louise Meriwether's *Daddy Was A Number's Runner*, Toni Morrison's *The Bluest Eye*, and Alice Walker's *The Third Life of Grange Copeland*. Meriwether's books is about a young girl growing up in the Harlem of the 1930's. Compared to the Harlems and other urban areas of the Sixties and Seventies, the book is revealing. Although it is the period of the depression, it is a far cry from the crime and drug laden Bronzevilles of a latter era. There is not the tension of the character being drowned in the evil that the ghettoes have come to represent. But more than the difference between the two Harlems is the difference in Meriweather's perspective. *Daddy* is an interesting contrast to the works by Black male writers which are set in the ghetto in this period, such as those of Baldwin, George Cain and Claude Brown. Here is an affirmation of the human spirit which refuses to be caught in the web of self-destruction.

Morrison's theme in the *Bluest Eye* echoes that of Gwendolyn Brooks' concerning the devastation of a sensitive young girl considered "Black and ugly." Unlike Brooks' characters, however, Pecola, who wishes for "blue eyes," goes mad. Morrison is able to render a certain intimacy between the character and the reader that few writers are capable of doing. Thus Pecola's ill-starred odyssey is even more painful to follow. Pecola, observes Arthur Davis, "is the most tragic victim of American racism to appear in recent fiction."[39] With the publication of her first novel, Morrison showed her poetic mastery of the language, including that of the Black folk with its special idioms and rhythm.

The second novel by Morrison, *Sula* (1973) is, as Davis notes, "a study in evil, and the fascination of evil as exemplified in the protagonist." The critic goes on to say that such a theme is new to Black fiction. The protagonist is a skillfully drawn character—so much so that Sula's evil takes on an epic quality.[40]

Sula's character exposes a theme prevalent in the new novels by Black women in this period: that of the suppression of the creative sensibility. From the beginning we see Sula's artistic temperament, but there is no place in the confines of Sula's world to express it. She thus becomes an artist without an art form, one of the potentially dangerous characters in any society. An urgent creative force cannot be entirely stemmed, only turned destructive—either outwardly or inwardly. In Sula's case it is the former. She is a free spirit loose in a conventional small town in Ohio. Sula feels no responsibility for her actions, and she wreaks havoc. This is shown through her relationship with her childhood friend, Nell. The relationship between women is another important theme of the book. The author has long felt the friendships of Black women have not been revealed adequately in fiction. Despite the disruption of Nell's life by Sula, who causes Nell and her husband to divorce, Nell discovers that her world is incomplete without Sula.

Morrison's most recent book, *Song of Solomon* (1977) was the most highly praised by establishment critics. *The New York Times*, for example, ranked it with *One Hundred Years of Solitude* and *The Tin Drum*. It was the first book since Richard Wright's *Native Son* (1940) to be a main selection of the Book-of-the-Month Club. *Song of Solomon* attempts to move out of the woman's chambers into the physical world of men. The protagonist of the novel is Milkman Dead, whom Morrison takes on both a real and symbolic journey to find his history and thus his emotional redemption. But the most interestingly drawn characters are women, particularly Aunt Pilate who is a mother earth figure, was born without a navel, wears a brass box for an earring, and carries around a bag full of human bones. In *Solomon* the most poignant scenes belong to the women, whether it is Pilate, who saves Milkman's life with the sacrifice of her own; his mother Ruth, whose emotional well-being has been sucked dry, or his sisters, who are on the verge of madness. His lover, Hager, has become maddened by her jealousy of him and hopes she can just keep herself from killing him, a possibility that she has no control over. Though highly praised, and brilliantly written, *Solomon* may be more a triumph of style than the emotional depth that Morrison achieved in her former works.

Alice Walker's first novel, *The Third Life of Grange Copeland*, contains two main themes: The first is the realization of Copeland during the height of the civil rights period that blaming whites for the lack of fulfillment in his life truly does make them the gods in the Black man's thinking. His shirking of any responsibility for the path of his own life emasculates him. Thus, there is another more detailed contradiction of the naturalist school of thinking. The second theme answers the matriarchal charge in works by Black men by stressing their mistreatment of women. Notes Mary Helen Washington, the central theme in Walker's work is "the belief that Black women . . . are the most oppressed people in the world." This oppression goes beyond physical abuse, for "the true terror is within," and involves the "mutilation of the spirit and the body."[41]

Walker's second novel, *Meridian* (1976) is the most profound fictional presentation of the civil rights period. The protagonist, after

Alice Walker (sitting) - novelist and essayist, with daughter Rebecca Leventhal

whom the book is named, is a more complex and profound character than those found in her previous novel. Meridian is self-directed and compassionate; she is committed and has a strong sense of her own identity. A characteristic of Walker's work is her total commitment to being the fictional chronicler of Black women's sensibilities and the evolvement of her female characters. Washington notes that through Walker's work "she sees the experiences of Black women as a series of movements from women totally victimized by society and by the men in their lives to the growing developing women whose consciousness allows them to have control over their lives."[42] There are three types of women in Walker's books: "the suspended" or totally victimized woman; the "assimilated" woman, more aware but alienated from her roots; and the most highly evolved, the "emergent" woman. Washington would call Meridian an "emergent" female character, one who has been influenced by the events of the Sixties, and thus has come to the edge of a new awareness. However, before they come to complete realization, they undergo a "period of initiation." For Meridian, that initiation was the movement itself. Through it she has seen loss of commitment, even integrity, especially by the Black men that she thought they had. The combination of her compassion and commitment take on the characteristics of a religious conversion, and she finds peace within herself.

Gayl Jones has written two important novels, *Corregidora* (1975) and *Eva's Man* (1976). Her works are the most emotionally devastating of any of the other writers, for her characters are trapped not only by their contemporary situation but by exigencies of their own personal histories. They are ruled not only by fate but their untempered physical needs. They are all suspended women. The first novel concerns the love-hate relationship between Ursa Corregidora and her first husband, Mutt Taylor. Corregidora is the last female descendent of a Portuguese slave master who sexually brutalized and fathered children by his own daughters and granddaughters. The story revolves around Ursa's preoccupation of her memories of the slaver and her sex life with Mutt and her second husband Tadpole. Ursa becomes depressed when she loses her womb and cannot have children. A primary theme seems to be the brutality of Black men toward women. James Baldwin characterized the novel as "A metaphor for Black (and white) sexual slavery that is both shocking and beautiful."

Eva's Man is written in a similar blues-like narrative of the first book. Sex and castration are seminal in the plot. Better written than the previous book, the portrait of Eve is called by Davis, "the most reticent, the most non-committal, the most enigmatic woman in recent Black fiction. She represents the accumulation of centuries of emotional pain,"[43] which she attempts to exorcise by castrating her lover. Jones' novels are the most vivid, if brutal, soundings of the echoes of the sexual oppression of Black women over the centuries, which come to the fore not with a whisper, but a scream.

The novels of Black women in this period have a common characteristic that makes them unique. Their female characters— more likely to be found outside the urban ghetto than those of their male counterparts—are self-directed, even if that direction is toward evil or madness. There is little blame placed on outside forces for their state of being. Unlike most male novelists, their tension is within, rather than from without. Even Petry's character Lutie, though fatalistically doomed by her environment, nonetheless fights it to the very end. In this way she is very different from her compatriot Bigger Thomas, who is thrown this way and that like a listing ship at sea. Black women novelists also affirm life, in most instances even going mad rather than being an acquiescent to forces which seek to control it. Particularly in the late Seventies, it is Black women who have written the modern Black novel, one which explores their sensibility as women, and is unafraid of the results. They have departed from the traditional Black novel in that their focus is to enlighten each other, not whites around them.

The Final Chord

"How was the creativity of the Black woman kept alive, year after year and century after century, when for most of the years Black people have been in America, it was a punishable crime for a Black person to read or write? And the freedom to paint, to sculpt, to expand the mind with action, did not exist,"[44] asks Alice Walker. Yet somehow it was, and the artistic expression of Black women in America, whose wellspring even predates the founding of this country, has been an extraordinary wonder to behold.

NOTES

[1] Lorenzo Johnson Greene, *The Negro in Colonial New England* (New York: Atheneum, 1968), p. 245.

[2] Cedrick Dover, *American Negro Art* (Greenwich, Connecticut: New York Graphic Society, 1960), p. 14.

[3] Merle A. Richmond, *Bid the Vassal Soar, Interpretative Essays on the Life and Poetry of Phillis Wheatley and George Moses Horton* (Washington, D.C.: Howard University Press, 1974), p. 19.

[4] Richmond, p. 24.

[5] Richmond, p. 3.

[6] William H. Robinson, *Phillis Wheatley in the Black American Beginnings* (Detroit: Broadside Press, 1975), p. 60.

[7] Robinson, p. 63.

[8] Eugene B. Redmond, *Drumvoices, the Mission of Afro-American Poetry* (New York: Anchor Press/Doubleday, 1976), p. 75.

[9] Rita B. Dandridge, "Male Critics /Black Women's Novels," *CLA Journal*, Vol. XXIII, No. 1, September 1979, p. 4.

[10] Dandridge, p. 4.

[11] Carol Watson, "The Novels of AfroAmerican Women: Concerns and Themes, 1891-1965," Diss. George Washington University, 1978, p. 8.

[12] Watson, p. 25.

[13] Watson, p. 22.

[14] Arthur Davis, *From the Dark Tower* (Washington, D.C.: Howard University Press, 1974), p. 94.

[15] Davis, p. 96.

[16] Alice Walker, ed. *I Love Myself When I Am Laughing: A Zora Neale Hurston Reader* with an Introduction by Mary Helen Washington (New York: Feminist Press, 1979), p. 14.

[17] Watson, p. 62.

[18] Walker, p. 16.

[19] Walker, p. 15.

[20] Walker.

[21] Redmond, p. 164.

[22] Roseann P. Bell, Bettye V. Parker, and Beverly Guy Shettall, *Sturdy Black Bridges* (New York: Anchor Books/Doubleday, 1979), p. 76.

[23] Bell, et al., p. 77.

[24] Bell, et al., p. 78.

[25] Redmond, p. 29.

[26] Redmond, p. 157.

[27] Davis, p. 138.

[28] Redmond, p. 215.

[29] Margaret Walker, *For My People* (New Haven: Yale University Press, 1942).

[30] Paula Giddings, "A Shoulder Hunched Against A Sharp Concern," *Black World*, Vol. XXI, No. 2, December 1971, p. 20.

[31] Davis, p. 185.

[32] Bell, et al., p. 158.

[33] Gwendolyn Brooks, *A Street in Bronzeville* (New York: Harper, 1945), p. 21.

[34] Patricia Meyers Spacks, ed., *Contemporary Women Novelists* (New Jersey: Prentice Hall, 1977), p. 108.

[35] Davis, p. 194.

[36] Spacks, p. 112.

[37] Davis, p. 192.

[38] Redmond, p. 334.

[39] Arthur P. Davis, "Novels of the New Black Renaissance," *CLA Journal* Vol. XXI, No. 4 (June 1978), p. 276.

[40] Davis, p. 476.

[41] Bell, et al., p. 135.

[42] Bell, et al., p. 137.

[43] Davis, p. 487.

[44] Alice Walker, "In Search of Our Mother's Gardens: The Creativity of Black Women in the South," *Ms* Magazine, May 1974.

SELECTED BIBLIOGRAPHY

Abdul, Raoul. *Blacks in Classical Music.* New York: Dodd, Mead and Co., 1978.

Abdul, Raoul. *Famous Black Entertainers of Today.* New York: Dodd, Mead, and Co., 1974.

Anderson, Marian. *My Lord, What a Morning: An Autobiography.* New York: Viking, 1956.

Andrews, Benny. "New Colors, Old Canvas." *Encore American and Worldwide News,* 23 June - 4 July 1975.

Angelou, Maya. *I Know Why the Caged Bird Sings.* New York: Random House, 1970.

Bailey, Pearl. *The Raw Pearl.* New York: Harcourt, Brace, and World, 1968.

Baker, Houston, Jr. *The Journey Back.* Chicago: University of Chicago Press, 1980.

Barksdale, Richard K. and Kenneth Kinnamon, eds. *Black Writers of America: A Comprehensive Anthology.* New York: Macmillan, 1972.

Bearden, Romare and Harry Henderson. *6 Black Masters of American Art.* Garden City, N.Y.: Doubleday, 1972.

Bell, Roseann P., Bettye V. Parker, and Beverly Guy Shettal. *Sturdy Black Bridges.* New York: Anchor Books/Doubleday, 1979.

Bennett, Lerone. *The Shaping of Black America.* Chicago: Johnson Publishing Co., 1975.

Bigsby, C.W.E., ed. *The Black American Writer.* Deland, Fla.: Everett Edwards, Inc., 1969.

Bogle, Donald. *Toms, Coons, Mulattoes, Mammies, and Bucks: An Interpretive History of Blacks in American Film.* New York: Viking Press, 1973.

Bond, Frederick W. *The Negro and the Drama: The Direct and Indirect Contributions Which the American Negro Has Made to the Drama and the Legitimate Stage.* Washington, D.C.: Associated Publishers, 1940.

Bone, Robert A. *The Negro Novel in America.* New Haven, Conn.: Yale University, 1968.

Bonetemps, Arna W., ed. *American Negro Poetry.* New York: Hill and Wang, 1968.

Boyer, Horace C. "Gospel Music Comes of Age." *Black World,* November 1973.

Braman, Constance Lee, compiler and arranger. *The Negro Sings.* Jacksonville, Fla.: Work Projects Administration of Florida — Professional and Service Division Statewide Recreation Project, 1940.

Brasmer, William and Dominick Consolo, eds. *Black Drama.* Columbus, Ohio: Charles E. Merrill, 1970.

Brawley, Benjamin, ed. *Early Negro American Writers.* New York: Dover, 1970.

Brawley, Benjamin, *The Negro Genius: A New Appraisal of the American Negro in Literature and the Fine Arts.* New York: Dodd, Mead, and Co., 1937.

Brendt, Joachim. *The Jazz Book.* New York: Lawrence Hill and Co., 1975.

Brewer, J. Mason. *American Negro Folklore.* Chicago: Quadrangle, 1969.

Brooks, Gwendolyn. *Report from Part One.* Detroit: Broadside Press, 1972.

----------------------. *A Street in Bronzeville.* New York: Harper, 1945.

Brown, Sterling A., Arthur P. Davis, and Ulysses Lee, eds. *The Negro Caravan.* New York: Dryden Press, 1941.

Brown, Sterling A. *Negro Poetry and Drama and the Negro in American Fiction.* New York: Atheneum, 1969.

Bryant, Linda Goode and Marcy S. Phillips. *Contextures*. New York: Just Above Midtown, Inc., 1978.

Bullins, Ed, ed. *New Plays from the Black theatre*. New York: Bantam, 1969.

Butcher, Margart Just. *The Negro in American Culture*. New York: Alfred A. Knopf, 1972.

Carruthers, Ben. "Shirley Verrett: I'm Singing With the Voice that Gid Has Given Me." *Encore*, 19 March 1979, p. 29.

Chappel, Steve and Reebe Garofalo. *Rock-n-Roll is Here to Pay*. Chicago: Nelson-Hall, 1977.

Clark, Edgar R., comp. *Negro Art Songs*. New York: Edward B. Marks Music Corporation, 1946.

Couch, William, ed. *New Black Playwrights*. Baton Rouge: Louisiana State University, 1968.

Cullen, Countee, "Elizabeth Prophet: Sculptress." *Opportunity,* July 1930.

Culp, Daniel Wallace, ed. *Twentieth Century Negro Literature*. Toronto: J.L. Nichols and Co., 1902.

Dandridge, Dorothy and Earl Conrad. *Everything and Nothing: The Dorothy Dandridge Tragedy*. New York: Abelard-Schuman Ltd., 1970.

Dandridge, Rita B. "Male Critics/Black Women's Novels." *CLA Journal*, September 1979.

Davenport, M. Marguerite, *Azalia: The Life of Madame E. Azalia Hackley*. Boston: Chapman and Grimes, Inc., 1947.

Davis, Arthur. *From the Dark Tower*. Washington, D.C.: Howard University Press, 1974.

Davis, Arthur, "Novels of the New Black Renaissance." *CLA Journal*, June 1978.

Dorson, Richard M. *American Negro Folk Tales*. New York, N.Y.: Fawcett, 1967.

Dover, Cedric, *American Negro Art*. Greenwich, Conn.: New York Graphic Society, 1960.

Driskell, David. *Two Centuries of Black American Art*. New York: Alfred A. Knopf, 1976.

Dunham. Kathrine. *Kathrine Dunham's Journey to Accompong*. New York: Henry Holt and Co., 1946.

--------------------. *Island Possessed*. New York: Henry Holt and Co., 1946.

--------------------. *A Touch of Innocence*. New York: Harcourt, Brace, and Co., 1959.

Emery, Lynne Fauley. *Black Dance in the United States from 1619 to 1970*. Palo Alto, Calif.: National Press Books, 1972.

Fax, Elton C. *Seventeen Black Artists*. New York: Dodd, Mead, and Co., 1971.

Fine, Elsa Honig. *The Afro-American Artists*. New York: Holt, Rinehart, and Winston, 1971.

Fletcher, Tom. *100 Years of the Negro in Show Business*. New York: Burdge and Co. Ltd., 1954.

Garland, Phyl. "The Lady Lives Jazz." *Ebony,* October 1979.

--------------------. *The Sound of Soul*. Chicago: Henry Regency Co., 1969.

Giddings, Paula. "A Shoulder Hunched Against a Sharp Concern." *Black World,* December 1971.

Giovanni, Nikki. *Gemini: An Extended Autobiographical Statement on My First*

Twenty-Five Years of Being a Black Poet. New York: Bobbs-Merrill, 1972.

------------------. *Night Comes Softly.* New York: Medic Press, 1970.

Gomes, Maxine Sims. "Problems of the Black Woman in Music." *Women's Time,* June 1976.

Graham, Shirley. *The Story of Phillis Wheatley.* New York: Messner, 1949.

Greene, Lorenzo Johnson. *The Negro in Colonial New England.* New York: Atheneum, 1968.

Gross, Seymour L. and John Edward Hardy. *Images of the Negro in American Literature.* Chicago: University of Chicago, 1966.

Hansberry, Lorraine. *To Be Young, Gifted, and Black.* Englewood Cliffs, N.J.: Prentice Hall, 1969.

Hare, Maud Cuney. *Negro Musicians and Their Music.* 1936; rpt. New York: DeCapo Press, 1974.

Harnan, Terry. *African Rhythm American Dance.* New York: Alfred A. Knopf, 1974.

Hemenway, Robert, ed. *The Black Novelist.* Columbus, Ohio: Charles E. Merril, 1970.

Herskovits, Melville J. "The Contemporary Scene: Africanisms in Religious Life." in *The Myth of the Negro Past.* Boston: Beacon Press, 1941, pp. 207-260.

Hill, Herbert, ed. *Anger and Beyond: The Negro Writer in the U.S.* New York: Harper and Row, 1968.

------------------. *Soon, One Morning: New Writings by American Negroes,* 1940-1962. New York: Alfred A. Knopf, 1963.

Holiday, Billie. *Lady Sings the Blues.* Garden City, N.Y.: Doubleday and Co., 1956.

Hoover, Velma J. "Meta Vaux Fuller: Her Life and Art." *Negro History Bulletin,* March–April 1977, p. 678.

Horne, Lena. Lena. Garden City, N.Y.: Doubleday, 1965.

Hughes, Langston and Milton Meltzer.*Black Magic: A Pictoral History of the Negro in American Entertainment.* New York: Bonanza Books, 1967.

Hurston, Zora Neale. *Dust Tracks on a Road: An Autobiography.* Philadelphia: J.B. Lippincolt, 1942.

Isaacs, Edith J. *The Negro in the American Theatre.* New York: Theatre Arts, 1947.

Jackson Harriet. "American Dancer, Negro." *Dance* Magazine, September 1966.

Jackson, Jesse. *Make a Joyful Noise Unto the Lord: The Life of Mahalia Jackson, Queen of Gospel.* New York: Thomas Y. Crowell Co., 1974.

Jackson, Mahalia and Evan McLeod Whylie. *Movin' on Up.* New York: Hawthorne Books, 1966.

Johnson, Helen Armstead. "Some Late Information on Some Early People." *Encore American and Worldwide News,* 23 June 1975.

Johnson, James Weldon. *Black Manhattan.* New York: Alfred A. Knopf, 1930.

Jones, LeRoi. *Blues People: Negro Music in White America.* New York: Morrow, 1963.

Kitt, Eartha. *Thursday's Child.* New York: Duell, Sloan, and Pearce, Inc., 1956.

Koegler, D.M. "John Neumeier's New Tour de Force; "Legend of Joseph." *Dance* Magazine, June 1977.

Lewis, Samella. *Art: African American.* New York: Harcourt Brace Jovanovich, 1978.

Locke, Alain, ed. *The Negro in Art: A Pictorial Record of the Negro Artist and of the Negro Theme in Art.* Washington, D.C.: Associates in Negro Folk Education, 1940.

Locke, Alain. *The Negro and His Music.* Fort Washington, N.Y.: Kennikat, 1968.

Loggins, Vernon. *The Negro Author: His Development in America to 1900.* Columbia University Studies in English and Comparative Literature, no. 103. New York: Columbia University Press, 1931.

Long, Richard. "Arts of the Black Peoples of the Americas." in *World Encyclopedia of Black Peoples.* Vol. I. St. Clair Shores, Mich.: Scholarly Press, 1975, pp. 16-32.

McDonagh, D. "Negroes in Ballet." *New Republic,* 2 November 1968, pp. 41-44.

McMillan, Lewick. "Mary Lou Williams: First Lady of Jazz." *Downbeat* 27 May 1971, pp. 16-17.

Majors, Monroe A. *Noted Negro Women.* 1893; rpt. Freeport, N.Y.: Books for Libraries Press, 1971.

Mapp, Edward. *Blacks in American Films: Today and Yesterday.* Metuchen, N.J.: Scarecrow Press, 1972.

Matthews, Geraldine O. et al., comps. *Black American Writers, 1776-1949: A Bibliography and Union List.* Boston: G.K. Hall and Co., 1975.

Maynard, Olga. "Judith Jamison." *Dance* Magazine, November 1972.

Miller, Jean-Marie. "Angelina Weld Grimke: Playwright and Poet." *CLA Journal,* June 1978.

Mitchell, Loften. *Black Drama: The Story of the American Negro in the Theatre.* New York: Hawthorne Books, Inc., 1967.

Moore, Carman. *Somebody's Angel Child: The Story of Bessie Smith.* New York: Thomas Y. Cromwell Co., 1969.

Morrison, A. "Women in the Arts." *Ebony,* August 1970, pp. 90-94.

Nash, Joseph. "Dancing Many Drums." *National Scene Magazine,* September-October 1976, p. 3.

The Negro Artist Comes of Age. A National Survey of Contemporary American Artists. Albany, N.Y.: Albany Institute of History and Art, February 11, 1945.

The Negro Heritage Committee. *Afro-American Women in Art: Their Achievement in Sculpture and Painting.* Greensboro, N.C.: The Negro Heritage Committee, 1969.

Newman, Shirlee P. *Marian Anderson: Lady from Philadelphia.* New York: Westminster Press, 1965.

Noble, Jeanne. *Beautiful Also Are the Souls of My Black Sisters.* Englewood Cliffs, N.J.: Prentice-Hall, 1978.

Oliver, Paul. *The Story of the Blues.* New York: Chilton Book Co., 1969.

"On Black Artists." *Art Journal,* Spring 1969.

Patterson, Lindsay, ed. *Anthology of the American Negro in the Theatre.* (International Library of Negro Life and History). New York: Publishers Co., 1970.

Patterson, Lindsay. *Black Film and Filmmakers.* New York: Dodd, Mead, and Co., 1975.

Pierre-Noel, L.J. "Black Women in the Visual Arts: A Comparative Study," *New Directions,* April 1976, pp. 12-20.

Pines, Jim. *Blacks in Films.* London: Cassell and Collier MacMillan Publ. Ltd., 1975.

Porter, Dorothy B. *North American Negro Poets: A Bibliographical Check List of Their Writings, 1760-1944.* New York: Burt Franklin, 1963.

Porter, James A. *Modern Negro Art.* New York: Dryden Press, 1943.

Rahman, Aishan. "To be Black, Female, and a Playwright," *Freedomways,* 1979, p. 257.

Redmond, Eugene B. *Drumvoices, the Mission of Afro-American Poetry.* New York: Anchor Press/Doubleday, 1976.

Richmond, Merle A. *Bid the Vassal Soar, Interpretative Essays on the Life and poetry of Phillis Wheately and George Moses Horton.* Washington, D.C.: Howard University Press, 1974.

Robinson, William H. *Phillis Wheatley in the Black American Beginnings.* Detroit: Broadside Press, 1975.

Rollins, Charlemae. *Famous American Negro Poets.* New York: Dodd, Mead, and Co., 1967.

Shapiro, Nat and Nat Hentoff, eds. *The Jazz Makers.* Westport, Conn.: Greenwood Press, 1957.

Shearer, Lloyd. "Cicely Tyson—From Slum to Stardom." *Parade* Magazine, 3 December 1972, pp. 10-12.

Shook, Karel. *Elements of Classical Ballet Technique as Practiced in the School of the Dance Theatre of Harlem.* New York: Dance Horizons, 1977.

Small, Linda. "Black Dancers, Black Travelers," *Dance* Magazine, October 1979.

Smith, B.H. "Women Artists: Some Muted Notes." *Journal of Communication,* Spring 1974, pp. 146-149.

Smythe, Mabel *The Black American Reference Book.* Englewood Cliffs, N.J.: Prentice   Hall, 1976.

Sobel, Mechal. *Trabelin' on the Slave Journey to an Afro-Baptist Faith.* Westport, Conn.: Greenwood Press, 1979.

Southern, Eileen. *The Music of Black Americans.* New York: Norton and Co., 1971.

------------------. *Readings in Black American Music.* New York: Norton, 1971.

Spacks, Patricia Meyers, ed. *Contemporary Women Novelists.* Englewood Cliffs, N.J.: Prentice-Hall, 1977.

Stevens, Janet. *Marian Anderson: Singing to the World.* Chicago: Encyclopedia Britannica Press, 1963.

Stewart-Baxter, Derrick. *Ma Rainey and the Classic Blues Singer.* New York: Stein and Day, 1970.

Subject Index to Literature on Negro Art. Selected from the Union Catalog of Printed Materials on the Negro in the Chicago Libraries. Federal Works Agency. Works Projects Administration. Chicago, Ill: Chicago Library Omnibus Project, 1941.

Thompson, Francesca. "Final Curtain for Anita Bush." *Black World,* July 1974.

Trotter, James. *Music and Some Highly Musical People.* 1881; rpt. New York, N.Y.: Johnson Reprint Corporation, 1968.

Ulanov, Barry. *A History of Jazz in America.* New York: DeCapo Press, 1972.

University of California, Santa Barbara. *An Exhibition of Black Women Artists: May 5   17, 1975.* Catalogue. Santa Barbara: University of California, 1975.

Vehanen, Kosti. *Marian Anderson A Portrait.* New York: McGraw, 1941.

"A Voice Like a Banner Flying." *Time* Magazine, 10 March 1961.

Walker, Alice, ed. *I Love Myself When I am Laughing: A Zora Neale Hurston Reader.* New York: Feminist Press, 1979.

Walker, Alice. "In Search of Our Mother's Gardens: The Creativity of Black Women in the South." *Ms* Magazine, May 1974.

Walker, Margaret. *For My People.* New Haven, Conn.: Yale University Press, 1942.

Waters, Ethel. *His Eye is on the Sparrow: An Autobiography.* Garden City, N.Y.: Doubleday, 1951.

Watson, Carol. "The Novels of Afro-American Women: Concerns and Themes, 1891 1965." Diss. George Washington University 1978.

Webster, Ivan. "A Woman Called Tyson." *Encore American and Worldwide News,* 6 November 1978.

Williams, Ora. *American Black Women.* Metuchen, N.J.: Scarecrow Press, Inc., 1973.

Work, Monroe N. *Negro Year Book.* Tuskegee, Ala.: Tuskegee Institute 1937.

INDEX OF BLACK WOMEN: THE ARTS

THE CONTRIBUTIONS OF BLACK WOMEN TO AMERICA:
MEDIA

Manuscript Writer
Janell Walden

Consultant
Sharon Bramlett, Ph.D.

Evaluators
Lois Alexander
Director
National Association of Media
Women, Inc.
New York, New York

Ed Bradley
CBS News Correspondent
CBS News
New York, New York

Hazel B. Garland
Consultant
New *Pittsburgh Courier*
Pittsburgh, Pennsylvania

Johnny Tolliver, Ph.D.
Chair
Department of Mass Communications
Jackson State University
Jackson, Mississippi

Sonia Walker
Director of Community Relations
WHBQ-TV
Memphis, Tennessee

Editor
Marianna W. Davis, Ed.D.

PART II

MEDIA
Table of Contents

INTRODUCTORY ESSAY

BLACK WOMEN IN MEDIA

There are among us yet, those old enough to recall the lamplighters who came around at dusk with their ladders to turn on the street lights. They were the illuminators of the night, and they held a certain mystique because of their function. Modern technology has replaced them. The lamplighters have faded into the nostalgia of things past, but the memory lingers on. It reminds us of our heritage: that "the past is prologue to the present."

This book on the Contributions of Black Women in Media illuminates the important, often unknown or often ignored contributions of a segment of society to the world of communications. These early Black women communicators were the lamplighters piercing the darkness through the power of the printed word. Their modern-day counterparts, sisters in the sophisticated art of tele-communications or the instant medium of transmitted words, are the inheritors of a tradition which deserved to be stamped indelibly in their memories.

For young, aspiring journalists, the book fulfills a need for role models of pioneers who went before them, lighting the way. Experience is the instructor for that which is about to be undertaken. It is the parent guiding the fledgling child's venturing first steps. And for those who thirst for a glimpse of the past, the book provides a refreshing view. It is an effort whose time has come, and we are all better for it.

If there were no Black women journalists in the early days of the struggle for freedom, the Lord would have had to invent them. The approximately 300,000 freed persons of color in the pre-Civil War period enjoyed only a modicum of independence. The constrictions of color and the cruelties that society inflicted upon these second-class citizens required strong voices to keep up the drum beat of protest.

In bondage, Black men suffered the indignities that denied them the right to full manhood, even among their peers. Black women endured the humiliation of inferior status, at the same time that they were treated as sexual conveniences to satisfy the appetites of white overseers.

The social mores demanded strict conformity with the customs of segregation. To stay alive necessitated going along with the rules of apartheid. Even the framers of the Constitution defined Blacks as three-fifths of a person. So it was that without the weapons to resist or the climate of sympathy to support their grievances that the journals of protest sprang up. The abolitionist movement was growing, but it had not reached its zenith. The printed word became the expression of pain as well as the armor against degradation of the spirit.

In the beginning, Black women were the forces behind their husbands, "helping out" in preparing the newspapers for circulation. Often they were the inspiration for the editorials that challenged the system and trumpeted the call to "let my people go." It was noted that the colored ladies of Philadelphia held bazaars in support of Frederick Douglass' papers, which he supplemented with contributions collected at the Negro conventions and other public meetings.

The advent of the Civil War brought heavier pressures than ever on the hopes and dreams of Blacks. Mary Ann Shadd Carey emerges in the book as the first Black woman to gain recognition as a journalist before the War Between the States. She was born October 23, 1863 in Delaware and was a strong advocate of Black migration to Canada. Her book, *Notes on Canada West,* urged Blacks to settle in the friendly climate of the neighbor to the North. We learn that her femininity and strong personality drew the attention of a leading Black editor in Canada, Samuel Ringgold Ward, publisher of the *Provincial Freeman.* He hired her as "public agent" which meant promoting subscriptions to the paper.

By the time of the first publication, Shadd was acting as both agent-financier and editor. The paper's total emphasis was on self-development programs for fugitive slaves with Canada West as their permanent home. She even suggested that the exiles should become British citizens. Her ideas clashed with the views of a rival paper, *Voice of the Fugitive,* which advocated only temporary residence in Canada for the fugitives with the hope that they would some day return to a free America.

Even then, Shadd was critical of Black leadership which she saw as confused and powerless. When the Dred Scott decision was handed down by the Supreme Court which nullified the rights of returned fugitive slaves, Shadd called for increased emigration to Canada as the only salvation for Blacks. "Your national ship is rotten and sinking, why not leave it?" she urged. While her preachments declined in favor, we are fascinated with the daring adventures of this early journalist—her association with abolitionist John Brown, recruiting for the Union Army and as contributing editor for the newspapers of Frederick Douglass and John Wesley Cromwell.

Shadd's life was a long chronicle of unusual achievements. She returned to Washington, D.C. to resume her teaching career, became the principal of three colored schools and went on to earn her law degree from Howard University in 1884. Mary Ann Shadd Carey has to be one of the great legends in the history of journalism.

The legacy which she left to Black women is contained in these words which appeared in the "New National Era" in 1872. " . . . For a people whose leaders seek to learn the tortuous ways of speculation and whose women are awed into silence, vital questions must for the time take back seats among the people . . . But our women must speak out . . . white women are getting to be a power in the land, and colored cannot any longer afford to be neutrals."

Shadd's impact was felt in the early days of the women's rights movement in this country. Many educated Black women supported the efforts of white women in the expectation that gains could be shared by Black women. Some strong Black feminine voices followed in the wake of Mary Ann Shadd Carey.

The role of the religious organs and Black women writers' contributions to these journals is worth noting. Among them were the *Christian Recorder* and the *A.M.E. Review*, publications of the African Methodist Episcopal Demonination. Frances Ellen Watkins (Harper), poet and lecturer, was one. She was a fiery suffragette and a passionate supporter of abolition. In the year of the Emancipation Proclamation (1863) there was a short hiatus in the publication of Black journals. Perhaps this time may be best described as a time for regroupings, a search for new directions. But with the challenges of an uncertain freedom, Black papers renewed publishing and there was a proliferation of general interest and church-sponsored periodicals.

There is scant evidence of Black women writers in the period of Reconstruction. Blacks had gained citizenship and voting rights under the Thirteenth, Fourteenth, and Fifteenth Amendments, and many were elected to State and Federal offices. The interlude of comparative freedom ended with the Hayes-Tilden Compromise of 1876. In return for the election of Hayes as President of the United States, the agreement was to withdraw Federal troops from the South in exchange for the votes of whites.

In the dark days of despair that followed crushed Black hopes of equality, the Black convention movement was revived, marked by formation of the Afro-American League, the Afro-American Press Association, and the Atlanta University Conference on Negro Problems. Blacks were absorbed in seeking education as an alternative way out of second-class citizenship. A record number of Blacks were enrolled in public and private schools. Church-sponsored institutions of higher education were in vogue.

In Louisville, Kentucky at the state university for Blacks, Dr. William J. Simmons, President, was editor of the *American Baptist*, the organ of the Negro Baptist congregations, as well as the founding editor of *Our Women and Children* magazine. The topics included child care, home managment, marital relationships, and the spiritual development of mothers and children. The primary sources of information for the articles were wives and mothers. "Many of the first Black women journalists wrote for the magazine," the book tells us. It was described as "giving the world a bright array of female writers upon different questions hitherto unknown to the literary world."

One of this group was Mary Britton who wrote under the pen name "Mab". She was born in Lexington, Kentucky about 1858. At age 19, she was published in the *Cincinnati Commercial*. A woman colleague applauded Britton for her excellent talent in comparing, explaining, expounding, criticizing, and upsetting politicians for their attacks against worthy Black citizens. Britton went on to become a leading newspaper editor and contributor to many periodicals. She was credited with influencing legislation which led to equal treatment for Blacks on Kentucky railroads.

It is interesting to note that the early Black women writers most frequently combined teaching careers with journalism. Thus, they played dual roles as educators and moulders of public opinion. However, by the 30's Black men dominated the newsrooms of the Black press. Women were generally relegated to writing social news possibly because conventional belief assigned a more genteel role for women writers, on the biased conviction that women were ill-equipped by training or sex to handle the rigors of hard news reporting. Moreover, the chronicling of social events had become a staple of Black newspapers, indeed one of its key sources of both news and income. Black people who were ignored by the general media, except for acts of crime, took satisfaction in seeing their names and pictures in the society columns of Black newspapers. Black women writers of more serious persuasion turned to the church periodicals as outlets for these energies.

One of the first Black women writers to break the print barriers in the general (white) media was Victoria Earle Matthews, who began her press career as a substitute reporter for a number of New York papers. In addition, her articles were well received in many publications around the country.

Ida B. Wells (Barnett) is the most famous of the early Black women journalists, often referred to as "Princess of the Press." She was born in 1862 in Holly Springs, Mississippi. After the deaths of her parents during a yellow fever epidemic, she assumed the responsibilities of rearing her younger brothers and sisters. They moved to Memphis, Tennessee where Ida pursued her studies at Fisk University and LeMoyne Institute, while continuing to teach.

A born firebrand and crusader, she rebelled at Jim Crow laws of segregation in travel and public accommodations. She sued the Chesapeake, Ohio and Southwestern Railroad and won, but the verdict was later reversed. Wells took the pen to write of her experiences in church organs and later established her own newspaper, the *Memphis Free Speech*. Her scorching editorials landed her on the enemies list of the white power structure. Eventually, the newspaper office was sacked and burned. Wells was in New York at the time, but because of the dangerous threats against her, she took the advice of friends and gave up trying to revive the paper.

Later, Wells moved to Chicago and was married to Ferdinand Barnett, a lawyer. She remained a powerful figure and legend in her time. Her daughter, Alfreda Duster, has written a sensitive biography of her famous mother.

Ida Wells' greatest impact was on the crime of lynching in this country in which Blacks were the majority of victims. She at least paved the way for the passage of anti-lynching laws. She championed the rights of Black sharecroppers, and at one point substituted for her husband in arguing before the bar in Cairo, Illinois for the dismissal of the county sheriff on the grounds of his complicity in a lynching. She won the case and the sheriff was released from his duties. Significantly, there were no further lynchings in the state of Illinois. She was a founder of the National Association of Colored Women. Her epitaphs include these words, "She told the truth in words so stirring that she forced the world to listen."

With the beginning of the so-called Modern Era of the 50's, Black women writers erased the unwritten taboos against them by some Black publishers and editors. Alice Dunnigan became the first Black woman accredited to the White House press corps. She represented the Associated Negro Press. Like most of her predecessors, Dunnigan was a former school teacher. She has written a book about her experiences, *From the Schoolhouse to the White House.*

Credit for pioneering an enlightened and more vigorous role for Black women writers should be assigned to John H. Sengstacke, publisher of the Sengstacke chain of newspapers; Louis E. Martin, former editorial director of the papers; Carl Murphy, publisher of the Afro-American newspapers; Carter Wesley, *Houston Informer*; and Mrs. C.W. Franklin of the *Kansas City Call*, to name a few. Sengstacke named Venice Tipton Spraggs to head his Washington Bureau. When Spraggs resigned to work full-time for the Democratic National Committee, she was succeeded by Ethel Payne of Chicago. Sengstacke later assigned Payne to cover the Asian–African Conference in Bandung, Indonesia in 1955 and again sent her to Ghana to cover the independence ceremonies in 1957.

Audrey Weaver of Chicago became the first Black woman to be named managing editor of a daily newspaper, the *Chicago Daily Defender*. Lucille Bluford was appointed managing editor of the *Kansas City Call*, a post she holds today. Frances Murphy, a daughter of the publisher, was a European correspondent in World War II.

The establishment of affirmative action programs across the spectrum of employment and education and the enactment of Title VIII of the Civil Rights Act, prohibiting discrimination on account of sex, triggered increased hiring of Black women in communications. The Equal Employment Opportunity Commission became the monitor for the progress of the new "emancipation." Fair access regulations of the Federal Communications Commission opened new doors in broadcast journalism.

Perhaps it should be noted that some analysts of recent employment trends in television have voiced concern with an apparent growing tendency to hire Black women as "twofolds"—thereby satisfying twin goals of race and sex. And while the substantial increase of Black women on camera and as reporters has been applauded, this recent hiring trend is under study to determine if Black male presence is restricted as a consequence.

In radio, progress continues, albeit at a gradual pace. This book points to some growth in Black women occupying executive-managerial positions and working as news readers and reporters.

In the print media and magazines, Black women have made strides. Some are on the staffs of national magazines. Ida Lewis is the editor - publisher of *Encore* Magazine. Marcia Gillespie is the editor of *Essence* Magazine, and her column "Getting Down" is widely read nationally. Ethel Payne pioneered as a commentator for six years on the CBS network opinion program, "Spectrum," the only Black woman to have held that spot.

Research shows there is a bright new group of women journalists emerging on the national scene—creative, innovative, and aggressive. Some are boldly advancing with publications and co-ownership and editorial partnership. Barbara Reynolds, a correspondent for the *Chicago Tribune*, Washington Bureau, also edits a new magazine that shows promise called *Dollars and Sense*, with Donald Woods as publisher.

This introduction does not attempt criticism of the book's content, the completeness and accuracy of the considerable research that has gone into it. While I hestitate to describe it as the *definitive* work on the contributions of Black women in media, I would describe it as a courageous, ambitious beginning of research in an area of activity woefully neglected by historians.

As Benjamin Quarles once wrote: "The story of the Negro in the United States is a combination of the tragic and the heroic, of denial and affirmation. But most of all, it is a record of a tidal force in American life."

We would hope—and should be encouraged—to continue serious efforts to unearth more of the rich heritage left by Black women writers to our contemporaries in media.

For her counsel and assistance in the preparation of this introduction, I wish to thank Ethel L. Payne, a true pioneer still charting new courses in journalism. And for the patience in awaiting delivery of this manuscript, I am deeply grateful to the director of this project, Dr. Marianna W. Davis.

William C. Matney
Editor-in-Chief
Who's Who Among Black Americans, Inc.

CHAPTER I
THE BEGINNINGS: THE PRINTED WORD

Black women have evolved a long, traditional, and proud history in the print media. When Black-owned and operated newspapers first appeared in early nineteenth century, the women were among their most vigorous and articulate supporters. They contributed directly to the production of these "mouthpieces of the race." It was not unusual to find women as editors, owners, and publishers.

The Birth of Freedom's Journal

An urgent call was sounded in New York's free, Black community early in 1827, and the men gathered quickly. Of chief concern was the sharply increasing number of attacks made against Negroes, particularly those mentioned in the pages of the *New York Enquirer*, a newspaper which loudly supported slavery and heaped scorn on free Blacks as well.[1] It attacked all Black demands for freedom and justice, and enjoyed considerable influence in the city. Adding fuel to the fire, was the American Colonization Society, a white group, which enthusiastically promoted the return of free Blacks to Africa as a solution to the "race problem." Combined with the *Enquirer's* threats and increasing dangers in the city's streets, freedmen faced an ugly, intimidating situation.

The men knew they must fight these forces somehow. For one thing, they had accumulated more than a million dollars in real estate holdings, and $500,000 in savings. Moreover, they had developed African free schools and were providing excellent education for their children.[2] Despite their shining examples of thrift, industry, and selfreliance—all the qualities held dear by Puritan-influenced people—they were still opposed by most Whites.

Blacks resolved that night to speak for themselves, their people, and the record. They would begin a paper of their own to campaign for their cause. It could also fan the then small fire of abolition. John Russwurm, the second Black to graduate from an American college, and another highly educated man, the Reverend Samuel E. Cornish, would edit the publication named *Freedom's Journal*.

Readers of the first issue, which appeared March 30, 1827, were greeted with an eloquent statement of purpose:

To Our Patrons:

We wish to plead our own cause. Too long have others spoken for us. Too long has the public been deceived by misrepresentations, in things which concern us dearly.

The first sustained voice for the 320,000 free Blacks in the country, the *Journal* preached the abolition of slavery and the rights of freemen as its articles of faith. It flourished for only two years, but other Black papers soon followed, complimenting those developed by white abolitionists. Thus began the tradition of an activist Black Press, which grew to become the most significant voice of protest and agitation for Black rights in America, and one of the agencies most committed to glorifying achievements of the race.

In name as well as content, other Black papers followed the *Journal's* lead, such as the *Colored American*, the *Elevator*, the *National Watchman*, and the *Mirror of the Times*. The *Ram's Horn* and the *North Star* were publications whose titles also referred to signals on the Underground Railroad. Collectively, these publications came to be known as the Black Press, and were proud promoters of a valiant fighting tradition.

The antebellum Black Press, typified by the Russwurm and Cornish example of highly-motivated editor-publishers, was controlled by free Blacks whose outrage with so-called "black laws" matched their disgust for the "peculiar institution." Both systems were built on the foundation of racial discrimination. The *Colored American*, the third Black paper published in America (1837), succinctly stated the case in this credo printed in an 1840 issue: "We believe the overthrow of the slave system will greatly be for the interest and advancement of the free colored population, inasmuch as all our obstacles to advancement in this country, and all our disabilities arise from that system."

The *Enquirer* diatribes that first sparked the organization of *Freedom's Journal* were merely some of the sharpest tips of an enormous racist iceberg. Throughout the North and South, free persons were subject to chafing regulations. By 1835, every state required free Blacks to work or otherwise face the threat of state-enforced servitude. In both the North and South, free persons were either disenfranchised outright or subject to meeting difficult property and/or residence requirements. So effective were the voting restrictions until there was no significant voting by Negroes anywhere after 1830. Also, by 1835, free Negroes were not allowed to immigrate to most southern states or even to several northern ones.[3] Only New England Blacks escaped such restrictive legislation.

More outrageous affronts remained. Whites could claim a Black was a slave and there was little with which to refute the charges, since Blacks were not allowed to testify against Whites. Similarly, Blacks without "free papers" could even be remanded to slavery once challenged to produce them. Kidnapping was also a danger. In the face of such unjust and unreasonable treatment, the Black Press was formed not a moment too soon to air Black grievances, demands, and desires. Black women during the Black Press infancy had participated to a limited extent.[4] In 1837, the Ladies Literary Society of the City of New York raised money for the *Colored American*, which by then was a champion of all Black organizational policy.[5] They also contributed to the New York Vigilance Committee, which provided shelter, food, and clothing for fugitives. One of several such groups formed by free Black women in major northern cities between 1830 and late 1840, the Literary women were "actuated by a national feeling for the welfare of [their] friends [and] thought it fit to associate for the diffusion of knowledge, the suppression of vice and immorality, and for cherishing such virtues as would render them happy and useful to society."[6] Clearly, the aims of these women were aligned with Black papers whose editorials hammered out messages of racial uplift, progress, and justice.

Likewise, the Colored Ladies of Philadelphia held bazaars in support of Frederick Douglass' papers, which he supplemented with contributions collected at the Negro conventions and other public meetings.[7] Apart from raising funds collectively, it is probable that some women subscribed to these early papers. It was during the eve of the Civil War, that Black women first gained recognition as journalists, editors, or publishers.

NOTES

[1] I. Garland Penn, *The Afro-American Press and Its Editors* (1891; rpt. New York: Arno Press, 1969), p. 28.

[2] Paula Giddings, "The Beginning: The Spirit of the Early Black Press," *Encore,* 20 June 1977, p. 17.

[3] John Hope Franklin, *From Slavery to Freedom,* 4th ed. (New York: Knopf, 1974), pp. 167-169.

[4] Benjamin Quarles, *Black Abolitionists* (New York: Oxford University Press, 1969), p. 195.

[5] Dorothy B. Porter, "The Organized Educational Activities of Negro Literary Societies, 1828-1846," *Journal of Negro Education,* October 1936, p. 569.

[6] Porter and Giddings, p. 17. Discusses the paper's split with Blacks who favored integrated organizations.

[7] Quarles, p. 87.

CHAPTER II

SHAPING OF THE BLACK PRESS BY CRITICAL EVENTS

The Antebellum Period

The early Black Press was a powerful tool of abolition. Even more than the Black church, the one other institution controlled by the race, "the press presented a united and consistent front against slavery . . . a more single-minded attack than could be expected from the clerical quarter," with its several denominations and hundreds of ministers.[1] No Black paper began operation without sounding the same chord: demanding freedom for the Black race. Furthermore, Black papers had the secondary effect of promoting the abilities and intelligence of the race. While permitting the expression of Black frustrations and fostering racial unity and uplift, they encouraged white appreciation for their often high caliber of literary achievement and moral argument. Whether they favored or opposed abolition, white readers of the antebellum Black papers were exposed to a far more capable race than was widely supposed. No lazy, shuffling, addle-brained folks were turning out these vociferous weeklies.

Concurrent with the emergence of the Black Press in the 1830's and 1840's, the American abolition movement took on a decidedly more outspoken and militant cast.

One aspect was the Black Convention Movement, which began in the North in 1830. National meetings were held annually through 1835 and sporadically after that, with southern sites included after Emancipation.[2] Enjoying their greatest prominence before the war broke out, these gatherings generally included the most distinguished leaders of the race—most of whom received word via Black papers— and yielded resolutions demanding justice for Blacks, which the Black Press also widely circulated. Forming an organized political base for the Black abolition effort, these meetings preceded the December 1833 Philadelphia Conference at which the three major white abolition groups convened with free Blacks for the first time.[3]

Organizing itself as the American Anti-Slavery Society, the group resolved "to . . . spare no exertions to bring the whole nation to speedy repentance," and began confronting the subject of Black bondage head-on, admitting its proponents would not concede the debate nor the issue fade away. Immediate emancipation was the new goal, and it was championed in the white abolition press. Dominant among its publications was *The Liberator*, edited by William Lloyd Garrison. The combined effects of increased white fears after the bloody slave rebellion led by Nat Turner in 1831, and unrelenting efforts to expand slavery into the western frontier, amply proved this revision of White abolition tactics was in order. Soon, many Whites were calling for immediate, not gradual emancipation of slaves.[4]

In the 1840's, sectional tensions escalated between the agricultural South and the industrial North. Northern and southern capitalists alike intended to expand their enterprises into the new western territories, but Garrisonian abolitionists and other sympathizers took up that decade's slogan, "no union with slaveholders" and complicated the business. The phrase underscored their belief that the Union perpetuated slavery and was, therefore, not worth preserving. It deserved to meet its fate through revolution, they said.[5]

When the 1850's dawned, a complicated compromise bill became the law of the land and, ironically, seemed to exacerbate rather than cool the regional differences. Addressing the need to govern westward expansion and update the federal interpretation of slavery, it admitted California to the Union as a free state but organized other territories without mention of slavery. It protected slaveholders' interests with a stringent Fugitive Slave Act, but ended the slave trade in the nation's capitol. Finally, it compensated Texas for lands ceded to New Mexico since the Mexican-American War.[6]

Rather than ultimately strengthening the slaveholders' hand, the overall effect of this law weakened it. The "passenger" volume of fugitive slaves transported by the Underground Railroad dramatically increased and the ranks of abolition sympathizers swelled as well. Joining their voices in the freedom song, the whites readily understood why fugitive and free-born Blacks alike depised the new rule, and felt that "in the spirit it ought to be violated with impunity."[7] Retroactively applied, it encouraged bounty hunters by making runaways unsafe even in the North, for it disregarded their having built new lives. It also absolutely denied fugitives due process of the law, and assumed their guilt. Jury trials were forbidden and the enforcers, federal officials, were encouraged to rule in favor of the claimants for larger fees. Thus, a decision in favor of the alleged runaways would not be in the commissioners' best pecuniary interests.[8]

Finally, the act legally put "free" Blacks everywhere on notice, for its provisions offered no redress for those wrongly accused of being fugitives.

Many of their number sought refuge in Canada, the northernmost frontier. Even Harriet Tubman, the celebrated Underground Railroad conductor who led more than 300 slaves to freedom, refused to "unload" her human cargo in the United States.

Having pointed the way earlier, the efforts of Blacks to combat slavery kept pace with those of Whites after 1850, but with more of the freemen sounding increasingly defiant. Many vowed to oppose the spirit *and* the letter of the law. In Boston that year, for example, Blacks attending a "reassurance" meeting following passage of the 1850 Compromise resolved to (1) call for repeal of the measure, and (2) agree they would "not allow a fugitive slave to be taken from Massachusetts." Already a tradition had been struck, for rescues of recaptured slaves had been carried out since 1833.[9]

The Black Press decried the infamous 1850 rule for its role in a larger plan to perpetuate slavery and racial discrimination in the expanding nation. The theme of emigration, whether to Canada, Haiti, or elsewhere, appeared on the pages of Black publications which grew in volume and intensity. This emigration "call" reflected the increasing sense of Black disillusionment that the Constitutional guarantees would ever be applied to them.[10]

Announcement of the Dred Scott decision in 1857 "fanned full sail" the militant spirit among Negroes, Quarles writes, for it approved slavery in the western territories and unashamedly stated that Blacks had no rights Whites were bound to respect. Faced with an important and unfavorable legal interpretation, Black sentiment swung farther left. Demonstrations and meetings were held and speakers such as prominent abolitionist Robert Purvis, vowed they "owed no allegiance to a government founded upon the position expressed in the Scott case."[11]

Would-be race liberator John Brown swept down to Harper's Ferry, Virginia in 1859, and Blacks and their stalwart white supporters quickly acclaimed the unsuccessful mission. The leader became "a martyr figure of unprecedented proportions" and the ultimate effect of this raid goaded pro-slavery and emancipation-minded Whites alike, toward squaring off on slavery in the arena of war.

The Black Press carried reports and interpretations of these and all major events impacting on the welfare of Black Americans. Much more strident in tone yet unwavering in its calls for resistance to injustice, its editors were counseled to soft-pedal their indignation and calls to action. The *Weekly Anglo-African* wrote soon after Brown's execution:

    . . . Our Anglo-African blood, at any rate, will not permit us to cease hostilities at that point. We must insist on going farther on, no more patching up of wrongs, no more compromises with wrong-doing. We must continue united, and never cease wrestling with the giant evil of Slavery till we have rid the land of it—till the bondsman shall stand free and disenthralled—a man. We must insist upon all this, before we shall be willing to ensure that peace and tranquility now so earnestly sued for. . . .[12]

The summer before the raid, the same paper ran another editorial addressing its critics. It was an eloquent summation of Black America's case and the Black Press cause:

. . . Cease agitation? Yes, when you repeal the Fugitive Slave Law, reverse the Dred Scott decision, and give us the right of citizenship in the free States, abolish slavery in the District of Columbia, break up the internal slave trade between the slave states, and guarantee unto us the privileges which the Federal Constitution guarantees to all men. Then, and not until then, may you expect us to be silent.[13]

A Voice in the Wilderness

The first Black woman to gain recognition as a journalist and editor gained fame before the Civil War as a major proponent of Canadian emigration.

Mary Ann Shadd (Carey) was born October 9, 1823.[14] She embarked on her newspaper career after writing, publishing, and promoting the highly successful *Notes on Canada West*, an 1852 booklet that urged Canadian resettlement for American Negroes taunted by slavery injustice. A timely response to one of the most hotly debated issues of the day, *Notes* was produced after Shadd, a free-born, Quaker-educated schoolteacher, left her native Delaware for the northern frontier where she reported on conditions and opportunities available.[15]

Historian Benjamin Quarles describes her as slender and somewhat tall, a woman who combined "an attractive femininity with an imperious manner, a combination enabling her to overawe a hostile audience or to outstare a segregation-minded streetcar conductor."[16] Her abilities, manner, and commitment to the Canadian experiment impressed prominent Black abolitionist Samuel Ringgold Ward. The owner and editor of *The Provincial Freeman*, Ward, enlisted her services as "public agent"—a latter-day promotion and subscription associate. The first issue appeared in Windsor, Canada in March, 1853, and was essentially an advertising tool. Well-edited and attractively presented, it attacked slavery, segregated Black settlements, begging (on behalf of fugitives), and anything else its management thought was designed to keep Blacks subservient.[17] They should reject all aid that "materially compromised our manhood by representing us as objects of charity," she wrote.[18] Another *Freeman* hallmark was its coverage of province-wide Black news.

To provide information for all "colored generally but especially to the fugitives from slavery," was the goal of this earliest Black Canadian paper. Its motto was "Self-reliance is the True Road to Independence."[19]

By the debut of the first full issue in March, 1854, Shadd was the true editor as well as financier. She had initially agreed to wear both editor's and publisher's hats for only the first issue, but it was actually 1856 before her responsibilities eased. In the meantime, the press moved to Chatham, Canada West, not far from Detroit and Windsor.

Shadd began her involvement with organized abolition activity when she became the only Negro among the American Missionary Association's 263 home missionaries.[20] Through her *Freeman* experiences she had developed firm opinions concerning resolution of America's race problem and the proper conduct of self-development programs among resettled Blacks in Canada. While at the publication's helm she headed a spirited debate with the *Voice of the Fugitive*, a competing paper. As its title suggested, the *Voice* appealed to fugitive slaves who considered their Canadian exile temporary, and who hoped to return to an emancipated America. In stark contrast, the *Freeman* urged Blacks to make the most of their present situation. Home, Shadd made clear, was now Canada West.[21]

All was not well with the Black Canadian resettlements, however. Dissention was rife over tactics and objectives, and material support for destitute refugees was difficult to obtain. Shadd regularly presented opinions in the *Freeman* calculated to calm the sullied waters. At one point she even urged fugitives to become British citizens. She said it seemed they could never officially become Americans. Britain, she said, had at least freed its slaves by then, and it ruled Canada, too.

Another important reason for her disillusionment was the disunity she saw among free American Blacks. To her mind, the many Black caucuses, conventions, and their resolutions highlighted their great confusion and powerlessness in the face of an unyielding foe.[22] What good were these meetings, she asked, when "the pretended leaders of the people" always had to return to them anyway.[23] Shadd made numerous trips across the border to promote emigration through her lectures. "Your national ship is rotten and sinking," she said upon hearing the Dred Scott decision. "Why not leave it?"[24]

The tenor of the times, coupled with the testimony of others who preached the Canadian gospel, complimented Shadd's own sincerity and intensity. By 1860 the Black Canadian population was past 15,000.[25]

Still, the *Freeman's* audience was limited to begin with and had little prospect of increasing circulation. Few of the emigrants could read and fewer still could afford the luxury of a newspaper. Complicating matters, Mary Shadd "served meat strong even for the time and few cared to digest it."[26] Besides denouncing the attempts of American Blacks to unite, she was guilty of accepting money from a missionary society for her school—while simultaneously disclaiming. Her attacks against several other aid societies and Josiah Henson, a Canadian emigrant and the man on whom the renown "Uncle Tom" character was based, were also well-known.[27] Unwavering in her caustic criticism, yet prone to gloss over the drawbacks to Canadian resettlement, Shadd's paper declined in importance by the time she relinquished major responsibility. Still, she would be remembered as "One of the best editors in the Province, even if she did wear petticoats."[28]

Married to Thomas F. Carey of Toronto in 1856, she remained an active supporter of abolition and kept her journalistic hand supple, compiling the notes of Osborn P. Anderson, sole survivor of the 1859 Harper's Ferry Raid.[29] Shadd met John Brown, leader of the ill-fated assault, in the previous year during his Chatham Convention.[30]

After her return to the United States during the Civil War, the fiery abolitionist was commissioned to recruit Black volunteers for the Union Army. Later, she regularly contributed to Frederick Douglass' *New National Era* and John Wesley Cromwell's *Advocate*, two of the most distinguished organs of the Black Press.

Finally, settling in Washington, D.C., Shadd resumed her teaching career, became principal of three large schools, and earned a law degree from Howard University in 1884. The third Black woman ever to achieve this distinction, she was in her sixties at the time but went on to enjoy a successful legal practice.

By the time of her death in 1893, it was clear that Mary Ann Shadd's pioneering legacy had laid the foundation for the tradition of outspoken and articulate Black women journalists. These crystals of her thought appeared in the *New National Era* on May 21, 1872, and are a heartfelt charge to Black women in view of the growing woman suffrage and women's rights movements:

> ... For a people whose leaders seek to learn the tortuous ways of speculation and whose women are awed into silence, vital questions must for the time take back seats among the people. ... [But] our women must speak out. ... White women are getting to be a power in the land, and colored cannot any longer afford to be neutrals.[31]

Many educated Black women became involved in the woman's rights movements, whether gathering under the banner of temperance or suffrage. Besides shouldering all the disadvantages of being Black, they shared all the social and political limitations of white women. When white women began to press forward with their concerns and demands in the mid-nineteenth century, a significant number of Black women urged them onward. Whether in the crowd's midst or on the sidelines, they hoped the triumphs would be shared.

Frances Ellen Watkins Harper was even more outspoken than her contemporary in calling for the enlightenment of women, and of Black women, especially. A lyrically eloquent speaker and poet, she was a commanding voice in many of the moral and political reform movements of the era, and enjoyed the respect and admiration of many Whites and Blacks. She took the greatest interest in meetings called exclusively for freedwomen, feeling their needs were far more pressing than those of any other class. She was also a great champion of women's rights saying, "It is the women of a country who help to mold its character, and to influence if not determine its destiny."[32] This is why she so strongly believed women were due encouragement and the opportunity to acquire educational benefits and exercise the political rights enjoyed by men.[33]

Frances Watkins Harper regularly contributed articles during the second half of the century to several prominent Black Press journals. Among them were the *Christian Recorder*, the *A.M.E. Review*, and the *Philadelphia Tribune*. Press historian I. Garland Penn called her the "journalistic mother" of the many Black women who entered the field after Reconstruction, despite Mary Ann Shadd's earlier contribution.

Reconstruction and Black Resurgence

Little is known of the few Black papers publishing by the time the Civil War commenced in 1861. The swirling events of the oft-foretold conflict seemed to have eclipsed the need for the press. By 1863, the Emancipation Proclamation became law and not much was heard of those papers that continued to publish. The *North Star*, for example, a loud voice of abolition heard since 1847 and commanded by Frederick Douglass, fell silent that year.[34]

By the war's end, however, the first two Black papers published in the South debuted, thus opening a new chapter in Black Press history. Accompanying the tremendous challenge after Emancipation to fashion a new and solid race awareness and pride, these papers joined other pioneers to swell the number of journals to ten by 1870 and thirty in another decade. The ranks increased five-fold, to 154, by 1890.[35] This group included general interest and church-sponsored periodicals. It was notably enhanced by the sterling contributions of Black women who followed Mary Shadd Carey a generation after she blazed the trail.

Now loosed from slavery's chains, Blacks throughout America understood that elevating the race was the task of the hour. Overwhelmingly deprived of material necessities, the freedmen needed employment for income with which they could construct better homes and buy or raise food.

Education, whether moral, social, spiritual, or practical, was also greatly desired. To counter the prevailing inbred racist sentiment of Whites and resulting feelings of inferiority among the darker brethren, schooled and unschooled Blacks alike rushed toward any opportunity to teach or learn. Armed with literacy and calculation skills, and steeled with the moral and religious sensibilities of their foreparents, they equipped themselves with practical and ethereal armor for the treacherous days ahead.

And difficult they were, as defeated Southerners maneuvered to rebuild a life in which the subjugation and exploitation of Blacks played an intrinsic part. In the first short years after General Lee's surrender, Blacks acquired the freedom, citizenship, and voting-rights provided by the Thirteenth, Fourteenth, and Fifteenth Amendments. Some were elected to state and federal offices, and some became landowners.

The Freedmen's Bureau led in the establishment of southern schools and relief services, and Blacks shared the benefits. Indeed, from all outward appearances, Negroes were finally to become first-class citizens in a country built with the aid of their slave labor.

But the same forces that fueled the Civil War explosion combined to continue the strife after surrender. Northern capitalists greedily eyed the agricultural riches of the South, while Southern Bourbons connived to maintain their dominance with less violence than before.[36]

After the "Revolution of 1876," when Rutherford B. Hayes agreed to withdraw federal troops and other sanctions from the South in return for Southern Republican votes, the lid blew off a boiling pot. Widespread intimidation of Blacks followed. From 1880 onward, "in order to earn a living the American Negro was compelled to give up his political power."[37] Southern legislatures enacted Black codes and the sharecrop system and threats of consignment to convict work-gangs sapped all personal freedoms. Terrorism by the Ku Klux Klan, the Red Shirts, and other "vigilante" groups ensured the turnabout.

The era's tangled and mournful melody carried few bright accents, but these were critical. They were the "sober, honest and capable leaders and public servants" developed from a people of scant resources and experience, wrote Benjamin Quarles.[38] W. E.B. DuBois was even more emphatic. "Had it not been for the Negro school and college, the Negro would, to all intents and purposes, have been driven back to slavery."[39]

Southern Black men and women first received instruction from Freedmen's Bureau programs, dedicated and philanthropic whites, and equally dedicated northern Blacks who came South. With it, they were able to fashion an "inner culture" that helped them adjust to their changing world and survive with a dignity the southern white world disallowed. Their examples offered the one bright and shining hope in a darkened world.

As self-reliance became the keyword during the 1880's and 1890's, Black self-help organizations blossomed under the direction of these leaders.

Black churches, already the pre-eminent institutions, increased their social commitments and sponsored orphanages, hotels, and employment assistance services, and publications. Fraternal orders, beneficial associations, insurance companies, and Black women's groups proliferated in a climate saturated with frustrated hopes and the myriad needs of a people only recently released from slavery. Additionally, the Black Convention Movement was revived then, marked by the appearance of the Afro-American League, the Afro-American Press Association, and the Atlanta University Conference on Negro Problems. All told, these cooperative efforts provided information and encouragement for continued Black resistance to the common foe of racial discrimination.

A New Day's Dawning

With the exception of Frances Ellen Harper, the Black women who distinguished themselves as journalists were products of the massive post-war development efforts. Born mainly in the years immediately preceding or during the war, they were old enough to directly benefit from the many schools funded by the Freedmen's Bureau and northern-based church programs. Negro schools were opposed by white southerners not nearly as much as other self-help agencies, perhaps because white society had not traditionally viewed teachers with the degree of respect it lavished on politicians or businessmen.

There seemed to be a greater willingness to tolerate the growing educational institutions than any of the other agencies Negroes established to improve themselves. Education's pursuit, therefore, came to be one of the great preoccupations of the race. Successfully gained, it was believed the greatest single opportunity to escape mounting proscriptions and indignities heaped on the race.[40] Testifying to their zeal, freedmen contributed $785,700 cash only five years after Emancipation to the sustenance of the nearly one hundred schools established by the Freedmen's Bureau. By 1870, nearly a quarter of a million pupils attended some 4,300 southern schools.[41] Contrasted with the severe limitations enforced against Black education, especially after 1850, these post-war efforts were heroic.

Once literate, Blacks could learn the country's laws and prepare themselves to vote, enter job contracts, and otherwise successfully handle all the rights and duties of citizenship. Black women were denied the franchise, as were white women, but they understood that even a rudimentary education would provide them new means of self-expression and a growing self- and cultural awareness. This they could share with others and use to advance their fight for the ballot and other rights of life, property, and the pursuit of happiness. "Our women have great work to do in this generation," journalist Gertrude B. Mossell would soon write. "The ones who walked before us could not do it, they had no education. The ones who come after us will expect to walk in pleasant paths of our marking out."[42]

Louisville Connection: Church
Publications Inspire Black Women

Of the late nineteenth century group of Black women journalists, several who made noteworthy contributions were from the Louisville, Kentucky area, where they lived and usually were also employed as instructors. Louisville was the site of the State University, founded in 1881 by Dr. William J. Simmons.

Simultaneously busy with church, press, and educational work, Dr. Simmons was president of the university and secretary of the Southern District of the American Baptist Home Mission Society. He edited several papers, including *The American Baptist*, organ of the colored Baptist congregations, before he became founding editor for *Our Women and Children* magazine in 1888.[43]

As its title suggest, *Our Women and Children* was primarily designed to inspire and educate its target audience. Child care, home management, spiritual development of the mother and child, and the marital relationship were major areas of coverage. And what better source of information in these matters than women themselves—the wives, mothers, and culture-bearers? Many of the early Black women journalists wrote for this magazine. A few years after its founding, one student of the black press wrote, "By the efforts of its editor, [*Our*

Women and Children] has given the world a bright array of female writers, upon different questions hitherto unknown to the literary world."[44]

One of the brightest stars in the galaxy was Mary E. Britton, who wrote under the pen name "Meb," and was born in Lexington, Kentucky about 1858. At 19, she was published in the Cincinnati *Commercial*, leading a fellow woman journalist to applaud her ". . . . excellent talent for comparing, explaining, expounding, and criticizing," and upsetting politicians [for] their attacks against "worthy [Black] citizens."[45]

Britton was first a teacher, but soon became a regular contributor to the journal and later, editor of the woman's column in the *Lexington Herald*. In line with the progressive women's thinking of the day, societal reformation was her standard theme. Temperance, the virtue of industrious work, woman's suffrage, practical instructions for child care, and the role models of preachers and teachers were her subjects. She contributed to a number of papers published in and around the Lexington area, including the *Courant*, an educational journal. "Miss Mary E. Britton is one of the brightest stars which shine in Dr. Simmons' great magazine . . . and the magnitude of those stars is national," boasted the *Christian Soldier*, a fellow Lexington publication. Other journals attest to her local celebrity, much of it derived from her exacting attitude as teacher—and her success in grooming accomplished students. One refers to her oratorical prowess, comparing her to Hallie Q. Brown, a nationally-known lecturer. A well-received paper, "Woman's Suffrage as an Important Factor in Public Reforms," appeared in the *American Catholic Tribune* (Cincinnati) in 1887.[46]

Apart from the thoroughly practical articles she prepared, Mary Britton also contributed children's articles to the *Ivy* of Baltimore, under the pen name "Aunt Peggy."

The *Cleveland Gazette* and *Indianapolis World* were to benefit from her contributions and later, Lucy Wilmot Smith, a contemporary, testified that Mary Britton had instigated ("with her pen") many of the reformatory measures allowing Blacks equal treatment on railroads in Kentucky.

Lucy Wilmot Smith, Mary V. Cook, Ione E. Wood, Lavinia B. Sneed, and Mrs. C.C. Stumm all taught or attended school in or near Lexington during the 1880's, and each contributed to *Our Women and Children*.

Lucy W. Smith, in fact, was private secretary to the educator

Simmons until 1884, when he encouraged her to handle the children's column in *The American Baptist*. She greatly enjoyed the work and shortly, Simmons had lost a secretary, gaining a fine reporter/ editor who became head of the woman's department at *Our Women and Children*. She contributed regularly to the *Baptist Journal*, the *Boston Advocate*, and the prestigious *Indianapolis Freeman*, the first and (at that time) only illustrated race paper, whose editorial and typographical quality was so superior until it was on the exchange lists of the nation's leading white papers.[47]

Smith was born November 16, 1861 in Lexington. She began teaching at 16, but managed to graduate from the Normal Department at the State University ten years later. Later, she joined the faculty. Early on, she correctly recognized women's lack of political status, and was an outspoken advocate of woman's suffrage as well as for the elevation of her sex, generally. "We are not sure that fifteen million women of voting age would say [they do not want to vote]; and if they did, majorities do not always establish the right of a thing. Our position is, that women should have the ballot, not as a matter of expedience, but as a matter of pure justice."[48]

One of the most thoroughly professional Black women journalists, Smith counted among her professional credits a series of profiles of Black women journalists written for a New York trade paper. She also maintained membership in the Afro-American Press Convention. These words give a lofty, seemingly idealized description of the relationship between Black men and women. However, her enthusiasm for journalism and the opportunities it offered her sisters is clear:

> Born and bred under the hindrance of slavery and the limitations of sex, the mothers of the race have kept pace with the fathers. They stand at the head of the cultured, educated families whose daughters clasp arms with the sons. The educated Negro woman occupies vantage ground over the Caucasian woman of America in that the former has had to contest with her brother every inch of the ground for recognition; the Negro man, having had his sister by his side on plantations and in rice swamps, keeps her there, now that he moves in other spheres. As she wins laurels he accords her the royal crown. This is especially true in journalism. Doors are opened before we knock, and as well-equipped young women emerge from the classroom, the brotherhood of the race, men whose energies have been repressed and distorted by interposition of circumstances, give them opportunities to prove themselves.[49]

"Grace Ermine" was Mary V. Cook's pen name, and it appeared in her columns for the *American Baptist* and the *South Carolina Tribune* (1887). She once served as editor of the educational department for *Our Women and Children*.

Small in stature and a tenacious fighter "for all that is due her," she became well-known for her pointed commentary supported by religious truth. Concerning the injustice perpetrated by the South against virtually defenseless Blacks, she once said:

> White faces seem to think it is their heaven-born right to practice civil war on Negroes, to the extent of bloodshed and death. . . . The Negro is still clothed in swarthy skin, and he is still robbed of his rights as a citizen, made dear and fairly wan to him by the death of those who fell in the late Rebellion. This outrage cannot endure. God still lives, and that which has been sown shall be reaped.[50]

Cook, one of the most outstanding faculty members at State University (Kentucky) was a Latin and mathematics professor and one of the few women to gain the A.B. degree by 1887. She held several positions in the Baptist Women's Educational Convention, including executive officer for the board of managers.

C.C. Stumm was the wife of Reverend C.C. Stumm, and who, in the curious fashion of the day, wrote under her husband's name. Born March 5, 1857, she was also a teacher and worked at the Hearn Academy (Texas) and at the Bowling Green Academy (Kentucky) where she first met Mary V. Cook, also an instructor there. Reverend Stumm, an accomplished journalist in his own right who once edited the children's column of the *American Baptist* and contributed to several other church- and politically-related publications, eventually teamed with his wife to produce *The Christian Banner*, a religious home journal begun in 1890.

In her journalistic career, Stumm was also contributor and agent for the *Hub and Advocate* of Boston and the *Bowling Green Watchman*. Later, she acted as Philadelphia agent for the *National Monitor* of Brooklyn, New York and *Our Women and Children*, contributing articles and also helping to distribute copies or solicit ads for the publications.

Two other journalists who gravitated to Louisville and the State University during this period were Lavinia B. Sneed and Ione E. Wood. Wood taught Greek after her graduation from the Normal department, and was described as an outstanding teacher by Gertrude (Mrs. N.F.) Mossell in *The Work of Afro-American Women*. She won a permanent position on the faculty after having taught successfully while working toward her Bachelor of Arts degree.

When only twenty-one years old in 1890, Wood was a stockholder in *Our Women and Children* and a regular contributor and editor of the temperance department. Like some of her contemporaries, she was a board member of the Baptist Women's Education Committee and the Women's National Suffrage Association.

Sneed confined herself to writing magazine and newspaper pieces aimed at the common reader, not the scholar, and thus addressed a group often missed by her colleagues. Another distinguished scholar, she earned her bachelor's degree in 1887 and was an original traveling member of the schools' concert troupe, which was modeled after the Fisk Jubilee Singers.

Other Contributors

Alice E. McEwen was the daughter of a prominent Nashville Baptist minister who edited the *Baptist Leader* (1887), the statewide organ of the 150,000-member Tennessee Baptist congregation.[51] She attended Fisk University, Roger Williams University, and Spelman Seminary. Her first article, "The Progress of the Negro," was published in the *Montgomery Herald* when she was sixteen. Born July 29, 1879, she became associate editor at the *Leader* after her graduation in 1888, and began presenting papers to several national groups, including the National Press Convention.[52]

It is not known whether or how she continued her career after 1893, but like Lucy W. Smith, she advocated journalism careers for Black women. She once told the press convention and the Women's Baptist State Convention, "There is no work which women can engage in that its influence will be brought to bear upon the public more than this. . . . America has furnished her share of noble women in this work, and they have done much in molding the national life."[53] She was probably thinking of many of the distinguished members of the Louisville sorority, who were journalists as well as staunch Baptists.

Some of Georgia Mable DeBaptiste's most impressionable experiences were strikingly similar to Alice McEwen's. Born in Chicago on November 24, 1867, DeBaptiste also enjoyed a prominent father who was an outstanding minister and newspaper editor.

Despite her father's influence, DeBaptiste was not inspired to write until she read an article written by a female friend. She tried her first piece with the *Baptist Herald* during high school. It was so enthusiastically received that she became a regular correspondent until its suspension two years later. Later she wrote for church journals such as the *Baptist Headlight*, the *African Mission Herald*, and the luminous *Our Women and Children*.

Wider Horizons: Secular and Literary Press Experience

Several of the crop of writers working in the latter part of the century placed their articles in a wider variety of papers—weekly and daily newspapers plus church-supported journals.

Josephine Turpin Washington's clipping file sported stories from the

New York Freeman, the *People's Advocate*, the *New York Globe*, and other Black Press weeklies, plus *A.M.E. (Church) Review* and *Christian Recorder* credits.

Her first story, an attack on the practice of selling wine at fund-raising affairs given by church members was published in 1877 by the *Virginia Star* when she was only 16. The reaction was favorable and inspired her to write occasionally for both news and opinion sheets.

Washington graduated from Howard University's college department in 1886 and later taught at Richmond Theological Seminary, Howard University and Selma University (Alabama). She was also a copyist under Frederick Douglass when he was Recorder of Deeds for the District of Columbia.

Among her most popular features were "Notes to Girls," a series of letters in the *People's Advocate*; and "Teaching as a Profession," a feature in the *A.M.E. Church Review*.[54]

Amelia E. Johnson, born in 1858, first wrote short poems and stories for the Black Press, but further distinguished herself by creating *The Joy*, an eight-page literary monthly for young people, in which Negro writers, especially women, could be published. Original fiction, poetry, and inspiring excerpts from the works of prominent Blacks formed the editorial content. *The Joy* was widely acclaimed. A white Baptist paper commended its editor for ". . . having done a good work, and shown the way for some other to follow."[55]

Johnson wrote stories and poems for the magazine, some of which were reprinted in the *National Baptist*, one of the largest white denominational publications in the country. By 1893, after the demise of *The Joy*, she also handled a "Children's Corner" column in *The Sower and Reaper* of Baltimore.

When the American Baptist Publication Society, one of the largest publishers in the country, produced *Clarence and Corinne or God's Way* in 1890, Johnson's career reached its zenith. Hailed by both the Black and white religious press as "must" reading for each household, her book was the first penned by a female author to be published by the Society, and the first Sunday School book published by a Negro. It was written "from affection for the race and loyalty to it, the author desiring to help demonstrate the fact that the colored people have thoughts of their own, and only need suitable opportunities to give them utter-ance."[56]

Westward expansion followed the employment and entrepreneurial opportunities available in the vast tracts of land lying West of the Mississippi River, and Kate D. Chapman's family was among the settling groups. Born in Mound City, Illinois on February 19, 1870, she was filling dispatches from Yankton, South Dakota territory by 1888, when her first poems and articles saw print. Besides writing for the most popular of the Black religious organs, she was a regular contributor to the great weekly, the *Indianapolis Freeman*, and she was included among the profiles Lucy Smith lined for *The Journalist*.

Editors of Note: Two Luminaries

The women with perhaps the widest newspaper experience of the period were Gertrude Bustill Mossell and Ann Victoria Earle Matthews. Both enjoyed a wide following and were published in the foremost Black and white publications. They were widely known as editors, as well.

During her career, Gertrude (Mrs. N.F.) Mossell edited the woman's departments of the *New York Age*, the *Indianapolis World*, and the *Woman's Era*, the national Negro clubwoman's magazine. Mossell initiated the woman's column for the *Age* and her first article, "Woman's Suffrage," appeared in 1885, attesting to her support of the movement. The piece suggested a reading list on human liberty and woman's rights, and lauded a United States Senator who had recently lobbied for universal suffrage.[57]

The scion of a prominent Philadelphia family of free Blacks, Mossell was a regular and long-time contributor to the *Philadelphia Standard Echo* and to the *Christian Recorder*, where she began her career. The *African Methodist Episcopal Review, Our Women and Children,* and *Ringwood's Journal* all were occasionally graced with her work.[58]

There is no mention of women writers or editors employed by daily publications until after 1870 when the country was busy forging its economic revitalization and expansion plans following the Civil War. By 1880, the first time a survey was taken, 288 women were found in editing and writing jobs by the United States Census.[59] This information probably does not reflect participation of Black women, but it spotlights the importance of Mossell's valuable seven-year experience writing for three of the most influential Philadelphia papers, the *Press Republican,* the *Times* and the *Enquirer*, when it was rare for *any* woman to have such wide exposure.

Still, Mossell noted that publications by and for women were proliferating in the last decade of the nineteenth century, meeting the demands of a more self-conscious audience. "The Women's Century," she wrote, arose with the "yielding of barriers," surrounding women's lives. "In the school, the church, the state, her value as a cooperative being is widely discussed. The co-education of the sexes, the higher education of women, has given to her life a strong impetus in the line of literary effort."[60] She also noted that any good writer would be given a chance to publish in "our best Afro-American journals." Reflecting her own experience, she allowed that opportunities were sometimes available with the larger white papers in northern cities.[61]

As one result of her own rich experience, Mossell learned business techniques she frequently urged Black Press members to adopt. These included market research to identify audiences and therefore attract advertisers, and information-trading through the creation of professional associations and news syndicates. She even urged some papers to hire newsboys to go find the readers and actively distribute the news.

With all her literary and business experience, Mossell proved a valuable asset to her husband, Dr. N.F. Mossell of Philadelphia, in the creation of his *Alumni* magazine.

Perhaps the most brilliant jewel in her crown of achievements was the production of *The Work of the Afro-American Woman*, one of the first books heralding outstanding Black women of the day. She strongly believed that the future of women, especially Black women, was in the work place, and she urged them to consider the alternative journalism offered to domestic work, teaching, or dressmaking, because of its creative outlet and potential to influence widely. Her professional advice was enthusiastic, although unlike Lucy Smith, she admitted certain career limitations:

> . . . Few [women] have become independent workers in this noble field of effort, being yet satellites, revolving around the sun of masculine journalism. . . . Women [yet] can do much to purify and strengthen life through the columns of the daily press or the weekly, or monthly journals. Right well do they seem to appreciate their opportunities; and a broad view of life and its purposes will come to them through this source. Let one who desired journalism as her life-work, [or] study . . . be alive to obtain what is news, what will interest. Let the woman select her *nom de plume* or take her own name, if she prefers, and use it always. . . . Write oftenest for one journal and on one subject; or on one line, at least, until a reputation has been established. Work conscientiously, follow the natural bent, and the future will not fail to being its own reward.[62]

> *Further*: To the women of my race, the daughters of an oppressed people, I say a bright future awaits you. Let us each try to be a lamp in the pathway of the co-laborer, a guide to the footsteps of the generation that must follow . . . let us feel the magnitude of the work, its vast possibilities for good or ill. Let us strive not to be famous, but to be wisely helpful, leaders and guides for those who look eagerly for the daily or weekly feast that we set before them. . . . Doing this, our reward must surely come. And when at some future day we shall desire to start a women's journal, by women, for our women, we will have built up for ourselves a bulwark of strength, we will be able to lead well because we have learned to follow.[63]

Of the multi-talented, energetic Black women to write for the press near the century's end, Ann Victoria Earle Matthews was published in the widest variety of papers and enjoyed the greatest popularity. Like her peers, she produced copy for secular and religious organs. But she also wrote dialect tidbits for the Associated Press, and her literary accomplishments included a novel, plus a series of historical textbooks for young people. Additionally, she edited the *Waverly* magazine.

Born a slave May 27, 1861 in Fort Valley, Georgia at the start of the Civil War, Matthews grew up in abject poverty. Her mother escaped to New York soon after Victoria's birth, leaving her with her siblings in the care of a much older woman until she was able to return for them. Once re-settled in New York, Matthews attended a grammar school until she was forced to take a job to help support the family.

Perhaps her tough childhood experiences helped increase her tenacity and spunk, because somehow, she continued her education and was able to start a press career as a "sub" (substitute) reporter for several large New York papers including the *New York Times*, *Herald*, *Mail and Express*, *Sunday Mercury*, the *Earth*, and the *Phonographic World*.[64] In time, Black Press organs like the *Boston Advocate*, *Washington Bee*, *Richmond Planet*, *Cleveland Gazette*, and the *New York Globe*, *Age*, and *Enterprise* would hope to receive copy from her typewriter. If one of Matthews' bountiful letters arrived, some are reported to have eliminated editorials to make space. Other papers and magazines like the *National Leader*, the *Detroit Plaindealer*, *South Christian Recorder*, and the *African Methodist Episcopal Review* hired her as their New York correspondent.[65]

Like Frances E.W. Harper, Gertrude Mossell, and other prominent Black women of the day, Matthews was intensely concerned with the welfare of her sisters. She traveled extensively to investigate their condition or lecture to them concerning their rights, responsibilities, and challenges for successful living in the post-war world. Active in the Afro-American women's club movement, she toured the South during the winter of 1895-1896 to report the status of Black women there for the Federation of Afro-American Women. During this journey, she stayed in Atlanta for a time to help her friend and occasional publisher, T. Thomas Fortune, edit the *Southern Age*, his latest acquisition.[66]

Press historian Penn wrote, "She is indeed entitled to the highest honor from her race by her efforts to dignify her work, and eminently prove Afro-American journalism to be the peer of any." Whether writing superior copy for Black or White journals, Matthews was an excellent example of a reporter not strictly confined within the woman's page margins. Another staunch supporter of women's rights, she was an active member of the Women's National Press Association, a mainly white group organized in 1885, and provided living inspiration for any girl thinking to seek a press career.

Not as widely known as her press work was Matthews' role as founder of the White Rose Mission, a shelter and training center in New York City. Here, she carried out the challenges addressed by the then-thriving colored women's club movement. Her home provided lodging and taught basic homemaking and literacy skills to the young Black women residents.

Specialty Editors

Lillian A. Lewis (a/k/a Bert Islew) distinguished herself from the rest of her contemporaries by developing a specialty area, much as Gertrude Mossell suggested. She won fame with her gossip column when a growing audience of women were being entertained by "sob sister" and other personal interest columns.[67]

Lewis grew up in Boston. She showed promise of becoming an outstanding writer, even when in grammar school, so for those who knew her, it was no great surprise that she completed a novel, *Idalene Van Therese*, soon after her high school graduation, or that she later enjoyed a successful career at the *Boston Advocate*.

Irreverent and witty, Lewis wrote and delivered several lectures while in high school, including "The Mantle of the Church Covereth a Multitude of Sins," which poked fun at the pious hypocrisy that seemed so fashionable in the corseted Victorian era. Abandoning the lecture route, she began her *Advocate* work as a contributor when the paper's circulation was low and its future uncertain. Eventually, she convinced the editor to give her a chance to establish a column that would attract readers of *all* ages and interests.

The "They Say" gossip column was the result and it was a stunning success. In two years' time it helped build the paper's popularity until "there [was] scarcely a colored family of intelligence in Boston that does not read the *Advocate* and Bert Islew's gossip."[68] Later, Lewis was handed the society page editorship and "They Say" news and views correspondingly increased.

In addition to her *Advocate* responsibilities, Lewis was a staff member of the *Boston Herald*.

Meta E. Pelham was another thoroughly professional newspaper staff member. Employed as a general writer for the *Detroit Plaindealer*, she was credited with being instrumental in the paper's success. Specific responsibilities were not detailed, but she kept busy with editorial as well as business matters, and worked closely with her two brothers who were the paper's business manager and editor. Pelham contributed many of the paper's features, although she never received a byline.

The *Plaindealer*, founded in May, 1883 during the Black Press' earliest boom years, was acclaimed as a first-rate operation whose business end was as level as its editorial quality was captivating—unusual for most of its competition.

Several female editors were not confined to church-sponsored publications, but were active in the last years of the century. A.G. Cooper controlled the woman's department of *The Southland*, a monthly first issued in February, 1880 at Salisbury, North Carolina, which was a principal exponent of various Black leaders' opinions. Adah M. Taylor edited the woman's department of the *Afro-American Budget*, a monthly from Evanston, Illinois that focused on personal management, and M.E. Lambert edited the *St. Matthews' Lyceum Gazette* in Detroit.[69] Julia Ringwood Coston published *Ringwood's Journal*, a women's-interest magazine which was similar to the *Ladies Home Journal*. *Light and Love*, a journal covering domestic and foreign African Methodist Episcopal missions, was published by Lida Lowrey and Emma Ranson.[70]

A.L. Tilghman, whose full first name is lost, was one of the handful of Black women to start publications in the Black Press heyday. Her ideas and energy gave birth to the *Musical Messenger* in 1885, a magazine "for musicians and music lovers," devoted to "the musical elevation of the race."[71]

Following suit with many of her journalistic sisters, she taught school after graduating from the Howard University normal department in 1871. During her fourteen years of teaching she also began a highly promising singing career that ended abruptly after an accident. Prevented from singing or teaching, she began studies at the Boston Conservatory of Music. Eventually she moved to Montgomery, Alabama, where she resumed teaching and staged a cantata based on the Biblical story of Queen Esther. Her musical and literary interests merged to result in *The Musical Messenger*.

Ida B. Wells: Princess of the Press

The one newswoman to emerge as a singular mover and shaker during this period and who remains the most dynamic and revered of all Black journalists was Ida B. Wells, the investigative reporter whose razor-sharp editorials and speeches were prime forces in focusing national and world attention on the outrage of the "lynch law." Her vociferous defense of Black people's right to equal treatment under the law continued throughout her long and active life, never wavering in intensity. T. Thomas Fortune, one of the most important publishers of the day, once described the diminutive Wells as having ". . . plenty of nerve . . . is sharp as a steel trap, and has no sympathy with humbug. No writer, the male fraternity excepted, has been more extensively quoted; none struck harder blows at the wrongs and weaknesses of the race. . . nor at the abuses of white society."[72]

Born in 1862 in Holly Springs, Mississippi, Wells was one of the first students to attend Shaw University (later, Rust College), the first local school established for Blacks by the Freedmen's Aid Society. In the next few years of "radical reconstruction," she listened to her father discuss politics with friends like Hiram Revels, the first Black elected to the United States Senate, and James Hill, who eventually joined the Mississippi Senate. No doubt, this early experience figured in her willingness to address political issues.

In 1878, both her parents and a brother died in a yellow fever epidemic. To earn money and keep the brothers and sisters together, she began teaching school under an assumed name for she was not old enough to legally take the job. In search of greater educational and social opportunities, she later moved the group to Memphis in 1884 and resumed her studies at Fisk University and LeMoyne Institute while continuing to teach.

Her own circumstances were slightly improved in relocating, but Wells was very much aware that there had been precious little improvement in Black people's general circumstances in her life time. For instance, segregationist practices took up where slavery once stood, denying Blacks public accommodations of every sort. In fact, after the 1875 Civil Rights Law forbidding discrimination in public places was overturned by the United States Supreme Court in 1883, an indignant Wells was thrown off a train for refusing to move from a first-class coach to a musty car reserved for Blacks and smokers.

Following the high court's provision for redress in the state courts, Wells sued the Chesapeake, Ohio and Southwestern Railroad in the first such case heard since the 1883 decision—and she won $500 in damages.

Elated at her success and at least the partial triumph of justice after all, she related her experiences for a Black church weekly, *The Living Way*. The resounding, enthusiastic reader response convinced her of the power of the press to educate and inspire large numbers of people, and to amplify the call for justice. ". . . There is no agency so potent as the press, in reaching and elevating a people," she wrote.[73] The printed page would be her medium, her tool for positive change, although she did not use it singlemindedly, until she lost her teaching job a few years later.

Before she left the schools, she wrote practical, simply-stated articles on handling everyday problems. Her articles on Tennessee country and city life were often reprinted, and editors and publishers in other parts of the country requested articles from her. Under the pen name of "Iola," Wells' byline eventually appeared in such prestigious journals as the *New York Age*, the *Detroit Plaindealer*, and the *Indianapolis Freeman*. She later edited the home department of *Our Women and Children*, and was a regular contributor to the *American Baptist* and the *Afro Methodist Episcopal Church Review*. "Iola's" pearls were also harvested by the *Gate City Press* of Kansas City, Missouri, the *Little Rock Sun*, the *Memphis Watchman*, the *Christian Index*, the *Fisk University Herald*, and the *Chattanooga Justice*.[74]

In 1887, her print prominence established, she was elected secretary of the Afro American Press Association—a position she would hold for many years. She was the first woman representative to attend the conclave, and there acquired the "Princess of the Press" sobriquet.

Wells became part-owner of the *Memphis Free Speech and Headlight* (later, the *Free Speech*) in 1889, and handled the paper's editorial operations. As a result of her typically frank commentary, she lost her teaching position for criticizing the racist school system. This move turned out to be a blessing in disguise, however, because she was inspired to transform the *Free Speech* into a truly profitable enterprise in order to increase her share of the profits. For the first time, she spoke at all kinds of public meetings promoting the newspaper and, likewise, the critical idea that knowledge would uplift and emancipate the race.

Simultaneously, and in stark contrast to her optimism, Wells was seeing first-hand that conditions were worsening for her people—even as Reconstruction was being suffocated. Before long, even Wells' railroad suit decision was reversed as justice's proverbial blindness seemed more handicap than assistance. "I had hoped such great things from my suit for my people generally," she wrote in her diary. "I have firmly believed all along that the law was on our side and would, when we appealed to it, give us justice. I feel shorn of that belief and utterly discouraged, and just now if it were possible would gather my race in my arms and fly away with them."[75]

When she joined the 1891 meeting of the Afro-American League convened by T. Thomas Fortune, her fighting spirit was rekindled—so much so that she was quite disappointed when this august body did not tackle the segregated railroad car issue head-on and propose strategies for doing battle. Her letter to Fortune criticizing the conference clearly displayed her sense of mission:

> We must depend for success upon earnest zeal and hard work to spread the truth of our cause. This history of the abolitionists shows that they kept up with tireless zeal, until that handful of men and women made themselves heard and people began to think. Surely we can do as much to make their work complete, as they did to begin it! . . . Yes, we'll have to fight, but the beginning of the fight must be with our own people. So long as the majority of them are not educated to the point of proper self-respect, so long our condition here will be hopeless.[76]

For her part, Wells saw to it that the *Free Speech* kept up a crusade against the Jim Crow cars. But when one of her dearest friends was lynched in 1892 for being "too successful" a businessman, all of Wells' missionary fervor was redirected and increased. She dedicated her creative energy to exposing lynching for the vicious, terrorist tactic it was, not the law enforcement tool it claimed to be.[77] It was designed to intimidate and eliminate Blacks from direct competition with Whites for goods, services, rights or privileges. "I have no power to describe the feeling of horror that possessed every member of the race in Memphis when the truth dawned upon us that the protection of the law was no longer ours," she wrote after her friend's death. Further venting her outrage, the fiery editor told her readers that they could only "leave a town which will neither protect our lives and property, nor give us a fair trial, but takes us out and murders us in cold blood."[78]

At least partly due to her editorial, some 2,000 Blacks then left Memphis in the following six months for Arkansas, Kansas and California with scouts like "Pap" Singleton. Others prepared to join the Oklahoma land rush, since the government land in the territory would be opened to settlers shortly.[79]

In an effort to stem the exodus and fearing the loss of income from Black customers, Whites circulated news that Oklahoma territory was a no-man's land. But Wells, much as did Mary Shadd Carey before her, traveled to this wilderness to give readers first-hand reports. Her reaction? Hearty approval, which was all some readers wanted to hear before they left Memphis.

Soon after her return, Wells realized that the Memphis lynchings were only part of a regional phenomenon. In classic investigative reporting technique, Wells sought out witnesses, relatives of the murdered men, and other news sources, to piece together damning evidence of what Blacks already knew: the common charge of raping a white woman was usually utter fabrication and cruel hyprocrisy, too, since white men regularly raped Black women with impunity. Fully aware of the indignation this challenge to the very underpinnings of a racist way of thought would arouse, Wells dared print in a May 1892 issue:

> Nobody in this section of the country believes the old threadbare lie that Negro men rape white women. If Southern white men are not careful, they will over-reach themselves and public sentiment will have a reaction. A conclusion will then be reached which will be very damaging to the moral reputation of their women.[80]

She traveled East soon after, attending a conference in Philadelphia as a guest of Frances E.W. Harper, the pioneering journalist and human rights crusader. By the time she reached New York, T. Thomas Fortune told her that the *Free Speech* offices had been vandalized, the paper was closed, and she was to be hanged if caught in Memphis. He also hired her on the spot to write a column for the *Age*. Through this paper Wells began a full-blown anti-lynching campaign. Here, writing in the North, she could speak freely.

The *Age* quickly published her seven-column article on lynching, complete with names, dates, and proffered charges of rape.[81]

Frederick Douglass and other prominent freedom-fighters immediately praised her work and courage. The white press, both North and South, took little notice.

It was with the support of Black women that Wells was first able to reach audiences through lectures and thereby substantially increase the attention that her campaign received. On October 5, 1892, leading women from New York (including fellow journalist Ann Victoria Earle Matthews), Boston and Philadelphia presented her at the Lyric Hall and raised $500 towards resurrecting *FreeSpeech*. The money was eventually used to expand the exemplary *Age* article into the *Southern Horrors* pamphlet, which was distributed at the many lectures Wells would give in coming months.

Traveling to Boston, her path crossed that of Josephine St. Pierre Ruffin, her host and that city's most prominent Black woman. Besides recruiting Black soldiers for the Civil War and working with Julia Ward Howe and others prominent in the woman's suffrage movement, Ruffin was an organizer for the "Kansas Exodus" effort and founder of the first Colored Women's Club in Boston, possibly the first such group formed in the country. Boston-born in 1842, she also founded *Women's Era*, a monthly magazine for Negro club women she ran with her daughter, Florida Ruffin Ridley.[82]

Like Ruffin, Margaret Murray Washington, second wife of Booker T. Washington, led a national club-women's group and founded a journal. Fifth president of the National Association of Colored Women, she created *National Notes*, the group's official publication.[83] She also knew Ida Wells Barnett.

Through Ruffin, Wells was introduced to white sympathizers who sponsored her on trips to England in 1893 and 1894, where she conducted extensive lecture tours. These appearances gained the attention of many British citizens prominent in the government or elite social registers who, she figured, could influence the messages emanating from America's white pulpits and newspapers.

Through her extended speaking engagements, voluminous correspondence, and piercing editorials and reportage, the "Princess of the Press" almost singlehandedly focused a blazing spotlight of national and world attention on the lynch law. Her book, *Red Record: Tabulated Statistics and Alleged Causes of Lynchings in the United States, 1892-1894*, was distributed after she returned to America. For a year she lectured, wrote, and organized anti-lynching leagues.

Wells married Ferdinand Barnett, a Chicago lawyer, in June, 1895. She purchased *The Conservator*, Illinois' first Black newspaper, from Barnett and his associates and proceeded to work as editor, publisher, and business manager. In the meantime, she raised a family of her own. When her husband was appointed assistant state's attorney for Cook County in 1896, Wells sold the paper and announced her first retirement from public life. Still, she never failed to stay abreast of important national affairs—like the founding of the National Association for the Advancement of Colored People in 1909, which she attended.

Not surprisingly, Wells' commitment to work for the improvement of her people would not retire gracefully, not as long as there was so much work to do. In late 1901, for example, she investigated a lynching in Cairo, Illinois in which she argued before the bar—in her husband's stead—that the county sheriff should be dimissed for allowing the deed to take place. She won the case, the sheriff was released from his duties, and there have been no lynchings recorded in the state since then.

Years later in 1922, Wells hit the road to investigate a 1918 massacre of Black sharecroppers in Phillips County, Arkansas. It was her first trip South since the demise of the *Free Speech*.

She wrote a series for the *Chicago Defender*, appealing for defense fund contributions, even before her journey.[84] She also determined to conduct her own investigation when she discovered that no other reporters actually talked with the prisoners or their families, so intimidated were they by lynching threats. Wells passed herself off as a "cousin from St. Louis," got her story, and contributed substantially to evidence that eventually freed the prisoners.

Thus, she lived to see another triumph of good over evil and of sensible, civilized living over brutality. Her longtime goal of seeing national anti-lynching legislation enacted never materialized, although between 1893 and 1897 at least six states (North and South Carolina, Georgia, Ohio, Texas, and Kentucky) enacted laws prohibiting lynching.[85] By the late Thirties, mob violence had dramatically decreased.

Before her death in March, 1931, Wells helped launch a number of organized efforts to uplift and advance Blacks, including the National Association of Colored Women, a movement sparked by such dynamic individuals as Frances E.W. Harper, and Josephine St. Pierre Ruffin, two women who helped organize her first lecture tour.

"Writing, speaking, spurring others on, Ida Wells-Barnett had told the truth in words so stirring that she had forced the world to listen."[86] As a direct result of her tireless commitment to fighting the particular offense of lynch law, and numerous general injustices levied against Blacks some said that the Afro-American had the ear of the civilized world for the first time since emancipation.[87]

NOTES

[1] Benjamin Quarles, *Black Abolitionists* (New York: Oxford University Press, 1969), p. 175.

[2] Martin E. Dann, *The Black Press: 1827-1890, The Quest for National Identity* (New York: G.P. Putnam's Sons, 1971), p. 17.

[3] Quarles, p. 14.

[4] Dann, p. 41.

[5] Morton Dillon, *The Abolitionists: The Growth of a Dissenting Minority* (DeKalb, Illinois: Northern Illinois University Press, 1974), pp. 152-153.

[6] John Hope Franklin, *From Slavery to Freedom*, 4th ed. (New York: Knopf, 1974), pp. 208-209.

[7] Hallie Q. Brown, ed., *Homespun Heroines and Other Women of Distinction* (1926; rpt. Freeport, New York: Books for Libraries Press, 1971), p. 26.

[8] Monroe N. Work, *The Negro Year Book, 1931-1932* (Tuskegee Institute, Alabama: Negro Year Book Publishing Company), p. 311.

[9] Quarles, pp. 203-204.

[10] Dann, p. 236. Entire chapter, "The Black Exodus," is most helpful for discussion of subject, complete with appropriate excerpts; pp. 236-291.

[11] Quarles, p. 231.

[12] Dann, p. 78.

[13] Dann, p. 74.

[14] Edward James, et al., eds., *Notable American Women: 1607-1950*, Vol. 1 (Cambridge, Massachusetts: Belknap/Howard University Press, 1974), p. 300.

[15] Brown, p. 92.

[16] Quarles, p. 217.

[17] Robin W. Winks, *The Blacks in Canada: A History* (New Haven, Connecticut: Yale University Press, 1971), pp. 394-395, 207.

[18] Winks, p. 207.

[19] Brown, p. 94.

[20] Quarles, p. 79.

[21] Winks, pp. 395-396.

[22] Winks, p. 396.

[23] Winks, p. 396.

[24] Quarles, p. 231.

[25] Quarles, p. 217.

[26] Winks, p. 396.

[27] Winks, p. 396.

[28] Dorothy Sterling, *Black Foremothers: Three Lives* (Old Westbury, New York: Feminist Press-McGraw-Hill, 1979), p. 74.

[29] Brown, p. 95.

[30] Winks, p. 267.

[31] Dann, p. 347.

[32] Bert Loewenberg and Ruth Bogin, eds., *Black Women in Nineteenth Century*

American Life: Their Words, Their Thoughts, Their Feelings (University Park, Pennsylvania: Pennsylvania State University Press, 1976), p. 245.

[33] See Loewenberg and Bogin, pp. 244-247 for address in its entirety.

[34] Penn, pp. 69-70.

[35] Penn, pp. 104-105.

[36] Giddings, p. 19.

[37] W.E.B. DuBois, *Black Reconstruction in America* (1935; rpt. New York: Atheneum, 1973), p. 693.

[38] Benjamin Quarles, *The Negro in the Making of America*, rev. ed. (New York: CollierMacmillan, 1969), p. 137.

[39] DuBois, p. 667.

[40] Franklin, p. 277.

[41] DuBois, p. 648; Franklin, p. 246.

[42] Gertrude Mossell, *The Afro-American Woman* (Freeport, New York: Books for Libraries Press, 1971), p. 99.

[43] Penn, pp. 120-121. Source material on virtually all nineteenth century journalists here mentioned was found in the Penn chapter on "Women in Journalism."

[44] Penn, p. 120.

[45] Penn, p. 415.

[46] Penn, p. 416.

[47] Penn, p. 336.

[48] Penn, p. 380.

[49] Penn, pp. 380-381.

[50] Penn, p. 374.

[51] Penn, p. 302.

[52] Penn, p. 398.

[53] Penn, p. 398.

[54] Penn, pp. 394-396.

[55] Penn, p. 424.

[56] Penn, pp. 425-426.

[57] Rosalyn M. Terborg-Penn, "Afro-Americans in the Struggle for Women Suffrage," Diss. Howard University 1977, pp. 111-112.

[58] Penn, pp. 405-406.

[59] Marion T. Marzolf, *Up From the Footnote: A History of Women Journalists* (New York: Communications Arts/Hastings House, 1977), p. 21.

[60] Mossell, p. 98.

[61] Mossell, p. 100.

[62] Penn, pp. 490-491.

[63] Mossell, p. 102.

[64] Penn, p. 375.

[65] Penn, p. 376.

[66] Emma Lou Scarborough, *T. Thomas Fortune: Militant Journalist* (Chicago: University of Chicago Press, 1972), p. 155.

[67] Marzolf, pp. 20-21.

[68] Penn, p. 382.

[69] Penn, p. 427.

[70] G.F. Richings, *Evidence of Progress Among Colored People*, (1900; rpt. Chicago: Afro-American Press, 1969), p. 424.

[71] Penn, p. 404.

[72] Sterling, p. 74; see also Penn, p. 408.

[73] Sterling, p. 73.

[74] Sterling, pp. 73-75.

[75] Sterling, p. 77.

[76] Sterling, pp. 77-78.

[77] Bettina Aptheker, "Woman Suffrage and the Crusade Against Lynching, 18901920," p. 13. Presented at the First National Scholarly Research Conference on Black Women, The National Council of Negro Women, Washington, D.C. November 13, 1979.

[78] Sterling, p. 79.

[79] Sterling, p. 80.

[80] Sterling, p. 82.

[81] Scarborough, p. 125.

[82] Mossell, p. 15.

[83] Elizabeth Lindsay Davis, *Lifting as They Climb: The History of the National Association of Colored Women* (1895; rpt. Washington, D.C.: National Association of Colored Women, 1933), pp. 171-172.

[84] Sterling, p. 113.

[85] Sadie I. Daniels, *Women Builders*, rev. and enlarged by Charles Wesley and Thelma Perry (Washington, D.C.: Associated Publishers, 1970), p. 279.

[86] Sterling, p. 116.

[87] Lerone Bennett, *Before the Mayflower: A History of Black America*, 4th ed. (Chicago: Johnson Publishing Company, 1969), pp. 285-286.

CHAPTER III

NEW ROLE FOR NEW CENTURY: 1900-1920

During the twilight period between the end of Reconstruction and the founding of the NAACP (1909), it became apparent to black Americans that they were not going to be integrated into the total fabric of American life. When white periodicals continued to insult black readers by playing up "black crime" and playing down black achievement, black Americans turned to an increasingly articulate black press for an interpretation of the world in which they lived.[1]

By 1910, nearly fifty years after Emancipation, seven of every ten Blacks were literate[2] and the growth of the press parallelled the expansion of the audience, as well as its ever-growing interest in the struggles and triumphs of the race. Economics also figured since freedmen were able to earn a bit more money and thus, could better afford the luxury of a weekly newspaper. The self-help theme remained paramount, and many a publisher/editor issued his paper, hoping to widely and helpfully influence his audience. Many of these visionaries founded their papers with the commercial venture prospects firmly in mind. They intended to feature news-as-entertainment, and not strictly operate their papers as organs of opinion.[3] Nevertheless, their sympathies were cast squarely for the race.

Some of the day's most important Black publications were started in the tumultuous period bridging the centuries. The *Philadelphia Tribune* (1884), the *Chicago Defender* (1905), the *Baltimore Afro-American* (1907) and the *Pittsburgh Courier* (1910), headed the list and remain outstanding examples of the genre. The National Association for the Advancement of Colored People's *Crisis* magazine (also 1910), conceived and directed by W.E.B. DuBois, immediately became an acclaimed journal of Black political and literary thought. Meanwhile, segregation laws were passed throughout the country and a practically unabated pattern of violence was highlighted by a wave of lynchings coupled with the increasing frequency of race riots. These developments called for vigorous and unified Black protest. As before, the Black Press would be the chief advocate for the race, amplifying all demonstrations and boosting campaigns of the emerging civil and political rights organizations.

Black reaction to the continuing insults and degradation galvanized during World War I, and fully half of the two dozen Black papers begun between 1900 and 1919 were started after 1914.[4] Many Black men who enlisted were eager to prove their worth in the armed services, to dispel any lingering doubts of their ability or loyalty. Likewise, plentiful readers wanted to read all about wartime events and issues. The papers generally recognized the contradictions facing Blacks who fought for freedom abroad when it was not guaranteed at home, but these sentinels also concluded that Black and white alike would suffer if the enemy won the battles. So Black men went off to war, and the papers led the fight for equality—at home and in uniform. To a far more impressive degree, Black newspapers became "the medium through which the yearnings of the race were expressed, . . .the coordinator of mass action which Negroes felt compelled to take, and a major instrument by which many Negroes were educated with respect to public affairs."[5]

A by-product of the war critical to the development of the Black Press, was massive migration to northern industrial centers. This swelled the local, urban audience. When the fighting interrupted the westward flow of European immigrants, northern industrialists subsequently looked South for their labor force. The Black labor pool, encouraged by such clarions as Robert S. Abbott's fledgling *Defender* took heed. Distributed through an informal network of Pullman porters and other agents who persisted despite threats and beatings, a phenomenal 230,000 copies of the paper circulated weekly by 1915.[6] Other Black news leaders reached sixfigure circulations during the same period.[7]

In the South, threats of lynch mobs and realities of the renewed slavery of tenant farming convinced many Negroes to consider, then opt, for the great adventure of the time. Thus, between 1900 and 1930 over three million left the South, with 500,000 resettling betwen 1915 and 1918, alone.[8] However, tribulations awaited the migrants in such forms as miserable housing conditions, segregated facilities of every sort, and race riots.

Urbanization and the Society Pages

The growth of the Black ghettos demanded a continued community-conscious press. Editors continuously attacked discrimination, but now they were obliged to increase coverage of "the minutiae of Black life"—the social events no other publishers would cover or appreciate.[9] Reports of births and deaths, engagements and weddings, club, church, lodge,and community meetings, out-of-town visitors, and parties appeared in greater numbers. Most often, they were written by women who, according to traditional practice, were social creatures. Men, conversely, were believed to be more political and business minded. The social items usually appeared on a social or "women's" page, while the remainder of the paper was devoted to crime reports and other news, editorials, church and sports reports, and the ubiquitous advertisements. "Hard news" by contrast, was the province of male reporters, with rare exceptions.

A 1911 *Pittsburgh Courier* featured a society page complete with correspondent news from nearby cities and towns, women's club news, and occasional features based on social welfare themes. In a 1912 paper, the society page ran stories on "How to Serve Tea," and "Christian Home for Boys Doing Good Work." Local and dispatch items filled the remainder of the page, along with ads for the Jenkins Industrial Home for Colored Girls, and for fashions and dry goods. Another how-to article instructed would-be seamstresses.

This concern for goings-on in the increasingly circumscribed Black community differed in expectations at least, from the pecuniary motives admitted by white publishers at the turn of the century. Publishers of metropolitan dailies conceived of these "specialty" departments strictly as attractions for new readers—who would, in turn, lure more advertisers.[10] Never favored with substantial advertising income, Black publishers incorporated women's and society news for the direct pleasure of its readers and the immediate benefit of increasing sales.

Still, it would be the next decade—the Roaring Twenties—before society and women's pages increased in volume and prominence, and the Black women contributions to their editors were more widely recognized. By then, a professional class of college graduates and tradespersons had increased its numbers to meet the needs of the race, and there was an increased demand for writers to report their activities.[11] More able to afford the trappings thought necessary to accompany "success," they often emulated the conventions of their white counterparts. Along with their intellectual and economic achievements, many also took pains to throw the grandest party, and be seen in whatever that community considered the "right" company. Through the society pages, they received the notice they desired.

In her history of "Black society," Gerri Major explains one time-honored practice in this light. Since Blacks were unwelcome in hotels and other public accommodations before the current decade, even the wealthiest and most prestigious members of the Black community were obliged to be house guests when they traveled. Thus evolved the practice of reporting a trip and the name of the hosts, as well. "It was . . . relatively easy to determine the status of the visitor by knowing whose hospitality they accepted," she explained.[12] And to a people accustomed to snubs, no matter how bright its accomplishments, such acknowledgements of one's "status" or "class" proved important—in certain circles, at least.

Wives of Publishers

Geraldine Pindell, born in 1872, married William Monroe Trotter, who was destined to become one of the three most influential Black men of the early Twentieth Century. His paper, the *Boston Guardian*, was a clear champion of the dignity and rights of Blacks and an extension of its uncompromising founder's National Equal Rights League (NERL). "Dennie" Pindell Trotter was drawn into active participation in the enterprise after her husband's arrest in a 1905 protest against Booker T. Washington, and became the office half of the partnership. She handled the bookkeeping, billing, subscription details, and edited the society columns, thus freeing Trotter to travel in connection with the National Equal Rights League and to write.

The niece of William Pindell, a leader in the fight to integrate Boston schools in the 1850's, Dennis was already accustomed, at least philosophically, to the demands of the equal rights struggle. Her devotion to Trotter and his enterprise afforded her the starker view, however. She worked diligently to maintain the paper, even after its operation had depleted the couple's savings. They were forced to leave far behind the "genteel life" they once enjoyed when Trotter sold real estate.

As if accounting for her change in circumstances, Dennie once offered these thoughts in a speech:

> This is the great lesson we Colored people should learn. Those of us who have had the advantages of education, who have seen life in its broadest light, [should] be willing to sacrifice and . . . to do for our own down-trodden people all in our power . . . . to make their cause our cause, their sufferings our sufferings. . . .[13]

Nannie Mitchell Turner co-founded the *St. Louis Argus* in 1912 with her husband, Eugene Turner, thus taking a more active role in the business from the start. Their city was the largest community west of the Mississippi, and the *Argus*, its pioneer Black newspaper.

After Turner's death, his wife inherited the publisher's role and began a regular column, as well. In a May 25, 1970 comment, she mentioned a feud between the St. Louis mayor and *Life* magazine, saying that she reserved final judgement until she actually read the piece. She also made this high-spirited remark:

> I suppose that the basic reason I like [the mayor] so much is that our paper, the *Argus*, opposed him so strongly when he first ran for office. But while we were right in his wheeling-dealing proclivities we were absolutely wrong as to his individual personality and great drive and determination to make St. Louis a great city and include Blacks on his team. This he has certainly done. Even those things

that some include as "fiascos" have earned our admiration. . . . Failures, maybe,
but when you walk up to the plate swinging hard you don't hit a homer every time.
Ask Richie Allen.

Praised as "First Lady of the Negro Press and Dean of Newspaper
Women" by the mayor, Turner received the Distinguished Editor
award from the National Newspaper Publishers Association in 1967.
She died in 1976 after 64 years in the profession.

Today with its circulation of some 25,000 copies weekly and its
attractive mix of interpretive news and features, the *Argus* ranks
among the more well-received Black papers.[14]

Turner's contemporary across the state, Ada C. Franklin, continues
to publish the *Kansas City Call* a weekly founded in 1919 by her
husband Chester A. Franklin. In the Black Press heyday of the Thirties
and Forties, the *Call* was regularly classed with the *Courier, Defender,
Afro-American*, and other leading exponents of the genre.

Other Figures of Note

Purveyors of the written word are fashioners of public opinion.
Although it is extremely difficult to launch and sustain a profitable
magazine, some Black women have succeeded in making inroads as
editors and publishers of popular magazines.

One of the early Black women editors and publishers during the late
1800's was Florida Ruffin Ridley, of Boston, Massachusetts. During
1894-1900, Ridley and her mother published the *Women's Era*, a
monthly magazine devoted to the interests of Black women. During the
presidential campaign of 1924, she worked for the Democratic Party,
visiting and speaking in many cities of the East.[15]

Carrie Elizabeth Bruce, born in 1890 in Philadelphia, Pennsylvania,
began her career as bookkeeper in the law office of E. Spence Miller
(white) in 1907. After seven years, she resigned and assumed charge of
property interests bequeathed on the death of her parents. She
became proprietor of a mail order business under the name of
Necessary Specialities Company and later was the editor of a women's
column in the *Philadelphia Tribune* and corresponding secretary of the
Business Clerks' Association of Philadelphia.[16]

NOTES

[1] Lerone Bennett, *Before the Mayflower: A History of Black America* 4th ed. (Chicago: Johnson Publishing Company, 1969), pp. 285-286.

[2] Roland E. Wolseley, *The Black Press, U.S.A.* (Ames, Iowa: Iowa State University Press, 1971), p. 30.

[3] Luther P. Jackson, Jr., "The Age of the Publisher, 1910-1954," *Encore*, 5 July 1977, p. 16.

[4] Vishnu Oak, *The Negro Newspaper* (1948; rpt. Westport, Connecticut: Negro University Press, 1970), p. 125.

[5] John Hope Franklin, *From Slavery to Freedom*, 4th ed. (New York: Knopf, 1974), p. 426.

[6] Wolseley, p. 38.

[7] Franklin, p. 426.

[8] Margaret Just Butcher, *The Negro in American Culture*, 2nd ed. (New York: Knopf, 1972), p. 246.

[9] Wolseley, p. 27.

[10] Marion T. Marzolf, *Up From the Footnote: A History of Women Journalists* (New York: Communications Arts/Hastings House, 1977), p. 205.

[11] Franklin, p. 427.

[12] Gerri Major, *Black Society* (Chicago: Johnson Publishing Company, 1973), p. 273.

[13] Stephen R. Fox, *The Guardian of Boston: William Monroe Trotter* (New York: Atheneum, 1970), pp. 211-212.

[14] Henry LaBrie, III, *The Black Newspaper in America: A Guide*, 3rd ed. (Kennebunkport, Maine: Mercer House, 1973), p. 49.

[15] Thomas Yenser, ed., *Who's Who in Colored America,* 6th Ed. (New York: Yenser Publishers, 1944) pp. 359-360.

[16] Letter received from Dr. Brenda E. Savage, Lincoln University, Pennsylvania, 23 April 1979.

CHAPTER IV

RENAISSANCE THROUGH DEPRESSION:
BETWEEN THE WARS

A "New Woman" for a New Day

In the 1920's, most of the reporting or editing jobs held by women
were on women's or society pages, in magazines, or in book
publishing—doubled the positions available in the Teens.[1] Specific data
are not available for interpretation, but it is likely that educated Black
women felt just as much a part of the "new woman" self-regard as did
white women, particularly after winning their voting rights—and full
citizenship. Coupled with the overall expansion and discovery
characteristic of wartime, a serious-minded approach to the profession
paid off notably in general reporting careers for some. No mistake
about it: this was an important formative period. "Not until the Forties
and the war years were opportunities again as good for women as they
had been in the 1920's" when 24 percent of all reporting or editing
positions were occupied b women.[2] This trend was supported by the
Black Press expansion after 1900 as circulations grew steadily. By the
Twenties, some 450 weekly newspapers and special interest journals
were available.[3] Surely, Black women figured in the growing workforce
needed to service the papers.

In the Black Press, as Gertrude Mossell and Lucy W. Smith
explained a half-century earlier, women were likely to be accepted by
the male editors and publishers if they could handle the jobs. Given the
opportunity for professional evaluation, some would shine brightly, but
they often were victims of typical male assumptions, as well. Women
were generally thought to be too fragile to stand the strain of deadline
pressure, or too inattentive to such details as vigorous language and
verification of facts to be worthwhile employees in "hard news"
positions. These misconceptions died hard. As late as 1942, at least one
Black publisher, unconvinced that women could produce satisfactory
newspaper work, admitted he would not hire one to perform "man's
work," even in an emergency.[4]

Ishbel Ross, a celebrated white reporter of the era, described the
professional standard against which women were measured:

> The woman reporter really has to be a paradox. She must be ruthless at work . . .
> genteel in private life . . . not too beguiling to dazzle the men and disrupt the work .
> . . . comradely with the male reporters . . . able to take the noise and pressure and
> rough language of the city room without showing disapproval or breaking into

tears under the strain of rough criticism. She must do her own work—asking no help or pampering, and make no excuses.[5]

Black America and the Black Press

The wartime experience forged a new Black America. Living in teeming urban communities, Negroes swapped stories of the "old" farm life, migration, military action, and their exposure to a much larger world than previously imagined. Booker T. Washington's admonitions of "lift up your buckets where you are," had fallen silent, and W.E.B. DuBois and others urged Blacks to let superior educations be their armor for the equal rights battle. Marcus Garvey appealed to the masses to return to the African homeland, boosting race pride all the while. Although lynch mobs continued their dirty work, and discrimination remained the rule at home and throughout the diaspora, scholars among the race said the excitement and expansion of the era resulted in "New Negroes" who were—

> . . .independent, popular, and often radical [spokesmen], unmistakable representatives of a new order. . . .Negroes in the Northern centers reached a stage at which, tutelage, even of the best-intentioned sort, had to yield to new relationships, and positive self-direction had to be reckoned with in increasing measure. The American mind had to accommodate itself to a fundamentally different idea of the Negro.[6]

This new breed contributed to an artistic and literary ferment spanning the years between World Wars I and II. Many of the group were drawn to Harlem, the "Black Mecca," and their vigorous activity was dubbed the "Harlem Renaissance." Jazz, that dynamic American sound, rocked the city, and writers, visual artists, speakers and preachers abounded.

Race papers benefited from this outpouring as they expanded their coverage of theatre news and featured more literary material, such as Alice Dunbar Nelson's syndicated column, "As in a Looking Glass."[7] Magazines filled with high-caliber social, political, and literary commentary and analysis such as *Opportunity*, journal of the National Urban League, were launched during this period.

Although an economic depression began for Blacks right after returning white soldiers hung up their uniforms and reclaimed their jobs, the entire nation was in shock by late 1929. Many Black presses, dependent on newsstand sales for their life-blood, folded when so many of their readers could no longer afford the luxury. Graced with strong management, some survived these lean years in good measure. Certain larger operations, like the *Afro-American* and the *Courier*, inaugurated regional editions or began combines of affiliate papers to build more solid national readerships.[8]

Throughout the period, they continued in their race crusading roles, as with their support of the Scottsboro Boys' trial defense and the "Don't Spend Your Money Where You Can't Work" campaign. They also capitalized on the big stories of race accomplishment and pride, like the Joe Louis heavyweight title win or Jesse Owens' 1936 Olympics coup.

The outbreak of World War II, with its call to action and attendant employment opportunities, tremendously stimulated newsstand sales, and the Black Press prepared to ride the cresting wave.

Renaissance Handmaidens

When rushing forth to publish their short stories, reviews, poems, and commentary during the Renaissance years, writers found Black women in key positions at certain magazines.

Jessie Redmon Fauset joined the *Crisis* in 1919 as literary editor, and was an unquestionably valuable addition to the staff.

Born to a socially-prominent "O.P." (Old Philadelphia) family about 1885, she studied at the Sorbonne and earned Cornell University undergraduate (1905) and University of Pennsylvania Master of Arts degrees. A "prolific and versatile contributor" to the *Crisis*, she produced poems, short stories, reviews, articles and translations. From 1920 to 1922, she was managing editor of *The Brownies' Book*, Dubois' magazine for children.[9]

Among Fauset's most notable *Crisis* features were: an essay on the European reaction to the second Pan-African Congress, which she covered (November and December, 1921); an article on artist Henry O. Tanner (April, 1924); and a biographical sketch on Martin R. Delaney (November, 1926).

Literary critic Arthur P. Davis evaluates Fauset as a "small but significant contributor to the literature and to the intellectual climate of the New Negro Renaissance, 'the time in which'. . .almost every young Negro in the streets of Harlem had a masterpiece or plans for a master piece. All of them felt that a new day had come and that there was a New Negro to seize it."[10] In her role as prime evaluator with one of the relatively few outlets for this creative outpouring, Jessie Redmon Fauset will also be remembered.

Maude Cuney-Hare controlled the music and art columns of the *Crisis* for seven years during the Twenties, contemporary with Fauset's employ. Born in Galveston, Texas in February 1879, she was an accomplished musician and music teacher whose writing credits included the *Christian Science Monitor* and the *Musical America* magazine, plus the 1913 biography of her father, Norris Wright Cuney.

Another editor at the *Crisis* during its early years, Mary Lee Newsome, born January 19, 1885, handled the journal's "Little Page."

The *Challenge* magazine was one of the dozen and a half Black–oriented magazines begun in the 1930's, and a Black woman, Dorothy West, worked as editor from 1934 to 1937.

Boston-born in 1910, West began her literary output in the Twenties when her short stories were first published. She attended the Columbia University journalism school and contributed to the *Challenge* before joining its staff.

West's novel, *The Living is Easy* (1948) received critical attention. In the 1970's, she again turned her hand to journalism, reporting news for the *Martha's Vineyard Gazette*.

Specialty Publishing

Successful Hairdressing, a magazine for the beauty trade, benefited from the overall boom in Black efforts toward self–sufficiency and the specific achievements of entrepreneurs such as Madame C.J. Walker. Walker's company sold hair straightening preparations and other beauty aids, and employed more than 500 agents nationwide. By 1915 she had become a millionaire.[11]

Katheryn Wilson, owner and operator of the first beauty culture school established between Omaha and California, edited the first edition of the early trade magazine, which appeared in 1925 and was distributed worldwide. Reared in a pioneering atmosphere, Wilson was born in 1870 in St. Joseph, Missouri, a famous stop on the Pony Express mail route.

Just as the Garvey movement was one guage of the growth of race pride, and self-reliant attitudes, so was the more conservative Black women's club movement. Club affiliates were mainly social welfare groups, not mere social organizations. Among the services they supported to aid the burgeoning mass of impoverished urban Blacks were day care centers, old folks' homes, counseling centers, basic hygiene and homemaking classes, and auxiliary support for schools.[12]

The *Half-Century* magazine was closely affiliated with the colored women's club movement. Katherine Williams Irvin edited the journal from 1916 to 1924, and during her tenure adopted the subtitle, "A Colored Magazine for the Home and the Homemaker." Possibly the change anticipated the mass appeal the recently formalized study of "home economics" would attract by mid-decade. Among the magazine's topics were race loyalty, the duties of a hostess and the rules of etiquette.[13]

Irvin switched to the managing editorship of the *Chicago Bee*, a popular Black weekly, in 1924. Her media experience also included contributing to the *Encyclopedia of Colored People* published by the Overton Hygenic Company, a Black-owned firm, in August 1921.

Unlike Irvin's *Half-Century*, the *Negro World* women's page appealed to the working class women who supported Marcus Garvey's Universal Negro Improvement Association (UNIA). It was highly political, and urged reforms in Black leadership as well as roles women played in Black life. The page had a distinctly feminist tone and never categorized the contributions of Black women, often urging them to step into leadership roles whenever necessary. In an editorial, Amy Garvey once issued this fervent charge:

> Be not discouraged black women of the world, but push forward, regardless of the lack of appreciation shown you. A race must be saved, a country must be redeemed, and unless you strengthen the leadership of vacillating Negro men, we will remain marking time until . . . we be forced to subserviency . . . or extermination.[14]

"Hard News" Assignments

Two Black women distinguished themselves primarily on the basis of their reporting and editorial contributions to Black Press weeklies during the "Roaring Twenties." Delilah L. Beasley and Fay M. Jackson also profited from exposure to the international angle.

Beasley's career spanned the centuries. Born in 1871 in Cincinnati, she wrote her first article when only twelve years old. By 1886, she had become a correspondent for the *Cleveland Gazette* and handled a column, "Masaics," in the Sunday edition of the *Cincinnati Enquirer*. Later, Dan Rudd, editor and publisher of the *Colored Catholic Tribune*, impressed with her work, allowed her to study the newspaper business in his Cincinnati plant. However, after the death of her parents, she was forced to find more lucrative work, including stints as a nurse, a teacher, and a masseuse.

Beasley eventually moved to California and contributed to the *Oakland Tribune*. By 1925 she had become involved on several fronts with the fight for human rights and world peace, and represented the *Tribune* as full delegate to the National Convention of Women Voters. Later, she was the *Tribune's* representative to the International Council of Women convention, and joined the fledgling League of Nations (for northern California) and the World Forum.

Apart from her internationally-aware political and social

commentary, Beasley led the battle during the 1920's to abolish the widespread use of "darky" and "nigger" for descriptions of AfroAmericans in the Bay Area daily press, and she succeeded in convincing many editors that their papers should avoid these offensive labels. Her column in the *Tribune's* Sunday edition was an audience favorite.

A footnote to Beasley's assault on name-calling turns up thirty years later in the 1952 edition of the *Negro Year Book*. Two pages in the report on the Black Press are devoted to a discussion of "Race and the News," but the concern is *when* to identify Blacks as Blacks in general descriptions, and not with the choice of a descriptive word. Evidently, Beasley's motion had carried by that time.

The Negro Trailblazers of California, a nine-year project hailed by prominent libraries, historians, and the United States government as an outstanding reference work, was another of Beasley's memorable accomplishments.

When Fay Jackson published *The Flash* in 1923, it was the first Black news magazine in Los Angeles in an era when both news magazines and magazines about Blacks were infant ideas.

After *The Flash* failed, Jackson joined the *California News* as editor, and later edited the *California Eagle,* then the oldest continuously published paper in the state since 1879. It was during her *Eagle* affiliation that she traveled to London's Westminister Abbey, becoming the first Black woman sent abroad to report a major story—this, the coronation of Britain's King George VI. [15]

While Fay Jackson prepared to launch *The Flash*, Beatrice Cannady Franklin was in the midst of a hard-fought campaign to influence public opinion in another Far West community.

Associate editor of Portland, Oregon's *Advocate* in 1922, Franklin led a successful campaign to repeal the state's discriminatory "Black Laws." Running pro-repeal editorials in six successive issues of this paper, whose masthead read, "Don't Ask for Your Rights, Take Them," she made a powerful appeal to reason. Often she reminded her readers that Southern Blacks still could not exercise the powerful right Oregon's Blacks took for granted.

Franklin won support from the community's churches, lodges, and social clubs, as well as from a significant number of area Whites who read the well-edited news-sheet. The repeal measure, previously defeated, passed by a comfortable 2-to-1 margin. [16]

A fellow Pacific coast editor was Eleane Dixon of Washington state's *Progressive Westerner*, which appeared later in the decade.[17]

"Society" Arrives

News items reflecting noteworthy slices from Black life were an established and necessary part of any Black weekly's success by the Twenties. Social and dispatch items that once filled a single page in the *Courier*, for example, frequently commanded three or more pages by 1925, when Thelma E. Berlack was an editor.

Born October 15, 1906 in Ocala, Florida, Berlack handled the New York society news along with her responsibilities as a New York University student. She blazed a new trail for would-be Black women writers as the first admitted to Delta Mu Delta, a journalist's equivalent to Phi Beta Kappa, the national honor society.

The April 11, 1925 edition of the *Courier* featured Berlack's byline under an "Everyday Etiquette" column on wedding anniversary giftgiving and celebratory tips. The May 23rd edition that year ran her "Chatter and Chimes" column, in which Berlack reported a New York testimonial dinner. Here, Paul Robeson and Walter E. White were honored by local "business, professional, and literary men of color."

Berlack held down society page responsibilities at the *New York Amsterdam News* during her association with the *Courier*, 1924–1926, which she terminated to become assistant managing editor for the *News*.

Andre Buni, biographer of *Courier* principal Robert L. Vann, includes an account of Thelma Berlack's invitation to join the staff. Vann asked George Schuyler, himself a columnist and New Yorker, to approach Berlack. "Since she covers Harlem for her own work, it will be easy to send [the news] to us," Vann opined.[18] Evidently, Berlack accepted the invitation, although she did not choose to write under an assumed name, as Vann also suggested.

Another socially active Harlem woman at the time was Bessye J. Bearden, who edited the New York edition of the *Chicago Defender*. Like Berlack, Bearden was an early journalism student and she took courses at the prestigious Columbia University school.

Across the continent, Kathryn Bogle kept busy gathering Oregon's social news for the *Courier* and writing a Black news column for the *Northwest Enterprise*, a Seattle paper that featured a page of Oregon news in each issue.

When H.L. Mencken, dean of American letters during the Twenties and Thirties, complimented Julia Bumbry Jones for writing "the best column of the kind in American journalism,"[19] he confirmed what her publisher knew and her readers suspected all along. Joining the *Pittsburgh Courier* staff in the late Twenties, she directed the women's and society pages through the next decade, and wrote the "Talk O' the Town" and "Jule's Soliloquy" columns. Jones also conceived and successfully promoted "Frog Week," seven days of go-for-broke social events designed to put Pittsburgh on the map.

In an August 1, 1929 issue of the *Courier*, she brought readers up to date after an absence. "Although this column has not appeared in several weeks, it is impossible to crush it the week of the celebrated "Frog activities." She admitted to suffering from "Frogite."

> That dark born taste, that feeling, that panicky palpitation of the heart everytime I hear the words *dance, cabaret* or *bridge*. If I didn't have a good boss, I would have been fired Monday morning. After being off duty since Wednesday, I labored into the office Monday morning instead of fluttering in the bright, happy employee who had had several days of rest.[20]

She proceeded to list the ten parties she had attended in the meantime, before getting on to the guest lists and other details.

When publisher Robert L. Vann decided to promote boxer Joe Louis even before he won the heavyweight title, Julia Jones actively participated in the campaign, going so far as to interview his new bride in their bedroom the morning after the wedding. Louis slept on, but Jones got a glimpse of his blue silk pajamas.

Jones truly enjoyed her active career, and this comment shows just how much. In her March 21, 1936 "Talk O' the Town" article, she answered the question, "What Would You Do If You Had Only 24 Hours to Live?"

> Well. . .my last 24 hours would be most precious. Methinks I would get up rather early. . .take a luxurious bath and groom myself with care. Then I would pray, earnestly, too. . .and then I would Write. What about? Who knows! But I can imagine it would be my very best work. My last day on earth would truly be my best day. . . . .

Publishing Ventures

At least two Black women wore the publisher's mantle in this decade.

Blossie Belvins Oldfield, like others in the journalism sorority, taught school when she started her career. But by 1925, she was helping her husband, John, establish the *Chattanooga* (Tennessee) *Defender*. As did Nannie Mitchell Turner, she assumed command of the paper after her husband's death. She was born in 1891 in Selma, Alabama.

Like others before her, Mary Ellen Vaughan recognized the power of the press to amplify her own concerns, and so founded the

Murfeesboro *Union* in this decade to ". . . help more of my people and get them interested in reading more and reading good books and good newspapers," she said.[21]

Vaughan, born in Montgomery, Alabama in 1893, worked as a nurse, then as a teacher before organizing her paper in that medium-sized Tennessee town. She reported her experience to Frederick Detweiler in 1922:

> Some of the best people of my race got together and thought [my idea] a fine movement, so I worked it up myself. . . . I put in $100 to start the paper and we have now 300 subscribers, so you can see that there is nothing to be realized out of it as yet. I struggle from day to day canvassing the town with my pad and pencil, trying to meet the printers' bill. . . . I went straight to the white folks in this section and knocked at the door of their conscience and they received me, and assured me of their loyal support.[22]

Added to these two publishers are two other Black women who were active in the publishing world. A poet and editor, Thelma Childs Taylor became publisher of the *Topeka Plaindealer*, Topeka, Kansas, in 1925. And in 1929, Olive Myrl Diggs of Mound City, Illinois, assumed the position of business manager and auditor of the *Chicago Bee* newspaper.[23]

NOTES

[1] Marion T. Marzolf, *Up From the Footnote: A History of Women Journalists* (New York: Communications Arts/Hastings House, 1977), p. 52.

[2] Marzolf, p. 52.

[3] Frederick G. Detweiler, *The Negro Press in the U.S.* (1922; rpt. College Park, Maryland: McGrath Publishing Company, 1968), p. 4. This figure includes 253 weekly newspapers, 83 religious journals and 31 magazines.

[4] Margaret Rose Davis, "A Survey and Analysis of the Opportunities for Negro Women in Journalism," Thesis, Kansas State College 1942, p. 23.

[5] Marzolf, p. 52.

[6] Margaret Just Butcher, *The Negro in American Culture*, 2nd ed. (New York: Knopf, 1971), p. 249.

[7] The Associated Negro Press (ANP), this column appeared occasionally in *Couriers*, 1929.

[8] Vishnu Oak, *The Negro Newspaper* (1948; rpt. Westport, Connecticut: Negro University Press, 1970), p. 128.

[9] Arthur P. Davis, *From the Dark Tower: Afro-American Writers, 1900-1960* (Washington, D.C.: Howard University Press, 1974), pp. 90-91.

[10] A. Davis, p. 94.

[11] Sylvia G.L. Dannett, *Profiles of Negro Womanhood*, Vol. 1, 1619-1900 (Yonkers, New York: Educational Heritage, Incorporated, 1969), p. 188.

[12] Gerda Lerner, *The Majority Finds its Past* (New York: Oxford University Press, 1979), p. 84.

[13] Mark D. Matthews, "Our Women and What They Think—Amy J. Garvey and *The Negro World*," *The Black Scholar,* May/June 1979, p. 8.

[14] Matthews, p. 8.

[15] "Is Matchless Calvacade of Brilliance," *California Eagle,* 21 May 1937, p. 1.

[16] Quintard Taylor, Jr., "A History of Blacks in the Pacific Northwest, 1788-1970," Diss. University of Minnesota 1979, p. 143.

[17] Taylor, p. 167.

[18] Andrew Buni, *Robert L. Vann of the Pittsburgh Courier* (Pittsbourgh: University of Pittsburgh Press, 1974), p. 137.

[19] George S. Schuyler, *Black and Conservative* (New Rochelle, New York: Arlington House, 1966), p. 234.

[20] "Talk O' the Town," *Courier,* 7 December 1935.

[21] Detweiler, p. 77.

[22] Detweiler, p. 77.

[23] Thomas Yenser, ed., *Who's Who In Colored America*, 6th Ed. (New York: Yenser Publishers, 1944), pp. 502, 158.

CHAPTER V

WORLD WAR II THROUGH THE FIFTIES: SEEKING THE AMERICAN DREAM

The Second World War forced editors and publishers into a new era of public advocacy. Paramount among the toughest issues was whether Blacks should risk their lives to defend freedoms and opportunities in a country that excluded them. Having learned a tough lesson in the previous conflict, the papers did not see this as sufficient reason to relax race vigilance, "especially when the armed forces' determination to maintain segregation became apparent."[1] Becoming more vocal than ever, they hammered home their indignant, insistent call for justice. The *Courier* even mounted a campaign naming "Double V" girls of the week, attractive women who posed for the press photographer with fingers of both hands aligned as two "V's." The double "V's" signified victory abroad *and* at home. So relentless was the combined force of this press protest that the Justice Department threatened some publishers with sedition indictments, or they found their operations circumscribed by sudden newsprint shortages.[2]

Acceleration of the wartime economy created more jobs in the war-related industries—all the better for women to fill once men returned to uniform. Additionally, Blacks as a whole were earning more money and thus, could better afford copies of their Black papers. Reporting the activities of Negroes in the war, the era's job opportunities, the renewed migration North, the strengthened possibilities of racial integration, plus the expanded role of women occasioned by unmet "manpower" needs, Black papers had seldom been so irresistible. Circulations soared through the late Forties. The (N.W.) *Ayer Directory* noted that the *Courier's* figures nearly reached 287,000 in 1947, up from some 127,000 copies in 1940. Likewise, the *Chicago Defender* and *Norfolk Journal and Guide* rose from 82,000 to 161,000 and from 30,000 to 68,000 copies, respectively.[3]

A wartime survey provides insufficient evidence to determine whether war-related conditions themselves encouraged the employment of Black women as journalists, but 96 worked in the field by 1942 in other than general office work or clerical positions.[4] It is clear that, had certain of the papers not been constrained by the economics of Black publishing, they would gladly have hired more women.[5] A contemporaneous study declared that "Negro women journalists were already commonplace; if one had the ability, she could land a job."[6]

Black women at Black newspapers were surely inspirations to the following generation. The *Defender* employed twelve in 1942; the *AfroAmerican*, eleven, and the *Courier*, seven. Most benefited only from good, basic writing skills and common sense, for very few Black women had received journalism training by that time. Segregation remained the rule—although there were exceptions—and the first two Black journalism schools did not begin operations until later in that decade. Still, the *Kansas City Call* proudly boasted having in its employ four college graduates with journalism degrees—and two others who held degrees in differing fields.[7]

Marguerite Rose Davis conducted the 1942 survey and concluded that Negro women would not receive greater journalism opportunities until a general economic improvement allowed Black publishers to flourish, expand their operations, and "give more professional opportunity to all Negroes interested in journalistic work." The white press was not interested in Black women, and respondents to Davis' questionnaires said so. That establishment was only then overcoming its own biases against female reporters, employing 32 percent in the total editing and reporting jobs by 1950.[8] Davis observed that the white press might welcome a few Black men, however.[9]

Postwar Developments

Integration seemed the popularly anticipated panacea for a variety of ills plaguing Black America. Proponents argued that integration of public accommodations, of educational institutions, and of the armed services, for instance, would defeat discrimination and segregation. In the wake of victory abroad, the time was ripe for demanding exactly this.[10]

The Black Press championed the social justice campaigns of the era and witnessed inspiring victories, such as the 1954 Supreme Court decision outlawing "separate but equal" schools, and the integration of the armed services. Surprisingly, however, its overall circulation declined after these signal victories. Even with developments like the rise of independent African nations and continuing struggles at home, it seemed to some observers that ". . .by fighting. . .injustices practiced against the Black citizen," the press was "helping bring about democratic conditions that would make the papers unnecessary."[11]

Press advocates dismissed this theory, however, observing that so long as Blacks did not fully assimilate into mainstream America, there would be a need for it to speak to them about themselves and to support their causes.[12] These stalwarts attributed declining circulations of the late Forties and Fifties to the incursions of the electronic media. Black-owned and oriented radio came of age during this time, as did television—itself the bane of establishment newspapers.

Community Press Champions

Not all crack women journalists have been known solely by the quality of their copy. Some have always carried the baton of activism an extra length in the run for first-class citizenship.

Lucile H. Bluford is a modern example of an outspoken Black woman in the writer/editor/activist tradition first defined by such leaders as Mary Shadd Carey and Ida Wells Barnett. The *Kansas City Call*, a midwestern weekly has been her work-post for more than forty years.

Bluford began her tenure there in the early 30's as a reporter under Roy Wilkins, who later became Executive Director of the National Association for the Advancement of Colored People. When the National Association for the Advancement of Colored People started its court attack on racism, orchestrated by lawyers like Charles Hamilton Houston, Bluford prepared to join the battle. A 1932 graduate of Kansas University, she sued the University of Missouri at Columbia in 1939 for denying her admission to its world-renown journalism school. Even with the support of white students who regularly attended the trial, and a valiant prosecution effort, Bluford lost the case. As one result, a journalism school was established in 1942 at Lincoln University, the Black state school. Segregationist forces won out, but they made a valuable concession. Until that year, no journalism training programs existed for Blacks.

Managing editor of the *Call* since the late Thirties, Bluford was cited in 1961 for her reporting and editing work by Lincoln University. In 1977 she became the only woman enshrined in the recently-established Gallery of Distinguished Publishers of the National Newspaper Publisher's Association (NNAP). Originally called the Negro Newspaper Publishers Association, twenty-one executives of Black weeklies organized NNPA in 1940. Designed "to improve and promote the Negro press [and] to increase the status of the Negro," it recognized Bluford's record of superior service to the race.

Another long-time press activist was Carlotta A. Bass, the editor and publisher whose work was reminiscent of Delilah Beasley's contributions.

Bass headed the *California Eagle*, a dynamic west-coast paper challenged during World War II for its strident objections to American racism at home. While at its helm, she vigorously participated in successful efforts to end job discrimination in the late Forties and early Fifties at the Los Angeles General Hospital, the Rapid Transit Company, Southern California Telephone Company, and the Boulder Dam Project—all large public service concerns that profited from Black-generated tax dollars and usage fees.

Born in 1890, Bass was keenly political-minded, and attended the historic 1919 Pan-African Conference convened by W.E.B. DuBois in Paris. Co-president of the Los Angeles branch of Garvey's United Negro Improvement Association during the early Twenties, she later helped promote the "Don't Buy Where You Can't Work" campaign, along with fellow editor/publisher Leon Washington of the *Los Angeles Sentinel*.[13]

Bass' concern for human rights and dedication to political action ran steady and deep, and few who knew her were surprised when she was chosen, at age 62, to share the 1952 Progressive Party ticket as VicePresidential candidate with Vincent Hallinan, a prominent California civil liberties lawyer. Thus, she became the first Black woman to run for one of the highest offices in the land and the "first woman named for high national office by any political party."[14]

The Progressives were never seriously in the running but their ticket offered voters a clear choice, for a change. Their party pledged to redirect Cold War hysteria and provide leadership to combat discrimination. It also opposed the country's foreign policy of containment and its obvious imperialist foreign investment philosophy, and articulated these positions clearly and forcefully. Criticizing short-comings of the Democrats and Republicans during the campaign and promoting the revolutionary nature of her own candidacy, Bass asked:

> Can you conceive of the party of Taft and Eisenhower and MacArthur and McCarthy and the big corporations calling a Negro woman to lead the fight in 1952? Can you see the party of Truman, of [Senator] Russell of Georgia, of [Representative] Rankin of Mississippi, of [Governor] Byrnes of South Carolina, or [Secretary of State] Acheson, naming a Negro to lead the fight against enslavement?[15]

Supported by such prominent Blacks as Paul Robeson and W.E. B. DuBois, Bass' candidacy in this largely sumbolic attempt to capture the attention of American voters prompted a group of Harlem women to say, "Because of you we can all hold our heads a little higher."[16]

It is a striking irony that the paper to which she devoted so much of her working life would eventually discuss her vice-presidential candidacy as mere "bait" for Black voters.

Charlotta Bass detailed her fascinating career in her autobiography,

Forty Years: Memoirs From the Pages of A Newspaper, which appeared in 1960.

Sarah McNeamer Henry made her mark as a journalist in the Thirties at white and Black papers. Born in 1900, she became the first female to edit the *Mississippi Enterprise*, a Black paper. Likewise, she was the first Black contributing editor for the *Jackson* (Mississippi) *Daily News.* Here, she covered events of particular interest to Negroes, which ran in the paper's "Black Star" edition. A generic term, "Black Star" papers were versions that included a page of race news— often substituted for the regular edition's business page and distributed only in the Black community. They were common in the South in the pre-Sixties.

Both Edna Louis Harrison and Carrie Hazard Blue made pioneering reporting efforts in the Boston area during the Forties.

Before graduation from Roxbury Memorial High School for Girls in 1934, Harrison freelanced for the *Boston Guardian.* She contributed to its "Poetry Corner," as well. In 1933, she began a drama column, "Close-Up," for the *Boston Chronicle,* a paper her brother once served as editor-in-chief.

Harrison's 22-year *Chronicle* tenure allowed her to interview all the promising Black stage and screen talents of the era. It also obliged her to fight for opening night press privileges in 1945 and 1946. Up to that time, Black newspapers were routinely denied press passes to theatrical events—a courtesy normally shown white papers for review purposes.

Harrison capped her newspaper career in 1954, when she became the first Black female to edit the *Boston Graphic.* After nearly ten years outside the media, she became the New England representative for *Jet* and *Ebony* magazines in 1964.

Carrie Blue was born February 26, 1905 to a distinguished Cambridge, Massachusetts family once involved in assisting fugitive slaves. An educator for most of her career, she worked as the first Black female reporter, from 1948 through 1956, of the Ayer (Massachusetts) *Public Spirit.*

Julia Scott Reed commenced her media career in the late Forties and has accumulated a number of "firsts" since then. A native of the Lone Star state, she was the first Black journalist employed as a columnist for a major daily newspaper in the Southwest. Her *Dallas Morning News* column focuses on Black activities and personalities throughout Texas, but her extensive reporting experience, both in newspapers and radio, has yielded stories on local and national judicial and political

events. She carefully covered Texas school integration in its early
stages during the Fifties.

Reed was the first Black to join the Press Club of Dallas and the first
admitted to the local Women in Communications chapter.

A Voice in Little Rock, Arkansas

Another Black woman who gained distinction for her effort to
cover—and make—the school integration story is Daisy Bates,
co–publisher of the (Little Rock, Arkansas) *State Press*. The campaign
waged there from 1957-1959 for the integration of Central High School
became the first critical test of the 1954 Supreme Court decision.
Bates, local director of the National Association for the Advancement
of Colored People at the time, admitted that, "This was not the first
really great fight waged by Negroes themselves for the validation of
their civil and political rights, but it was certainly the most
spectacular."[17] The glare of the television cameras and the huge
national press corps on hand saw to that. All the while, Bates' paper
continued its tradition of championing the Black cause, until loss of
advertising revenue—a direct result of Bates' refusal to terminate or
postpone the integration campaign—forced the plant to close.

L.C.Bates, her husband, convinced her to pool her savings with his,
soon after they married, in order to start a paper. That took some
doing, as she recalled, for she realized "Such a project required
possibly more money and effort than the two of us had to give."[18] The
couple leased the plant of a church paper and issued the first volume of
the *State Press* in 1941. It grew steadily until advertisers abruptly
cancelled contracts in the spring of 1942. The only Black paper in the
area, the *State* decided to make a strong comment to condemn the
slaying of a respected Black sergeant based at a nearby military
installation. Daisy Bates wrote:

CITY PATROLMAN SHOOTS
NEGRO SOLDIER
Body Riddled While
Lying on Ground

One of the most bestial murders in the annals of Little Rock occurred Sunday
afternoon at 5:45 o'clock at Ninth and Gaines Streets, in front of hundreds of
onlookers, when Patrolman A.J. Hay shot and mortally wounded Sergeant
Thomas P. Foster. . . . When Sgt. Foster asked the Military Police why they had
Pvt. Albert Glover . . . in custody, City Policeman Hay interfered and struck Sgt.
Foster with his night stick. A scuffle ensued, whereupon Policeman Hay threw
Sgt. Foster to the ground and then fired five shots into his prostrate body. Sgt.
Foster died in the University Hospital five hours later. . . .[19]

Despite the hardships they faced, the couple decided to continue
their work by appealing directly to their readers for support. World

War II was on, and they believed, "The Negroes supposedly fighting a war in the name of freedom had, through our paper, found a voice to express their feelings."[20]

The gamble worked. Not only did the Black community rally behind the *State*, but it began to exert political and economic pressure "against violations of fundamental rights guaranteed all Americans under the Constitution." By 1945, Daisy and L.C. Bates celebrated the victory by purchasing printing equipment for the *State*.

In 1946, while her husband enjoyed, a long-deserved vacation, Daisy Bates decided to write an article critical of a judicial decision involving striking mill workers.

FTA STRIKERS SENTENCED
TO PEN BY A
HAND-PICKED JURY

Three strikers, who by all observation were guilty of no greater crime than walking on a picket line, were sentenced to one year in the penitentiary yesterday by a "hand-picked" jury, while a scab who killed a striker is free.

The prosecution was hard pressed to make a case until Judge Lawrence C. Auten instructed the jury that the pickets could be found guilty if they aided or assisted, or just stood idly by while violence occurred. Motions to quash the indictments were overruled by the judge. These motions included protests to the fact that there were no Negroes on the jury in accordance with the law.

Appeal bond was fixed at $2,500 each. The usual bond in such cases is $1,000.[21]

As a result of this protest against another miscarriage of justice, Bates and her husband were arrested for contempt of court. Found guilty initially, they were later exonerated by the State Supreme Courtbut not until the *State* confirmed its dedication to freedom and justice, once again.

The final challenge to the Bates' courageous enterprise was delivered by a white woman who said she represented a group of southern Christian women. She asked if Daisy Bates would withdraw the Black students' applications from Central High School so the women could "prepare" the community for integration. If not, she threatened, "You'll be destroyed—you, your newspaper, your reputation. Everything!"

Wondering if she "had the guts to tell the bigots to go to hell," Bates fought with her conscience. But she finally decided that "in the struggle for freedom there could be no turning back, no strategic withdrawals, subterfuges, or compromises. What I was going to tell my "Southern Christian" friend was now perfectly clear."[22] L.C. Bates agreed.

Although, it seemed, the *State* was a sacrifice in the equal rights fight, Central High School was successfully integrated. Like so many other

Black publishers and journalists before her, Daisy Bates remembered the words of Ella Wheeler Wilcox:

> To submit in silence when we should protest makes cowards out of men. The human race has climbed on protest. Had no voice been raised against injustice, ignorance, and lust, the inquisition yet would serve the law, and guillotines decide our least disputes. The few who dare must speak and speak again to right the wrongs of many.[23]

Federal, City Correspondents

Since the days of the great congressional debates on slavery, the nation's capitol has been the focal point for most of the lobbying in behalf of Black Americans. Here are found the headquarters of agencies and individuals largely charged with interpreting and upholding the laws of the land.

The Washington-based national correspondents for the Black Press, then, have played important although indirect roles in sparking the Black protest movement. Henry LaBrie, the Black Press historian, credits their "presence and pursuit of the news [as being] indirectly the genesis of positive social change," for they exposed certain legislators and bureaucrats—for the first time—to professional Blacks who directly confronted the issues most affecting their race.[24] The correspondents, in short, made Blacks more visible to exactly the power-brokers who needed to see.

LaBrie also credits Claude Barnett's Associated Negro Press (ANP) news service as a bonding factor in racial unity efforts. Because the Associated Negro Press fed stories to its subscribers simultaneously, it helped to coordinate the continuing national Black protest movement, and provided editors across the land with copy of national significance—whether it originated in Washington or not.

Working in Washington as an Associated Negro Press correspondent from the mid-Forties, Alice D. Dunnigan was in a sensitive, demanding, and exciting position.

After taking the job, she quickly discovered that the first thing she needed to do was get press credentials for the Capitol galleries. She took a full dose of bureaucratic rigamarole before becoming the first Black woman (and only the third Black reporter) so cleared. Soon after, she was accredited by the White House and the State Department, the other major stops on her "beat."

In her press career, Dunnigan contributed to the *Chicago Defender*, the *Pittsburgh Courier*, and the *Norfolk Journal and Guide*, as well as to the *West African Pilot* of Nigeria. She was the first woman to cover a presidential election campaign, traveling with Harry Truman's train in 1948.

For a time, Dunnigan was the only female journalist in Washington filing sports stories. She originally was denied admission to cover boxing matches because of her sex, so male colleagues designed stationery and organizational plans for a "Negro Boxing Writers' Association." Dunnigan was identified as librarian of the group. Reluctantly, the boxing commission gave her the necessary press credentials, and she filed her Associated Negro Press stories without further incident.

Despite the discrimination she encountered, Dunnigan firmly believes the Black Press offered her every opportunity to expand her journalistic horizons and never attempted to limit the scope of her coverage—a complaint often issued by white women journalists on staff at metropolitan dailies.[25]

Fannie Granton, Johnson Publishing Company's associate editor who has worked in the Washington Bureau since the 1950's, describes Washington-based Black Press reporters as generic, which probably accounts for their wide exposure. "There is no one, particular, beat that we follow to the exclusion of others. We cover everything."[26] Plagued by limited advertising revenues and ever-increasing costs, Black papers have traditionally made the most of their staffs. One reporter, for instance, may not be in several places at once, but she must often try.

Like her Kentucky journalist foremothers, Dunnigan began her career as a teacher. She worked in that state's public schools before taking a civil service job in Washington in 1942. Her memories are gathered in A Black Woman's Experience From Schoolhouse to White House (1974), and she is currently working on a history of Blacks in Kentucky.

Several other Black women have prominently figured in relaying news from Washington, like Venice Tipton Spraggs, the Washington bureau chief of the Chicago Defender, from 1943 to 1953, and Ethel Payne, who followed her in that job.

The second Black woman accredited to cover the White House, Spraggs supplied a popular column, "Women in the National Picture." It covered significant trends and news of government activities important to Blacks. In a September 1944 clip, titled "You, Inc.," she spoke of dislocations in the war industries that would surely follow in peacetime, and solemnly reminded readers that "Negro women, the newest of the industrial workers, always are among the first to go."

For her distinguished service, Spraggs became the first Black initiated into Theta Sigma Phi Sorority of Women in Journalism (later known as Women in Communications, Inc.). In 1946 she was one of twelve initiates to the National Council of Negro Women's honor roll for her "Outstanding work in the field of Journalism."

Marjorie McKenzie, a *Courier* columnist, also was Washington-based. Politically-oriented, her commentary appeared on the feature page along with that of George S. Schuyler and others, and was as logically-developed and articulate as any other worthy of the name. McKenzie was the only female writer appearing on the "Feature Page" at that time.

In her May 30, 1942 column, titled "People are Far Ahead of Leaders in Discussion of America's War Aims," she chastized readers for meekly accepting misguided leadership. Although specifics were not mentioned, she wrote:

> As Negroes, we have been trying to evolve some techniques that would get us into things. Discouraged by an initial lack of success, we have taken refuge in a retirement that has been overdramatized by certain leaders. . . . We shall have to get over this idea of ours that all of our problems are unique. . . .

Her August 22nd essay spotlighted the myriad problems confronting the young, single, Black women living in Washington and making their living as stenographers in the recently-desegregated capitol pool. Hemmed-in by Jim Crow housing patterns and public accommodations, they must often have wondered why they were ever excited about this great adventure in the first place, she sympathized.

Other columns appearing in the 1942 *Couriers* carried heads like: "Selfish Greed of Some Industrialists May Jeopardize War Efforts of Allies," "The Elections Proved Need for Alignment to Oust Tories from Power." In the latter she commented:

> It means nothing to the Negro people that one of our leaders announces that he is going to throw the support of a hundred thousand people in his organization to the Republican party because the Democratic party has failed to do thus and so for us. Neither the Republicans nor the Democrats as such are going to do anything for us. The conservative elements in both are in control, and they are operating for themselves. . . . we owe support only to individuals within both parties who fight for universal freedom and justice.[27]

Not far from Washington in Baltimore, Elizabeth Murphy Moss prepared to travel to England during the war, in order to report a series on the Black troops stationed there. Slated to become the first Black woman war correspondent, she took ill and missed the opportunity.

The granddaughter of John H. Murphy, founder of the *Afro-American,* Moss stuck with the business. She continues to pen her long-lived

"If You Ask Me" column under her pen name, Bettye M. Moss, and she is today vice-president and treasurer of the Afro-American Company.

John H. Murphy, Sr. bought the business in 1892 with a $200 loan from his wife.[28] The enterprise remains family-owned and has the second largest circulation of any general distribution Black newspaper. Like the *Courier*, it produces national and regional editions.

The Black Image in the Black Press

In the postwar years, the conditions that threatened the vitality of Black newspapers encouraged editors to retreat from the standard protest diet attacking discrimination and the miscarriage of justice. Proportionately more emphasis was given to social and entertainment features, instead.[29]

Rather than abandoning the struggle for equality out of despair, they resolved to align themselves with the public sentiment.

Integration forces had long been at work when the 1954 Supreme Court decision heralded an idea whose time had—finally—arrived. The forces for positive change increased momentum with prominent victories such as the desegregation of the armed forces, and now noisy protests were swiftly toned down. As literary critic Arthur P. Davis explains, "the spiritual commitment and climate" out of which full integration could develop was highly evident in Black America. "The Negro literary artist," an interpreter of the human condition, recognized and acknowledged that climate; he accepted it in good faith; and he resolved to work with it at all costs.[30] So did the Black Press.

Expansion of society news and coverage of successful and distinguished Blacks was a by-product of the integration movement. Seventy-five percent of race editors believed "the social pages have always been, and will continue to be the most important part of the Black newspaper."[31] So increased coverage of Blacks who were sharing somehow in the American Dream reflected reader interest.

Rightfully so, the field of society editors whirled during the Fifties. If press reaction to slipping circulations and the public opinion barometer increased this activity, so did the entry of the Johnson Publishing Company's periodicals with their competitive spark. A 1950 edition of *Ebony* devoted an article to this unique press corps, encouraging skeptics to re-evaluate their opinions of this sorority. Said one advocate:

> No one in America is closer to the pulse of colored life than the society editors of the Negro press. Through their columns and news items about the most intimate phases of Negro life, they do more to interpret the social patterns of the

community than the sociologist or psychologist and do more to dignify colored womanhood than the reformer or do-gooder. [32]

High praise, this, but now without cause.

"To be a social editor, you must have a strong constitution, cast iron stomach, a private income, lots of good clothes, and the ability to say 'dahling'."[33] So said Toki Schalk-Johnson, who followed Julia Bumbry Jones as *Pittsburgh Courier* society editor. Gerri Major added that any society or women's editor also ". . . knows her people, her columns, her pages, and will develop a following loyal to the death."[34]

Johnson graduated from Boston College and compiled the "Beantown" column for the *Courier* while there. A 1942 "Women at War" feature carried her byline. In the meantime, she produced copy for the popular and confession magazines. In 1944, she was hired as a full editor at the *Courier* and soon, she established her trademark—a collection of "incredible" hats.

Marion B. Campfield, born in 1910, worked in the Black Press for forty years. City editor of the *Chicago Bee* while Olive Diggs held the managing editor spot, she later joined the *Defender* as its women's editor. Then, she managed four assistants and produced a ten-page local section.[35]

Campfield began her long love affair with the Black Press when she married into the Mitchell family of the *St. Louis Argus* in 1928. She died November 3, 1973 and received a special tribute in *Ebony's* "Backstage" department.

Pearl Cox, another long-time women's editor who favored memorable hats, began "Pearlie's Prattle" with the *Washington Tribune* in 1933 and continued it after its purchase by the Afro-American Company.

Gladys Mills Makel (Johnson) first handled society pages for the Detroit edition of the *Courier* in 1946. By the Sixties, she was editor of the Detroit paper, commanding a staff of twenty people. Her "most memorable society story caused her to get locked in all night at a birthday party for the renown Prophet Jones."[36]

A competitor, Myrtle Gaskill, handled the women's pages for the *Michigan Chronicle*.

Lula Jones Garrett edited women's pages for all editions of the *Afro-American*—Baltimore, Washington, New Jersey, Richmond, and National—and penned two society columns as well, while Jessie Mae Beavers of the *Los Angeles Sentinel* enjoyed the willing assistance of her four sisters and mother in gathering her news.

Beavers received the Ida B. Wells Woman of the Year Award for 1968, from the National Association of Media Women, and was one of the first Blacks to join Women in Communications.

Other notable women's and society page editors of the postwar years were: Betty Granger of the *New York Age* and the *Amsterdam News*, to which she contributed Long Island's reports; Ora Brinkley of the *Philadelphia Tribune*; Hennie Mae Cisco, who edited the *Chicago Courier's* women's page from 1939; Camille Hood, who held a Cincinnati position for twenty years; and "Eve Lynn," pen name of the woman with the 22-year tenure (by 1950) at the *Philadelphia Courier*.[37] Odile T. Elias reported for the *New Orleans Louisiana Weekly*.

In the Seventies, Theresa Fambro Hooks, women's editor of the *Chicago Defender*, and one-time president of the National Association of Media Women (NAMW), would imitate Ora Brinkley's fashion show promotion idea. Eunice Johnson, wife of John H. Johnson and vice-president of the Johnson Publishing Company, directs that company's highly successful fashion show, which tours nationally. Like other such press-sponsored events, it promotes the sponsor and thus encourages subscriptions and overall sales.

Johnson Publishing Company and Other Periodicals

When many Black publishers greeted the integration age with a reduced volume and intensity of racial protest copy, and greatly expanded coverage of race pride and achievement themes, John H. Johnson took the trend a step further. In 1945 he began *Ebony* magazine, a heavily-illustrated monthly devoted to "emphasizing the bright side of Black life and reporting successes by Black people in any endeavor."[38] Except for a brief fling in the Fifties with sexier articles and pictures designed to boost newsstand sales—which backfired when many religious subscriber households objected—it has hewn closely to the mark. Today, *Ebony* is Johnson's biggest success story. Flagship of the Johnson fleet, its circulation of 1,250,000 sets it squarely in the select group of American magazines whose circulations exceed the one-million mark.

Ebony's success spawned new ventures, the most successful of which is *Jet*, a pocket-sized weekly filled with brief news items and photos. Other projects are *Black Stars*, reporting the activities of entertainment and show-business personalities; and *Ebony Jr.*, a children's magazine. *Black World*, a digest of often militant social commentary and literary works began as *Negro World* in 1942, was phased out in the mid-Seventies. *Tan*, originally *Tan Confessions* and modeled after *True Confessions*, continues to please its female audience.

All these publications have opened important new employment opportunities to Black women journalists and editors, and several of their award-winning staffers and alumnae figure prominently here.

Johnson Publishing Company Editors

One of the best-known names in the Black world of journalism belongs to Gerri (Geraldyn) Hodges Major, the doyenne of "Black Society." Born on July 29, 1894, her career as a society editor spans sixty years, much of it in conjunction with the Johnson empire.

Major grew up in Chicago and taught in Chicago and Missouri before moving to New York. She began this career in 1925, contributing New York social news to the *Pittsburgh Courier* in "Through the Lorgnette." She wrote "In New York Town" for the *Chicago Bee* and organized the Geraldyn Dismond Bureau of Specialized Publicity by 1928. Disenchanted with this profession, she remembered her favorite aunt's advice to select a career she could enjoy—one that would benefit her intellectually and materially—Major decided to write.

The same year she took on the managing editorship of the *Interstate Tattler*. Here, she enlarged her scope, reporting society, sports, and political news, theater and entertainment stories, and gossip. She even learned page make-up, delighting in handling the type elements, taking the copy to press, and watching completed pages roll off. The *Tattler* was one of her "most exhilarating experiences as a journalist," where two regular columns, "Social Snapshots of Geralydn Dismond" and "Between Puffs by Lady Nicotine," added to her extensive responsibilities. Her "New York Social Whirl" column appeared in the *Baltimore Afro-American* in 1928, as well, and its title probably comes closest to describing Major's life in those heydays.

She remained with the *Tattler* until 1931, but it was during the late Twenties that Major began developing a national following. "I wrote my columns for the local readership, whether it was Baltimore, New York, Pittsburgh or Chicago," she explains.[39]

Living on "Striver's Row," one of the most fashionable Blacks in Harlem, and being there during the "Roaring Twenties," Major found herself surrounded by many of the most colorful, talented Blacks of the age. Her memories are of Who's Who of Black culture, business, and politics: James Weldon Johnson and brother J. Rosamond Johnson; Walter White, W.E.B. DuBois; Claude McKay and Langston Hughes; Florence Mills and A'Lelia Walker. She saw Sissle and Blake in "Shuffle Along" and Charles Gilpin in "Emperor Jones," and she witnessed Bert Williams' funeral.

In the Thirties, Major held the women's editor spots at both the *New*

York Daily Citizen for six months, and the *Amsterdam News* for longer. In 1953 she joined Johnson Publishing Company as society editor of *Jet* and senior editor for *Ebony*—positions she still holds.

The "piece de resistance" offered her by John H. Johnson was the opportunity to cover the coronation of Britain's Queen Elizabeth II, certainly *the* event of the generation. Here, she described the activities of a fascinating crowd of heads-of-state and assorted dignitaries:

> Africa and the West Indies were well represented in London. . . . One [person] who did not attend was the Ashantiene of Kumasi, who was voted 30,000 pounds by his tribal council to attend but decided not to go because one local organization objected. . . . The fabulous 60-year-old ruler was supposed to have had so many jewels that he seldom went out because it took him too long to dress. . . . It cost the Gold Coast chieftain, Nii Kwabena Bonne, an extra 12 cents taxi fare to transport his umbrella, which was six feet in diameter. It was purple and green with a silver fringe and topped with a gold pineapple. . . . At an informal supper party, Herbert McDermot, who once lived in New York but was then selling prefabricated houses in Africa for a British firm, served up pigs' "trotters" to add a homey touch for American visitors. Josephine Baker and some African guests won eating honors. . . . Marie Bryant, the American entertainer, responded [to an offensive political act] by singing nightly a song at London's Hippodrome which poked fun at Malan and had the nationalist [South African] government leader fuming in London. The tune, "Don't Malign Malan" stirred up as much talk as coronation pageantry.[40]

And on the fountain flowed.

Some time later, after excitedly recounting her first year with *Ebony* and *Jet* to Mary McLeod Bethune, Major remembered the great lady quietly saying, "Daughter, don't ever forget to be humble."[41]

Major's columns "always had a heavy sprinkling of items about the international set" from then on—featuring Americans traveling abroad and Third World people, Africans and West Indians involved in stateside events. Thus, she kept in step with an audience whose horizons had been expanded by war, the news of the worldwide assault on racism and the rise of colored peoples. In late 1967, publisher Johnson assigned Major to the Paris bureau for six months where she produced her "Paris Scratchpad" column in this favorite city for Blacks traveling in Europe.

Returning to America in 1968, the society pro has continued her worldwide travels, and received several awards from foreign sources. Among them are the National Decoration of Honneur et Merite from the Republican of Haiti, and a diploma and Medal of Honor from the Centro Studi E Scambi Internationali of Rome. The Global News Service of New York once cited her for her "record of superior achievement," as did the Dominican Press Association of the Dominican Republic.

Major, along with *Ebony* colleagues Era Bell Thompson and Moneta

Sleet, played goodwill ambassador to the Dominican Republic when General Trujillo held power. Interested in enhancing his image among American Blacks, the General agreed to take a lifetime subscription to *Ebony*, which Major would present. The magazine's staffers would also produce an article on Dominican life under Trujillo.[42]

Gerri Major celebrated her eightieth birthday in 1974 with a three-month-long round of activities that belied her age, as does her continuing work for the Johnson publications. "My legs say they want to stop, but my heart and head say, 'Keep going,' and I do. It is the spirit that has brought my people out of the darkness of slavery into the light of a brighter day. I am grateful for having been a part of it."[43]

In 1976 her life story and those of many who compose her treasuretrove of old-line, Black middle-class contacts was published in *Black Society*, a survey of this American group in text and photographs.

Era Bell Thompson joined the infant Johnson Publishing Company more than thirty years ago. Today she is the dean of Black women magazine journalists and *Ebony* International Editor. In the position since 1964, she primarily reports on issues and personalities prominent in the global arena and travels abroad frequently. Earlier, Thompson served as managing editor of the magazine.

Thompson has been a pioneer even in the traditional American use of the word, having moved from her Des Moines, Iowa birthplace in 1917 to homestead in North Dakota with her parents. She graduated from Bismarck High School in 1924 and went on to study journalism at the University of North Dakota, where she also set five intercollegiate women's track records and tied two national records. Later, Thompson was one of the first Negro coeds to graduate from Morningside College, which she attended after her years at the University.

The seasoned reporter has written several books in addition to her articles, including *Africa, Land of my Fathers: American Daughter*, the story of her early life in Iowa and North Dakota, and *The Fifth Estate*, which chronicles her experiences in the Black Press.

Among her latest achievements is her honorary Doctor of Humane Letters degree granted by the University of North Dakota. In 1965 she was named the Outstanding Woman of the Year by Iota Phi Lambda, and honored by the North Dakota Press Women for her distinguished service in the public interest in 1966.

Asked about the inspirations and beliefs that successfully carried her from the rough, Dakota territory to the fast-paced, influential world of national and international journalism, Thompson said:

> I was inspired by my father, who gave me faith in myself and the learned ability to keep my mouth shut, while accomplishing obstacles others were still talking about doing.
> What I didn't have in worldly goods (and I had nothing), I made up in ingenuity.
> [I] turned my negatives into positives. You'd be surprised how being a small black girl—and plain—were really advantages.
> I have always believed that I could do anything I wanted to do, if willing to make the necessary efforts and sacrifices.[44]

Era Bell Thompson, (right) EBONY's International Editor, with Mrs. Kaatje de Vries, wife of the Governor of Surinam
(photo courtesy of EBONY)

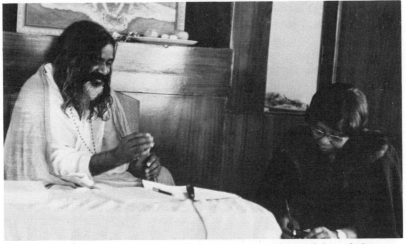

Era Bell Thompson interviewing Maharishi Mahesh Yogi in Asham, India
(photo courtesy of EBONY Magazine)

A third distinguished Johnson staffer active in the postwar years is E. Fannie Granton, associate *Jet* editor and assistant *Ebony* editor since 1956. Based in the Washington, D.C. bureau, she has figured in most of the Federal City dispatches and features—as resource person, researcher, or reporter.

Winner of the 1978 National Achievement award from the National Association of Media Women, and the Freedom's Journal award, she has been further honored by the United Black fund of America's creation of a scholarship to the Howard University School of Communications in her name.

Among Granton's most memorable assignment, she counts her tours to Africa and South America with former First Lady Pat Nixon.

Active in Capitol Hill professional associations, Granton was the first Black to hold office in the Washington Press Club, which she served as parliamentarian in 1971-72 and recording secretary from 1975-76.

Other Contributors: Publishers and Editors

At least one Black woman started a magazine in the Forties. Victoria Lillian Cumber, born February 5, 1920 in San Antonio, Texas, published the *Sepia Hollywood* magazine from 1941 to 1945, when new publishing ventures were discouraged by paper shortages and other war-related problems. Later, she pursued her performing arts interest by working as a Hollywood theatrical agent for her own firm, and in 1967 she began as a columnist for the *South West Wave* newspaper of Southern California.

Today's magazines are often very specialized offerings whose featured subjects appeal to a specifically-defined readership. Following this design, editors and publishers can now make their strongest sales pitches to potential advertisers because they can more accurately determine their readers' needs and interests.

This wedding of marketing and readership-base projection has become a sophisticated proposition in the last few years, thanks to advanced polling and computing techniques. But long before the advent of these new research methods, astute publishers knew their publications must adequately serve their readers or be damned to low circulations and financial failure.

Lyda V. Merrick of Durham, North Carolina identified a distinct and neglected market for a service magazine in 1952. The resultant *Negro Braille* magazine now has a circulation among 400 or more devotees, many of whom live outside the United States or are not even Black.[45]

Merrick worked as sole editor until 1969 when Charlotte Hackett assumed the responsibility.

The founder's editorial formula was to create a digest—reprint articles that appeared in nationally-known Black-oriented periodicals on national and international news, history, editorials, and entertainment topics.

Thelma Gorham's career spans almost forty years in print media and journalism education. She made her first major contributions as a magazine editor.

Born February 21, 1913 in Kansas City, Missouri, she started as a newspaper reporter in 1931, contributing smart, brief pieces to the *Kansas City Call*, or working in other editorial capacities for that paper until 1937. In the meantime, she earned her undergraduate journalism degree at the University of Minnesota. Soon after she became the only female editor for the *Apache Sentinel*, an official United States Army Publication at Fort Huachuca, Arizona, where Black troops and WAACs trained during World War II.

In the next decade, she taught journalism at Lincoln University (Missouri), earned her master's degree and served as executive editor and publisher of *Step-Up*, a Saint Louis-based forerunner of today's *Black Enterprise*. *Step-Up* addressed the needs and spotlighted the achievements of Black Midwestern businessmen and women.

Other positions Gorham held in the Fifties included managing editor for the *Oklahoma Eagle*, executive editor for the *Black Dispatch* (Oklahoma City). Later, she was an instructor at Southern University.

Honors and recognition abound for this Ford Foundation Mass Media Fellowship winner and "Foremost Woman in Communications," who is writing her doctoral dissertation on Supreme Court Justice Thurgood Marshall, the first Black to sit on that bench.

This topic is actually an extension of the spirit that crystallized in her reporting. "I have always been interested in Negro life and history," she said during a *Tallahasse Democrat* interview. "Blacks made so many contributions to different cultures that were never publicized until recently." So Gorham has dedicated herself to recounting positive Black accomplishments through the media. As a child she says she realized that the only reporting on Black affairs she saw or heard concerned murders and robberies, with nothing positive or uplifting, unless she saw a Black newspaper. She decided then to work with the Black Press.

Ever since her Southern University tenure, Gorham has taught

communications at the University of Minnesota and at Florida
Agricultural and Mechanical University. One of the very few Black
women so engaged, her experience bears out Marguerite Rose Davis'
hope that Black women would someday find greater opportunities as
journalism instructors. Prophetically, Thelma Thurston Gorham was
listed in the study as a recent graduate—one of fifteen to finish from
major universities belonging to the American Association of Schools
and Departments of Journalism.[46]

NOTES

[1] Harry A. Ploski and Warren Marr, II, comp. and eds., *The Negro Almanac: A Reference Work on the Afro-American* (New York: Bellwether, 1976), p. 916.

[2] Ploski and Marr, p. 916.

[3] Roland E. Wolseley, *The Black Press, U.S.A.* (Ames, Iowa: Iowa State University Press, 1971), p. 56.

[4] Marguerite Rose Davis, "A Survey and Analysis of the Opportunities for Negro Women in Journalism," Thesis, Kansas State College 1942, p. 46.

[5] M. Davis, pp. 19-20.

[6] Lewis H. Fenderson, "Development of the Negro Press, 1827-1948," Diss. University of Pittsburgh 1948, p. 74.

[7] M. Davis, p. 19.

[8] Marion T. Marzolf, *Up From the Footnote: A History of Women Journalists* (New York: Communications Arts/Hastings House, 1977), p. 52.

[9] M. Davis, p. 43.

[10] John Hope Franklin, *From Slavery to Freedom*, 4th ed. (New York: Knopf, 1974), pp. 463-465f.

[11] Wolseley, p. 322.

[12] Wolseley, p. 326.

[13] Sharon Harley and Rosalyn Terborg-Penn, eds., *The Afro-American Woman: Struggles and Images* (Port Washington, New York: Kennikat Press 1978), p. 110.

[14] Harley and Terborg-Penn, pp. 110-111.

[15] Harley and Terborg-Penn, p. 113.

[16] Harley and Terborg-Penn, p. 118.

[17] Daisy Bates, *The Long Shadow of Little Rock: A Memoir by Daisy Bates* (New York: David McKay, 1962), pp. 220-221.

[18] Bates, p. 33.

[19] Bates, p. 36.

[20] Bates, p. 37.

[21] Bates, p. 41.

[22] Bates, p. 175.

[23] Frederick G. Detweiler, *The Negro Press in the U.S.* (1922; rpt. College Park, Maryland: McGrath Publishing Company, 1968), p. 134.

[24] Henry LaBrie, III, ed., *Perspectives of the Black Press: 1974* (Kennebunkport, Maine: Mercer House, 1974), p. 196. In his essay, "World War II and the Black Press," John D. Stevens terms this Black presence "problematical." While it might have been noted in the executive branch, a *Chicago Defender* survey refuted any significant influence on lawmakers. See p. 33, *Perspectives.*

[25] Marzolf, pp. 57-58, and elsewhere in text.

[26] Fannie Granton Johnson, "Mass Communications," A Panel, First Scholarly Research Conference on Black Women, The National Council of Negro Women, Washington, D.C., November 12, 1979.

[27] *Pittsburgh Courier*, 22 August 1942.

[28] *The Black Press Handbook*, 1977, pp. 60-62.

[29] Ploski and Marr, *The Negro Almanac*, p. 916.

[30] Arthur P. Davis, *From the Dark Tower: Afro-American Writers, 1900-1960* (Washington, D.C.: Howard University Press, 1974), p. 138.

[31] LaBrie, *Perspectives*, p. 199.

[32] "Society Editors: They Work Hard to Chronicle Gay Doings of the Cadillac Set," *Ebony*, March 1950, p. 52.

[33] "Society Editors: . . .," p. 52.

[34] Gerri Major, *Black Society* (Chicago: Johnson Publishing Company, 1973), p. 357.

[35] "Society Editors: . . .," p. 53.

[36] "Society Editors: . . .," p. 54.

[37] "Society Editors: . . .," p. 52.

[38] Wolseley, p. 63.

[39] Gerri Major with Doris E. Saunders, *Gerri Major's Black Society,* (Chicago: Johnson Publishing Company, Incorporated, 1976), p. 338.

[40] Major, *Black Society*, pp. 361-364.

[41] Statement received from Gerri Major, 1 March 1980.

[42] Major, *Black Society,* pp. 367-368.

[43] Major, *Black Society,* p. 393.

[44] Statement made by Era Bell Thompson for Contributions Questionnaire, 29 February 1980.

[45] Wolseley, pp.160-161.

[46] M. Davis, p. 30.

CHAPTER VI

THE SIXTIES: BLACK REBELLION AND BEYOND

The hopeful attitude of the Fifties built added measures of courage in young "Freedom Riders," marchers, and sit-in or jail-in participants who tested local and state governments' commitment to enforce the rules. They also attempted to show just how ridiculous and energy-wasting stubborn opposition was in the face of impending change. The demonstrators dramatically appealed to society's moral conscience, trusting that if pushed a bit, the best of mankind's instincts would win out. Integration could then become the rule, not the exception.

By 1963, a century after Emancipation, however, true freedom was as elusive for Negroes as ever. Demonstrators began to press for equal employment opportunities as well as public accommodations and voting rights, and hit the root reason for racism's stranglehold. Civil Rights and Voting Rights bills passed Congress, while an unpopular war took more lives and tax money than ever. Overall employment and improved housing opportunities remained beyond reach of the Black masses, and hundreds of ghettos exploded in frustration between 1964 and 1968. Meanwhile, the Black press renewed its loudest calls for racial unity, protest, and fortitude, and chronicled the rise of Black Nationalism and a new militant spirit. Even Ebony began to reflect more of the decade's struggle and championed the Black cause.[1]

President Lyndon Johnson called the "Kerner Report" issued by the National Advisory Commission on Civil Disorders ". . . the most important report that has been made to me since I've been President," for ". . . the conclusion that it reaches about the cause of our problems in this country evolving primarily from white racism."[2]

The report carried a scathing criticism of the establishment media:

> The media report and write from the standpoint of a white man's world. The ills of the ghetto, the difficulties of life there, the Negro's burning sense of grievance, are seldom conveyed. Sights and indignities are part of the Negro's daily life, and many of them come from what he calls "the white press" —a press that repeatedly, if unconsciously, reflects the biases, the paternalism, the indifference of white America. This may be understandable, but it is not excusable in an institution that has the mission to inform and educate the whole of our society.

Further, the report accused the profession of being ". . . shockingly backward in seeking out, hiring, training, and promoting Negroes."

White Press vs. Black Press

Even before the Kerner report circulated, the white-owned media began hiring more significant numbers of Black reporters who, they reasoned, could gain confidence to "get the story" on Black protests as no white reporter could. It also seemed a sensible public relations move. The riots and demonstrations were among the top stories of the decade, and no editor, regardless of his prejudices, could afford to miss the most interesting angles.[3]

One *Washington Post* staffer admitted this. "I got a newspaper job because people threw a lot of bricks in 1968," he said, adding ". . . I feel an obligation to work my ass off to make the paper more sensitive to coverage of the Black community."[4]

Since the establishment press first reported the activities of Black people, the images presented were unavoidably negative. The outright practice or lingering tendency of the white press has been to report only stories of crime or poverty, even when there are many more sides to Black life.

Robert Maynard, former *Washington Post* associate editor and editor of the *Oakland Tribune*, describes the concerns of Black reporters on white papers: "We seek portrayal of our communities as places inhabited by real people, not pathological fragments. We are not asking to be romanticized. Where there is disease, report disease; crime, report crime. But where there is health, report health; creativity, report creativity.[5]

Charlayne Hunter-Gault amplifies:

> . . . People aren't asking you for handouts and they aren't asking you to do press releases or public relations, they just want you to tell the truth. They want you to call it like you see it. The time when the black community gets most upset is when they get misrepresented in the press, which happened an awful lot prior to the riots and still does to some extent. . . .[6]

For Black staffers on white-owned papers, it is ironic now that the volcanic passions accompanying mass protests and insurrections have cooled, most publications are no longer interested in "civil rights" stories or even in more general coverage of Blacks. Yet more Black journalists have sought press jobs in the Seventies than ever before. "This is the time of the cross-over reporter," says *Washington Post* staffer Dorothy Butler Gilliam, "but a cruel joke is that minority news does not get covered in its full complexity."

For exactly this reason proponents believe the offspring of *Freedom's Journal* will be around for quite some time. The Black Press owes its existence to satisfying the readers' thirst to know more about themselves and the way the world treats them. So long as racism exists, the argument goes, Black people will need a voice of their own.

With the climate change of the 60's, however, many of the venerable

Black Press beacons ". . . which had molded . . . so many . . . Black writers, fought for integration only to become one of its victims when talented newcomers, as well as veterans, deserted the reportorial ranks for the greener pastures of mainstream media."[7]

Salaries there are more competitive, and the prestige accrued and opportunities for future accomplishment are greater. Black and other minority-group journalists are concentrated on a small number of papers with 38 percent employed by only 34 dailies. Two thirds of the nation's 1,762 daily papers do not employ any of the 1,700 Black news professionals.[8]

Another obstacle lies on the road to advancement. The time-honored tradition is for newcomers to start at small-town dailies and there gain the experience and seniority that leads to editing jobs. Transfers to larger markets in the largest cities—where Black populations are concentrated—may come later. The inherent problem with going by these rules is that even once reporters make the sacrifices, some say white editors simply refuse to share power. Even when all professional standards are met, racism and sexism override these considerations, with rare exceptions. "White management is unwilling to place coverage decisions in the hands of people whose values and perspectives may differ from their own," reported a writer who interviewed the only four Blacks—all men—who held positions as assistant city editor or higher in the white press hierarchy by 1976.[9]

Prominent Newspaper Contributors

When Hazel Garland became the first Black woman to work as editor-in-chief of a newspaper chain, her achievement capped a rich, thirty-year career at the *Pittsburgh Courier*. Presently a consultant and public relations representative for the journal, she continued to produce her long-lived columns, "Things to Talk About," social commentary and "Video Vignettes," begun in 1946 and 1955, respectively.

Some dozen years of her career were spent on the paper's women's page, first as assistant editor under Toki Schalk-Johnson (1947-1952), and later as women's editor from 1965 to 1972.

Garland started with the *Courier* in 1943 as a stringer, but landed a full-time position as a general assignment reporter in 1946, early in the postwar era. *Mademoiselle's* job editor wrote that the war's end ushered in a bad time for women hoping to land metropolitan-desk reporting jobs on daily papers. Even those already handling straight news were being shifted to departments with women's angles. If they quit, men replaced them.[10]

But what holds for white dailies does not necessarily hold true in Black Press practice. By 1946, *Courier* editors must have decided Garland's blossoming talent, was far more important to them than any trivial sex considerations. Besides, "thinking has no sex," asserted an early twentieth century journalist.[11]

In 1952, she was given the responsibility of co-editing a new magazine section. Armed with a magazine writing/editing course, plenty of mother wit and some hard-nosed newspaper experience, she charted the course for its single year at sea. Ever-climbing, Garland moved up to the city editor's spot after her stint as woman's department head before moving into the top editorial spot.

Garland, the 1975 Headliner Award winner of Women in Communication, Inc., is half of the only prizewinning mother–daughter journalist duo. Phyl Garland is the other.

Had Elizabeth Moss made her wartime trip to London, she would have been the first Black woman war correspondent.

The distinction of becoming the first Black woman war correspondent was claimed by Ethel L. Payne. Payne went to the Vietnam war front and became one of the most seasoned of national or foreign correspondents-Black or white, male or female. For twenty years, 1953–1973, she rant he Washington bureau of the Sengstacke newspaper chain until her return to the Chicago home office as associate editor. During her days on "the Hill" she made valuable contacts that enabled her to accompany government heads on foreign tours, and to cover some of the biggest news stories of the decade.

Payne went to the *Defender* shortly after graduation from the Medill School of Journalism at Northwestern University. Within her first year on staff, she was transferred to the Washington bureau to replace Venice Tipton Spraggs. Spraggs, as Payne admits, "was a formidable person to follow," and had run the office since 1943. It was her sympathy, hospitality, and "thorough indoctrination course" in the ways of Washington that helped Payne get firmly established in one of the most exciting and demanding reportial roles of all, where the endless round of press conferences and cocktail parties leading to establishment of news and background sources for stories, were all essential to the job. Payne was most apt to cover beats that included the White House, Capitol Hill, the Labor Department, Housing and Urban Development Department (HUD), the State Department, and such independent agencies as the Equal Employment Opportunity Commission (EEOC), and the United States Information Agency (USIA). All create or enforce policies that directly bear on Black people. She also kept in close contact with the African embassies, whose news was of increasing interest to observers of the struggle to end white domination here and in the Black ancestral homeland.

From the very first, once she was accredited to cover the various agencies and departments, Payne spoke up. The first question she ever posed at a presidential press conference was later picked up by all the major media. It concerned a Republican Day celebration in which the Howard University choir was prevented from participating with the Emory and Duke University groups. Diplomatically, the President replied that he would be "the first to apologize," if it were true.

Ethel L. Payne, newspaper Correspondent
and first Black woman war correspondent

Another time Payne's question probed a much more sensitive area. She asked Eisenhower what he intended to do to end segregation in interstate travel—a reminder of Ida B. Wells and her reportorial blows against segregation in passenger train cars sixty years before. Payne recalled that Ike bristled. "I will do what I believe is in the best interest of the country," he said. This response deflected the probe at a time when the National Association for the Advancement of Colored People was busy fighting the critical legal battle of *Brown vs. the Board of Education,* and "massive resistance" to change was mounting on all sides. Throughout the land, Blacks undertook legal and civil disobedience campaigns to win admission to segregated educational institutions. Meanwhile, the *Washington Evening Star* reported, "Negro Reporter Angers Ike," on its front page.

Payne was snubbed for about a year as a result of her insistence on posing questions, as she puts it, "on issues of vital concern to minorities."[12] Nearly a century after Emancipation, White America was still unwilling to seek or face equitable solutions to the many pressing problems inherent in a divided society.

In 1955, the indefatigable reporter covered the historic Asian-African Conference at Bandung, Indonesia, which became the first in a series of celebrated foreign assignments. In 1957, she traveled to West Africa with Vice-President Richard Nixon for ceremonies creating the new nation of Ghana. Later she traveled from DaNang to the Mekong Delta in Viet Nam to report on the activities of Black soldiers at the front. On her way home in 1967, she sent dispatches from other spots in the Far East including Tokyo. Stories on the World Council of Churches Assembly in Upsalla, Sweden (1968), the Nigerian civil war (1969), and the goodwill tours she made with Secretary of State Henry Kissinger are notable additions to her clipping file.

Ethel Payne has twice won the Newsman's Newsman Award of the Capitol Press Club, and she served as organization president in 1970. In 1973 she was named winner of the Ida B. Wells Media Woman of the Year Award by the National Association of Media Women.

Black Women Journalists Organized

Rhea Callaway organized the National Association of Media Women in October 1965. Then women's editor of the *New York Age,* she joined Evelyn Cunningham, city editor of the New York Edition, *Pittsburgh Courier,* and Sarah Slack, education editor for the *Amsterdam News* to promote the group and recruit members.

Today, with chapters in a dozen major cities extending from Los Angeles and San Francisco to Atlanta and New York, the National Association of Media Women is the largest and oldest national organization of Black women in the mass media. "To create a new climate of understanding," is the group's motto, and it bestows several awards each year on Black women journalists and others with distinguished media achievement, including the Ida B. Wells Media Women of the Year citation. Jessie Mae Beavers of Los Angeles (1968), Vicki Lucas of New York (1971), and Ruth Kendall, also Los Angeles (1972) are some recent recipients of the Ida B. Wells award.

Amplifying the group's motto are these words, taken from the group's tenth anniversary booklet: "Just as a mother passes the soil of the earth from her hands to her child's, may we pass our creative talents and skills to young people who are seeking careers in the total industry of mass communications."

Lois K. Alexander was national president of the National Association of Media Women from 1971 to 1975 and received the Association's Founder's Cup in 1971 and the President's Plaque in 1978. A long–time freelance writer, and consultant, she was one of the highest communications officers in the New York regional office of the Department of Housing and Urban Development. During the Fifties she edited the Washington edition of the *Courier*, served as vice–president of the Capitol Press Club and edited the *Tattler Magazine*.

A reporter making a stellar ascent in both print and the electronic media is Charlayne Hunter-Gault, born February 27, 1942 in Due West, South Carolina.

Gault made important news before she reported it when, at age seventeen she became the first black women and one of the first Blacks ever to attend the University of Georgia. Earning a bachelor's degree in journalism she quickly became a writer for the "Talk of the Town" section of the *New Yorker*, perhaps the best-read section of this epitome of literary magazines. This job overlapped with her 1967 stay in Washington as a Russell Sage scholar, when she edited transcripts for a magazine, and worked with an investigative news team and as co-anchor for the news show at WRC television, the NBC capitol city affiliate.

By 1968, Gault was at the *New York Times* heading the Harlem bureau, whose creation accompanied the social upheaval wrought by Black America's uncompromising demands for freedom and justice. Gault remained at the *Times* until 1977, when she joined the "MacNeil/Lehrer Report," a weeknight program that investigates nationally or internationally-significant events by devoting entire shows to single issues. A correspondent, she handles all special assignments and works as anchor, interviewing guests when the executive associate editors are on assignment. For fifteen months before joining the Public Broadcasting Service (PBS) program, Gault was a director of the Michelle Clark Fellowship Program for Minority Journalists at

Columbia University. (The Clark program was spawned in the wake of the Kerner Commission report.)

Realizing her career path as most unusual, Gault has emphasized that her trailblazing road has not been an easy one to follow. She acknowledges that the present and next generation of writers will probably find positions in the white press every bit as difficult to capture as at present.

Charlayne Hunter-Gault - PBS News Correspondent

I was brough up that you don't let anybody get you down and you don't let anybody get the best of you. That's just how it was. . . .If there is anything I've noticed in comparing young Blacks to young Whites. . .white kids move into situations as if they expect to become the editor of the newspaper, or the news director of the station. . . .That's a tradition with them. They all grow up thinking that they can be the head of it. . . .It's a matter of attitude, sooner or later we will be able to succeed, and we have to be ready when the time comes.[13]

Gault won several Publisher's Awards while at the *Times*, plus a Lincoln University (Missouri) Unity Award for an in-depth article on teenage unemployment. In 1977 she also served as a juror on the Pulitzer Prize selection committee.

Another renown Black woman writer, Sandra Clark Haggerty, is also one of the few women to have commanded a nationally-syndicated column. From 1969 thru 1977, her weekly observations on urban concerns—as viewed from her Black woman/mother/single parent/educator's perspective—appeared in 110 papers served by the *Los Angeles Times* Syndicate.

Concurrently, Haggerty lectured at colleges, universities, and before social and civic organizations on such subjects as: "Myths About Black Womanhood," "Transracial Adoption," "Black English," "The Black Press," "Black Inventors," and "Parallels of Sexism and Racism." Combined with her experience as an associate professor in the Department of Communications at the University of Utah, she seems a modern-day version of the journalistic foremothers so actively concerned with women's and children's rights.

Born July 26, 1939 in Oakley, Kansas, Haggerty received the prestigious Headliner Award from Women in Communications in 1977, and in 1975 won a Unity Award in Media for Excellence in Minority Journalism.

On the International Beat

The one reporter who most closely followed Fay Jackson's lead as international correspondent was Marguerite Cartwright, who covered the 1951 Zagreb Conference in Yugoslavia, and interviewed President Marshal Tito when Cold War tensions between western democracies and Communist lands were building during escalation of the Korean conflict.

Cartwright has been a United Nations reporter and international affairs columnist for the *Pittsburgh Courier* and a stringer for the *Chicago Sun-Times*, as well as a liaison officer for the United Nation's Department of Public Information. She holds a doctorate from Boston University and is presently a member of the Hunter College faculty in New York City.

Laura Parks, another United Nations Press Corps member who uses the name Loretta Pauker in her stage career, is an accomplished dramatic reader and concert singer who has performed throughout the United States, the Soviet Union, and East and West Africa, where she has been the personal guest of several heads of state. Her entertainment travels have well-complemented her United Nations reporting for the *Afro-American* newspaper chain since the early 1960's.

Community Press Standouts

The *Washington Post* launched its pioneering "Style" section in 1969 in a daring effort to update its women's page by eliminating it altogether. Inspired by the changing sexual roles heralded by the "Women's Lib" movement, the paper decided instead to create a section appealing to common interests of men and women. It would tell "about the private life of Washington and probe the quality of this life and the kinds of things happening elsewhere that affect it." Book reviews, crossword puzzles, the leisure calendar, arts features, fashion news, and food articles are now the section's diet.

Dorothy Butler Gilliam,
Journalist with the WASHINGTON POST newspaper

Dorothy Butler Gilliam, a Memphis native, has been an associate editor for this popular section since 1972. She arrived after a stint at WTTG-TV (Washington) where she produced and hosted the "Panorama" show since 1967. The author of *Paul Robeson, All*

American (1976), which was hailed as one of his most impressive biographies, she once won an Emmy award from the Academy of Television Arts and Sciences for "the Panorama" work, and was named Journalist of the Year by the Capitol Press Club, a Black journalist's organization.

Gilliam has also won the Anne O'Hara McCormick Award of the Newspaper Women's Club, given in honor of the first woman to sit on the *New York Times* editorial board.

Lynn R. Dunson also hails from Washington where she had been a metropolitan reporter for the *Star* since 1970. Before commencing her *Star* career, she built an impressive record in Indiana as editor of the daily Indiana University campus newspaper in 1965–1966 and an *Indianapolis Star* reporter for the next two years.

For her professional promise and achievements, she received the William Randolph Hearst Award in 1965 and the Casper Award in 1967 and 1969. Also in 1969 Dunson worked as a Ford Foundation Fellow at the Washington Journalism Center.

Peggy Mitchell Peterman, a Tuskegee native born October 6, 1936, had not been on the *St. Petersburg* (Florida) *Times* long before admitting to herself that she detested the very idea of the paper's "Negro Community News Sheet." It was 1965 and demonstrations against racial discrimination and segregation were giving full vent to protests throughout the South.

Peterman soon fired off a fourteen-page memo to the management, telling why she believed Black news should be distributed throughout the paper, like any other "news," and not confined to the special insert. She left the paper soon after on maternity leave, but returned to win a spot as feature writer in the women's department, thus becoming the first Black to work there. Later, Peterman became the first Black to join the Florida Women's Press Club, which has since become the Florida Press Club, a professional organization for men and women.

Peterman has twice been cited for outstanding feature writing by the state group and is currently working on a book entitled *Ain't Nothing Changed*, an evaluation of the South since the 1960's.

Two contemporary Motor City writers of distinction are June Brown Garner and Marie Teasley.

Born July 19, 1923, Garner is a columnist with the *Detroit News* just as widely known for her popular lectures on Black philosophy and Black culture's effect on current events. The National Newspaper Publisher's Association citation for Best Original Columns (1968-69) and the Michigan Press Club's Best Expression of Editorial Opinion, won in 1972 and 1974 are among her press achievements.

In addition to her writing workload, Garner hosts a Detroit television talk show.

Teasley, woman's editor of the *Michigan Chronicle*, has written for publications since she was fourteen. Her career reached a pinnacle in 1975 when she won top honors for the *Chronicle's* women's pages. She also won the Ida B. Wells Award from the National Association of Media Women that year.

Society editor of the *Denver* (Colorado) *Weekly News* since the early Seventies, Betty Wilkins was the first Black woman to work in Denver media when she began an eighteen-year career editing the Denver edition of the *Kansas City Call*.

Wilkins won the 1968 Harriet Tubman Distinguished Service Award, awarded by the state Association of Colored Women's Clubs. The first Black admitted to membership in the Colorado Women's Press Club, she once hosted two radio shows—a gospel program on KIML-AM and the "Honey Bee Show" on KDKO-AM.

Further north, Connie E. Bennett edits the *Tacoma* (Washington) *True Citizen*. Winner of the National Newspaper Publisher's Association Merit Award for composing the best news story of 1974, Bennett is also a monthly reporter for the ABC-TV outlet in Seattle.

Teaching the Craft

A category of modern journalism just opening up under pressure for women is in teaching the journalist's craft. Only eight percent or 73 of the total personnel employed in journalism education were women, according to a 1971-1972 survey, and fewer than a dozen nonwhite professors teach at white journalism schools.[14]

Higher education administrators in journalism would have had ample justification for the low number of women on their faculties, if the pool of teaching candidates was as limited as supposed. But further investigation by a group of female journalism school educators discovered that between 1968 and 1972 some forty doctoral degrees had been awarded to women in mass communications, with many others in the pipeline. There are no statistics on Black women so distinguished, but available data suggest that there are more qualified to serve on journalism school faculties than commonly thought. Lillian S. Bell, a South Bend, Indiana native, earned undergraduate and doctorate degrees from the Medill School in 1945 and 1973. She was chairman of the journalism department and the first Black woman professor at St. Joseph's Calumet College in East Chicago, Indiana, and was the only Black journalism professor at Northern Illinois University during her tenure.

Before earning her doctorate, Bell taught journalism courses at Medill in 1970 and 1971. A contributor to the *Post Tribune* and *Info* of Gary, Indiana, she was a judge in a recent Illinois Press Woman's Association student writing contest.

Thelma Gorham, a long-time journalism instructor, has only to complete her dissertation to finish her doctoral requirements. She and Phyl Garland, another distinguished college-level journalism instructor, are mentioned elsewhere in this book.

Women Executives

As is true in virtually every profession save teaching, management positions are almost exclusively filled by men. Print journalism is no exception. A representative reflection is offered in a recent American Society of Newspaper Editors survey. This organization, whose members manage news staffs and determine policy, could list only seven of its 749 members as women.[15] The racial minority overview is even bleaker. A 1979 *Columbia Journalism Review* feature noted that more than 99 percent of all editors are white.[16] Considered simultaneously, these statistics hint why Black women who have risen to fill management positions in the white press hierarchy are nearly non-existent.

After a spectacular career as reporter and editor in metropolitan daily newspapers and magazines, Barbara Ann Reynolds is now Washington Bureau Chief of the *Chicago Tribune*, a standout among high achievers.

After her graduation from Ohio State University in 1966, where she participated in a variety of campus publications, Reynolds worked at *Ebony* magazine as an associate editor for a year. From 1969 to 1974 she was a writer for *Chicago Today*, and later in 1974 she signed on as urban affairs writer for the *Tribune*. In 1976 she was the Headline Award winner for Women in Communications the same year her controversial book, *Jessie Jackson: The Man, The Myth, and the Movement*, was published.

A dynamic communicator, Reynolds has served as a *National Observer* correspondent and editor of two books: *Black Book Minority Business and Reference Guide* and *Dollars and Sense*. She is also currently a commentator for the Chicago CBS radio affiliate, WBBM.

Recounting her major motivations to success Reynolds declared that "Racism from whites and condemnation from Blacks in Columbus, Ohio, where I was born were my great inspirations. When I was growing up I often heard adults prejudge me. They would say she will never amount to much. . . ." Later, when she took a journalism course for a change of pace from the workload of a pre-med major "I decided to become a journalist," she said. She had been writing from the age of twelve, but had been discouraged from pursuing the discipline since, at that time and place, it was not considered a profession for Black women.

When Reynolds told her professor, as a joke, that she intended to become a journalist, he admonished her to "Be a school teacher, like the rest of them."

"I swore then that no one would ever define me, but me. And no one has since then," she remembered.

"... The belief that one person can still make a difference—as a role model to youth, as a writer who feels a mission to stand up against the powerful for the powerless, and as a servant of God," is what she now credits as her greatest inspiration.[17]

Even in the Black Press, women's participation has been somewhat limited. It was only in the early 1970's that the *Chicago Daily Defender* named its first female managing editor. A contemporary, Hazel Garland, became the first female editor-in-chief at the *Pittsburgh Courier* about the same time.

Audrey Turner Weaver, a Racine native born July 11, 1913, attended the University of Wisconsin journalism school. She has followed a press career since 1943 when she started at the *Afro-American*. During a ten-year tenure, she worked in a variety of positions as reporter, copy editor, and layout aide. A brief stint as *Jet* associate editor preceded her employment at the *Defender*, where she has worked since 1955.

In 1969, she was named the Ida B. Wells Woman of the Year, by the National Association of Media women and in 1977 she won the Distinctive Imprint Award bestowed by the National Association of University Women.

Weaver was one of the first women to work as a Pulitzer Prize juror, participating from 1971, the first year women served, to 1974. Melba Sweets of the *St. Louis American* joined the selection committee for the 1978 awards.

Two top-level managers who exert both editorial and fiscal decision-making clout, unusually enough, work with Black Press weeklies that are head-on competitors in the Minnesota twin cities area.

Jeanne Cooper is editor and publisher of the *Twin City Observer* and the *St. Paul Sun*, both founded in 1941. She was executive manager before becoming publisher in 1967.

Mary James Kyle was a columnist/reporter for the *Twin Cities Observer* from 1947 to 1952, but joined the Minnesota Sentinel Publishing Company, parent organization of the *Twin City Courier*, in the late Sixties. By 1967, she was editor and associate publisher, and the next year she became company president. Kyle has since stretched her media wings even further and worked as commentator for two local radio shows in 1969.

Other women who made a conscious career choice to work in the Black Press and who now hold management positions are: Ruth Washington of the *Los Angeles Sentinel*; E.P. Alexander of the *Los Angeles Herald-Dispatch*; Claire Paisner of the New York *Voice*; Mildred Brown of the *Omaha* (Nebraska) *Star*; Dickie Foster of the *Dallas Post-Tribune*, and Marjorie Parham of the *Cincinnati Herald*.[18]

In general, women continue to be a small minority among the ranks of writers and editors, even in the Black Press. The reasons do not necessarily include sex discrimination, says Wolesley, but there is a tendency to give men the job advantages, even if their inclination is less marked than in white-run press rooms.

Wolseley attributes the proportion of Black women staffers to the nature of the calling itself. "They too have heard of long hours and low salaries. But the romantic view that some persons have ink instead of blood in their veins exists for Black journalism as well, with the result that some women have made a reputation for themselves in his occupation." Rather than simply "ego-tripping," the entire history and tradition of the Black Press suggests that for the women who have found career fulfillment, more is involved than the desire to see a byline and report the news. The dedication to a struggling enterprise stems from a commitment to work on behalf of race uplift and against racial injustice, not merely from some romantic literary notion.

As indicated elsewhere in this book, Black women have become publishers following the deaths of their husbands. Henry LaBrie lists five of this number who are also active Black Press leaders: Elouise Banks of the *Phoenix Arizona Tribune*; Ophelia Mitchell of the *Columbus* (Georgia) *Times;* Dorothy Leavell of the (Gary, Indiana) and *Chicago New Crusaders;* and Mrs. Julius Carter of the (Houston) *Forward Times.*[19]

Periodical Contributors

Black women have been involved in the production of Black-owned magazines since Frances E.W. Harper contributed to the African Methodist Episcopal Church's *Christian Recorder*, a monthly publication founded in 1852.[20]

The social upheaval of the Sixties apparently influenced the thinking of managers at some of the nation's most popular general interest and women's magazines. White newspapers and magazines seriously considered talented Blacks for jobs.

In the early Seventies, at least three new national Black magazines were launched. Coupled with the newfound interest on the part of establishment periodicals, Black journalists could justly be excited by the possibilities.

Ponchitta Ann Pierce, born August 5, 1942 in Chicago has established her expertise in more than one medium, but with the magazine as her primary expressive vehicle.

Ponchitta Pierce, roving editor with the READER'S DIGEST

She began her career at *Ebony* in the early Sixites and attended the first Asian-American Women's Journalists Conference in Honolulu in 1965. By 1968 she was promoted to Bureau Chief of the New York *Ebony* office. Soon thereafter, she became a special correspondent for Columbia Broadcasting System (CBS) news, one of a handful of women in network news spots just when the male-dominated management was beginning to understand that women could compile impressive reports on subjects other than children's matters and human interest features.

Pierce has successfully worn broadcast and print media hats ever since. She served as a contributing editor for *McCall's* magazine from 1972-1977 and also began a stint as co-host and contributor for WNBCTV's "Sunday" show (in New York) in 1972. Since 1977 she has been a *Reader's Digest* "roving editor."

As her several awards attest, the scope of Pierce's reporting is matched by its insight and appeal. In 1967 she won the first annual Penny Missouri magazine award given for the best reporting, editing, and feature writing on women's pages. In 1968, she won the New York Urban League's John Russwurm Award, named for the pioneer Black Press editor. The Los Angeles chapter of Women in Communications presented her with its 1969 Woman Behind the News citation. Pierce was also the 1970 Headliner Award winner and the 1974 AMITA (Italian-American award) recipient "for distinguished achievement in communications."

One of the most prolific and entertaining Black writers to grace the pages of a magazine is Phyl Garland. Daughter of a career journalist (see Hazel Garland), she has ably fashioned her own distinct and exceptional reputation.

Born in McKeesport, Pennsylvania on October 26, 1935, Garland tasted enough of the newswriting cuisine as a young woman to decide to prepare for a career as master chef. She earned a journalism degree at Northwestern University and was the only Black to graduate in the class of 1957. She was also weary of the whole field by then. Her college experience with establishment "objective" journalistic technique taught her that, "There was no room for journalists who also wanted to be 'writers,' and it could not contain the passions of those driven to act out their convictions."[21]

After school she spent several months at menial jobs until she attended an interview with the *Courier* editor. He gave her a test assignment to write a history of the Black Press for the paper's anniversary issue. Then, she recalled, "I first saw the history of my people as I looked through the back files and books. It turned me into a journalist." Garland's talent and enthusiasm won her a reporting position she was to hold until joining *Ebony* in 1966.

Keeping abreast of the times, Garland's reported trends for *Ebony* that were the pulse-beat of the late Sixties: Black liberation, nationalism, and civil rights; even "natural" hair styles, plus penetrating interviews with political leaders and musical innovators. Garland also regularly contributed record reviews to *Ebony*, even after leaving in 1971 to teach at the State University of New York at New Platz. Later, she was invited to teach at the Columbia University School of Journalism, where she is the first woman, Black or White, on staff.

"The Lady Lives Jazz," one of her latest *Ebony* pieces, appeared in the October 1979 issue and is a profile of the singular jazz musician, Mary Lou Williams. Her book, *The Sound of Soul*, was published in 1969 and traces the development of Black popular music. Garland's byline regularly appears in the record review pages of *Stereo Review* magazine.

Garland received the Golden Quill Award in 1962 for outstanding feature writers, and in 1971 she was the Headline Award winner for Women in Communications.

Negro Digest, John H. Johnson's first magazine, appeared in 1942 and featured articles on Black literature, history and culture. Deactivated for a time, it reappeared in 1961 and was rechristened *Black World* in 1970 to bring it "into full harmony with the times." Admired and respected for the quality of its content and maverick protest spirit, it often published unknown poets and writers.

Carole A. Parks served as *Black World's* associate editor until it was disbanded in the mid-Seventies. She left for Atlanta with Hoyt G. Fuller, *Black World's* managing editor, to edit a new magazine. *First World* was conceived to resume where *Black World* left off. Despite the support of a small but enthusiastic audience, *First World* did not survive.

Johari Amini is managing editor of the *Black Books Review*, another publication born in the Seventies, whose material tends to literary, cultural, or historical themes. It is published quarterly and distributed nationally by the Chicago-based Institute for Positive Education.

Black women editors at white-oriented publications were virtually unheard of before the Seventies, when a bumper crop of Black college graduates arrived on the job market. Teens during the Sixties upheavals, they sought jobs in these previously unapproachable areas. Two, Stephanie Stokes and LaVerne Powlis, were among the first to break the color barrier. Stokes was hired as a feature writer in 1974 for the fashion and arts departments of Conde Nast publications, the giant firm that includes such surveyors of "good taste," style and fashion as *Vogue*, *Glamour* and *Brides*. Before the year was out, Stokes was named a beauty editor—the first Black woman ever. A Seattle native, she is an honors graduate of Howard University. Most recently, Stokes was working with the "Contemporary Living" department of *Essence*.

Powlis is beauty and health editor for *Brides*. After leaving *Family Circle* for the Conde Nast operation, Powlis began by writing a monthly column, "Living Black," which covered fashion, health, and food with the Black woman in mind. This was the first column of its kind in a national publication—*Essence* excluded—and was a big hit with Black readers who, before her arrival, had never been specifically addressed.

Faith Daryl Berry, has pursued a good deal of her journalism outside the editorial offices, choosing to produce more copy as a free-lancer, all the while enjoying a wide variety of writing jobs. Born May 29, 1939 in Cincinnati, Ohio, Berry has worked the media with great facility, performing a variety of tasks in as many different spots. After a stint as editorial assistant at the *New Yorker*, she moved to Paris and successfully free-lanced as a writer, translator, and editor for such publications as *Black World*, *Jeune Afrique*, and the *New York Times Magazine*.

Returning to America in 1968, she worked as copy editor for the *Congressional Quarterly*, and by 1969 she had earned a degree in linguistics at Georgetown University. In 1971 Berry became senior editor for the Dispatch News Service International, well-armed for the spot with her degree and experience abroad. Through 1975 she kept busy editing the *Uncollected Social Protest Writings of Langston Hughes* (1973) and continued her free lancing. She was the 1974 "Decision-maker in Communications" for the National Association of Media Women.

Taking perfect advantage of a sparkling opportunity, Berry won a minority training grant from the Corporation for Public Broadcasting for 1975-77, and worked as staff writer/associate producer for WETA-TV, the Washington public broadcasting outlet.

NOTES

[1] Roland E. Wolseley, *The Black Press, U.S.A.* (Ames, Iowa: Iowa State University Press, 1971), p. 118.

[2] Wolseley, pp. 120–122.

[3] The obvious exceptions were southern papers. See discussions in *Race and the News Media*, ed. by Paul L. Fisher and Ralph L. Loewenstein (F.O.I. Center, University of Missouri, 1967), pp. 22–54.

[4] Nick Kotz, "The Minority Struggle for a Place in the Newsroom" *Columbia Journalism Review*, March/April 1979, pp. 28–29.

[5] Kotz, p. 28.

[6] Kalamu Ya Salaam, "A Career in Journalism," *The Black Collegian*, October/November 1979, p. 110.

[7] Henry LaBrie, III, ed., *Perspectives of the Black Press: 1974* (Keenebunkport, Maine: Mercer House, 1974), p. 170.

[8] Kotz, pp. 23–24.

[9] Kotz, pp. 23–24.

[10] Marion T. Marzolf, *Up From the Footnote: A History of Women Journalists* (New York: Communications Arts/Hastings House, 1977), p. 75.

[11] Marzolf, p. 57; quoting Doris Fleeson, an early female political reporter with the *New York Daily News*. A champion of employment equality, she once feared bright women would leave the field if denied greater access to top-level management positions.

[12] LaBrie, p. 156.

[13] Salaam, p. 112.

[14] Marzolf, p. 259. N. Kotz reports that an unwritten "benign neglect" policy for Black students accompanies the dismal employment rates of black faculty in journalism.

[15] Marzolf, p. 95.

[16] Kotz, p. 24.

[17] Statement received from Barbara Ann Reynolds, 1 March 1980.

[18] LaBrie, p. 198.

[19] LaBrie, p. 198.

[20] Wolseley, p. 155.

[21] Phyl Garland, "Staying With the Black Press: Problems and Rewards," in *Perspectives of the Black Press* by Henry LaBrie, III, p. 177.

CHAPTER VII
THE SEVENTIES: PUBLISHING AND ELECTRONIC
VENTURES

Two current Black magazines are proudly headed by Black women. *Encore Worldwide and American News* is a current-affairs biweekly commanded by Ida E. Lewis, and *Essence* is a monthly steered by Marcia Ann Gillespie.

Encore sports the title of a Black music magazine that appeared in the Twenties, but that is where all similarity ends. Published continuously since 1971, it is the only national Black news magazine in the country. As such, it is considered an important barometer of the readers' attitudes and a similarly strong influence on their political opinions. News clips, in–depth international and national analyses, profiles of prominent newsmakers, and reviews of singular cultural events and trends, are basic ingredients in the editorial mix.

Lewis, born October 22, 1935 in Malverne, Pennsylvania, has been *Encore's* editor and publisher since its birth. By 1975, when her successful fight to lead the journal through its delicate formation period was recognized, she received the International Benih Award for her contribution to Black people throughout the world.

Ida Lewis, (right) Publisher of ENCORE magazine, with her assistant, Betty Cooper

A contemporary of Phyl Garland, Lewis finished her undergraduate communications degree in 1956 at Boston University. In the early Sixties she worked as financial editor of the *New York Age*, T. Thomas Fortune's brainchild. Later she was a staff writer for *Life* magazine in the mid-Sixties when Blacks were all but unheard of in major white magazine establishments.

In 1967, Lewis signed on with the prestigious British Broadcasting Corporation (BBC) where she was a writer broadcaster, and from 1968-71, she worked as a correspondent for *Jeune Afrique*. During this time she was approached by the organizers of a proposed service magazine for Black women. They knew of her expertise and wanted her to serve as editor-in-chief of the new publication. Lewis consented and consequently led *Essence* on a maiden voyage that overlapped with her *Age* commitment, in 1970-71.

Lewis left *Essence* and joined *Encore American and Worldwide News* in 1972, as publisher and editor-in-chief of Tanner Publications, Incorporated, the parent organization for *Encore* and two newer publications in the group: *Good Living*, a guide to health and well-being and *Eagle and Swan*, a magazine for Blacks in the armed services. Each issue of *Encore* reaches 150,000 readers.[1]

Marcia Gillespie, first hired by Lewis, has been editor–in–chief of *Essence* since Lewis' departure. Born July 10, 1944 in Rockeville Centre, New York, she reached the *Essence* offices via a four-year stint at Time-Life Books and *Life* magazine.

Gillespie earned her undergraduate degree at Lake Forest College in American Studies, and has gained a wide and devoted following with her incisive, politically-charged editorials, the regular "Getting Down" column, which is uniquely and prominently presented in the body of the magazine and not in the first pages, as is the common practice.

Meanwhile, *Essence*, "the magazine for today's Black woman" as the subtitle proclaims, has grown tremendously to its present circulation, increasing its base at least seven-fold since Gillespie's takeover. It is easily the most important single advertising medium reaching Black females between 18 and 35 years of age.[2]

The Broadcast Media

Television and radio are unquestionably powerful instruments. These fascinating purveyors of information can transmit messages instantaneously to millions of people nationally or even globally (with aid of shortwaves and satellites). No special skill is needed to receive the messages: literate and illiterate alike can turn the sets on, listen, and look. They need not be still or set aside time to peruse a paper, magazine, or book. Discerning members of the audience will refuse to accept all presentations as gospel, evaluating them with critical eyes and ears. But most will happily file the receipts, never questioning their accuracy.

The nation's nearly 8,000 commercial radio stations fill the airwaves with such sounds as rock, rhythm and blues or "soul," top-40, disco, country and western, or middle-of-the-road (MOR) music, plus public affairs, religious and all-news shows. Of these, the 1979 *Broadcasting Yearbook* lists 208 AM and FM radio stations that describe their principal formats as "rhythm and blues" or "soul," industry labels covering most styles of Black popular music. In 1970 only sixteen were Black-owned and operated.

Many of the giants in the area of Black-oriented programming are owned by Southern white interests. Promoting Black community interests is not of paramount concern, but such coverage is important in Black radio, "the only medium through which the Negro, himself, believes he can receive the happenings of the day as they happen, and he feels they should be reported."[3]

Beaming both sounds and images to viewers, television's dramatic, attention-getting potential outranks radio. If pictures say a thousand times more than any words can muster, presentation of what appears to be the "whole story" make it relatively simple for viewers to accept the images as truthful and complete. After all, they seem realistic. Nevertheless, "The feeling is that the impact of television coverage is a reflection of the power of the medium, not necessarily of the journalistic wisdom or imagination of the news organization."[4]

Whether evaluated from the news and information perspective or the entertainment armchair, both presentations are limited and ultimately deceptive. The tragedy lies in the realization that American Blacks so greatly need to be better understood by white America, whose misconceptions feed racism and self-deceit. Following the example of the Black press, Black ownerships of broadcast outlets is highly desirable, for they would benefit the race and the nation.

Given the economic disadvantage under which Blacks have historically labored, including the difficulty of securing adequate financing, it is little wonder there are so few Blackowned broadcast licenses. Recent encouragements, however, such as the Minority Broadcast Ownership Program established by the Carter Administration on January 31, 1978, have already resulted in a 65 percent increase in minority-owned stations since then.[5]

Television Imagery, Bias, and Black Women

Most noticeable of the changes network television was undergoing by 1968 was the rash of Black characters regularly appearing in its entertainment fare.

The reasons commonly given for this change are the success of Bill Cosby in "I Spy," the pressures of social change, the murder of Martin Luther King, Jr., the Kerner Commission report, which called for more Black actors on television, recognition of Negroes' buying power, and a willingness on the industry's part to further the cause of social justice as long as it is in vogue and doesn't cost.[6] So Diahann Carroll became the first Black woman to star in a television series; Leslie Uggams enjoyed a short-lived variety show; Gail Fisher appeared in "Mannix;" Nichelle Nichols became "Star Trek's" Lieutenant Uhura, and Ruby Dee went to "Peyton Place."

The trouble with all these female characterizations was that none made significant statements about what it meant to be a Black woman, and thus, they contributed to established distortions.

Sheila Smith Hobson, a writer who once worked with the "Black Journal" TV show, observed by 1970 that the news shows were ". . . hardly the result of an industry that has seen the light. . . . .Watch your TV screen closely . . . it will be empty of 'soul' shows and black–oriented shows . . .with the possible exception of Diahann Carroll's and Bill Cosby's. That type of soul sells, and besides, you can even forget they are Black."[7]

Such programming results contribute nothing to improved understanding of Black men or Black women. "Race and gender . . . stereotyping has long been a fact of American occupational life and our fiction has often reflected it. To the extent that television serves as a creator or reinforcer of beliefs about the kinds of occupations and characters that are appropriate for people, it plays a negative role in regard to minorities and women."[8]

Further, an analysis of prime time television drama conducted from 1969 through 1974 discovered that fewer minority female characters appeared than majority (white) males, majority females, or minority males.[9] Black women appeared least often on the small screen, and when they did, their roles did not offer insight or depth sufficient to alter popularly-held impressions.

Similarly, sex and race bias operate on the news side of the coin. Since the Federal Communications Commission ruled in 1969 that the employment opportunity provisions of the 1964 Civil Rights Act applied to broadcasters, some 80 percent—roughly 650 of the nation's television stations, have been subject to its provisions. Discrimination based on color, religion, or sex by stations employing twenty-five or more people is banned. Blacks and other minority women have been significantly more visible in and on television as a direct result. Even so, Hobson criticized the phenomenon thusly:

> The medium is the message. Give other black women something to make them think they've arrived . . . [It's really a] double cop-out. You get your token woman and your token Black in one foul swoop. You use that "black" woman as your front to other blacks. [10]

Indeed, many viewers erroneously believe that Black women in television have an easy time of things. But a woman producer at the Public Broadcast System (PBS) pointed out that women are still conspicuously absent from news assignment, line production, or key policy positions. [11]

Recalling the impact of television and the distortions it can create, it is understandable how viewers might conclude that all Black women, represented by news reporters, are happily enjoying the society's fruits and "have it easy." Statistics, however, reveal otherwise. The overwhelming majority of (network) correspondent appearances in 1977, for example, were made by white males. Minority men and white women were both seen about 8.9 percent of the time, and Black women, not at all, even though several are employed as correspondents. [12]

One impression this situation casts is that white males are thought more able in the role of news-gatherers and reporters, even though Vernon Stone's study of "Attitudes Toward Television Newswomen" disputes this. It reported that a correspondent's sex alone did not reduce audience acceptance or understanding of the delivery. (The racial factor was not surveyed.) That neither women nor Blacks have yet held the focal "anchor" position in prime time network television, further attests to the continuing dominance of white males in broadcast news. [13]

The opportunities for Black women to influence programming and policy provisions, in order to improve minority representation, is also limited. Mal Johnson, the Black woman director of community affairs for Cox Broadcasting, explained at the "Kerner Plus 10" conference:

> The problem today is that minorities who have been in the business for several years need to be moved up. The pipeline is clogged. . . . The indictment of broad-casters comes not in their hiring practices, so much as in their promotion, programming, and policy-making positions. [14]

Figures supporting Johnson's claims show that in a 1977 study of forty television stations across the nation, only 4.4 percent of the officials and managers were Black women, while 5.2 percent were Black men—contrasting with 64.9 percent of the white males and 21.3 percent white females and other minorities comprising the remainder.[15]

Statistics at the network headquarters level are more discouraging, especially when it is remembered that network-level decisions affect the programs aired nationally. In most cases, significantly lower percentages of minorities are employed at the higher levels than is true at local stations. Additionally, Black women were singled out as having the lowest employment rate in the category: only two percent.[16]

Despite race and sex bias, Black women in television have compiled an impressive record of contributions. Allowed to handle more and different responsibilities, they hold great promise for improving the images and broadening the range of ideas currently provided the viewing audience.

Television Pioneers

The years immediately following World War II saw white women in a variety of important television-station and studio roles. Their numbers were not large but they worked as engineers, producers, directors, writers, editors, and announcers. The "magic boxes" were selling rapidly and the audiences and stations to supply them, proliferated. But just as these expanding job opportunities snapped back to their prewar positions in the press and radio, women in television were stung when, in the mid-Fifties, they realized they would not be encouraged to share equal opportunity in station management. In general, the most they could look to was running local women's interest programs.[17]

Black women were not involved, with the possible exception of Willie Cosdena Thomas Gideon Gunn. A Seneca, South Carolina native born in 1926, she narrated two television series produced in Michigan in the 1950's on the activities of Nancy Williams, wife of a former Michigan governor. In 1976, she won the Media Woman-of-the-Year Award from the Flint chapter of the National Association of Media Women. In 1965 Gunn narrated a Negro history series sponsored by the National Association for the Advancement of Colored People. If racism prevented encouragement of Black women's talents even in radio, it most definitely accounts for their continuing neglect by small screen editors and producers.

Black women first appeared regularly on television in the mid-Sixties —before the shock waves of the ghetto rebellions hit shore, but after significant numbers of white women had gained more television exposure, experience, and respect.

It was 1960 when the three major networks (ABC, CBS, NBC)

assigned women to news teams covering the Democratic and Republican conventions. This was the first time so many women had been simultaneously involved in such important coverage.

Sexism in the news did not cease, but at least the executive powers were beginning to more fully appreciate the skills women could bring to the field. Award-winning women professionals were among the pre-Sixties trailblazers who insisted on hard-news assignments and handled them admirably. The "education" of men continued, and by the end of the decade, some two dozen women were employed as network producers, assistant producers, reporters, and correspondents.[18]

While white women were gaining experience as network professionals, the first Black women reporters were hired. Joan Murray, born November 6, 1941 in Ithaca, New York, was probably the first Black newswoman at a major television station when she joined WCBS, New York in April 1965. The Civil Rights Movement was in fullstride by then-the March on Washington, the integration of several major southern schools, and the passage of the 1964 Civil Rights Bill. And it was high time for television's powerful stream of ideas to allow for a Black presence and influence apart from protest activities.

Murray entered the field before "affirmative action" was coined, getting her start as personal secretary to Allen Funt of "Candid Camera" fame. She next tried writing scripts for an aborted "Woman on the Move" program. Later, she joined New York's WCBS-Television, as a secretary. The next year she won an audition and was soon handling human interest features and general reporting for two daily newscasts.

Murray's experience gives testimony to another Black woman journalist's advice:

> Get the basic skills at the local broadcast level. . . . Then take any entry job you can get and once inside keep after them to try you out; audition for any openings. You have to be aggressive to get the job you want. You can move up from secretary, but you do have to push.[19]

Two other Black women assumed similar posts in Philadelphia in 1966. Trudy Haynes was an "Eyewitness News" staffer for KYW-Television; she handled features and news. Edith Huggins of WCAU-Television did likewise. Huggins switched to the news side after enjoying some success as an actress in "The Doctors," a daytime show.

In 1966, Haynes was quite optimistic about her new career, remarking that, ". . .the especially pleasing thing is that careers in the industry are based on ability and talent, rather than on color and sex."[20]

Broadcasting 'Round the Globe

Where Alice Dunningan, Venice Spraggs, and Ethel Payne were print journalists in the inner circle of White House correspondents, Mal Johnson won White House credentials in 1974, becoming the first Black woman broadcaster so distinguished. She accompanied former President Richard Nixon on his historic 1972 Russian trip, following Payne's lead. Today, Johnson is director of community affairs and senior correspondent for the Cox Broadcasting Company in Washington. She was the company's first female national correspondent. As a result of her international affairs and media experience in the capitol, she was commissioned by the State Department in 1974 to help organize the first communications school in Lesotho, a small but independent country surrounded by the Republic of South Africa.

Johnson has produced documentaries in Europe, the Middle-East, and Israel, and has been a monthly guest reporter for "Overseas Mission," on WAMU-FM and WAMU-TV in Washington. She was one of the 2,000 Outstanding Women of the Year for 1970; commended participant on the 1972 Presidential trip to Austria, the Union of Soviet Socialist Republics (U.S.S.R.), Iran, and Poland; and Outstanding Female Decision-maker of the Year for 1974.

Mal Johnson of Cox Broadcasting Corporation,
reporting on Capitol Hill, Washington, D.C.

When asked what or who inspired her to achieve, Mal Johnson replied:

> There are women whom I have encountered in my lifetime, those whom I have read of, some whom I have known intimately, and still others whom I would like to meet that have set the examples for me daily. . . . To be inspired by Blackness is to be inspired by a Dr. Mary McLeod Bethune. . . . To be inspired by womaness is to be inspired by Mrs. Eleanor Roosevelt. But most of all, I am inspired by the reverent respect I have for my race and the mothers of my race.[21]

The copper-rich African nation of Zambia is a very long way from the freeways of Los Angeles, but Glenda McCoo Wina's media career has well-acquainted her with both.

While pursuing her undergraduate degree at the University of California at Los Angeles, she was employed at the *Los Angeles Tribune*, the area's major daily. In 1963, during the post-war colonial retreat that permitted the creation of dozens of independent African states, she landed a job as a newswriter and interviewer for TV Zambia, following her strong interest in African affairs, her undergraduate minor.

Wina was in Zambia until 1971, and during her stay she freelanced for the *London Times* and various African papers and periodicals.

Later that year, she joined CBS-Television, becoming host/reporter of the "Noontime" show in Los Angeles, a position she presently holds.

In 1977 Wina was an Emmy award nominee for individual achievement as "Noontime" hostess, and she was the Conference of Black Elected Officials' honoree for outstanding media service in 1973. The Los Angeles Soroptimists also named her as Outstanding Media Woman in 1972.

Network Correspondents

Black women have appeared as correspondents since the early Seventies. Those employed in this specialty are among the most recognizable women in the country. Frequently on assignment in distant spots, they beam their on-camera reports to anchor desks in New York City.

Although a relatively recent addition to the network ranks, Norma Quarles has the greatest broadcasting background. Entering the field in Cleveland, Ohio, she worked in a jazz station that featured an all–female "D.J." contingent. Next, she moved to New York and joined the NBC flagship station, WNBC.

Quarles remembered that there was only about one woman per station on the air, and none behind the scenes except secretaries to executives, when she joined WNBC in the early Seventies.[22] Now, she reports there are at least eight or nine women on staff, including a camerawoman, sound woman, electrician, and film editor. Executives are still rare, but she believed the lower-level changes would naturally evolve with promotions.

Norma Quarles - NBC Network Correspondent
(photo courtesy of Ebony Magazine)

Today, Quarles is an NBC network correspondent covering the Midwest.

Lee Thornton, Carole Simpson, and Renee Poussaint are correspondents for preeminent news organizations.

Thornton has been a full-time Columbia Broadcasting System Washington, D.C. correspondent since 1976. She joined the network in 1974 after working two years in the news operation of a midwest station. She holds a doctorate degree in mass communications and has taught speech classes.

She considers herself fortunate to have worked as a reporter-assignment editor in her first network position. Two days a week she worked on the assignment desk, while the rest of her week was spent on general assignment reporting. On the desk, she was able to suggest stories—a function usually the exclusive domain of editors.

One idea she happily remembers concerned a successful voluntary busing program in Boston, which finally aired as a feature. The Black teenager chosen as narrator spoke of the new scenery he saw on his daily trip, "trees and apples growing." Thornton framed her story with the youth's images. "When I go home at night I don't think about the dirty streets and the drug addicts down the street," he closed.

Thornton believed this brand of journalism ". . . tells the world what kind of lives people are living and how they meet their challenges. And these stories are remembered. This is a touch that many women have. . .good hard news judgement plus human interest. A terrific com-bination."[23]

Carole Simpson joined the National Broadcasting Company as a Washington, D.C. correspondent in 1975. Previously, she was a correspondent for WMAQ-Television (Chicago), for five years, and had worked as a reporter in a variety of settings. One-time stringer for the Voice of America and editor for the information bureau at Tuskegee Institute, the Chicago native, born December 7, 1940, has worked for three radio stations, including Chicago's WBBM-AM.

Jayne Kennedy, a feature sports commentator for the Columbia Broadcasting System who previously appeared in feature films, now enlivens late-afternoon play-by-play details with commentary for the National Football League broadcasts.

Becoming a network correspondent is normally the greatest aspiration of television newscasters, usually reached via entry positions in smaller markets and promotions to stations in the largest cities.

Unlike many others, Carol Ann Jenkins worked up to the top, but then chose to work in a local assignment. Since 1973 she has held a variety of broadcasting assignments at WNBC-TV, including anchoring the evening news.

Jenkins, a Montgomery, Alabama native born November 30, 1944, moderated the "Straight Talk" program on WOR-TV, New York for several years. Between 1970 and 1972, she co-anchored and reported news for the station. At ABC in 1972 and 1973, she appeared on the "Reasoner/Smith Report."

Training Program Alumnae

After working for the Ford Foundation as a representative to the networks and undergoing a training program at the San Francisco

Examiner, Gail Christian joined KQET-TV in that city. Soon, she decided that a career in commercial television was what she really wanted, so she applied to the Summer Program in Broadcast Journalism for Minority Groups conducted at the prestigious Columbia University Graduate School of Journalism, probably the largest program of its type. After completing the ten-week hands-on course in 1970, she began a reporting job for KCET-Television in Los Angeles and was soon appointed news director there, the first Black to hold the position. Most recently Christian has been a National Broadcasting Company correspondent, specializing in urban affairs.

The American Broadcasting Company (ABC) also sponsored a training program that began in 1968, and was a direct result of the agreement that networks would participate in training minorities for various jobs in news divisions. Fronza Wood graduated from their third class and started as a network researcher soon thereafter. Women have traditionally been assigned researcher posts, and Wood was determined to move up to a more challenging and powerful job, or move out. After considerable lobbying in her behalf, she was named associate producer for the religious documentary program "Directions" in 1971.

The future seemed bright for Columbia Broadcasting System correspondent Michele Clark, before she died in an airplane crash in 1972, just two years after her graduation from the Columbia University summer training program.

The program was quickly renamed the Michele Clark Fellowship Program for Minority Journalists. Before its demise after the summer of 1974, 227 minority men and women had been trained for print and electronic media jobs, giving the program the distinction of having produced nearly twenty percent of the total minority journalists employed nationally in 1974.[24]

The Columbia Broadcasting System television network has further distinguished itself with the employment of Barbara Jean Flack and Marquita Pool, both associate producers.

Pool works with the "CBS Evening News" show. Commonly known as the "Walter Cronkite Show," for years it has probably been the most popular national newscast.

Flack handles documentaries for "Magazine," a "60 Minutes"-type program airing Thursday mornings. It often deals with such issues as unnecessary hysterectomies, rape, and divorce, and it is aimed at the large number of female viewers tuning in at that time of day. Despite its boast of having all female associate producers, "Magazine" is still headed by a male executive producer.

With Syndicates

Two other Black women broadcasters whose efforts have made a national impact are Alice Demery Travis and Darlene Hayes. Both work with independently-produced syndicated shows.

Beginning in late 1977, Travis hosted "For You, Black Woman," a half-hour discussion-format series. Designed to present a forum for the instruction of viewers, it covered important social topics such as child abuse, teenage sex, alcoholism, education of the children, and the relationships of Black mothers to their sons.

Hayes, a Topeka, Kansas native, became an associate producer on the "Phil Donahue Show" in 1975. She started there in 1969 as a clerktypist, when the production was located in Dayton, Ohio, and was rewarded with the promotion when the show moved to Chicago. Known today simply as "Donahue," the audience-participation, talk show is the "hottest on television" and outranks the "Today," "Merv Griffin," "Tonight," and "Dinah Shore" gabfests by reaching an audience in some six million homes daily.[25]

Darlene Hayes, Associate Producer
of the "Donahue Show," with Phil Donahue

Public Broadcasting

Since the Civil Rights Movement hit full stride, only four Black–oriented presentations have made a dent in the public broadcasting shield. "Black Journal," a controversial show first aired in the late Sixties, featured a magazine format and interviews with nationally-known Black spokespersons. Conducted by Tony Brown, it aired under the auspices of the Public Broadcasting System (PBS).

"Soul!," another nationally-aired program, was primarily an entertainment vehicle showcasing the best in Black performing artists. Produced by Ellis Hazlip, it folded when it failed to secure adequate funding for the 1974-1975 season. "Black Journal" and "Soul!" represented the first generation of Black-oriented Public Broadcasting Service fare.

"Tony Brown's Journal," an incarnation of the original show, has been independently-produced and sponsored by Pepsi-Cola in national, commercial syndication since 1977. It is the first Black show to be so developed. It was removed from PBS syndication after increasingly fewer member stations agreed to carry it.

"Black Perspectives of the News" enjoyed acceptance by ninety percent of the 139 PBS stations in 1974, but later only 77 of 276 stations carried it.[26] Today, their views/interviews program, featuring Black journalists who give their analyses of various world and national developments, is the only Black-oriented program offered by the Public Broadcasting System.

In the PBS network, station managers decide what will air, and all but one are white males at the national level. Only six minorities of 583 are station managers in local markets.[27]

Despite the scarcity of Blacks and women in PBS programming operations two Black women served with distinction during their tenure at "Black Journal."

Hazel V. Bright was the managing editor at one point, and Peggy Pinn was an associate producer in the program's heydays—prior to 1974.

Pinn took her involvement and knowledge of production and broadcasting a step further when she founded the National Education Television (NET) training school, which prepared Blacks in a variety of technical skills essential to the production of television shows. Tired of being asked to recommend "qualified" Black technicians for production workcrews, particularly after the assassination of Dr. Martin Luther King, Jr. and the release of the Kerner Commission

Report, she committed herself to "fill the industry with beautiful, talented, creative, and knowledgeable brothers and sisters so that I would never again have to hear those words, 'we would hire some but we can't find any who are qualified'."[28]

By 1972, the school offered year-round classes and could proudly point to some forty alumni, the vanguard of Black behind-the-scenes television workers. At that time it was financed by nearly $125,000 from the Corporation for Public Broadcasting and the New York State Labor Department—a far cry from the $5,000 grant Pinn started the program with in 1969.

Pinn began her television career as a secretary at American Broadcasting Company and Columbia Broadcasting System networks, where in seven years she learned as much as she possibly could about the industry's filmmaking requirements. She was a "Black Journal" staffer for three years.

Local Scenes: Public
Affairs and News

Findings of the 1977 update of the United States Commission on Civil Rights report on the status of women and minorities in the broadcast industry found that local stations reflect a higher percentage of women in all job classifications than do network headquarters. A turn of the dial during the local news hour in most major cities, for example, will show at least one Black, often a woman, reporting.[29] Whether network affiliated or not, local stations enjoy a great degree of autonomy and are able to provide their audiences with a unique and appealing local identity.

Black women have figured in creating this image in recent years, from hosting public affairs shows, producing documentaries of special interest to their communities, or reporting news for daily round-ups.

Xernona Clayton [Brady] was the first Black woman to host a television show in the South for WAGA-Television in Atlanta. Since 1969 she has deftly mixed entertainment with guests who discuss topics of interest to the Black community.

Born August 30, 1930 in Muskogee, Oklahoma, Clayton is also a columnist for the *Atlanta Voice* and organizer and past president of the Atlanta chapter of the National Association of Media Women. Her active career has included teaching in the Chicago and Los Angeles public schools, and photographic and fashion modeling.

A vibrant, engaging personality, Clayton won the 1969, 1970, and 1971 Georgia Associated Press Awards for Superior Television

Programming. She was the 1973 Founder's Cup winner of the National Association of Media Women, and former Georgia Governor Jimmy Carter appointed her to the State Motion Picture and Television Commission, where she served from 1972-76. In 1977 she was elected president of the National Association of Media Women.

Quida Hogan Lindsey is a *Chicago Sun-Times* columnist and hostess of the popular local "Soul Searching" television show, which investigates the relationship of Black culture to the media. Lindsey is also a noted lecturer and recognized expert in promoting human relations studies, appearing at race relations/human relations workshops in high schools and colleges throughout the country. She is author of such books as *If You Are Going to Teach Black Children* and *Prejudice and the Young Child*.

In an age characterized by retreats from sincere and courageous remedies to racial discrimination, this media woman's efforts to promote mankind's ability to solve its greatest social problems has been duly recognized: in 1974 she received the Chicago Media Women's Certificate of Merit, and the Female Decision Maker in Communications award of the National Association of Media Women.

Like Carol Jenkins, Melba Toliver is a popular New York broadcast journalist who tasted the network correspondent fare and then decided to work in a local station.

Toliver, a Rome, Georgia native, earned a nursing degree in New York. Soon thereafter, she took a job as a secretary in the broadcast industry. Her correspondent experience followed. In a local New York assignment, she once co-hosted "Like It Is," an award-winning Black–oriented public affairs show, with producer Gil Noble. Toliver has been a reporter on WABC-TV's "Eyewitness News" and co–anchor for the Sunday evening news report.

Roberta Byrd Barr, a Wilberforce University graduate who became Seattle, Washington's first woman high school principal, is also a fine speaker whose talents are often in demand. The inauguration of her "Face-to-Face" public affairs show in 1965 seemed a satisfying compromise to her admirers. In twelve years on the air, Barr has also hosted "Let's Imagine," another talk show. She received the Matrix Award from Women in Communications in 1972.

Although not trained as a teacher, Rebecca Buard won the admiration and respect of a statewide teaching organization for her 1978 coverage of public education in Florida. The recipient of the Florida Teaching Profession of the National Education Association (FTP-NEA) Newsmaker Award, she is currently an associate producer and reporter/editor for Florida Public Broadcasting Community Television, Incorporated in Tallahassee.

Rebecca Buard, television editor and reporter
at WTVT in Tampa, Florida

Buard was born October 25, 1953 in Los Angeles, California and was news director, newscaster, and public affairs coordinator for WYLD-AM and FM in New Orleans in late 1977. Previously, she produced, wrote, and hosted the "Dimensions" TV magazine show for WVUE-TV in New Orleans, and won the 1976 New Orleans Press Club Award and United Teachers of New Orleans Media awards for her efforts.

While there are no nationally broadcast anchor women for news programs, Beverly Payne is one of the few local anchors. Seen on "TV 2 News" in Detroit, Payne co-hosted "Focus" in 1973, and appeared on "Toyko Eleven: PM" where she taught English on Japanese television.

Carol Davis Randolph and Sue Booker both have received national recognition for their broadcast production work.

Randolph frankly told participants in a media workshop that she was hired by a Washington, D.C. television station in the early Seventies when pressure was turned high to employ Blacks and females. Since 1971 the St. Louis, Missouri native has appeared as co-host of the popular "Harambee" show, where she currently serves as executive producer. What may have begun as tokenism, she seized as a ring of opportunity, and by 1976 Randolph had won the George Foster Peabody Award for achievement in public service programming.

Other Randolph credits include co-hosting the "Everywoman" show from May 1974 through June 1976, and co-hosting the ninety-minute morning show, "Morning Break," from January 1975 through May 1977.

Born in Jersey City, New Jersey on March 25, 1946, Sue Booker tucked her master's degree from Columbia University's Graduate School of Journalism under her arm and headed for Los Angeles. Ever since, she has been building an impressive broadcast career as a writer, producer, and director.

The first Black woman to join the Directors Guild of America, she won an Emmy Award as producer of "As Adam Early in the Morning," a dramatic special originally prepared for KNBC-TV in 1972. (The Emmy is awarded by the Academy of Television Arts and Sciences for outstanding achievements broadcast to fifty percent or more of the national nighttime audience.) Booker also received an Emmy citation as a contributing producer to the "L.A. Collective," which first appeared on KCET-TV.

Her other broadcast accomplishments include writing, producing, and directing "Compton: A Restless Dream," a documentary, and scripting a history series for KNBC-TV in 1974; and producing and directing "The Black Frontier" historic film series in 1969 for PBS in Lincoln, Nebraska.

A true multi-media creator, Booker has written articles for the *Los Angeles Times* and *Los Angeles Sentinel.* Co-author of two books, she worked as an associate professor in the Department of Radio and Television, California State University at Long Beach in 1973.

The Atlanta International Film Festival has awarded Booker the Gold Medal and Grand Jury Award for her work as co-producer of "Soledad," (KCET-TV). Her production of "Cleophus Adair: His Life, His World," received the "Best Documentary" stamp from the Associated Press.

Station autonomy prevails on the local level, and it is unusual to find big city stations that do not have at least one Black-oriented program. Typically, talk shows, but sometimes designed as news or documentary presentations, they invariably battle for recognition while pitted against the worst time spots and hampered by limited budgets.[30]

Judy Gambrell works for the now-progressive National Broadcasting Company affiliate in Jackson, Mississippi, WLBT-TV. She is the first Black woman in the state ever to win an award for a documentary presentation.

WLBT first won national attention in 1969 when its license was revoked. This action followed a successful renewal challenge mounted by local citizens and influential supporters long active in human rights and communications affairs. In addition to its lopsided employment policies, WLBT was noted for such travesties as dropping segments of nationally-aired shows that starred Blacks, or substituting "Sorry, Cable Trouble" signs during network interviews with leading civil rights spokespersons: this in a community in the deep South with a large Black population, during the white heat generated by the civil rights movement.[31]

Peggy A. Cooper, born April 7, 1947 in Mobile, Alabama, won the 1976 George Foster Peabody Award for "excellence in public affairs production," and was a finalist in the 1977 National Emmy Award selections. She has received the John D. Rockfeller II International Youth Award, and has also been named "Washingtonian of the Year."

Although a lawyer with multiple involvements in the arts, including her contribution as developer—and founder—of the (Duke) Ellington High School of Fine and Performing Arts in Washington, she garnered invaluable broadcast knowledge during a stint as special assistant to the president of the Post-Newsweek Stations, Incorporated, a communications conglomerate that includes the *Washington Post* and *Newsweek* publishing giants and three television stations.

Black Women in Radio

By World War II, network radio news was an American institution whose audiences had been weaned on presidential "fireside chats," reports from war-beclouded Europe, and presidential conventions and campaign updates. Since it was still a youthful medium, its executives undertook abundant market research to get hints on likely programming successes. One result was the proliferation of women's programming during mornings and afternoons. Features on fashion, food, beauty, health, babies, housekeeping, culture, and education aired, and women ran them.[32]

This development encouraged white women to enter the field, whereas previously, they had been dissuaded. Since radio sets did not pleasantly reproduce feminine voices then, masculine timbre-generally more resonant—was much preferred. With the improvement of technology, this excuse for bias dissolved and the participation rate of women improved.

Black women, in contrast, did not participate in radio in appreciable numbers until the late-Sixties and Seventies. Otherwise, they appeared as performers, but in stereotyped roles, at that.

Alice Dunbar Nelson, a distinguished writer once married to poet Paul Lawrence Dunbar, "premiered" at KADN-AM in Wilmington, Delaware in 1931. Possibly she read from her literary work.

Artie Belle McGinty enjoyed a vaudeville career, appearing with Fred Waring's Pennsylvanians, C.W. Parks' Smart Set, and the International Sweethearts of Rhythm in Washington, D.C. She had also played summer stock in Ogonquit, Maine, a favorite resort of the rich.

Once, after auditioning for the part of Madame Queen in the renown "Amos 'n Andy" show, McGinty "was found to be too good," the October 18, 1941 edition of the *Amsterdam News* reported. The part went to Fanny May Baldridge, a white woman with whom the white actors cast in the title roles felt comfortable.

About the time McGinty was making her mark in radio, Lillian Randolph also aired. Winning the part of Mammy on the Al Jolson Show in 1936, she later appeared with Edward G. Robinson in "Big Town." "Lulu and Leander," a National Broadcasting Company network show reportedly built around her talents, aired for over two and a half years.

Black women did not enter the announcing field until well after the structure of radio had changed. As television came of age during the late Forties and early Fifties, radio was forced to abandon many of its hallowed attractions such as situation comedies and drama and live music.

Combining the appeal of radio and film, television could handle these presentations far more effectively.

Thus, radio producers turned increasingly to music as the entertainment coincident with the rise of the hot new commodity "rock and roll" and the increased popularity of recorded music generally.

This period also increased the need for announcers who would spin records, handle station identifications, and perhaps, deliver newscasts. Black dee jays, or D.J.'s, as announcers were soon called, first appeared on white-owned rhythm and blues stations located mainly in the South.[33]

The continuing migration of southern Blacks to northern metropolises during the war years presented broadcasters with an expanded market of Black wage-earners, so white stations began devoting a portion of their air time to rhythm-and-blues music. This development allowed the entry of professional Black announcers, an all-male fraternity—at least until the mid-Fifties.

Gretchen Flippin Jackson, born November 13, 1918 in New Rochelle, New York, became the first Black female in New England—and perhaps the country—to broadcast a sustained radio program, "The Gretchen Jackson Show." It aired on WVOM (later WBMS-AM) until 1964.

In adition to her broadcast credits, Jackson is a columnist of wide experience, contributing to the *Boston Chronicle, Pittsburgh Courier*, Johnson Publications, and *Fame* magazine of Bermuda.

She was named Foremost Woman in Communications in 1970.

The next announcer of record, Merri Dee of Chicago, did not air until 1966, when she hosted a music/interview program, announced news, and worked as a woman's editor.

After 1972, Dee's experiences included a stint as talk-show hostess at WSNS-TV. She soon returned to the audio world, however, and hosted WSDM-FM's "Merri Dee Show." Born in October 1936, Dee has been an announcer, editorial voice, and women's editor for WGN television and WGN-AM in Chicago. Widely known as "the voice of WGN," Dee won the Chicago Chapter of the National Association of Media Women's Pioneer Award in 1975 for her broadcasting contributions.

Other announcers who pioneered in the Sixties were Bea Moten, a Selma, Alabama native who claims the distinction of being the first Black radio announcer at the United Nations when she began interviewing African ambassadors in 1962, and Loretta Craft of Chicago, who became a dee jay with WSID-AM, Baltimore in 1968.

Moten eventually left radio for television, and currently moderates "African Profiles," a weekly show in Indianapolis. Craft has worked for a number of radio stations, but keeps her pen in motion as a feature writer for the *Chicago Daily Defender* and other area papers. Before signing on as announcer with WSID, she attended an electronics school in preparation for a radio career. She received the Outstanding Lady Disc Jockey of the Year citation in 1971 from a local group, and the Television and Radio Personalities Award from the Staple Singers in 1970 and 1972.

That Black women remained largely neglected resources in radio well into the Seventies is seen no more clearly than in New York, one of the largest and most volatile radio markets. It was 1971 when Vy Higgensen joined WBLS-FM, whose playlist is one of the strongest and most progressive Black-oriented presentations in the country deftly mixing top 40, rhythm and blues, jazz, disco, and even "easy listening" music. Until 1974 she was the only woman announcer on a staff headed by Frankie "Hollywood" Crocker, and her distinctive, honey–dipped voice attracted a wide following. Higgensen was the first Black woman to announce a prime time radio show in the city, and proved to be a major factor in raising the station's position to number one in the ratings.

Higgensen left to join WRVR-FM, a jazz station, where she hosted the "Saturday Night Special" show in 1975. During that time she also co–hosted "Positively Black," the local NBC affiliate's public affairs show; worked as an *Essence* contributing editor; and produced and announced the nationally–broadcast Army ROTC "Soul Line" program.

In the midst of all her other activities, Higgensen founded *Unique New York*, a guide to local Black–oriented entertainment that included fashion and grooming tips and other practical advice. It folded in 1978.

Glamour magazine recognized Higgensen in 1977 as one of the "Ten Most Outstanding Women in America." She continues to lecture on new careers for women, business development, and the art and power of successful mass communications.

Apart from finding the female voice inappropriate for "serious" speaking, some broadcast news directors have held fast to other prejudices. Women supposedly could not handle assignments requiring transport of heavy equipment, nor could they separate personal and emotional problems from the performance of their jobs. With slight variation, this same litany of inadequacies rolls off whenever women are denied equal employment opportunity. At the network level, Black women simply did not announce news, records, weather. Only a handful of white women were doing so, even though during World War II as many as 20 to 35 percent of all jobs in the industry were held by women.[34]

In 1972 only eight percent of the entire national radio staff was female—up from 4.7 percent in 1965[35]—although a government survey pointed out that radio stations were much more numerous than television facilities by then, and should have offered many more entry-level positions. These spots ideally, could have been filled by women, but that idea has not panned out. In 1971 there were nearly 8,000 AM and FM radio stations and the employment patterns had not substantially changed.

Not until 1976 did Black women break into "establishment" network radio news. Jane Tillman Irving won a newscaster spot with WCBS-FM (New York), the flagship station of the Columbia Broadcasting System. Twice daily on weekdays, she delivers a two-minute series devoted to urban and minority affairs. Her half-hour report produced by Fred Mattingly, airs on Saturday evenings.

Irving's work focuses on situations of particular interest to the burgeoning minority population typical in many urban locales. Citizen advocates for more responsive media had often attacked the myopic programming concerns of white media on numerous fronts by 1976. One CBS broadcast group president even complained that paid executives were ". . . putting . . . decision-making power affecting the interests of the community as a whole into the hands of a small minority. . . ."[36] Despite (or because of) the trouble such vocal and persistent groups may have caused this executive, observers within the industry have admitted that "the citizen advocates have heightened [the decision-makers'] awareness of the medium's power to do psychic harm by consistently airing only one view of an issue, if any." This is exactly the sort of enlarged perspective Irving's work has provided. Another national newscaster, Audrey June Taylor, reporter for the National Black Network in the mid-Seventies, became a familiar name to many. NBN is the nation's only Black-owned broadcast web, and has 82 affiliates in 23 states and the District of Columbia.

Managers

The institutional bias against women in broadcast news positions is well-documented, as is their scarcity in management ranks. As late as 1976 only five percent of the print or broadcast media's policymakers were women.[37] At least three Black women hold commanding positions at Black stations. Dorothy Brunson was until recently general manager at New York's WLIB-AM, and WBLS-FM, both primary components to the blossoming Inner Cities Broadcasting group. She was the premier representative to the board of directors for the stations, and their top decision-maker in the day-to-day station business.

Brunson has been in the business for over twenty years and is a noted radio authority. She founded *Airwaves* magazine, a monthly reporting news of interest to minorities in the radio, television, and recording industries, and provides such news as listings of radio frequencies that are for sale.

Joyce L. James is the Station Manager for WWWS-FM in Saginaw, Michigan, and her role parallels Brunson's. She was promoted to the spot after successfully filling the public affairs directorship.

Bernadine C. Washington is the vice-president of Black-oriented but white-owned WVON-AM in Chicago, one of that city's powerhouse stations. In 1973, she was the Chicago Chapter of the National Association of Media Women's Radio Woman of the Year.

Across the state line, Lillian Jones is the national sales director at WLTH-AM in Gary, Indiana and responsible for arranging air time for advertisers' products and services—and bringing in the revenue.

Radio's Black women include a station president and owner among their number. Mary P. ("Ma") Bell, a Nashville, Tennessee native, heads the Bell Broadcasting Company of Detroit. Comprised of WCHB-AM, WJZZ-FM, and Bell Outdoor Advertisements, it was founded by Bell's husband and a partner in 1956. She reluctantly assumed command of the closed corporation upon his death in 1974. "I didn't really want to assume the responsibility. . .but I did it because I knew what my husband wanted to accomplish. I think he'd be pleased to see how far we've come now."[38]

Mary Bell was the 1974 Detroit Chapter of the National Association of Media women's Communications Award winner.

Black women professionals and management employees are still rare in a medium that commands 93 percent of the Black audience,[39] but recent developments are encouraging.

The trend toward increased Black ownership of radio stations signaled by a growing interest in controlling powerful mediums for their own benefit, plus government incentives provided by the Minority Broadcast Ownership Program, promises new opportunities for the employment and promotion of Black women. The half-dozen or so Black-owned stations noted in 1969 grew to thirty by 1973, including publishing magnate John H. Johnson's purchase of WGRT-AM (now WJPC-AM) for $1.8 million, and the Inner City Broadcasting acquisition of WLIB-AM.[40]

Today there also exists a bargaining tool to encourage a greater commitment to affirmative action and equal opportunity guidelines among the white stations comprising roughly the largest ten percent of the nation's radio broadcasters.[41] The general public was granted both the right and duty to challenge license renewals for stations whose policies and programing were not serving "the public interest, conscience, and necessity." No longer would the arena be reserved strictly for fellow broadcasters. Fully 200 challenges to radio and television licenses were filed between 1969 and 1972, and 26 of these were withdrawn after the station owners offered new minority training programs, employment opportunities, or more relevant and informative programing.[42]

Other Black Women of Note In Publishing

One of the youngest publishers in the United States, Lenora Carter, of Houston, Texas, is the prime motivating force behind *Forward Times*, one of the largest Black newspapers in the South. Prior to becoming publishers, Carter was the newspaper's business manager and advertising director. Carter's astute business skills have enabled the paper to thrive and prosper. She has continued an editorial policy of making *Forward Times* the voice of the Black community and the inspiration of 400,000 Houston Blacks who, according to Carter, "need to know those things that are happening that directly affect their lives.[43]

The Robert S. Abbott Publishing Company is the publisher of more than ten newspapers throughout the country, including the *Chicago Defender, Michigan Chronicle, Tri-State Defender*, and the *Pittsburgh Courier*. Myrtle E. Sengstacke, executive vice-president of the Board of Directors, has been associated with this publishing business for more than thirty years.

In 1975, the National Baptist Convention, USA, Inc., with a constituency of 6,300,000 members, elected the first lay person and the first woman to the position of executive director of its Sunday School Publishing Board. The person elected was Cecelia Adkins of Nashville, Tennessee. In her job she directs the multitude of publishing efforts performed by the board to keep the people of the National Baptist Convention informed and vocal within their religious communities.

While the road to her executive position has not always been easy or without discrimination, Adkins' career with the publishing board is marked by several firsts.

She says, "Every job I have ever had I was the first woman to have landed it. When I was made chief accountant, I was the first woman in that position. I was the first woman to be fiscal manager. I was the first woman to be executive director. I am the only woman in the world to hold this position in a religious publishing house, and I am convinced that because I never took advantage of the fact that I was a woman for special favors, accounts for my success. If it was necessary to work all night, I did. This is the kind of thinking and sacrificing you have to do."[44]

Jacqueline Pinckney is manager of publications in the urban and public affairs operation of General Electric's Aerospace Corporation in Valley Forge, Pennsylvania. She feels that a Black woman in business has two handicaps, her race and her sex. "Black women have to prove constantly to others that they are intelligent, competent, and not afraid of hard work," she says. "And they also have to cope with anti–feminists." She sees only one way to solve such problems and that is to do the job as effectively and efficiently as possible, since results are what count.[45]

The Johnson Publishing Company of Chicago has a number of Black females who serve in top editorial positions in the magazine industry.

Gertrude Johnson Williams, former vice-president of Johnson's, was the mother of John H. Johnson, the firm's founder. Born in 1891 in Lake Village, Arkansas, she and her son went to Chicago in 1933 and found business opportunities there that enticed them to make Chicago their home.

Gertrude Johnson Williams,
Vice-President of Johnson Publishing Company
(photo courtesy EBONY Magazine)

June Acie Rhinehart serves as assistant to the publisher of *Jet, Ebony, Black Stars, Black World,* and *Ebony, Jr.* magazines. Her work involves administration of departments—including editorial, advertising, personnel, and financial.

Ariel Perry Strong is managing editor of *Black Stars,* a Johnson publication. Originally from Social Circle, Georgia, Strong became the first woman to head *Tan* magazine as managing editor in 1963.

Kathleen F. Banks is a publicist with the National Broadcasting Company television in Burbank, California. She handled publicity for the "Flip Wilson Show" and "The Dinah Shore Show." As a journalist, she has worked as a newswriter and feature writer for several network news programs and the *Los Angeles Times.*

Candance Caruthers, a former researcher and associate producer at New York's WNET-television in New York; Caruthers is now editorial director for WABC-television station.[46]

NOTES

[1] *1979 Ayer Directory of Publications* (Philadelphia: Ayer Publishing Company), p. 1031.

[2] *1979 Ayer Directory* lists a 600,461 circulation, second only to *Ebony* in black-owned (monthly) periodicals. See p. 600.

[3] Roland E. Wolseley, *The Black Press, U.S.A.* (Ames, Iowa: Iowa State University Press, 1971), p. 283.

[4] William B. Monroe, Jr., "Television: The Chosen Instrument of the Revolution," *Race and the News Media*, ed. Paul L. Fisher and Ralph J.L. Lowenstein (New York: Praeger, 1967), p. 96.

[5] The Washington, D.C. Office of Louis Martin, *Minority Supplement/Fact Sheet 107*, October 1979, p. 1.

[6] Richard Lemon, "Black is the Color of TV's Newest Stars," *Saturday Evening Post*, 30 November 1969, p. 42.

[7] Shelia Smith Hobson, "Women and Television," *Sisterhood is Powerful*, Robin Morgan, ed. (New York: Random House, 1970), pp. 73-74.

[8] United States Commission on Civil Rights, *Window Dressing on the Set: An Update*, January 1979, p. 17.

[9] United States Commission on Civil Rights, p. 7.

[10] Lawrence S. Fanning, "The Media: Observer and Participant," *Race and the News Media*, p. 108.

[11] Hobson, p. 74.

[12] The sample of appearances analyzed was a composite week of news broadcasts randomly selected between March 1974 and February 1975. See United States Commission of Civil Rights, *Update*, pp. 27-28.

[13] Ed Bradley of CBS has appeared in the anchor spot, but not in prime time (weekday evening) broadcasts. Max Robinson, an ABC national newscaster, appears during prime time, but shares the spotlight with two newsmen who report from different "desks." Charlayne Hunter-Gault, when substituting for either of the McNeil-Lehrer news team principal, comes the closest of any Black woman to anchoring a prime-time news show.

[14] United States Commission of Civil Rights, *Update*, p. 34.

[15] United States Commission on Civil Rights, *Update*, p. 35.

[16] United States Commission on Civil Rights, *Update* p. 42.

[17] Marion T. Marzolf, *Up From the Footnote: A History of Women Journalists* (New York: Communications Arts/Hastings House, 1977), p. 157.

[18] Marzolf, p. 164.

[19] Marzolf, p. 193.

[20] "TV News Hens," *Ebony*, October 1966, p. 45.

[21] Letter received from Ms. Mal Johnson, March 13, 1980.

[22] Marzolf, p. 193.

[23] Al DeLeon, "Showdown on Morningside Heights," *Black Enterprise*, September 1974, p. 33.

[24] DeLeon, p. 19.

[25] H.F. Waters, et al., "Talk of Television," *Newsweek*, 29 October 1979.

[26] E. Holsendolph, et al., "Shame of Public Television; Report of the Task Force on Minorities in Public Broadcasting," *Black Enterprise*, February 1979, p. 37.

[27] Holsendolph, et al., p. 37.

[28] "Mrs. Mastermind of TV's Black Tech School," *Ebony*, May 1972, p. 103.

[29] Marzolf, p. 176. Costello also reports that by 1972 alone, some 34 Black women were employed as newscasters, up from 3 in 1968 (p. 630).

[30] Jacob Wortham, "In With the Big Boys," *Black Enterprise*, September 1974, p. 23.

[31] C. Johnson, "WLBT—A New Look in TV," *Vue South,* May/June 1979, p. 31.

[32] Marzolf, p. 125.

[33] Steve Chapple and Reebee Garofalo, *Rock'n Roll is Here to Pay: The History and Politics of the Music Industry* (Chicago: Nelson-Hall, 1977), pp. 54-55.

[34] Marzolf, p. 141.

[35] Marzolf, p. 183.

[36] "Television," Update, *Newsweek,* 25 June 1976, p. 79.

[37] *Media Guidelines Proposed by the National Committee on the Observance of International Women's Year* (Washington, D.C.: Department of State, July 1976), L-1.

[38] "Minorities Gain in Broadcasting," *Business Week*, 10 March 1973, p. 168.

[39] *Black Enterprise,* July 1978, p. 22.

[40] Wolseley, p. 284.

[41] The 1964 Civil Rights Act bans discrimination on the basis of color, sex, and religion, by operations of twenty-five or more people. Since 1968, this rule has been applied to the broadcast industry. "FCC, WBLT, and Negroes," *Nation,* 5 August 1968.

[42] "Minorities Gain in Broadcasting," p. 168.

[43] Garland A. Smith, ed., *Black Texans of Distinction* (Austin: Garland Smith Associates, 1979), p. 16.

[44] "Cecelia Nabrit Adkins, '43," *Fisk Profile,* Fisk University, Nashville, Tennessee, 1976.

[45] John S. Morgan and Richard L. Van Dyke, *White-Collar Blacks, A Breakthrough?* (New York: American Management Association, 1970), p. 122.

[46] *Black Enterprise,* September 1976, p. 14.

BLACK WOMEN IN MEDIA: AN OVERVIEW

Black women in the press, in radio, and in television have been discussed in this book on Media. Their contributions have been not without struggle, but even so, they now stand among others of American history as models. In this book, therefore, media embraces the contributions of these women in the areas of newspapers, journals, magazines, radio and television.

Since the newspaper is the oldest of these areas of mass communications, its history is much more revealing of the trials, tribulations, and successes of Black women in the press. The Black press began March 16, 1827, with the publishing of *Freedom's Journal*, and by 1945, there were 155 Black newspapers in the United States. Also in 1945, there were 100 Black periodicals, covering general, religious, and educational fields of reporting. By 1977, more than 200 Black newspapers with an annual combined circulation of over two million copies existed.

The function of the Black press, since its beginning, is the promotion of the welfare of Black people. To accomplish this, the press has a responsibility to objectively report the news, to fight opression, to give voice to community events, and to record the historical progress and contributions of Black people to the society in which they live and work.

Black women entered journalism during post-Reconstruction and they continue to be positive forces in all aspects of print media. As early as 1865, notes of the affairs of Black women, including social, cultural, religious, and educational items, were reported in the Black press.

In the October 19, 1891 edition of *The New York Age*, the following item was listed under "Personal":

> Mrs. John L. Waller of Kansas, the courageous and talented wife of Honorable John L. Waller, the United States Counsel at Tamatave, Madagascar, and her little daughter, reached New York from Bellefontaine, Ohio, Friday afternoon of last week, and were met by the editor of *The Age* who took them to Mrs. Hill's in West 40th Street where they were handsomely cared for. On Friday evening the two travelers went aboard the Cunard Steamship "Eutria" (sic), which sailed early Saturday morning for Liverpool, en route for East Africa. . . .

The above item illustrates how the Black press responded to social news, including those about Black women.

News about births, marriages, birthdays, and deaths were also extensively reported in the Black press. Often the writers were women. The March 17, 1888 edition of *The New York Age*, in reporting on such events, carried headings such as "Buffalo Brevities," "Albany Annals,"

"Springfield Sprays," "Jersey City Items," "Poughkeepsie Pointers," "New Bedford News," "Doings Down In Delaware," and "New London Notes."

A December 5, 1891 item in *The Age* is a clear example of the importance of reporting historical news in the Black press:

> "Talk Of The Week" - Mrs. Eunice Davis, the only surviving member of the Women's Anti-Slavery Board of Boston, recently celebrated her 91st birthday at Dedham, Massachusetts.

Again, noted here is significant news about a Black woman and about Black history.

In 1895 and 1896, Margaret Black wrote a weekly column entitled "Women's Column" in the *Afro-American* newspaper. She covered cultural, social, business, religious, and educational items about Black women in Baltimore, Maryland, as well as in surrounding states and communities.

The Ledger, another Black newspaper in Baltimore, not only included numerous items on Black women, but also wrote complimentary columns about them. The June 11, 1898 editorial was entitled "The Eloquence of Afro-American Women."

By 1977, Black women had become reporters in the white press, owners of newspapers, and publishers of magazines. They had also become editors as well as managers. However, Black women still are at the bottom of the ladder in employment in all aspects of print media. Though highly trained and qualified, they rank below Black males, white females, and white males. On the job, the Black woman is paid less than her white counterpart and considerably below the income of both Black and white men. (See "A Statistical Portrait of the Black Woman Worker" by Alexis M. Herman in *The Black Collegian*, June 1978.)

Radio and television are indeed powerful instruments of communications. Yet, given the 1969 ruling of the Federal Communications Commission on employment opportunity, Black women are still conspicuously absent from news assignment, line production, or key policy positions. The January 1979 report of the U.S. Commission on Civil Rights *(Window Dressing On The Set: An Update)*, p. 62 shows three important findings about television network and about network-owned stations:

> The proportion of minority and female newsmakers declined in 1977, while the proportion of white male newsmakers increased significantly, from 78.7 percent to 88.4 percent.
> No significant increase in the percentages of minorities and women employed as officials and managers in the 40 station sample occurred between 1975 and 1977.

The employment status of minorities and women who work at the headquarters level of each of the networks is significantly lower than at the stations owned by ABC, CBS, and NBC.

Beyond the paucity of employment opportunities in both print and electronic media, Black women have, as always, done what they have to do. They have "created" their own unique opportunities in order to advance the cause of all Black people, and they have overcome far too many struggles in order to advance the cause of humanity. This book, therefore, has cited their contributions and their gifts to American society - a society where they shall be models for the young and old alike, for years to come.

SELECTED BIBLIOGRAPHY

Aptheker, Bettina. "Women Suffrage and Against Lynching, 1890-1920." A paper presented at the First National Research Conference, Council of Negro Women, Washington, D.C., November 13, 1979.

The Associated Negro Press (ANP). This column appeared occasionally in *Couriers*, 1929.

1979 Ayer Directory of Publications. Philadelphia: Ayer Publishing Co., 1979.

Bass, Charlotta A. *Forty Years: Memoirs From the Pages of a Newspaper*. Los Angeles: n.p., 1960.

Bates, Daisy. *The Long Shadow of Little Rock: A Memoir by Daisy Bates*. New York: David McKay, 1962.

Bearden, Jim and Linda Jean Butler. *Shadd: The Life and Times of Mary Ann Shadd Carey*. Toronto, Ontario (Canada): The NC Press, Ltd., 1977.

Bennett, Lerone. *Before the Mayflower: A History of Black America*. Chicago: Johnson Publishing Co., 1969.

Black Enterprise Magazine, September 1976.

"Blacks vs. the News Media." *Encore*, 19 May 1975, p. 48.

Brown, Hallie Q., ed. *Homespun Heroines and Other Women of Distinction*. 1926; rpt. Freeport, N.Y.: Books for Libraries Press, 1971.

Buni, Andrew. *Robert L. Vann of the Pittsburgh Courier*. Pittsburgh, Pa.: University of Pittsburgh Press, 1974.

Butcher, Margaret J. *The Negro in American Culture*. New York: Knopf, 1972.

"Cecelia Nabrit Atkins, '43." *Fisk Profile*. Fisk University. Nashville, Tennessee, 1976.

Chapple, Steve and Reebee Garofalo. *Rock'n Roll is Here to Pay: The History and Politics of the Music Industry*. Chicago: Nelson-Hall, 1977.

Collins, Lisa. "Women Behind the News." *Sepia*, October 1977.

Daniels, Sadie I. *Women Builders*. Rev. and enlarged by Charles Wesley and Thelma Perry. Washington, D.C.: Associated Publishers, 1970.

Dann, Martin E. *The Black Press, 1827-1890: The Quest for National Identify*. New York: Putnam, 1971.

Dannett, Sylvia G.L. *Profiles of Negro Womanhood: 1619-1900*. Vol. I. Yonkers, N.Y.: Educational Heritage, Inc., 1969.

Davis, Arthur P. *From the Dark Tower: Afro-American Writers, 1900-1960*. Washington, D.C.: Howard University Press, 1974.

Davis, Elizabeth L. *Lifting as They Climb: The History of the National Association of Colored Women*. 1895; rpt. Washington, D.C.: National Association of Colored Women 1933.

Davis, Marguerite Rose. "A Survey and Analysis of Opportunities for Negro Women in Journalism." Thesis Kansas State College 1942.

DeLeon, Al. "Showdown on Morningside Heights." *Black Enterprise*, September 1974.

Detweiler, Frederick G. *The Negro Press in the U.S.* 1922; rpt. College Park, Md.: McGrath Publishing Co., 1968.

Dillon, Morton. *The Abolitionists: The Growth of a Dissenting Minority*. DeKalb, Ill.: Northern Illinois University Press, 1974.

Douglas, Pamela. "An Inside Perspective on the Black Woman TV Executive." *Contact*, Spring 1974, p. 46.

DuBois, W.E.B. *Black Reconstruction in America*. 1935; rpt. New York: Atheneum, 1973.

Dunnigan, Alice. *A Black Woman's Experience: From Schoolhouse to White House*. Philadelphia: Donance and Co., 1974.

------------------------------------. "Early History of Negro Women in   Journalism." *Negro History Bulletin*, May 1965, pp. 178-179.

Emery, Michael C. and Ted C. Smythe. *Readings in Mass Communication: Concepts and Issues in the Mass Media*. Iowa William C. Brown Co. Publishers, 1974.

"FCC, WBLT, and Negroes." *Nation*, 5 August 1968.

Fenderson, Lewis H. *Development of the Negro Press, 1827-1948*. Diss. University of Pittsburgh 1948.

Fisher, Paul L. and Ralph J.L. Lowenstein. *Race and the News Media*. New York: Praeger, 1967.

Foster, Vera Chandler and Jessie P. Guzman. "The Negro Press" in *The Negro Year Book*. Tuskegee, Alabama: Department of Records and Research, 1949.

Fox, Stephen R. *The Guardian of Boston: William Monroe Trotter*. New York: Atheneum, 1970.

Franklin, John Hope. *From Slavery to Freedom*. New York: Knopf, 1974.

Giddings, Paula. "The Beginning: The Spirit of the Early Black Press." *Encore*, 20 June 1977, p. 16.

Harley, Sharon and Rosalyn Terborg-Penn, eds. *The Afro-American Woman: Struggles and Images*. Port Washington, N.Y.: Kennikat Press, 1978.

Hobson, Sheila Smith. "Women and Television." In *Sisterhood is Powerful*. Ed. Robin Morgan. New York: Random House, 1970.

Holsendolph, E., et al. "Shame of Public Television; Report of the Task Force on Minorities in Public Broadcasting." *Black Enterprise*, February 1979.

"Is Matchless Calvacade of Brilliance." *California Eagle*, 21 May 1937.

Jackson, Luther P., Jr. "The Age of the Publisher, 1910-1954." *Encore*, 5 July 1977, p. 16.

Jacobs, Donald M., ed. *Antebellum Black Newspapers*. Westport, Conn.: Greenwood Press, 1976.

James, Edward, et al., eds. *Notable American Women: 1607-1950*. Vol. I. Cambridge, Mass.: Belknap-Howard University Press, 1974.

Johnson, C. "WLBT—A New Look in T.V." *Vue South*, May-June 1979.

Kotz, Nick. "The Minority Struggle for a Place in the Newsroom." *Columbia Journalism Review*, March-April 1979.

LaBrie, Henry G., III *The Black Newspaper in America: A Guide*. Kennebunkport, Maine: Mercer House, 1973.

------------------------------------. *The Black Press in America*. Iowa: Institute for Communication Studies, University of Iowa—School of Journalism, 1970.

------------------------------------. *Perspective of the Black Press: 1974*. Maine: Mercer   House Press, 1974.

Lemon, Richard. "Black is the Color of TV's Newest Stars." *Saturday Evening Post*, 30 November 1969.

Lerner, Gerda. *The Majority Finds Its Past*. New York: Oxford University Press, 1979.

Lewis, Ida. "The 150th Year of the Black Press." *Encore*, 20 June 1977, p.4.

Loewenberg, Bert and Ruth Bogin, eds. *Black Women in Nineteenth Century American*

Life: Their Words, Their Thoughts, Their Feelings. University Park, Pa.: Pennsylvania State University Press, 1976.

Major, Gerri. *Black Society*. Chicago: Johnson Publishing Co., 1973.

Marzolf, Marion. *Up From the Footnote: A History of Women Journalists*. New York: Hasting House Publishers, 1977.

Matthews, Mark D. "Our Women and What They Think—Amy J. Garvey and the Negro World." *The Black Scholar*, May-June 1979.

Media Guidelines Proposed by the National Committe on the Observance of International Women's Year. Washington, D.C.: Department of State, July 1976.

"Minorities Gain in Broadcasting." *Business Week*, 10 March 1973, p. 168.

Morgan, John S. and Richard L. Van Dyke. *White-Collar Blacks, A Breakthrough?* New York: American Management Assoc., 1970.

Mossell, Gertrude. *The Afro-American Woman*. Freeport, N.Y.: Books for Libraries Press, 1971.

"Mrs. Mastermind of TV's Black Tech School." *Ebony*, May 1972.

Oak, Vishnu V. *The Negro Newspaper*. Westport, Conn.: Negro Universities Press, 1970.

Penn, Irvine Garland. *The Afro-Americans in the Struggle for Women Suffrage*. Diss. Howard University 1977. Ann Arbor, Mich.: University Microfilms, 1977.

Penn, Rosalyn T. *The Afro-Americans in the Struggle for Women Suffrage*. Diss. Howard University 1977. Ann Arbor, Mich.: University Microfilms, 1977.

Ploski, Harry A. and Warren Marr, III, comps. and eds. *The Negro Almanac: A Reference Work on the Afro-American*. New York: Bellwether, 1976.

Porter, Dorothy B. "The Organized Educational Activities of Negro Literary Societies, 1828-1849." *Journal of Negro Education*, October 1936.

"The Press." *Encore*, 23 June-4 July 1975, p. 74.

Pride, Armistead. *The Black American and the Press*. Los Angeles: Ward Ritchie Press, 1968.

--------------------------------------. *The Black Press—A Bibliography*. Jefferson City, Mo.: The Association for Education and Journalism, 1963.
--------------------------------------. *The Black Press—A Bibliography*. Jefferson City, Mo.: The Association for Education and Journalism, 1963.

Quarles, Benjamin. *Black Abolitionists*. New York: Oxford University Press, 1969.

--------------------------------------. *The Negro in the Making of America*. Rev. ed. New York: Collier-Macmillan, 1969.

Rawles, Beth. "The Media and Its Effects on Black Images." Unpublished paper. West Hartford, Conn.: Office of Public Affairs, WVIT-Television, 1979.

Richings, G.F. *Evidences of Progress Among Colored People*. Philadelphia: George S. Ferguson Co., 1896.

Salaam, Kalamu Ya. "A Career in Journalism." *The Black Collegian*, October-November 1979.

Scarborough, Emma Lou. *T. Thomas Fortune: Militant Journalist*. Chicago: University of Chicago Press, 1972.

Schuyler, George S. *Black and Conservative*. New Rochelle, N. Y.: Arlington House, 1966.

Smith, Garland, ed. *Black Texans of Distinction*. Austin, Texas: Garland Smith Associates, 1979.

"Society Editors." *Ebony*, March 1950, pp. 52-56.

Stein, Meyer L. *Blacks in Communications; Journalism, Public Relations and Advertising*. New York: Julian Messner, 1972.

Sterling, Dorothy. *Black Foremothers: Three Lives*. Old Westbury, N.Y.: Feminist Press-McGraw-Hill, 1979.

"TV News Hens." *Ebony,* October 1966, pp. 44-50.

"Talk O' the Town." *Courier*, 7 December 1935.

Taylor, Quintard, Jr. *A History of Blacks in the Pacific Northwest, 1788-1970.* Diss. University of Minnesota 1977. Ann Arbor, Mich.: University Microfilms, 1979.

"Television." Update. *Newsweek,* 25 June 1976.

The Ledger Newspaper, Baltimore, Maryland. 11 June 1898.

The New York Age Newspaper, 10 October 1891, 17 March 1888, 5 December 1949.

Thurman, Sue Bailey. "The Negro Woman in the Magazine Press." *The Afro-American Woman's Journal,* Spring 1940, pp. 7, 26.

United States Commission on Civil Rights. *Window Dressing on the Set: An Update.* January 1970.

United States Library of Congress. *Negro Newspapers on Microfilm*. Washington, D.C.: ACLS Committee on Negro Studies, 1953.

"Upsurge in TV News Girls." *Ebony*, June 1971, pp. 168-170.

Waters, H.F., et al. "Talk of Television." *Newsweek,* 29 October 1979.

Winks, Robin W. *The Blacks in Canada: A History*. New Haven, Conn.: Yale University Press, 1979.

Wolseley, Roland E. *The Black Press, U.S.A.* Ames, Iowa: Iowa State University Press, 1971.

Wood, Bill. "Black Women in Television News." *Essence*, July 1972, pp. 30-31.

Work, Monroe N. *The Negro Year Book, 1931-1932.* Tuskegee Institute, Ala.: Negro Year Book Publishing Co., 1933.

Wortham, Jacob. "In With the Big Boys." *Black Enterprise*, September 1974.

Yenser, Thomas, ed. *Who's Who in Colored America*. 6th Ed. New York: Yenser Publishers, 1944.

INDEX OF BLACK WOMEN: MEDIA

THE CONTRIBUTIONS OF BLACK WOMEN TO AMERICA:
BUSINESS AND COMMERCE

Manuscript Writer
Alba Myers Lewis, Ph.D.

Consultant
Mary Clay Torian, Ed.D.

Evaluators
Alfred L. Edward, Ph.D.
Director of Research
Graduate School of Business
University of Michigan

W.J. Musa Foster
Metropolitan State University
St. Paul, Minnesota

Stephen H. Fuller
Vice-President, Personnel
General Motors Corporation

James F. Hansley
President
Vanguard Investment Company
Winston-Salem, North Carolina

Barbara Proctor
President
Proctor & Gardner Advertising, Inc.
Chicago, Illinois

Editor
Marianna W. Davis, Ed.D.

PART II

BUSINESS AND COMMERCE
Table of Contents

INTRODUCTORY ESSAY

BLACK WOMEN IN BUSINESS

Black women, according to W.E.B. DuBois in his June 1921 article in the *Pacific Review*, have been pioneers voluntary and involuntary in American life and culture. More than "any other group," says DuBois, "the United States colored women are self-supporting, with nearly 39 percent of colored women being gainfully employed as compared with 18½ percent of white women."

Though gainfully employed, Black women, by 1977, were still paid less than other working groups and were underemployed across all occupations. The history of American business attests to this neglect of Black women and men in their efforts to be business achievers.

Without equal, America has long reigned as the leading capitalist nation in the world; however, the beginnings of the American economic system were far more humble. Like burgeoning offspring, American business developed in the wake of British capitalism, especially during the Colonial Period when the colonies depended primarily on their economic ties to England. Even after America gained its political independence, British capitalists continued to invest heavily in the economy. As America moved rapidly from an agrarian society to an industrial nation, and as the practice of free enterprise unleashed individual initiative and accelerated America's exploitation of its natural resources, the evolution of the system we know today as American business began. As in beginnings of American business enterprise, the roots of Black commerce in America stretched deep into foreign soil. Africans brought with them the business experiences gained in their native land and, with these, they became active participants in the economic transformation of America. When the first twenty Blacks (three of whom were women) arrived in the New World, therefore, participation in business enterprises was not a new experience for Blacks. Even after the South instituted slavery to meet the growing demands for cheap labor, some slaves, because of a shortage of white skilled labor, were trained in the handicraft trades. Some of them, already skilled in crafts, readily adapted their skills as coopers, carpenters, shoemakers, tailors, bricklayers, painters and plasterers. In some instances, where they were permitted to hire themselves out, enterprising slaves earned enough money to buy their freedom.

In the Northern colonies, Black women became skilled in knitting, spinning and weaving, while Black men artisans adapted their skills to such crafts as cabinetmaking, ropemaking, goldsmithing, and carpentry. Given the Black population in America during the seventeenth and eighteenth centuries, it is reasonable to conclude that Blacks, both women and men, engaged in far more business activities than have been recorded.

Unlike the growth of American business enterprise, however, the evolution of Black business was severely circumscribed by retarding social and economic forces. In the South, the development of Black businesses was restricted primarily by the prohibitions of slavery; in the North, open competition with larger businesses and a limited Black population controlled their proliferation. Despite the prohibitions of slavery and the social and economic restrictions, however, a number of business enterprises operated by Blacks managed to survive, especially those operated in such cities as New Orleans, Savannah, Boston, Philadelphia, Charleston and Richmond. Usually, these business ventures were undertaken by two loosely distinct groups of entrepreneurs, one composed of free Blacks who, accumulating capital, started a variety of small businesses, and the other consisting of slaves who, through thrift, ingenuity, and industry, developed small businesses under extremely adverse circumstances.

In the South, where most Blacks were slaves and could neither trade nor purchase goods freely, a few Blacks exhibited business acumen which enabled them to achieve success in spite of restrictive laws and customs.

Although many of the outstanding achievements of Black entrepreneurship in ante-bellum America went unrecorded, the few extant records are testimonials to the exceptional efforts and determination of Black business pioneers. While their efforts to acquire wealth through commercial enterprise were restricted, free Blacks achieved no little command of property and money. Acquisition of real estate seemed to provide the best business opportunities, for as early as 1836, free Blacks in the South had accumulated property valued at $2,462,470. In states such as Virginia and Louisiana, for example, free Blacks amassed significant property holding, some becoming wealthy enough to buy large tracts of farmland and to hire workers.

Black women, according to the 1850 Population Schedules of the Seventh *Census* of the United States, were very active in occupations in the South. These women, according to the *Census*, also owned property of high value. For example, in Charleston, South Carolina, "Sylvia Garret, age 40, was a seamstress; Nancy Bonneau, age 50, was a shop-keeper; Mary Green, age 28, was a stable manager; and Caroline Claucey, age 40, was a pantry cook." The record also shows that in Charleston, "Annett Elliott, age 57, owned property valued at $2,000, while 49 year old Henrietta McNeill's property was valued at $5,000."

Other Blacks that prospered while America was still predominantly agrarian were those Black farmers who either rented or owned land and planted their own crops. Thus, the free Black farmers in some Southern states generally enjoyed better conditions than Blacks in other areas of economic activity. Included in the number of Black farmers in Ante-bellum South are Black women who helped farm the lands.

Black business ventures in America before the Civil War were obviously small in comparison to American business enterprises, but the variety of Black business enterprises was far more comparative. In the North, where Blacks enjoyed a better political status, this was especially the case. One of the earliest known Black businessmen was Emanuel Bernoon, an emancipated slave who bought his freedom about 1730, and later, with the experience he gained as a servant, operated a catering service and ale and oyster house in Providence, Rhode Island. And in Wilmington, Delaware, according to Mrs. Alice Dunbar-Nelson, speaking to the Silver Jubilee session of the National Negro Business League, (See *The Southern Workman*, August 1927) "Aunt Sallie Shadd of Delaware invented a delicious concoction — ice cream." Later, Sallie Shadd gave the recipe to Dolly Madison who was hailed as the "inventor" of the recipe. The true history was never told. Like early American business people, therefore, Blacks were courageous in the development of business enterprise, albeit they were severely handicapped by a dearth of capital, limited credit, and the relatively poor customers who patronized them.

Inseparable from the development of Black business enterprise in America were the organization and conduct of secret and beneficial societies. The first of these, the Free African Society, was established in Philadelphia in 1787 by two of that city's prominent Black community leaders, Absalom Jones and Richard Allen. In successive years, other mutual aid societies sprang up in both Northern and Southern cities where large Black populations were concentrated. Mrs. Maggie Draper Walker formed the Saint Luke's Bank and Trust Company in 1903, becoming the first Black woman bank president. Her bank, also, was a mutual self-help organization which offered financial incentives for Blacks to save and to invest.

Established to promote cooperative aid among Blacks, these societies, served as the centers of social and religious activities, were extremely influential factors in the economic lives of free Blacks, and provided fundamental and important business experiences for many of them. Recognizing that the segregated isolation in which most Blacks were forced to live could be economically beneficial, Black leaders operated these effective financial institutions with an eye toward achieving the goal of economic stability within Black communities. By the Civil War, for example, Blacks in Philadelphia had accumulated real estate holdings valued at nearly one million dollars. Perhaps as equally significant as their attempts to achieve economic stability was the corollary result that these financial efforts by Blacks established the foundation for the building of what are still among the largest, most successful and most enduring of Black businesses — insurance companies and banks.

After the Civil War, aspiring Blacks continued the uphill struggle to succeed in the economic arena, but with the additional burden of doing so amidst the shattered national economy that followed the War. The Emancipation Proclamation, while it freed Blacks physically from slavery, altered neither the conditions indigenous to a slave society nor the lack of sufficient capital; consequently, the number of business ventures initiated by Blacks during the decades immediately after 1865 did not increase substantially over the number existing before the War, despite even the radical difference in Black-white relations. In fact, in some instances, this drastic political transformation in American society mitigated against the growth of Black business, for some Blacks who established first businesses in hostile communities were doomed to fail. Yet, with all these obstacles impeding their progress, Black business enterprises survived the great watershed of American history and continued to expand.

Quite understandably, the abolition of slavery altered the status of Black business in the North much less than it did in the South. Apart from their gaining civil rights which had been withheld, Northern Blacks did not realize any substantial change in economic advantages. Many noteworthy entrepreneurial efforts by Blacks, however, were typical of the continued efforts to gain economic leverage. The Chesapeake and Marine Railway and Dry Dock Company, organized in 1865 by a group of Baltimore Blacks and created to protect Black mechanics from the competition and discrimination of whites, is an example of these new ventures. Capitalized at $40,000, the company became prosperous enough to purchase a shipyard in 1870 and survived until 1883. Black women were continuing to form their own businesses. On the pages of Black-owned newspapers such as the *Afro-American* (August 3, 1895) and the *New York Age* (November 16,

1889), the ads of these businesses are printed: "Mrs. Scott wishes the patronage of her many friends and the public generally at her National Laundry and Employment Service." "Mrs. Cooley's Boarding House, 62 Phillips Street, Boston, Massachusetts."

In the South, the abrupt emancipation of thousands of slaves was problematic for the economy. Not only were there legal and monetary difficulties for Blacks seeking business opportunities, but perhaps the most serious blow to the efforts of newly emancipated Blacks was the collapse of the all-important Freedmen's Savings Bank and Trust Company. Blacks all over the country had come to believe that this bank, organized by an act of Congress in 1865, was a government institution created on their behalf; therefore, by 1872, there were in excess 70,000 depositors. When the bank closed in 1874, many Blacks suffered devastating financial setbacks. This economic defeat precipitated a renewed effort by Blacks and the more far-sighted among Black leaders envisioned the need to establish banks of their own.

Consequently, during the latter half of the nineteenth century, Blacks pioneered in addition to lesser business ventures, two major financial institutions, Black banks and insurance companies. The first black-owned and operated banks, the Capital Savings Bank and the Grand Fountain United Order of True Reformers (Savings Bank), were founded in 1888 in Washington, D.C. and Richmond, Virginia, respectively. Between 1888 and 1934, 134 such banks were established; however, when measured in terms of permanancy and profit, most of the institutions were not notably successful. The failure of these financial institutions was not due solely to the inexperience of Blacks in finance, but encompassed a variety of other factors, including the absence of large Black commercial and industrial firms and the accompanying restricted investment and earning power of Black banks. Closely associated with Black ventures into the world of finance were other efforts involving credit unions, industrial loan associations, and building and loan associations. Created mainly to serve as depositories for fraternal orders, these financial institutions, though most were short-lived, were evidence of the initiative and resourcefulness of the organizers of these business enterprises and their efforts became the foundation of a vital legacy to succeeding generations of Blacks.

As with the rise of Black banks in America, the organizational impetus for Black insurance companies can be found in the benevolent societies, fraternal orders and Black churches. The early insurance experiments by Blacks, like the banking ventures, were generally doomed to failure; however, other companies succeeded them, the proliferation continuing at such a pace that by 1936 there was a total of fifty-four companies. The more stable of them survived for many years, some down to the present: the Order of St. Luke, founded by Mrs. Maggie Lena Draper Walker; Pilgrim Mutual Aid Association of Augusta, Georgia, organized by T.J. Hornsby, the Afro-American Insurance Association of Jacksonville, Florida, founded by J.M. Waldron; Atlanta Life Insurance Company by P. James Bryant; North Carolina Mutual Insurance Company by C.C. Spaulding; and Standard Life of Atlanta, Georgia, by Herman E. Perry.

There has perhaps been no greater testimony of Black Americans' belief in Democracy than their unceasing efforts to make their way in the American capitalistic structure, espite the many social, racial, and economic restrictions. By the dawn of the twentieth century, Black Americans, fewer than fifty years removed from slavery, had demonstrated admirably their commitment to American business. The first survey of Black businesses, conducted in 1898, revealed a total of 1,906 businesses with an average capital investment of $4,600. Though the majority of these was small by any standards of comparison today, this number of Black-owned and operated businesses was considered impressive; and their existence provided the impetus for the continued expansion of Black business enterprise in the twentieth century. Convinced that their communities, isolated socially and economically from mainstream American business, could in fact sustain Black business. Black Americans held steadfastly to their vision of business and real estate as a way out of poverty. With this climate for business, Booker T. Washington called in 1900 for the organization of the National Negro Business League (NNBL), whose express purpose was the promotion of business among Blacks; by 1907, the NNBL had recorded the organization of 300 additional business leagues in cities and towns throughout America. Thus, Black Americans ushered in the twentieth century with an optimistic outlook toward the growth and expansion of their businesses.

Any chronicle of Black business in America, however, would be highly distorted without the inclusion of the contributions of the Black businesswoman. Like that of the American woman in general, the Black woman's place in American history has been grossly neglected and misrepresented. Until recently, she has been relegated to virtual obscurity in the annals of American history. W.E.B. DuBois' research, reported in the July 23 *Homiletic Review*, illustrates the number of

Black women gainfully employed in 1910. A few examples are worth noting:

Agriculture	1,051,137
Mining	84
Manufacturing and Hand Trades	81,285
Transportation	2,083
Business	8,384
Domestic and Personnel Service	871,008
Public Service	457
Professional	30,071

This over-due study, *Contributions of Black Women in Business and Commerce*, with nine companion studies, will lay the foundation for the rectification of this inexcusable historical ommission. From the beginning, the Black woman emerged as a veritable mainstay of her people. It was the Black woman's strength and determination to make a better world that helped Black people survive the grinding heel of chattel slavery. It was she who held the family together when the boulder of racial oppression rolled down the mountain of opportunity, making it difficult for Blacks to reach the summit of equality. It was she who helped Black men push the boulder back up the mountain, and she who refused to give up though the boulder rolled down many times again. Indeed, strength and determination have manifested themselves not only in the struggle for freedom from slavery and racial oppression, but also in the struggle for equal economic opportunity.

The profile of the Black woman in business in America from 1776 to 1977, or until now, is one of unsung pioneers who, in the face of the most adverse circumstances, stoutly persevered. Though the weight of her visions and the fruits of her labors have gone largely unrecorded, the Black woman's legacy in business enterprise in America illustrates this fact. Consistent with the traditional roles of women during antebellum America, Black women were severely limited in their occupational outlook. They were further restrained by racial and social customs. Before the Civil War, therefore, free Black women in the North were restricted primarily to various types of domestic work, serving as cooks, house servants, and launderers. In the South, the situation was slightly different, reflecting the dominance of a slavery economy. Neither the American Revolution nor the subsequent abolition of slavery nor the rise of an industrial economy had a significant effect on their occupations. An 1859 survey of Philadelphia showed, for example, that eight out of every ten Black working women were domestic servants and that most of the skilled Black women were seamstresses. In the South, more than 5,000 slaves, mostly women, worked in cotton and textile mills; however, they also worked in turpentine camps, sugar refineries, food and tobacco processing plants, rice mills, foundries, saltworks, and at a number of other slavery-related jobs. Free Black women in the South, like their Northern sisters, were usually relegated to domestic jobs.

There were, of course, exceptions, which this study of the Black woman in business addresses. Even with the triple oppression of race, sex and custom, these Black women managed to contribute to the economic development of America. As described by Joyce Ladner, the Black woman in business, as in other areas of American life, was not to be denied:

> One of the major characteristics which defines the Black woman is her stark realism as this relates to her resources. Instead of becoming resigned to her fate, she has always sought creative solutions to her problems. The ability to use her existing resources and yet maintain a forthright determination to struggle against the racist society in whatever overt and subtle ways necessary is one of her major attributes...Still, under the most rugged conditions, she has managed to survive and to offer substantial contributions to society as well.

And survive they did! Nettie Elizabeth Mills, Biddy Mason, "Dutchess" Quamino, Clara Brown, Sarah Gordon. Each of these women has two things in common — they are Black and they are a part of this country's business heritage. They and others like them were visionaries who saw that their future and the futures of Black people in America were inextricably tied to economics. Each one of these and the other Black women in this volume achieved a notable degree of economic success at a time when being Black and female almost always guaranteed failure in the business arena.

Before the abolition of slavery, Biddy Mason was one of the earliest Black women to succeed in Business. As a slave, she began the trek from Mississippi to California behind her master's 300-wagon caravan when she was thirty-two years old. Her job was tending the livestock. After the caravan arrived in Los Angeles in 1854, her master decided to return to Mississippi, but Biddy Mason, seizing her opportunity, pleaded her case with the local sheriff and won freedom for herself and her three daughters. She worked hard, acquired large parcels of land and made shrewd investments that brought her wealth. Before she died, she donated her land for the construction of schools, churches, and a nursing home.

Clara Brown, another shrewd businesswoman, became one of the leading citizens of Central City, Colorado. After purchasing her freedom, Mrs. Brown talked her way into a cooking job with a gold prospecting party headed West. At age 59, she found herself sitting on the back seat of a wagon on her way to Denver. Eight weeks later, the thirty-wagon caravan arrived. She then migrated to Central City where she hoped to earn enough money to purchase her husband, two daughters and son, all of whom had been sold to other owners. Mrs. Brown opened up a laundry and worked as a nurse. Despite her generosity in helping others, she managed to save $10,000 in seven years and made investments in mining claims. She located thirty-four relatives in her search for her family and brought all of them to Denver.

The end of the Civil War brought the release of approximately 1.9 million Black women from slavery, but for most of them, opportunities to work in the free market were not much different than when they were slaves. The majority of these former slaves continued to work as household domestics or on the farm as wage earners, sharecroppers or tenant farmers. During the post-Civil War period, however, there developed a cadre of Black professional women, the dominant professions being teaching, social work, and nursing. Though these were important professions in their own right, they often spawned Black businesswomen of note. Some of these women, like Nettie Elizabeth Mills, exhibited amazing business skills and acumen. She, for example, became the first woman, Black or white, to own and operate an oil drilling rig. Another Black woman who initiated a significant business venture before the turn of the twentieth century was Sarah McWilliams Walker (Madam C.J. Walker). Through her hair preparation business, she became the first Black woman millionaire in America. Like Black men, however, Black women in business were handicapped primarily by the twin retardation of unavailable credit and limited capital investment.

The mass migration of Blacks from the South, reaching one of its highest peaks in the 1920's, created ready markets for Black businesses in Northern cities. Many businesses were established, not all being small retail and service oriented businesses. In the South, the expansion of Black business occurred more slowly. The financial holocaust of the Thirties severely stunted the spurts of growth that Black business had enjoyed; however, later decades would again prove more favorable, especially the decades of the Civil Rights era. The goal of equal access to business opportunity for Blacks has not been realized; Black business in numbers and sizes are yet too few. In America today, Blacks own fewer than 200,000 firms, and 60 percent of these are in retail trades and services. Although they are still retarded by many of the same social and economic problems which have hampered their development for two hundred years or more, there is ample evidence today, however, that Black business is moving toward corporate enterprise, however slowly.

Black businesswomen, along with their Black male counterparts, have achieved considerable success during the twentieth century. Though most of the businesses operated by Black women are in retail — primarily cosmetics, jewelry, and apparel, in 1979 Black women in business held 21.8 percent of the Black retail market. Overcoming racial and sexual barriers that have limited their employment options, many Black women today are finding careers and businesses in such nontraditional fields as banking, advertising, investment, and manufacturing. Some, like Milicent V. Boney of California, have succeeded in finance; or like Freddye Henderson of Atlanta, Georgia, in travel service; or Helen T. Jones of Chicago in the milk distribution business. With such a current expansion of opportunities in business, Black women will no doubt continue to make inroads into the world of American business.

Since the segregated enrivonments in which Black businesses have traditionally survived are of less import today than in the past, Black women and men must of necessity explore other options for business enterprises. The opportunities to go into business will remain, but Black Americans who elect these options will be forced to move toward corporate business and service to the whole community. As they do so, Black women in business will write the final chapters to pioneering volumes of research on Black women such as this one. They will assuredly become twentieth century pioneers as indeed their predecessors were pioneers. If they follow the example of Black women progenitors in business, they too will rebound from all attempts to crush them and achieve against what may seem to be impossible odds. To them, as to the imposing roster of Black high achievers cited in this volume, Black Americans will be able to trace that indomitable faith and spirit of a people — their own.

Thomas B. Shropshire
Senior Vice President
Miller Brewing Company

CHAPTER 1

FROM SLAVERY TO ENTREPRENEURSHIP

Despite slavery, there were always some Blacks involved in business. "The economic system of the South was such that a few learned by observation and a still smaller number by actual participation in business." And throughout other sections of the country there were "many 'free persons of color' from 1790 to 1860 engaged in every necessary line of work, entering the trades and becoming successful in business."[1]

Along with Black businessmen in the 18th century, there were also a number of Black business women. Documented records show that during the ante bellum period "A free woman of color ran one of the most popular taverns in New Orleans...while others of her group had stores of all descriptions."[2] And other records note that between 1780 and 1820, Cornelia Gomez and Katie Ferguson were successful caterers in New York City.[3]

For the most part, it was free Blacks who managed to operate business prior to the Civil War, but after 1865 a few more, albeit slowly, became business owners and operators. DuBois pointed out in his 1899 study that "it [was] probable that there were at least 5,000 Negro businessmen at that time".[4] Grocery store owners, general merchandise dealers, barbers, druggists, builders, and contractors are examples of some of the kinds of businesses Blacks operated. In Virginia a group "organized a Home Building Fund and Loan Association," and, in addition, to those operating as caterers and restaurant keepers, a few others entered the poultry, ice cream manufacturing, tailoring and real estate business.[5]

Although history books and other recorded information generally cite Black men who advanced in business, one historical account does credit "The wife of H.L. Sanders, of Indianapolis, [with] actually starting his whitejacket manufacturing business" in the 19th century. The jackets she made for him "to wear at the hotel were so superior that others seeing them brought her their trade." To a great extent, the early successes in businesses run by Black men were due to the hard supportive work of their wives and children.[6]

Historians such as DuBois, Woodson, and Harmon have recounted the problems and gains Blacks faced as they sought to enter more conspicuously the business world after emancipation. As with other aspects of American society, there were obstacles. In addition to having to find enough capital to invest, working long hours, often at home and at a business, and maintaining customers, Black women had to contend with race and sex barriers as they engaged in business ventures.

Serrenna Palmer of Milford, Delaware, was another 19th century Black business woman. She "began business in 1889 with a cash capital of seven dollars which she invested in notions. She had wonderful success, and in addition to a good sized stock of goods...paid for two houses."[7] DuBois' 1896 study of the occupations of Blacks in Philadelphia also identifies several women in businesses such as candy and notion shops, funeral homes, caterering and dressmaking.[8]

Along with Cornelia Gomez, Katie Ferguson, and Mrs. Henry L. Smith, were notable examples of Black women who succeeded in business in the 19th century back to Serrena Palmer.

There were also some Black women involved in the mining business in the 19th century. The Colorado Gold Rush in the early 1850's was joined by a number of Blacks in quest of gold and adventure. Many of the prospectors in this endeavor were Blacks who had been slaves. Some had bought their freedom, and others became part of the gold rush after Emancipation. Among these westbound pioneers was Clara Brown, "Angel of the Rockies," a former slave from Kentucky who became the owner of several gold mines. Another who acquired substantial wealth as the owner and operator of the Whig and Chloride mines near Pitkin, Colorado was "Old Aunt Ony Combs."[9]

During the 1880's, Minnie Ringhold, known as the "Black Bonanza Queen," established a reputation in Montana as a prospector, hotel proprietor, and mine owner. About this same time Catherine Blake was the sole owner of a $150,000 hotel in Albany, New York, and one of the richest Black women of this period was the wife of James Thomas of St. Louis, Missouri, who owned and operated the "Lindell." Mrs. Thomas, in her estate holdings, accumulated property worth over $300,000. Also during the early 1800's, Mary Pleasant owned eight homes in San Francisco, a ranch in San Mateo, and $100,000 in government bonds. In Dallas, Texas, Happy Thompson, a highly successful real estate agent, was reputed to be worth $30,000.[10]

At the beginning of the twentieth century, Madame C.J. Walker, discoverer of a new hair dressing process, was the first black woman in this country to accumulate a million dollars. In the early 1900's, a major Black-owned insurance company was founded by Gertrude Geddes Willis, and the celebrated educator, Mary McLeod Bethune, was a land developer and director of substantial Florida businesses.

A number of Black business women of the twentieth century have asserted themselves in different areas of business such as controlling finances, handling sales and services, directing the total operation of firms, acting as sole proprietors, directing governmental departments, and working within multi-million-dollar white-owned corporations. Not only have many of them been able to engage themselves in numerous and exciting business careers but many have also succeeded in holding families together against overwhelming odds. "Unlike many white women in this country, Black women were brought up with the thought that having some kind of job in addition to rearing a family was expected of them." As a result, working is not a new phenomenon for Black women. While far too many Black women still hold low-paying jobs, there are "thousands (more) pursuing careers in business and making advances. . . where few. . . have preceded them."[11] The impetus toward achievement in the business world has been enhanced by the back-to-back thrusts of civil rights and women's liberation. Today there are a good number of Black female entrepreneurs using their shrewd and hard-working capabilities to engage in new and exciting business areas.

NOTES

[1] J.H. Harmon, Jr., Arnett G. Lindsay, and Carter G. Woodson, *The Negro As A Business Man* (College Park, Maryland: McGrath Publishing Co., 1969), p. 1 and 41. See also W.E. Dubois *The Negro In Business* (New York: AMS Press, 1971).

[2] Harmon, Lindsay and Woodson, p. 3.

[3] Booker T. Washington, *The Negro In Business* (Chicago: Afro-American Press, 1969), p. 38.

[4] W.E. Burghardt Dubois, *The Negro In Business* (New York: AMS Press, 1971). p. 6.

[5] Harmon, Lindsay, and Woodson, p. 911.

[6] Harmon, Lindsay, and Woodson, p. 14-15. See also Washington, *The Negro In Business*, p. 31.

[7] G.F. Richings, *Evidences of Progress Among Colored People* (Chicago: Afro-American Press, 1969), p. 413-414.

[8] W.E. Burghardt Dubois, *The Philadelphia Negro* (New York: Benjamin Bloom, Inc., 1967) p. 117.

[9] W. Sherman Savage, "Colorado Gold Rush," *New Day*, No. 5 (1947), p. 12.

[10] *Cleveland Gazette*, 23 October 1887, p. 1, Cols. 3-4.

[11] *Black Enterprise*, November 1971, p. 35.

CHAPTER II

BEAUTY CULTURE, FASHION, AND MODELING

Willie Smith, an award winning Black designer, commented in the December 1972 issue of *Black Enterprise* magazine, "There is more fashion excitement stimulated from the Black community than any place else." Rarely credited, Black women have always been style setters. From the Black women in their church finery to the scarfed, headwrapped, women in the fields or the kitchen; from the smartly dressed school teacher to the chicly suited Black businesswomen; from the strutting sisters out for a social event and on to the ribboned, rubber-banded, braids of little Black school girls, there is something about the way Black women dress, use make-up, and carry themselves which shouts beauty and style. As another Black designer puts it, one sees color and style when one looks at a Black woman. No matter what their condition, Black women have always been concerned about their looks and have known how to take what they had and create beauty and fashion. "When they purchased clothes, they did it generously. . . And when they had to make do with hand-me-downs and cast offs, they accepted [them] and pieced together, hooked up, and altered things in such a way that not a soul could tell the difference. [There is no denying the fact that] Blacks have had a tremendous influence on the fashion industry. Fashion editors [have had to] acknowledge that certain looks, such as headwraps and types of hairstyles, were created by Black women and eventually became trends reported in major fashion magazines."[1] Many enterprising Black women have parlayed their sense of fashion and beauty knowledge into successful businesses.

Perhaps the most famous Black woman in the history of beauty culture is Madame C.J. Walker, originally from Delta, Louisiana, who amassed a fortune from her invention of the straightening comb and other beauty products.

Walker was born Sara Breedlove McWilliams on December 23, 1867, to improverished ex-slave parents. She was left an orphan at the age of fourteen and became widowed at twenty with a child to educate. After the death of her husband, Walker, a beautiful and ambitous woman, started a new life for herself in St. Louis where she worked as a laundress. In 1905, she married Charles J. Walker, a newspaper man from Denver, Colorado, and thereafter became known as Madame C.J. Walker. It was in St. Louis that she discovered the hair straightening formula which was to make her a fortune.[2]

Gifted in mixing herbs and natural products, she invested some of her meager earnings in special ingredients which she mixed and tested on herself and her daughter until she developed a formula for hair and skin treatment. In 1900, Walker started selling her hair and scalp ointments door-to-door teaching women to care for their hair and skin. Moving from city to city, she traveled to the South and Midwest selling her products — even riding the train in order to toss advertising leaflets to Black people standing on the platform. As she traveled, her name and products became better known. Walker soon worked with her daughter to establish a correspondence course in beauty culture. For $25.00, women learned skin and hair care and upon graduation, they received diplomas and contracts.

At first, Walker's process was ridiculed by both Blacks and whites. However, because she had confidence in her product, she ignored these reactions and in 1910, in Indianapolis, began to manufacture hair preparations as well as a complete line of cosmetics. She purchased a house, built an adjoining factory and laboratory, and on September 9, 1911, filed the Articles of Incorporation with the State of Indiana. She continued to travel, setting up schools in a number of cities to teach her system of beauty culture and to sell her beauty products.

Walker's daughter encouraged her mother to stop working so hard and to move to New York. While there, she decided to build a home and contracted a Black architect. She purchased land in Irvington on the Hudson River and built a twenty room mansion, complete with pipe organ, swimming pool, and sunken garden. Her home was later named "Villa Ledwardo" by Enrico Caruso, the famed operatic tenor. Her husband, whom she had divorced in 1912, but who remained a good friend, wrote to her when she moved into the mansion: "I must give you praise for your womanhood, your pluck, your push and determination. You have reached the highest place in society and wealth among our people, a place you rightly deserve."

By 1915, hers was the largest business in the state owned by a Black person, employing more than 500 agents throughout the United States. She was the world's first Black in modern times to build a large manufacturing enterprise.

Despite her financial success, Walker was always concerned about her lack of formal education and always tried to help with educational projects for Blacks. She became a good friend to Mary McLeod Bethune, whom she admired, and helped her and others with financial and moral support. She believed in education for Black youth and encouraged the development of their skills.

Madame C.J. Walker is best known for her contributions in developing beauty products designed for the Black woman. Her proficiency and organization in business laid the foundation for the cosmetics industry among Blacks.

Madame C.J. Walker, businesswoman

The American Black woman is "indebted to the genius of Madame C.J. Walker as a pioneer inventor-manufacturer in the field of hair care products for the Black woman. Singlehandedly, [she] created ways and means for [Black women] to care for [their] hair . . . Among other things, she invented the hot iron comb and founded a beauty culture business that still employs hundreds of thousands of Black women around the globe. She died, the first female Black millionaire, in 1919."[3]

Another pioneer in the field of beauty culture was Annie Turnbo Malone, a self-made millionairess from Metropolis, Illinois, who developed in 1906 a hair preparation called "The Wonderful Hair Grower," copyrighted as "Poro." The business was originally founded in Illinois but was located in St. Louis, Missouri, during the early part of the twentieth century.

Malone was one of eleven children who was orphaned during early childhood. Under the care of older siblings, she obtained a basic education in the Illinois public schools. As a young child, she seemed to have a flair for hair grooming and an aptitude for chemistry which she studied in high school. Talent and ability enabled her to develop the hair preparation, "Wonderful Hair Grower."

In 1900, she began to manufacture this product in her home in Illinois. By extensive advertisement and efficient management, the business expanded still further and the founder moved to a more spacious office building which served as headquarters for "Poro College" in St. Louis, Missouri. The business became by far one of the more outstanding manufacturing establishments in the West. In the early 1900's, Malone's business was valued over a million dollars.

At the turn of the twentieth century, Fannie Kay Burns, formerly of Cincinnati, Ohio, established one of the most thoroughly equipped hairdressing, facial massage and allied lines of business in Syracuse, New York. Her patrons included people of wealth in Syracuse and its vicinity.

Still another early pioneer in the area of beauty culture was Sara Spencer Washington, originally of Princess Ann County, Virginia. In 1913, in Atlantic City, New Jersey, she founded a small hairdressing establishment where she worked as an operator and taught her system. She spent her evenings taking her products from house to house. In 1920, she organized *Apex News and Hair Company*. In 1937-39 in Atlantic City, she built her own laboratories where she manufactured seventy-five different kinds of beauty preparations. As the director of Apex Beauty Colleges she employed 215 regular employees. At one time, there were more than 35,000 Apex agents throughout the country.

Washington's philanthropics are pronounced. She endowed a home for girls devoted to the educational features of the National Youth Administration Program, and she gave 20 acres of her farmland as a camp site for Black youth.[5]

Another well-known pioneer in the area of beauty culture was Kathryn Wilson of St. Joseph, Missouri, who, in the early 1900's, established the oldest school between Omaha and the Pacific Coast, the California Beauty School. Her graduates are some of Omaha's most outstanding hairdressers, white and Black. In 1925, she edited the first edition of *Successful Hairdressing*, which was a big seller and was distributed over the world.

In Orangeburg, South Carolina, in 1918, Julia Breeland, who studied under Madame C.J. Walker, opened the Elite School of Beauty Culture, the first beauty school in the area. In 1935, she organized the South Carolina Beauticians' Association and was elected the first president. This organization still meets annually to perpetuate the original prupose: to keep the beauticians in the state informed about the developments in the field.[7]

Outstanding among the pioneers in beauty culture in Alabama was Ruth P. Jackson, born in Gasden, Alabama, 1898. Through her efforts in raising the professional standards of beauticians in Alabama, the Alabama Association of Modern Beauticians was established. Jackson, at 81 years of age, is still active in many civic, community, and church activities.

In West Hynannisport, Massachusetts, Margaret Cardoza Holmes established in 1937 the first Black hairdressing business in the area. Her establishment, known as Cardoza Hairstylists, is valued at more than a million dollars. She was one of three Cardoza sisters whose grandfather was the Secretary of State in South Carolina during the Reconstruction period.[8]

In 1948, Carmen Murphy opened her "House of Beauty" in Detroit, Michigan, and as it grew she saw a need for a new line of beauty products designed to complement Black women. Three years later, she founded Carmen Cosmetics, a company manufacturing cosmetic products which were sold exclusively at the House of Beauty. Today Carmen Cosmetics are sold throughout the world.[9]

Rose Morgan, born in Shelby, Mississippi, is an internationally noted pioneer in modern beauty culture for Black women. Her beauty salon in New York City, Rose Morgan House of Beauty, is managed by the Rodelia Corporation of which she is the president and founder.

Rose Morgan supervises a chain of beauty salons operating in New York, Detroit, and Chicago. She has traveled widely, speaking and providing commentary on fashion, trade shows, and beauty clinics. She also manages a national and international mail order business, Rose Morgan Enterprises. Feature stories concerning her business enterprises have appeared in many magazines in the United States of America and abroad.[10]

Stacey Jones of Boston, Massachusetts, is an example of the current-day entrepreneur in the area of cosmetology and hair designing. Jones has found time to manage her own beauty salon, Stacey's Coiffures, in downtown Boston while actively presiding as president of the Boston Hair Fashion Guild. Her activities in the hair fashion and cosmetology worlds have brought her to prominence as a guest on many television and radio talk shows in the Boston area. Jones is an example of the dynamic young business woman of today who is making changes in the world of beauty culture.[11]

Also on the contemporary scene in the area of cosmetology is Lucille Andrews Troupe, a native of Denison, Texas. For more than twenty years, she owned, operated and was instructor of the only Black beauty college in the northern area of Oklahoma. Originally owned by the Wallar Company, Troupe's Beauty College was purchased by Troupe in 1950 and became well-known all over the state of Oklahoma under her ownership. She graduated and placed well over 1,000 men and women on jobs during the time her school was in operation. She also gave over $10,000 in scholarships to deserving young seniors to attend beauty school. Troupe has written a book on cosmetology pioneers and has received numerous awards for her community service and many professional contributions.

In the cosmetic sales aspect of the beauty business field, Ruell Cone in Atlanta, Georgia, has become one of the more successful business women in America. As an independent national sales director of Mary Kay Cosmetics, Inc., she has worked her way to the top to achieve this select position. Only 17 of 70,000 women in Mary Kay Cosmetics have reached this status. Each year, since she first joined the company in 1973, her sales group has placed numbers 4, 3, 7, and 1 in sales through-out the nation. In 1976 when Cone's group was number one, she broke the entire record of Mary Kay Cosmetics by setting a record of over $700,000 in sales for the year. Although Cone has received numerous awards and citations for her achievements, she says that her greatest joy and satisfaction is showing what a group of Black women can do in the world of business.

Cone says, "I am a builder of women — I build their self-confidence, their self-image, their positive attitude, their self-motivation and their persistence. I help them to become the very best they can become in their individual business."[13]

Fashion

Historically, the role of Blacks in fashion extends beyond their position as consumers. In the early 1800's in many cities of the country, Blacks were major producers of clothing as seamstresses, tailors, and hatters. These businesses, along with others, such as barbering and catering, were among the most successful for early Black entrepreneurs. DuBois' 1896 study of Black female occupations in Philadelphia cities a number of women employed as skilled dressmakers and notes that one dressmaker "runs a dressmaking school."[14]

One interesting personality in the early days of American fashion was Elizabeth H. Keckley, born in Virginia, in 1820. She was the daughter of slave parents, and was herself a slave, who, after years of suffering and physical punishment, went to St. Louis with her master and mistress. There she became a seamstress and dressmaker for the leading ladies of the city. With the assistance of one of her patrons, Keckley received permission from her master to buy her freedom for herself and her son for $1,200.

As a free woman in the spring of 1860, Keckley went to Washington, D.C. where she was employed as dressmaker by the wife of Jefferson Davis. Her desire to work for the ladies of the White House was realized when she became dressmaker to Mary Lincoln, the wife of President Abraham Lincoln. She made Mary Lincoln's clothes throughout the Lincoln administration and became the First Lady's confidante, accompanying her on many trips.

In 1862, Keckley was instrumental in forming the Contraband Relief Association and was able to receive contributions from the Lincolns as well as many philanthropists in America and from England.

Elizabeth Keckley never became a rich woman, despite her connection with people of means, but this did not seem to be of importance to her. In the conclusion of her book of reminiscences, *Behind the Scenes*, or *Thirty Years a Slave, and Four Years in the White House*, she wrote, "I close the imperfect story of my somewhat romantic life. Though in worldly goods, I am rich in friendships, and friends are a recompense for all the woes of the darkest page of life."[15]

It was not until the latter part of the nineteenth century that the position of Blacks in clothes production was reduced. This was due mainly to the industrialization that was revolutionizing the garment business and to immigrants from Europe who provided cheaper labor and in time dominated the industry.[16]

One of the earliest Blacks to engage actively in the fashion business was Emma L. Pitts who was born in Athens, Georgia, in the early 1900's. She conducted dressmaking and millinery stores in Macon and in Albany, Georgia. Later Pitts trained many Black women in the art of dressmaking and millinery in New York. She organized The Vogue, a school for training young women in the art of dressmaking, millinery, and beauty culture. She had the distinction of being the oldest woman member of the National Negro Business League, and she attended and spoke at the second meeting of that League, held in Chicago, Illinois.[17]

Annie Grantland Horner was one of several dressmakers who in 1903 obtained work experienced with exclusive shops near 42nd Street in New York City. In 1923, she went into partnership with Carrie Wallace, and they opened up a shop at 30 West 51st Street.

Horner never had formal training. Taught to sew by her grandmother and aunt, she came to New York about 1900 highly recommended by people for whom she had worked in her native Macon, Georgia. At that time, most of the Black people were employed as domestics and she was not able to get a job. To survive, she, temporarily, took the job of an ill friend and worked as a maid in Jersey City. When her employer found out Horner could sew, she gave her a job making clothes for the family after the regular maid returned. This job led to another job as a draper for a shop run by Madame Charlesworth at 43rd Street and Lexington Avenue in New York City. Horner was sent to see a play starring Ina Claire and was asked to copy the gown Claire wore. Her copy of the design was so good that her job with Madame Charlesworth became secure.

After working for Charlesworth for a while, Horner took a fitting job at another large and exclusive shop in the same neighborhood where she worked for 12 years, directing 32 women of almost every nationality. In 1921, Horner opened her own shop at 2311 Seventh Avenue. During the time she was in Harlem, her shop made clothes for the play "The Fool," and several individual Broadway stars.[19]

Carrie Wallace started her business in her apartment at 220 West 133rd in New York City. Her work became so well known that she was soon doing work for several Broadway and picture stars. She was born in Virginia and moved to New York when she was young. She had no formal training as a seamstress. The firm she and Annie Horner ran employed 12-20 people and made clothes for concert singers as well as many wealthy people in New York.

Perhaps the first Black woman to open her own business in the shopping district of New York was Madame C.B. Reed, who was in business for 16 years. The first shop was on West 45th Street near Sixth Avenue for nine years. In 1923, the shop relocated to 61 West 55th Street. It employed 10-15 women and sold mostly to wealthy people. Madame Reed primarily made gowns, but did make some hats. She was born in Virignia and grew up in New York.[20]

Since the Black women who pioneered in the fashion world in the 19th and early 20th Century, many others entered the fashion business. Each town and city can no doubt boast of some Black women whose skills have gone unheralded by the industry. Using their sense of fashion and style, Black women have also entered other areas of the fashion industry. One 20th Century woman who has made a name for herself in the fashion show area is Eunice W. Johnson.

Eunice Johnson, a native of Selma, Alabama, is director and producer of the Ebony Fashion Fair, a touring fashion show which appears in many cities throughout the United States. Her duties as director of the Ebony Fashion Fair have taken her around the world, and the reponses to her efforts are hailed with enthusiasm. Her shows are examples of the most fashionable designs on the market.[21]

Naomi Sims, a native of Oxford, Mississippi, is another very succesful businesswoman in the world of fashion. Sims, a former top model and a writer in the fashion world, was the first Black woman to be featured in a multi-colored magazine spread in *Vogue* and *Harper's Bazaar*. She has also appeared on the cover of *Life* and *Ladies Home Journal*. She has contributed articles to numerous magazines in which she states her desire to be of service to Black women. She has written a best selling beauty and health book for and about Black women, *All About Health and Beauty for the Black Woman*, which provides a number of tips on fashion, grooming and health.

Naomi Sims is president of her own manufacturing company which she formed after helping to develop *Kanekalon Preselle*, a patented fiber that closely duplicates the texture and sheen of Black women's straightened hair. Today Naomi Sims' wigs are sold in thousands of department stores throughout the United States, the West Indies, England, and Africa.[22]

In response to the question, "What inspired or who inspired you to achieve in your field," Sims replied,

My major inspirations were: 1) Stubborness (my own) and 2) Negative Reinforcement (from others). Kind, experienced, well-meaning family and friends constantly told me what I could *not* achieve because I was both Black and female. "You can't be a high fashion model," "You can't write books about health and beauty," "You can't start and run your own company." I refused to accept this kind of advice and listened only to myself. What I *did* accept was that I could not take the orthodox roads to these goals so I blazed my own trails by first doing the job and then seeking its application. In other words, first I got on the cover of a fashion magazine *then* I went to an agency; first I developed my fiber for life-like wigs for Black women and *then* searched for financing to put together a company; first I spent five years at my own expense and time in perfume laboratories testing my first fragrance *then* found a company to manufacture and market it; and so on. If you are Black and female and you tell the world you can do something or are going to do it. they will at best smile politely and show you the door. But if you *do it*. they can't argue.
    Historically I would say that Madame C.J. Walker was my greatest inspiration; she worked entirely within the structure of Black American society to establish a beauty product empire that owed nothing to the white world.
    In general terms I would like to add simply that it is all well and good to give applause to a handful of high-achievers as myself and hope we'll be an inspiration

to other Black women who desperately need hope but to my mind the Black women of today who are really making the greatest contribution to America are all those mothers across this nation who, despite absent spouses, welfare cuts, job insecurity, inflation, crime and sheer drudgery are nonetheless struggling to bring up their children with a Christian sense of decency, dignity and regard for all women and men. The future of Black society in America is not going to be determined by the handful of us who get our names in the news or achieve high office, academic honors or political office but by the *average* Black family, its strength and weakness. Any Black adult committed to "family life" in this day and age deserves all the credit.[23]

Many Black women have become successful in the fashion business by setting up their own stores and boutiques. The exclusive La DeCouverte Boutique in the Beverly Hills section of California operated by twin sisters, Denice and Denette Richardson, is one such example. The boutique carries women's apparel, designer fashions, and accessories. In 1977, the four-year-old business brought in $70,000 in sales and with the auxiliary businesses it has generated earnings of close to $80,000.[24]

Denice and Denette Richardson, owners of La Decouverte Fashions in Beverly Hills

Lu Willard Enterprises of New York City is a jewelry design and manufacturing firm that specializes in custom-made jewelry for individual clients and retail department stores. The firm's founder, Lu Willard of Charlotte, North Carolina, has been in the jewelry business for twenty years. Willard employs a staff of seven and counts among her clients entertainers including Aretha Franklin, Dick Gregory,

Richard Pryor, Isaac Hayes, the Isley Brothers, the Dells, the Jackson Five, and Andy Williams, as well as civil rights activists Coretta King and Jesse Jackson.[25]

A recently organized company, International Costumes headed by Ruthie West of Los Angeles, has been successful in designing costumes for the entertainment industry. West creates many of the costumes for the Jackson Five, the Miracles, and many other singing groups associated with Motown. West feels that this area of fashion is one that has wide opportunities for Blacks.[26]

In Manhattan, New York, Jackie Lewis owns and operates two successful boutiques which cater to women who seek high fashion casual and evening wear. Lewis estimates that her stores gross between $150,000 to $200,000 annually. She says her clothes appeal to the vanguard woman, the one who appreciates quality and uniqueness.[27]

Two women who have gained success in specialty clothing are Dorothy Drummer and Sandy Jones. Dorothy Drummer was an expert seamstress at age 10. At age 18 she began working with furs in a large Chicago department store. In 1979, she owned a fur store, "Furs by Dorothy," located in the heart of the Loop.[28]

Sandy Jones is co-owner of the M.D. Northe Company in Philadelphia which carries an extensive line of Italian-made clothes, accessories, and leather goods. Jones gave up her career as a school teacher to devote her full time to business. Her goal is to manufacture clothing under the company's label and eventually to franchise in other cities.[29]

Modeling

"The Black model, like many other successful Blacks, struggled for many years in a society that chose to ignore her."[30] Unless they were hired by Black magazines, they generally could not find work. There have, of course, always been beautiful and photographically perfect Black women, but "until 1945 virtually no Black faces appeared in ads. Then they began to appear regularly in the Black publication *Ebony* but only to tout hair products and eventually cosmetics, cigarettes and liquor."[31] It was not until 1964 that the first Black female model appeared on the cover of a fashion magazine. That woman was Donyale Luna, from Detroit, Michigan, who strode confidently into New York City in 1964 and within three months hit the cover of *Harper's Bazaar*. With that photo cover, she also became the first Black model to earn top fees.[32]

Before Donyale Luna, there was Helen Williams who was really the first Black successful model. But while Williams was "the Black model of the 1940's" and was identified in 1959 as the most photographed Black model in the country, she was primarily confined for most of her career to Black magazines because she was "too dark."[33] Still, Helen Williams, from Riverton, New Jersey who began modeling as a child in New York City, is credited by other successful Black models with opening the door for them. An article on her notes that Helen Williams was "every Black girl's dream come true in their aspirations to model. She [was] the first dark model to gain acceptance in the industry and has opened the doors for all women of darker than olive complexion. Her exquisite Budweiser Beer and Modess ads became a trademark."[34]

By the mid-70's Williams was working in New York City as a fashion coordinator and stylist and was "responsible for hiring hundreds of models to feature in the Sears Catalog. She also helps many Black models to get catalog work and to launch their careers." Reflecting on her career, Williams said in 1975, "When I started modeling, I was out there alone. It was fun for me, a challenge. Every time a door closed, I wanted to find out why until it opened. I kept on fighting. The industry just wasn't ready to accept the idea of a dark-skinned model. Over the years, more doors have opened, but it is still a constant struggle for our women. I can't understand why there must be one beauty for each year. There are too many beautiful Black women to give one as an example for the Black race. We should have more beauty commercials and be on more covers and in more publications."[35]

In October 1959, *Ebony* magazine carried an article noting that big business, capitalizing on the increasing importance of the purchasing power of Blacks, was beginning to use an increasing number of "brown models to sell its products." These Black models included Janie Burdette from Los Angeles, Mease Booker, a native of Waco, Texas, Marlene Fitzhugh and Josie Cain from Chicago, and Joyce Jones of New York. They were primarily used to sell soft drinks, toothpaste, rice, radios and cosmetics often at salaries which alone could not support them. Donyale Luna's appearance on the cover of *Harper's Bazaar* and her subsequent earning power were real breakthroughs for other aspiring Black models.

In 1967 Naomi Sims hit the fashion magazines and became the first "Black model superstar, flanked by the twin attendants of fame and fortune. Within two years from the time she began modeling, Sims was on the cover of *Life*, described simply as 'top model'." She has appeared in virtually every fashion magazine in the world.[36]

"In 1973 after setting a precedent in runway modeling (she would get standing ovations wherever she appeared), Sims shelved her numerous awards, certificates, and titles and retired." She then launched her highly successful Naomi Sims Collection of wigs and hairpieces and wrote an equally successful beauty and health book for Black women.[37] Sims is the most vivid example of a Black woman who rose from supermodel to superbusinesswoman.

Naomi Sims, model and cosmetologist

When Black models began to crack the fashion industry in the mid-60's, photographers, designers, and modeling agencies were wildly excited about the glamour they brought to clothes. Said one photographer, "If you put a fairly ordinary dress on a brunette and then on a blonde, not too much happens. Put the same dress on a Black girl and it becomes something really wonderful."[38] "The real breakthrough for more Black models came in the 70's with the advent of black designers like Stephen Burrows who launched Alva Chinn and hired Bethann Hardison." The civil rights movement also effected some changes in the attitudes of modeling agencies although most firms sought to deny this, claiming instead that making money was what was important to them.[39] And there was no doubt that once they got hired, Black models made money for the agencies.

Some of the top Black models in the early 60's included Mozella Roberts; Beverly Valdes, a Harlem-born one-time beautician; LaJeune Hundley; Liz Campbell; and Bethann Hardison. Hardison was both a house model (used by top designers for their collections), fashion coordinator, and business associate from whom others in the industry sought advice on what women want to wear. There were also a number of other early Black models who earned high salaries. These include Madelyn Sanders and Charlene Dash. Sanders was one of the first Black models to appear in a television commercial and Dash was signed by the Ford Model agency, one of the most prestigious agencies, in 1968. In a year's time she became a top money-maker, doing television commercials for firms like Clairol cosmetics.[40]

Sherri Brewer from Chicago has modeled for television. Pat White of New York is a magazine and television commercial model who has earned up to $75 an hour and has appeared in newspapers, catalogs, magazines, and on posters and billboards in every Black community. Norma Jean Darden from Newark, New Jersey, "has appeared in every major American and Foreign fashion publication and has worked for nearly every top designer in the world." In addition to modeling and acting, Darden has written, with her sister Carole Darden, a best-selling cookbook, *Spoon Bread and Strawberry Wine: Recipes and Reminiscences of a Black Family*.[41]

"Black female models are credited with dramatically changing the manner in which clothes are introduced at "trade-only" fashion shows. Until the mid-sixties, when designers began using Black models, the high fashion mannequin was stiff, lifeless — almost other worldly. But beginning with Donyale Luna, Naomi Sims, Norma Jean Darden, Billie Blair, and Pat Cleveland fashion shows began to change. Black models danced and strutted. They brought to the runway an attitude that delighted fashion editors and buyers alike. And they made designers and manufacturers happy because they helped boost sales."[42]

The May 5, 1975, edition of *Newsweek* magazine called attention to the stunning style of Black models. Commenting on that year's fall fashion show in Paris, *Newsweek* said that "when the two Black American models sashayed on. . . they brought the *maison* down." The two models were Pat Cleveland from New York City and Alva Chinn from Boston. The article further noted that "the new bevy of Black models makes dresses move like they'll never move again." Another of the top runway models who captured the attention of designers and fashion magazines is Billie Blair from Flint, Michigan. Blair has also appeared in major magazines and worked for top designers.

After Sims, the top, superstar, highfashion Black model is Beverly Johnson. Johnson, a former Championship swimmer from Buffalo, New York and criminal justice major while attending Boston's Northeastern University, walked into the offices of *Glamour* magazine in 1971 and was hired immediately. She worked steadily thereafter, and in August 1974 she became the first Black woman to appear on the cover of *Vogue*, one of the world's most prestigious fashion magazines. She is also the first Black woman to appear on the cover of the French magazine, *Elle*, and has appeared on the cover of numerous other magazines including *Glamour* where she has appeared over six times. Beverly Johnson began her modeling career "making $60.00 an hour, with her rate increasing to $75.00 in four months and finally to $100.00 per hour, no questions asked." Like Sims, Johnson has begun to launch her career in other directions including acting, singing, and writing. But she remains a top model, earning in 1975 between $100,000 to $200,000.[43]

Even models have to learn certain techniques and have to acquire agents. Many Black models have been helped in developing their skills through the work of people like Ophelia DeVore. DeVore, originally from Edgefield, South Carolina, has for many years stood out as a giant in the modeling and charm business. At age sixteen, she became a model in New York City, and at age 18 she organized one of America's first Black-owned modeling agencies which pioneered in the development of counseling and placement of non-white models. In 1947, DeVore founded one of the nation's first Black-owned charm schools which vigorously promoted image-building and self-determination among Blacks.

DeVore has served as a consultant to industry for many years. She acts as a counselor in areas of marketing, product development, research, advertising, public relations and distribution to retailers, consumers, and the media. The DeVore cosmetics that she developed have been widely known for over two decades.

Of the ten thousand students who have attended her charm schools, many have reached fame. Among these are actresses Gail Fisher, Diahann Carroll, and Ellen Holly; television news correspondents Joan Murray, Melba Tolliver, and Lucille Rich; and models Mozella Roberts, Helen Williams, and LaJeune Hundley.

DeVore has also made equal contribution to the communication media. She owns the *Columbus Times*, a newspaper in Columbus, Georgia. She is secretary of the National Newspaper Publishers Association, serving as one of the five officers and also a Board member. This Association represents over one hundred eighty publications, including *Jet* magazine.

Beside DeVore, there are other Black women who have established modeling and charm businesses. A former assistant buyer and model for I. Magnin and Company in San Francisco, Barbara Davis, along with Millie Carter, is the owner of "The House of Black Elegance." This business enterprise is a fashion and charm school where everything is taught with the Black woman in mind.[45]

In New York City, Bettye Williams is one who is determined to speed things up for the Black fashion model. As a member of the Models Association of America, she is the prime mover in the "Shades of Black," a touring fashion show. Williams operates the Bettye Williams Finishing School for Black models and has opened her own agency for the placement of models and artists.[46]

Another person who has been instrumental in developing young Black women in modeling is Frances Huff of San Francisco. At one time her House of Elegance, Charm and Modeling School and Agency awarded over 150 scholarships to Black teenagers in the Bay area.[47] Elaina Brooks, former model and head of the Black American Model Agency in New York, is also a pioneer in the field and a main spokeswoman for the Black male model.[48]

After many years of apparent blindness, Madison Avenue, the nation's advertising capital, has discovered the beauty of Black. For hundreds of Blacks, this means a new and exciting life in the glamorous world of modeling.

NOTES

[1] "Moving Ahead In Style: Blacks in the Fashion Industry," *Black Enterprise,* *September 1976, p. 35.*

[2] Sylvia G.L. Dannett, "The Business Builders, Maggie Lena Mitchell Walker," in *Profiles of Negro Womanhood, Negro Heritage Library,* Vol. 1(Philadelphia: Goodway, Incorporated, 1964), pp. 188-195. Unless otherwise noted, all text information regarding Walker is taken from pages cited here.

[3] Naomi Sims, *All About Health and Beauty for the Black Woman* (Garden City, New York: Doubleday and Company, 1976), p. 57.

[4] Herman Preer, "Negro Leadership in St. Louis: A Study of Race Relations," Diss. (University of Chicago, 1975), pp. 132-134. See also J.H. Harmon, Arnett Lindsay, and Carter G. Woodson, *The Negro As A Business Man* (College Park, Md: McGrath Publishing, 1969), p. 22-23.

[5] Harding B. Young, "The Negro's Participating in American Business," *Journal of Negro Education,* Fall 1963, pp. 390-392.

[6] *Omaha Star,* 11 April 1952, p. 1.

[7] Carrie Shuler, "The Magnificent Story of Mrs. Julia E. Breeland," Unpublished paper, Orangeburg, South Carolina, n.d.

[8] Alpha Kappa Alpha Sorority, Incorporated, Heritage Series #3: *Women in Business,* 1970, p. 12.

[9] Alpha Kappa Alpha Sorority, p. 15.

[10] *Ebony's 1,000 Successful Blacks,* Vol. I (Chicago: Johnson Publishing Co., 1973), p. 228.

[11] *Ebony's 1,000 Successful Blacks,* p. 172.

[12] *Ebony's 1,000 Successful Blacks,* p. 392.

[13] "Mary Kay's Sweet Smell of Success," *Reader's Digest,* November 1978, pp. 5-6.

[14] *Black Enterprise,* September 1976, p. 35. See also W.E.B. Dubois, *The Philadelphia Negro,* (New York: Benjamin Bloom, Inc., 1967), pp. 103 and 119.

[15] Dannett, pp. 176-178.

[16] *Black Enterprise,* September 1976, p. 35.

[17] *Ebony's 1,000 Successful Blacks,* p. 235.

[18] *New York Age,* 10 November 1923, p. 43.

[19] *New York Age,* p. 44.

[20] *New York Age.*

[21] Alpha Kappa Alpha Sorority, Inc., p. 11.

[22] "From High Fashion to Big Business," *Black Enterprise,* September 1976, p. 41. See also Frederick Murphy, "Naomi Sims: Entrepreneur Extraordinaire," *Encore* April 1976, pp. 25-27.

[23] Personal statement received from Naomi Sims, 20 March 1980.

[24] *Black Enterprise,* May 1979, p. 43.

[25] *Black Enterprise,* January 1978, p. 17.

[26] "From High Fashion in Big Business," p. 6.

[27]"From High Fashion to Big Business," p. 27.

[28]*Black Enterprise*, October 1979, p. 34.

[29]*Black Enterprise*, September 1976, p. 28.

[30]"Have Black Models Really Made It," *Ebony*, May 1970, p. 158.

[31]"Black Models Take Center Stage," *Life*, October 1969, p. 36.

[32]*Ebony*, May 1970, p. 152.

[33]*Ebony*, May 1970, p. 158. See also "Dark Glamour" *Newsweek*, September 3, 1962, p. 69.   [34]Frederick Murphy, "Black Models Have Their Say," *Encore*, April 7, 1975, p. 33.

[35]Murphy, p. 33.

[36]*Black Enterprise*, September 1976, p. 41.

[37]Murphy, *Encore*, April 7, 1975, p. 32. See also, Frederick Murphy, "Naomi Sims: Entrepreneur Entraordinaire," *Encore*, April 19, 1976, pp. 25-27.

[38]*Life*, October 1969, p. 36.

[39]"Those Sleek Black Beauties," *Newsweek*, May 5, 1975, p. 68.

[40]*Life*, October 1969, p. 36. See also *Ebony*, May 1970, p. 152.

[41]Murphy, *Encore*, April 7, 1975. pp. 32-33. See also *Newsweek*, May 5, 1975, p. 68.

[42]*Black Enterprise*, September 1976, p. 35.

[43]Murphy, *Encore*, April 7, 1975. See also Ted Morgan, "I'm the Biggest Model, Period," *New York Times Magazine*, August 17, 1975, pp. 12-14, 16, 18, 20, 22.

[44]Alfred Duckett, "The Legend of Ophelia DeVore," *Equal Opportunity*, Vol. 11, No. 3 (1978), pp. 30-36.

[45]*The Sun Reporter*, San Francisco, 12 August 1972, p. 27.

[46]*The Sun Reporter*, San Francisco, 27 May 1972, p. 19.

[47]*The Sun Reporter*, San Francisco, 10 June 1972, p. 32.

[48]"Moving Ahead in Style: Blacks in the Fashion Industry," *Black Enterprise*, September 1976, p. 36.

CHAPTER III

BANKING, SAVINGS & LOAN,
ACCOUNTING, AND REAL ESTATE

World War I changed conditions considerably for Blacks in business. As people learned to cooperate in general, Blacks realized their physical and financial strength and "began to enter business in a larger measure." Between 1910 and 1920, rapid strides were made by Blacks in all forms of commercial enterprise. "Real estate dealers became an unusually important factor in the development of Negro business in connection with banks and other financial institutions." In order "to promote progress in real estate, Blacks organized and successfully conducted in most of the large cities of the South enterprising building and loan associations which. . .decidedly stimulated home buying.[1]

It would, however, be inaccurate to cite the World War as the starting date for Blacks engaged in real estate and banking. Although they did not deal exclusively in private banking or selling of land and houses, there were a number of "free persons of color" who, as early as 1833, had "accumulated enough wealth to make investments, to make 'personal loans'," and to engage to a limited extent in real estate and brokerage. After the Civil War, many of the freed persons became more interested in some form of systematic saving as they began general improvement of their economic conditions. Thus, established banks for Blacks came into being. Such establishment "was made somewhat easy by the large number of 'free persons of color' who even before the war had accumulated wealth and property."[2]

As with any business ventures, the early efforts by Blacks to establish financial institutions met with varying degrees of disappointment and hope, failure and success. The more successful efforts were those responsible for the establishment of several banks. It is in fact through one of them, the Independent Order of Saint Luke of Richmond, Virginia, that the first Black female made a significant entry into banking. Maggie L. Walker formed the St. Luke's Penny Savings Bank, later changed to Saint Luke's Bank and Trust Company, in 1903. She was "the first woman bank president in America," and the first Black female to hold such a position.[3] Maggie Lena Draper Walker, the daughter of a house slave, was born in 1867. At the time of her birth, her mother was a cook in the household of a wealthy spinster. Walker attended school in Richmond and entered Richmond's Armstrong Normal School (high school), graduating at the age of sixteen. After graduation, she became a teacher in the Lancaster schools. While teaching she was a part-time student in accounting and sales. She was held a part-time job with the Women's Union, an insurance company. This relationship advanced her interest in the United Order of Saint Luke — a mutual self-help organization which she had joined at the age of fourteen. Due to her interest and leadership qualities, she became secretary to a council of the Order and was a delegate to a national convention.[4]

In 1886, she married Armstead Walker, a man several years her senior. He was associated with her father in the contracting and construction business in Richmond. As a young wife and mother of two sons, she remained active in the Independent United Order of Saint Luke. While holding office in the Order, she noted that the organization was in dire financial straits. When she was promoted to grand secretary, an office she held until her death, she inaugurated many new ideas of self-help. Feeling the need for further activity and service, she founded the Saint Luke Penny Savings Bank, chartered and managed by the United Order of Saint Luke. The bank offered financial incentive for Black women to save.

Walker also established a Black newspaper, the *St. Luke Herald*, to enhance employment for Black workers; she contributed to the establishment of a Richmond, Virginia, department store offering merchandise catering to Blacks. This latter endeavor was her only failure and caused her to remain concerned about ways of educating Blacks in business endeavors.

In the next decade, despite personal tragedies involving a handicapped knee and the death of her husband, Walker founded and was president of the Richmond Independent School for Black girls; raised money for the Black Tubercle Bacillus Sanitorium; promoted the establishment of a Black community center for better health care for Blacks; and served on various boards of civic institutions.

The merger, in the 1920's, of two Black banks in Richmond changed the name of the merging banks to the Consolidated Bank and Trust Company, and Walker became chair of the board and retained that title until her death in 1934.

The Virginia Union University of Richmond awarded Walker an honorary degree in 1925, and, in her native city, a street, a theatre, and a high school bear her name. Her successor as executive secretary-treasurer of the Independent Order of Saint Luke, Hattie N.F. Walker, the widow of her elder son, inherited a strong organization with chapters in fourteen states, a fully owned home office, and a record of over $3,000,000 in paid claims — and this notwithstanding the fact that changing economic and social conditions by the 1930's had reduced considerably the role of small-scale fraternal insurance cooperatives like the one to whose success Maggie Walker contributed so greatly.

Maggie Lena Draper Walker, banker

As founder of the oldest surviving bank owned and operated by Blacks in America, Maggie Walker exemplifies the role of minorities in the growth and development of this country. The Horatio Alger style in which she rose from poverty to affluence is a source of inspiration to all young Americans, and is especially an inspiration to young people of minority and ethnic groups.

Jeanette G. Harris, born July 18, 1934, in Philadelphia, enjoys the distinction of being the first Black female bank manager in Philadelphia. She is a banking officer and bank manager for the First Pennsylvania Bank and is a member of the Philadelphia Black Bankers' Association. Harris has also served as treasurer of Merchants Association for Progress Plaza Shopping Center.[5]

The first Black woman to be appointed second vice-president of a major Chicago bank is Challis Lowe. She serves as manager of a branch facility of Continental Illinois National Bank and Trust Company, the seventh largest bank in the United States. Lowe was born in Chicago and obtained her early education in the local schools. She received the Bachelor of Arts degree in communications from Southern Illinois University and the Master of Business Administration from Northwestern University.

She began her career as a buyer's assistant at Sears, Roebuck and Company in 1967 and entered the banking business as a senior customer service representative in 1971. Lowe joined Continental Illinois National Bank and Trust Company in 1971 and was promoted to second vice-president in 1976. In this position she was responsible for coordinating the activities surrounding the planning and the building of Continental's first remote banking facility. This assignment included the development and implementation of a marketing plan which would penetrate the Chicago North-Loop deposit market. She is also responsible for the hiring and training of a staff which can function across traditional departmental lines. For the first time at Continental, high net worth individuals and retail and commercial customers could be serviced under one management. The management of this banking facility of forty employees includes the task of administering an annual expense budget of approximately $2,000,000.[6]

Emma Carolyn Chappell, bank Vice-President

In the 1970's many other Black women began holding lay positions in banking and other money management institutions. In Philadelphia, Pennsylvania Emma Carolyn Chappell serves as vice president of Continental Bank. Prior to attaining this office in 1974, she moved through the ranks as commercial teller, new accounts clerk, executive secretary, administrative assistant, executive trainee, credit specialist, and assistant treasurer.[7]

Lillian Frances Warren, born in Pleasant Hill, Louisiana, is the personnel banking representative for the First National Bank of Minneapolis, Minnesota. She was a former columnist for the *Twin Cities Courier*, and executive secretary of the Minneapolis Urban League. She was the Equal Opportunities coordinator for the First National Bank in 1969-1975.[8]

The First Bank National Association of Cleveland, Ohio was established in 1974 with Carole Hoover as deputy organizer. Now, with assets totaling more than $34 million, the bank ranks sixth among Black banks in the United States. Currently, Hoover holds the positions of vice president, secretary, and member of the institution's governing board.

Hoover is a leader in the area of Black economic development in Cleveland. She heads the Greater Cleveland Growth Corporation, a business development association formed to provide minority businesses with financial, managerial, and technical assistance. As chief executive officer of the Growth Corporation, she has full responsibility for the operations of the organization. The corporation has aided more than 400 minority businesses since its inception, and in 1976 alone, 167,000 loans totaling $8 million were processed.[9]

At Bryn Mawr Trust Company in Philadelphia, Pennsylvania, Henrietta Bright serves as assistant treasurer in the institution's general banking department.[10]

A number of Black women have become leaders in other lay areas of money management. For example, Eunice Elaine Winston, a lawyer from San Diego, California, serves as treasurer of the city of San Diego. She formerly was fiscal manager, deputy director, and administrator of San Diego Model Cities Program. Winston was also budgetary and enterprise accountant for the city of San Diego, and the legal accountant for Einstein, Lustig, Harris and Single, Incorporated.[11]

Patricia Staunton Davis has been an economist with the Federal Reserve Board in Washington, D.C. since 1976. From 1973-75 she was a management consultant with Booz, Allen and Hamilton, and she was senior programmer and marketing representative for Urban Institute in 1970-71.[12]

Geraldine D. Green, an attorney specializing in corporate finance, serves as State Commissioner of Corporations in California. Green gave up a $65,000 a year job as senior counsel of Atlantic Richfield Company to take the $46,000 a year post heading the department in which 350 employees are under her authority. The Department of Corporations, which Green heads, polices the sale of securities, credit unions, real estate and other retail franchises, check cashing companies, escrow companies, industrial loan brokers, personal property loan brokers and prepaid health plans. Green serves as president of the Beverly Hills-Hollywood branch of the National Association for the Advancement of Colored People.[13]

Victoria Lynn Sanders, Chicago's first Black woman stockbroker, has been a registered representative with Gore Forgan, William Staats, Inc. since 1969. Sanders is unique in that she thrives in what has previously been an exclusively male enclave. "Managing 50 blue-chip portfolios can be an exciting job," she says, "especially when the ratio of men stockbrokers to women stockbrokers is approximately 500 to 9." However, Sanders sees significant potential in her job. Referring to the Black community she says, "There's a market here that has to be explored."[14]

Savings and Loan

A number of Black women has achieved in various kinds of financial institutions since Maggie L. Walker exerted her guiding influence as the first female and first Black woman president of a bank. One such institution where Black women have made some progress in upper management is savings and loan firms. Two 20th century Black women who have upper level positions in savings and loan are Louise K. Quarles and Wilma J. Sutton.

Louise K. Quarles is secretary and managing officer of the Illinois Federal Savings and Loan Association, a $27 million institution. She earned a Bachelor of Science degree in business administration from Alcorn College in Mississippi and joined Illinois Federal after working for the Federal Wage Stabilization Board. She became the first woman on the Board of Directors for Illinois Federal in 1963 and was elected secretary and managing officer in 1965. Quarles thinks that "the field of business is opening wider for women executives and it is most necessary that we take the opportunity to prove ourselves capable of handling any position we accept."[15]

Wilma J. Sutton worked for several years with Chicago Title and Trust Company before joining the Hyde Park Federal Savings and Loan Association of Chicago in 1964. Today she is a vice president and manager of the mortgage department at Hyde Park Federal. She is one of the few women ever to become a chief loan officer in Chicago savings and loan associations. Sutton had previously spent eleven years at the Chicago Title and Trust Company before joining Hyde Park Federal in a clerical position.[16]

Certified Public Accountants

The accounting profession has grown rapidly in the past several decades. This progress has been because of the increased use of accounting information in business management, the greater use of accounting services by small business organizations, the complex and changing tax systems, and the growth in size and number of business corporations required to provide financial reports to their stockholders.[17]

Between 1945 and 1976 the membership of the American Institute of Certified Public Accountants (AICPA) increased from 9,000 to over 150,000.[18] Despite the recent growth in the accounting profession, however, the number of minorities and women in the field is small. Although women represent 22 percent of all persons working as accountants, only 3 percent of the certified public accountants (CPA's) in this country are women.[19] Moreover, Blacks make up only 0.3 percent of the total CPA's in the United States. According to a 1976 survey of CPA's, 450 of the total 150,000 were Black. Although this number appears small in comparison to the total, it represents more than twice the number of Black CPA's identified in 1969. Black women are entering the profession at a faster rate than Black men. Black women represented 8.8 percent of the identified Black CPA's in 1968 and 11.5 percent of those identified in 1976.[20]

One writer commenting on women and minorities in accounting points out that "Even though the percentage increase of Blacks in the CPA profession has been greater than most other professions because of the small base from which it is measured, the percentage representation of Blacks in the CPA profession still falls behind Black representation in other key occupations such as medicine and law."[21]

In 1970, an American Institute of Certified Public Accountants' survey showed 13 Black certified public accountants (men and women) in the nation's major public accounting firms, but by 1972 that number had increased to 41. The total number of Black professionals employed in major accounting firms increased from 197 in 1969 to 764 in 1972.[22]

The 1975 survey of these firms showed 118 Black certified public accountants and 1,026 Black professionals employed by major accounting firms.[23] Progress for Black women in accounting has come about slowly and almost painfully, but there is evidence of their advance.

Mary T. Washington, born in Vicksburg, Mississippi in 1910, became in 1939 the first woman certified public accountant of her race. She received her degree in business from Chicago's Northwestern University and in 1939 she started her own accounting firm in Chicago with the idea of attracting more young people to the profession. As her business grew, young men and women entered the firms for apprenticeship and experience. Fifteen of them received their certified public accountant certificates, and many others have gone on to become highly successful in other careers.[24]

Washington belongs to a number of professional societies; among them are The American Institute of Certified Public Accountants, The

Mary Washington Wylie - Certified Public Accountant

Illinois Society of Certified Public Accountants, The National Association of Cost Accountants, associate member of the American Institute of Management, and the National Association of Minority Certified Public Accounting Firms. She served on the Governor's Auditing Advisory Board of Illinois from 1963 to 1965, and on the President's Council on Youth Opportunity under President Lyndon B. Johnson in 1967. She has been honored as a pioneer in her field by numerous organizations.

Ann Vickers Beasley, born in Orlando, Florida, is a public accountant, owner and manager of the Active VIP Bookkeeping, Incorporated in New York City. She was formerly the comptroller of Bathgate Community Housing Development Corporation and the auditor and consultant for St. Nicholas Park Management Corporation. Beasley, a real estate saleswoman, was also an auditor for the City of New York Housing Development Administration.[25]

In 1962, Ruth Coles Harris became the first Black woman to pass the examination for certified public accountants in the Commonwealth of Virginia. Harris received her Bachelor of Science degree in business administration from Virginia State University, her MBA degree in accounting and management from New York University, and her Ed.D. in higher educational administration from the College of William and Mary in Virginia. Beginning as an instructor in the Department of Commerce at Virginia Union University in 1949, she has been promoted through the ranks and is now director of the Sydney Lewis School of Business Administration at Virginia Union University. She is a co-author of an elementary accounting textbook, *Principles of Accounting*, published by Putnam Publishing Company, 1959.[26]

In Chicago, Illinois, Beverly Gina Garrison is an accountant and auditor with Central City Marketing, Incorporated. She was formerly the chief accountant of RCA Service Company and the senior auditor of Touche Ross and Company of Chicago. She also worked in system analysis at Standard Oil Company.[27]

Another accounting executive in Chicago, Kathie Price Leaner, is with CBS-WBBM Newsradio 78. She also served as accounting executive with WBEE Radio.[28]

In 1969, Carolyn Lee Smith became the first Black woman to pass the Certified Public Accountant examination in Washington, D.C. Smith is now auditing manager of Cooper and Lybrand Company in Washington, D.C.[29]

Carolyn L. Smith, Director of Finance and Revenue,
Government of the District of Columbia

Kathleen Copeland, now a self-employed attorney and accountant in Highland Park, Michigan, was the former owner and public accountant of Allen Bookkeeping Service in Highland Park.[30]

Since 1965, Mary L. Harper, of Pomona, California, has been a self-employed accountant and tax consultant.[31]

Carmen Snaggs, in 1944, established a public accounting practice in New York City, under the name of Carmen Medford, and today her business continues to be successful.[32]

Several Black women in colleges and universities have been responsible for the development of many budding certified public accountants. Outstanding among these educational leaders are Larzette Golden Hale, head of the Department of Accounting, Utah State University, and Sybil Mobley, dean of the School of Business, Florida A & M University. To be noted also are Johnnie Clark,

Professor of accounting at Atlanta University, and Ruth Harris, director of the Sidney Lewis School of Business Administration.[33]

Larzette Golden Hale, with a B.S. degree from Langston University in Oklahoma, holds a Ph.D. degree in accounting from the University of Wisconsin and she is a certified public accountant. For more than ten years, she served as head of the Department of Business Administration at Clark College while also maintaining her own CPA Office in Atlanta, Georgia.

Serving as the vice-president of the American Society of Certified Public Accountants, Hale also holds national office in five other professional groups. In Logan, Utah she is active in community affairs, serving as trustee at the United Presbyterian Church, as state treasurer of the American Association of University Women, and as a member of the Governor's Commission on Status of Women. She is a past national president of Alpha Kappa Alpha Sorority, Inc., the first Black national service sorority with present membership of more than 70,000 college women and graduates.

Larzette G. Hale - Certified Public Accountant
and college administrator

Hale, widow of a college president and mother of one son and three daughters, is also recognized for her activities in public education. She is an active member of the National Citizens Emergency Committee to Save Our Public Libraries, and she is the author of nine recent publications on accounting and higher education.

Sybil Collins Mobley
Certified Public Accountant and College Dean

Sybil Collins Mobley, born in Shreveport, Louisiana, holds a B.A. degree from Bishop College in Texas, the M.B.A. from the Wharton School of Finance and Commerce at the University of Pennsylvania, and the Ph.D. in accounting from the University of Illinois. She is also a certified public accountant. With more than eighteen publications to her credit, Mobley has work experiences at International Business Machine Corporation, Union Carbide Corporation, Price Waterhouse and Company, and the Chase Manhattan Bank. An active member of nine professional organizations, including the American Institute of Certified Public Accountants and the National Association of Black

Accountants, Sybil Mobley serves as vice-president of the American Accounting Association; a director of the Southeast First National Bank of Miami, Florida; member of the Florida Tax Reform Commission; and President of the International Association of Black Business Educators.

Married and mother of three children, Mobley is also recognized as an international scholar in accounting. In 1974 and 1976 she was appointed Special Consultant to the United States Agency for International Development. For outstanding contributions to her profession, Mobley was presented the Robert Russa Moten Leadership Award by the National Business League in October 1975 in Boston.

Real Estate

Since antiquity land has been recognized as the only really permanent form of wealth. Land forms the backbone of the economic structure of every nation. And while Blacks have owned land in America from the early periods of history, it is evident that Blacks have not generally possessed this form of wealth in proportion to their numbers. Nevertheless, records on Black population and occupations show that there were some Blacks in real estate in the early 18th century. Between the early 1900's and the mid-1920's "real estate dealers became an important factor in the development of Negro business in connection with banks and other financial institutions." Some years later when there was a marked migration by Blacks to industrial centers where housing was a problem, an unusual opportunity was offered to Black real estate brokers, many of whom "established realty corporations in most of the largest cities with large Black populations."[34]

One of the early Black female property owners was Clara Brown. Brown was born a slave in Kentucky and secured her freedom at age fifty-five after long years of toil. She joined the procession of gold seekers in Gregory Gulch, where from a mining camp she reaped unusual returns which enabled her to bring thirty-eight of her relatives from the old plantation in Kentucky to Colorado.

In her early years in Colorado, "Aunt Clara Brown, the Angel of the Rockies" as she was known, was a cook and laundry woman. She arrived in Denver with one of the first wagon trains. Clara Brown was noted for her generosity and charity because she fed and loaned money to destitute pioneers. She also grub-staked numerous prospectors and became well-to-do from the half shares of their mines when they made promising strikes. It was with the money she made that she was able to return to Kentucky. She bought many of her friends and relatives out of slavery and provided sponsorship to two wagon trains of Black families traveling from Leavenworth, Kansas to Colorado.

Brown succeeded in securing mines of her own and was frequently seen in camps looking after some of her property. She was one of the first Blacks elected as a member of the Colorado Pioneer Association. She was elected to membership while in her seventies and was buried with honors by that association.

Brown was also very active in the early organization of the Methodist Episcopal Church in the mining regions of early Colorado at Central City, and she aided in the founding of the Union Sunday School. She was the only female who took part in the early Union Sunday School Conference meetings.[35]

Other early property owners include Lillie G. Taylor, "Old Aunty Combs," Lucy Phillips, Biddy Mason, and Mary Ellen Pleasant. In 1869, Lillie G. Taylor became what is believed to be one of the richest Black women in the world when the Massachusetts Supreme Court ruled that a vast tract of land in southwestern Claiborne County, Louisiana, that was rich in oil and gas and estimated to be worth not less than $20 million, belonged to her.[36]

In 1890, another Black woman, "Old Aunty Ony Combs" struck it rich. It is not known where she was born or when she moved to Pitkin, Colorado. In addition to earning part of her living working at the washtub, she investigated mining claims and secured interest in various prospects. Sometimes she prospected on her own efforts and labor and sometimes by the grub-staking of her husband. Among the properties which she owned was the Whig Mine, an extension of the Chloride Mine, located three and one-half miles southwest of Pitkin and to which she secured a clear title just before the turn of the twentieth century.[37]

In the mid-1800's, in Cheyenne, Wyoming, Lucy Phillips, a laundry woman by profession, was able to accumulate several land parcels throughout Cheyenne. She was instrumental in the establishment of the African Methodist Episcopal Church in Wyoming and donated land for the site of the church. She was also one of the first to help write the church's laws and to participate in church planning.[38]

Biddy Mason was a slave who "rose to a position of affluence after winning her freedom in the California courts." This Black woman pioneer arrived in San Bernadino, California in 1851 with a caravan of wagons, having walked from Hancock County, Mississippi. She not only herded cattle and other livestock during the long trek West, but she also had responsibility for the care of her three young daughters.

When her master decided to return to the South with his slaves in 1856, Biddy Mason appealed to the local sheriff and was successful in winning freedom for herself and her daughters.

Moving to Los Angeles, she worked assiduously as a confinement nurse at the rate of $2.50 per day, until she saved enough money to buy property in what was then the city of Los Angeles. Apparently realizing the potential of growth for the city, she continued to acquire property and to teach her children to value it. Before she died in 1891, Biddy Mason had become a wealthy widow who sold off parcels of land as the value of property increased dramatically. A *Los Angeles Daily Times* article of February 12, 1909, reported her daughter Ellen's real estate holdings as being worth $300,000.[39]

Biddy Mason, like so many successful Black women, was a humanitarian. She was generous with her time and her money, visiting and feeding prisoners in jail and helping the homeless and unfortunate. In the early 1800's when the Los Angeles area was struck by a disastrous flood, Biddy Mason arranged and was responsible for an "open account" at a local grocery store to be used for food supplies for flood victims. Her concern for human beings, regardless of race, made her a legend in Los Angeles County.[40]

Mary Ellen Pleasant is one of the more interesting early Black female financial geniuses. Numerous accounts credit her with being the best business person (male or female) in San Francisco during the early Gold Rush days. She described herself as "a capitalist by profession" to an 1890 census-taker.[41] Her exact origin remains questionable. One theory is that "she was born in slavery, either in Louisiana or Virginia or Georgia. [But] in 1901, she said, 'I was born in Philadelphia, at number 9 Barley Street'."[42]

Whatever her origin "almost everyone agrees that she settled in San Francisco during the Gold Rush and made a fortune by speculating in the stock market and by operating a string of ultra-fashionable boarding houses. While she was doing this with her left hand, she was supporting, with her right, the struggle for Black liberation, aiding and hiding fugitive slaves, and challenging the Jim Crow laws of California. In her spare time, she busied herself with the problems of women, supporting and maintaining a long line of Black and white protegees. . ."[43]

For several years after her arrival in San Francisco, Pleasant worked as a housekeeper for a succession of merchant princes. While working as a housekeeper, she speculated in the stock and money markets. . . [She] was sensationally successful in these ventures, partly because she had a genius for financial speculation, partly because she had developed almost infallible sources of information. . .The grand outcome was that Mary Ellen Pleasant soon knew more about the business secrets of the West Coast than the leading bankers and stock experts. By 1855, she owned a string of laundries."

Mary Ellen Pleasant, "Mother of the Civil Rights Struggle
in California"
(photo courtesy The Society of California Pioneers)

In 1867 or 1868 Mary Ellen Pleasant opened her first boarding house and "Pyramiding her profits, she soon became the managing director of several boarding houses and restaurants. In 1890 and 1891, she bought and created the 1,000 acre Beltane ranch in Sonoma County, California. After a series of tangled legal affairs, and questionable events involving people in her life, Mary Ellen Pleasant died in January 1904.[44] It is apparent that this Black woman wielded a great deal of power through her wealth of prime property in the areas of Bakersfield and Fresno because she counseled and influenced men of wealth and power.[45]

Another Black woman who amassed quite a fortune in real estate holdings in the early part of the 20th century was "Pigfoot Mary." Mary, whose real name was Lillian Harris, arrived in New York in 1901.

> Within a week after her arrival she had earned five dollars as a domestic. Mary spent three dollars of the amount for a dilapidated baby carriage and a large wash boiler and invested the other two in pigs' feet. Then she wheedled the proprietor of "Rudolph's," a popular saloon near Sixty-first Street on Amsterdam Avenue, into allowing her to boil the delicacy atop his cookstove. Mounting the steaming boiler of pigs' feet on the baby carriage, she wheeled all her worldly wealth through the swinging doors of the saloon and set up business at the curb in front.
>
> The pigs' feet business soon showed a profit, and hog-maws, chitterlings, and corn-on-the-cob were added to the menu. Pig Foot Mary, now a licensed peddler, presided over a specially constructed portable steam-table, which she had designed herself. Pleasant-faced, deep-voiced, her enormous proportions neatly swathed in starched checked gingham, she was at her stall from early morning until late at night. Her personal needs were few; she owned two cotton dresses and lived in a small furnished room. Her bank account mounted, for Mary was saving money against her old age. She often explained that she intended to have enough to buy a place for herself in an old folk's home for respectable colored people. Nothing else interested her.
>
> After more than sixteen years at her Amsterdam Avenue stand, Pig Foot Mary was forced to trail her migrant customers to Harlem. This time she rented a tiny booth, an appendage to a newspaper and shoe shine parlor, at Lenox Avenue and 135th Street. In less than three weeks she married the stand's owner, John Dean. As Mrs. Dean, Pig Foot Mary's concern about her old age lessened and she allowed herself to be persuaded to invest her savings in Harlem properties. Her first venture was the purchase of a $44,000 Seventh Avenue apartment-house building, which six years later she sold to a Negro undertaker, Adolph Howell, for $72,000. Her subsequent dealings in real estate were equally successful, and at one time her total holdings were valued at $375,000.
>
> Regarded as one of the community's shrewdest business women, Pig Foot Mary could neither read nor write. She died in California in 1928 at the age of fifty-eight.[46]

Other Black women involved in early real estate holdings include Amanda Eubanks, Zula Swanson, Mary McLeod Bethune, and Margarite Reed Syphax. Amanda Eubanks became one of the wealthiest women in the country when a 1921 decision by the Georgia Supreme Court declared her entitled to the $500,000 real estate holdings left to her by her white father in his will.[47]

When Zula Swanson, a former Alabama cotton plantation worker, moved in 1929 from Portland, Oregon to Anchorage, Alaska, Anchorage was a frontier town of only 3,000 inhabitants to which fishermen and gold prospectors came to have a good time. For $2,000, Swanson bought a burned building and a piece of land along the town's one main street. She rebuilt the structure into a rooming house and further spread her estate holdings to the extent that she was considered Alaska's richest Black of her time. Today, a multi-million-dollar Penney's Department Store stands on one corner of the intersection where Swanson ran her rooming house, and a modern office building on another. She reportedly turned down an offer of a quarter of a million dollars for her corner. All of the twenty or so pieces of property she owns have become more and more valuable as population and industry have mushroomed.[48]

Mary McLeod Bethune, educator and political activist
(photo courtesy Schomburg Center
New York Public Library)

Mary McLeod Bethune is well known as an outstanding educator, advisor to presidents, and as the only Black woman to establish what is today a four-year accredited college in Florida. Perhaps less well known is the fact that she was also a land developer and director of substantial Florida businesses.

Margarite Reed Syphax of Arlington, Virginia, has received many awards for her excellence in business and community endeavors. She is secretary-treasurer of W.T. Syphax Enterprises, an umbrella corporation of property management, development, and construction firms owned by Margarite Syphax and her husband, William T. Syphax.

Syphax, who heads the management aspects of the company, once spent her lunch and evening hours supervising the carpenters, plumbers, electricians, and other workers back in the days when the Syphaxes first began in the field. Their business of making repairs on old homes eventually snowballed into a development and construction operation, forcing them to devote full time to the business which now grosses more than $4 million annually.

In the 27 years they have been in business, Syphax has built hundreds of units, both single and multiple dwellings, and, in the process, has employed hundreds of people in the area. The Syphaxes are channeling their resources into the development of an institution, for unemployed people who want to work in the building trades and property management.[49]

Celestine Strode Cook, a native of Teagus, Texas, became president of the estate of her first husband who was one of the wealthiest Black men in Texas. Under the administration and trusteeship of First Hutchings-Sealy National Bank, she became manager of his holdings in Texas and Illinois.

When she married Jesse Cook, owner of Good Citizens Life Insurance Company, Celestine Strode Cook moved to New Orleans. In 1959, she became the director of personnel and public relations at Good Citizens Life Insurance Company. She is currently a member of the board of directors of Liberty Bank and Trust Company, the only minority owned and operated bank in New Orleans. She is also a management consultant to Security Industrial Insurance Company.[50]

Another prominent Black woman involved in real estate management is Callie Broxton Watkins, owner of the Broxton Apartments in Chicago, Illinois. Watkins, an Alabama native, attended Chicago Business College and studied business administration. After the death of her father in 1955, she assumed the leadership of the family business.[51]

Flaxie Madison Pinkett, a native of Washington, D.C., started her career in the real estate business after her graduation from Howard University. She worked her way through each level of employment and is now president and treasurer of a Washington, D.C. real estate brokerage and general insurance company. Pinkett was elected a member of the Board of Directors of John R. Pinkett, Incorporated in 1942 and became its president in 1958.[52]

Lottie Watkins, Atlanta, Georgia, born and bred, started her business, Lottie Watkins Enterprises, in that city in 1960. Her firm, in 1976 listed as a $4,500,000 operation, specializes in real estate management, sales, and loans. Watkins "has been called the 'Tireless lady tycoon' by *Atlanta* magazine." She is cited in the international *Two Thousand Women of Achievement* and has served on a number of civic, political, and professional boards and organizations.

In 1961, Mary Hutson Landon began her business career with the Harris Hanby Real Estate Company in New Castle, Delaware. Securing Federal Housing Administration and Veterans Administration financing for urban Blacks prior to the 1963 "open housing" legislation was one of Landon's most challenging career efforts. She was the first Black female real estate broker in the State of Delaware and was a co-founder of the New Castle County Board of Realtors.[54]

Anne W. Toliver is an administrator who serves as executive director of the National Association of Real Estate Brokers, Incorporated (NAREB) in Washington, D.C. Toliver, a native of Atlanta, Georgia, directs and supervises administrative programs of the National Association of Real Estate Brokers and plans and coordinates its national conventions, conferences, and special meetings. She is the founder and owner of her own real estate firm, Reliance Realty Company, in Washington.[55]

Banking and Other Financial Institutions and Women

Since Maggie Draper Walker, the first female and first Black woman president of a bank, exerted her guiding influence in making a bank successful, a number of Black women have been involved in various areas of financial institutions. The increase in employment of Black females in banks and other financial institutions started in 1940 along with the overall increase in female employment. But Black females are still underrepresented in upper level positions, i.e. officials and managers, professionals, and in sales and technical positions. "The top banking jobs are still predominantly white male, the middle jobs predominantly female [non-black] and the blue collar jobs predominantly Black males."[56]

"It was not until the mid-1960's that employment opportunities for minority group members began to increase significantly, in part because of social protest and stronger legislation, including the 1964 Civil Rights Act. An Equal Opportunity Commission summary report for the banking industry showed that by 1975, 16% of all employees were minority women."[57] But since that 16% includes Black, Hispanic, and other non-white females, the picture of Black females in banking is not as sanguine as it should be. Considering the statistics, the Black women who have become successful in the financial industry deserve high praise.

NOTES

[1] J.H. Harmon, Jr., Arnett G. Lindsay, and Carter G. Woodson, *The Negro As a Business Man* (College Park, Md.: McGrath Publishing Co., 1969), pp. 24-26.

[2] Harmon, et al, pp. 41-47.

[3] Harmon, et al, pp. 57-63.

[4] American Mothers Committee, Bicentennial Project, *Mothers of Achievement: 1776-1976* (Rutland, Vermont: C.E. Tuttle Publishers, 1976), pp. 552-557. Unless otherwise noted, all subsequent text information regarding Mrs. Walker is taken from this source.

[5] William C. Matney, ed., *Who's Who Among Black Americans: 1977-1978*, 2nd ed. (Northbrook, Illinois: Who's Who Among Black Americans, Inc., 1978), p. 386.

[6] Alpha Kappa Alpha Sorority, Inc., Heritage Series #3, *Women in Business*, 1970, p. 12.

[7] Matney, p. 157.

[8] Matney, p. 228.

[9] *Ebony*, August, 1977, p. 43.

[10] "Names in the News," *Black Enterprise*, September 1976, p. 14.

[11] Matney, p. 987.

[12] Matney, p. 224.

[13] *Variety*, 18 December 1979.

[14] *Beacon-News*, Aurora, Illinois, 22 August 1970.

[15] Alpha Kappa Alpha Sorority, p. 17.

[16] Alpha Kappa Alpha Sorority, p. 20.

[17] Stephen A. Schneider, *The Availability of Minorities and Women for Professional and Managerial Positions: 1970-1985* (Philadelphia: University of Pennsylvania, 1977), p. 76.

[18] Gary John Previts, "The Accountant in our History: A Bicentennial Overview," *Journal of Accountancy*, Vol. 142 (July 1976), p. 50.

[19] *Occupational Outlook Handbook*, 1974-1975 Edition, Bulletin 1785 (Washington, D.C.: Government Printing Office, 1974), p. 128.

[20] Bert N. Mitchell, "The Status of the Black CPA—An Update," *Journal of Accountancy*, Vol. 141 (May 1976), p. 52.

[21] Schneider, p. 81.

[22] William R. Gifford, "Black Accountants," *Price Waterhouse Company Review*, Vol. 18 (1973), p. 44.

[23] Schneider, p. 79.

[24] Letter received from Dr. Mary Clay Torian, Head, Department of Business, Savannah State College, Georgia, 3 March 1980.

[25] Matney, p. 52.

[26] Dr. Mary Clay Torian.

[27] Matney, p. 321.

[28] Matney, p. 321.

[29]Matney, p. 825.

[30]Matney, p. 191.

[31]Matney, p. 381.

[32]Matney, p. 838.

[33]Mary Clay Torian.

[34]Harmon, *et al*, pp. 25-26. See also Roi Ottley and William Weatherby, *The Negro in New York: 1626-1940* (New York: Praeger Publishers, 1967), pp. 183-188.

[35]W. Sherman Savage, *New Day*, Vol. 5, December 1947, p. 12.

[36]Mabel M. Symthe, *The Black American Reference Book* (Englewood Cliffs, New Jersey: Prentice-Hall, Inc., 1976), p. 131.

[37]Savage, p. 12.

[38]Savage, p. 18.

[39]Savage, p. 14.

[40]*Drumtalk*, Vol. 1, No. 2 (July/August 1978), p. 22.

[41]Lerone Bennett, Jr., "The Mystery of Mary Ellen Pleasant," *Ebony*, April 1979, p. 90.

[42]Lerone Bennett, Jr., "The Mystery of Mary Ellen Pleasant," *Ebony*, May 1979, p. 72.

[43]Bennett, *Ebony*, April 1979, p. 91.

[44]Bennett, *Ebony*, May 1979, pp. 74, 76, 82, 86.

[45]William Loren Katz, comp., *Guide to Black Studies Resources* (New York: Education Design, Incorporated, 1970), p. 162.

[46]Roi Ottley and William J. Weatherby, Ed. *The Negro In New York* (New York: Praeger Publishers, 1969), pp. 187-188.

[47]Symthe.

[48]Letter received from William Cody, Anchorage, Alaska, 10 December 1979.

[49]*Ebony*, November 1975, pp. 124-125.

[50]Elneita Dever, "Celestine Strode Cook," Unpublished paper, North Texas State University, Denton, September 1979.

[51]Alpha Kappa Alpha Sorority, p. 21.

[52]Alpha Kappa Alpha Sorority, p. 17.

[53]Dorothy Gloster, "The Tireless Lady Tycoon," *Essence*, March 1976, pp. 61-62, 90, 96, and 116.

[54]Karla Froman Wright, "Black Women: Challenge for the 1980's," Presentation at the Black Women's Conference, Saturday, May 2, 1979, Radisson Wilmington Hotel, Wilmington, Delaware.

[55]*Ebony's 1,000 Successful Blacks*, Vol. 1 (Chicago: Johnson Publishing Co., 1973), p. 307.

[56]Armand Thieblot, Jr. and Linda Pickthorne Fletcher, *Negro Employment In Finance* (Philadelphia: University of Pennsylvania, 1970), p. 37. See also *Women and Minorities in Banking*, Wendy C. Schwartz, Ed., (New York: Praeger Publishers, 1976), pp. 21-34.

[57]Schwartz, p. 25.

CHAPTER IV

INSURANCE, ADVERTISING, MARKETING AND MANAGEMENT, SALES, BOOKING AND RECORDING AGENCIES

Insurance businesses among Blacks grew out of church benevolent societies and Black fraternal organizations such as the Masons and the Odd Fellows. These societies and organizations obligated themselves to take care of the sick and to bury the dead, and somewhat later they began giving the heirs of the dead a certain amount of money. This was an important step toward actual endowment.

As such organizations increased and, by necessity, began to employ business management techniques, something like the modern insurance business began among Blacks. The first association to approach an insurance basis was the Grand United Order of True Reformers of Richmond, Virginia. This order "enabled other societies to learn by observation." In fact, the bank headed by Maggie Draper Walker, the first woman bank president in America, also had an insurance department (and published a newspaper). "Under her direction the Independent Order of St. Luke with more experience and better trained workers. . .overcame the difficulties" which caused the undoing of other banks and fledgling insurance companies.[1]

The first insurance company started for that purpose alone by Blacks was established in Philadelphia in 1810. It, however, did not last and the first successful firm, The Southern Aid & Insurance Company, was organized in 1893 in Virginia. At the time that this company was started, records show that other benefit societies (which usually provided "insurance" benefits) were growing. One, in particular, was the Order of Good Shepherds, presided over by Ora Brown Stokes, a Black woman.[2] So from at least 1893 on, insurance businesses owned and operated by Blacks began in earnest.

As the Black insurance industry slowly evolved from the self-help groups and mutual aid societies established to meet the needs of the time, insurance grew to be the most important business concern for Blacks during the first half of the twentieth century. In the early 1920's Black businessmen, alarmed at the discrimination Black people faced in attempting to secure coverage, realized the necessity of converting small firms into legal reserve life insurance companies. These businesses, which began largely as family enterprises, were quick to draw upon the resources of their women family members and a large number of Black women were given employment in the field.

Ebony magazine reported in a 1977 article on women in business that many of the current female executives of Black firms today started as clerks, secretaries, and insurance agents, while others inherited their positions or were appointed administrators by virtue of family ownership of the company. Women now are clearly visible in management positions."[3]

Throughout the United States, numerous Black women are holding prominent positions in the insurance industry. In Louisiana, Ida M. Edwards is a board member and vice-president of Lighthouse Securities and Investment Companies of Shreveport. Celestine Strode Cook is a stockholder and corporate secretary of three corporations: Good Citizens Life Insurance Company; Good Citizens Funeral System, Incorporated; and Good Citizens Realty Corporation, Incorporated, all in New Orleans, Louisiana. Also located in New Orleans is the Gertrude Geddes Willis Life Insurance Company and the Gertrude Geddes Willis Funeral Home, founded by Willis in 1940. Martha B. Ballory is second vice-president and office manager of the corporation. The National Service Industrial Life and United Fidelity Victory Insurance Companies of New Orleans are headed by Sandra Rhodes Duncan, vice–president, and Joan Rhodes Brown, sister of Duncan, who is also executive vice-president of National Service Industrial Life Company; Marion Gundy Hill is vice-president of Purple Shield Life of Baton Rouge.[4]

Alabama also has its share of Black women in the insurance business. Minnie L. Gaston is first vice-president of Booker T. Washington Insurance of Birmingham and Lucille G. Fletcher is vice-president and agency director of Bradford's Industrial Insurance Company. Also in Birmingham, the Protective Industrial Insurance Company is a third generation family business. Madeline Harris Davis worked her way through the ranks and is now executive secretary and director of the corporation. In Mobile, Alabama, Lillian M. Lovett and her daughter, Cassaundria, own and manage Lovett's Life and Burial Insurance Company. Lovett serves as board chairwoman and president; Cassaundria is vice-president and secretary.[5] Also in Mobile, Pearl Madison is president of the Christian Benevolent Burial and Insurance Company. Madison, who founded the business in 1929, employs more than seventy people in a variety of positions within the insurance and funeral directing branches of the business.[6]

As president of Hornsby-McCoy Realty Company in Augusta, Georgia, Hattie B. Hornsby heads a multi-faceted company, underwriting various types of insurance as well as handling rental property sales and property management. Another Georgian, Helen J. Collins, has a career with Atlanta Life that spans 40 years. She was named vice-president in 1973 and also serves on the Board of Directors.[7]

Hilda Hall Butler, active in insurance work since 1939, is vice-president and secretary at Mammoth Life and Accident Insurance Company of Louisville, Kentucky. She is the daughter of Henry Hall, the company founder.[8]

In California, Amanda G. Lockett served as president, corporate secretary, and director of data processing at Golden Gate Mutual Life in Los Angeles.[9] Born in Shreveport, Louisiana, she began her career with Golden Gate in 1942.

Also associated with Golden Gate of Los Angeles was Verna Alvis Hickman who retired in 1974 after 47 years with the company. She held the position of vice-president, secretary, and treasurer. In that position, she was responsible for custody of corporate records, bank funds, bonds and securities. Hickman designed and released the first Black insurance company's advertising to appear in *Ebony* magazine. The ad has been credited as being the opening wedge for the then fledgling magazine to procure advertising from national corporations. She also initiated one of the first advertising logos using the initials of the corporation's name, a medium now in general usage by major national corporations. The company received a series of awards for the logo design and its use from a number of graphic arts shows and organizations in the United States and Europe.[10]

In Chicago, Illinois, Martha H. Frye holds the position as vice-president of mortgage accounting with the Supreme Life Insurance Company of America. She was formerly a founder, board member, and comptroller of Dunbar Life of Cleveland, now a part of the Supreme Life Company of Chicago. At the American Woodmen's Life Insurance Company of Kansas City, Kansas, Lillie Anne Owens serves as vice-president, corporate secretary-treasurer.[11]

In Boston, Massachusetts, in 1963, Erna Ballantine Bryant became the first Black female to hold a quasi-administrative level position at any bank in New England. She is the head of Boston Five Cent Savings Bank and Life Insurance. Bryant is responsible for the promotion and sale of Savings Bank Life Insurance. In recent years, she has sold one-half million dollars of insurance annually.[12]

One of the pioneers in the insurance business was Florence Madison Hill, formerly of Essex County, Virginia. She established and operated a real estate business and insurance company in Philadelphia, Pennsylvania. Hill was a charter member of the National Association of Real Estate Brokers.[13]

Patricia Walker Shaw, a native of Little Rock, Arkansas, is a civic and professional leader in Memphis, Tennessee. Shaw, a research analyst, is vice-president and associate comptroller for Universal Life Insurance Company. In 1971, she became the first woman and the second Black commissioner of the Memphis Utility Board.[14]

In 1971, Glenda L. Copes was appointed as manager of Urban Affairs at Aetna Life and Casualty Company in Hartford, Connecticut. In this position, she maintains close liaison with the community, provides technical assistance to senior management involved in urban affairs, proposes new programs and coordinates and motivates participation of Aetna employees in community activities.[15]

V. Alyce Foster is co-owner with her husband of the H.C. Foster Insurance Agency and the H.C. Foster Real Estate Company of Dallas, Texas. Her company is the mortgage loan correspondent for Golden Gate Mutual Life Insurance Company of Los Angeles, California. This agreement helped to broaden the home-buying outlets for Black people in the Dallas area.[16]

In New York, Ernesta G. Procope has established herself as one of the most outstanding Blacks in the insurance business. She serves as president of the largest Black-owned insurance brokerage firm in the nation, the E.G. Bowman Company, Incorporated, founded in 1953 in Brooklyn, New York. Her business grosses over $10 million annually. Procope has received many state and national honors and awards as a leader in the business world. She is a member of the boards of directors of Avon Products Incorporated, Urban National Corporation, Equitable Community Home Service Corporation of Equitable Federal Savings and Loan Association, and the Salvation Army. She is a director of the Chubb Corporation of New York City and was elected to the boards of the Federal Insurance Company and the Vigilant Insurance Company, both subsidiaries of Chubb Corporation.[17]

Ernesta Procope says, "Although we have physically moved our main operation from the ghetto to Wall Street, our company's goals and objectives remain the same. To achieve those goals, we must be a part of economic mainstream America. It is not an easy task, especially being small and Black. We believe in perseverance, competence and dedication in building an effective and meaningful business, which happens to be Black owned but an equal opportunity employer. Our managers are committed to this concept. We, therefore, act and think in unison, for this is our philosophy."[18]

In Dallas, Texas, a young woman has spiraled to the top to become an insurance executive. She is Susie Tindell, who works for Phoenix

Mutual Life Insurance Company. In less than a decade, her earnings have jumped from well under $10,000 a year to an income reaching into the six-figure bracket. She started her career marketing cosmetics for a small firm, then for herself and subsequently for Revlon. She made the transition into business insurance and estate planning for Phoenix Mutual Life Insurance Company, then expanded to independent brokering for her own firm, Tindell and Associates. During her first year as a Phoenix Mutual agent, Tindell did $7.5 million dollars worth of business, thus earning a top rating among all the company's agents.[19]

Advertising

The creation of new markets and the stimulation of lagging markets through the use of advertising is a major business activity. Several Black women have carved out for themselves notable positions in this booming industry.

Barbara Proctor of Chicago, Illinois, is a leading business-woman in the field of advertising. This creative president of Proctor and Gardner Advertising, Incorporated, set out to establish an advertising agency based on a philosophy of community service. Although one of the top Black advertising firms in the nation, Proctor and Gardner is a small agency with twenty-two full-time employees doing $8 million a year in business. The firm specializes in marketing to Black communities on a local, regional, and national basis, and it selects clients whose products and services are constructive influences in the consumer communities. For example, two of her clients, Kraft, Incorporated, and Jewel Food Stores, a Chicago-based area chain, have shown their commitment by withdrawing sponsorship from violent television programs. Proctor admits that such selectivity has somewhat restricted the company's client list. As the chief policy-maker regarding client acquisition, she will turn away business if she deems it contrary to her philosophy of social responsibility.

Proctor, born in Asheville, North Carolina, came into the advertising business in 1963, after leaving a recording company as a writer and jazz critic. After seven years and two advertising agencies, she formed Proctor and Gardner in 1970 with the aid of loans from a local bank and the Small Business Administration. When Proctor began her business, she had what is traditionally considered to be three strikes against her — her race, her sex, and her age. To run a successful enterprise, she believes actions must be taken and decisions be made independent of the western ethic. "Our strength," she says, "will not be in numbers. We must become more expert in economic matters to make ourselves viable and necessary."[20]

Reflecting on the two people who inspired her most, Proctor says, "I was reared by my grandmother in the backhills of North Carolina. I have no idea how I came about, and I've never tried to find out. My grandmother had the greatest influence on my spiritual formation. . . . Her strength and faith in me became my spiritual backbone and I have never stopped building on it."

Barbara Proctor, (standing) President of Proctor-Gardner Advertising Company

Beyond the inspiration that her grandmother gave, Proctor says that "My absolute super inspiration for every thing in the whole world in terms of what you can be and do was Lena Horne. Way, way back in Black Mountain, when I was running around barefooted, ignorant, and Black, in the South, Lena was all we had." She goes on to say, "I like to think that some young person will look out at my example, the way I've looked at those who inspired me and, develop a drive to win."[24]

Caroline Robinson Jones, born in Benton Harbor, Michigan, is an advertising executive of Mingo, Jones, Guilmenot, Incorporated, a New York based agency specializing in marketing to the Black community. This corporation, established in 1977, is a full-service, Black-owned advertising agency started and staffed by high-level advertising professionals. Mingo, Jones, Guilmenot, Incorporated (MJM) was the first domestic affiliate of the Interpublic Group of Companies, Incorporated, which claims to be the world's largest advertising and marketing communications network providing services to both general and Black consumer markets.

As a founder, vice-president and creative director of Mingo, Jones, Guilmenot, Incorporated, Caroline Jones has spearheaded the firm's billings into a five million dollar annual business which has attracted accounts from top corporations interested in zeroing in on the $100 billion Black consumer market. Among the major clients from whom the firm creates Black–oriented advertising campaigns are Miller Brewing Company, Uncle Ben's Rice, L'Oreal, International, Cutty Sark, Kentucky Fried Chicken, Philip Morris, Incorporated, and International Mill Service.

Since leaving the University of Michigan in 1963, Caroline Jones has been establishing herself as a professional in the field. In 1963, she began her career as secretary-copywriter trainee at J. Walter Thompson Company (JWT), New York headquarters. (J. Walter Thompson is the world's largest advertising agency.) Within three weeks she was promoted to secretary for the creative director of J. Walter Thompson's largest account. As one of eighteen out of four hundred contestants she competed successfully in all-female competition for J. Walter Thompson's famous Copy Class. At J. Walter Thompson, Jones was promoted to copywriter and subsequently helped to write the "100 Years of Advertising: The J. Walter Thompson Story," the principle trade publication for the industry.

In 1969, Jones joined Zebra Associates, Incorporated, as senior copywriter and as a member of the founding group, in 1970 she was promoted to creative director and elected vice-president of the firm. In 1973, Jones became a partner and creative director of the Black Creative Group, Incorporated (BCG) established in New York City. The Black Creative Group was a marketing/creative service for major corporations and advertising agencies to create more intelligently positioned and relevant advertising for the Black consumer market.

Before joining Mingo, Jones, Guilmenot in 1977, Jones, by then an award-winning copywriter, held the position as vice-president and creative supervisor of one of the nation's largest advertising agencies, Batten, Barton, Durstine and Osborn, Incorporated. In 1975, she was elected to the board as the first Black female vice-president of a major advertising agency.

"Today advertising is a great field for women," says Jones, "especially since more than 50 percent of all consumers are female — a fact that many advertisers overlook. What is needed are women in management — women who come from account supervision and marketing rather than just the creative area — the route that most women take to get into the field."[22]

The Washington, D.C.-based company, Pride Environmental Services (PES), is headed by Mary Treadwell Barry who has created and guided to maturity a company which is literally turning trash into dollars. Pride Environmental Services provides trash containers for the city of Washington in return for the exclusive rights for all advertising on them.[23]

Barry says that advertising revenue is the key to making the business run and to paying off the initial seed capital which was borrowed to begin the firm. Under its agreement with the city, Pride Environmental Services has to buy, distribute, and service the environmental containers (called kiosks), and eventually place ten thousand of them on the city's streets. In addition to Pride Environmental Services and Kiosk Advertising, Barry also heads P.I. Properties and Pride Economic Enterprises, both of which are involved with housing management and ownership ventures.[24]

Another prominent Black woman in advertising is Amelia Grunstead of New York. She was elected as a vice-president of the J. Walter Thompson Company in 1976. She joined the New York-based advertising agency in 1967 and has served as a media planner and an associate supervisor.[25]

Joel P. Martin is the manager and owner of her own advertising firm on Madison Avenue, New York City, called J.P. Martin Associates, Inc. She began her business in her home in 1973 in Wingdale, New York. She moved to Madison Avenue in 1975. The firm provides clients with marketing analysis and research, media strategy and purchases, corporate recruiting and consumer advertising campaigns, promotional programs and public relations campaigns. She specializes in the Black and female market. The bulk of her money comes from employment advertising for the government and corporate clients.[26]

Marketing and Management

Black people have always been involved in the general process of moving goods from producers to consumers. But until very recent years, this involvement has most often been peripheral. A number of Black females have now carved out careers for themselves in marketing.

One such person is Joan M. Bryan, a resident of St. Albans, New York, who is manager of Special Marketing Affairs for Eastern Airlines of New York. Throughout the United States, Canada, Mexico, and the

Caribbean, Bryan directs promotional and community relations programs which are aimed principally at minority and women's markets. She is involved with market research, sales promotion, and direct sales. Her responsibilities include the dissemination of information to the special markets about Eastern Airlines' sales programs, promotional fares, tours, equipment, passenger as well as community affairs, has held research positions with Sara Lawrence College and the Decision Center of Marketing Research.[27]

Since 1973, Darlene Thompson of Detroit, Michigan, has been director of public relations and consumer affairs at Tom Cleveland and Associates (TCA), a Detroit-based marketing and advertising company. She heads a staff of professional people in marketing, sales and public relations.[28]

In 1977, Mary M. Farrington joined *Interspace Personnel* in New York City, as the director of recruitment and client development for marketing and sales personnel. Prior to joining *Interspace*, she was executive vice-president of Farwood Company, a sales agency for educational services.[29]

Karen Johnson, a Charleston, South Carolina native, reared in New York City, owns the Female Employment and Management Company (FEM), which offers job placement in a wide range of fields. FEM provides a comprehensive and personalized service and works with the client from the first steps in the job process to final placement. Ninety-five percent of FEM's clients are women and seventy percent are Black. Prior to establishing her own firm, she was employed for a number of years as vice-president of personnel for New York State Urban Development Corporation.[29]

Also making a name for herself in New York City is Margaret L. Richardson, a marketing and management specialist who is the executive director of National Minority Purchasing Council (NMPC), a quasi-public corporation formed in 1972 to increase the purchases of goods and services from minority-owned firms.

Richardson has served as executive director of the New York-New Jersey Regional Minority Purchasing Council, the largest of the thirty-eight regional councils that make up the National Minority Purchasing Council's national network. An advocate of minority economic development for many years, Richardson is well-known for her promotional projects and is an entrepreneur in her own right, having owned and managed three diverse companies.[30]

In 1974, with an initial investment of $600, Carol A. Bonds founded C.A. Bonds and Associates, a management and consulting firm in

Springfield, Illinois. After only a year in business, she secured more than seventy thousand dollars in contracts.

In 1974, Bonds resigned from her job as a computer programmer with the Illinois Department of Registration and Education, and in only one year, she more than quadrupled her annual income. She employs a staff of professional associates who work on a contract-to-contract basis in their field of business expertise. She offers clients a highly specialized consulting service in areas of records management, personnel training, public attitude surveys, and a variety of other business-related areas.[31]

Adrienne Frye was site office manager for Paschen Contractors, Incorporated of Chicago. The job included purchasing construction equipment and supplies, approving payment to suppliers and subcontractors, handling payroll for workers, and making reports to building owners. One of the projects she was involved with was a Federal building in the Loop of Chicago's business district.[32]

In 1973 Vernice McGriff, who earned her Bachelor of Science in marketing from New York University, was manager of corporate business planning for RCA in New York City. The job included assessing and reviewing the annual business plan for each division of RCA (NBC, Hertz, and Banquet among others), and providing market planning and strategy.[33]

Betty Proctor Brown joined the General Electric Company's Neutron Devices Department in 1968 and currently serves as manager of personnel relations. She is responsible for all employment activities, salary and wage administration, performance appraisal programs, and other personnel practice programs for the plant's 1,200 employees.[34]

Nancy L. Lane of New Brunswick, New Jersey was appointed in 1977 as vice-president of personnel and a member of the Board of Directors at Ortho Diagnostics, Inc., Raritan, New Jersey, a division of Johnson and Johnson Company.

Prior to joining Ortho, Lane served as vice-president of personnel with the New York City Off-Track Betting Corporation; second vice-president, Chase Manhattan Bank, New York City; and project manager for the National Urban League.

A trustee of Wilson College in Chambersburg, Pennsylvania and Benedict College in South Carolina, Lane is also on the board and Executive Committee of A Better Chance, the Studio Museum of Harlem, the United Way of Central New Jersey, and the National Black M.B.A. Association. She is also a member of the advisory committee of the National Urban League Black Executive Exchange.

One of her recommendations while working on an Urban League program for Black colleges and corporations led the American Bankers Association to establish centers for business education at Howard University and Texas Southern University.[35]

Judith Price, as sole owner and founder of AMATISTA Import Ltd. of New York City, was the first Black woman in the United States independently to organize and receive approval to operator a wholesale business in the beverage alcohol industry.

Prior to organizing AMATISTA, Price was vice-president and director of the Beam Distilling Company's import subsidiary, headquartered in New York. She joined the Beam organization in 1965, was elected to the board of directors in 1969[36] and held the positions of import manager, corporate secretary, and administrative director before her election as vice-president in 1972.

Over the course of her career in the highly regulated wine and spirits industry, she traveled to England, Scotland, Germany, Italy, and Portugal, coordinating vendor, warehouse and agency operations, evaluating physical distribution systems, and directing foreign suppliers in product conformance. Her experience includes extensive operations with state-controlled monopolies, domestic and overseas military procurement activities, export commercial trade and price stabilization and marketing practices in the alcohol industry.[37]

Lucille Mason Rose, born in Richmond, Virginia, became the first director of the Bedford-Stuyvesant Manpower Center in New York. Mayor Lindsay appointed her first deputy commissioner of the Manpower and Development Agency in 1970. In 1972, she was named Commissioner of Employment for the city of New York. Under Rose's direction, the city's employment agency locates employment openings and then trains people on the job. "Our main concern," says Commissioner Rose, "is to get poor people into jobs."[38]

Helen I. Barnhill, president and founder of Barnhill, Hayes and Crosby, Incorporated, a management and consulting firm in Milwaukee, Wisconsin, has been active in affirmative action and civil rights programs for most of her professional career. Barnhill, Hayes, and Crosby, founded in the early 1970's, is designed to assist corporate management with all aspects of affirmative action program planning and implementation and to help corporations make substantial progress toward compliance with government affirmative action programs.[39]

A management consultant who is an outstanding example of a successful Black woman in the world of business, is Geraldine Henry

Rickman, president of Rickman Associates, San Diego, California. Geraldine Richman Associates provides total consulting services to Black businesses, including marketing, personnel systems evaluation, and review of office systems. They evaluate all aspects of the business and recommend appropriate changes and training programs.

In recent years, her company has been the recipient of substantial contracts directed toward job search assistance. The company re-programs individuals who consider themselves failures in life because of years of unemployment. The program, designed and tested by Rickman, gives people the opportunity to control their own lives, market themselves and enhance their self-image and self-respect. The majority of the program's enrollees have gone out and obtained jobs in the private sector. Rickman is nationally known as a consultant, lecturer, and writer and has been recognized for her "linking pin session" and bridge-building, which seek, through carefully designed meetings, to bring people of all races and political persuasions together. She strongly believes that coalitions around issues are possible if individuals communicate more directly with one another on issues of mutual concern and impact.[40]

A business executive with Philip Morris, Incorporated, New York City, Carole E. Johnson serves as manager of Employee Career Program and Planning. She has been with Philip Morris since 1972, serving as Urban Affairs information analyst.[41]

In 1973, E. Marie Johnson, president and owner of E. Marie Johnson and Associates — a multi-service consulting agency concerned with researching excellence in the social and psychological sciences, included among her clients some of the top 500 companies in the country.[42]

Sales

Although many women may have been initially deterred from select-ing careers in sales due to racism and sexism, there is a history of Black women involved in buying and selling. Evidence of the activities of Black females in the areas may be traced back to the late eighteenth century.

The daughter of an American Indian woman and an African slave, Eleanor Eldridge, born in 1785 in Warwick, Rhode Island, was the owner of a weaving, soap boiling, and spinning business. Later, she established, with her sister, a white-washing, papering and painting business in Providence, Rhode Island.[43]

"Mammy Chloe" Bland, was born a slave in the service of Mary Lee

Bland in Cumberland County, Kentucky. When the eldest daughter of the Bland House married a Morman missionary, Dr. William Ewell, Chloe Bland was given to the bride by her mother. She later accompanied Mary Bland Ewell and her family to their new home in Missouri. Dr. Ewell died, but Chloe Bland remained with the widow Ewell, caring for her six children. They made the long trek to Salt Lake City, arriving in 1849. The Ewell family had no means of support and Chloe Bland taught the Ewell mother to spin and weave materials for clothes, to make carpets and quilts, and to weave straw hats. Chloe Bland then sold these items to stores and individuals, and with the finances received supported this family until the children were grown.[44]

In Milford, Delaware, Serrena Palmer began business in 1889 with a cash capital of seven dollars which she invested in notions. Palmer did a successful business and was the owner of two homes which she bought and paid for.[45]

In his 1896 study of Black occupations in Philadelphia, DuBois noted that a number of cigar stores, candy and notion shops were businesses run by women.[46] Quite early, then, Black women were operating various kinds of sales.

Flower shops are also business enterprises which have a history of Black women owners. The florist business showed an increase among Blacks during the mid-1920's. Since Blacks spent considerable sums on flowers (primarily for funerals), it apparently seemed reasonable as a business venture. In a study of Blacks in business for the Association for the Study of Negro Life and History, one writer notes that "Many of the most successful. . . florists are women, [with] one of the neatest shops in the country operated in Indianapolis, Indiana, by Miss Dora Oma Atkins."[47]

As the founder and manager of Weaver Floral Company, established in 1911, Bessie May Weaver became the only Black florist in Kansas City, Missouri during that era. She successfully competed with white florists and was a prominent member of many business and cultural organizations in Kansas.[48] Gwendolyn Hooker of Portland, Oregon, was the first Black woman to establish a florist shop in Oregon. She founded the business in 1938 and continues to operate it at age 78.

Black women have been successful in various other businesses involving buying and selling. Some own dress shops; others own and operate unusual firms like cab companies and security firms. Sylvia Hill Alridge, born in 1884, Broward County, Florida, was the county's first Black resident. She was also one of its most generous citizens, and she probably provided more Black people with jobs than any other individual in the country.

At first, Alridge worked as a domestic. She saw that there was plenty of work to be had, but that many Blacks did not know how to go about getting it. This led her into her primary business and public service, Sylvia's Employment Agency around 1906. It was the city's first such business and for many years it was the only agency for domestic help. Later, she started Sylvia's Victory Cabs to drive many of her clients to work. She was a benefactor and trustee of Bethune-Cookman College and was active in many civic and professional organizations.[50]

As a business woman and community leader for more than half a century, Susie B. Green was a familiar figure in Washington, D.C. She operated the Unique Printing Shop according to her own motto: "Don't make excuses, find a way or make one." A native of Montgomery, Alabama, Green went to Washington in 1914 and took courses in printing. She became the first licensed woman printer in the United States. She was founder, two-term president, and trustee of the Business and Professional Women's League and at one time published *The Negro Women's World*. Green was one of the few Depression pioneers in Washington, D.C.'s up-town business who made it to the 1970's.[51]

In Jackson, Mississippi, Thelma Sanders, a community and civil rights' activist, is the owner and manager of Sanders Women's Apparel. She has operated the business for more than twenty years and was one of the pioneers in Black-owned retail clothing stores in Jackson.[52]

Helen Thorton Jones operates the Joe Louis Milk Company of Chicago, the first and only Black-owned milk distributing company in Chicago. The business' annual sales figures exceed three million dollars. Jones is especially interested and active in working with underprivileged children and in organizations dedicated to this cause.[53]

In 1965, Ann Howard Lacewell and her husband moved from New York to Baltimore, Maryland, where they purchased a Fuller products distributorship. Today, forty full-time self-contracted salespersons are supplied through Lacewell's distributorship.[54]

Roberta Lewis of Pittsburgh, Pennsylvania, was able to get a Small Business Administration loan in 1967 in order to open a frozen food manufacturing company. Her company, the House of Roberta, is now a successful business enterprise, supplying frozen food and other food specialists to department stores, individual customers and an airline company. In 1968 Lewis was chosen from more than 200,000 small business entrepreneurs in Pennsylvania to be named "Small Businessman" of the Year.[55]

In Baltimore, Maryland, Doris Banks had worked in the fur trade for twenty years before a chain of events shifted her from manager of Selenkow Furs to owner of the business. She has owned the business since 1967 and was the first Black in Baltimore to own a fur business.[56]

Cora Walker had been trying for a long time to sell the idea of a cooperative supermarket in Harlem before anyone seriously began to listen. With the aid of community residents and other interested parties, the Harlem River Consumers Cooperative was organized in 1968 with Walker as coordinator and legal counsel. The cooperative is a community-owned supermarket supported by more than 4,000 shareholders. Its development affords many Harlemites the opportunity to share in the profits of an expanding business enterprise as well as the chance to learn the fundamentals of supermarket operation.[57]

Afram House of Florida is a mail-order company owned and operated by Black people and designed to serve the Black community. It was begun in 1968 with Blanche Calloway as president. The company specializes in cosmetics and is headquartered in Opa Locka, Florida. Besides operating as a mailorder house, the company's Afram Cosmetics are also sold in variety and department stores throughout the country.

In addition to being the president of Afram House, Galloway is also executive director of WMBM, a radio station in Miami. She has also worked as a real estate saleswoman.[58]

In Washington, D.C., Helen Greenwood Allen is secretary-treasurer of the Greenwood Transfer and Storage Company, one of the oldest Black-owned businesses in D.C. Under her direction, the firm has tripled its yearly income and expanded considerably. Allen runs the business, although her seventy-four year old mother, Cathrine Greenwood, is president.

In 1975, *Ebony* magazine, highlighted Saint Charles Lockett as one Black woman making a success in the American corporate scene. Lockett, founder and president of Ethnic Enterprises in Milwaukee, Wisconsin, heads a packaging and assembly company which also manufactures illuminator lights used to show X-rays. Her company, which was also a sub-contractor for American and General Motors, grossed approximately $1 million per year. Most of Ethnic's employees are women who were former welfare recipients.[59]

In 1972, Madeline Bunch of Santa Rosa, California and other

members of her family began the Bunch Products Company which manufactures Old South Brand beef and pork sausages. The family had made sausages in the basement of their home because they could not find a store product which suited their tastes. The fledgling business had a rough time in its beginnings. For nearly two years, all of the family, including some who had relocated from Connecticut, worked without pay because of a shortage of money. The business received a boost when they received a $40 million contract and they were able to promote Old South Brand in supermarkets. Today the business is thriving and has developed into a lucrative family-owned manufacturing company.[60]

Fannie Lou Hamer, Civil Rights Activist
(photo courtesy Schomburg Center
New York Public Library)

Fannie Lou Hamer, known mostly as a civil rights activist, was the founder of Freedom Farm Cooperative and a garment factory which provided food and jobs for residents of Ruleville, Mississippi. Born in Ruleville, she was the youngest of twenty children in a poverty-stricken family. In the 1960's, her efforts at voter registration brought arrests, evictions, and threats. Although the delegation she led in the 1964

Democratic National Convention failed in its effort to be seated, she was one of twenty-two Blacks that unseated the regular (white) Mississippi delegation in the Chicago 1968 Convention.

Hamer once read that pork had more nutritional value for children than most meats, so she started a pig farm in 1968 with the financial backing of the National Council of Negro Women. She believed that some measure of economic independence is a prerequisite to building political strength in the Black community.

With further help from the National Council of New Negro Women, she bought an old building in Doddsville near Ruleville, Mississippi in 1970 and converted it into a garment factory. Her plan was to employ 25 women who would be trained to operate the machinery. The factory included a day-care center for the young children of those working at the factory.

In 1969, Hamer began her Freedom Farm Cooperative with the objective of buying tracts of land — over 600 acres which eventually would be used for housing and raising vegetables. The concept also included a plan to package and can the beans, okra, potatoes and corn that would be grown.[61]

Barbara Jean Carter of Chicago serves as executive vice-president of Key Systems, Incorporated, a supplier of temporary office services. At age twenty-one, she owned her own secretarial service. Since that time, she has worked as an account executive with the *Chicago Sun-Times* newspaper and the Harris Bank in Chicago, but the highlight of her career has been her appointment to the vice-presidency of Key Systems.[62]

Willie Lewis of Oakland, California is one woman whose knowledge has propelled her full force into the business world. Lewis is comptroller at Aladdin Electric, Incorporated, an electrical contracting firm, owned and operated by Blacks in Oakland. She keeps financial tabs on the firm, making sure the company's $2 million annual gross is managed properly.[63]

In 1964, Annie B. Rodger began her Village Maid Service, Incorporated in Chicago with the idea of uplifting and improving the status of household employees. Today, her employees do household work by contract in high-rise apartment buildings throughout the Chicago area. She also has the same services available in Washington, D.C., and plans to expand to other cities.

Rodger, a native of Norristown, Pennsylvania, spent nine years as a social worker at the Abraham Lincoln Center, a settlement house in Chicago. While there, she helped in the development of special programs for teenagers and organizations for senior citizens. Dedicated to the advancement of Black people, Rodger feels that Black people must establish an economic power base within their communities. These beliefs have prompted her attempts to organize Black businesses as a force to combat racism.[64]

One of the top executives in merchandising is Yolanda H. Chambers of Detroit, Michigan, director of executive and staff development at Bullock's, a division of Federal Department Stores in Southern California. Chambers was previously director of training at Bullock's. Before joining Bullock's, she was vice-president of personnel and training for Federal's, Incorporated, served on the Detroit Housing Commission and has spent years in private law practice. An active member of the American Society for Personnel Management, the National Retail Merchants Association and the American Management Association, she was recognized.and awarded the key to the city of Detroit in 1963 and a certificate of commendation from Mayor Jerome P. Cavanaugh.[65]

As the president of the Safe Bus Company of Winston-Salem, North Carolina, Delphine Webber Morgan became the largest stockholder of the company in 1959. That year the company boasted of carrying three million passengers. The white-owned city bus line took note of the desegregated operation of the Black company and followed suit and after 1969, there was no color pattern in seating on any of the Winston-Salem buses. A historical review of the situation written up in *Ebony* magazine brought nationwide attention to the Safe Bus Company.[66]

One Black woman who has engaged herself in a rather unusual business is Wanda Babin of Los Angeles, California. Babin is founder and president of the Eagle Guard Security and Patrol Service which she began in 1972. Her first year gross from the business was $75,000. In 1977, she grossed $500,000 and employed a staff of 25 security guards.[67]

In 1969, Milicent V. Boney became the first Black woman in the United States to own and operate an investment company. Boney was a real estate broker in Los Angeles, California, before achieving this distinction.[68]

In the world of business and commerce, Freddye Scarborough Henderson of Atlanta, Georgia stands out as a woman of many talents. In 1955, Henderson and her husband, Jacob R. Henderson, opened the Henderson Travel Service, Incorporated of Atlanta. Henderson, currently the executive vice-president of Henderson Travel Service, has been designated as a certified travel counselor, the highest professional distinction of excellence in the travel field.

Freddye Scarborough Henderson, Vice-President of Henderson Tours

Prior to opening the travel service, Henderson was assistant professor of Clothing and Applied Art in Spelman College in Atlanta. She has also owned a dressmaking business, hosted a radio program, and was the travel editor for the *Pittsburgh Courier*. Her sculpture has been exhibited in Atlanta University and she has sold greeting card designs to the Hallmark Cards Corporation. She has traveled extensively throughout the world and is a noted authority on both travel and fashion.[69]

Henderson received her master's degree in fashion merchandising — the first Black woman to do so. Her travel agency has also won a number of "firsts." It was the first travel agency, Black or white, to operate group tours to West Africa, beginning in 1957 when Ghana gained independence; the first Black firm to receive the Africa Trophy (in 1972, for excellence in African tour production and operation); and the first to gross $1 million. Henderson was also the first Black to be appointed to the U.S. Travel Service.[70]

Black women throughout the country have been founders and directors of business colleges.

One of the pioneers in such a venture was Minnie Gaston of Birmingham, Alabama, who not only has served as owner and director of the Booker T. Washington Business College since 1943, but is also the first vice-president of Booker T. Washington Insurance Company. Working with her well-known husband in the business, she has achieved recognition in her own right as an outstanding contributor to the multi-faceted business enterprise and as a leader in civic and fraternal organizations.[71]

Another owner of a business college is Willa Mae Blayton who retired as president and owner of the Blayton Business College in Atlanta, Georgia, after heading the business since its organization in 1947.[72]

Peninsula Business College, established in 1952 by Jessie M. Rattley, is a highly successful enterprise in Newport News, Virginia. The Detroit Institute of Commerce, a private school founded by R. Louise Grooms, helps to qualify Blacks for occupational training in accounting, bookkeeping, secretarial science, and related fields.[73]

Booking and Recording Agencies

Many Blacks with well-known names are on the creative side of the entertainment industry, but few have reached the top-level of influence on the business side of entertainment. One of the few who has been successful is Ruth Bowen, founder and president of Queen's Booking Corporation in New York, the largest Black-owned talent agency in the United States.

Born in Danville, Virginia, and reared in Brooklyn, New York, Ruth Bowen studied business administration at New York University and at the University of California, Los Angeles. After marrying Billy Bowen, one of the original Inkspots, she began to gain show business experience by handling her husband's business affairs.[74]

A confidante and friends of the late singer, Dinah Washington, Bowen was convinced by the entertainer to organize her own public relations' agency which later evolved into her present corporation. Queen's Booking Corporation now handles over one hundred top acts, securing booking dates in clubs and theaters throughout the country and around the world. Included among her clients are such superstars as Ray Charles, Aretha Franklin, James Cleveland, Gladys Knight and the Pips, the Isley Brothers, Sammy Davis, Jr., and Richard Pryor.

Starting from a net worth of $500 and a few employees, the Bowen firm has grown to a staff of over thirty full-time employees and total assets valued at nearly $3 million.

Ernestine McClendon Enterprises is a theatrical agency in Los

Angeles, California. Its owner, Ernestine McClendon, born in Norfolk, Virginia, has appeared on television and live theater. She was one of the first in her field to be sanctioned by all unions as a theatrical agent. She represents over one hundred clients, including actors in television, radio, theater, and movies. Her agency has been largely responsible for getting Blacks into television commercials.

Esther Gordy Edwards has worked with her brother, Berry Gordy, Jr., since 1959 when he began Hitsville, U.S.A. Today, she is senior vice-president of the Motown Records Corporation, a Gordy enterprise, and the largest manufacturer and supplier of 45 RPM phonograph records in the country. In addition to her responsibilities at Motown Records, she is corporate secretary of Motown Industries and Motown Productions. She also plays a major role in an artist management corporation, which is a subsidiary of Motown as well as directing the company's international operations. Her duties take her throughout the United States, Europe and the Far East, setting up the distribution of Motown records and arranging engagements for famous entertainers.

Esther Gordy Edwards, Senior Vice-President
of Motown Record Corporation

Edwards, in a personal letter, says that her parents, Bertha and Berry Gordy, Sr., "instilled into us, their eight children, what the ultimate benefits and rewards of hard work were. They taught us, by way of example mainly, what work and thinking for yourself really meant." She continued, writing that both her mother and father inspired and motivated their children "to think, think for ourselves; have faith and believe you can do anything anybody else can do."[75]

Suzanne de Passe has advanced up the corporate ladder to become one of the recording industry's magnates at Motown. de Passe directs the operations of the largest division of the multi-faceted firm, overseeing everything from talent acquisition to the quality of recordings.

In 1965, Gloria E.A. Toote, an attorney from Englewood, New Jersey, opened the Town Sound Recording Studios. The studios are housed in one of the city's oldest buildings, which she remodeled with the aid of a Small Business Administration loan, money from friends, and her personal savings. Town Sound has been hailed as being one of the most modern recording studios in the East.[76]

Irene Gandy, the associate directress of Press Information and Artist Affairs for CBS Records, handles public relations for the company. This means that all the Black recording artists who appear on CBS Records' various labels receive publicity and advertising campaigns through her department. She arranges press conferences, advance and post-performance media coverage, and tailor-made sales campaigns according to the unique needs of each artist.[77]

Gandy became the first and only Black woman to be registered with the Association of Theatrical Press Agents and Managers (APAM) after satisfying the three-year Broadway apprenticeship requirements.

NOTES

[1] J.H. Harmon, Jr., Arnett G. Lindsay, and Carter G. Woodman. *The Negro As a Business Man* (College Park, Maryland: McGrath Publishing Co., 1969), pp. 92-96. *See also* Armand J. Thiebolt, Jr. and Linda Pukthorne Fletcher, *Negro Employment In Finance* (Philadelphia: University of Pennsylvania 1970), pp. 124-125.

[2] Hamon, et al, pp. 97-98.

[3] *Ebony*, August 1977, p. 132.

[4] Alpha Kappa Alpha Sorority, Heritage Series #3, *Women in Business*, 1970, pp. 5, 7, 10, 13, 17, 20, 23-24.

[5] *Ebony*, August 1977, p. 132.

[6] Alpha Kappa Alpha Sorority, p. 13.

[7] Alpha Kappa Alpha Sorority, p. 10.

[8] *Ebony*, August 1977, p. 132.

[9] *Ebony*, August 1977, p. 132.

[10] Letter received from Elneita Dever, North Texas State University, Denton, February 1980.

[11] *Ebony*, August 1977, p. 132.

[12] Letter received from Ann Chandler Howell, Wellesley College, Massachusetts, 8 October 1979.

[13] Letter received from Elaine Witty, Norfolk State College, Virginia, 18 August 1979.

[14] *Forward Times* Newspaper, Memphis, Tennessee, 9 March 1971, p. 19A.

[15] *Ebony's 1,000 Successful Blacks*, p. 79.

[16] Alpha Kappa Alpha Sorority, p. 7.

[17] *Black Enterprise*, August 1977, p. 8.

[18] Letter received from Ernesta Procope, 2 February 1980.

[19] Casey M. Cohen, "Insurance Executive Tells How She Reached Six-Figure Income," *Texas Woman*, April 1977, pp. 21-23.

[20] *Ebony*, August 1977, p. 122.

[21] Letter received from Barbara Proctor, 2 February 1980.

[22] Karin Abarbanel, "Caroline Jones, Vice President and Creative Director of Mingo, Jones, Guilmenot, Inc.," *The Executive Female Digest*, May-June 1979, p. 37-39.

[23] *Black Enterprise*, January 1976, p. 32.

[24] *Ebony*, August 1977, p. 33.

[25] *Black Enterprise*, "Names in the News" September 1976, p. 14.

[26] *Black Enterprise*, October 1979, p. 34.

[27] *The Afro-American*, 28 April 1973.

[28] *Black Business Digest*, April 1973, p. 42.

[29] Vincent A. Capozzi, ed., *Black Business Digest* (Philadelphia: Compeers, Incorporated, April 1973), p. 42.

[29] *Encore American and Worldwide News*, 4 October 1976, p. 14.

[30] *The Afro-American*, 31 October 1978.

[31] "Making It," *Black Enterprise*, 11 January 1976, p. 12.

[32] *Ebony's 1,000 Successful Blacks*, p. 68.

[33] *Ebony's 1,000 Successful Blacks*, p. 114.

[34] Letter received from Leanor B. Johnson, Florida State University, Tallahassee, 6 August 1979.

[35] *New York Amsterdam News*, 21 December 1974.

[36] Letter received from Thomas Shropshire, Senior Vice President, Miller Brewing Company, Milwaukee, Wisconsin, 8 February 1980.

[37] "Blacks in the Liquor Industry," *Black Enterprise*, September 1975, p. 48.

[38] Letter received from Elaine Witty, Norfolk State College, Virginia, 20 September 1979.

[39] Branhill-Hayes Management Company, Brochure, Milwaukee, Wisconsin, p. 2.

[40] Letter received from Frances S. Foster, San Diego State University, California, 7 July 1980.

[41] Matney, p. 479.

[42] *Ebony's 1,000 Successful Blacks*, p. 176.

[43] Rowena Stewart, "Elleanor Eldridge," Unpublished paper, The Rhode Island Black Heritage Society, Providence, R.I., October 1979.

[44] Kate B. Carter, *The Story of the Negro Pioneer* (Salt Lake City, Utah: Daughters of the Utah Pioneers, 1965), p. 182.

[45] G.F. Richings, *Evidences of Progress Among Colored People* (Chicago: Afro-American Press, 1969), pp. 413-414.

[46] W.E.B. Dubois *The Philadelphia Negro* (New York: Benjamin Bloom, Inc., 1967), p. 117.

[47] Harmon, et al, p. 31.

[48] *Ebony's 1,000 Successful Blacks*, p. 176.

[49] Letter received from Addie Dunlap, Black Women's Caucus, Seattle, Washington, 18 September 1979.

[50] *Black Pioneers In Broward County: A Legacy Revealed*, Links, Inc. 1976.

[51] "Susie B. Green: Pioneer Printer," *Washington Afro-American* 1 December 1979.

[52] Alpha Kappa Alpha Sorority, p. 16.

[53] Alpha Kappa Alpha Sorority, p. 12.

[54] Alpha Kappa Alpha Sorority, p. 11.

[55] Alpha Kappa Alpha Sorority, p. 12.

[56] Alpha Kappa Alpha Sorority, p. 1.

[57] Alpha Kappa Alpha Sorority, p. 22.

[58] Alpha Kappa Alpha Sorority, p. 2.

[59] Carol A. Morton, "Black Women In Corporate America," *Ebony*, November 1975.

[60] Capozzi, p. 42.

[61] *Ebony's 1,000 Successful Blacks*, p. 137.

[62] Alpha Kappa Alpha Sorority, p. 3.

[63] *Ebony*, November 1975, p. 11.

[64] Alpha Kappa Alpha Sorority, p. 18.

[65] Alpha Kappa Alpha Sorority, p. 18.

[66] Letter received from Bertha L. Maxwell, University of North Carolina, Charlotte, 10 August 1980.

[67] *Sepia* Magazine, April 1977.

[68] Martin Rywell, ed., *Afro-American Encyclopedia*, Vol. II (North Miami: Educational Book Publishers, Incorporated, 1974), p. 264.

[69] Alpha Kappa Alpha Sorority, p. 10.

[70] *Ebony's 1,000 Successful Blacks*, p. 268.

[71] Alpha Kappa Alpha Sorority, p. 8.

[72] Alpha Kappa Alpha Sorority, p. 1.

[73] Alpha Kappa Alpha Sorority, p. 18.

[74] *Black Enterprise*, September 1976, p. 22.

[75] Letter received from Mrs. Esther Gordy Edwards, Detroit, Michigan, 28 February 1980.

[76] Alpha Kappa Alpha Sorority, p. 21.

[77] Deborah Guillarme, "Taking Care of Business at Black Rock," *Black Enterprise*, September 1975, pp. 29, 39.

CHAPTER V

FUNERAL HOMES AND CATERING

Funeral Homes

Booker T. Washington recounts the story of a Black man in Montgomery, Alabama, who got started in the undertaking business when he noticed that the corpses of Blacks were being taken to the cemetery in rough wagons. Disturbed by this, he bought a hearse and went into the business himself. This example is similar to others which caused the secret organizations like the Masons, the Independent Order of St. Luke, and other fraternal organizations to include burial of the dead among their services. Burials and caring for the sick became prominent features of such organizations and they helped to create a special business opportunity for Blacks.[1]

"The demand by Blacks for solemn, decent, and sometimes elaborate burial services" caused the burial business to be one of the very early businesses in which Blacks were most numerous and successful.[2] DuBois' 1896 study of occupations of Blacks in Philadelphia identified two Black women who conducted successful undertaking establishments. He pointed out that theirs were old establishments — "six to thirty-three years." And as other historians were to do, DuBois' noted that Blacks had "evinced much push, taste, and enterprise" in the undertaking business.[3]

G.F. Richings in a 1900 publication identified "two very successful [Black women] undertakers in Philadelphia, in the persons of Henrietta Duterte and Addison Foster." He noted that Duterte was in fact the oldest Black undertaker in the city.[4] The January 15, 1927 issue of *The Tuskegee Messenger*, commenting on Black women in business, noted that "nearly 200 qualified as undertakers."

In 1929, an astute businesswoman of Atlanta, Georgia, Geneva Moton Haugabrooks, became the founder and owner of one of Atlanta's oldest Black-owned funeral homes, the Haugabrooks Funeral Home, located on Atlanta's famous Auburn Avenue. Haugabrooks began her business with a loan of $300, and later became the third largest Black funeral service owner in Atlanta. Like others, she attributed her success to much hard work, determination, and sacrifice. Before her death in 1977, at age ninety, Haugabrooks continued to direct her enterprise. Her staff of one in 1929 had increased to over thirty workers and her business was worth over $200,000 at the time of her death.[5]

One of the first Black women of Kansas to attend a school of Mortuary Science and become a licensed embalmer and funeral director was Xavia Hightower Howard of Coffeyville, Kansas. Howard, owner and president of Citizens Funeral Home of Wichita, has been associated with the funeral business for over thirty years.[6]

Clarie Collins Harvey of Jackson, Mississippi, the owner and president of Collins Funeral Home and Insurance Companies, is a generous contributor to a number of Black colleges and institutions. Her businesses, worth over a quarter of a million dollars, employ forty people. In 1974, she became the first Black member of the Board of Trustees of Millsaps College, a white private college in Jackson, Mississippi. She is the author of *Stars at Your Fingertips*, 1976, and *From Caterpillar to Bufferfly*, 1979, a study in prosperity consciousness.[7]

Clarie Collins Harvey, funeral home owner

As an educator, civic leader, and the owner-president of Jackson Funeral Home in Houston, Texas, Thelma L. Gordon is the recipient of many outstanding awards in the area of funeral directorship, business leadership, and community awareness.[8]

In Beaumont, Texas, Bessie M. Knighton owns and operates the Knighton Funeral Home and the Knighton Funeral Benefit Association. As a licensed funeral director and embalmer, she has won the esteem of Golden Triangle citizens over a wide area of Texas. The two Knighton firms have twice outgrown their physical plants. In 1973, a new facility was built which provides a total area of 11,000 square feet and includes modern conveniences for its patrons.[9]

In 1921, Mayme Diggs and her husband founded Michigan's largest Black funeral home. The House of Diggs in Detroit has beautiful chapels located within fifteen minutes from any part of the city. Diggs, treasurer of the corporation, says her main interest is helping young people develop into useful citizens, and eventually to become successful.[10]

Another successful woman in the funeral business is Emma Wilburn. A native of Tennessee, she was the founder and owner of a highly successful funeral home and the New Park Cemetery of Memphis.[11]

Catering

Along with the undertaking business, the catering business was historically the most successful early business ventures for Blacks. In fact, for many years Blacks dominated the catering business.[12] The credit for the successful entry of Blacks into catering belongs to Black women as they were the first ones to enter the business. Booker T. Washington points out that "The catering business in New York seems to have begun with [Black] women. Among the most notable of these early women caterers, who held sway in New York somewhere between the dates of 1780 and 1820, was Cornelia Gomez. Her successor was Katie Ferguson who kept the business until about 1820."[13]

Another successful Black woman caterer was Mrs. W.H. Smith who, along with her husband, had a catering business which was used by banks and other companies along Wall Street in New York City. And in Westchester County, one of New York state's wealthiest counties, Fannie J. Alston Moultrie, and her husband, Francis J. Moultrie, operated in 1878 the largest catering establishment in the county. Moultrie, originally from Charleston, South Carolina, had carried on a small catering business from her home in the beginning years while her husband had accepted employment with private families as they sought enough capital to establish their own business. She always had "direct charge of the wares to be sold or to be served, as well as the manufacture of all confections."[14]

DuBois reported 18 Black women caterers in his 1896 study of Black female occupations in Philadelphia.[15] And G.F. Richings identifies a Mrs. Henry F. Jones of Philadelphia as a successful Black woman engaged in a large catering business.[16]

Julia Wyche Boggs, originally from Henderson, North Carolina, became a successful and respected caterer in Washington, D.C., after working in private homes for a number of years.[17]

In Omaha, Nebraska, Helen Mahamitt and her husband founded a catering business in 1905. She studied at Farmer's School in Boston and one of the finest schools in Paris, France, in 1927. She taught advanced cooking and catering in a private school which she organized — the only school of its kind in Omaha, or for that matter, west of Chicago. Mahamitt, who died in 1956, was one of the founders of the Northside Young Women's Christian Association of Omaha.[18]

Another Black woman who has been successful in another area of the food business is Lucille Bishop Smith, a resident of Fort Worth, Texas. She has had a long and notable career as a teacher and business leader. Through research and experimentation, she developed and published many original ideas on the culinary arts. She reportedly developed the first hot roll mix in the United States; set up the first Commercial Foods and Technology Department at the college level with an apprenticeship training program at Prairie View A & M College; published a cookbook, *Lucille's Treasure Chest of Fine Foods*, and at age 82, founded and became president of her family corporation, Lucille B. Smith's Fine Foods, Incorporated.

Much of the success of the Texas Hotel and Motel Association's cooperative training program for cooks and bakers is due to the dedicated efforts of Smith. *Treasure Chest*, her cookbook file, was copyrighted in 1941 and is a collection of recipes she has tried and used many times. In addition to providing recipes for foods that will lend variety and taste to meals, Smith hoped the recipes would make the task of preparing the foods easier and more enjoyable and that waste would be reduced through better food consumption.[19]

NOTES

[1] Booker T. Washington, *The Negro In Business* (Chicago, Afro-American Press, 1969), pp. 94-96. See also J.H. Harmon, et al, *The Negro As A Business Man* (College Park, Maryland: McGrath Publishing Co., 1969), p. 92.

[2] Washington, p. 94.

[3] W.E. Burghardt DuBois, *The Philadelphia Negro* (New York: Benjamin Bloom, Inc., 1967), p. 118.

[4] G.F. Richings, *Evidences of Progress Among Colored People* (Chicago: Afro-Am Press, 1969), p. 118.

[5] Letter received from Jane Browning, Spelman College, Atlanta, Georgia, 18 September 1979.

[6] Letter received from John C. Gaston, Wichita State University, Kansas, 23 May 1979.

[7] Letter received from Lou Holloway Bolden, Tougaloo College, Mississippi, 23 August 1979.

[8] Garland A. Smith, ed., *Black Texans of Distinction* (Austin: Garland Smith Associates, 1979), p. 38.

[9] Smith, p. 66.

[10] Alpha Kappa Alpha Sorority, Inc., Heritage Series #3, *Women In Business*, 1970, p. 6.

[11] Letter received from Jessie C. Smith, Fisk University Library, Nashville, Tennessee, November 1979.

[12] See DuBois, *The Philadelphia Negro*, pp. 35-36, 119-120 and Washington, *The Negro In Business*, Chapter IV.

[13] Washington, pp. 38-39.

[14] Washington, pp. 40, 43-46.

[15] DuBois, p. 104.

[16] Richings, p. 424.

[17] Sally Quinn, "The Last Great Lady," *The Washington Post*, 12 November 1978, Col. 2, p. F2.

[18] Letter received from Donna Polk, Lincoln, Nebraska, 17 March 1979.

[19] *The Fort Worth Press*, 17 November 1966.

AN OVERVIEW: BLACK WOMEN IN BUSINESS

"Simply holding down a responsible job is an old story for Afro-American women. . .Black women were brought up with the thought that having some kind of job in addition to rearing a family was expected of them."[1] So it is not just because they work but because they are businesswomen — owners, managers and executives — that the Black women cited here deserve recognition for their contributions to America. They and the many other unnamed Black women in business have charted courses for other women to follow. Most often without role models and far too frequently with little encouragement, they have overcome the dual barriers of racism and sexism, to name two of their obstacles, to advance themselves in business.

Black women have made strides in fields as varied as advertising, stockbrokerage, real estate, banking, and as heads of their own businesses. Yet, the success of these women is only part of the history of Black women in business. For one thing, past historical accounts have failed to give proper credit to those who quite early understood capitalism and triumphed as business leaders in the towns and cities across the United States. We know, for example, far too little about the 12,000 Black women engaged in trade mentioned in the January 15, 1927, issue of the *Tuskegee Messenger*. (3,200 of that number were retail dealers and 1,300 of them owned and conducted grocery stores, according to the article.) For another, there are still far too few Black women with top-level executive positions in major American corporations. A November 1, 1971 *Time* magazine article headlined "Black Capitalism: The Rarest Breed of Women," pointed out that "Black businesswomen were practically nonexistent in the executive suites of major corporations." And three years later, *Black Enterprise* Magazine cited statistics which still gave a "sobering overview of career opportunities for most Black women in the national work force." The article noted that "Though the proportion of minority women employed in professional and technical jobs between 1960 and 1973 rose from 7 to 12 percent. . .minority women are still likely to be more heavily concentrated in low-skill, low-wage occupations than white women. . ."[2]

The civil rights movement of the 1960's was a major national force in opening up many business opportunities for Blacks. But even as it helped some gain a foothold in business, there were, less than a decade later, still too few Blacks in professional and managerial positions. "In July 1976, 46% of all white workers had blue collar or service jobs, while 64% of all 'Black and other' workers were employed in such jobs. In contrast, 50% of all white workers but only 34% of all minority workers were white collar employees. . .a [dubious] improvement from 1964, when 73% of all minority workers were in the lower level jobs, and only 19% held white collar positions."[3]

While Black women have always worked, they have consistently historically earned less than other workers, male or female of any race. "In 1969 more than half of all employed Black women still earned less than $3,000 a year (the official poverty level). . ."[4] "In 1975, the median wage or salary income for Black women employed full-time year-round was $7,932. The 1975 level represents 96% of the $7,737 that white women were making at the same time, but just 75% of the $9,848 that Black men earned, and only 55% of the $13,459 that white men were averaging."[5]

Such statistics are sobering and cause for pause especially when one thinks of the potential for Black women in business, a potential born out of a history of past accomplishments by Black women in business. There have always been Black women in this country who have been in various areas of business, and their successes must be viewed not solely in terms of accumulated wealth but also in terms of their achievements, despite the odds.

The women cited in this book and the other Black business women, far too numerous to name, have earned high distinction as role models for other women to have careers in the business world.

NOTES

[1] "Black Professional Women," *Black Enterprise*, November 1971, p. 35.

[2] Karen DeWitt, "Black Women In Business," *Black Enterprise* August, 1974, p. 16.

[3] Wendy Schwartz, *Women and Minorities in Banking* (New York: Praeger Publishers, 1976), p. 21.

[4] Charmeynne D. Nelson, "Myths About Black Women Workers In Modern America," *Black Scholar* March 1975, p. 13.

[5] Schwartz, p. 24.

SELECTED BIBLIOGRAPHY — BUSINESS AND COMMERCE

Abaranel, Karin. "Caroline Jones, Vice President and Creative Director of Mingo, Jones, Guilmenot, Inc." *The Executive Female Digest*, May-June 1979.

Abbot, E. *Women in Industry: A Study in American Economic History*. New York: D. Appleton, 1970.

Aery, W.A. "The Negro in Business." *Southern Workman*, October 1913, p. 522.

Alexander, Rodney. *The Shortchanged: Women and Minorities in Banking*. Port Washington, New York: Dunellen Publishing Co., 1973.

Alpha Kappa Alpha Sorority. *Women in Business*. Heritage Series #3. Chicago: Alpha Kappa Alpha, 1970.

America, Richard and Bernard Anderson. *Moving Ahead: Black Managers in American Business*. New York, N.Y.: McGraw-Hill, 1978.

American Mothers Committee. Bicentennial Project. *Mothers of Achievement: 1776-1976*. Rutland, Vermont: C.E. Tuttle Publishers, 1976.

"As Six of Them See It: Black Women Executives Discuss Their Lives and Careers." *Black Enterprise*, August 1974, pp. 20-23.

Bailey, Ronald W., ed. *Black Business Enterprise*. New York: Basic Books, Inc., 1971.

Basil, D.C. *Women in Management*. New York: Dunellen Publishing Co., 1972.

Bennett, Lerone. "The Mystery of Mary Ellen Pleasant." *Ebony*, April 1979, pp. 90-96.

Bennett, Lerone. "The Mystery of Mary Ellen Pleasant." *Ebony*, May 1979, pp. 71-86.

Bird, Caroline. *Enterprising Women*. New York, N.Y.: Norton, 1976.

_____. "Women in Business: The Invisible Bar." *Personnel*, May-June 1968, pp. 29-35.

"Black Capitalism: Rarest Breed of Women." *Time*, November 1971.

"Black Fashion Designers: With Brash Self-Assurance Young Stylists Make the Fashion Scene." *Black Enterprise*, December 1972, pp. 16-18.

"Black Models Take Center Stage." *Life*, October 1969, p. 36.

"Black Professionals: Progress and Skepticism." *Manpower*, June 1973, pp. 9-13.

"Black Professional Women, Forging New Careers Despite Dual Standards and Doing Quite Well, Thank You." *Black Enterprise*, November 1971, pp. 35-39.

"Black Women in Business." *Contact*, Fall 1972.

"Black Women in Business and Public Life." *Black Enterprise*, August 1974.

"Blacks in the Liquor Industry." *Black Enterprise*, September 1975.

Brandies, L.D. *Women in Industry*. New York: Arno, 1969.

Carson, Lester. "Black Directors." *Black Enterprise*, September 1973.

Carter, Kate B. *The Story of the Negro Pioneer*. Salt Lake City, Utah: Daughters of the Utah Pioneers, 1965.

Capozzi, Vincent A. *Black Business Digest*. Philadelphia: Compeers, Inc., April 1973.

Cash, William L., Jr. and Lucy R. Oliver, eds. *Black Economic Development: Analysis and Implications*. Ann Arbor, Mich.: University of Michigan Press, 1975.

"Cecelia Nabrit Adkins, '43." *Fisk Profile*, Fisk University, Nashville, Tenn., 1976.

The Census of Negro-Owned Businesses. Philadelphia: Drexel Institute of Technology, 1964.

Cheyney, A.S. "Negro Woman in Industry." *Survey*, 23 April 1921, p. 119.

Cohen, Casey M. "Insurance Executive Tells How She Reached Six-Figure Income." *Texas Woman*, April 1977.

Coleman, Ronald G. "Blacks in Utah History: An Unknown Legacy." *The Peoples of Utah*. Helen Z. Papanikolas, ed. Salt Lake City, Utah: Utah Historical Society, 1976.

"Colored Women in Business." *Messenger*, Tuskegee, Ala., 15 January 1927, p. 2.

"Colored Women in Industry in Philadelphia." *Monthly Labor Review*, May 1921, pp. 1046-1048.

Danbey, Wendell Phillip. *Maggie L. Walker and the I.O. Saint Luke: The Woman and Her Work*. Cincinnati, Ohio: Danbey, 1927.

Dannett, Sylvia G.L. "The Business Builders, Maggie Lena Walker." In *Profiles of Negro Womanhood*. Vol. I. Philadelphia: Goodway, Inc., 1964.

"Dark Glamour." *Newsweek*, September 3, 1962, p. 69.

Davis, Lenwood G. "Newspaper Publishers and Editors." In *The Black Woman in American Society*. Boston: G.K. Hall and Co., 1975.

DeWitt, Karen. "Black Women in Business." *Black Enterprise*. August 1974.

Donahue, M.P. "Female Labor Force in the United States." *Geographical Review*, July 1971, pp. 440-442.

Douglass, Pamela. "An Inside Perspective on the Black Woman TV Executive." *Contact*, May 1974.

DuBois, W.E. Burghardt. *The Philadelphia Negro* New York: Benjamin Bloom, Inc., 1967.

DuBois, W.E. Burghardt, *The Negro In Business* New York: AMS Press, 1971.

Duckett, Alfred. "The Legend of Ophelia DeVore." *Equal Opportunity*, Vol. II, No. 3, Spring 1978.

Dyson, E. "Help Wanted: Minorities and Women in the Retail Industry." *Economic Priorities Report*, 1974, pp. 1-58.

Ebony's 1,000 Successful Blacks. Vol. I. Chicago: Johnson Publishing Co., 1973.

Epstein, C.F. "Positive Effects of the Multiple Negative: Explaining the Success of Black Professional Women." *American Journal of Sociology*, January 1974, pp. 24-28.

Epstein, Edwin M. and David R. Hampton. *Black Americans and White Business*. California: Dickenson Publishing Co., Inc., 1971.

Fox, Stephen R. *The Guardian of Boston*. New York: Atheneum Co., 1970.

Frazier, E. Franklin. *The Negro Family in The United States*. Chicago and London: University of Chicago Press, 1968.

"From High Fashion to Big Business." *Black Enterprise*, September 1976.

Fuentes, S. "Job Discrimination and the Black Woman." *Crisis*, March 1970, pp. 103-108.

Gifford, William R. "Black Accountants." *Price Waterhouse Company Review*, Vol. 18, 1973.

Ginsberg, Eli, ed. *The Negro Challenge to the Business Community.* New York: McGraw-Hill, 1964.

Ginsberg, Eli and M. Yohalem. *Corporate Lib: Women's Challenge to Management.* Baltimore: Johns Hopkins University Press, 1973.

Gloster, Dorothy. "The Tireless Lady Tycoon." *Essence,* March 1976, pp. 61–62, 90–96, 116.

Green, B.M. "Upgrading Black Women in the Supervisory Ranks." *Personnel,* November-December 1969, pp. 47-50.

Guillarme, Deborah. "Taking Care of Business at Black Rock." *Black Enterprise,* September 1975.

Haddad, William F. and G. Douglas Pugh, eds. *Black Economic Development.* Englewood Cliffs, N.J.: Prentice-Hall, Inc., 1969.

Harmon, J.H., Jr., Arnett G. Lindsay, and Carter G. Woodson. *The Negro as a Business Man.* College Park, Md.: McGrath Publishing Co., 1969.

Harris, Abram L. *The Negro as a Capitalist.* Brooklyn, N.Y.: Negro Universities Press, 1969.

"Have Black Models Really Made It?" *Ebony,* May 1970, p. 158.

Holdredge, Helen. *Mammy Pleasant.* New York: Putnam Co., 1953.

Hunter, G.C. "Women Executives: The New Breed." *Tuesday at Home,* May 1975, pp. 4-6, 8, 15.

Hurwood, D.L. "More Blacks and Women in Sales and Marketing?" *Conference Board Record,* February 1973, pp. 38-44.

Irvin, H.B. *Conditions in Industry as They Affect Negro Women.* Proc. of a National Conference on Social Work, 1919.

Jackson, Jacquelyne Johnson. *Career Options for Black Women, 1975-76.* Washington, D.C.: National Institute of Education, 1976.

Jackson, Luther P. *Free Negro Labor and Property Holding in Virginia, 1830-1860.* New York: Appleton-Century, 1942.

Jensen, Beverly. "Black and Female, Too." *Black Enterprise,* July 1976.

Katz, William Loren, comp. *Guide to Black Studies Resources.* New York: Education Design, INc., 1970.

Keyes, J.B. "Big Business for Negroes." *Southern Workman,* April 1915, p. 239.

Kilson, Marion. "Black Women in the Professions." *Monthly Labor Review,* May 1977.

Kinzer, Robert H. and Edward Sagarin. *The Negro in American Business.* New York: Greenberg, 1950.

Lyle, Jerolyn. *Women in Industry.* Lexington, Mass.: Lexington Books, 1973.

"Making It." *Black Enterprise,* January 1976.

"Mary Kay's Sweet Smell of Success." *Reader's Digest,* November 1978.

Matney, William C., ed. *Who's Who Among Black Americans.* Northbrook, Ill.: Who's Who Among Black Americans, Inc., 1976, 1978, 1981.

Mitchell, Bert N. "The Status of the Black CPA — An Update." *Journal of Accountancy,* Vol. 141, May 1976.

Morgan, John S. and Richard L. Van Dyke. *White-Color Blacks, A Breakthrough?* New York: American Management Association, 1970.

Morgan, Ted. "In The Biggest Model Period." *New York Times Magazine*. August 17, 1975. pp. 12-14, 16, 18, 20, 22.

Morton, Carol. "Black Women in Corporate America." *Ebony*, November 1975.

"Moving Ahead in Style: Blacks in The Fashion Industry." *Black Enterprise*, September 1976.

Murphy, Frederick. "Black Models Have Their Say." *Encore*, April 7, 1975, p. 33.

Murphy, Frederick. "Naomi Sims: Enterpreneur Extraordinaire," *Encore*, April 19, 1976.

Mydal, Gunnar. *An American Dilemma*. New York: Harper, 1944.

"Names in the News." *Black Enterprise*, September 1976.

"Negro Business." *Outlook*, September 9, 1914, p. 66.

"The Negro in Business." *Southern Workman*, October 1914, p. 523.

"Negroes Enter the Labor Union." *Literary Digest*, June 28, 1919, p. 12.

"Negroes in Industry." *Survey*, 27 September 1919, p. 900.

Nelson, C.D. "Myths About Black Women Workers in Modern America." *Black Scholar*, March 1975, pp. 11-15.

Occupational Outlook Handbook. 1974-1975 edition. Bulletin 1785. Washington, D.C.: Government Printing Office, 1974, p. 128.

Ottley, Roi and Weatherby, William, ed. *The Negro In New York: An Informal Social History, 1626-1940*. New York: Praeger Publishers, 1969.

Payne, Ethel L. "Black Women in Business: Can We Overcome the Barriers?" *Contact*, Fall 1974.

Pierce, Joseph A. *Negro Business and Business Education*. Westport, Conn.: Negro Universities Press, 1947.

Placing Minority Women in Professional Jobs. Washington, D.C.: U.S. Department of Labor, 1978.

Preer, Herman. "Negro Leadership in St. Louis: A Study of Race Relations." Diss. University of Chicago, 1975.

Pressman, S. "Job Discrimination and the Black Woman." *The Crisis*, March 1970, pp. 103-108.

Previts, Gary John. "The Accountant in Our History: A Bicentennial Overview." *Journal of Accountancy*, Vol. 142, July 1976.

Procope, E.G. "Real Estate: An Investment for Women." *Black Enterprise*, August 1974, p. 43.

Quinn, Sally. "The Great Lady." *The Washington Post*, 12 November 1978, p. F2.

"Rarest Breed of Women: Black Businesswomen in the Executive Suites." *Time*, 8 November 1971, pp. 98-102.

Richardson, Clement. "The Nestor of Negro Bankers." *Southern Workman*, November 1914, p. 607.

Rickman, Geraldine. "Continuing the Search for Greater Horizons: Black Women in Business." *Contact*, Fall 1972.

Rywell, Martin, ed. *Afro-American Encyclopedia*. Vol. II. Miami: Educational Book Publishers, Inc., 1974.

Savage, W. Sherman. "Colorado Gold Rush." *New Day*, No. 5, 1947, p. 12.

Schneider, Stephen A. *The Availability of Minorities and Women for Professional and Managerial Positions: 1970-1985.* Philadelphia: University of Pennsylvania, 1977.

Schartz, Wendy, *Women and Minorities in Banking.* New York: Praeger Publishers, 1976.

Scott, Patricia Bell. "Preparing Black Women for Nontraditional Professions: Some Considerations for Career Counseling." *Journal of National Association for Women Deans, Administration and Counselors,* Spring 1977.

Seder, John and Berkeley G. Burrell. *Getting It Together.* New York: Harcourt, Brace, Jovanovich, Inc., 1971.

Shepherd, W.G. and S.G. Levin. "Managerial Discrimination in Large Firms." *Review of Economics and Statistics,* 1973, pp. 412-422.

Shuler, Carrie. "The Magnificent Story of Mrs. Julia E. Breeland." Unpublished paper, Orangeburg, S.C., n.d.

Sims, Naomi. *All About Health and Beauty For The Black Woman.* New York: Doubleday, 1976.

Smith, Garland, ed. *Black Texans of Distinction.* Austin: Garland Smith Associates, 1979.

Smythe, Mable M. *The Black American Reference Book.* Englewood Cliffs, N.J.: Prentice-Hall, Inc., 1976.

Stead, Bette Ann. *Women in Management.* Englewood Cliffs, N.J.: Prentice-Hall, 1978.

Styles, Fitzhugh Lee. *How to be Successful Negro Americans.* Boston: Christopher Publishing House, 1941.

"1977 Survey of Minority-Owned Business Enterprises." U.S. Department of Commerce, Bureau of the Census, Economic Survey Division.

Taylor, L. "Women in Business." *Essence.* March 1971, pp. 50-55.

Thieblot, Armand J., Jr. and Linda Pickthorne Fletcher. *Negro Employment in Finance.* Philadelphia: University of Pennsylvania, 1970.

"Those Sleek Black Beauties." *Newsweek.* May 5, 1975.

Walker, Ernestein. "The Black Woman." In *The Black American Reference Book.* Mabel M. Smythe, ed. Englewood Cliffs, N.J.: Prentice-Hall, Inc., 1976.

Walker, T.C. "Negro Property Holding in Tidewater Virginia." *Southern Workman,* November 1913, p. 622.

Washington, Booker T. *The Negro in Business.* Chicago: Hertel, Jenkins, and Co., 1907.

_____. "Negro Disfranchisement and the Negro in Business." *Outlook,* October 9, 1909.

Weaver, Robert C. *Negro Labor.* New York: Harcourt Brace and Co., 1946.

"Women in Business." Report of Hearings Before the Subcommittee on Minority Enterprises and General Oversight of Committee on Small Business, U.S. House of Representatives. Washington, D.C.: U.S. Government Printing Office, 1977.

"Women: On the Way Up." *Survey of Business,* May-June 1975.

"Women Owned Business 1972." U.S. Department of Commerce, Bureau of the Census and the Office of Minority Enterprise, WB 72.

"Women Seek Equal Changes in Business: First National Conference for Minority Businesswomen Produces Keen Insights." *Commerce Today,* July 10, 1972, pp. 4-7.

Wright, Karla Froman. "Black Women: Challenge for the 1980's." Presentation at the Black Women's Conference, Radisson Wilmington Hotel, Wilmington, Delaware, May 2, 1979.

Young, Harding B. "The Negro's Participation in American Business." *Journal of Negro Education*, Fall 1963, pp. 390-401.

INDEX OF BLACK WOMEN: Business and Commerce

THE CONTRIBUTIONS OF BLACK WOMEN TO AMERICA:
LAW

Manuscript Writer
Dewaran M. Johnson, J.D.

Consultant
Kenneth W. Gaines, J.D.

Evaluators
Willis Brown, Esquire
Director
Albany Urban League
Albany, Georgia

Gilroye Griffin, Esquire
Vice President - Employee Relations
Bristol-Myers Company
New York, New York

Attorney Alfrieda Harrell
Legal Department
Harper & Row Publishers
New York, New York

Attorney Sadie Jordan
Community Development Agency
Charlotte, North Carolina

Brown Hugo Payne, Esquire
Beckly, West Virginia

Editor
Marianna W. Davis, Ed.D.

PART IV

LAW

Table of Contents

INTRODUCTORY ESSAY
BLACK WOMEN IN LAW

The Black woman in America has been celebrated for her courage, her persistence, her stamina, her resiliency. She has seemed not to recognize the threat of defeat, nor to heed the omnipresence of rejection. In an article entitled "Double Jeopardy: To Be Black and Female," Frances M. Beal referred to the Black woman as a victim of a "double jeopardy"—a victim of being both Black and female. But the Black woman in America has refused to resign herself to being a victim, and instead, has viewed obstacles as challenges to be met, barriers as frontiers to be penetrated.

Of the numerous professional frontiers in America that Black women have labored to penetrate, the field of law has been one of the most resistant. Having subscribed to the premise that by their nature women and law were incompatible, the profession for a long time tended not to encourage women to join its ranks and this exclusion was felt most poignantly by Black women. At the turn of this century only about 558 of all lawyers in this country were female, and less than two percent of these were Black females. The picture has gradually grown brighter through the years. In 1970 there were approximately 376 Black women lawyers; in 1977, of the 6,000 Black lawyers practicing in the United States, one-third were women.

Black women lawyers today deserve high commendation and respect for their accomplishments. They bring to their profession some of the finest training and credentials available in the field. The fruits that these lawyers enjoy today, however, must be credited in part to the relentless efforts of their forebears in the profession. Prior to 1872 no Black woman in this country could boast of holding a law degree or bar membership, but there were those who succeeded in spite of overwhelming odds in making their voices heard in the legal arena.

Prior to the 1800's a number of circumstances and laws conspired to restrict Black participants in the legal system. As chattel, Blacks had neither status nor freedom to voice their opinions publicly. Laws prohibited them from citizenship and due process of law. Even religion was sometimes misconstrued as a means to keep Blacks in bondage. As early as the middle 1700's, many courageous Blacks felt compelled to fight against the legal system that oppressed them and denied them full citizenship in the United States. During this period Black women began to emerge in positions of leadership in the fight for freedom.

Note: The author of this essay was assisted by Dr. Ruby W. Watts of Columbia, South Carolina.

In the mid-1700's there was a number of Black women who overtly protested the unfair treatment of Blacks, and oftentimes demanded that they be given their rights. One of the most prominent figures of this era was Lucy Terry Prince, a slave woman who defended her right to happiness. Stolen from her native Africa, Mrs. Prince took her first step toward gaining her freedom in 1775. For reasons that are unclear, it appears that Lucy Prince and the other members of her family were being threatened by their white neighbors. Mrs. Prince immediately filed suit with the Governor's Council in Vermont, requesting that she and her family be protected by law against violent attacks by their white neighbors. The Council granted her request, thereby decreeing that the Prince family be protected by men selected by the Governor's Council.

The Princes had six children, one of whom Lucy Prince attempted to get enrolled in college. Having failed in her attempt, she filed suit against Williams College charging that her son had been denied admission based on his race. According to George Sheldon, the historian of Deerfield, "The indignant mother pressed her claim before the trustees in an earnest and eloquent speech of three hours, quoting an abundance of law and gospel, chapter and verse, in support of it, but all in vain."

In would appear that Lucy Prince had lost her case before the Trustee Board of Williams College. However, continuing remarks from Sheldon contend that "Before the trustees of Williams College, she had lost her case, but somewhat later, before the Supreme Court of the United States, she triumphed with eclat."

Lucy Prince's case heard before the Supreme Court was based on an issue which involved Eli Bronson. Apparently, Bronson attempted to steal a lot that was owned by the Prince family. Prince later filed suit against Bronson. To represent her, she retained Isaac Tichenor, who at that time was a lawyer in Vermont. Lucy, however, argued the case and won. This magnificent woman died at age 91.

During the early years Black women suffered in spite of the law, and mainly because of the law. Elizabeth Freeman, better known as "Mum Bett," was one who suffered because of the law. Freeman and her sister were purchased at an early age by Colonel Ashley of Massachusetts. At the Ashley plantation, they encountered problems with the Mistress. One day in a state of outrage the Mistress, using a heated shovel, viciously struck at Mum Bett's sister. Mum Bett, however, threw her arms in front of her sister to protect her from the shovel. From that day to the day of her death, the scar reminded her of that awful day at the plantation. After this terrible event took place, Mum Bett left the master's house without any intention of returning. Ashley felt it necessary to pursue the matter, for he believed that both Mum Bett and her sister were rightly his, and sought to recover his slaves by appealing to the law. Having been informed of Ashley's intent, Mum Bett obtained Theodore Sedgwick, a young lawyer, to represent her.

Mum Bett's suit soon became a historic case. She based her call on the "Bill of Rights — all were born free and equal." Finally, the case was argued by Sedgwick. After the arguments were heard, the jury ruled in favor of Mum Bett, and the court ordered Ashley to pay her thirty shillings for damages. This historical case settled the question that the Bill of Rights was introduced as a measure to abolish slavery in Massachusetts.

According to *The Black Presence in the Era of the American Revolution: 1770-1800,* in an abolitionist lecture at the Stockbridge Lyceum in Massachusetts, Thomas Sedgewick cited Elizabeth Freeman as his prime example. Sedgewick said, "If there could be a practical refutation of the imagined superiority of our race to hers, the life and character of this woman would afford that refutation. . .She had nothing of the submissive or subdued character, which succumbs to superior force."

As early as 1832, Black women were involved as amateur lawyers in the judicial system. Sylvia Dannett's *Profiles of Negro Womanhood* includes an account of one such pioneer. Born 1785 in Warwick, Rhode Island, Elleanor Eldridge was the first Black woman in her native state to obtain the title "amateur lawyer." Her achievement is indeed historical, for during this time Blacks still owned nothing, slaved day and night for whites, were classified as the lowest class of human beings, and were beaten by vicious white plantation owners who strongly believed that slaves had no rights.

These circumstances of history led Ms. Eldridge to a keen interest in law. At the age of ten, she was forced to become independent. Her mother died, and although her father, brother, and sisters were alive and well, Ms. Eldridge learned to depend upon herself.

She was hired by the Bakers, a family for whom her mother worked before her death. In this employment, Ms. Eldridge managed for five years on the meager salary of twenty-five cents per week. At age 16, she went to work for Benjamin Green as a spinner and a dairy woman.

Ms. Eldridge's lifestyle soon changed. During this time her brother George was selected for three consecutive terms as "Governor of the Colored Election." George's position was unique inasmuch as it gave him the power to oversee the affairs of other Blacks. Hence, George

Eldridge became the voice for many slaves who could not speak out freely against discrimination and violence.

Elleanor Eldridge grew fond of her brother's position, an affection visible during the political and social events held in his honor. She felt that her brother's job gained her much respect among the other slaves. The political activities of George Eldridge's job may have triggered Eleanor's interest in becoming an amateur lawyer.

Prompted by a desire to pursue a more fruitful life, Ms. Eldridge decided to move to Providence, Rhode Island. Upon her arrival there she established her own business, a white-washing, papering, and painting business. The business was successful, and she became financially able to purchase a home of her own.

Life prospered for Ms. Eldridge. Then word reached her of her brother's imprisonment in Warwick. She was astonished to hear that her brother, well-respected in Warwick, was being held for horse-beating a man on a highway. Apparently, Ms. Eldridge had not lost her ambition to become an amateur lawyer. Upon receipt of the letter about her brother, she readied herself to prepare his defense case.

To get to Warwick, she sent for a handsome horse and carriage, determined to go in a style that suited "the dignity of her mission," and on arriving at the jail, immediately posted a 500 dollar bond for her brother's release. As soon as he was liberated, she took over the entire management of his case. The case finally came to trial in October, 1833.

George Eldridge was acquitted, as nothing could be proved against him. This was the first law suit in which Eleanor Eldridge engaged. She had no previous legal education and no schooling whatsoever.

These accounts highlight the early struggles of Black women and their attempts to become professionals in a field where their presence was and, in many cases, still is unwanted.

Nevertheless, to fully understand the struggles of Black women to win favor in the legal system, it is important to further explore the conditions under which they have gained a foothold in the legal society of the United States.

This extended exploration of the struggle and the eventual fruition are what constitute the chapters of this volume. The second phase of the chronicle of the Black woman in law embraces the abolitionist activities that served as a platform for pioneer Black female lawyers. The various anti-slavery societies and the women's right societies provided forums for the voices of such Black women as Maria Stewart, Laetitia Rowley, and Frances Watkins Harper. Others such as Harriet

Tubman and Sojourner Truth became known as dynamic lecturers for the cause of both the abolitionist movement and the women's rights movement. The contributions of still other nineteenth century pioneer lawyers — including Ellen Craft, Ida B. Wells, and Mary Church Terrell — provide a further record of the Black woman's rights in this country.

Despite the groundwork laid by her predecessors, the first credentialed Black woman lawyer was not destined to find her law career a "crystal stair." This woman, Charlotte Ray, was the first Black woman to earn a law degree and to be admitted to the bar. While she was recognized as a lawyer of impressive ability, she found that society and the profession were not ready to accommodate her unique abilities.

Having been forced by these conditions to abandon her law practice, Ray went into teaching but continued her active involvement in the women's suffrage movement.

The second Black female lawyer in the United States was Mary Ann Shadd Cary, an 1883 graduate of Howard University's School of Law. Following Mrs. Cary, there were other Black women who distinguished themselves in the uphill journey of Black women lawyers. The turn of the twentieth century found these women still barred from full participation in their profession but emerging, nevertheless, as more aggressive participants. Several national legal organizations, formed during this period, were instrumental in promoting acceptance of Black women into the law field.

Following World War II, Black women gained increased visibility as lawyers, judges, and civil rights activists, as well as in other occupations that required a legal background. Among those who distinguished themselves during this period were: Hannah Byrd, Pennsylvania's first Black woman magistrate; Myrtle B. Stryker, first Black woman assistant attorney-general of the state of Illinois; Pauli Murray, recipient of a doctorate in law from Yale University; Barbara Morris, former Assistant General Counsel of the NAACP; Julia Cooper Mack, Judge of the District of Columbia Court of Appeals; Geraldine Green, Commissioner of Corporations in the state of California; Margaret Bush Wilson, chairperson of the Board of Directors of the NAACP; and Patricia Roberts Harris, first Black woman ambassador for the United States, who later became secretary of the U.S. Department of Housing and Urban Development and, still later, Secretary of Health, Education, and Welfare. One of the best known outstanding women lawyers is Constance Baker Motley, now a U.S. District Judge for the Southern District of New York. Another outstanding Black woman lawyer, Jewell S. LaFontant, became a Deputy Solicitor General of the United States.

The 1960's and 1970's saw Black women lawyers gaining footholds in the higher echelons of their profession. Having exemplified their capabilities before the courts, 48 Black women were rewarded with election or appointment to judgeships, the most prestigious positions in the legal profession. The first Black woman to enjoy such an honor was Jane Matilda Bolin of Poughkeepsie, New York. Her appointment helped pave the way for the elevation of other Black women to judgeships at the federal, state, and local levels.

By mid-1980, seven Black women in the United States were serving as Federal judges: Norma Holloway Johnson, Amalya L. Kearse, Mary Johnson Lowe, Gabrielle K. McDonald, Constance Baker Motley, Anna Diggs Taylor, and Anne E. Thompson.

At the state and local level, the register of "first" judgeships included: Marjorie M. Lawson, first Black woman to receive a presidential appointment to a judgeship (appointed by President John F. Kennedy, 1962); and Juanita Kidd Stout, first Black woman to win an election to a judgeship in the United States. Other pioneers and otherwise distinguished Black women who made names for themselves as judges are discussed at length in this volume.

The final chapter of *Contributions of Black Women in Law* looks at Black women lawyers in the 1970's and describes them as "assertive and challenging." A 1966 study showed that between 1940 and 1970 the number of Black lawyers and judges increased 107 percent. Yet, "in 1970 there were only 376 Black women lawyers in the United States as compared to the total lawyer population of 260,066, and as compared to 13,000 white women lawyers."

The statistics above suggest that in spite of the superb quality of their participation in the field, Black women lawyers were still somewhat restricted in terms of their numbers. Nevertheless, following the principles and examples of their predecessors, they continued to assert themselves in the face of "subtle hostility and the burdens of racism and sexism." Reminiscent of an earlier era, they determined that organized unity would be beneficial to them individually and collectively. Thus, in 1972, the National Association of Black Women Attorneys came into being, with attorney Wilhelmina Jackson Rolark as its founding president.

With sustained fervor Black women lawyers of the 1970's persisted in their efforts to surmount the obstacles between themselves and full participation and acceptance in their chosen profession. Each "First" achievement was a meaningful victory for that particular woman and for all Black women in the field. The final pages of this volume chronicle the story in full.

From the 1700's to the 1970's is a success story for Black women lawyers in America. True, the story embodies episodes of rejection, of frustration, of setbacks, but its more weighty episodes are of courage, of determination, of triumphs. Lucy Terry Prince, Sojourner Truth, and Charlotte Ray would surely agree that they presented a fine case for the inclusion of the Black woman in the field of law.

In the July, 1979 issue of *Black Enterprise*, Keven Dillworth noted that: Blacks are making slow yet steadfast gains in climbing up and permeating the ranks of the traditionally white legal profession. There are about 8,000 Black attorneys in the nation. Today's Black attorneys are getting a bigger piece of the legal economic pie. Municipal bond law, corporate and international law, bankruptcy, real estate, government, patent, labor and tax law, telecommunications law, and even establishment of legal clinics are some of the things Black attorneys have hold of today. (p. 38).

True to the tradition of those who preceded them, Black women lawyers across the country today assert themselves in this progressive movement. In the Northeast, for example, Renee Jones Weeks, head of the Women's Division of the National Bar Association, is a corporate attorney for a major insurance company based in New Jersey. A California trio of Black women — Corlette, Jeffries, and Thomas — run a firm geared toward corporate business matters. Their projections include involvement also in international law. And in the Southwest, Evelyn Briggs is a member of the firm Briggs, White, and Bonner, which serves the needs of small Black businesses as well as offers specialized counseling in the areas of consumer affairs, entertainment and athletics management, and workmen's compensation.

After 200 years of persistent efforts, the present and future prospects are more promising than ever for the Black woman lawyer in the United States.

Matthew J. Perry
U.S. District Judge
South Carolina

CHAPTER I

ABOLITIONIST ACTIVITIES:
A PLATFORM FOR BLACK WOMEN

An Early Activist: Maria Stewart

In 1831 the Abolitionist Movement was born. The organization's birth was indeed unique, for it was the first time in history that women would be allowed to speak publicly. Additionally, the birth of the movement was considered a "new spirit of abolitionism," for a number of anti-slavery societies were also formed. This movement, it appears, served as an awareness training ground for Black women who would later become enmeshed in the legal aspects of slavery, racism, and suffrage.

Shortly thereafter, female abolitionists societies were formed. Women were urged by the American Anti-Slavery Society, based in Philadelphia, to form their own abolitionist groups. "The public," contended renowned historian Benjamin Quarles, "held that reformists activity was defeminizing and that a woman reformer had somehow unsexed herself." The shout, "Go home and spin," often greeted a woman on the public platform. It was this reason, among others, that women formed their own groups.

Black women did not stay at home to spin. Before the Female Anti-Slavery Society was formed, a Black woman, Maria Stewart, had been employed as a full-time activist for the Maine Anti-Slavery Association. She thus became the first Black woman to publicly express her views on the issue of slavery.

Born in 1803 in Hartford, Connecticut, Stewart was orphaned at age five. She was later adopted by a clergyman and his family and remained with this family until she was fifteen years old. Stewart received no formal training in education; however, she did have access to the family's library, and she also attended the Sabbath School. Having been reared by a minister, she developed a religious conscience. At age 23, she married James W. Stewart, a mulatto from Connecticut. Shortly thereafter, she was widowed. In 1830, she was converted to Christianity and consecrated her life to the will of God. After her conversion, she became a well-known public speaker, delivering four speeches in a day during a time women were forbidden to speak publicly.

Stewart's speeches conveyed a religious and indeed a biblical style. But while her speeches were low-keyed, they carried much impact, urging free Blacks to educate themselves and press charges for violations of their rights. "She had apparently long been concerned for the plight of her people when William Lloyd Garrison's interest in them turned her concern into 'a holy zeal' for the cause."[1]

It was fortunate for Stewart, however, that Garrison started his publication of the *Liberator* in 1831, for in it a number of Maria Stewart's essays and speeches were published. The published materials included her essays entitled, "Religion and the Pure Principles," "The Sure Foundation on Which We Must Build," "Meditations," which were presented to the African Baptist Church Society in Boston, and "While My Hands Are Toiling for Their Daily Sustenance." Three major addresses delivered by Stewart at Franklin Hall in 1832, one to the African-American Female Intelligence Society during the same year, and one at the African Masonic Hall in 1833, were also published.

It was during 1833 that Stewart moved to New York City where she joined the Female Literary Society in an attempt to further educate herself. While in New York, she taught in the public schools.

In 1878, a law passed that granted widows whose husbands had served in the War of 1812 the right to receive a pension. Stewart, as a widow received a pension of eight dollars a month from Congress, and was able to finance the second edition of her speeches and essays entitled *Meditations From the Pen of Mrs. Maria W. Stewart* (1879). She died December 17, 1879.

Formation of the Female Anti-Slavery Society

The Female Anti-Slavery Society was chartered in Philadelphia in 1833 to help combat slavery. Although the leader of this society was Lucretia Mott, it is significant to note that four Black women, Harriett Purvis, Sarah Mapps Douglass, Sarah Forten, and Margaretta Forten, were charter members of the Society.

Because the women's rights movement was not as popular as the abolitionist movement, female abolitionists continued their quest to gain women's rights on the same platform with male abolitionists.

Thus, "with the coming of the abolitionist movement, many budding women's righters found an outlet for their energies," for, "it was the struggle for the rights of Black people that many Northern white women first became aware of their own oppression."[2] As a result, the purpose of the Society became two-fold. Its leader not only spoke out against the issue of slavery but also attempted to win support for the women's movement.

While white women were becoming aware of their oppression and while the abolitionist movement was not in full swing, Black women had managed to establish reputable characters for themselves.

The Formation of the Boston Female Anti-Slavery Society

In 1833 the Boston Female Anti-Slavery Society was formed. The prominent person in this society was Susan Paul. Soon after its formation in Boston, it was decided that the society should communicate with the Female Anti-Slavery Society in Philadelphia, a venture that proved to be fruitful. As a result, the first anti-slavery convention was held. The convention was unique for it was the first time in history that a group of women assembled together on a platform to address the issues affecting both slaves and women. This convention led to a second convention in Philadelphia in 1838, where Susan Paul was elected as a vice-president, and Sarah Douglass elected as treasurer.

Apparently the women's anti-slavery societies had gained momentum as well as impact. The speeches were being heard, and women felt very strongly about the issues they addressed. This momentum stirred a number of women and as a result, the third women's convention met with opposition. During the third convention, white women were urged to refrain from holding meetings and to disassociate themselves from Black women. The women's organization instead drafted "An Appeal to American Women on Prejudice Against Color."

The appeal not only urged that racial bias be unlawful, but also stirred the emotion of women as well. One such person was Clarissa C. Lawrence, president of the Colored Female Religious and Moral Society of Salem, who said: "It is worth coming all the way from Massachusetts to see what I see here."

Consequently, the new abolitionist movement united Black and white women — white women were primarily concerned with suffrage and Black women with abolition. The new movement, therefore, was an integrated force.

Formation of the Self-Help Societies

Aside from the involvement in the abolitionist movement, Black women were also responsible for forming self-help societies in the early 1800's. Two of the societies were the Daughter's of Allen Society and the African Benevolent Society which was formed in Rhode Island in 1808.

Since the question of slavery was being raised by the abolitionists, these self-help societies disapproved the purchasing of products made by slaves. Hence, the societies patterned themselves after the Quakers, who were the first to engage in such a practice. Nonetheless, products produced by slaves were displayed by the Colored Female Produce Society which was formed in 1831. The society, headed by Judith James and Laetitia Rowley, was formed to raise money for anti-slavery societies. It promoted displays of free labor products at the Broadway Tabernacle, charging money for admission and for food.

The Free Produce Movement was the attempt to strike at the slave-holding system by a boycott of the products of slave labor. The free produce societies had about 1500 members, mostly Quakers. But only about 6,000 people attempted to purchase free labor goods, and the movement was not very successful. However, abolitionists, such as Frederick Douglass, endorsed the free produce movement, for they believed it rendered an important moral impetus to the struggle against slavery.

One of the most prominent figures in the movement that boycotted "free produce" was Frances Watkins Harper, who later became one of the forerunners in the abolitionist movement. She was the speaker for the first boycott ever held by a group of Blacks. What is even more important is the fact that Black women* were steadily becoming involved with politics and the legal implications of slavery mainly as platform speakers. And of historical significance is the fact that Black women such as Frances Harper and Maria Stewart were voicing their opinions even before the Thirteenth Amendment was passed.

Anti-slavery did not mean anti-racism. Blacks, including Black women activists, found that whites still discriminated against them. Even the anti-slavery societies debated among themselves the question of whether or not to extend membership to Blacks — an ironic debate.

During the first two national anti-slavery conventions held by women, the same problem existed. The convention, held in New York, denied Black women the right to participate. Realizing that this was an act of prejudice, a year later the members of the New York Anti-Slavery Society drafted a plea against such acts of prejudice in 1837.

Although the Black self-help societies met with a number of obstacles, they proved helpful, yielding opportunities for Blacks to be actively involved in their economic struggle. "The advent of the new

*For further discussion of Frances and Maria Stewart, see *The Afro-American Woman: Struggles and Images* by Sharon Harley and Rosalyn Terborg-Penn, 1978 and *Black Women in Nineteenth-Century American Life* by Bert J. Loewenberg and Ruth Bogin, 1976. Also see the companion volume in this series, *Black Women in Civil Rights in America: 1776-1977.*

abolitionists," according to Quarles, "coincided with, and doubtless stimulated, an increase in Negro-self-help organizations."

The Birth of the Women's Rights Movement

After controversy over women's rights within the anti-slavery movement diminished, the first women's rights convention was held in Seneca Falls, New York in 1848. It was during this convention that a number of women assembled themselves in New York to discuss the status of women and to take the first step to obtain rights for themselves.

The feminists explained and justified their attacks on traditional practices by pointing to the injustices of these practices; at the same time many participants in the women's movement had taken advantage of new opportunities available and new attitudes toward woman's role in society.[3] Nevertheless, by 1848, the question of women's rights was still being debated, and the women's role in the anti-slavery movement was also still very much alive. The question of women's rights was one of the issues that caused dissension of the abolitionists. Since the abolitionists failed in their attempt to gain the support of religious groups, they turned to political activism instead. Thus, the anti-slavery movement became politically-oriented, promoting women to public platforms and legal activities.

After years of controversy, the American culture became feminized during the 1940's. Medler contends that "although this change did not persuade every aspect of the national life, effecting all social classes and geographical areas in the same degree, it brought to the arts, social practices, education, and reform work, an influence and a spirit which were distinctly feminine." Women were beginning to enroll in institutions of higher learning, becoming educators, and therefore, the status of women was being elevated. They were gaining recognition and influencing politics.

Black Women Lecturers

"The women's movement, according to Margaret Walker, has been a parallel struggle for freedom, peace, and human dignity. Even in pre-Civil War days, Black women stood in the vanguard for equal rights, for freedom from slavery, for recognition of women as citizens and co-partners with men in all of life's endeavors."[4]

Among the earliest of Black women lecturers who participated in both the abolitionist movement and the women's struggle were Harriet Tubman and Sojourner Truth. Sojourner's famous "And Aren't I a

Woman?" speech is often times cited as an example of her dedication and active engagement in the women's movement.

Frances Watkins Harper, an antebellum Black woman, an educated poet and novelist, worked as hard for women's rights and temperance as she worked for the abolition of slavery.[5]

Walker also contends that "because of the nature of American history, and particularly because of the institutions of slavery and segregation, the names and lives of Black women leaders are all but unknown in American society — Black as well as white. The names of a handful of Black women leaders of the past may be familiar — Harriet Tubman, Sojourner Truth, Mary McLeod Bethune. The names and accomplishments of recent civil rights leaders — Fannie Lou Hamer of Mississippi, Daisy Bates of Arkansas, Gloria Richardson of Tidewater County in Maryland and Virginia — have scarcely reached the ears of American school children."[6]

Walker further states:

> Three great Black American women were fighters for freedom — freedom from slavery of the mind and the spirit as well as freedom of the body from the despicable use of a human being as a piece of property or thing. All three women — Ellen Craft, Ida B. Wells, Mary Church Terrell — were born in the nineteenth century. All three were women of great beauty, character, and ability. Although their circumstances were very different — Ellen Craft grew up as an unlettered slaved, Ida Wells scrimped pennies for an education, Mary Church Terrell, the daughter of the South's first Black millionaire — they were equally indomitable and courageous. Taken together, these three lives span one hundred and twenty-eight years — from 1826, the year of Ellen Craft's birth, to 1954, the year of Mary Church Terrell's death.[7]

Terrell, Wells, and Craft shared the same views about the concerns of Black women and their active roles in politics, and they used the public platform and the law to bring attention to their concerns, thereby creating a positive image of the Black woman.

NOTES

[1] Edward James, ed., *Notable American Women 1607-1950*, Vol. III (Cambridge, Massachusetts: Harvard University Press, 1971), p. 377.

[2] Gerda Lerner, *The Majority Finds Its Past: Placing Women in History* (New York: Oxford University Press, 1979), p. 97.

[3] Keith E. Melder, "The Beginnings of the Women's Rights Movement in the United States," Diss., 1963, p. 5.

[4] Margaret Walker, "Introduction," in Dorothy Sterling's *Black Foremothers* (New York: McGraw-Hill Co., 1979), p. xiv.

[5] Walker.

[6] Walker.

[7] Walker.

CHAPTER II

BLACK WOMEN SEEK STATUS IN LAW

The first decade after the Civil War saw Black women still struggling to win the battle against discrimination and unfair treatment. To help under-privileged and uneducated Negroes, the Freedmen's Bureau was established.

W.E.B. DuBois, in his 1901 scholarly essay, "The Freedmen's Bureau," called the Bureau the "most singular and interesting of the attempts" of the United States to "grapple" with the race problems. With Paul S. Pierce of Boston as the "founder" of the Bureau at Port Royal, South Carolina in 1861, it actually lasted "legally from 1865 to 1872."[1]

The greatest success of the Freedmen's Bureau was its free schools for the children of former slaves as well as those of free Negroes. According to DuBois, by 1870, "150,000 children were in school."

On the other hand, the greatest failure of the Freedmen's Bureau was its legal or "judicial functions." Former slaves, including women, were daily beaten, raped, intimidated, and butchered. And beyond the normal concern of human life was the deep-seated fear of Black men for their women — the threat of rape, and of torture.

In 1875 this feeling was echoed poetically by the Mississippian, John R. Lynch, Negro member of the United States House of Representatives (1873-1878), when he spoke before the House about public rights, including the right of public transportation. Speaking about Negroes being forced to ride the train with drunkards and criminals, he said, in reference to Negro women: "Our wives and our daughters, our sisters and our mothers, are subjected to the same insults and to the same uncivilized treatment."[2]

Later, however, Negro women in the North joined their white sisters in the battle for temperance, higher education for all women, humane enterprises, and the right of all women to vote. But the greatest battle of all for the Negro woman was the battle for her race. These women worked tirelessly to open up greater opportunities for Negro youth. They founded their own normal schools and colleges; they became college deans, doctors, writers, musicians, singers, orators, business executives, painters, sculptresses, morticians, chiropodists, and lawyers.[3]

The achievements of these women during this period stems in part from the impact of the Women's Christian Temperance Union

Movement. Organized in 1874 in Hillsboro, Ohio, the Movement soon spread abroad.

Having taken an evangelical approach during the Movement, Blacks, including Black women, took to the streets, praying and singing in churches as well as saloons. Within a remarkable short span of time, according to Flexner, in her book *Century of Struggle*, "the Movement had reached into every state in the Union, and claimed to speak for more than two hundred thousand women. . .

Its wide appeal was attested by the variety of able women whom it drew into activity and leadership at some period during their lives: the labor organizer Leonora Barry, the Negro lecturer and author Frances Harper, . . .Mary McDowell, and many others."

This historical period, the Reconstruction Era, was especially important to Blacks, including Black women, for the Thirteenth, Fourteenth, and Fifteenth Amendments to the United States Constitution were ratified. However, both Blacks and women were soon to learn that ratified amendments did not mean rights, freedoms, and full citizenship in America.

Following ratification of the Fourteenth Amendment in 1872, "the Supreme Court of Illinois refused to grant to Myra Bradwell a license to practice law in the courts of that state, on the ground that females are not eligible under the law of Illinois. The United States Supreme Court held that such a decision violates no provision of the federal constitution."[4]

The Illinois Court declared:

> It is sufficient to say that, in our opinion, the other implied limitations upon our power, . . .must operate to prevent our admitting women to the office of attorney-at-law. If we were to admit them, we should be exercising the authority conferred upon us in a manner which, we are fully satisfied, was never contemplated by the legislature.[5]

The State of Illinois, in the Bradwell case, concluded that ". . . the paramount mission of women is to fulfill the noble and benign offices of wife and mother. This is the law of the creator."

The First Black Woman Lawyer in the United States

Even though the Thirteenth, Fourteenth, and Fifteenth Amendments establishing citizenship rights of Blacks had been passed by Congress, the legal status of Blacks and women hung in suspension. Reconstruction politics, only four years before the Hayes Compromise, was already showing signs that Blacks would eventually be abandoned by Federal protection, leaving them vulnerable to the malicious tentacles of white supremacy. In addition, white feminists had embarked on a campaign to show that they, rather than Black men and women, should be enfranchised by the Constitution. Their rhetoric certainly did not alleviate the increasing acts of wholesale terrorism directed against Blacks attempting to exercise their human rights. Thus, Black women lawyers were especially welcomed at this moment in history.

Charlotte Ray, daughter of an abolitionist, graduated from Howard Law School in 1872, thus becoming the first Black woman to graduate from a law school. Born in 1850 in New York City, she was one of seven children born to Reverend Charles B. Ray and Charlotte Augusta Burroughs Ray, a native of Savannah, Georgia.

In her youth she attended the Institution for the Education of Colored Youth in Washington, D.C. Having completed the requirements of the institutions, Ray became an instructor at Howard University in 1869, during which time she was also a student at the University. Described as "an apt scholar," a contemporary visitor to the law school was impressed by a "colored woman who read us a thesis on corporations, not copied from the books but from her brain, a clear incisive analysis of one of the most delicate legal questions."[6]

A few months after Ray graduated from the law school, she was admitted to the District of Columbia Bar, becoming the first Black woman to be admitted to that bar.

Ray later opened a law office in Washington. A Wisconsin lawyer, Kate K. Rossi, said "Ray. . .although a lawyer of decided ability, on account of prejudice was not able to obtain significant legal business and had to give up active practice." After giving up her law practice, Ray taught in the public schools in Brooklyn, New York. However, she remained actively involved in the suffrage movement, attending the 1879 National Women's Suffrage Association meeting in New York City. At age 60, Charlotte B. Ray died of acute bronchitis.

According to the May 1975 issue of *The Crisis*, Ray received her law degree in the same year (1872) that the *Bradwell vs. Illinois* case was upheld by the United States Supreme Court, denying women the opportunity to practice law, reasoning that "the natural and proper timidity and delicacy which belongs to the female sex evidently unfits it for many of the occupations of civil life." While the court applauded "the humane movements of modern society which have for their object the multiplication of avenues for women's advancement, and of occupations adopted to her condition and sex. . .," nonetheless, it was unwilling to say that women should be permitted to pursue a career which the court characterized as ". . .requiring highly special qualifications and demanding special responsibilities. . ."[7]

Since 1872, Black women lawyers have effectively demonstrated to deal with those special responsibilities that the court described.

The Second Black Woman Lawyer

Eleven years had elapsed before Mary Ann Shadd Cary became the second Black woman to receive a law degree in the United States. She graduated from Howard University's School of Law in 1883.

A native of Wilmington, Delaware, Mary Ann Shadd Cary was the first of thirteen children born to Abraham D. and Harriet P. Shadd, free Blacks.

Cary's family as a whole inspired and motivated her to dedicate her life to the cause of the freedom and liberation of Black people. Her brother Isaac, a newspaper publisher, served in the Mississippi Legislature from 1871 to 1874. And another brother was a lawyer. Her father was a prominent citizen, for he held a seat at the 1835 and 1836 American Anti-Slavery Society Convention. He served as president of the National Convention for the Improvement of Free People of Color in the United States in 1833. He was also a member of the Township Council in Chatham, Ontario, Canada.

At the age of ten, Cary attended a school for free Blacks which was sponsored by the Quakers. Having completed her studies in 1839, she taught in the Wilmington, Delaware school system.

In 1850 she became a noted spokeswoman for Blacks who had fled to Canada during the Fugitive Slave Act of 1850. Cary's concern for the fleeing Blacks inspired her to establish a school to help them. Later, she received support from the American Missionary Society, and established the school.

In 1853, she became involved with a publication committee which later founded the *Provincial Freeman*, the first Black newspaper. This was a newspaper dedicated to the interest of Black people, and Cary used this publication to inform and educate Blacks.

By 1878, she was a part of the suffrage movement, serving as one of the principal speakers at the National Woman Suffrage Association Convention.

After the Civil War, Cary settled in Washington, D.C. where she headed an American Missionary Association school. Later, while in her forties, she enrolled in law school. Following her graduation, she "practiced law for ten years until her death in 1893."[8]

Two Activists in the Late 1800's

From 1868 to 1879, progress was gradually increasing for Blacks in the United States. As economic conditions improved so did the conditions of women and of Blacks. Wyoming, Colorado, Utah, and Washington were states that established women's suffrage, and women became even more politically active.

Black women, during these years especially, supported Black men in politics, as they (Black women) became more and more educated about the legal process in the United States. Ida Platt and Ida Wells Barnett were two such Black women who were activists in legal proceedings and in other human rights movements.

Ida Platt of Chicago received the honor in 1892 of being the only representative of her race practicing at the bar. At the early age of sixteen, she had finished a high school course, taking first rank among the students of the institution.

At a later date, this studious young lady entered an insurance office, acting in the capacity of stenographer and private secretary where the correspondence required proficiency in German and French. Following this, she entered a prominent law office as a stenographer and later established an independent office of law reporting and stenography. Eventually Platt entered the Chicago Law School from which she graduated, richly deserving unstinted praise for her courage and perseverance. Although busy at her usual work during the day, she had only the evening hours in which to pursue her chosen profession and yet ranked among the best students of her class.[9]

A prominent journalist, among other talents, Ida Wells Barnett also helped to pave the road for the twentieth century woman to obtain favor in the legal profession. Wells is nationally known for her suit against the Chesapeake and Ohio Railroad.

In 1883, the Supreme Court ruled that the Civil Rights Act of 1875 was unconstitutional. According to Dorothy Sterling, author of *Black Foremothers*, "The Supreme Court [had] declared that railroad corporations are free to force us into smoking cars or cattle cars; that hotel keepers are free to make us walk the streets at night; that theater managers can refuse us admittance to their exhibitions." In spite of the Supreme Court decision, however, Barnett was determined to reverse the decision. The incident which led her to sue the railroad took place in Memphis, Tennessee. Having been accustomed to riding first-class as a passenger on the train, Barnett sat in the first-class car as usual. But a commotion started when the conductor refused to accept her ticket. The fact that she was sitting in the "wrong" car did not persuade her to move when asked by the conductor, and she refused. The conductor then pulled her arms to drag her out of the seat, and Ida Wells Barnett bit him, and remained seated. It took three men to remove Barnett from the car, although she fought a hard fight. During the incident, she was bruised and her clothes were torn. Ida Wells Barnett was outraged by the fact that the white passengers applauded the three men as they dragged her to the car reserved for Blacks. Upon her return to Woodstock, she hired a lawyer and sued the railroad company. Barnett was successful in her suit, and the court awarded her five hundred dollars in damages. The ground for the decision was based on the fact that Blacks were no longer wards of the United States, but citizens of individual states.

"The case of *Wells vs. Chesapeake and Ohio Southwestern Railroad*," according to Sterling, "was the first to be heard in the South since the demise of the Civil Rights Act. . .While the railroad appealed the decision, Barnett, flushed with her victory, wrote an account of the case for *The Living Way*, a Black church weekly." This case, however, did not overrule the previous Supreme Court decision that declared the Civil Rights Act of 1875 to be unconstitutional.

NOTES

[1] W.E.B. Dubois, "The Freedmen's Bureau," *Atlantic Monthly*, January 1901, pp. 354-356.

[2] George Alexander Sewell, *Mississippi Black History Makers* (Jackson, Miss.: University Press of Mississippi, 1977), p. 39.

[3] Sylvia Dannett, *Profiles of Negro Womanhood* (Chicago: Educational Heritage, Inc., 1964), p. 55.

[4] Karen DeCraw, *Sexist Justice* (New York: Random House, 1974), p. 30.

[5] DeCrow, p. 31.

[6] Edward James, ed., *Notable American Women: 1607-1950*, Vol. I (Cambridge, Massachusetts: Harvard University Press, 1971), p. 121.

[7] Joyce A. Hughes, "The Black Portia," *The Crisis*, May 1975, p. 167.

[8] Eleanor Flexner, *Century of Struggle* (Cambridge, Massachusetts: Harvard Univ. Press, 1959), p. 129.

[9] Gertrude Mossell (Mrs. N.F.), *The Work of the Afro-American Woman* (1894; rpt. New York: Books for Libraries Press, 1971), pp. 19-20.

CHAPTER III

THE TWENTIETH CENTURY BLACK
WOMAN EMERGES IN LAW

Against a background of contrasting political viewpoints, of war and
Reconstruction, of reaction to and loss of recently acquired rights, the
Black woman emerged as the great mainstay of the Negro race. "Many
Negro men," [through the years], have given her credit for leading the
race in its struggle for better things.[1]

Law, one of the last of the learned professions to accept women
practitioners, accepted the premise that law and women had little in
common. It was written that: "Law is logical, women are intuitive; law
requires long, sustained application; women excel in short spurts. . .By
1910 there were only 558 women lawyers in the United States."[2]

"In 1900 among female lawyers, Blacks were 1.9 percent; among
male lawyers, 0.6 percent."[3]

Among the annals of American jurisprudence is the name Sadie
Tanner Mossell Alexander, a native of Philadelphia, noted for her
pioneering efforts. Born 1898, she was the first Black woman to earn a
Ph.D. degree in the United States (University of Pennsylvania, 1921),
and the first Black woman to be admitted to the bar in the State of
Pennsylvania.[4]

This great pioneer struggled under unusual conditions to accomplish
what she wanted most in life. Upon graduation from high school,
Alexander was awarded a scholarship to attend Howard University.
However, her mother decided that she wanted her daughter to attend
the University of Pennsylvania. While at the University of Pennsylvania,
Alexander found the studies there extremely difficult. Realizing that
she was inadequately prepared for the studies at the school, Alexander
considered leaving only to be greatly encouraged to stay by her
teachers. Completing a four-year course in three years, she graduated
as one of the University's most distinguished students.

Being naive about racial discrimination while in college, Alexander
later tasted the bitter buds of that social phenomenon while seeking
employment. She kept the faith, however, and later became an
assistant actuary for the North Carolina Mutual Life Insurance
Company in Durham, North Carolina.

Alexander's interest in law stemmed from her father, Aaron Mossell,
the first Black to receive a law degree from the University of
Pennsylvania.

In 1924, Alexander entered the University of Pennsylvania Law School, and later became a member of the Law Review Board. Upon graduation from law school, she was appointed assistant city solicitor for the City of Philadelphia. She served in that capacity for six years. Afterwards, she formed a partnership with her husband, Raymond Pace Alexander, also a lawyer. This husband-wife team, one of the earliest of its kind, lasted for twenty-six years.

Alexander served on the Board of the Urban League for twenty-five years, and as chair of the Commission on Human Rights for more than twenty years.

According to Sylvia Dannett (*Profiles of Negro Womanhood*), Alexander took over the Commission on Human Rights in one of the most trying periods of American life when "we were in a revolution." She continues: "The fact that there have been no sit-ins in Philadelphia is largely due to the work of the Commission."

Also among the annals of American jurisprudence is the name Edith Sampson. Sampson was born in Pittsburgh in 1898, and when she was 18, associated charities in that city sent her to the New York School of Social Work. While there, Sampson performed outstandingly in a law course, which led to her interest in the field. However, it was not until she later moved to Chicago that she decided to pursue the study of law. She attended John Marshal Law School and was awarded a Bachelor of Laws in 1925. Later, she earned a Master of Laws from Loyola University, becoming the first Black woman to receive the degree from Loyola.[5] She was admitted to the Illinois Bar in 1927. Later that year, she also was appointed an Assistant State Attorney in Chicago and in 1950, President Harry S. Truman appointed her as an alternate delegate to the United Nations General Assembly, becoming the first Black in America to receive this appointment.

Sampson was elected an Associate Judge of Chicago's Municipal Court in 1962. When her term expired she was elected Judge of the Circuit Court of Cook County. From 1964 to 1965, she served as a member of the Advisory Committee on Private Enterprise in Foreign Aid. She was also a member of the American Bar Association, Chicago Bar Association, Women's Bar Association of Illinois, and the National Association of Women Lawyers.

Edith Sampson died during the fall of 1979, months after retiring from the bench.

Both Black men and women depended on the government to protect them as well as recognize them as citizens, capable of voicing their opinions on political issues. Since legislative decisions had a significant effect on Blacks, it was only politically sound that Blacks be involved in political decisions and in those legal proceedings that determined laws in this country.

-Nevertheless, as late as the early 1900's it was quite obvious that Black women were still being denied full participation in the political decision-making process. And by this time, it was also quite obvious that Black women were beginning to talk less and act more.

Born in 1900, Ollie M. Cooper holds the distinction of being one of the first Black women in the history of the nation to enter practice with a partner in a private firm owned and operated by women. She is also one of the founders of Epsilon Sigma Iota Legal Society.

Cooper attended the public schools in the District of Columbia. In 1921, she graduated magna cum laude with the Bachelor of Letters in Law from the Howard University School of Law. Cooper, spending some time as acting secretary of the Howard University Law School, served as a law clerk from 1918 to 1928. Years later, the Washington Bar Association established the Ollie May Cooper Award in her honor in August 1978.[6]

From 1905 to 1912 Black women were becoming even more active in the judicial system. They were no longer called "amateur lawyers."

Born in Lincoln, Nebraska, around 1905, Zanzye Hill became the first Black co-ed at the University of Nebraska Law School and the first Black female attorney in the state. She received the Bachelor of Arts degree from the College of Arts and Sciences and graduated from the law school in 1929. Soon after graduation, Hill became the legal counsel for the Woodmen of the Union Insurance Company at Hot Springs, Arkansas, the largest insurance company for Negroes in the nation at that time. Ill health forced her to resign, and she died in 1935 in Jackson, Mississippi.[7]

One who has also made considerable contributions to the field of law is Mahaila A. Dickerson. Born 1912 in Alabama, she holds the distinction of being the first Black woman admitted to the Alabama and the Indiana Bars. Dickerson was also the first Black attorney to practice law in the State of Alaska.[8]

She attended Fisk University, where she received the Bachelor of Arts degree. In 1948, she received the Bachelor of Laws degree from Howard University.

Organizations Form Legal Bases

A half-dozen national organizations formed to promote Black

progress during the early part of the twentieth century. These organizations included the Equal Rights League, the National Urban League, the Negro Independent Movement, the National Negro Business League, and the National Association for the Advancement of Colored People. Although these organizations had been developed, the program initiated by the National Association of Colored Women was still very much alive, and organizers realized that the decades ahead would yield considerable progress for Black women. Therefore, these organizations continued to encourage Blacks to become politically active in the fight for women suffrage.

All of these organizations, however, paved the way for Blacks in the legal arena.

Despite the efforts of these organizations and the women's movement, Blacks were still faced with a number of obstacles, such as the Ku Klux Klan. To fight the Klan, Blacks, in most cases, turned to the law and the courts. Needless to say, the attempt to eliminate discrimination and to fight for the right to life, liberty, and the pursuit of happiness through the courts ended with little success. Blacks, however, continued their struggle for human dignity.

According to Albert Blaustein and Robert L. Zangrando in *Civil Rights and the American Negro*, "the voting rights granted the Negro under the Fifteenth Amendment were merely a paper guarantee. For nearly a century, a vast arsenal of legislative devices was created to keep the Negro from the polls."

One of the legislative devices used to eliminate the Black vote or render it ineffective was the establishment of literacy tests. In the states of South Carolina, North Carolina, Oklahoma, Georgia, Louisiana, and Alabama, the "grandfather clause" was the establishment of literacy tests. In the states of South Carolina, North Carolina, Oklahoma, Georgia, Louisiana, and Alabama, the "grandfather clause" was also introduced as an attempt to serve the same purposes. John Hope Franklin, historian, states that:

> Where possible, the legislatures, controlled by zealous White Supremacy Democrats, helped to disfranchise Negroes. Areas with a heavy concentration of Negroes were divided by a system of gerrymandering which rendered the Negro vote ineffective. Poll tax requirements, elaborate and confusing election schemes, complicated balloting processes, and highly centralized election codes were all statutory techniques by which Negroes were disfranchised. . .South Carolina and Virginia were not alone in devising ingenious schemes to render the Negro vote ineffective. All Southern states used some device or another.[9]

Attention was diverted, however, from segregation and elimination of the Black vote during the war. Blaustein and Zangrando wrote, "confronted with the peculiar disruptions of World War I, which had noticeably accelerated the migration of Blacks from rural and southern areas to northern and mid-western metropolitan centers, the National Association for the Advancement of Colored People set a new course." The course taken by this organization involved working through the legislature and courts to rule on the various discriminatory acts against Blacks.

Hence, during the first-half of the 1930's, the Supreme Court began to assert its power toward civil rights and individual liberties. The Supreme Court, according to Benjamin Quarles, "began to go behind the formal law as stated in order to discover whether it was being fairly applied. It began to look beyond the laws enforcing segregation to see whether the separate facilities provided for Negroes were in fact equal to those of whites."

Having investigated these areas, the Supreme Court later handed down numerous rulings in regards to discrimination in housing and voting. According to Quarles, one of the most significant cases handed down concerning discrimination in housing was that of *Shelley vs. Kramer*. The Supreme Court ruled in 1948 that "restrictive covenants — private agreements to exclude persons of a designated race or color from the ownership or occupation of real property — were not enforceable by the judiciary."

While the Supreme Court had settled the issue of housing discrimination, there still remained an ever more significant issue to be ruled on — education. Consequently, the Supreme Court from 1938 to 1950 handed down rulings on a number of cases pertinent to education. One such case was that of *Gaines vs. Missouri* in 1938. Quarles wrote: "The court ordered that a Negro applicant be admitted to the law school of the University of Missouri since there was no other acceptable way for him to get a legal training within the state. Ten years later the Court ordered Oklahoma to provide Ada Louise Sipuel, a Black woman, with a legal education."

Blacks were making a come-back the latter part of the 1920's and early 1930's, for the Supreme Court rulings had given them and many civil rights organizations a boost, and they were encouraged to continue their struggle for human dignity and human rights.

Despite these advancements during the early 1930's, the Depression, in more ways than one, caused the positive changes for Blacks to decrease or to become meaningless. During the Depression, Blacks were actually retrogressing.

Meanwhile, it was 1938 that the first Black woman was elected to a state legislature in the United States. Crystal Bird Fauset acquired this distinction when she was named to the Pennsylvania House of Representatives.[10]

NOTES

[1] Sylvia Dannett, *Profiles of Negro Womanhood* (Chicago: Educational Heritage, Incorporated, 1964), p. 53.

[2] *Time Magazine*, 24 May 1937, p. 44.

[3] Gilbert Ware, *From the Black Bar* (New York: G.P. Putnam's Sons, 1976), p. 29.

[4] Thomas Yenser, *Who's Who in Colored America*, 6th ed. (New York: Thomas Yenser Publications, 1942), p. 20.

[5] Alpha Kappa Alpha Sorority, *Negro Women in the Judiciary*, (Chicago: AKA, 1968), p. 15.

[6] J. Clay Smith, "Washington Bar Association Establishes the Ollie Cooper Awards," Washington, D.C., 1978.

[7] *Lincoln Star*, 5 April 1935 (n.p.)

[8] Romeo B. Garrett, *Famous First Facts About Negroes* (New York: Arno Company, 1972), p. 186.

[9] John Hope Franklin, *From Slavery to Freedom: A History of Negro Americans* (New York: Alfred A. Knopf, 1947), p. 334.

[10] Garrett.

CHAPTER IV

BLACK WOMEN LAWYERS
BECOME ACTIVISTS: 1940's-1960's

Gaining Visibility

World War II propelled young Blacks into professional fields where the GI Bill helped to finance the educational expenses of those who would later become engineers, doctors, dentists, teachers, accountants, and lawyers. Among the fields, however, law stood out as an area for the political activist, and the Black woman became visible as lawyer, judge, and civil rights activist.

Leonard writes in his widely accepted publication that "by 1940, more than 1,900 Black lawyers were practicing in the United States."[1] However, this represented only 0.8 percent of the total number of lawyers in America.

National Black figures in law served as models and as mentors for young Blacks who wanted to become lawyers. Charles Hamilton Houston was such a figure. Full-time lawyer for the legal defense council of the National Association for the Advancement of Colored People, Houston provided the incentive for many aspiring lawyers who eventually became well-known in their own rights.

Regardless of the thirst for legal training, young Blacks would find many barriers to their ambition in the 1940's. To begin, in the South, only three law schools accepted Blacks: Simmons University in Louisville, Kentucky; Virginia Union University in Richmond, Virginia; Howard University in Washington, D.C. Secondly, bar examinations, especially in the South, appeared to carry racial tones, and thirdly, after becoming lawyers, Blacks found that they were denied membership in law societies, including the American Bar Association.

But prior to the 1940's, Black lawyers saw the need to form their own professional organization in order "to strengthen and elevate the Negro lawyer in his profession and in his relationship to his people; to strengthen his standing at the bar, and to create a bond of true fellowship among the colored members of the Bar of America for their general uplift and advancement and for encouragement of the Negro youth of America who will follow their choice of this profession."[2]

Visibility for Black lawyers moved to a high plane in the 1950's — the shaping of the civil rights thrust. Although a few, including Black women, had claimed posts in fields of law other than general practice or civil rights, these Blacks were few in number. According to Clark,[3] few or no Black lawyers held significant posts as government lawyers, judges, attorney generals, legal consultants, or seats in prestigious firms, including white firms.

By the beginning of the 1960's Black lawyers, emerging from civil rights struggles, including those for equal opportunity, increased their numbers in the legal departments of large companies and industries.

Even the all-white American Bar Association extended membership invitations to Black lawyers. But having an interest in the welfare of the Black community, Black lawyers as a whole stayed with their own National Bar Association. And those who worked in the corporate world brought their skills to groups such as the National Bar Association, where young aspiring Blacks could become motivated.

Black Women Practitioners

During the 1950's and 1960's, an increasing number of Black women, holding law or other degrees, entered vocational fields such as governmental service and law enforcement where law was central to the job. One such woman was Hannah Elizabeth Byrd.

In 1950, Byrd became the first Black woman magistrate in Pennsylvania. Having been appointed by Governor James H. Duff to fill her husband's vacancy, she served with distinction for two years.[4] Byrd attended the Philadelphia public schools and graduated from Duncan's Business College. She was a member of the Philadelphia Congress of Councils, the Pennsylvania Council of Republican Women, and she served as a state committeewoman.

But, more importantly, those who attained legal degrees became outstanding lawyers. And these professional Black women achieved in community activities — giving time, for example, to the improvement of the Black community and its people.

A noted pioneer in the field of law is Gertrude E. Rush, who, in 1950, held the distinction of being the only Black lawyer who had ever practiced in Iowa. The *Registrar Tribune* states that "court officials sometimes call her the 'Sunday School lawyer'." Rush firmly believes "the Golden Rule and the Ten Commandments will work, particularly in those cases involving young persons." As far as race and her profession are concerned, Rush said: "Race has not been any particular professional handicap, but in my fledgling days 31 years ago, it was pretty hard to be a woman. Court officials and police officers always have been cooperative, but clients too often were brutally frank." Active in community organizations, she established a charity league for women and girls in Des Moines, and it remained open for thirteen years.

In 1946, Myrtle B. Stryker was awarded the Bachelor of Laws degree from John Marshal Law School. In 1947, she was admitted to practice law in Illinois. In 1953, she was cited by Iota Phi Lambda Sorority as Outstanding Woman of Achievement of the Year. Ten years later she practiced before the United States Supreme Court. When she was appointed attorney for the Cook County Public Administrator, she was the first Black so appointed. Later, Stryker was appointed assistant attorney-general of the State of Illinois, the first Black woman to receive such an appointment. In 1960, she ran for Judge of the Municipal Court of Chicago, another first, for no other Black woman in Illinois had ever entered any judicial race. She was unsuccessful in a campaign that was made difficult by her husband's serious illness. In 1966, she was given the Merit Award for Distinguished Service to the Legal Profession by the Cook County Bar Association.[5] Myrtle B. Stryker, in 1966, was also sworn in as a magistrate in the Circuit Court of Cook County, the only woman in a selected field of twenty-two magistrates. During the course of her career, she has achieved many "firsts" in her hometown and in the state of Illinois.

"Watergate," says Pauli Murray, is the reason she dramatically switched from law to the Ministry. "I was teaching young people law as an instrument of social change at Brandeis University in 1973. Then came Watergate, a breakdown in the profession at the highest level, and I felt that law no longer held the answer."[6]

Murray, a trained attorney, was ordained in 1976 as the first Black woman priest of the Episcopal Church.

Born in Baltimore and raised in Durham, North Carolina, Murray earned a Bachelor of Arts degree from Hunter College, taught adult education, and became interested in the legal profession after being denied admission to a segregated University of North Carolina in 1935, where she had hoped to pursue graduate studies. She filed suit with the aid of Thurgood Marshall, who was then an attorney for the National Association for the Advancement of Colored People, and lost on the grounds that she was an out-of-state resident.

After being arrested in 1940 for refusing to move to the back of an interstate bus in the South, she firmly decided that law was to be her avocation. Upon entering Howard University Law School, she ran into another obstacle. She was the sole female enrollee. "I came out of Howard University a convinced feminist," she says. "Up until that time I had not been aware of discrimination against women. The school was entrenched in sexism. But all of my life I have tended to accept challenges; setbacks sharpen my determination. So I suppose my strategy there was simply to excel."[7] And that she did, graduating at the top of her class in 1944. After Howard, she went to the University of California for a Master's degree in law; in 1965, she was awarded a doctorate in law from Yale.

Pauli Murray, Civil Rights Activist, in Episcopal vestments, preaching at Virginia Theological Seminary on "Absalom Jones Day"

Invited by President Benjamin F. Payton, Murray accepted the position of Vice-President for Educational Plans and Programs at Benedict College in South Carolina in 1967, serving there for one year. Her experiences, however, as a lawyer led her to new horizons in civil rights, education, and human rights issues.

Following her graduation from the University of California, she became an attorney for the Commission on Law and Social Action of the American Jewish Congress. In 1948, she entered into private practice in New York City, maintaining this office until 1960. Because of her skills as a lawyer, she won two notable awards as Woman-of-the-Year: In 1946, one from the National Council of Negro Women, and in 1947, one from *Madamoiselle* Magazine. In 1956, Murray joined the distinguished law firm of Paul, Weiss, Rifkind, Wharton, and Garrison in New York City. This position was followed by her appointment as Senior Lecturer of Constitutional and Administrative Law at the Ghana Law School in Accra, Ghana, West Africa in 1960. She then became a lecturer in law at the Boston University School of Law. From 1968 to 1973, she was the Louis Stulberg Professor of Law and Politics at Brendeis University in Massachusetts. Holding seven honorary doctorate degrees, Murray has also published in the field of law. Pauli Murray, outstanding lawyer, is also widely acclaimed internationally as "priest, poet, teacher, revolutionary, feminist, and civil rights activist."

Patricia Roberts Harris, the first Black woman to hold such a diplomatic rank — Ambassador to Luxembourg — now serves as the newly appointed Secretary of the U.S. Department of Health and Human Services. Prior to this, she was the second Black person to hold the cabinet post of Secretary of the Department of Housing and Urban Development.

Briefly, Harris was Dean of the Howard University Law School, resigning rather than submitting to demands by students for a more important role in running the school. She then became a partner in the prestigious Washington law firm of Fried, Frank, Shriver, and Kampleman. Previously, Harris served as program director for the Young Women's Christian Association for the Chicago area. She also served under John F. Kennedy as co-chair of the National Women's Committee on Civil Rights, and was later named to the Commission on the Status of Puerto Rico, 1964-66.

Born 1924, the daughter of a pullman porter and a school-teacher, Harris attended Howard University and graduated summa cum laude. She did graduate work at the University of Chicago and the American University. She received her Doctor of Laws degree from George Washington University Law School in 1960. The recipient of 32 honorary degrees, Harris heads the District of Columbia Law Revision Commission.

"Women's rights and equality for Blacks are not diametrically opposed," Florynce (Flo) Kennedy believes. "I adhere to the philosophy that human rights are indivisible. We cannot play one set off the other without both sides losing. I don't think we'll wipe out racism unless we wipe out sexism."[8] At age 61, Flo Kennedy is still speaking her mind. "I'm still rebellious, still making a fool of myself, and most people still don't agree with what I have to say. The big difference is that now they pay me to say it anyway."

Florynce "Flo" R. Kennedy, Activist Lawyer,
Civil Rights Advocate, and Feminist

In the early sixties, the political activist, feminist, author, and attorney turned lecturer, became disillusioned with law practice and took to the picket lines. Since then, her unrelenting attacks on big business, the media, the church, marriage, motherhood and other institutions, have made her a celebrated thorn in the thumb of the establishment and a big attraction on the college campus lecture circuit. Later, after attending several women's rights conferences, including the National Women's Conference in Houston in 1977, Kennedy strongly states: "It must be realized that racism is more serious than sexism. Black people are often killed for no reason other than they are Black. Racism is to sexism what cancer is to a toothache."[9]

Born in St. Louis, Missouri, the daughter of a pullman porter who went into the taxi business, she explains her initial attraction to the legal profession: "I went into law because I learned from my daddy — who once bought a house in a white neighborhood and then had to defend it against the Klu Klux Klan — that you do not go to the place the enemy has set up for you to go."[9] A graduate of Columbia University in 1948, she decided to attend the Columbia University Law School. After graduating in 1951, she landed a job as an assistant to a bookkeeper in a law firm. In 1954, she opened her own law office, handling matrimonial and few criminal cases of interest.

On August 4, 1978, J. Clay Smith and the Washington (D.C.) Bar Association Board of Directors approved the Creation of the "Ollie M. Cooper Service Award." The award was named in honor of one of the association's most distinguished members, Ollie M. Cooper. Cooper's service to the Bar dates back nearly to its inception. She has served the association in numerous capacities, including that of vice-president. But her service to the bar extended beyond the Washington Bar Association, because for years Ollie M. Cooper was actively involved in the affairs of the National Bar Association as well. She, and other Black women attorneys, gave substantial time and service, yet to be fully recognized in the struggle and the survival of Black lawyers in the nation. She also held the position of assistant secretary in the National Bar Association.

Black women have chosen many paths when addressing the struggle and survival of Black lawyers. One avenue for Black women was education and more education. The career path of Inez Reid exemplifies educational gains which have resulted in diverse policy making position. Inez Reid received a B.A. from Tufts University in 1959, followed by an LL.B. from Yale University, followed by an M.A. from UCLA, culminating with a Ph.D. from Columbia University in 1968. Although currently practicing as an attorney, Reid served as a Professor of Political Science at Barnard College, Columbia University, and at Brooklyn College. Attorney Reid became a general counsel for the New York State Division for Youth in 1976 and currently serves as deputy general counsel, regulations review, for HEW.

Reid has served on the board of trustees of Antioch College, the board of governors for Antioch School of Law, as well as the boards of Wildcat Corporation, Black Women's Community Development Foundation, and Homeland Ministeries.

Another outstanding attorney during this period of time was Frankie Muse Freeman. Freeman was awarded an LL.B. degree from Howard University in 1947. Before obtaining her law degree, Freeman served as

general counsel for the St. Louis Housing and Land Clearance
Authorities, as a clerk for the U.S. Treasury Department, and as a
Statistician for the Office of Price Administration. Practicing law as a
private attorney from 1949-1956, Freeman interrupted her law career
to teach business at the College of the Fingerlakes in New York.
Frankie Freeman has been instrumental in developing organizations
such as the National Council of Negro Women and Delta Sigma Theta
Sorority. She is presently a member of the U.S. Commission on Civil
Rights, continuing her struggle for equal opportunities.

Frankie Muse Freeman - lawyer and U.S. Commissioner of
Civil Rights, with M. Maceo Nance, President of
South Carolina State College

Other Black women pioneers in the field of law deserve mention:
Cassandra E. Maxwell, of Orangeburg, South Carolina, the first Black
woman to pass the South Carolina Bar; Mrs. L. Martin Poe, of Newport
News, Virginia, the first Black woman admitted to practice in the
Commonwealth of Virginia, 1925; Isadora A. Letcher of Washington,

D.C. believed to be the first Black woman lawyer admitted to practice in the state of Michigan; Jewel S. LaFontant, the first Black woman Deputy Solicitor General of the United States; and Julia Cooper Mack, the first Black woman to sit on the District of Columbia Court of Appeals; Elreta Melton Alexander, general court judge in Greensboro, North Carolina; Theresa Doss, judge of Common Pleas Court in Detroit, Michigan; Golden Elizabeth Johnson, city judge of Newark, New Jersey's Municipal Court; Consuelo B. Marshall, superior court judge in Los Angeles, California; and Edith Miller, a family court judge in New York City.

NOTES

[1] Walter J. Leonard, *Black Lawyers* (Boston: Senna and Shih, 1977), p. 119.

[2] Gilbert Ware, *From the Black Bar* (New York: G.P. Putnam's Sons, 1967), p. xxxiv.

[3] Christine P. Clark, *Minority Opportunities in Law* (New York: Law Journal Press, 2974), p. 46.

[4] Alpha Kappa Alpha Sorority, *Negro Women in the Judiciary* (Chicago: AKA, 1968), p. 7.

[5] *Negro Women in the Judiciary.*

[6] Resume and Letter received from Pauli Murray, 16 February 1980.

[7] Pauli Murray.

[8] Telephone interview with Florynce Kennedy, New York City, 26 May 1980.

[9] Florynce Kennedy.

[10] Florynce Kennedy.

CHAPTER V

BLACK WOMEN PRESIDE OVER COURTS

In 1977 the National Bar Association reported that 6,000 Blacks were actively engaged in the practice of law. Nearly a third of these practitioners were women; but only 400 of the total number were judges.[1] Judicial posts, long bastions of male dominance, have rarely been commanded by Black women. Nonetheless, after receiving law degrees and practicing the profession before the courts, Black women increasingly assumed roles of judges such that the 1970's saw some 48 Black women either elected or appointed to judgeships. Judicial appointment or election is usually regarded as the crowning glory in any attorney's career, for to be a judge is to hold one of the most prestigious positions in society. The job carries the tremendous responsibility of ruling upon points of law dealing with trial procedure, presentation of evidence, and the law of the case. If a case is tried without a jury, the judge alone determines the facts as well as perform the aforementioned duties.

Born in 1908 in Poughkeepsie, New York, Jane Matilda Bolin became the first Black American woman judge in the United States.[2] A 1928 grduate of Wellesley College in Massachusetts, Bolin received the Bachelor of Laws degree from the Yale University Law School in 1931. She was later admitted to the New York Bar. From 1931 to 1937, Bolin embarked on private practice. In 1939, New York's Mayor Fiorello LaGuardia appointed her as head of the Court of Domestic Relations.

Bolin's appointment as judge helped to change the circumstances for Black lawyers in the United States, for it opened the doors for other Black lawyers. Bolin's professional affiliations include: the New York State Association of Family Court Judges, National Council of Juvenile Court Judges, and the Harlem Lawyer's Association.

Federal Judges

As of May 1980, seven Black women sat as Federal Judges in the United States: Norma Holloway Johnson, U.S. District Court, Washington, D.C.; Amalya L. Kearse, U.S. Court of Appeals, New York, N.Y.; Mary Johnson Lowe, U.S. District Court, Southern District, New York, N.Y.; Gabrielle K. McDonald, U.S. District Court, Houston, Texas; Constance Baker Motley, U.S. District Court, Southern District, New York, N.Y.; Anna Diggs Taylor, U.S. District Court, Detroit, Michigan; Anne E. Thompson, U.S. District Court, Trenton, N.J.

Judges Constance B. Motley and Norma H. Johnson are the only two Black women Federal judges appointed prior to 1977.

Constance Baker Motley, U.S. District Judge,
New York, New York

In response to demands for justice and equal opportunity during the 1960's President Lyndon Johnson nominated Constance Baker Motley for a Federal judge for the Southern District of New York. She was confirmed by the U.S. Senate and became the first Black woman Federal judge.[5] Prior to her appointment, Motley had gained acclaim as a superlative trial attorney, handling civil rights cases. In 1963 she became the first Black woman elected to the New York State Senate, and was the only woman among that session's 58 members.[4] She was born in 1921 in the State of Connecticut. At age 15, she entered high school where she encountered her first experience with racial discrimination. While still in high school, she was elected president of the New Haven Youth Council, and later secretary of the adult New

Haven Community Council, organizations established to promote civil rights.

Motley graduated from high school in 1939 and was able to attend college through the goodwill of Clarence Blakeslee, who heard her speak at a public gathering and immediately recognized her extraordinary oratorical talent. When asked why she was not in college, Motley replied candidly that she simply did not have the money. Without hesitation, Blakeslee offered to finance her education. During 1941 and 1942 she attended Fisk University. In 1943, however, she received the Bachelor of Science degree in economics from New York University.

Motley was first attracted to the legal profession and to its usefulness in fighting civil rights as a teenager.

> What sparked my interest in law was the 1938 Lloyd Gaines case. I was in high school in New Haven at the time when the Supreme Court ruled that Mississippi could not send Blacks outside the state to law schools since they were not permitted to atend the University of Mississippi Law School. It was a major decision, the first civil rights case in our time. But that decision did not knock out segregation. Mississippi set up a separate law school for Blacks.[5]

In pursuit of her interests, Motley attended law school at Columbia University from which she received her law degree in 1945.

In 1970, former President Richard Nixon nominated Norma Holloway Johnson for a seat on the U.S. District Court in Washington, D.C. She won that nomination.

Johnson, a native of Lake Charles, Louisiana, graduated magna cum laude from the District of Columbia Teachers College in the class of 1955, of which she was also valedictorian. She begun studies toward a master's degree in education from 1956-1957, but chose to forego the advanced degree to enter law school. She received her J.D. degree in 1962 from Georgetown University Law Center in Washington, D.C. Although admitted to the bar in December 1962, Johnson did not engage in the practice of law until August 1963 when she became associated with the firm of Arthur Reynolds, Esquire. In November 1963, she left the firm for employment with the Department of Justice until February 1967, at which time she was appointed Assistant Corporation Counsel. She remained in this position until her appointment to the bench in 1979.[6]

Mary Johnson Lowe,[7] Federal Judge of the U.S. District Court, Southern District, New York, is a native New Yorker. Born June 10, 1924, she attended the public schools and received a bachelor's degree in political science from Hunter College in 1952. Her law degrees were earned at the Brooklyn Law School and Columbia University's School of Law.

Recipient of numerous academic awards and honors, including the John Hay Whitney Fellowship for graduate school, Lowe was appointed to the Criminal Court of the City of New York in December 1971, and served until March 1973, when she then became Acting Supreme Court Justice in New York. In 1975, she was named County Supreme Court Judge, Bronx, New York, and in November 1977, Lowe was elected Justice of the Supreme Court, State of New York. She presided here until July 27, 1978, when she was inducted as Judge, U.S. District Court as a Federal Judge.

Gabrielle Kirk McDonald,[8] Federal Judge, U.S. District Court, Houston, Texas, was born in St. Paul, Minnesota, April 12, 1942. Educated at Boston University and Hunter College, McDonald received her law degree from Howard University, graduating as first in her class in 1966.

Gabrielle K. McDonald
Judge U.S. Southern District of Texas

During her years in law school, she served as Notes Editor of the *Howard Law Journal*, and received the Kappa Beta Pi Legal Sorority's award for academic excellence.

From 1966 to 1969, McDonald served as staff attorney for the NAACP Legal Defense and Educational Fund, Inc. For the next ten years, she engaged in private law practice and taught law at Texas Southern University and the University of Texas. On May 11, 1979, Gabrielle K. McDonald was appointed Judge of the U.S. District Court, Southern District, State of Texas.

Anna Johnston Diggs Taylor,[9] Judge of the U.S. District Court, Eastern District of Michigan, was appointed to the federal bench by President Jimmy Carter on November 2, 1979.

Anna Diggs Taylor, Judge, U.S. District Court,
Eastern District of Michigan

Born December 1932 in Washington, D.C., Taylor was educated at Barnard College-Columbia University and at Yale University's School of Law, receiving her LL.B. degree in 1957. She also holds a degree in mortuary science from Wayne State University.

Married and the mother of two children, Taylor held several posts in the law field prior to her nomination to the federal bench. She served as attorney for the U.S. Department of Labor for three years, as assistant Wayne County prosecutor for a year, and as an assistant U.S. attorney in 1966. From 1970 to 1975, she was a partner in the law firm of Zwerdling, Maurer, Diggs, and Papp. While serving as corporation counsel for the City of Detroit, Taylor taught law at Wayne State University's School of Labor and Industrial Relations.

A board member of the National Lawyers' Guild, Taylor is actively involved in 16 professional groups, including the District of Columbia and Michigan Bar Associations and the Detroit Committee for Seven Eastern Women's Colleges. She also belongs to 35 community organizations, including the Board of the Home for Black Children, the Episcopal Society for Cultural and Racial Unity, the United Community Services Board, and the Detroit's Women's Opera Committee.

Anne Elsie Thompson,[10] U.S. District Judge in Trenton, New Jersey, received her LL.B. degree from Howard University's College of Law in 1964, where she served as Notes Editor of the *Howard Law Journal*. She also holds a B.A. degree from Howard University and an M.A. degree from Temple University in Philadelphia.

Prior to her appointment on November 20, 1979 to the federal bench by President Jimmy Carter, Thompson held several law posts in New Jersey. A staff attorney in the U.S. Department of Labor in Chicago in 1965, she moved to Trenton where she was hired to draft a proposal for a free legal service project for the Trenton Anti-Poverty Agency. Later she became prosecutor for the Township of Lawrence. In 1972 she was Municipal Court Judge for the City of Trenton, and prior to her federal judgeship, she was prosecutor of Mercer County.

Thompson serves on 13 boards and commissions, including the Board of Trustees, Criminal Law Section, New Jersey State Bar Association. She also holds membership in three bar associations, including the American Bar Association.

Amalya L. Kearse[11] was appointed to the United States Court of Appeals, Second Circuit, New York City on June 21, 1979 by President Jimmy Carter.

Born June 11, 1939 in Vauxhall, New Jersey, Kearse received her B.A. degree in philosophy in 1959 from Wellesley College. In 1962, she received her J.D. law degree (cum laude) from the University of Michigan's School of Law, where she was a member of the Order of the

Coif. Serving as *Law Review* editor, she was responsible for articles and comments in the areas of commercial law, property law, and civil procedures. For her work on the *Law Review*, she was awarded the Jason L. Honigman prize.

While in law school, Kearse also served as research assistant to Professors John W. Reed, Samuel D. Estep, and Alan N. Polasky. Member of the New York State Bar and certified to practice before the U.S. Districts Courts in New York; U.S. Courts of Appeals, second and fourth circuits; and the Supreme Court of the United States. Kearse has also served as lecturer at the New York University's School of Law, and she has authored more than five publications on law.

In 1977, she was voted to a two-year seat on the Board of Directors of the NAACP Legal Defense and Educational Fund, Inc. Presently, she serves on the Committee of Visitors, University of Michigan Law School; Fellow, American College of Trial Lawyers; member, American Law Institute; member, American Bar Association.

Kearse is also very active in community organizations and projects. She has served on the Board of Directors, National Urban League; Board of Trustees, YWCA of the City of New York; Board of Directors, Big Sisters, Inc.

She is a master bridge player and has authored five books on bridge including the Third Edition of the *Official Encyclopedia of Bridge*.

State and Local Judges

Born in 1912 in Pittsburgh, Marjorie M. Lawson is noted for being the first Black woman appointed to a judgeship by the President of the United States, President John F. Kennedy. This was in 1962. Lawson also holds the distinction of being the first Black woman to be approved by the United States Senate for a statutory appointment.[12]

Lawson practiced law along with her husband, Belford V. Lawson, Jr., until her appointment to the bench. From 1943 to 1946, she served as assistant director and later director of the Division of Review and Analysis of the President's Committee on Fair Employment Practices. In addition to her legal background, Lawson wrote a weekly column for the *Pittsburgh Courier* for fifteen years.

Edith Sampson, early Black woman judge fashioned a distinguished career in the Illinois state attorney general's office, and made history as an alternate delegate to the United Nations.

Edith E. Sampson, Judge,
Circuit Court of Cook County, Chicago

Another Black woman among the firsts in the law profession is Juanita Kidd Stout. During an interview with Sylvia Dannet in 1963, Stout referred to herself as a "product of the Depression, and not only that, I'm a product of the state (Oklahoma) in which, in those days, there were no integrated schools." After receiving her first degree in music, she taught for three years at Booker T. Washington High School in Sand Springs, Oklahoma, and then moved to Washington, D.C. Upon her arrival, Stout applied for the position of a junior professional assistant with the National Housing Authority. The job required that the applicant pass an examination. After passing the examination, Stout was still denied the job. Upon making an inquiry, she was told that she had "majored in music and that $1,800 a year was a lot of money for a colored girl." Being aggressive, Stout immediately resigned. Shortly thereafter, she accepted employment with the Houston, Houston, and Hastie Law Firm.

In 1942, Juanita Kidd married Otis Stout, who after being discharged from the army, enrolled in Indiana University to complete his master's studies and obtain the doctorate degree. During the same time, Stout enrolled in the University's law school. Later, she and her husband graduated from Indiana University in 1949 where she was awarded the Doctor of Jurisprudence degree. In 1954, she was awarded the Master of Law degree, specializing in legislation.

Juanita Kidd Stout, Judge,
Court of Common Pleas in Philadelphia

With the appointment of William H. Hastie, of Houston, and Hastie law firm, as judge of the United States Court of Appeals, Third Circuit in Philadelphia came the opportunity for Stout to work with him in Philadelphia. After succesfully completing the Pennsylvania Bar, Stout became Assistant District Attorney for the Family Court Division. She served in this capacity for approximately nine months. She was then appointed Chief of Appeals, Pardons and Paroles Division in the District Attorney's Office in Philadelphia. She remained in this position for three years, during which time she simultaneously conducted a private practice. In 1959, Stout was appointed the County Court Judge in Philadelphia, a position that had been vacated due to the death of her immediate predecessor. This appointment, however, ended within two months. Nevertheless, Stout was determined to retain the position and became a candidate for election. This courageous fighter won the election and became the first Black elected woman judge in the United States.[13]

Stout is also recognized for her published articles, "Separate But Equal Theory," "Shall We Recommend," and "Cases on Constitutional Law."

Margaret Haywood, a Knoxville, Tennessee native, born October 8, 1912, graduated from Washington's Robert H. Terrell Law School in 1940. Until her federal appointment as Judge of the District of Columbia Superior Court, she maintained a general legal practice, in which she gained the respect and admiration of many.

Named one of America's Outstanding Women in 1951 by the National Council of Negro Women, she was cited by the Sigma Delta Tau Legal fraternity in 1957 for outstanding professional service. She won the National Bar Association award in 1968, and another peer group, the Women's Bar Association, voted her the Woman Lawyer of the Year in 1972, the year of her ascent to the bench.

Haywood, who once served as Grand Basileus (1948-52) of the Lambda Kappa Mu Sorority, Inc., also holds honorary doctorates from three colleges.

Julia P. Cooper Mack, an associate judge in the Capitol's largest court, was born in Fayetteville, North Carolina. She received her LL.B. in 1951 from the Howard University Law School, and began a career as trial attorney in the Appellate Section, Criminal Division of the Department of Justice in 1954. By 1968, when America was in the midst of a social upheaval, she moved to the newly-formed Equal Employment Opportunity Commission for which she served as associate general counsel from 1968 to 1973. She then became a deputy general counsel there and held that position until appointed as a federal judge.

Among Mack's citations are the EEOC Award for Distinguished Service, 1971, and the Justice Tom C. Clark Award for the outstanding federal career lawyer, bestowed in 1974.[14]

Julia Cooper Mack, Judge,
District of Columbia Court of Appeals

Charlye O. Farris of Wichita Falls, Texas made history in July 1954 when she served as Wichita Judge Pro Tem for three days during the absence of the regular County Judge. It was a first in the South. Farris again served temporarily in 1973 for approximately two weeks as a Federal district court judge.[15]

A Wichita Falls natvie, Farris graduated from Prairie View University in 1948 and earned her law degree by 1953 from Howard University. She holds the additional distinction of being the first woman admitted to the Texas Bar.

Lucia T. Thomas, mentioned in an early *Ebony* article on Black women lawyers, was a civil rights and patent law specialist who wanted to enter politics. By 1947, she had been admitted to practice before the U.S. Supreme Court.[16] Today, Thomas and colleague Blanche M. Manning are judges of the Cook County (Illinois) Circuit Court, and have taken up the mantle of Edith Sampson.

The first Black woman in Mississippi to be appointed a Municipal Court Judge in the town of Rosedale was Alma Campbell. A native of Mount Bayou, Mississippi, one of the oldest Black towns in the United States, she received the bachelor of Arts degree from Tougaloo College in 1968, and the law degree from the University of Illinois, Champaign, in 1975.[17]

Sara J. Harper holds the distinction as being the first woman to serve as a justice for the U.S. Marine Corps, one arm of the national defense force. When interviewed after the 1973 appointment, Harper told a reporter, "I really love my country, I love being a woman, I love being Black, and this is a chance to make a contribution to all three."[18]

Already a municipal court judge in Cleveland, Ohio since 1970, Harper became interested in joining the Marines' court when she learned of the need for Black judges in the military justice system, and of the racial inequities therein. A Marine reserves major, she studied military law at the University of New Hampshire Naval Justice School. The military bench appointment allows her to maintain her position with the City of Cleveland.

Harper has held a series of highly challenging positions within the Cleveland legal apparatus, beginning with her role as chief attorney with the city's Legal Aid Society from 1966 to 1968. In 1969 and 1970, she was assistant director of law for the city's law department. Posts handled before her court appointment were chief attorney positions with the Air Pollution and Control Department and the Department of Human Resources and Economic Development.

Held in high esteem by the electorate as well as the governor who appointed her to the court, Harper won election to a six-year bench term in 1971.

In 1977, 22 of all federal judges were Black.[19] By 1978, six of the overall total were women — roughly 1.1 percent.[20] Despite their late entry into the legal profession, Black women have compiled an impressive record in the federal judicial ranks. As pointed out by Wade McCree, U.S. Solicitor General, Blacks on the federal bench are stellar examples who offer powerful incentives to other Blacks hoping to excell in the legal profession. Of equal importance is the fact that they, through participation in Judicial Conference committee work — where federal bench policy is made — can influence "some of their white peers who . . . still [stonewall] on desegregation and other civil rights issues."[21]

Born in 1944, Margaret A. Burnham holds the distinction of being the first Black female judge in Massachusetts.[22] Judge Burnham was admitted to the New York and the North Carolina Bars in 1970, and to the Massachusetts Bar in 1973. From 1972-73 she served with the Roxbury Defenders Committee as a staff attorney, responsible for criminal litigation in the Roxbury District Court and Suffolk Superior Court. She also represented criminal defendants in numerous jury trials as well as handled routine district court matters. In 1978, Judge Burnham was the recipient of the Massachusetts Black Lawyer Association Award and the Justice Resource Institute's Community Service Award.

Margaret Burnham, Associate Justice, Boston Municipal Court, with Governor of Massachusetts (photo courtesy of Ellen Shub)

In December 1977, Barbara Merriweather Sims became the first Black woman to hold the position of Associate Judge of the City Court of Buffalo, New York. Following her interim appointment, in 1978 Judge Sims was elected to a full 10-year term. She was the only woman among 12 associate judges.[23] A native of Buffalo, New York, she graduated from the State University of New York at Buffalo Law School, and later became the first Black female member of the faculty at the law school. She later served as assistant to the President of State University of New York, and also served as the Assistant Attorney in Buffalo. Judge Sims also organized the Buffalo chapter of the National Bar Association, and was one of the founders of the National Association of Black Women Attorneys. Also included among the founders were Wilhelmina Jackson Rolark, Gwendolyn Cherry, and Ruth Chassity.

Another prominent Black woman judge is Alice A. Bonner,[24] a native of New Orleans, Louisiana. She was admitted to the practice of law in Texas in 1967. She received both her Bachelor of Arts and Doctor of Law degrees from Texas Southern University. Having specialized in Family Law, she engaged in private practice in Texas until 1976. She also attended the National Judicial College and the American Academy for Judicial Education. In 1975, she organized the Black Woman Lawyers Association in Texas. She was appointed judge of the Harris County Criminal Court in June of 1977 and served until December of 1978.

Alice A. Bonner - State Judge in Texas
(photo courtesy of Houston Chronicle)

A former legal columnist for the *Forward Times* newspaper and co-host for the KYOK Community Talk Show, Bonner is a member of many civic and social organizations, including the National Council of Negro Women and the Young Women's Christian Association.

In 1978, Bonner was cited by *Focus* Magazine as the "Most Influential Black Woman" in Houston. Presently, she is a judge for the 80th Civil Judicial Court for the state of Texas.

In 1977, Florida appointed its first Black female judge. Mary Ellen Whitlock Hicks, a Texas native, was the first Black and the first female to hold this position.[25] Born 1949, Judge Hicks graduated from the Texas Woman's University, Denton in 1970 and the Texas Tech School of Law in 1973. In 1977, she was the recipient of the "Trailblazer of the Year" award. She was also the recipient of an Outstanding Young Women in America award in 1976 and was listed in the 1979 edition of *Who's Who in Black America*.

The first Negro woman to serve as a Municipal Court Judge in Los Angeles, California was Vaino Spencer.[26] She was appointed in 1961. Spencer graduated summa cum laude from the Los Angeles City College in 1949, and earned the Bachelor of Laws degree from Southwestern School of Law in 1952. Spencer was admitted to the California Law Revision Commission in 1960, and to the attorney general's Advisory Committee on Constitutional Rights for two consecutive terms. Being the recipient of numerous awards, she received the Trailblazer Award from the National Association of Business and Professional Women in 1962, and was also named Distinguished Citizen in the field of Civil Rights by the Coca Cola Company. Los Angeles City College named her its Most Distinguished Alumni in 1966.

In spite of the obstacles that often hinder Black women from running for office, Geraldine Ford won and now sits as Judge of Recorder's Court in Detroit, Michigan.

Ford's judicial campaign was unique. Although her qualifications equaled or exceeded those of other candidates, she was considered very nice, an able and experienced attorney — but still a woman, with little chance of being elected.

Born in Detroit, Ford attended Wayne State Universty Law School, and was awarded the Bachelor of Letters in Law in 1951. Since that time, she has practiced with the family firm, Bledsoe, Ford and Bledsoe, for ten years. Ford later served as assistant United States Attorney for the Eastern District of Michigan.

The first Black woman judge in the state of Louisiana was Joan B. Armstrong.[27] In 1974, Armstrong was appointed judge of the Orleans Parish Juvenile Court, Section A. A native of New Orleans, she received the Bachelor of Arts degree from Xavier University, and was awarded a Doctor of Laws degree from Loyola University School of Law in 1967. Since Judge Armstrong's graduation from law school, she has been active in many organizations. She was past president of the Community Relations Council of Greater New Orleans and the Louisiana League of Good Government. In 1974, Armstrong was cited for outstanding achievement and was awarded the Distinguished Service Award as the outstanding young woman in New Orleans by the city's Jaycees. She also received the Greyhound Company's Silver Bowl Award in recognition of her services to the New Orleans' community. On two occasions, 1975 and 1976, she was selected as outstanding woman in the field of law by the Women's Committee of the Federal Executive Board of New Orleans.

History was made when Harriet L. Murphy became the first Black woman to be appointed for a term as judge in the state of Texas. She also holds the distinction of being the first Black woman to be appointed as a Municipal Court Judge in Texas, and the first Black woman to serve as a presidential elector in Texas. Born 1927, in Atlanta, Georgia, she was appointed for a two-year term as a judge by the Austin City Council in January 1974. And in 1976, Murphy served as one of Texas' 26 electors in electing the President of the United States. A 1949 graduate of Spelman College, she received a Bachelor of Arts degree in History and Government. In 1952 she obtained the Master of Arts degree in Political Science from Atlanta University. Murphy later studied at Columbia University and the School of Advanced International Studies of Johns Hopkins University. She received the Doctor of Laws degree in 1969 from the University of Texas Law School. Having practiced law, she is presently an Associate Judge of the Austin Municipal Court. Judge Murphy was also appointed by the Austin City Council to serve on the city's first Energy Study Commission, 1972. In 1973, the Austin chapter of Zeta Phi Beta Sorority presented her with the Woman in Law Award.

Lillian Walker Burke serves as Municipal Judge in Cleveland, Ohio. She received her law degree from the Marshall Law School following her undergraduate degree from Ohio State University. A former school teacher, Burke serves as a board member of the American Association of University Women. Serving on the Governor's Commission on the Status of Women, she is also an active member of the Women Lawyers Association, and the Black Judicial Council of the National Bar Association.

In 1970, Burke received honors and a salute from the American Woodmen for being the first elected Black female judge in Cleveland.

Black women judges, though few in number, have set examples in courts, in family, community, and civic activities that underline their professional qualifications as well as their human qualities.

Lillian Walker Burke, Judge,
Municipal Court, Cleveland, Ohio

NOTES

[1] "Alexander, Harris, Kennedy, Motley, & Murray; Attorneys at Law," *Black Enterprise*, August 1977, p. 19.

[2] William C. Matney, ed., *Who's Who Among Black Americans* (Illinois: Who's Who Among Black Americans, Incorporated, 1978), p. 78.

[3] *Ebony*, May 1974, p. 22.

[4] Sylvia Dannett, *Profiles of Negro Womanhood* (Chicago: Educational Heritage, Incorporated, 1964), p. 327.

[5] *Black Enterprise*, August 1977, p. 23.

[6] Letter received from Norma H. Johnson, 6 May 1980.

[7] Telephone interview with Rosa Weir, secretary to Judge Mary Johnson Lowe, 16 June 1980.

[8] Telephone interview with Ella Smith, secretary to Judge Gabrielle K. McDonald, 16 June 1980.

[9] Resume of Anna Diggs Taylor, 1980.

[10] Resume of Anna Elsie Thompson, 1980.

[11] Resume of Amalya L. Kearse, 1980.

[12] Alpha Kappa Alpha Sorority, *Negro Women in the Judiciary* (Chicago: AKA, 1968), p. 13.

[13] John P. Davis, *The American Negro Reference Book* (Englewood Cliffs, N.J.: Prentice-Hall, Incorporated, 1966), p. 522.

[14] "Black Woman Nominated for Appeals Court Judgeship," *Jet*, 24 July 1974, p. 12.

[15] Letter received from Jewel Prestage, Southern University, Baton Rouge, Louisiana, 18 April 1980.

[16] *Ebony*, August 1947, p. 19.

[17] *Tougaloo News*, Tougaloo College, Spring 1979.

[18] "Cleveland Woman Becomes Marines' First Woman Judge," *Jet*, 24 May 1973, p. 32.

[19] *Black Enterprise*, August 1977, p. 19.

[20] *Women's Political Times*, National Women's Political Caucus, Spring 1978, p. 1.

[21] Diane Camper, "Still Too Few Black Federal Judges," *Dollars & Sense*, June/July 1979, p. 11.

[22] Resume of Judge Margaret A. Burham, 1979.

[23] Resume of Judge Barbara Merriweather, 1979.

[24] Resume of Judge Alice A. Bonner, 1980.

[25] Letter received from Elneita H. Dever, North Texas State University, 18 May 1979.

[26] *Negro Women in the Judiciary*, p. 11.

[27] Letter received from Thelma M. Cobb, Southern University, Baton Rouge, Louisiana, 20 April 1979.

CHAPTER VI

THE 1970's: BLACK WOMEN LAWYERS — ASSERTIVE AND CHALLENGING

Black law students — female and male — continue to view legal education as a route to political power and socio-economic status. And since the time of law school desegregation, the enrollment of Black students has increased dramatically. A 1966 Howard University study reported that the number of Black lawyers and judges increased 107 percent between 1940 and 1960.

One reason for the dramatic increase in law school enrollment of Black students is the strengthening of traditionally Black law schools at Howard University; Southern University in Baton Rouge, Louisiana; Texas Southern University in Houston; North Carolina Central University in Durham.

Another reason for the upswing in Black enrollment is the additional funding given by foundations and other private groups. For example, the Ford Foundation gave Howard University 1.8 million dollars in 1964 for its law school, and most of this money was earmarked for scholarship aid. Along with the Ford's effort is that of CLEO — the Council on Legal Education Opportunity, an organization that raises funds for recruitment and scholarship and for Black law students.

But even with these efforts, in 1970 there were only 376 Black women lawyers in the United States as compared to the total lawyer population of 260,066 and as compared to 13,000 white women lawyers.

Yet, in the ranks of achievers one finds the names of Black women lawyers. Toiling under subtle hostility and the burdens of racism and sexism, they have maintained the same sturdy values as their fore-mothers: keeping families together, stressing moral values, and maintaining faith in their God. These lawyers have also used their legal education to assist them in other related occupations as well as in their movements toward community building.

In 1972, however, the women decided that organizational unity would provide for them a stronger voice in the legal profession and in efforts to attract more Black women to the field. Attorney Wilhelmina Jackson Rolark became founding president of a group that carries the name The National Association of Black Women Attorneys, formed November 1972.

The organization's general purpose includes (1) advancing the practice of law; (2) increasing opportunities for participation of Black women at all levels of justice; (3) increasing the number of Black women practicing law by developing programs for recruitment and for scholarship; (4) advancing the causes of civil and human rights of all citizens in the United States.[1] As a result of this unification in the 1970's, Black women lawyers became more assertive, more highly visible, and national change-agents.

Wilhelmina J. Rolark received both the bachelor's and master's degrees from Howard University. In 1944, she received the Bachelor of Letters in Law from the Terrell Law School. Elected to a four-year term as member of the District of Columbia City Council, she is the recipient of many awards, including the Phyllis Wheatley Award in 1966.

Gwendolyn Sawyer Cherry, born in 1923 in Miami, Florida, graduated cum laude from the Florida A&M University Law School in 1965. In 1970, she became the first Black woman ever to serve in the Florida Legislature, following her election in Dade County.[2] Holding a college degree in biology and chemistry from Florida A&M and a master's degree in Human Relations from New York University, Cherry was the Dean of Democratic Women in the Florida Legislature in 1974.

One of the founders of the National Association of Black Women Attorneys and a former U.S. Coast Guard attorney, Cherry was honored with more than 46 awards for community services in law, education, and politics from 1965 to 1976.[3]

On February 9, 1979, Cherry met an untimely death in an automobile accident, leaving a husband, a daughter, and a son to mourn her passing.

Wyvetter H. Younge,[4] born 1930 in St. Louis, Missouri, spent ten years in successful private law practice in St. Louis before becoming Executive Director of the East St. Louis Housing Corporation in 1968.

A 1951 graduate of Hampton Institute in Virginia, Younge holds the J.D. degree in law from St. Louis University of Law and the master's of law degree from the Washington University School of Law, 1972.

Active in community affairs, focusing on programs for the poor, Younge, married and the mother of three children, was elected to the Illinois Assembly in 1972, representing the 57th District, East St. Louis.

Not only have Black women been active politically and as legal counselors, but also many lawyers have contributed to the academic field by preparing young people for law careers. Joyce A. Hughes, a noted educator, is presently a professor at the Northwestern

University School of Law, and Sallyanne Payton is on the faculty of the University of Michigan School of Law.

Joyce A. Hughes, a native of Gadsden, Alabama, graduated magna cum laude from Carleton College in Northfield, Minnesota in 1961. From 1961 to 1962, she attended the University of Madrid in Spain, and in 1965, she received her law degree (cum laude) from the University of Minnesota School of Law. Having served as special consultant to organizations such as the Ford Foundation in New York City, the U.S. Congress-Office of Technical Assessment, the Auerbach Corporation of Philadelphia, and Peterson & Holtze of Minneapolis, Minnesota, Hughes has maintained close ties between her teaching of law and practicing of law. She is a member of Phi Beta Kappa and a recipient of numerous awards, including the Fulbright Scholarship and the John Hay Whitney Fellowship. A vice president of the National Urban League and of the Chicago Forum, Hughes is an example of active Black women in both professional and community circles.

Sallyanne Payton, native of Los Angeles, California, served as a White House aide under President Jimmy Carter. She holds the B.A. and law degrees from Stanford University in California. A former social caseworker for Los Angeles, Payton is a member of the Bars of both California and the District of Columbia. A former staff assistant to former President Gerald Ford, she served the Federal Government in various capacities before accepting the position at the University of Michigan School of Law.

Eleanor Holmes Norton, a lawyer who in 1977 became head of the Equal Employment Opportunities Commission at the Federal level, once said that "there are certain substantive principles that I believe in strongly, one is racial equality, the other is free speech. As it turns out, if I want to implement the principle of equality, I do it through participation in the civil Rights Movement. To implement my belief in free speech, I represent anyone whose free speech has been infringed."

Having graduated from Antioch College and from Yale Law School in 1964, she became a lawyer for the American Civil Liberties Union (ACLU), specializing in First Amendment cases. During the sixties, Norton was one of three lawyers who wrote the brief for the Mississippi Freedom Democratic Party. She also wrote a brief for Julian Bond, a Georgia legislator, who was denied his seat because of his opposition to the Vietnam War.

Norton replaced Simeon Golar as head of the New York City Human Rights Commission in the Spring of 1970. As head of the city's principal anti-discrimination agency, Norton was also the highest-ranking Black in the administration of New York's Mayor John V. Lindsay. Upon acknowledging her appointment, Norton characterized the function of the Commission as one of assuring that irrational criteria of race, religion, or national origin be eliminated as grounds for evaluating the personal merits of job applicants. Norton included sex among the irrational factors which sometimes caused discrimination and pledged to remove this consideration from the list of acceptable job criteria. In 1968, while serving as a Civil Liberties Attorney, Norton demonstrated her dedication to principle by pressing for the right of George Wallace to hold an outdoor rally at Shea Stadium in New York. She followed through on her stand, despite stiff opposition from the Mayor and noisy protest from other liberal quarters.[5]

Another aspect of Norton's legal philosophy is women's rights. As former Human Rights Commissioner, Norton was determined "to provide a forum for the particular problems of Black women, who have had to contend with both racial and sexual discrimination."

In 1977, Paulette Sullivan Moore became the first Black woman to be admitted to the Delaware Bar. A native of Delaware, she graduated from Wheaton College, and she received a degree in law from Rutgers University. Moore is also a member of the Board of the Moot Court and the Washington, D.C. Bar. She presently holds the position of Managing Attorney at the main office for Community Legal Aid.

In 1976, Irma Brown founded the Black Women Lawyers Association of California, and served as the association's president from 1976 to 1978. She was also the founder and secretary for the California Association of Black Lawyers. Her professional affiliations include the John M. Langston Bar Association, and the Los Angeles County Bar Association. Brown graduated from Loyola University School of Law in 1973.

A native of Bennettsville, South Carolina, Marian Wright Edelman became the first Black woman to be admitted to the Mississippi Bar. This was in 1966. Edelman was educated at Spelman College in Atlanta and received her law degree from Yale University. Having worked with the National Association for the Advancement of Colored People Legal Defense and Educational Fund, she became very proficient in her knowledge of "welfare war." When she went to Washington, D.C. Edelman became the Southern Christian Leadership Conference Congressional liaison. In 1968 she pushed for the jobs bill, a repeal of repressive welfare legislation, and a major resolution of the hunger issue.

Edelman now sits as a trustee at her alma mater, Spelman College, and is also the Director of the Children's Defense Fund of the Washington Research Project, Incorporated. She is also a board member of the NAACP Legal Defense and Educational Fund.

The first Black female member of the Hennepin County Minnesota Bar Association was Lena Smith. Smith served on the Minneapolis Urban league's Board of Directors from 1931 to 1942 and as president of the National Association for the Advancement of Colored People. She is also a member of the National Association of Women Lawyers.

The first Black woman to be elected president of the Law School Council at the University of Virginia was Linda Howard.[6] As a Black woman who defeated four white men in competition where there was approximately 90 percent white and male voters, Howard attributed the victory to her platform. According to the *Richmond Times-Dispatch*, "she questioned the absoluteness of the honor system, called for more women and Black professors in the law school, and proposed a broader view of job placement." As far as more Black and women professors, Howard said: "We have the money and we have the prestige to draw women and Blacks as qualified as the people we have on our staff now, and I think we should do it."

A Black woman noted for her achievement in the field of law is Patricia Ruth Hardiman Long. Long became the first Black female president of the American Bar Association, Law Student Division (ABA/LSD).[7] A third year law student at Boston College Law School in Massachusetts, Long was elected a division delegate by the American Bar Association in Chicago. In the field of six candidates for the position, Long was the front runner and was declared winner by a landslide victory.

As a result of the American Bar Association's activities at Boston College Law School, Long was awarded the Silver Key Plaque, the highest award given to the American Bar Association Law Student Division members. Long recently distinguished herself by being selected as a member of the Massachusetts delegation to the White House Conference on Handicapped Individuals held in Washington, D.C.

Long received an undergraduate degree from the University of Illinois, Urbana and a master's degree in education from Boston University. She holds national membership in the American Association of University Women, and Zeta Phi Eta (the National Professional Communications Arts and Sciences Fraternity).

Patricia Hardiman Long - lawyer, with Michael R. Hollis (left) and
Chief Justice Warren Berger (right)

Constance Ione Harvey became the first Black ever to graduate from
the University of Mississippi School of Law (1970). She was also the
first woman and the first Black ever to sit as special chancery judge in
the Second Chancery District, Scott County (Forest), Mississippi.[8]
Aside from these achievements, she is also founder and Executive
Director of the Southern Legal Rights Association. In 1973 Harvey was
also selected as a "Found Woman" by *Mississippi Magazine*. She
serves on many national and regional boards.

Born 1950 in Jackson, Mississippi, Attorney Harvey was also the first
female president of the Student Government Association at Tougaloo
College, where she received the Bachelor of Arts degree in 1967.

The first Black female lawyer in Fort Pierce, Florida was Pamela
Fort.[9] Born 1954, Fort is presently a public defender in Fort Pierce. She
is a member of the League of Justice Society and the Black Americans
Law Students Association (BALSA).

Jacquelyn R. Bullock, in 1977, became the first Black woman to
serve as Assistant Attorney General for the predominantly Black
Harlem community. Long before this time, she demonstrated her
administrative abilities and concern for others. While a student at the
City College of New York, she helped found that school's first day-care
center and later worked there as a family counselor. At Brooklyn Law

School, Bullock was vice-president of the Black American Law Students Association, as well as a member of the Student-Faculty Relations Committee. After graduation, she worked with the Harlem Assertion of Rights Committee, and with the Brooklyn Legal Service where she was a staff attorney, specializing in housing matters.

In addition to her administrative duties, Bullock works to raise consumer consciousness by appearing at local tenants' councils, churches, senior citizen centers and health organizations. "There is a need for a shift in the thinking of the Black community," says Bullock. "It is appalling that the residents of the poorest communities in this country have the least knowledge of their consumer rights."[10]

Mary Frances Berry - lawyer, teacher,
Federal Administrator

Mary Frances Berry, notable lawyer, received her B.A. degree from Howard University. From the University of Michigan, she holds three degrees: M.A. and Ph.D. in history and the law degree, receiving the

latter in 1970. A native of Nashville, Tennessee, Berry has been associated with the U.S. Civil Rights Commission since 1972. A former
chancellor at the University of Colorado, she also served as Assistant
Secretary of Education in the U.S. Department of Health, Education,
and Welfare. Berry is noted across the United States for her scholarship in both law and in history.

At 27 years of age, Beverly Anita Spencer[11] had received the Doctor
of Laws degree (cum laude) from Howard University School of Law.
Earlier, when 22 years old, she graduated cum laude as a biology major
from Stephen F. Austin State University in Nacogdoches, Texas.

Beverly Anita Spencer - attorney for oil company in Texas

Born in 1948 in Gladewater, Texas, Spencer was outstanding as a
student and is now rated as a notable Black woman lawyer in a major
American industry.

Before attending Austin University, she enrolled in Tyler Junior
College at her hometown of Tyler, Texas. There, she was an honor
student and the recipient of numerous awards, including the Brook-
shire Scholarship. Spencer graduated magna cum laude in Biology in
1968.

At Austin, she founded the Afro-American Club, serving as its vice
president. She was also responsible for the institution of the Black

Studies Program at the university. Holding membership in national and local honor societies, Spencer was rated as one of the most outstanding students in the history of the institution.

At Howard's School of Law Spencer was still an honor student. She was the associate editor of *The Howard Law Journal* and was named as one of the Outstanding Young Women in America in 1974. While in law school, she published an article, "De Funis V. Odegaard — the Aftermath and Effects of an Unresolved Issue."

While a law student, she worked as a law clerk in the Arnold and Porter Law Firm in Washington.

Spencer holds membership in the National Bar Association, the American Bar Association, Black Women Lawyers' Association, National Association of Black Women Attorneys, the State Bar of Texas, and the American Association of Blacks in Energy.

Holding interest and having skills in the areas of energy, environmental law, and corporate law, Spencer is presently staff attorney for the Exploration and Production Division of Exxon Company in Houston, Texas. Additionally, she is Adjunct Professor at the South Texas College of Law.

The poignant words of Patricia Stephens Due seem appropriate here. While a student at Florida A&M College in Tallahassee in the early 1960's, she was arrested for participating in the sit-ins. Writing in the Leon County Jail, where she, her sister, and six other students were serving 60-day sentences, Patricia Due was determined to accept the test of staying in jail, and refused to be released on bond. Says Due, "Priscilla (her sister) and I both explained this to our parents when they visited us the other day. . .We made it clear that we want to serve out our full time." She further stated, "There is plenty of time to think in jail and I sometimes review in my mind the events which brought me here."[12]

So it is with Black women lawyers — serving full time, paying dues, and reflecting on the events that brought them to their levels of achievement.

From Charlotte Ray to Beverly Spencer, Black women lawyers have paid unlimited dues. They continue to assert themselves to benefit the Black community as well as other oppressed peoples. This action, perhaps, is the single most satisfying thread between the symbols of success and the conscience of sensitive Black women. A willingness to turn imperfection to perfection, to bring hope when despair has set in — these are the special talents of assertive Black women. And the legal profession seems a very logical route to take them from here — this moment in American history — to the future — a time of achievement and success without regard to race or sex.

NOTES

[1] *The National Black Monitor*, January 1978, p. 4.

[2] Allen Morris, *The Florida Handbook*, 1971-72, p. 171.

[3] Resume of Gwendolyn Sawyer Cherry, 1979.

[4] Alan J. Dixon, ed., *Illinois Blue Book* (Springfield: Illinois Assembly, 1977-78), p. 180.

[5] Harry A. Ploski and Roscoe C. Brown, Jr., comps., *The Negro Almanac*, 1st ed. (New York: Bellwether Publishing Company, 1967), p. 883.

[6] *Richmond Times-Dispatch*, 28 February 1972, Section B.

[7] *Lexington Minuteman*, September 1979 (n.p.).

[8] *Tougaloo News*, Tougaloo College, February 1976.

[9] Personal interview with Pamela B. Fort, 21 March 1979.

[10] *Essence Magazine*, September 1979, p. 30.

[11] Resume of Beverly Anita Spencer, 1980.

[12] Lettie Austin, Lewis Fenderson, Sophia Nelson, "Achievement Against Odds," in *The Black Man and the Promise of America,* (Glenview, Illinois: Scott Foresman Company, 1970), p. 357.

APPENDIX-A

BLACK WOMEN FEDERAL AND STATE JUDGES*

Federal Judges

Name	State
1. Norma Holloway Johnson	D.C.
2. Amalya L. Kearse	N.Y.
3. Mary Johnson Lowe	N.Y.
4. Gabrielle K. McDonald	Texas
5. Constance Baker Motley	N.Y.
6. Anna D. Taylor	Michigan
7. Anne E. Thompson	N.J.

*This list was submitted by the Honorable Russell R. DeBow, Supervising Judge, Pretrial Section, Law Division, The Richard J. Daley Center, Chicago, Illinois. Judge DeBow is also Chair of the Judicial Council of the National Bar Association which is responsible for the research of this information, May 26, 1980. Attorney Gail J. Wright of the NAACP Legal Defense and Education Fund, Inc. in New York City was also helpful in compiling the information on Black women judges.

State Judges

	Name	State
1.	Shelli F. Bowers	D.C.
2.	Margaret Haywood	D.C.
3.	Julia Cooper Mack	D.C.
4.	Annice Wagner	D.C.
5.	Jean F. Williams	Ariz.
6.	Candice Cooper	Calif.
7.	Dawn B. Girard	Calif.
8.	Holly Graham	Calif.
9.	Consuelo B. Marshall	Calif.
10.	Florence Pickard	Calif.
11.	Elizabeth Riggs	Calif.
12.	Ivy G. Roberts	Calif.
13.	Vaino Spencer	Calif.
14.	Maxine F. Thomas	Calif.
15.	Arleigh Woods	Calif.
16.	Thelma W. Cummings	Ga.
17.	Louise Hornsby	Ga.
18.	Edith J. Ingram	Ga.
19.	Earlene Montgomery	Ga.
20.	Romae Turner Powell	Ga.
21.	Rosilyin L. Toulson	Del.
22.	Blanche M. Manning	Ill.
23.	Lucia T. Thomas	Ill.
24.	Willie M. Whiting	Ill.
25.	Joan Armstrong	La.
26.	Mabel H. Hubbard	Md.
27.	Sylvania W. Woods	Md.
28.	Margaret Burnham	Mass.
29.	Joyce London	Mass.
30.	Geraldine Bledsoe	Mich.
31.	Evelyn Cooper	Mich.
32.	Theresa Doss	Mich.
33.	Jeanne C. Harbour	Mich.
34.	Vera Massey Jones	Mich.
35.	Carroll Little	Mich.
36.	Claudia Morcum	Mich.
37.	Frances Pitts	Mich.
38.	Jessie P. Slaton	Mich.
39.	Lucille Watts	Mich.

40.	Irma L. Inge	Miss.
41.	Rita Montgomery	Mo.
42.	Elizabeth D. Pittman	Nebr.
43.	Betty Lester	N.J.
44.	Dorothy A. Cropper	N.Y.
45.	Edith Miller	N.Y.
46.	Barbara M. Sims	N.Y.
47.	Joscelyn E. Smith	N.Y.
48.	Elreta M. Alexander	N.C.
49.	Karen Galloway	N.C.
50.	Joan T. Breland	Ohio
51.	Carol Buggs	Ohio
52.	Lillie W. Burke	Ohio
53.	Jean Murrell Capers	Ohio
54.	C. Ellen Connally	Ohio
55.	Lillian Green	Ohio
56.	Sara J. Harper	Ohio
57.	Alcie O. McCollum	Ohio
58.	Josephine Walker	Ohio
59.	Mercedes F. Deiz	Oreg.
60.	Duanne Darkins	Pa.
61.	Doris M. Harris	Pa.
62.	Juanita Kidd Stout	Pa.
63.	Thelma Cook	S.C.
64.	Verbena DeLee	S.C.
65.	Hattie Sims	S.C.
66.	Nancy Starks	W.Va.
67.	Alice Bonner	Texas
68.	Aldrinette Chapital	Texas
69.	Bonnie Fitch	Texas
70.	Maryellen Hicks	Texas
71.	Carolyn D. Hobson	Texas
72.	Veronica Morgan	Texas
73.	Harriet M. Murphy	Texas
74.	Frances Williams	Texas
75.	Joan Winn	Texas

APPENDIX-B

CURRENT MINORITY ADMISSIONS
AND LEGAL CAREERS

"The nation's law schools must bear a substantial part of the collective social responsibility for the general exclusion of non-whites from the legal profession and legal institutions as a result of myriad legal, social and educational discriminations over hundreds of years. If these myriad social inequities and injustices have left disproportionate numbers of non-whites ill equipped to compete in a strict credentials contest, then the law schools must reject strict credentialism in favor of a system which guarantees admission to a substantial number of otherwise qualified non-white applicants."

Amicus brief, U.S. Supreme Court DeFunis, Rutgers Univ. pp. 9-10 in Ginger, DeFunis versus Odegaard, 2: 785-86.

Since the inception of integrated legal education, Blacks have been under-represented in law schools and the legal profession. Blacks comprise approximately 11 percent of the population but less than 2 percent of the legal profession. Nationally, Blacks represent 1.3 percent of law school students and one-half of that number is enrolled in Black law schools. An even further disparity is the percentage of Black lawyers. By 1970, there were about 4,000 Black lawyers, representing one percent of the legal profession. Currently, there are 11,000 Black lawyers, comprising less than 2 percent of the collective bar.

According to Allan P. Sindler, author of Bakke, Defunis, and Minority Admissions, during the period of time from 1965 to 1977, Black enrollment in ABA approved law schools increased from a low .65 percent to 4.3 percent in 1969-70 to 8.2 percent in 1976-77. As a result of special admissions programs, affirmative action commitments, and special recruiting programs, minority enrollment increased 225 percent as compared to a total enrollment increase of 85 percent. Law school enrollment of minorities has stabilized between the years of 1975 and 1980 with a total minority enrollment of approximately 10,000 students, 5,300 of which are Black.

The Bakke decision has had a significant impact on the number of minorities applying to law school. Prior to Bakke, recruitment of minority law applicants was at a maximum. In 1975-76, 8.3 percent of Black college graduates applied to law school compared to 7.3 percent white applicant rate. For example, a study conducted by the National Law Journal notes that minority applications decreased from 20 percent at Stanford to 63 percent at Minnesota Law School, resulting in an overall applicant decline of 14 percent after the Bakke decision.

Within the legal profession there currently exists a need for more minority and women lawyers. Of the 11,000 Black lawyers in this nation, employment categories are as follows:*

Federal/State Government	3,500
Federal/State Judges	400
Corporations/Non-legal and Legal	2,300
Public interest law firms	500
Law teachers	300
Non-legal jobs or employment	2,500
Private practice	1,500

The majority of Black lawyers are working in the government and corporations, with fewer electing to go into private practice. Unfortunately, statistics are not yet available for Black female law students independently. In 1970 there were 376 Black female lawyers which increased to 2,000 for 1977. It is still a struggle for the Black female to work her way through the legal education system, pass the bar examinations, and obtain gainful employment or self employment. The facts speak for themselves. Black women have had to face extreme adverse conditions and Black women have not only survived, but have made significant impact on the legal system.

SURVEY OF MINORITY GROUP STUDENTS ENROLLED IN J.D. PROGRAMS IN APPROVED LAW SCHOOLS

		1st Year	2nd Year	3rd Year	4th Year	Year Not Stated	Total
Black	1979-80	2,002	1,647	1,438	170	0	5,257
American	1978-79	2,021	1,565	1,572	192	0	5,350
	1977-78	1,946	1,648	1,508	203	0	5,305
	1976-77	2,128	1,654	1,488	233	0	5,503
	1975-76	2,045	1,511	1,452	119	0	5,127
	1974-75	1,910	1,587	1,329	145	24	4,995
	1973-74	1,943	1,443	1,207	101	123	4,817
	1972-73	1,907	1,324	1,106	74	12	4,423
	1971-72	1,716	1,147	761	55	65	3,744
	1969-70	1,115	574	395	44	0	2,128

Published by the American Bar Association Section of Legal Education and Admissions to the Bar.

*From a paper presented by Dr. J. Clay Smith, Jr., Commissioner EEOC, before the Annual Convention of the Old Dominion Bar Association, Lynchburg, Virginia, May 6, 1979.

SELECTED BIBLIOGRAPHY

Ainsworth, M. "Women in Law." *Essence*, August 1975, p. 78.

"Alexander, Harris, Kennedy, Motley, and Murray; Attorneys at Law." *Black Enterprise*, August 1977.

Alexander, Saddie T.M. *Who's Who Among Negro Lawyers*. Philadelphia: National Bar Association, n.d.

_____. "Women as Practitioners of Law in the U.S." *National Bar Journal*, July 1941.

Alpha Kappa Alpha Sorority. *Negro Women in the Judiciary*. Chicago: Alpha Kappa Alpha, 1968.

Austin, Lettie, Lewis Fenderson, and Sophia Nelson. "Achievement Against Odds." In *The Black Man and the Promise of America*. Glenview, Ill.: Scott Foresman Co., 1970.

Banner, Lois W. *Women in Modern America — A Brief History*. New York: Harcourt Brace Jovanovich, Inc., 1974, pp. 45, 60, 171.

Bennett, Lerone. *Before the Mayflower: A History of Black America*. 4th ed. Chicago: Johnson Publishing Co., Inc., 1969, pp. 29-30.

_____. "No Crystal Stair: The Black Woman in History." *Ebony*, August 1977, p. 164.

"Black Woman Nominated for Appeals Court Judgeship." *Jet*, 24 July 1974.

Blaustein, Albert and Robert L. Zangrando, eds. *Civil Rights and the American Negro*. New York: Trident Press, 1968.

Burke, Joan Martin. *Civil Rights*. 2nd ed. New York: R.R. Bowker Co., 1974.

Camper, Diane. "Still Too Few Black Federal Judges." *Dollars & Sense*, June-July 1979.

Clark, Christine P. *Minority Opportunities in Law*. New York: Law Journal Press, 1974.

"Cleveland Woman Becomes Marines' First Woman Judge." *Jet*, 24 May 1973.

Contee, Clarence G. "Macon B. Allen." *The Crisis*. February 1976, p. 67.

Dannett, Sylvia. *Profiles of Negro Womanhood*. Vol. I. Chicago: Educational Heritage Inc., 1964.

Davis, John P. *The American Negro Reference Book*. New Jersey: Prentice-Hall, Inc., 1966, pp. 414, 461-63, 522, 582.

DeCrow, Karen. *Sexist Justice*. New York: Random House, 1974.

Dixon, Alan J., ed. *Illinois Blue Book*. Springfield: Illinois Assembly, 1977-78.

DuBois, W.E.B. "The Freedmen's Bureau." *Atlantic Monthly*, January 1901, pp. 354-356.

The Ebony Handbook. Chicago: Johnson Publishing Co., Inc., 1974, p. 366.

Ebony Pictorial History of Black America. Vol. II. Tennessee: The Southwestern Company, 1971.

Flexner, Eleanor. *Century of Struggle*. Massachusetts: The Belknap Press, 1959, pp. 142, 179, 248.

Garrett, Romeo B. *Famous First Facts About Negroes*. New York: Arno Company, 1972.

Harley, Sharon and Rosalyn Terborg-Penn. *The Afro-American Woman — Struggles and Images*. New York: Kennikat Press, 1978, p. 29.

Horne, P. *Women in Law Enforcement*. Springfield, Ill.: C.C. Thomas, 1975.

Hughes, Joyce A. "The Black Portia." *Crisis*, May 1975, p. 167.

"Ida B. Wells — Voice of a People." In *Black Foremothers — Three Lives*. Ed. Dorothy Sterling. New York: The McGraw-Hill Book Co., pp. 60-117.

James, Edward, ed. *Notable American Women: 1607-1950*. Cambridge, Mass.: Harvard University Press, 1971.

Kaplan, Sidney, ed. *The Black Presence in the Era of the American Revolution, 1770-1800*. Washington, D.C.: New York Graphic Society, Ltd. in association with the Smithsonian Institution Press, 1973, pp. 209-211, 214-217.

Kennedy, Florynce. *Color Me Flo: My Hard Life and Good Times*. Englewood Cliffs, N.J.: Prentice-Hall, Inc., 1976.

Klemesrud, Judy. "For a Remarkable Judge, A Reluctant Retirement." *The New York Times*, December 8, 1978, p. A22.

Kluger, Richard. *Simple Justice*. New York: Alfred A. Knopf, 1976.

"Lady Lawyers: 70 Carry on Battle for Sex and Race Equality in Courts." *Ebony*, August 1947.

Ledner, Joyce A. "The Black Woman Today." *Ebony*, August 1977, p. 33.

Leonard, Walter, J. *Black Lawyers*. Boston: Senna and Shih, 1977.

Lerner, Gerda, ed. *Black Women in White America*. New York: Vintage Books, 1973.

_____. *The Majority Finds Its Past: Placing Women in History*. New York: Oxford University Press, 1979.

Lynch, John K. "Civil Rights and Social Equality." A speech — delivered in the U.S. House of Representatives, February 3, 1875. In *Masterpieces of Negro Eloquence*. Ed. Alice Moore Dunbar Nelson. New York: Bookery Publishing Co., 1914, pp. 89-94.

Matney, William C., ed. *Who's Who Among Black Americans: 1977-1978*. 2nd ed. Illinois: Who's Who Among Black Americans, Inc., 1978.

Melder, Keith E. "The Beginnings of the Women's Rights Movement in the United States." Diss. 1963.

Mossell, Gertrude. (Mrs. N.F.) *The Work of the Afro-American Woman*. 1894; rpt. New York: Books for Libraries Press, 1971, pp. 19-20.

Ploski, Harry A. and Roscoe C. Brown, Jr., comps. *The Negro Almanac*. 1st ed. New York: Bellwether Publishing Co., 1967.

"The Politics of Alertness: A Tribute to Attorney Wilhelmina Jackson Rolark and the National Association of Black Women Attorneys." *National Black Monitor*, January 1978, pp. 4, 7, 12-13.

Quarles, Benjamin. *The Negro in the Making of America*. London: Collier-MacMillan Ltd., 1964, p. 56.

Sewell, George Alexander. *Mississippi Black History Makers*. Jacksonville, Miss.: University Press of Mississippi, 1977.

Smith, J. Clay. "Washington Bar Association Establishes the Ollie M. Cooper Award." Washington, D.C.: Washington Bar Association, 1978.

Sterling, Dorothy. *Black Foremothers: Three Lives.* Old Westbury, N.Y.: Feminist Press-McGraw-Hill, 1979.

Stewart, Maria W. *Meditations from the Pen of Mrs. Maria W. Stewart.* Washington: Enterprise Publishing Co., 1879.

Walker, Margaret. "Introduction." In *Black Foremothers.* Ed. Dorothy Sterling. New York: McGraw-Hill Co., 1979.

Ware, Gilbert. *From the Black Bar.* New York: G.P. Putnam's Sons, 1976.

Wesley, Charles H. *The Quest for Equality From Civil War to Civil Rights.* New York: Publishers Co., Inc., 1968, pp. 5, 8.

Yenser, Thomas. *Who's Who in Colored America.* 6th ed. New York: Thomas Yenser Publications, 1942.

INDEX OF BLACK WOMEN: LAW

PART V

THE CONTRIBUTIONS OF BLACK WOMEN TO AMERICA: **SPORTS**

Manuscript Writer
Janell Walden

Consultant
Miriam Calhoun Gilbert, Ph.D.

Evaluators
Kenneth D. Gibson, Ph.D.
Associate Professor
Athletic Department
Old Dominion University
Norfolk, Virginia

Nell Jackson, Ph.D.
Assistant Director of Athletics
Department of Intercollegiate Athletics
Michigan State University
East Lansing, Michigan

Tiny L. Laster, Jr.
Coordinator of Women's Sports
Tuskegee Institute
Tuskegee, Alabama

William Partlow
Director of Athletics
San Francisco State
University, California

Carolyn Gibson
Creative Strategies for
   Physical Education
Women's Center
Rutgers University
New Brunswick, New Jersey

Editor
Marianna W. Davis, Ed.D.

PART V

SPORTS
Table of Contents

INTRODUCTORY ESSAY

BLACK WOMEN IN SPORTS

Even in an enlightened twentieth century, there is still evidence that girls and women continue to be denied the joy and challenges of competitive sports. Although Title IX has had a notable impact on the participation in sports by females, society continues to question the self-concept of the female that wishes to excel in sports, demonstrates a highly competitive personality, and wants to win in what is still referred to as a male-dominated sports world.

Although a review of history will reveal that the Spartan girl received physical education and sports training similar to that given to the Spartan boy, the state supervised program for girls had a different objective from that of the boys. The girls' program was geared for "weight control and physical conditioning in preparation for mother-hood." The girls' program was usually discontinued at the age of 20. The Spartan girl was an attractive physical specimen and her beautiful skin and body were the envy of all women in Greece. However, partici-pation in physical activity and sport beyond the age of 20 was considered the exclusive domain of males.

So carefully guarded was the right of men to participate in sports that women could not attend nor view the ancient Olympic Games under the penalty of death. After centuries of this strict law, women were eventually allowed to see the Olympic Games. Under the Romans, women developed their own Olympic Games — Hereae — held in honor of Hera, wife of Zeus, these games were held every four years when no Olympic Games were staged for men.

It was the advent of the 20th Century that women first participated in the modern Olympic Games; six females participated in lawn tennis in the Paris Games. There were no women sports in the 1904 games in St. Louis, Missouri. Archery, figure skating, swimming, fencing, and track and field were added in the 20's.

The characteristics that are admired in the male and which are necessary for high-level competition — aggressiveness, self-confidence, assertiveness, and the willingness to take risks — are not especially appreciated in women. The prejudice and misconceptions which have prevented girls and women throughout history from participating in vigorous activity and sports played an even more dramatic role in limiting the participation of Black women in sports.

The emergence of Black women in sports was delayed not only by the Femininity Dimunition Syndrome which blighted the emergence of the white female, but their appearance on the sport scene was also seriously limited by the social, economic, and educational status of Blacks. Black women, no doubt, received some spin-off benefits from the three periods during which time sports took on a different meaning in our society: 1) 1833-1890 — Oberlin, Vassar, and Wellesley were founded; Mt. Holyoke and Smith took the lead in education for women; 2) 1891-1900 — sports instruction was included as a part of physical education instruction for women; 3) 1901-1910 — a complete acceptance of sports as a part of physical education instruction; and there was a gradual turning away from gymnastics and calisthentics toward sports for women. However, many years passed after the founding of Oberlin (1833), Vassar (1865) and Wellesley (1875) before the impact on Black women could be seen.

Leroy Walker
Former Olympics Coach
North Carolina Central University
Durham, North Carolina

CHAPTER I

THE EARLY SPORTS SCENE

Nineteenth-Century Women in Sports

Before Black women were exposed to organized sports in the Black colleges, White women were already participating in this activity in the eastern women's colleges. The most significant women's sports developments of the century, these programs accompanied the rising national interest in public health, as well as an increasing respect for sanitation and medical care. Educators at men's and women's colleges had only recently acknowledged that robust, vigorous health could exist simultaneously with optimum intellectual and spiritual growth. In fact, they said, since sports helped build the stamina necessary for successful attention to schoolwork, they logically should be added to the curriculum.[1]

So committed were the founders of Vassar and Wellesley to these ideas that they specifically mandated the establishment of sports programs there.[2] Initial school recreation programs taught calisthenics or programed exercises. Sports were added later. By 1890 some fourteen — from ping pong and fencing to golf and swimming — were energetically pursued in the private women's colleges, in the co-ed schools, the state run universities, and the normal (teacher's) colleges, as well.[3]

Although educators upheld the idea that healthy, physically fit students were the best students, they likewise endorsed limited sports for women. After all, stringent "Victorian" era ideals held sway. This code, named for the British queen whose reign spanned the century, considered the highest form of womanhood fragile and passive. Only home and family were to be the woman's domain. She neither understood nor cared for the "proper" concerns of men. Women were enshrined as graceful, skillful creatures.

Two of the few recreational activities that Victorianism condoned were archery and ice-skating. In these activities, skill and grace were primary components, not the masculine perogatives of strength, endurance, and the will to win.

Educators therefore promoted activities favoring the Victorian concept of womanliness. They avoided endurance and body-contact sports, which were more likely to produce injuries. Instructors also preferred individual sports to team games for the same reason. When the team sport of basketball, for example, was finally introduced, its rules were extensively modified or "properly regulated" to reduce the possibility of injuries.[4]

Other sports modifications emphasized playing style over substance. Disdaining the emotional outbursts that normally accompany vigorous sport exertion, some instructors required players to display neat appearances over all. One wrote that ". . .disagreeable expressions. . . squealing and yelling, crying, masculinity," had all been dealt with in her classes, boasting that "the absence of all these are the result of emphasizing the aesthetic feature of the games. . ."[5] The quality of the games probably suffered as a result.

Outside the institutional setting, women whose status allowed for leisure activities played gentle games like croquet and bowling. Like the students, they also enjoyed golf and tennis, although they were handicapped in their pursuit by the restrictive clothing deemed fashionable at the time; breathtaking corsets, full length petticoats and skirts, and long-sleeved blouses were de rigueur.

In time, sportswomen would successfully introduce styles more accommodating to their movements. At first, however, the only recourse was for women's sports departments to stage contests off-limits to men. Here, the women could dress more comfortably and not necessarily be labeled "wanton or lewd."[6] A woman "should always preserve her inborn sense of modesty and innocence; she must never be seen by the opposite sex when she is likely to forget herself," warned a critic.[7] Antithetical in concept and practice to the time's imagery of women, sports threatened to develop "aggressive (masculine) characteristics. . .(that) added nothing of the charm and usefulness [women] needed and were not in harmony with the best traditions of the sex."[8] The powerful offices of the clergy and the press adopted these thoughts and preached them far and wide. To challenge the prevailing attitudes for the gratification of urges to display strength or physical skill took a measure of courage and determination most women were loathe to admit. They received their greatest opportunities to flex their muscles and engage in sports on college campuses.

Ironically, the vast majority of nineteenth-century women, including Black women, were greatly occupied with strenuous work — either in the home or in industry. They had opportunity to pursue a college education and be exposed to sports on campus. Additionally, they enjoyed the luxury of leisure time that could be filled with sports. Yet, Victorian mores of propriety and "women's place" were brandished at these women all the same.

The beginnings of widespread female sports involvement gave rise to adverse opinion and three enduring reasons why women were counseled to avoid sports. The beliefs that they risked bodily harm if they engaged in strenuous activity, that they would suffer psychologically if exposed to the stress of athletic competition, and finally, that they would not be feminine if they participated in organized games, have come close to expiring only in the last decade.[9] Here, a renewed women's movement, encouraged by an atmosphere of protest and societal reevaluation, arose to loudly challenge these old bogeys.

Looking back, Leanne Schreiber, an editor of *Women's Sports* magazine noted:

> Women have been systematically encouraged to divorce their identities from their bodies and in so doing they have been divorced from the most basic sense of power and the most basic source of power.

> Because I genuinely believe that the physical discrepancy between men and women is the root and source of all later forms of discrimination — economic, political, educational, sexual — it's going back to that root and reestablishing a sense of control that is ultimately going to be the most potent means of women reclaiming a sense of their own value. And sports is the route for physicality in this country.[10]

Sports are able to cultivate self-confidence, leadership abilities, and strength to fight for what one believes in — all essential ingredients in the concept of "success." As American sportswomen have claimed, at least since the "Victorian Century," they stand to benefit from sports involvement every bit as much as men do.

Black College Sports Activity

While physical education and athletic programs developed at the college level for white women, administrators of Black schools were necessarily preoccupied with the firm, overall establishment of their institutions. Designed to enlighten a people recently freed from slavery and enforced ignorance, most curricula focused on (1) elementary studies with an emphasis on agriculture, the trades, and teacher-training courses at the lower level; and (2) raising the standards and offering higher-level teacher-training courses. Educating cadres to help uplift the race was the paramount challenge at hand.[11]

Additionally, the Black schools were often obliged to adjust their course offerings in order to qualify for urgently-needed foundation and endowment assistance.[12] Physical education was not a specifically recommended course of study.

Still, administrators recognized all their students' recreational needs. No. 70 of the "Regulations for Howard University" (1872) decreed that "From time to time, certain portions of the University grounds will be designated for purposes of recreation for each sex, and all out-of-doors recreation will be confined to these limits."[13]

Recreational activity eventually encompassed organized sports — for male students, at least. Major regulatory organizations such as the Inter-Scholastic Athletic Association (1906) and the Colored Inter-Collegiate Athletic Association (1912) emerged when an abundance of school teams clamored to compete among themselves.[14] There is no documentation of Black female students' involvement in organized sports activity, however, until the late Twenties when the climate encouraged development of women's track and field teams.

World War I, Migration North, and the Postwar Era

The advent of the first World War spurred the participation of Black and white women in sports.

When the conflict interrupted the flow of emigrants from Europe, the industrial demand for workers remained, and millions of impoverished Blacks moved North in a tremendous rush. Encouraged by the Black Press and their ever-gleaming hopes of finding dignity and a comfortable life, they wound up paced into the poorest, most ill-kemp neighborhoods of the "promised" land — the ghettos.

Here, conditions were typically depressing. Infant mortality rates were high. Services such as street lighting, sewer systems, and refuse disposal were haphazard, if operating at all. Overcrowded housing and the dangers therein — from fires to exaggerated mental strain — were part of the inhabitants' everyday tribulation. As Florence Henri wrote in her study of the phenomenon:

> Mental and physical health in the ghettos suffered from an almost total lack of wholesome recreation, particularly needed where home was so cramped and depressing, that no one cared to spend time there. The Urban League, social agencies, and churches tried to provide for this need, but existing public facilities were as inadequate as existing housing to accommodate the influx of migrants. Also, although there was no legal Jim Crow, there was plenty of a menacing unofficial kind at parks, beaches, theaters, and dance halls.[15]

One Black agency devoted to the race's welfare, the Young Women's Christian Association's (YWCA) Negro branches, blossomed during the war. Before long, they developed some of the most exciting athletes around of either race or sex.

The first colored branch was chartered in 1893, but the establishment of other outlets was painfully slow. The outbreak of the war proved catalytic, however, for Black YWCA branches tripled in number, from 16 in 1915 to 49 by 1920. "Y" work in military camps had been extended to Black soldiers, and women were eager to join to help the men in the war effort.[16]

Recreation and athletic programs were already in full swing in the YMCAs by this time. Given the pressing recreational needs of the Black communities, it is possible that the organization's growth there logically extended to providing some sort of organized sports.

The Black middle-class grew during the exodus North and provided yet another impetus to Black sports developments beneficial to Black women.

The large and segregated Black communities needed an abundance of services that professional men and women, and others in service occupations could deliver. This knowledgeable group consequently earned more money and, hence, commanded more privileges, such as leisure time for the pursuit of sports.

One indicator of the trend, the American Tennis Association (ATA) was organized in 1916, not yet fifty years after the court game debuted in this country.[17] Soon after its inception, the first Black woman to win acclaim for her sports prowess achieved the distinction through its tournaments.

In the larger picture, elements combined to alter significantly the national perception of women and their proper roles. Most important was achievement of woman's suffrage in 1919, which encouraged women and men to recognize the female sex in a compelling new light. Women's increasing activity in the workplace, where many filled in for men during the war and remained afterward, also worked to expand traditional ideas about women.

Taking advantage of the Twenties' climate change, many women celebrated by bobbing their hair, wearing shorter skirts and flesh-colored stockings, and smoking cigarettes in public — all previously taboo. Sports historian Ellen Gerber writes that ". . .the increased social freedom that came from the belief that suffrage symbolized equality of the sexes, and the model of the daring and successful women such as the suffragettes and the adventuresses like the aviatrixes, all served to alter the social milieu. The restrictiveness of the Victorian ideal gave way to the uninhibitedness of the jazz age."[18]

The story of Bessie Coleman's rise — and fall — highlights this time, giving testimony to the tremendous courage exhibited by some of the "new" women.

Coleman was an aviatrix and the first Black — man or woman — to become a licensed pilot.

Born January 26, 1893 in Atlanta, Texas, she was the twelfth of thirteen children. Ambitious, she spent a semester in college after arriving in Chicago, and worked as a manicurist and restaurant manager until she was able to find a way to realize her dream of learning to fly.

Robert S. Abbott, publisher of the *Chicago Defender*, suggested that she travel to France, where women were learning to become pilots. This she did, after saving her money for the trip and learning French.

Walking nine miles a day to school and steadfastly continuing the course, even after seeing a student killed in a crack-up, she eventually graduated barely twenty years after the Wright brothers proved humans could fly. She received advanced flight training, and then returned home to begin flying in earnest.

On Labor Day, 1922, she gave her first exhibition on Long Island. Loop-the-loops, figure eights, and the like were her stock-in-trade, along with daredevil parachute jumps from planes.

Coleman was not able to end segregation and discrimination at the air shows, which piqued her since more of their audiences included Black viewers as her reputation grew. Neither did she realize her other dream of establishing a flight training school for Blacks. But in 1926 she was asked to perform at a May Day celebration in Jacksonville, Florida, on behalf of the Negro Welfare League. Elated by the opportunity, she hoped to impress wealthy Blacks on hand with the need for a Black flight school. As fate would have it however, Coleman lost her life when her plane malfunctioned and crashed en route to the show.

Despite the many changes of the "Emancipation Era," sports historian Margaret A. Coffey notes that during the period, the basic female roles of wife, mother, and homemaker still reigned supreme. Gerber concurs, saying that marriage and *not* careers remained the life goal. All the same, the winds of change brought refreshing breezes to women who dared seek definition outside traditional parameters.

This exciting time surrounding the first World War gave birth to the black sportswoman. Still on the bottom rung of the American earnings/prestige/opportunity/status ladder, the Black woman defied the odds and not a few conventions to carve a distinguished place in the record books. Prejudice and racism remained to plague her, but on the field of play as nowhere else, her individual ability became the supreme arbiter of her worthiness.

NOTES

[1] Ellen W. Gerber, Jan Felshin, Pearl Berlin, and Wareen Wyrick, *The American Woman in Sport* (Reading, Massachusetts: Addison-Wesley, 1974), pp. 49-50.

[2] Gerber, et al., pp. 50-51.

[3] Gerber, et al., p. 50.

[4] Margaret Ruth Downing, "Women's Basketball: An Historical Review of Selected Athletic Organizations Which Influenced its Ascension Toward Advanced Competition in the U.S.," Diss. Texas Women's University, 1973, p. 40.

[5] Gerber, et al., p. 12.

[6] Gerber, et al., pp. 58-59.

[7] Gerber, et al., p. 12.

[8] Gerber, et al., pp. 12-13.

[9] Patsy E. Neal and Thomas A. Tutko, *Coaching Girls and Women: Psychological Perspectives* (Boston: Allyn and Bacon, 1975), p. 17.

[10] Joanna Bunker Rohrbaugh, "Feminity on the Line," *Psychology Today*, August 1979, p. 42.

[11] Dwight O.W. Holmes, *The Evolution of the Negro College* (1934; rpt. New York: AMA Press, 1970), p. 85.

[12] Holmes, pp. 167-168.

[13] Ocania Chalk, *Black College Sport* (New York: Dodd Mead, and Co., 1976), p. 40.

[14] Edwin B. Henderson, *The Negro in Sports*, rev. ed. (Washington, D.C.: Associated Publishers, Incorporated, 1949), p. 280.

[15] Florette Henri, *Black Migration: Movement North, 1900-1920* (New York: Anchor-Doubleday, 1976), p. 114.

[16] Gerda Lerner, ed. *Black Women in White America: A Documentary History* (New York: Pantheon, 1972), p. 478.

[17] Henderson, p. 206.

[18] Gerber, et al., p. 18.

CHAPTER II

TENNIS: THE SPORT OF ACES

Chronology

1874   Tennis imported from Europe to America

1890   Tennis introduced as a sport at Tuskegee Institute, Alabama

1898   Tennis tournament play began in Philadelphia, Pennsylvania

1916   Founding of the American Tennis Association (ATA)

1917   First national championships, Baltimore, Maryland, where Lucy B. Slowe clinched women's singles title.

1922   Isadore Channels becomes ATA champion

1927   Lula Ballard becomes ATA champion

1928   Ora Washington becomes ATA champion, holding title for 12 years

1944   Sisters, Roumania and Margaret Peters of Tuskegee Institute, win women's singles in ATA tournament

1957   Althea Gibson wins Wimbledon's crown in women's singles

1977   Leslie Elayne Allen on professional circuit as winner of ATA's women's singles

The grand aristocrat of ball games was imported to America from Europe in 1874, and the cities of Philadelphia and Chicago established courts prior to 1880. Blacks were involved with the game soon there-after, in the early 1890's with some enthusiasts claiming they first played it at Tuskegee.[1]

Tournament play commenced in 1898 and 1899 in Philadelphia, and by 1900 these inter-city matches were staged on Washington, D.C. courts, as well. As segregation of the races was the law of the land, early Black players soon conceived the idea of organizing a national coalition of tennis groups to promote the game among Blacks and motivate players. The result, the American Tennis Association (ATA) was born in Washington in November, 1916, and its founders pledged to encourage the building of courts, the formation of clubs, and promotion of the game among Black youth.[2]

Coming to prominence while an expanding Black middle-class group benefited from war-related opportunities, the American Tennis Association grew rapidly to include some fifteen regional tennis associations with 134 individual clubs by 1949.[3] In time their national contests attracted entries in women's doubles, mixed doubles, veteran's singles, and junior's (under 16) categories.

Although some early court standouts developed in YMCA training programs and Black colleges, the Black tennis clubs recruited and modeled by far the preponderance of Black tennis talent.

The first national championships took place in Baltimore in August, 1917, and some 23 eastern-seaboard clubs participated. Lucy B. Slowe, a native of Baltimore, clinched the women's singles title and became the first Black woman athletic champion.

That same season, she won five other cups, including one for the New York championship — her second in as many years. Possessor of the Philadelphia ladies' singles title and its doubles cup, (along with Florence Brooks) she also won the mixed doubles title of Philadelphia and New York, with the assistance of Talley Holmes.[4]

An inspiration to thousands of girls and women, whether on or off the courts, Slowe served as principal of the first junior high school established in Washington, D.C., and was once Dean of Women at Howard University.

In Chicago, another tennis birthplace, Mrs. C.O. Seames played a pivotal role in the development of the Black tennis scene as early as 1906. She learned the game herself when she was past thirty-five. "Ma" Seames did not develop into a tournament-rank player, but she worked hard to get many a young player into the tournaments, and popularized the game in the Windy City.[5]

Isadore Channels, another Chicagoan, won the American Tennis Association Championship in 1922, 1924, 1926, and 1934, and possibly benefited from "Ma" Seames' early proselytizing. Records show that about the time of Channels' tennis ascendency, she also was leader and star of the Chicago Romas professional tennis and basketball team.[6]

Lula Ballard, a Cleveland schoolteacher, spoiled Channels' attempt to hold the ATA title five years running. Channels regained the crown in 1926, but Ballard wrested it away in 1927 and held it through 1928. After a long silence, Philadelphia-born Ballard returned to dominance in 1936.

Premier Racket Queen: Ora Washington

Ballard's formidable opponent was the legendary Ora Washington, a fellow Philadelphian sportswoman. According to sports historian A.S. Young, Washington was suffering from sunstroke the day she met Ballard for the ATA championship. Otherwise, she probably would have chalked up her ninth singles tournament win. No matter: before she retired, Washington amassed the stupendous record of twelve undefeated years on the courts, and unheard-of 201 trophies in tennis and basketball, her second sports strength.[7]

From 1928 through 1936, she also supplied one-half of the ATA women's doubles championship team. On six occasions she shared the honors with Ballard, and once she paired with Blanche Winston, the 1947 veterans singles winner. Anita Gant, one-time top black woman singles player in the Capitol City, shared the ATA doubles championship with Washington in 1933. In 1929 and 1930 she held the mixed doubles title.

With her aggressive net game, the most outstanding net queen of the era among Blacks, Washington keenly wanted to face Helen Wills Moody, the top-ranked white racket star. Like other white champions, however, Moody flatly refused to play a Black.

Ora Washington, Tennis Star
(photo courtesy Schomburg Center
New York Public Library)

Many of Washington's fans thought the fact that she had held her title for twelve years, compared to Moody's seven-year tenure, was the true reason Moody avoided her, and not the color of her skin.[8]

Emma Leonard, Lillian Hines, and Frances Giddens were among Washington's top-seeded opponents, but none managed to get the best of her. The ATA singles winner in 1938, 1939, 1941, and 1942, she once gave the Black Press plenty of good copy when Flora Lomax angrily challenged Washington to come out of retirement and defend her title. Moved to respond, Washington picked up her racket and let Flora Lomax know she remained superb and superior by beating her soundly.[9]

A onetime member of the Germantown (Philadelphia) and Jersey City, New Jersey YWCAs, Washington, born in 1900, carved out a second competitive athletics career in basketball. For many years she started as center on the famed *Philadelphia Tribune* team.

Washington began her sports whirl in 1924 when, at the persistence of an instructor at the Germantown YWCA, she took up a sport to allay her grief after a favorite sister's death. "Courage and determination were the biggest assets I had," she later admitted when asked to comment on her amazing abilities. "I'd rather play from scratch and warm up as I went along," which is roughly how she started her career.[10]

Until the advent of a tennis champion whose unparallelled achievements included capturing the most-coveted American and international trophies, two sisters from Tuskegee were the biggest names in the ATA. Roumania Peters, women's singles champion in 1944 and 1946, teamed with Margaret Peters to command the doubles throne from 1938 through 1947 with these exceptions: The 1942 outing went to Flora Lomax and partner Lillian Van Buren, and no ATA tournaments were held in 1943, a war year. The year before the Peters' dynasty began, Lilyan Spencer of Jacksonville, Florida and Bertha Isaacs of Nassau, the Bahamas were winners. Roumania Peters also played varsity basketball and tennis while a Tuskegee Institute student, and briefly assisted the famed women's track team after graduation.[11]

Preparation Meets Opportunity: Althea Gibson

The easing of institutional barriers to Blacks in the war industries and armed services during the Forties and early Fifties quickened Black America's desire for desegregation and integration. Simultaneously, the first big wave in a renewed movement demanding human rights and full equality hit shore. The 1954 Supreme Court decision condemning "separate but equal" schools, and the successful Montgomery bus boycott of 1955 were part of it. In major organized golf, bowling, boxing management, basketball, and tennis Blacks gained entry.[12] During this social upheaval, Althea Gibson, one of the world's greatest court stars, commented honestly:

> I am not a racially conscious person. I don't want to be. I see myself as just an individual. I can't help or change my color in any way, so why should I make a big deal out of it? I don't like to exploit it or make it the big thing. I'm a tennis player, not a Negro tennis player. I have never set myself up as a champion of the Negro race. Someone once wrote that the difference between me and Jackie Robinson is that he thrived on his role as a Negro battling for equality whereas I shy away from it because it would be dishonest of me to pretend a feeling I don't possess.[13]

She did not belittle Robinson's achievement as the first Black to play professional baseball.

> I'm not insensitive to the great value to our people of what Jackie did. If he hadn't paved the way, I probably never would have got the chance. But I have to do it my way. I try not to flaunt my success as a Negro success. It's all right for others to make a fuss over my role as a trailblazer, and of course, I realize its important to others as well as to myself, but I can't do it.[14]

Despite criticism aimed at her position, Althea Gibson remained widely-respected for the talent, skill, and determination she wielded to become the first Black winner of the U.S. Open national tennis championship at Forest Hills, New York and the Wimbledon international championship.

Born August 25, 1927 in Silver, South Carolina, Gibson grew up in Harlem after the family moved North in search of a better life. An impetuous, fun-loving child, she was also brash, cocky, and quick to accept a challenge. All these qualities contributed to her ultimate racket success.

Against parental admonitions and discipline attempts, she left school after a year of junior high and spent the next four in a variety of jobs, from waitress to mail clerk. She enjoyed the independence of commanding her own income and living away from home, but realized that she still wanted to distinguish herself in some sort of meaningful way.

These vague stirrings soon gained focus after a city recreation supervisor spotted her playing paddle ball in the Harlem streets. Immediately impressed with Gibson's raw talent, he bought a couple of tennis rackets and encouraged her to try hitting tennis balls against a nearby park wall. Buddy Walker, she remembered, "got very excited about how well I hit the ball and he started to tell me all about how much I would like the game, and how it would be a good thing for me to become interested in because I would meet a better class of people and have a chance to make something of myself."[15]

Off and running, Gibson soon impressed members of an uptown tennis club where members raised money for her lessons. In 1941, when she was only fourteen, she won her first tournament, beating out a white girl. Ironically, a few years later, she could not find a white challenger.

Thus began the Harlem prodigy's trek on the long road to success. After seeing her perform in her first ATA women's singles championship in 1946, two doctors agreed Gibson would profit immensely from greater experience and instruction. Together, they offered her the opportunity to live with Dr. Hubert A. Eaton and his family in Wilmington, North Carolina during the school year. She would travel the ATA tournament circuit with Dr. Robert W. Johnson of Lynchburg, Virginia in the summer. Her benefactors' only conditions were that she do her very best on the courts and in school.

Grateful for the chance to learn, although skeptical about leaving New York's relative freedom of movement for the South and all the rock-hard segregation and violence she had heard of Gibson arrived in time to start high school in September, 1946 at age nineteen.

> I suppose now, that I think hard on it (the doctors) were hoping that I might just possibly turn out to be the Negro player they had been looking for to break into the major league of tennis and play in the white tournaments. Although they never said so to me — not for a long time.[16]

The next summer, Gibson won eight mixed doubles tournaments with Dr. Johnson and repeated her national singles win — a feat she duplicated through the next eight years. Outclassing all comers, Gibson's unquenchable thirst for a good challenge took hold. She wanted to square off with the ranked white players.

As it turned out, Gibson's sponsors had quietly been working with other American Tennis Association members to arrange just such an opportunity for her. By 1949, Jackie Robinson's contribution to major league baseball was no longer news. "They felt that the time was right, historically, and they felt that in me they had the key they had been looking for to open the door. They hadn't wanted to kick up a fuss until they knew they had a player good enough to back up their argument.[17] Gibson soon was accepted at the Eastern Indoor Championships, and played well enough to reach the quarter-finals before losing.

Next, she accepted an invitation to play the National Indoor Championships. Dr. Reginald Weir of New York, another ATA star, preceded her in that tournament. "But I felt that I was on my way, that I was getting my fair chance, and I couldn't ask for anything more than that."[18]

The 21-year old lasted until the quarter-finals, once again, and she rightfully felt good about being the first woman of her race invited to play in that tournament. Later in the year, she graduated from high school and accepted an athletic scholarship to Florida A&M University in Talahassee.

Much to her disappointment but not entirely to her surprise, Gibson was not invited to any of the important outdoor tennis meets that year. Perhaps the tournament sponsors feared public reaction to a Black woman's presence in these more popular matches.

It took a devastating, probing article by women's champion Alice Marble, appearing in the official U.S. Lawn Tennis Association organ *American Lawn Tennis*, to make the entire racket world overcome its discrimination.

> I think it's time we faced a few facts. If tennis is a game for ladies and gentlemen, it's also time we acted a little more than gentlepeople and less like sanctimonious hypocrites [Althea Gibson] may be soundly beaten for a while — but she has a much better chance on the courts than in the inner sanctum of the community, where a different kind of game is played.[19]

Marshalling arguments based on Gibson's ability and the ridiculous notion that a player's skin color had anything to do with meeting the challenge of top-flight tennis, Marble predicted the entrance of Blacks into big-league tennis was as inevitable as in baseball, football, and boxing. She challenged her readers to "rise up en masse to protest the injustices perpetrated by our policymakers. Eventually — why not now?"[20]

Her point made, Marble saw Gibson invited to the National Clay Courts Championships later that year, where she qualified for the Nationals. After this coup, barriers tumbled everywhere. In 1951, Gibson competed in Miami's Good Neighbor Match. It was the first time a Black had competed in any mixed tournament in the Deep South.[21]

Now a nationally-ranked contender and qualified to compete in Wimbledon, the college student readied herself with lessons from Jean Hoxie, one of the country's superlative instructors. Proud of Gibson's achievements, Detroit's Blacks raised $770 toward the cost of her Wimbledon challenge. Heavyweight champion Joe Louis even gave Gibson a round trip ticket to London and arranged for her to stay in his personal suite at that city's Gotham Hotel.

Gibson did not win at Wimbledon that year, even though the

experience was invaluable. This defeat marked the beginning of a particularly frustrating two-year stretch when she seemed unable to break through in the big matches. After graduation in 1953, she took a job as a physical education instructor at Lincoln University in Missouri, all but convinced that she simply could not win the critical matches. Even *Jet* magazine ran a story on her entitled, "The Biggest Disappointment in Tennis."

Then Sydney Llewellyn, an amateur coach and avid tennis fan, offered his services. He not only managed to talk Gibson out of quitting the game, but helped put together the game and attitude that finally fulfilled her dreams.

In 1956, the U.S. State Department invited Gibson to make an eight-month goodwill tour of Asia, then Europe. When the dust settled, she held sixteen international titles, including those of France and Ceylon. Once more the pioneer, she was the first Black to win any of the world's major singles championships.

With newfound confidence, she returned to Wimbledon, but lost again. Forest Hills also escaped her clutch, but she correctly identified her mistakes and renewed her personal promise to win the titles.

The next year she successfully defended her Ceylon and Southeast Asian championships, and traveled in three other continents, perfecting her skills as she went. When time for the next Wimbledon showdown, her gown for the victory ball and acceptance were as ready as her court game. Confident with good reason, she took the singles championship at long last in July 1957. While posing for photographers with her trophy, Gibson thought of a previous Wimbledon champ's words: "My feelings, when that final. . .match was mine, I cannot describe. This was the prize for all the games I have ever played since I was a little girl."[22]

That night her words returned, and she took center court again, entertaining guests with a rendition of "Around the World in Eighty Days."

Gibson's triumphant return home included a tickertape parade and receipt of the key of the city of New York. The old Harlem neighborhood rocked with joy, for one of the local kids had grown up to become "somebody." Once the noise died down, Gibson crowned her achievement by winning the U.S. title at Forest Hills. Fittingly, she beat the same opponent she first lost to on that same occasion in 1950. At thirty, Gibson was the proud champion of every tennis match worth winning.

Her story of discovery, encouragement, tremendous hard work, and determination in the face of repeated and sometimes frequent setbacks, is shared by virtually all other world-class athletes. Her achievements in the world of an aristocratic sport — so far from her youth in the Harlem streets, are also a testimony to the devotion of supporters who helped pay for the lessons, tournament entry fees, and other expenses far beyond the reach of most Black youngsters, and who bolstered her own determination when necessary.

Althea Gibson · professional tennis star
(photo courtesy of EBONY Magazine)

Gibson's subsequent achievements include her 1959 tennis tour with the renowned Harlem Globetrotters and her work as a recreation supervisor and tennis program director since 1970. A member of the New York State Recreation Commission in 1964, she had served New Jersey in a similar capacity since 1975. "Woman Athlete of the Year" in the 1957 American Press Poll and Sullivan Trophy winner as the AAU's Amateur Athlete of the Year, she is also an inductee of the Lawn Tennis Hall of Fame and the Tennis Museum.

The first black woman to gain spectacular national and international recognition for her athletic prowess while her race pressed forward with the struggle for equal opportunity and equal rights, Althea Gibson ignited the imaginations of millions with her triumph in a sport once deemed the exclusive domain of elite Whites.

Heiresses to Tradition

No Black women tennis players have yet achieved Althea Gibson's prominence but several have distinguished themselves as extraordinary players since her trailblazing days. Considering the excitement generated by the one-time Wimbledon champion, it is curious there have not been more to follow.

Renee Blount of St. Louis has been mentioned as a possible success to the Gibson mantle. Seasoned in national competition against the likes of Chris Evert, one of the top-seeded American players, she rates as Wimbledon or U.S. Open material. Born in 1958, she began tennis lessons as a young child. In her teenage years, she won the Missouri Valley Titles for 12, 14, 16, and 18 year-olds. Sugar Bowl, Easter Bowl, and Orange Bowl wins followed.[23]

Educated at Hampton Institute (Virginia) and the University of California-Los Angeles, she played with the Hampton men's varsity tennis team and the renowned UCLA women's team.

Today, after several major victories in Europe, Australia, and on the Avon Futures pro tour, Blount ranks in the low 50's nationally. Her previous rating was #146, and she no longer must qualify to play in any tournament.

The only Black woman currently on the professional tennis circuit is Leslie Elayne Allen, a White Plains, New York native who helped lead the University of Southern California at Los Angeles to a national championship. Turning pro after graduation in 1977, the 5 ft. 10 in. athlete is one of the top-ranked professional women players in the East and winner of the 1977 ATA women's singles and 1977 Australian Women's Tennis Association crowns. Her accomplishments are all the more astounding, because she only seriously took up the sport in 1974. Twenty years after Gibson's worldwide triumphs Allen expects to travel extensively and compete in Swiss, Swedish, and more Australian contests.

Ann Koger graduated from Morgan State University and once spent two years on the Virginia Slims pro tour. A fellow Morgan alumna, Bonnie Logan, played well enough to win the number two berth on the men's varsity tennis team in 1976, and keep it for 1977.

Leslie E. Allen · professional tennis player

Another promising contender for the Eighties is Diane Morrison, a Stanford University graduate sure to qualify for Wimbledon competition. She is one of the very few Black women to advance to the third round of the U.S. Open since Althea Gibson's lead.[24]

Andrea Whitmore, who began singles tournament play at sixteen, and Kim Sands are traveling the same road.

NOTES

[1] Edwin B. Henderson, *The Negro in Sports*, rev. ed. (Washington, D.C.: Associated Publishers, Incorporated, 1949), p. 204.

[2] Henderson, p. 206.

[3] Henderson, p. 208.

[4] "The Horizon," *The Crisis*, October 1917, p. 315.

[5] Henderson, p. 217.

[6] A.S. "Doc" Young, *Negro Firsts in Sports* (Chicago: Johnson Publishing Company, 1963), p. 198.

[7] Young, p. 194.

[8] Young, p. 195.

[9] Young, p. 195.

[10] Young, p. 195.

[11] Nolan A. Thaxton, "A Documentary Analysis of Competitive Track and Field for Women at Tuskegee Institute and Tennessee State University," Diss. Springfield College 1970, p. 156.

[12] Young, p. 116.

[13] Althea Gibson, *I Always Wanted to be Somebody* (New York: Harper & Row, 1958), p. 158.

[14] Gibson, p. 158.

[15] Gibson, p. 27.

[16] Gibson, p. 38.

[17] Gibson, p. 53.

[18] Gibson, p. 55.

[19] Young, p. 192.

[20] Young, p. 189.

[21] Gibson, p. 66.

[22] Gibson, p. 135.

[23] Aloma "AJ" Barnes, "Renee Becomes Tennis Princess," *Black Tennis*, May-June 1979, p. 8.

[24] Marcus A. Freeman, Jr., "Tips of the Iceberg," *Black Tennis*, September-October 1979, p. 5.

CHAPTER III

TRACK AND FIELD: THE STRONGEST SUIT

Chronology

1928   Cleveland L. Abbott initiates track and field at Tuskegee Institute in Alabama

1929   Tuskegee Relays Carnival initiated at Tuskegee by Abbott

1936   Black women compete in AAU National Outdoor Meet

1937   First Black team wins the AAU crown

1937
1953   Tuskegee women collect 21 national titles in track and field

---

1926   Era Bell Thompson establishes five women's track records

1929   Elizabeth Robinson wins 50-yard sprint meet in Chicago and sets new track record in 50-yard dash in 1932

1932   Louise Stokes of Massachusetts and Tydie Pickett of Illinois qualify for games in Los Angeles and Stokes also qualified for 1936 Olympics

1935-
1942   Christine Evans Petty guides Tuskegee's women's athletics

1938   Lula Mae Hymes performs in AAU contest for Tuskegee

1939   Alice Coachman enters the AAU nationals becoming a prize-winning Tuskegee athlete in the 1948 Olympics

1940   Jean Lane wins 50 and 100-meter dashes in AAU meet

1942   Jeannette Jones wins 50-meter dash in outdoor nationals

1944   Tennessee State University hires first women's track coach — Jessie Abbott

1953   Edward Temple takes helm of women's track at Tennessee State

1955   Tigerbelles of Tennessee State University win Women's Amateur Athletic Union Track and Field Championship

1956   Tennessee State University wins national AAU title

1956   Earlene Brown wins South Pacific AAU shotput title

1960   Wilma Rudolph wins in Olympics in Rome

1962   Vivian Brown wins national AAU meet

1968   Madeline Manning wins at Mexico City and performs in 1972 and 1976 Olympics

1972   Cheryl Toussaint performs at the Olympics in Munich

1976   Chandra Cheeseborough wins first place in national AAU 100-yard dash.

In no other area of sports have Black women achieved as great a degree of success as in the track and field events. The lists of national and world record holders in sprints and middle-distance running are studded with their names, and they have frequently turned in spectacular jumping performances. Even in the throwing events, where

European women have always dominated the field, at least one Black woman has won an Olympic medal. So overwhelming have their achievements been overall, until race critics and champions alike dare attribute their winning ways to a "natural" superiority, much as some observers regard the similar athletic record of excellence established by Black men.

Development Through the 1920's

The track and field events, as developed in the ancient Olympic games were designed to demonstrate and encourage the physical prowess of Grecian men. Hand-to-hand combat, the standard form of warfare, required warriors to be in top physical condition to meet and overcome the opposition's challenge. Little wonder then that the Greeks regarded the Olympics as a sacred occasion. Women were forbidden to attend them, and were threatened with execution if they disobeyed the rule.[1]

As nineteenth-century women emerged from their Victorian cocoon to participate in the sports programs initiated at Smith, Vassar, Oberlin, and other progressive institutions, they soon discovered that the track and field events were all but ignored. Since running, jumping, and throwing skills were basic tools in the primeval hunter's kit, it made sense for men to pursue these activities for they developed manly qualities. At least, so thought the physical educators and theorists who advanced a Darwinian approach to the matter.

> The case is very different with women. . .They cared for the home. They carried on the industries. They wove the cloth, made the baskets, tilled the soil, cared for the domestic animals, reared the children, prepared the food, made the clothing, and performed the other numerous duties which centered about the home. It was not the women who could run, or strike, or throw best who survived. . .The qualities of womanliness are less related to success in athletics than are the qualities of manhood.
>
> The important question is raised whether it may not be true that in view of the wide competition into which women are coming in the modern world, it would not be wise for them to have the discipline that is afforded by athletic sports... However much women may take work at which presently is done chiefly by men, their success will not be due to their ability to imitate the work and manner of men.[2]

Luther H. Gulick, deliverer of these words and an eminent physical educator around the turn of the century, summed up his thoughts: "I believe. . .that athletics for women should for the present be restricted to sports within the school; that they should be used for recreation and pleasure; that the strenuous training of teams tends to be injurious to both body and mind; that public, general competition emphasizes qualities that are on the whole unnecessary and undesirable."[3]

Baron Pierre de Courbertin, chief architect of the modern Olympic movement, carried this reasoning another step. He opposed the participation of women in his grand scheme altogether — except as members of the audience. "Female applause" would be the just rewards of the gallant male competitors.

Despite de Courbertin's inclinations, six women competed in the 1900 games' tennis meet. Archers and swimmers first appeared in the 1908 and 1912 meets, respectively. By 1924, women were secure in the Olympic lineup, but their participation remained circumscribed, partially because they were discouraged from entering the track and field events.

During the Twenties a relaxed national attitude, encouraged by the recent victorious wartime adventure, promoted the excursions of women athletes and other "adventurers" such as the aviatrixes. Armed with suffrage rights, many women felt free to flex their muscles in new ways. One popular method involved their becoming avid players on the many industrial teams formed for the entertainment of factory employees and their families.[4]

Rather than benefit from this overall excitement of women for sports, the track and field activities remained pariahs in the arena. The 1923 Conference on Athletic and Physical Recreation for Women and Girls, organized in response to the public enthusiasm, effectively discouraged track and field activities on the college level. Its summary statement was supported by most athletic organizations involved in women's sports with the notable exception of the Amateur Athletic Union (AAU). Its philosophy governed women's collegiate sport competition until the Fifties.[5]

Among the positions taken, physical educators and trainers agreed they would endeavor "To discourage athletic competition which involves travel," and "to eliminate types and systems of competition which put the emphasis upon individual accomplishment and winning rather than upon stressing the enjoyment of the sport and the development of sportsmanship among the many." On the other hand, they hoped, "To stress enjoyment of the sport and the development of sportsmanship, and to minimize the emphasis placed on individual accomplishment and the winning of championships."[6]

A measure of the participants' motivation stemmed from their support of some Victorian notions. They believed the female physiology extraordinarily vulnerable to injury and strain. It took research announced in the next decade to prove that the female reproductive organs were, if anything, more protected from sports-connected injuries than those of the male.[7]

Co-signers of the declaration also believed the stress of intensive competition a threat to the supposed "delicate" emotional nature of women.

Another, far more practical motive for their stance by modern standards, concerned possible abuse of the athletes themselves. Some male coaches had already utilized win-at-all-costs tactics "with their apparent disregard for the health and welfare of the participants" — in basketball, for instance, another highly-competitive sport. Conference participants did not want female participants exposed to such rough handling.[8] They found the traveling required to sustain intercollegiate competition unattractive because it constituted another measure of wear-and-tear on girls and women.

Paternalism also colored their views. Competition intended to separate "the best from the rest," and many of those attending the 1923 meeting wanted sports programs that could help *all* their girls, they said, not merely the Olympic hopefuls.[9]

A final consideration carried over from the Victorian era deemed women downright unattractive and therefore unfeminine in their pursuit of track and field achievement. The intense, individual competition which characterizes the sport not only encouraged a high degree of aggressiveness — commonly considered a masculine trait — it was also thought to develop unsightly "hardened" muscles.

Introduction to Black Colleges

Segregation being the rule of the day, sports development for Black women students occurred independent of white schools' programs. Scarcity of program funds and the differing educational emphasis appear to have contributed to the lack of institutional athletic programs for Black women. Confirming the general male tendency to relegate females to occupations and entertainments thought appropriate for their sex, however, men's football and baseball teams existed even in the last century and were soon followed by track programs.[10]

Another hindrance to female sports growth was a widespread lack of enthusiasm on the part of students. Some of the women who wanted to participate in the early days of track and field competition on Black campuses, for instance, refrained because they feared being ostracized by their peers. Others, imbued with traditional concepts, like many whites, simply believed it improper for women to take up vigorous sports.

The advent of Major Cleveland L. Abbott, Director of Physical Education and Athletics at Tuskegee Institute from the mid-Twenties until his death in 1955, gave many Black women their first great opportunity to participate in organized sports. His vision created a vehicle by which they would gain regional, then national recognition for their talent, skills, and dedication. It encompassed the track and field events, and was fueled by the unbridled enthusiasm of girls and young women eager to test their abilities and be part of an exciting new movement.

Abbott was but one of a coterie of Black men who played varsity sports at major white colleges during the Twenties. Some, like himself, later began careers as coaches in Black schools. Here they put their wide experience to good use.

Both Abbott and Ross C. Owen, who would become a coach of several sports at Tuskegee, played at South Dakota State University.[11] Sol Butler, a contemporary, starred at Dubuque (Iowa) and organized the Chicago Romas, a professional women's basketball team, in the Twenties.[12]

Owen, who is now retired from Tuskegee, recalled Abbott's organizing philosophy:

> . . .he felt that the colored girls did not get. . .all of the publicity that they should. . . So the results was [sic] that after we started the Relays. . .in 1927, a couple of years following that, he felt that the program for girls should be instituted and then began to invite not only. . .our girls here to come out and participate, which were very few at that particular time. . .Following that he began to bring in the high school girls with the idea in mind. . .these girls should, sooner or later, participate in the national Amateur Athletic Union meets. That was his basic objective for getting the girls' program started.[13]

Unmentioned but quite possibly in Abbott's mind were these additional considerations. First, Tuskegee already owned a good outdoor track. Given the minimal equipment requirements, mounting a track and field program probably seemed the most accessible manner of building a women's sports program.

Secondly, Abbott understood the chilling effect of the 1923 conference rulings upon the collegiate woman's presence in track and field and in competitive sports. AAU track competition commenced that same year, and participants were mainly affiliated with independent track clubs, such as the Black Mercury Athletic Club of New York.[14] Were the Tuskegee women to compete, their presence would throw a bright spotlight on the whole issue of women's ability to successfully compete in vigorous sports and the desirability thereof. More importantly, it would project the image of successful Black women to the American public.

A popular personality on campus whose judgment and budget requests were well-respected, Abbott developed a women's competitive division of the Tuskegee Relays Carnival in 1929. It was the only college-sponsored relay in the country to include women contestants.[15] That year 225 students attended from 25 Black schools.[16]

Alabama State University, Fort Valley State (Georgia) College, and Prairie View A&M College (Texas) sponsored similar relays between 1929 and 1968, but not on a regular basis.[17] All the schools, along with Wilberforce University, often fielded teams for the Carnival. They were joined by a host of mainly Tuskegee-area high school girls, some of whom attended the summer track and field clinics, where fundamentals were taught. In time, students attended these popular gatherings from as far as Oklahoma, Kansas, and West Virginia.

Only two events appeared on the 1929 program for girls and women: the 100-yard dash and the 440-yard relay. The next year the 50-yard dash and discus throw were added. In time the program expanded to cover many of the events listed in the AAU program, consonant with Abbott's intention of allowing the Tuskegee girls to compete there. Since no other colleges sported sustained and organized competitive track and field programs for women, the Carnival was the best opportunity Tuskegee women had to sharpen their competitive talents before traveling to the national AAU meets.

Its visibility and eventually its reputation for producing top-notch women athletes made Tuskegee particularly attractive to many college-bound girls, although it was several years after inception of the women's athletic program before sports scholarships could be offered.

Despite his responsibilities as physical education instructor, administrator and coach of several other school teams, Abbott remained devoted to the women runners and jumpers. In 1936 the team competed in the AAU national outdoor meet for the first time and posted a second-place finish. The following year they returned to sweep the meet.

> The athletic world was just beginning to become accustomed to the onslaught of male Negro athletes on the records and to Negro champions in sport, when up from the South came Tuskegee's track and field girls to win the national AAU women's track and field championship. It is not conservative to say that press dispatches created a sensation.[18]

And sensational they were. Scoring in ten of eleven events, the women amassed 33 points on September 24, 1937, to become the "First colored team to win the crown in the fourteen years that women's meets have been held," reported the *Afro-American* newspaper.

So began a dynasty. Between 1937 and 1953, Tuskegee women collected seventeen national outdoor titles and four indoor crowns.[19] Only the Ascendancy of Tennessee State University's Tigerbelles in the Fifties and Sixties would match the brilliance of the Tuskegee record.

Outstanding Early Tracksters: Midwestern, Tuskegeean, and Others

Not all the early Black women track stars were Tuskegee products, although the Tuskegee contribution to the overall development of Black women athletes cannot be denied. Even before Tuskegee women occupied the center stage, however, two others from the mid-central states won acclaim for their sports performances.

Era Bell Thompson, today the globe-trotting international editor of *Ebony* magazine, established five state women's track records and tied two national intercollegiate records — including the 60-year hurdles mark — as early as 1926. Born to parents who homesteaded in North Dakota territory in the early years of the century, she continued the pioneering tradition, as one of the few Blacks enrolled at the University of North Dakota. When the *Grand Forks Herald* proudly proclaimed her victories in its May 9, 1926 issue, it recognized her pioneering role in women's competitive sports, as well: "University of North Dakota athletics threaten to assume national prominence, but not through the efforts of its husky sons. It has remained for the women to flaunt the pink and green before the eyes of the world, for today Era Bell Thompson, colored freshman co-ed, looms as a national track champion."

Thompson bettered the school marks in the standing and running broad jumps at that meet, reaching 7 ft., 10½ in., and 15 ft., 10¼ in., respectively.

Elizabeth Robinson made news by July 1929, when she won the 50-yard sprint event in a Chicago meet. By June 1931, she set new American records of 5 4/5 seconds in the 50-yard dash and 25.1 seconds in the 220-yard run.[20]

Women were first permitted to compete in Olympic track and field events in 1928 and competed in the 100-meters, 800-meters, 400-meters relay, high jumps and discus.[21] Four years later, Louise Stokes of Massachusetts and Tydie Pickett of Chicago apparently qualified for the showpiece games in Los Angeles, with fourth and fifth-place finishes in the 100-meters qualifying race. Sports historian Ocania Chalk reports that the two were mysteriously replaced by two white athletes, even though they had run in a field that allowed six to qualify.[22]

Stokes, for one, was undaunted. By her high school graduation in 1933, she had set a world record of 8 ft. 5¾ in. in the standing broad jump and chalked up new marks in the 50-meters, 100- and 200-yard dashes, and the high jump.

Born October 27, 1913 in Malden, Massachusetts, and one of six children, she began her triumphant strides when only a sophomore and a star member of the Onteora (Massachusetts) Track Club. She collected the largest percentage of medals garnered by any individual in the history of the group. Clinching national titles in the 50-meter outdoor sprints in 1933 and 1935, she qualified for the 1936 Munich Olympics.[23]

Stokes also excelled in basketball during her youth, and bowled professionally in later years, after her marriage to Wilfred Fraser. The New England Amateur Athletic Union honored her in 1974 with a "Louise Stokes Fraser Day" held at Boston University. Prizes were bestowed in her name for the outstanding 50-yard dash performances. She died on March 3, 1978, following retirement as a clerk for the Massachusetts Taxation Department.

By far, the majority of Black women athletes developed before the Fifties trained at Tuskegee. Several women coaches were actively involved in the team development during this time as Abbott always attempted to have a woman coach. His own responsibilities prevented him from personally overseeing every aspect of the team's development. Most prominent among the women coaches were Christine Evans Petty, who joined the team in 1935 and assisted until her death in 1942, and Nell C. Jackson, who guided the team in the late Fifties and early Sixties.

The tracksters at Tuskegee made history for women athletes as they set records not to be forgotten, as well as history for this Black college.

Lulu Mae Hymes was the first all-around star in the Tuskegee galaxy. Her 100-meters, 400-meter relay anchor leg, and running broad jump performances in the 1938 AAU contest were major factors in the school's victory. She was elected the "Outstanding Athlete of the Meet." Even in the team's initial Nationals appearance in 1937, Hymes took the broad jump. Before her 1939 graduation, she equalled the world record in the 100-meters with an 11.5 second run.

The report in the October 1, 1937 *Baltimore Afro-American* gave

Hymes her due in its exuberant coverage:

> Aided by the mid-summer climate. . .and scoring in ten of eleven events, the
> Tuskegee Institute team romped off with the National Amateur Athletic Union
> Women's Track and Field Championships here Saturday afternoon. . .
>
> Led by Lulu Hymes, the Institute's all-around star, the fleeting-foot Alabama
> unit became the first colored team to win the crown in the fourteen years the
> women's meets have been held.

Hymes set a new American record of 18 ft., 1½ in., in the running
board jump at the 1939 Nationals.

Cora Gaines tied with Hymes for individual wins at the year's
Nationals, clinching both the 80-meter hurdles and the running high
jump. An outstanding individual performance recorded even earlier
was Mable Blanche Smith's soar in the running broad jump at the 1936
meet. The eighteen-foot jump qualified her for an Olympic berth, but
she never made the trip. Her event was not included in the women's
track and field program until 1948.[24]

Hester Brown, like Smith and a number of other Tuskegee
tracksters, graduated from the Booker T. Washington High School of
Atlanta, Georgia. With Celestine Birge, Jessie Abbott, and Lula Hymes
(at anchor), Brown contributed to a super-powered 400-meter relay
squad. It won the National crown in 1938 after posting a second-place
finish in 1937. Rowena Harrison, Lelia Perry, Lucy Newell, Lillie
Purifoy, Nell Jackson, and Alice Coachman were among other
members of this critical component in the Tuskegee strategy. Whether
the dependable unit won, as from 1938-1942 and 1945-1948, or only
placed, it contributed points to the team total. Combined with
individual first-place events, it explains how the team could run up
totals of 33 points in 1939, for example — double the score of their
closest competition.

Lelia Perry, a hurdling and high jump sensation, arrived at the
Institute in 1939. Lucy Newell, a Laurel, Mississippi native, turned in
consistently superior performances in the 50-meters and the broad
jump. Lillie Purifoy, a hurdler from Snow Hill, Alabama, first showed
promise in the Carnival's junior division competition. Together, Perry,
Newell, and Purifoy accounted for all the individual firstplace wins
chalked up by the school between 1939 and 1941, with the notable
exception of Alice Coachman.[25] Though not a first-place winner in the
1939 nationals, Rowena Harrison, a student on the Tuskegee High
School team, equalled the world record in the 100-meters with her
11.5-second yard dash in the annual school relays. Therefore, she
delivered dependable, strong finishes in national competition.

The prize-winning Tuskegee recipe's final, essential element was the phenomenal Alice Coachman, winner of 22 individual events in nine years of indoor and outdoor track and field competition.*

Born November 10, 1921 in Albany, Georgia, Coachman first entered the AAU nationals in 1939. Until her 1948 Olympic appearance, she gained fame for her high jump and sprint performances. In 1944 she equalled the 6.4 seconds record in the 50-meters. Then the next two national meets she defeated the formidable Polish-American champ, Stella Walsh, in the 100-meters (outdoors).[26]

In the shorter races Coachman placed first on ten occasions, and in the 1945 contest alone, she swept clean the 50-, 100-meters, and the running high jump. The relay unit also shared her strength.

As already noted, Tuskegee Institute, despite its dominance of the field, was not the only track club boasting superior talent in the Thirties and early Forties. The West Philadelphia Athletic Club participated in the 1937 national AAU meet, where Lucille Harris tied for third place in the high jump.

That renowned New York team, the Mercury Athletic Club, maintained high-class representation throughout the period. Coached by LeRoy Alston, it blazed the track in two notable 1938 contests. Gertrude Johnson, Esther Dennis, Ila I. Bynce, and Ivy Wilson carried the 800-meter relay and 880-yard relay in 1 minute 49.6 seconds at a meet held October 16 in Jersey City, New Jersey.[27]

Later that year they traveled to Toronto, Canada and posted a record meet time of 52.7 seconds in the 440-yard medley. Their 880-yard relay team beat all challengers in another record time — 1 minute, 49.6 seconds. Standouts here were Wilson, Johnson, Edwards, Dennis, Ramona Harris, Ida Bynce, Pearl V. Edwards, and Etta Tate.

Back home, Edwards, Bynce, Gertrude Johnson and Esther P. Dennis ran the staggered 50, 60, 110, and 220-yard components of the 440-yard medly relay to set yet another American record. They swept the event in 52.4 seconds at a June 26, 1939 New York meet.[28]

Mercury's team provided its noteworthy representation at the era's national AAU meets where Ivy Wilson excelled in the 50-meters, and Gertrude Johnson set a new AAU championship record at the 1937 outdoor meet with her 26 seconds time in the 200-meters.

At least one young woman, Jeannette Jones, proudly carried the Harrisburg Amateur Athletic Association's banner. Between 1939 and

*Note: Coachman competed under the Tuskegee banner from 1939 through 1946 before transferring to Albany State College.

1942, she placed in a variety of spring events, and won the 50-meter dash in the 1942 outdoor Nationals.

Jean Lane, hailing from Wilberforce University, made a spectacular premier appearance in the 1940 AAU meet. As the *Baltimore Afro-American* reported it: "A slender, medium-built lass. . .broke the domination Stella Walsh, famed Polish sprinter, has held over the women of the world here Saturday when Jean Lane snatched victories from her opponents with heart-pulsing triumphs in the 50- and 100-meter dashes in the National Women's Track and Field Championships on Recreation Field."[29]

Earlier in Cincinnati on May 29, 1940, Lane established a new American record (indoor) in the 100-meters in 10.9 seconds.[30] She retained her rank in the 1941 Nationals by adding wins in the 50- and 200-meters to her chain of accomplishments. She also swept the outdoor sprints that year.

Handing Off: Early Olympic Triumphs and the Rise of the Tigerbelles

In 1940 and 1944 the Olympic games were cancelled by the interruption of the Second World War. American track and field competition focused on the center ring of the national Amateur Athletic Union meets more than ever. Tuskegee maintained its superiority (outdoors) through 1951. Meanwhile, the club entered its first indoor meet in 1941 and won the 1945, 1946, and 1947 contests.

During this time of increased concentration on stateside competition, another mighty track and field club was in the making. Jessie Abbott, one-time Tuskegee team member and daughter of the Tuskegee head coach, signed on as the first women's track coach at Tennessee State University in 1944. School President and former Tennessee State University football coach Walter S. Davis strongly supported the idea of sports programs for women and brought Abbott in to launch one.

Davis felt that "good physical training. . .and discipline would be good for (the girls) rather than harmful. . .We knew that there was nothing to prove that (competitive sports) was harmful. And we decided to go into it. . .We had seen Abbott win the AAU with Negro girls, and being a geneticist I know that individuals are born equal. . .and it's the environment that makes the difference. We had at least two things to go on — what Abbott's girls had done in previous years and my knowledge of genetics."[31]

Jessie Abbott remained at Tennessee State University through 1945, when the school first competed in the Tuskegee Carnival Relays.

Volunteers filled in until Thomas Harris set the pace. Edward S. Temple took the helm in 1953. A Tennessee State University alumnus who led his prep school team to two state track championships, he proceeded to attract and develop women athletes whose accomplishments have gained an unprecedented amount of attention for the U.S. track and field contingent in general, and for American Black women, in particular.

The Tennessee State University Tigerbelles won their first national Women's Amateur Athletic Union Track and Field Championship in 1955, thus beginning a tradition that extended at least until 1968. Comprised of the most stunning record of international competition compiled by any women's track and field club in the country, it accounts for 25 of the 40 American women's track and field Olympic medals garnered through 1968; 15 gold, 6 silver, and 4 bronze.[32]

Even in its embryonic stages, the Tennessee State University team managed recognition as the sponsoring unit for two of the six Black women who competed in the Olympic Games for the first time. Emma Reed, a Mississippi native, was already on the Tennessee State University campus when Coach Harris arrived. Audrey "Mickey" Patterson, became a willing recruit from Texas via Wiley College. Both won berths in the 1948 London contests.

In competition preceding the Olympic qualifying meet, Patterson set a new American record in the 200-meters at the 1948 outdoor Nationals. She ran the distance in 25.4 seconds and surpassed Jean Lane's previous best time of 26 seconds flat. Reed, a high jump specialist, cleared the bar at four ft., 10 in., to capture first place. By the Providence, Rhode Island eliminations, Patterson maintained her superiority in the 200-meter dash and finished second in the 100-meters. Reed made the team with a running broad jump leap of eighteen feet, 4⅝ in., and a third-place high jump finish.

Another Tennessee State University trackster did not qualify for the trip, but she tied the world record in the 50-meter dash in 6.5 seconds at that year's Tuskegee Carnival Relays. Thus, the teenager shared honors with the perennial high jump queen Alice Coachman and Clara Isicson of Long Island University.

Tuskegee, still the dominant track and field club, sent three representatives to the London games: Mabel Walker, Theresa Manuel, and Nell C. Jackson. Alice Coachman hoisted the Albany State College banner since she recently transferred there.

Although Mabel Walker's 200-meter times were better than those of five other competitors in the semi-finals, she failed to get to the finals.

Other criteria were used in determining line-ups, it seemed. Jackson, a Tuskegee native who also excelled in swimming and basketball, encountered a similar situation. Her time in her 200-meters heat equalled that of the second-place finals qualifier, but Olympic rules decreed that only the two top contestants in any heat could reach the finals.

Emma Reed did not reach the broad jump finals, but Tennessee State University colleague Audrey Patterson won a bronze medal for her third-place finish in the 200-meters. Alice Coachman put up a valiant fight for the high jump gold medal. In high wind and rain she eventually disposed of the English champion at 5 ft., 6¼ in. before a crowd of 65,000 that remained to view the outcome after all other competition was completed on this final day of track and field events.

Coachman, perhaps, showed more than the requisite Olympian measure of determination in this meet. She says: "I had to train an additional four years before going to the Olympics, and that was because the countries were torn up from World War II. It took a lots [sic] to stay in training but I had made my mind up to do or *die* and I made it because I always carry God along with me."[33]

Alice Coachman (Davis), Olympics Gold Medal Winner

Twenty-six years old and possessor of the national high jump champion's crown since 1939, Alice Coachman was more than a little eager to prove herself in the limelight of global attention. For her efforts, she gained the added distinction as the only member of the American women's track and field squad and its first Black to win a gold medal. Later, Black Americans would proudly recall her achievement and Jackie Robinson's 1946 "crossing professional baseball's color line" in the same breath.

Overlapping Achievements:
The International Arena, 1950's

From the very beginning of his Tennessee State University tenure, Coach Edward Temple limited his focus and "played to win." Cleveland Abbott, however, seemed to have followed a philosophy that would "provide a medium whereby Negro girls would be able to exercise athletic talents in this particular activity," recalled an assistant.

Records show that over two hundred Black girls and women participated in the Tuskegee program. The inspiration and example it provided these sportswomen and thousands more throughout the South and elsewhere attest to Abbott's pioneering success with Black women in sports.

Temple's approach, however, primed his chosen few for the most demanding world-class competition. As a result, in just over a decade the Tigerbelles would become legendary American and international performers.

In the period following the 1948 Olympics and preceding Abbott's death in 1955, TSU rapidly increased its status as a training ground for top-notch women athletes. The team won its first national AAU title in 1956. The Tuskegee contingent continued its winning ways at the Nationals, but lacked the number of consistent, first-class performers it enjoyed in the past.

The creation of the Pan-American Games in 1951 appealed to foreign policy students and sports fans alike. Both had been educated by the recent war and liked the idea of this new-style competition.

Tuskegee's Nell Jackson, the Olympic 200-meter veteran, and Evelyn Lawler, a high jump specialist, attended the Buenos Aires pageant. Jean Patton, a 1949 Tennessee State University recruit who recalled that ". . .training [was] a very lonely experience because most of the time I was the complete team," represented her alma mater. These three were the only American women on hand representing colleges and universities.[34] College administrators and educators still overwhelmingly considered athletics inappropriate for their female students.

Holder of the national AAU (indoor) record in the 100-yard dash with her smoking 11.1-second time, Patton finished second in the event. At the urging of her Tennessee State University manager-coach, Evelyn Hall, she also did battle in the 200-meters, "a race she had never run before." Much to her surprise, she nosed out Jackson for first place. Earlier in 1949, Jackson set a new American record in 24.2 seconds, besting Polish-American champ Stella Walsh and Tennessee State University rival Audrey Patterson.

At the Pan American Games, Nell Jackson shared the United States' 400-meter relay victory with Patton at anchor.

In the high-jump, Evelyn Lawler cleared the same height as the winner — 4 ft. 9½ in., but she only qualified for sixth place. Her greater number of misses at that height diminished the value of her achievement, according to the governing rules. Lawler also placed sixth in the 80-meter hurdles.

The lineup of world-class tracksters changed completely for the 1952 Helsinki, Finland Olympics. The women's track and field squad included Mae Faggs, Barbara Jones, Janet Moreau, and Catherine Hardy, all from Tennessee State. Together they commanded the 400-meter relay field and set a new world and Olympic record in 45.9 seconds. Theirs was the only U.S. win in a disappointing overall performance.

Mae Faggs, later referred to as "the Human Rabbit" in an *Our World* article, soon became the first of the Tennessee superstars. Earlier that year she won the national AAU (indoor) 100-yard dash, and since 1949 had reigned supreme in the nationals' 200-yard sprints.

Barbara Jones of Chicago originally ran with the famed Catholic Youth Organization team developed by Joseph Robichaux. She, too, would later prove a key component of the Tennessee machine in its most important triumphs between 1955 and 1960.

Catherine Hardy, of Fort Valley State (Georgia) College claimed one of the best national performances in the 50-meters that year with a 6.4 second sweep.[35]

At age seventeen, Mary McNabb astonished spectators at the 1951 national AAU outdoor meet by running in fourteen races to win five individual titles in junior and senior division. She even competed in the heat and final of the 400-meter relay with the defending champion

Tuskegee relay team. Still, she finished fifth in the 100-meter Olympic qualifying race and was forced to settle for an alternate's berth.

Mabel Landry, another of the Chicago Catholic Youth Organization (CYO) alumnae, Mae Faggs, and Marjorie Larner, were the only individual American performers to even qualify for the finals. Landry finished seventh in the running broad jump. Faggs took sixth in the 100-meters and Larner posted a thirteenth-place finish in the javelin throw.

Lucile Wilson, manager-coach of the 1952 U.S. women's track team eventually filed a report with the American governing committee decrying the team's treatment. Feeling that the overall conduct of their training left a lot to be desired, Wilson suggested the following:

1. A woman should be selected to fulfill the duties of manager-chaperone, and another to act as coach.
2. Appointment should be made of a male coach, who has been active in national women's track to develop women's tracksters; he should be on the administrative committee as advisor to the women's track and field team.
3. The Olympic tryouts should be held at least one week previous to debarkation date.
4. Women competitors in this country should be provided with more national and international competition.[36]

Wilson's request that greater attention be given to the development of the women's squad was heeded, as the results of the next Olympiads bore witness. For one, Nell C. Jackson, outstanding Tuskeegee performer, coached the 1956 women's Olympic track team.

The years 1953 and 1954 were quiet for Tennessee and Tuskegee, compared to the excitement surrounding the school's athletic corps during 1951 and 1952. Now forced to actively compete with Tennessee State University for the best available female talent, the Alabama school seemed to depend only on Jeannette Cantrell and Mildred McDaniel, both high jumpers and sprinters, for winning performances. It posted its last national AAU meet win in 1951.

Nell Jackson began a professional sports career with the Tuskegee faculty in 1953 and coached the women's team. First attracted to Abbott's program by the summer track and field clinics in the mid-Forties, she remained at the school as an instructor — coach until 1960. Returning in 1962 after earning her physical education doctorate, she departed in 1963.

Meanwhile, an intensive building program was underway at Tennessee State.

Like other Black schools, Tennessee State University began a track clinic program in 1954, which taught would-be athletes basic track skills and exposed them to the Tennessee State University atmosphere, as well. The TSU relays commenced in 1955. Later that summer the Tigerbelles ran off with their first national AAU title.

At the same outing Tuskegee's Mildred McDaniel set a new American record in the high jump. Clearing 5 ft. 6½ inches, she exceeded Alice Coachman's 1948 Olympic Performance.

The 1955 Pan-American Games in Mexico City's rarified mile-high altitude served as tough international competition prior to the 1956 Olympics. Nine of the sixteen-member American squad were Black. Several, such as Hazel Watkins, Isabel Daniels, Barbara Jones, and Mabel Landry once ran with the Chicago Comets Track Club.

Outclassing all competition, McDaniel added another first-place prize to her burgeoning collection. Barbara Jones won the 100-meter dash. Jeannette Cantrell took fourth in the high jump, while Jones returned with Mabel Landry, Mae Faggs, and Isabel Daniels, to blaze the 400-meter relay trail in a record Pan Am time of 48.7 seconds. Patricia Monsanto, a shot putter, also traveled with the team.

Melbourne, 1956

As mentioned, the American Olympic committee's attitude toward women tracksters improved considerably by the 1956 preliminaries. Besides naming Nell Jackson women's coach, administrators arranged for a pre-Olympic training period. Thaxton reports officials even mounted a press campaign to "alter the attitude of the public in regards to women's track" — for the better.

Black women traveling to the Olympics included Mae Faggs, a one-time runner with the New York Police Athletic League; Lucinda Williams and Isabel Daniels, 100-meters specialists; Willye B. White and Margaret Matthews in the long jump; Mildred McDaniel, and Wilma Rudolph. Willye White and Wilma Rudolph were only in high school, but they had already shown their considerable talent while students of the Tennessee State track and field summer clinics.

At the Washington, D.C. Olympic qualifying meet, Tennessee State University teammates Isabel Daniels, Mae Faggs, and Lucinda Williams swept the 100-meter dash with 1-2-3 finishes. Faggs and Rudolph then placed first and second in the 200-meters, and Matthews leapt 19 ft., 9¼ in. to clear the long jump competition. All these performance marks anticipated good things to come, but the final outcome took unexpected twists.

Lucinda Williams (left) - track star, with Margaret Matthews and Isabelle Daniels
(courtesy-Tennessee State University)

First, Willye White "surprised everyone" with her 19 ft., 11¾ in. long jump, which set a new American record, and earned a silver medal. Margaret Matthews, the favorite, failed even to qualify for the finals.

The American 400-meter relay unit placed third in the finals, behind first-place Australian and British teams. These were amazing results since even the U.S. team performance bettered the previous world record.

Earlene Brown of Los Angeles became the first Black woman to distinguish herself internationally in the shot-put when she threw the metal ball far enough to capture sixth place. She also placed fourth in the discus.

Never before had an American woman competed so well in these events, yet the press ignored Brown's athletics. They reported on her Olympic Village celebrity for giving other athletes dance lessons, instead.[37]

Mildred McDaniel, following Alice Coachman's lead, was the only team member to clinch a gold medal. An Olympic committee observer described the contest:

> Mildred McDaniel sparkled as she high-jumped her way to new world and Olympic records with a leap of five ft. 9¼ in. before the spellbound stadium crowd in Melbourne. For the only time during the Games, what was usually a three-ring

circus became a one-athlete show as other events were completed. Millie's competition fell by the wayside, thus putting her alone in the spotlight with some 110,000 people to groan when she knocked the bar down and then stand up and cheer as she went over the top to become the greatest woman high jumper in the world.[38]

The empress of the horizontal bar competed in two-post-Olympic Australian events along with other teammates, but retired from competitive track and field thereafter. Coach Nell Jackson ". . .tried to encourage her to jump, but [McDaniel] felt that she didn't want to. . . Her best performance was in Australia. . .And she was improving on an average of three inches a year and I think perhaps if she had continued to jump the next year, she probably would have been the first woman to clear six feet.[39]

Isabel Daniels, another Black American who excelled in the post-Olympic Australian meetings, clinched the 100-yard race against women of New South Wales. Timed at 10.5 seconds, she claimed the fastest time ever recorded the distance by an American woman.[40]

European Ventures

The frequency of dual track meets, such as between America and the Soviet Union, or the several highly-publicized tours of East-European nations made by American athletes, attests to the symbolic significance of sports competition. Understood much as a universal language, these contests of skill, strength, endurance, and determination became highly popular entertainments following the 1956 Olympics and escalation of Cold War tensions. Black women, now recognized as superb sports achievers, played central roles therein.

Seven members of the Tennessee State squad traveled with the U.S. team through Moscow, Warsaw, Budapest, and Athens in 1958. These were Barbara Jones, Lucinda Williams, Margaret Matthews, Willye White, Martha Hudson, Annie Lois Smith, and Isabel Daniels. Tennessee State University coach Edward Temple served as the U.S. advisor that summer.

Despite the caliber of competition they faced, the Tennessee State University women held their own admirably. Willye White broke her own American long-jump record set at the Melbourne games when she spanned 20 feet, 2.52 inches on the tour. Daniels held her speed and set a new U.S. record of 23.9 seconds when she beat all comers in the 200-meters at Warsaw. It was the fastest time recorded for that event during the tour.

At the Moscow meet, Daniels, Matthews, Jones, and Williams set another U.S. record with their 44.8 finish in the 400-meter relay, an even swept by the Americans in each host city.

In a *New York Times* dispatch of August 7, 1958, Willye White received praise for producing the "best showing," winning the women's 80-meter hurdles and the broad jump within twenty minutes — before running with the victorious 400-meter relay team.

Eight Tennessee State University students participated in the 1959 summer meet between the United States and Russia before heading to the Pan-American games. Here, Lucinda Williams reasserted her authority, taking the 200-meters in 24.1 seconds for a new meet record. Isabel Daniels tied the meet record of 7.4 seconds in the 60-meters, while others, like Annie Lois Smith, won their events.

Earlene Brown, the 220-pound "natural athlete," representing the Southern Pacific AAU, heaved shot-put and discus far enough to post first-place finishes in both events and predict her upcoming 1960 Olympic performance. From 1956 through 1961 she held the national AAU shotput title; likewise, the baseball and basketball throw top marks were hers in 1957 and 1958, respectively. She even held the discus record from 1958 through 1961.

On the home front, Tennessee State University tracksters consistently dominated the indoor and outdoor field from 1957 at least through 1968.

Fifties Postscript

In 1956, *The Negro Woman's College Education* by Jeanne Noble was published. The study surveyed attitudes of Black women students in Negro and white co-ed colleges and universities, such as the University of Chicago and Michigan State University; in Black women's schools, such as Bennett and Spelman Colleges; and at the exclusive white women's schools, like Vassar and Barnard.

Under the heading "Amount of Attention Graduates Thought College Should Give to Selected Life Adjustment Areas," only 47 percent of the respondents replied that the achievement of "satisfying recreational pursuits" should receive "much attention," the lowest percentage response. This suggests that as of 1956, Black women still overwhelmingly felt sports or athletic activity was not of great consequence in personal development. The stellar performances of the "Tigerbelles" and of the Tuskegee, Prairie View, Wilberforce, and other women's track teams believed this mood, however. By the opening of the next decade, their splendid example of the character-building assets derived from a vigorous athletic program proved inspirational to growing numbers of Black girls and women who took up sports in the late Sixties and Seventies.

Sixties Standard-Bearers

If by 1960, any citizen had not heard of the Tennessee State Tiberbelles' track exploits, they were informed of their prowess by year's end. In large part, Wilma Rudolph was the reason why.

Born in Clarksville, Tennessee on June 23, 1940, she earned the title of the "World's Fastest Woman" for her electrifying performances in the 1960 Rome Olympics. It was a ten-event women's field, and USSR athletes claimed six victories, but nineteen-year-old Rudolph ran away with three of the remaining four. In the 100- and 200-meters, she produced 11-second and 24-second times, respectively. The amazingly swift 100-meters time, although an Olympic and world record, was unofficial since a strong wind was blowing at the time. Her win in the 200-meters was the first ever by an American woman.[41] The next year, 1961, she retained the NAAU championship, winning in a breathtaking 11.2 seconds.

Rudolph took her third gold medal in the 400-meter relay race. Here, she and teammates Martha Hudson, Lucinda Williams, and Barbara Jones delivered a new Olympic and world-record time of 44.5 seconds. Running the final anchor leg, Rudolph got off to a poor start but then she "poured elegantly" over the track, described one spectator. "Such was the acceleration of this long-legged girl that even her poor starting could not aid her rivals."

In Rome, Rudolph picked up two new nicknames, largely because of a "flowing stride that made the rest of the pack seem to be churning on a treadmill." The Italians called her "La Gazelle Nera" (the Black gazelle), and she was "La Chattanooga Choo Choo" to the French contingent. More than one American reporter said that she had "stolen" the Olympic show — some feat for a woman crippled by double pneumonia and scarlet fever at age four, and who did not learn to walk normally until age seven.

The seventeenth of nineteen children, she soon learned to run fast, she once said, because she wanted to get to the dining table first.

Imbued with a rock-hard determination to succeed, no matter the odds, Rudolph determined to make up for lost time. By high school she was averaging thirty points per game for the girl's basketball team. Here, she picked up the tag "Skeeter" because she "buzzed around the court like a mosquito" on her six-foot frame, and attracted the attention of Tennessee State track coach Ed Temple. Soon she was

Wilma Rudolph - Olympics track star
(courtesy, EBONY Magazine)

training as sprinter in the Tennessee State University summer camp, and in 1956 when she was sixteen, she performed well enough to win a berth on the Olympic track team.

As the first American woman to win three gold medals in track and field, Rudolph was the second Black woman — after Althea Gibson — to win the Associated Press' annual woman Athlete-of-the-Year award in 1960. The United Press International Athlete of the Year European Poll honors also befell her, as did the "World's Fastest Woman" nametag. In 1961, she became the third woman ever to win the Sullivan Trophy, given annually to the amateur athlete of the year who "by his or her performance, example and influence as an amateur, has done the most for sportsmanship during the year."

By the early 1970's observers recorded an unusual interest in women's track with AAU registration figures jumping nearly two-fold from 9,800 to some 18,000. Qualifying standards have since been adopted for national championships, where as late as 1956, only 200 women entered the meet.[42] The first sprouts in this movement can be traced to Wilma Rudolph's spectacular 1960 accomplishments, which as A.S. Young noted, loudly proved women can excel in much more than those traditional "women sports" of swimming, ice-skating, archery, and gymnastics. Her contributions went a long way toward convincing doubters that females could be vivacious *and* splendid athletes, as well: a reassuring note for all would-be women athletes fearing training would detract from their comeliness and sex appeal.

Marie Hart, writing on the overall position of women in sports, once cited Rudolph while discussing what appeared to be the Black community's more appreciative attitude toward its sportswomen:

> In startling contrast (to the white community's receptivity of its women athletes) is the Black woman athlete. In the Black community, it seems, a woman can be strong and competent in sport and still not deny her womanliness. She can even win respect and status; Wilma Rudolph is [but] one example.[43]

What Hart did not mention is the historical context of the Black woman's experience. Abused for centuries, she is not a stranger to extreme physical taxation, somewhat akin to that required in fiercely competitive athletes. Despite her antebellum labors in the fields or the "big houses," she was expected to care for her family, as well. Yet no Blacks thought her any less a woman for her vigor. Victorian ideals sifted down to affect the way Black women were viewed by others and themselves, but perhaps Lucy Wilmot Smith, a nineteenth-century journalist, best describes this basic difference in perception Hard observed:

> Born and bred under the hindrance of slavery and the limitations of sex, the mothers of the race have kept pace with the fathers. They stand at the head of the cultured, educated families where daughters clasp arms with the sons. The educated Negro woman occupies vantage over the Caucausian woman of America, in that the former has had to contest with her brother every inch of the ground for recognition; the Negro man, having had his sister by his side on plantations and in rice swamps, keeps her there, now that he moves in other spheres. As she wins laurels he accords her the royal crown.[44]

Despite all the acclaim Wilma Rudolph received for being a spectacular and beautiful Olympic medalist, she was denied one benefit of Olympic competition, until recently: financial gain. It took seventeen years for an idea-parched television network to consider her a good film subject. This recognition, in turn, has spawned an autobiography, a series of television commercials promoting cosmetics for Black women, and a Black woman's beauty book.

None of this is coming too soon, she recently admitted:

> Honestly, after winning three gold medals, I thought I would be a star. But I was forgotten. Maybe I expected too much. . .I thought I would be able to make it on television, or as a broadcaster. . .or maybe endorsing products. But nothing ever happened.
>
> But then I saw Mark Spitz (winner of seven gold medals in the 1972 Olympics). He got everything I always hoped I would get. Then I realized: He's a white man. I'm a Black woman.
>
> To this day, Black women athletes are on the bottom of the ladder. White women — Billie Jean King, Chris Evert, Donna De Verona. . .they all make it on the front cover of magazines. The Wilma Rudolphs don't. That's my challenge.[45]

Not since Tuskegee Institute's Hattie Turner won the national AAU (outdoors) discus and baseball throw events in 1944 had any Black woman excelled in power throwing competition. However, Earlene Brown changed this record in the late Fifties when she ruled these events. After her respectable finishes in the 1956 Olympic discus and shotput outings, it seemed only a matter of time and opportunity before she improved on the record.

These elements met in 1960 when she captured a bronze medal in Rome with a 53 ft. 10-2/3 in. heave of the shotput. Brown became friends with Wilma Rudolph in the 1956 games, and was inspired by the sprinter's success. "I was so happy when Wilma started winning her three gold medals. After her first medal I hugged her and went out and threw the shot for the bronze medal."[46] With this effort, Brown distinguished herself as the first American woman to win a medal in the event. She also became the only other American woman to win a medal for an individual track and field performance that year besides Rudolph.

Returning for a third Olympics performance in 1964, Brown finished a distant twelfth in the shotput.

Born in 1936 to a father who played Black league professional baseball and a mother who also was "big and strong" and Texan, Earlene Brown played and traveled with a women's softball team by age 11.

When a gym teacher later offered her instruction in the basic track and field skills, she readily accepted. Although tall and already weighing 186 pounds as a teenager, she ran anchor for her high school team's 440-yard relay unit, as well as in other sprints. The baseball and basketball games and all the jumping events were also part of her regimen.

Years later, when that same teacher encouraged Brown to train for the 1956 Olympics, the athlete accepted her husband's ultimatum that she should not return home if she left to compete. So, for six months Brown trained in the shotput, lived with her mother, and worked as a domestic to support herself. During the qualifying meet for the 1960 contests, she ate canned goods because she could not afford cafeteria food. Later, between Rome and Tokyo, she worked on an assembly job and studied cosmetology. Thus, she attempted to make ends meet for herself and her son, and allowed herself the freedom to compete.[47]

Earlene Brown - champion of shotput and discus

Despite her struggles, the Olympian emphatically says they were well worth it. "I've done it all, seen it all, had it all, got it all." This includes a seven-year tour in professional roller derby between 1969 and 1976, where she once earned $500 weekly. Now what she would most like to do is open a sports center for children in Watts, where she grew up. Apart from its physical benefits, she sees a variety of additional and important reasons for pursuing athletic enjoyment.

Sports teaches you to have patience and tolerance. It takes away ignorance and gives you survival. In sports you learn about different people — their attitudes, personalities, the rich, and the poor. You get to evaluate your position in the world.[48]

Once described as a "jolly, 226-lbs.," Brown once was honored by the 100 Per Cent Wrong Club of Southern California, a Black sports group founded in the late Fifties to promote interracial sports participation. Here, she admitted that she once was ashamed of her size. Happily involved in women's athletics, however, she told the crowd, "I never thought my size and strength could make me feel proud. But I feel proud now."[49]

Other Black women who traveled to the 1960 games were hurdlers Shirley Crowder and JoAnn Terry, and Annie Lois Smith, a broad jumper. Neomia Rodgers, a Tuskegee track club member and another high jumper, also qualified.

1961-1963: Between Olympics

Plenty of track and field activity kept all ranked runners and field competitors busy in these intervening years.

Wilma Rudolph broke the American Record for the 100-meters with an 11.2 second performance against Russian, Polish, German and English teams during the 1961 summer. Willye White, Vivian Brown and Ernestine Pollard reset the world's 400-meter relay mark at 44.3 seconds.[50]

In 1962, Vivian Brown set her own record time of 22.5 seconds for the 220-yard dash during the national AAU indoor meet, while JoAnn Terry did likewise, flying over the 70-yard hurdles in 9.2 seconds. Brown repeated her noteworthy performance outdoors at Los Angeles in 24.1 seconds. Later in 1962, Edith McGuire, the Atlanta speedster, and Wyomia Tyus, from Griffin, Georgia debuted. Immediately apparent that both possessed extraordinary athletic ability, they would often finish 1-2 in the sprints.

No other national or international meet records fell after Vivian Brown's 23.9-second performance in the 200-meters at the 1963 Sao Paulo, Brazil Pan-American Games. Here, she retired Lucinda Williams' 1959 mark. Later that year Edith McGuire smoked in the 100-yard dash at the Tennessee State University Volunteer Games in an astounding 10.5 seconds, to establish her new American record.

Tokyo, 1964

Wilma Rudolph was not among the American women track and field team members in the next Olympic meet, but at least four other Tigerbelles represented the United States, and well. They accounted for the four individual medals garnered by the American team, and the 400-meter relay unit.

Wyomia Tyus, Edith McGuire, and Marilyn White finished 1-2-3, blasting with 100-meters with 11.2, 11.4, and 11.6 times. The powerful image of three Black women straining to cross the finish line, and later mounting the three-tiered awards platform to receive their medals, must have been an inspirational sight to the many thousands viewing the satellite transmissions of the proceedings.

Tyus and McGuire frequently battled for top honors in this event. For example, Tyus clinched the Milrose Games title earlier in the year but McGuire bested her in the 1964 Russian-American meet.

McGuire earned her fourth Olympic medal when she finished the 200-meters in 23-seconds flat, barely arriving at the finish before Polish and Australian challengers.

Willye and Marilyn White, McGuire and Tyus carried the baton for the 400-meter relay machine's silver medals.

This Olympiad yielded Willye White's last medal, even though she would qualify to return to the 1968 and 1972 meets. "I have been the grand old lady of track for twenty years," she said later while reflecting on her start in the competition in 1956.

Born in 1940, White grew up on a Mississippi Delta cotton plantation where she began picking the fluffy crop at age eight. Athletically precocious, she played varsity basketball for the high school team when she was in the fifth grade, and by thirteen, she ran track for the Tigerbelles' club team.

In the Seventies, she was electd to the Black Hall of Fame.

Other Black participants in this Olympiad were Rosie Bonds, a Los Angeles challenger who took eighth in the 80-meter hurdles, and Eleanor Montgomery, who placed eighth in the high jump competitior with a 5 ft., 7¾ in. attempt. Estelle Baskerville also competed in that event.

More international meets followed the Olympics for the fortunate few chosen to compete. Edith McGuire, who had intended to retire from competition in 1966 after her college graduation, geared up for the grind after her loss in what was to have been her "last" race. Her pride would not let her end in defeat. "I can't quit now because I have to redeem myself," she said. True to her word, she took the 200-meters at the All-American Invitational Meets in the summer. While at it, she took third place in the 100-meter race.

In 1967, the Pan-American Games were held in Winnipeg, Canada.

Here Eleanor Montgomery, high jump standout in the 1966 dual meets, and Wyomia Tyus were joined by Martha Watson, a long jumper, and Madeline Manning, Montgomery's "home girl" from Cleveland. Manning set a new Pam American record of 2:02:03 seconds in the 800-meters — a middle distance race rarely attempted by Blacks or American women, for that matter. Tyus won the 200-meters and Watson took fourth place in the long jump finals.

Wyomia Tyus, Olympic Track Star
of Tennessee State University
(photo courtesy Coach Ed Temple)

Afterward, Montgomery, Manning, and Tyus stayed in Canada to face off against selected European athletes in a special meet held in conjunction with Montreal's Expo '67, the World's Fair.

Mexico City, 1968

While the world's best athletes were busily concentrating on turning in their best performances and capturing gold medals, Black America was in the throes of a "revolution," as historian John Hope Franklin described it. After years of concerted efforts, including some of the most hotly debated resolutions ever brought to the House and Senate floors, Congress passed a Civil Rights Act in 1964. Street demonstrations reminded America that equality of opportunity was still not a reality for its Blacks. The first urban rioting in a number of years erupted in several ghettos, where the frustration of living in a land of many other free, brave and successful second and third generation emigrants had proven too much for young and disillusioned Blacks to stomach.

There were many demonstrations, legislative battles, and confrontations designed to confront White America with "the imperfection of its social order and the immorality of its human relationships," by the time of the 1968 Olympics. That meet, infused with the politics of protest, was marked by several demonstrations by Blacks against racism at the games.

In one, Tommie Smith and John Carlos, first and third place winners in the men's 200-meters, ran their race wearing black knee-length socks, signifying their devotion to Black people, they said. When they approached the victory platform, Smith wore a black scarf and Carlos, a black shirt. Both raised black-gloved fists a la the "solidarity salute" at the playing of the "Star Spangled Banner," and stood barefoot while holding their shoes in the free hand. They also stared at the ground during the anthem and gave their salute once more while leaving the platform.

Loudly denounced and soon rejected from the games for their actions, the men were joined in spirit by the women's 400-meter relay team, which dedicated its gold medals to them.[51]

Barbara Farrell of Los Angeles and Margaret Johnson Bailes of Portland, Oregon raced in the 400-meter relay with Mildred Netter, a Rosedale, Mississippi native, and Wyomia Tyus, who was making her second Olympic appearance. Together they set another world record, cutting the time to 42.8 seconds.

Netter, an Alcorn State University graduate born in 1948, received the Outstanding Athlete-of-the-South award from the Southern AAU and the Most Outstanding Female Athlete award from Atlanta's 100 Percent Wrong Club, after the Olympics.

Both Farrell and Bailes ran the 100- and 200-meters in Mexico City, but only Farrell captured an individual medal — a silver medallion for her 11.1 seconds finish behind flash Wyomia Tyus. Tyus' 11-flat time established yet another world record, but so did her performance. No other athlete ever — man or woman — had won gold medals for the same event in consecutive Olympics.[52] Without a doubt, Tyus was the "Fastest Woman in the World."

Born August 29, 1945, she started running "because I liked it. First around the house and then around the block, and pretty soon in school." At thirteen she was training under Ed Temple's watchful eye and with Wilma Rudolph, five years her senior.

A logical successor to Rudolph, Tyus, like the several other world-class Black women tracksters following Rudolph's lead, has been ignored — save on the day of their triumphs. An *Ebony* reporter offered this observation of the athletes' dilemma:

> Their accomplishments, in most cases, have had the perverse effect of perpetu-ating the "all blacks can run" stereotype, rather than leading them to national celebrity. Wilma Rudolph escaped that fate, but only by pulling off one of the most spectacular sports coups in Olympic history — at precisely the right moment, although in so doing she diminished the importance of every woman sprinter who followed...Unlike the male-dominated sports where heroes are produced on a yearly basis to replace fallen heroes (Joe Louis for Jack Johnson; Muhammad Ali for Joe Louis, etc.) the female "heroine" seems a one-shot affair.[53]

Another gold-medal winner in 1968 was Madeline Manning, a 20-year-old Tigerbelle from Cleveland, Ohio, who set a new Olympic and world record for the 800-meters when she scorched the track with a winning time mere split-seconds over the two minutes mark: 2:00:9.

Ironically, her win, the first in which an American bested European women in an event they had dominated for years, did not truly contribute to the "all Blacks can run" stereotype — at least, not in the usual sense. In fact, Manning recalled in her autobiography that she started receiving anonymous phone calls after her highly successful 1967-68 season in which she won medals at the Pan-American and European meets. "What makes you think a nigger can beat white girls in the half mile? It isn't a nigger's event," they would snarl. And it is true the stereotypical evaluation allows Blacks to excel in the sprints for they supposedly cannot deliver in the middle-or-long-distance races.

Significantly, Manning's triumph forced doubters to give Black athletes more credit as *individuals* whose levels of determination, drive, and stamina make all the difference. Her encounter with a local Cleve-land reporter in Mexico City immediately prior to her qualifying heat illustrates her reaction.

> Here I was, ready to go to the track, and he was asking me if I thought I could make it through the race. It was as if he were saying, "You've already done all anyone in Cleveland would have expected." I was hurt and angry.
>
> Look, I said, "everybody who comes to the Olympics comes to win, and I'm no

different. I'm sure not going out there to lose. I'm going to qualify right now, and I'm going to win the finals."[54]

And so she did.

Manning, like so many of the other outstanding Black women in track and field, "always was fast." A standout on her elementary school track team, she later ran for her high school and the Cleveland Track Club under whose auspices she thrilled spectators when, at seventeen, she won the women's division finals in the half-mile at the (Toronto) Maple Leaf Games. It was her first middle-distance attempt.

Among her many medals and awards, Madeline Manning (Jackson) qualified for and attended three Olympic meets: 1968, 1972, and 1976. At one point she had given up competition running altogether to be a wife and mother, but she may well seek a 1980 comeback. Just before she last announced her retirement from competition in order to devote herself full time to a Christian ministry, she broke her American record in the 800-meters by two full seconds, lowering it to 1:57:09. She was then 28 years old.

Despite the abundant criticism of American organized sports, many Black athletes, from Ora Washington and Althea Gibson to Earlene Brown, attest to the challenge and "salvation" they have found in pursuit of these activities.

Jarvis Scott, who qualified for the 1968 Olympics and ran sixth in the 400-meters, remembers that she was "raised under the worst of conditions," in the Los Angeles Watts ghetto. Here, violence, frustrations, and hopelessness were ways of life. "I had a choice. I could get married at 18 and have babies or I could run."

She chose to run with the Los Angeles Mercuryettes, a long-time developer of female track talent, and produced the fastest time in the 400-meters by an American woman in 1968: 52.9 seconds. Scott was the first American woman to ever qualify for the Olympic finals in this event.

Today, she holds a law enforcement degree, coaches in the Jesse Owens Track and Field Program, and assists the University of California-Los Angeles track team. Additionally, she lectures to youth, motivating them to seek inspiration for lifetime success in sports. Admitting the problems, particularly in the Olympics, since America does not subsidize its athletes and "forgets all about you if you don't get a gold medal; there are no Wheaties commercials then."[55] Scott still believes the pros outweigh the cons.

The Latest Generation

The fifty-year-old tradition of Black women competing in track and field events is maintained today by a corps of young athletes whose racing speeds and leaping distances steadily increase. Inspired by many an outstanding example of Black achievement, encouraged by recent efforts to achieve between men and women's sports programs in the school, and instructed in the discipline's skills by ever-growing ranks of experienced competitors, they cannot help but continue breaking national and world records.

"Probably, it is the most remarkable women's track organization extant."[56] This is how a sportswriter summed up Fred Thompson's brainchild, born in the hallway of a ghetto school in 1944, when he "noticed that everyone emphasized the boys, so I picked out some girls." Operated for years with little more than faith, a full load of talent, determination, and whatever credit its coach could obtain, the Brooklyn Atoms Club boasts an Olympic medalist among its alumnae. Others of its runners have achieved national ranking. Most importantly, as any Atoms' graduate will attest, club members gain the confidence, self-respect, and motivation to obtain first-class education and passports out of the slums.

Cheryl Toussaint is the best-known Atom. In the 1972 Munich Olympics, she ran the anchor leg of the 4 x 400-meter relay race. The American team finished second in 3:25:03 to win silver medals in the first staging of the event in an Olympic meet.[57]

Earlier Toussaint toured Europe with an American team in the summer of 1970. She also starred with the Atoms' mile relay team, which broke a world record in a trial heat of the national AAU championships held in Los Angeles. The group then outdid itself, breaking the new record in the final.

Her own story is a profile in courage. Bored with being champion of practically all girls' sports in her neighborhood, Toussaint wandered into a track meet at Brooklyn Boy's High School in 1965. She managed to finish fourth against three Atoms, although wearing sneakers too large for her feet.

She was accepted for practices but remained invisible to Coach Thompson, who regularly ignores new prospects until convinced they have more motivation than the desire for an Atom's uniform.

Given the opportunity to test her mettle, Toussaint spared nothing. Running the mile in a local meet, she sped off as though sprinting and ignored Thompson's warning to "slow down or burn out."

With a hundred yards to go, the bomb of oxygen debt hit her. The long stride
flattened. She began to wobble. Nearing the finish, she staggered. Her head
ached. Currents of nausea struck her. A few yards from the tape she fell weeping.
Dizzy, crying, Cheryl Toussaint crawled across the finish line. Someone, only one
runner, rushed past her. In tears and pain, she had won second place by crawling
home.[58]

That's when Thompson realized she really was "something special."

Other outstanding members on the Atoms' roll are Carmen Smith,
an Olympic-class hurdler, Shelly Marshall, and Patricia Hawkins, one-
time national AAU hurdles champion. Lorna Ford, a recent two-time
indoor/outdoor champion in the national AAU competition who is
looking toward the 1980 Olympics, has been a Colgate Women's
Games champion four times.

The Colgate-Palmolive Company has sponsored the games since
1975, when it accepted Fred Thompson's idea to multiply the Atoms'
effect for thousands of New York area girls. More than 18,000 girls from
elementary schoolers to college co-eds, participated in the most recent
production.[59] Sprints, middle-distance races, hurdles, and the high
jump are featured events.

Another prize-winning Atom is Audrey Reid, who did not attend the
1972 Olympics but set a new American record in the women's high
jump that year when she cleared 6 ft. ½ inches. By 1974 Deborah
Sapenter revised the world record in the quarter-mile (440 yards) with a
52.2-second finish. In the 1975 national AAU meet she tied the
American record in the 400 meters in 51.6 seconds.

In the mid-Seventies, several superb tracksters gaining acclaim
hailed from the South. Kathy McMillan soared to international
prominence in the 1976 Montreal Olympics when she won a silver
medal in the long jump, landing only inches behind the winner.
Previously, the 18-year-old broke the old national AAU meet record in
the event with a 22 ft. 3 in. leap.

Born in Radford, North Carolina in 1958, McMillan was the high
school state champion in her specialty as well as in the 100-yard dash,
and the half-mile. She graduated and accepted an athletic scholarship
to Tennessee State University.

Chandra Cheeseborough from Jacksonville, Florida also posted
wins in the 1976 national AAU outings, clinching first place in the 100
yard dash. A 1975 member of the American squad attending the Pan-
American Games in Mexico City, she ran the 200-meters in an
eyebrow-raising 22.77 seconds.[60]

One of the best hurdlers anywhere is Mary Ayers of the Prairie View

University Pantherettes. In 1975 and 1976 she won the Association of Intercollegiate Athletic Women's (AIAW) national championship's hurdling event, and is holder of the meet record of 59.7 seconds in the 440-yard intermediate hurdles.

Ayers also runs on the school's mile relay team and has greatly contributed to the school's mile relay team and has greatly contributed to the Pantherettes — by 1976 — unbroken string of 155 regular season victories.

Another Texas track legend is Jacki Elaine Mays, who set a state and national high school record when she triple-jumped 39 ft. 11½ in. at the State Girls' University Interscholastic League Track Meet in May 1977 at Austin.

Born January 12, 1960, in Stamford, Texas, Mays was the subject of a *Sports Illustrated* article in the June 6, 1977 issue, following her record-breaking jump. Long jump winner with a 19 ft. 2¾ in. effort, she claimed the 100-yard dash in a 10.8 second burst of speed.

Mays won a full athletic scholarship to Angelo State in San Angelo, Texas.

Coaches and Administrators

Title IX attempts to define the difference between physical education and intramural athletic programming, which helps keep the distinction between coaching and administrative professions clear. In the U.S. Department of Education and H.E.W. Compliance Overview of Title IX and Physical Education, the distinction is spelled out:

> Although physical education and athletics are frequently linked in popular discussion and sometimes linked in their implementation and staffing in education agencies and institutions, they are treated separately within the regulation to implement Title IX, in the administrative policies and structures of most education agencies and institutions, and in the platform statements and position papers of the profession. According to these statements and papers *physical education* is that integral part of the total education which contributes to the development of the individual through natural medium of physical activity — human movement. In it, regular instruction and practices are provided in a variety of physical activities (leading up to and including athletics) that are suited to the nature and needs of the students depending on age and development of an adequate level of physical fitness.

> The *intramural* athletic program provides opportunities for students to utilize, in organized competition with their schoolmates, the knowledge and skills acquired in the basic physical education program. The interscholastic (or intercollegiate) program provides opportunities in secondary schools (or colleges and universities) for students with superior athletic ability to develop and utilize fully this talent through organized competition with students of similar ability from other schools.

Perhaps the preeminent Black woman in this area is Nell C. Jackson, former Tuskegee 200-meters specialist and women's track team coach. Uniquely qualified, she has, on at least two notable occasions, been the "woman of the moment" in American sports. After Lucile Wilson called for improved coaching and training of the U.S. women's squad following the 1952 Olympics, Jackson was appointed team coach. When Black athletes issued their grievances during the 1968 Olympics, the governing committee sought out Jackson, who already sat on the women's board of the U.S. Olympic Development Committee. As a result, she became the first Black to sit on the U.S. Olympic Committee, board of directors, 1969-1972.

Chair of the AAU Women's Track and Field Committee from 1967-71, she has held a variety of top-level positions within administrative circles of women's sports governing associations. They include: chair, U.S. Olympic Committee Women's Track and Field Committee, 1968-72; Division of Girls' and Women's Sports Liaison Chair, 1966-68; and she presently heads the Association for Intercollegiate Athletics for Women (AIAW), held since 1977.

Nell C. Jackson - sports administrator and former track star

Jackson holds a doctorate in physical education from Iowa State University. She managed the U.S. Women's National Track and Field Team that toured Europe in 1969, and she coached the team attending the World University Games the same year. Manager of the U.S. Track and Field Group for its 1966 European tour, she worked with the 1969 European tour for the AAU, and both coached and managed the 1972 tour to Martinique. Her latest Olympic coaching assignment was with the 1972 women's squad in Munich.

Among Jackson's most talented students have been Mildred McDaniel, high jump gold medalist (1956); Neomia Rodgers, another high jumper who competed in the 1960 Olympics; and Maeoper West, winner of the AIAW Collegiate Track and Field championships (1973) and member of that year's World University Games Team. Before swinging onto the national team coaching circuit, Jackson organized and coached the Illini Track Club for Girls.

Currently professor and Assistant Director of Athletics at Michigan State University, this all-around woman in sports has created a motivational film, "Grace in Motion," in connection with the U.S. Olympic Development Committee. She is the author of numerous articles on track and field, and wrote *Track and Field for Girls and Women*, which provides a clear introduction to track and field mechanics.

Nationally and internationally respected as an athletic expert, the Tuskegee native is a popular lecturer and workshop organizer. At a recent meeting of the National Women in Sports Conference at Howard University, she spoke on "The Ladder to the Top: Athlete, Coach, Administrator," perhaps a summary of her lifetime experience.[61] In it, she emphasized the necessity of women fusing practical experiences with education and their development of a sport philosophy — particularly concerning the sports-related myths commonly held in mind by men about women.

Jackson was inducted into the Black Athletes Hall of Fame in 1977.

Agnes Tilley Wheaton and Donnis H. Thompson are two other examples of Black women who have figured among the superior coaches working with women's track teams. Mary Reed Mabry, in contrast, has won distinction molding a *male* track club.

Agnes Wheaton was born March 4, 1907 in Portsmith, New Hampshire. Later, after she moved to Cambridge, Massachusetts, she became the first Black woman to coach and manage the oldest track team in the state, the Red Diamond Athletic Club. Over the years she has coached some 400 girls, some of whom competed in the National

AAU contests. The Red Diamond 400-meter relay squad and 100-meter dash entries placed in the 1941 outdoor meet.[62]

When the state needed an experienced person to produce the second annual Massachusetts state high school track and field meet in 1968, it called on Wheaton's capable knowledge.

A pioneer in the promotion of state track and field development, Wheaton was honored on July 26, 1975 when the second invitational relay meet, sponsored by the Boston Opportunity Industrial Center (OIC), was named for her.

Donnis Thompson is the pioneer physical education administrator who became the University of Hawaii's first full-time director of women's intercollegiate athletics, having organized the division in 1972. Holder of a physical education and administration doctorate from the University of Northern Colorado, she also shares Nell Jackson's experience as track coach, having directed the American women's team the competed against Russia and Poland in 1962. Also, she coached the first track and field team organized at the University of Hawaii.

Author of several books and tracts on physical education for women, Thompson is prominent in national women's athletic organizations, particularly the Association of Intercollegiate Athletic Women and the Amateur Athletic Union.

Her many awards include the 1976 Female Educator of the Year Citation from the University of Northern Colorado Alumni Association, the 1962 Distinguished Service Award from the Hawaii Athletic Union, and the 1974 Distinguished Service Award of the Hawaii State American Association of Health, Physical Education, and Recreation.

Shirley Johnson, another outstanding women's intercollegiate athletics director, is on staff at the University of California at Los Angeles.

Mary Reed Mabry did not start out with the idea of coaching men's track and field when she was a physical education major at Claflin College in Orangeburg, South Carolina. Falling in love and getting married, however, shifted her focus. Because her husband was a distance runner, she found herself quite interested in the subject of track. Between her instructors and her husband, Mabry learned "everything, from how to get off the starting blocks to pace in distance running."

For any who question her qualifications, she says "her background is as solid as many male coaches I've met in their field."

Since 1975 Mabry has been the head coach at Inkster (Michigan) High School, the first Black woman to hold the position. Under her leadership, the track team won the state Class B track and field championship that year, and any lingering doubts of her ability have evaporated.

Born July 21, 1941, in Orangeburg, she was honored by the Detroit chapter of the Black Women's Association of America in 1975 for her sensational coaching achievement.

Dorothy L. Richey and Alpha Vernell Alexander are two other administrators in women's athletics. Richey, educated at Tuskegee Institute in Alabama, holds a master's degree in Physical Education from Indiana State University and a Doctor of Education from Nova University. From 1974 to 1977, she was athletic director of men and women's intercollegiate athletics at Chicago State University in Illinois. Prior to this position, she served as coach-manager of the USA Track and Field Team in the World University Games in Rome, Italy, as coach-manager of the USA Jumping Team in Japan, as coach-manager of the USA Track and Field Team in Australia. Her professional responsibilities also placed her in key roles in national and international athletic organizations. In 1975 she served as a member of the U.S. Collegiate Sports Council Board of Delegates, and in 1976 she completed seven years of service as Delegate to the AAU conventions, representing Indiana Association, Region VI. Richey, popular among athletes around the world, has been featured in several magazines, including the June 1975 *Ebony* and the 1974 *Black Sports* magazines.

Dorothy L. Richey - administrator of sports programs
(photo courtesy of EBONY Magazine)

Alpha V. Alexander, native of Nashville, Tennessee, received her bachelor's degree in physical education from The College of Wooster in Ohio. Holding both a master's degree and doctorate degree from Temple University in Philadelphia, she became Assistant to Women's Athletic Director at Temple in 1976. Moving through various positions at Temple and gaining additional experience with professional groups in athletics, such as the NCAA Summer Camp Program, Alexander later became Assistant Athletic Director for Women at Temple University. Acclaimed as the youngest Black female in the USA to be an Assistant Athletic Director at a large, major American university, Alexander has published and has spoken at major professional meetings on athletics and sports.

NOTES

[1] Melvyn Watson, comp., *The Encyclopedia of Athletics* (New York: St. Martin's Press, 1977), p. 200.

[2] Ellen W. Gerber, Jan Felshin, Pearl Berlin, Wareen Wyrick, *The American Woman in Sport* (Reading, Massachusetts: Addison-Wesley, 1974), p. 70.

[3] Newspaper Enterprise Association, eds., *The Good Housekeeping Woman's Almanac* (New York: Newspaper Enterprise Association, 1976), p. 411.

[4] Gerber, et al., p. 39.

[5] Gerber, et al., p. 73.

[6] Gerber, et al., pp. 72-73.

[7] Newspaper Enterprise Association, p. 412.

[8] Margaret Ruth Downing, "Women's Basketball: An Historical Review of Selected Athletic Organizations Which Influenced its Ascension Toward Advanced Competition in the U.S.," Diss. Texas Women's University 1973, p. 43.

[9] Gerber, et al., p. 73.

[10] Edwin B. Henderson, *The Negro in Sports*, rev. ed. (Washington, D.C.: Associated Publishers, Inc., 1949), p. 280.

[11] Henderson, p. 160.

[12] A.S. "Doc" Young, *Negro Firsts in Sports* (Chicago: Johnson Publishing Company, 1963), p. 198.

[13] Nolan A. Thaxton, "A Documentary Analysis of Competitive Track and Field for Women at Tuskegee Institute and Tennessee State University," Diss. Springfield College 1970, p. 66.

[14] Henderson, pp. 438-458 and NAAU results.

[15] Thaxton, p. 207.

[16] Ocania Chalk, *Black College Sport* (New York: Dodd, Mead and Co., 1976), p. 328.

[17] Thaxton, p. 234.

[18] Henderson, p. 230.

[19] Thaxton, pp. 290-291.

[20] Henderson, p. 400.

[21] Lord Killanin and John Rhodda, eds., *The Olympic Games* (New York: Macmillan, 1976), pp. 235-236.

[22] Chalk, p. 356.

[23] "Welcome Back to Miss Louise Stokes," *Malden Evening News*, Malden, Mass., 10 September 1936, p. 1, Col. 8.

[24] Thaxton, p. 100.

[25] Thaxton, pp. 109-110.

[26] Henderson, pp. 450, 452.

[27] Henderson, p. 400.

[28] Henderson, p. 400.

[29] Henderson, p. 441.

[30] Henderson, p. 400.

[31] Thaxton, p. 128.

[32] Thaxton, p. 6.

[33] Thaxton, p. 169.

[34] Thaxton, p. 177.

[35] Nell C. Jackson, *Track and Field for Girls and Women* (Minneapolis, Minnesota: Burgess Publishing Company, 1968), p. 41.

[36] Thaxton, pp. 183-184.

[37] Karen Folger Jacobs, "Earlene Brown: Down From Olympia," *Essence*, May 1979, p. 12.

[38] Thaxton, p. 200.

[39] Thaxton, p. 201.

[40] Thaxton, p. 243.

[41] Killanin and Rhodda, p. 235.

[42] Gerber, et al., p. 131.

[43] Gerber, et al., p. 267.

[44] Irvine Garland Penn, *The Afro-American Press and Its Editors* (1891; rpt. New York: Arno Press, 1969), pp. 380-381. For further reading on the effects of distorted victorian imagery on Afro-American Women, see Lerner, pp. 437-471; also, other documents on the Black Women's Club Movement.

[45] "Wilma Rudolph Changes Gold Medals to Dollars," *Jet*, 12 January 1978, p. 52.

[46] Jacobs, p. 16.

[47] Jacobs, p. 16.

[48] Jacobs, p. 16.

[49] Young, p. 261.

[50] "The Black Amateur & Professional Athlete," *Reference Library of Black America*, Book III (New York: Bellwether, 1971), p. 214.

[51] Jack Orr, *The Black Athlete: His Story in American History* (New York: Lion Books, 1969), pp. 110-111.

[52] Newspaper Enterprise Association, p. 428.

[53] *Ebony*, August 1977, p. 64.

[54] Madeline Manning Jackson, *Running For Jesus* (Waco, Texas: Word Books, 1977), p. 84.

[55] Eric Gale, "Former Olympian Benefits Tech Trac," *Lubbock Avalanche Journal*, October 1979, p. 78.

[56] Roger Kahn, "Sports," *Esquire*, July 1974, p. 14.

[57] Killanin and Rhodda, p. 235.

[58] Kahn, p. 14.

[59] William S. Lewis, "The Colgate Women's Games V: And They're Off," *Encore*, 19 March 1979, pp. 42-43.

[60] Watson, p. 142.

[61] "Peter Harris," *Afro-American*, 15-19 January 1980.

[62] Henderson, p. 444.

CHAPTER IV

OF TEAM SPORTS: PLAYING GAMES TOGETHER

The most widespread and exciting development of the current era's sports scene for women revolves around the resurgence of interest in team sports. While track and field events, for instance, are often discussed in terms of team totals and team efforts, individual performances may occur at different times and places and in totally differing events — high jumping as opposed to sprinting, to cite an example. In contrast, each member of a basketball unit or rowing crew must learn to function most effectively together with her teammates. Together, they all pursue some one strategy to outplay the opposition.

This strict team function is absent from most of the sports women have traditionally pursued, like tennis, ice skating, or gymnastics, where grace and agility are more evident than strength and agressiveness. Since team sports, "with their emphasis on both physical aggression and teamwork are sometimes regarded as the crucible in which boys become men," it is understandable how male administrators of sports programs formerly did not even consider team sports and women simultaneously.[1]

Physical educators in the eastern women's colleges of the late nineteenth and early twentieth centuries instructed their charges in field hockey and basketball, but only with modifications. Players were thought more likely to injure themselves in the team sports, if only because there were enough of them in the area to increase the probability of collisions. General rules were adopted by instructors, independent of other schools. In basketball, at least, the proliferation of these guidelines resulted in a mish-mash of team experiences and expectations that discouraged intercollegiate competition.[2]

The injuries that so concerned nineteenth century educators could adversely affect feminine biology, they reasoned. Actually, by 1931 the uterus was proved practically jolt-proof an thereby free from any ill-effects associated with vigorous activity.[3] Apart from physical considerations, sports officials also wondered if women could bear the emotional stresses borne of vigorous competition.

To avoid injury, short of skipping games altogether, instructors discouraged student boisterousness and raw aggressions as "unladylike" and contrary to the accepted standard behavior for women. Still, in the early twentieth century the physical education curriculum was increasingly devoted to sport, although the educational emphasis fell on imparting the sport skills. The underlying idea was to promote various social values derived from group interaction, and to get vigorous education. Basketball, field hockey, volleyball, soccer and lacrosse were all taught in eastern women's colleges by 1910.

Despite this activity, critics persisted and reminded listeners that women's previous primary competitive activity involved snaring mates. "Why should they want to compete for anything else?" they intoned. Implicit was the assumption that women had no other legitimate reason for competing.

A resolution emanating from the 1923 Conference on Athletics and Physical Recreation for Women and Girls affirmed that women competing in college-level activities, at least, would do better to avoid highly competitive athletic contests for their own good.[4] By then, concerns over the possible exploitation of female athletes' health and welfare seemed to outweigh any devotion to Victorian edicts. The net result proved quite discouraging to would-be women sports participants, however.

Only since the 1960's have girls and women become much more aware and convinced that the joys of movement, challenge, achievement and success derived from competitive — and often, team-based — sports are not limited to men.

The feminist movement of the late Sixties and early Seventies accompanied the general upheaval in American society. Contemporaneous with the Black protest movement and the spirited opposition at the nation's Vietnam War involvement, it clarified several wideranging aspects of the culture undergoing transformation. For instance, increasing numbers of women went to work as self-images altered and a working woman's income became not merely a luxury, but a necessity for maintaining personal and family lifestyles. Strictly from the standpoint of functioning most effectively and successfully in the world of work, then, learning to play team sports would be an important experience for girls and young women. Betty Harragen, author of *Games Mother Never Taught You*, spelled it out:

> Once you work for pay, you are involved in a structure whose rules are modeled on competitive team sports. Businesses look for people who can play on a team, who can follow the rules, who know how to get along with all kinds of people, who have learned that you never disparage your teammates and you don't talk back to the coach. That holds for the office, the bank or the beauty parlor.[5]

Such experience will affect society, in turn, by molding more fearless and confident female citizens. One result could be that:

> Women who have had the regular experience of performing before others, of learning to win and to lose, of cooperating in team efforts, will be far less fearful of

running for office [or] better able to take public positions on issues in the face of opposition. . .[6]

Long workers outside the home, Black women can benefit from increased sports socialization every bit as much as white women. Discriminated against because of their color and sex, they stand to benefit from any competitive edge available.

Title IX and Equality of Opportunity

There may be worse (more socially serious) forms of prejudice in the U.S. today, but there is no sharper example of discrimination than that which operates against girls and women in competitive sports. No matter what her age, education, race or talent, the female's right to play is severely restricted. The funds, facilities, coaching and rewards allotted women are grossly inferior to those alloted men.[7]

The implementation of Title IX, the popular name given section 901(a) of the Education Amendments of 1972, has been largely responsible for the increasing accessibility of sports programs for girls and women in schools and colleges. Since the passage of Title IX of the Education Amendments of 1972 and the issuance of its implementing regulation in June of 1975, the implications of Title IX for the Physical Education programs of elementary and secondary schools and institutions of post-secondary education have been the focus of considerable attention. Title IX provides that: "No person. . .shall, on the basis of sex, be excluded from participation in, be denied the benefits, or be subjected to discrimination under any education program or activity receiving Federal financial assistance."[8] These major socializing institutions now provide programs more numerous and varied than ever before, and participation therein has skyrocketed. Title IX's mandate certainly has contributed to that escalation of participation. The number of women involved in college-level intramural sports programs increased more than 100 percent between 1971 and 1976, compared with the overall institutional population growth of 39 percent.[9]

Title IX forbids sexual discrimination denying citizens the benefits of any educational program or activity that receives Federal aid. "One of the most significant legislative results of a newfound women's movement, it specifically aims to increase opportunities for women to participate in competitive athletics.[10] Enforcement of the rule has been painfully slow, and most recent trends indicate that continuing vigilance on the part of students and other concerned citizens must continue in order for improvements to follow suit.[11]

With the boom in sports enrollments in 1971-1972 and the creation of new opportunities for instruction, more girls and women, Black and

White, were exposed to a wider selection of activities and encouraged to take part more than ever before. In secondary schools inter-scholastic sports programs for girls have increased six-fold since 1970, and a significant proportion thereof can be attributed to Title IX.

The Association for Intercollegiate Athletic Women (AIAW), founded in 1971-72, replaced the Commission on Intercollegiate Athletics for Women (CIAW). Today it is the premier supervisory body in women's athletics. Its advent nearly accompanied passage of the 1972 Amendment, and it claimed 278 charter members, all of which sponsored varsity sports programs for women.[12]

By 1979-80 the group planned to sponsor thirty national champion-ships in fourteen sports, including badminton, golf, skiing, track and field, basketball, field hockey, softball, and volleyball. Lacrosse and fencing championships will join the list by 1980-81.[13]

The AIAW and other women's groups have already petitioned the U.S. Commission on Civil Rights for stricter interpretation of Title IX provisions. The original five-year grace period allowed for implementa-tion of the changes has passed, and a number of institutions have taken little or no action to complete with regulations.[14]

Some of the delay can be traced to the concerns parents and educators alike have raised. Must locker rooms be co-ed? Must girls play ball with boys? There has also been consternation and dismay in administration offices, since budgets were ordered created to satisfac-torily support new or larger women's athletic programs.

Title IX does not force girls and women to compete against boys and men in contact sports, such as football, hockey, and basketball, although technically girls may now do so. A recent *Jet* magazine article suggests, however, that older females especially, would reject this opportunity. As one 250-lb., 5 ft., 11 in. girls high school basketball team member said, "No way I'll play on a boys' basketball team; the boys are just too rough."[15] Conversely, men eligible to compete on women's teams may be unwilling to compromise their masculine egos by doing so.

Despite the problems in interpretation and the implementation lag, Title IX has greatly increased the opportunity for women's organized sports participation. Yet while Black girls and women are profiting from this pendulum swing, the numbers actually benefitting remain disappointing. Of 4.6 million under-graduate college women counted in 1976, 573,00 were Black. Of these 17,000 were athletes in AIAW insti-tutions, but only 1,000 were Black.[15] Moreover, in only badminton, basketball and track and field was the minority participation rate above ten percent.[17]

These figures were compiled by the AIAW Commission on the Status of Minority Women, a group that will make recommendations of ways to increase minority representation in campus sports programs. Alpha Alexander, Commission member and instructor at Temple University, said that there are several reasons for the low rate of minority participation in college sports including, "lack of money for lessons and equipment, and lack of racial role models, and the availability of rental facilities." She added that "among minority women college athletes there are additional problems not generally faced by white women athletes like the need for child care, (and) the need for a job to support themselves and additional study time."[18]

Despite the problems impeding full distribution of Title IX benefits, the measure has taken a giant step in the right direction, increasing women's "sporting chance" to exceed their grasps.

Black Women on the Hardcourt

Today, one of the most popular sports among men is also one of the most popular among women. The sport is basketball.

Invented in 1891 by Dr. James A. Naismith as a diversion for students during the long winter months, the game caught on quickly enough in Black communities to support club teams in Washington, D.C., New York, Brooklyn, and Jersey City, New Jersey by 1906. There was a team for nearly every school, elementary and high, by 1911.[19] Men teams in the Black colleges organized about this time, but spectator attention was directed mainly to the club teams. The most popular and successful of these, the New York Renaissance (Rens) Club, developed a style later adopted by the world-famous Harlem Globetrotters.

The earliest Black women basketball stars, likewise, gained recognition through club teams, particularly the YWCA's and various privately sponsored groups.

Isadore Channels of early tennis fame led one of these teams. The Chicago Romas were organized by Sol Butler, one of the early Black athletes to star at white colleges. "For a long period after the First World War," Henderson records that the Romas "sparkled on the basketball courts," and remained undefeated the entire time.[20]

Channels played with Corinne Robinson, Mignon Burns, Lillian Ross, Virginia Willis and Lula Porter, another tennis standout, in this invincible unit.

Meanwhile, Anita Gant of Washington had cultivated her athletic skills and began reaping the fruits. Women's singles champ in Capitol City tennis in 1925 and 1926, she shared the ATA mixed doubles title in 1929 and 1930. Three years later she teamed up with the legendary Ora Washington for the ATA women's doubles championship.

As agile in water as on land, Gant sprinted for acclaim in 1928 as high-point scorer and meet champion in the first inter-city swim contest held in Washington.

In the late Thirties she provided essential offensive and defensive skills for the city's Phyllis Wheatley YWCA basketball team. Captain for nine years, she led the group to victory in all but three inter-city games. Her teammates were Fanny Orfut, Louise "Tiny" Johnson, Lil Plummer and Helen Smith.

One of the losses came against the *Philadelphia Tribune* team in a championship match. Led by Ora Washington, the sports sensation from the city of Brotherly Love, it probably was the most capable outfit among the nation's all-girl hoop crews. Between 1931 and 1940, the *Tribune* women lost only six games to opposing Black teams that played boys' rules. Gladys Walker, Virginia Woods, Lavinia Moore, Myrtle Wilson, Rose Wilson, Marie Leach, and Florence Campbell composed the unit.[21]

Washington, already possessor of a dozen ATA titles, was top scorer for both the *Tribune* squad and the Germantown (Pennsylvania) Hornets. Her playing philosophy of warming up to the game as she progressed held true for both her basketball and tennis approaches. She commanded the *Tribune's* center position for eighteen years and earned lasting recognition as one of the greatest pioneering inspirations for Black women athletes.

Not until the first Black woman made the national AAU women's team in 1953 could the women's basketball galaxy spot another star. She was Missouri "Big Mo" Arledge, who thrilled audiences at the Philander-Smith (Arkansas) College hoop games. The cager averaged 21 points per outing during the regular season.

No one followed Arledge's lead by joining a nationally-rated all-star unit until the 1970's when the advent of Title IX opportunities and an increased appreciation of women's athletic abilities fueled an explosion in the development of new talent. Black women hardcourt players stepped into the limelight. In no other discipline, save track and field, has their participation been as extensive.[22]

Lusia Harris of Mintor City, Mississippi heads the lineup. Although the national media recently fussed over Ann Myers' contract offer from the Milwaukee Bucks, Harris received overtures from the New Orleans Jazz pro club two years earlier. The first Black woman ever drafted by a National Basketball Association (NBA) team, she politely refused the 1977 offer although she and scores of sport fans appreciated the gesture. She received her eightround offer even before Dave Speicher, a Toledo University star, but passed it up because "There's no way a woman can compete with a man's team," she said simply.[23]

The hoop queen's considerable prowess and success belies her statement. Perhaps the most highly-honored woman ever to play organized basketball, she scored the first basket in the women's Olympic game in 1976 and led the U.S. team to a second-place finish. Others who shared the silver medals on the integrated squad were Pat Roberts of Monroe, Georgia, Charlotte Lewis of Peoria, Illinois, and Gail Marquis of St. Albans, New York. Two years later, the Association for International Intercollegiate Athletics for Women awarded Harris its first Broderick Cup for being the Outstanding Woman Athlete of the Year.

Currently working in admissions and coaching at Delta State University, her alma mater, Harris was named the Number One Female Athlete in College Basketball for Females, the Number Two Female Athlete of the Year, and the Number Two Sportsperson of the Year when she graduated in 1977. She scored an average of 31.2 points per game, and it was said the tops of her shoes wore out from being stepped on faster than the bottoms.

Another Black woman good enough to be drafted by the pros is Pearl Moore, who grew up just outside Florence, South Carolina and played sports with her brothers when she was a child. The training sharpened her natural talent, and the 5 ft. 7 in. Moore eventually set the women's single-game scoring record with 60-points to become the nation's all-time leading college basketball scorer. Her record of 4,061 points throughout her four-year college career even surpasses that of Pete Maravich, celebrated NCAA career scoring leader, and Travis Grant, scorring wonder from Kentucky State.

Moore played all four years with Francis Marion College, (South Carolina) and she was named the national small-college Player of the Year by the South Carolina Sports Media Association. She also received the Order of the Palmetto award from the governor of South Carolina.

Like Pearl Moore, Nessie Harris ". . .could be found on the playground, practicing one-handed bank shots and doublejump fadeaways," reported one interviewer.

Pearl Moore - basketball star at Francis Marion College

Pearl Moore (left) - basketball Stand-out

Pearl Moore (left)

Pearl Moore (left) - hooks another basket

Pearl Moore - basketball star
performing in AIAW Small College Tournament

"I played against boys all the time. There were no girls. I don't know what my girl friends were doing. But they weren't playing ball," Harris confirmed.

All that childhood activity has definitely paid off handsomely, for "Nessie is the best all-around player in the state, hands down," says Harris' coach at the College of Charleston (South Carolina). "I'm not just saying that because I'm her coach. I've seen the best women players in the United States and Nessie can play with anyone. She's that good."[24]

The 5 ft. 10 in., 144 lbs. miss from Aiken, South Carolina began playing organized basketball in the seventh grade, and in Aiken High School she started three years and led her teams to near-perfect records, a State AAAA championship, and a runner-up spot. She was the high school female athlete of the year in 1975.

During her college career, she has served as team leader for two seasons and squad captain. Nessie Harris was the second leading scorer and rebounder in the state, averaging 24.3 points and 15.1 rebounds. Perhaps her most outstanding single performance occurred in 1977 when she exploded for 54 points in a single game.

The hoop queen hopes to play for the American women's team in the 1980 Olympics, or in the recently-formed Women's (Professional) Basketball League.

Lynette Woodward, born August 12, 1959 in Wichita, Kansas, also enjoyed a spectacular basketball career in high school before enrolling at the University of Kansas on an athletic scholarship. Leading the Wichita unit to the 5A State championships in 1975 and 1977, she was a member of the Kansas "Grand State Team" in 1975 and was cited for All-State honors from 1975 through 1977.

Woodward made the *Parade* All-American Team in her senior year, received a *Sports Illustrated* Merit Award, and was honored by the Kansas State Senate.

The first recipient of the Muhammad Ali Black Women's College Player of the Year Award was Vivian Green, a Norfolk State College student. Sponsored by the recently-formed National Black Association for Women's Sports (NBAWS), the citation recognizes Green's college performance and her outstanding achievements as compared to the sixteen other members of the Muhammad Ali Black Women's All-American Team.

Organizers of the NBAWS believe it will ensure Black women to receive the publicity "they deserve for their excellence in sports," since those who play for predominantly white institutions are usually the only ones to be recognized.

Coaches and Administrators

Black women coaches and administrators are a relatively new breed in the sports aviary. In basketball as elsewhere, they have mainly become visible since 1970. While affirmative action plans designed to increase minority employment statistics took root after the Sixties' rebellions, Title IX provisions encouraged women physical education instructors and athletes to pursue coaching or administrative career options.

Shirley Johnson is a former Olympian and worked as Women's Intercollegiate Director of sports at the University of California-Los Angeles. UCLA has one of the most outstanding collegiate reputations for development and promotion of top women athletes, and Johnson wanted to increase this by being "a woman who is going to try to make UCLA as formidable in women's sports as it is in men's."[25] Traditional ideas die hard, however, and as late as 1973 Johnson continued to battle against policies designed to discourage vigorous athletic recruiting among women or charging admission to women's sports events.[26] The need for competitive sports programs for athletically talented girls and women has been recognized, but the AIAW and similar organizations continue to discourage equal application of practices common to men's athletic programs such as recruitment.[27]

Marian Washington was the first director of women's athletics at the University of Kansas, and like Missouri Arledge, was a member of the AAU All-American basketball team, 1972-1974. The previous three years, 1969-1971, she played for the women's national basketball team.

Among the outstanding basketball tutors are Vivian Stringer at Cheyney State College, LaRue Fields at Morgan State, Bessie Stockard of the University of the District of Columbia, and Carol Clark, sports head at Essex Community College in New Jersey.

Fields, who earned her master's degree in physical education from Salisbury College, notes that she is only a few years older than most of her charges and a very accessible role model. Her Lady Bears have competed in the AIAW national Division II tournaments twice since she joined the college. Asked about her basic advice to the players, she said "I want them to be ladies at all times and to think. I tell them if another team plays better than you, fine, but they should never out think you."[28]

Bessie Stockard, who has had experience in dealing with responsibilities to potentially professional athletes as coach of the AIAW's third-leading scorer and rebounder, recently addressed a National Minority Women in Sports Conference. "Have pro players who've done well and who have not done well come and talk to your players," she advised.

Another successful basketball coach is Alfreda Ramsey Harris, head of the program at the Roxbury Community College in Boston. Since she took the helm at the team's 1975 inception, it has won the National Junior College Athletic Association (NJCAA) regional championships twice; 1975-76 and 1976-77. The Roxbury unit also took back to back state championships in 1976-77 and 1977-78.

The team has received citations from the Massachusetts Black Caucus, the Governor, and both houses of the State legislature. Accordingly, Harris was named Coach of the Year for her contributions in 1977-78.

Team Stars, Continued

Two Black players perform with the recently-formed six-team Women's Professional Softball League. They are Alice Henderson and Brenda Gamlin, both of the San Jose (California) Sunbirds. Evidently, popular interest in this widely-played ball game is on the rise, and more women can look forward to playing it for profit.

Records do not reflect the existence of professional women's baseball teams, but they do yield the story of Toni Stone, of Oakland, California via St. Paul, Minnesota. In 1953 when she was 22, she signed to play professional baseball with the Indianapolis Clowns team, the Negro American League champions.

Stone began playing baseball with boys when she was 15, because softball was too slow to hold her interest. After a short college career, she dropped out once convinced playing ball was the one thing she did best and most wanted to pursue. Her affiliation with an interracial Wall Post American Legion Team helped win for it the California State American Legion championship.[29]

Stone played with the San Francisco Sea Lions, an interracial semi-pro team, for three months, and commanded the infield for the New Orleans Creoles, another Negro minor league team, for two years before going to the Clowns.

Toni Stone - professional baseball player
(photo courtesy of EBONY Magazine)

Prior to working with any of these clubs, the 5 ft. 7 in., 148 lb. Stone convinced the former catcher/manager of the St. Louis Cardinals and proprietor of a baseball skills school, that he should give her a chance to study with him. Gabby Hayes thought her a big joke and told her so, but once he found he could not shoo her away, he gave her a chance to show what she could do. Much to his surprise, her fielding was up to par, she displayed a keen eye at the plate, and rapped out long flies, line drives, and "grass clutters."

The Street training, coupled with her own native ability and determination, paid off. Stone had developed a .265 batting average, and the Clowns' organization was glad to have her. Earning $12,000 yearly, she traveled with the team on a bus — she likened it to the experience of women singers with jazz bands — and was respected by her coach, teammates, and fans as a dependable second basewoman.

A reporter once asked of her ambitions after all this success:

> Maybe I'll be the first woman to play minor league baseball. At least, I may be the one who opens the doors for others. A lot of things can happen, you know. There's always got to be a first in everything. Before 1946, nobody thought Negroes would be in the big leagues. But we've got 'em in there today. A woman player might have a chance, also. Maybe it will be me.[30]

The other most unlikely team sport for women, particularly because of its unbridled aggression and hard-hitting tactics, is football. At least one Black woman, Linda Jefferson, distinguished herself on the playing field by leading the Toledo (Ohio) Troopers to the 1976 National Women's Football League Championship.

In four seasons of play in the league, Jefferson averaged fourteen yards per carry and scored 72 touchdowns.

Volleyball has enjoyed a tremendous boost in popularity among women's sports programs since the spectacular performances of the Japanese and Russian teams in the 1964 Olympics. It has a big promoter in Flo Hyman who stars on the U.S. Women's Volleyball team and the University of Houston unit. Like Anita DeFrantz, she looks forward to competing in the 1980 Olympics.

Lacrosse is a ball game originally developed by Native Americans. It has been played in eastern women's schools since the first decade of the century. Among its standouts is Tina Sloane-Green, who in 1969-70 became the first Black woman to compete on the U.S. National Lacrosse team. She continues her interest in the game by coaching the Temple University squad. Sloane-Green is also a member of the AIAW Commission on the Status of Minority Women in Sports. She is Temple's field hockey coach.

Rowing, a sport in which two, four, or eight persons dip oars to propel a boat through water, has been greatly publicized by the rise of Anita DeFrantz. Bronze Medalist of the 1976 U.S. Women's Rowing Team, she has been national champion once in the eight-member crew, twice in the pair, and three times in the four.

DeFrantz grew up in Indianapolis and earned a law degree from the University of Pennsylvania. She first pursued rowing as a 19-year-old student at Connecticut College, where she majored in political philosophy. "I did not begin to be athletic until college — largely because I grew up. . .at a time when it seemed that no one was interested in creating sports opportunities for Black girls."[31]

Rowing proved appealing because it put the 5 ft. 11 in., 155 lb. athlete in water, which she much prefers to running and other forms of land training. Through it, she learned what competition meant.

> In grade school we had been taught not to compete. Either you were smart, or you weren't. Either you could sing or you couldn't. Either you were strong or you weren't. The idea of learning a skill through training and discipline didn't reach me until my senior year at Connecticut College when I realized I wanted to try to make the Olympic team.[32]

She proceeded to structure her life around that goal, and applied to and attended the University of Pennsylvania law school. Located in Philadelphia, it is near the Vesper Boat Club, host to the best women's rowing in the country. Working nights to support herself, enduring six-day-a-week training, and cramming law school in between, she managed to reach her goal. "One spends a great deal of time practicing and often free time is spent thinking about practicing," she says.

Difficulties increased when there was no one from a similar background and commitment to which she could relate her joys or frustrations. There are very few Blacks in rowing. Howard University was the last predominantly Black school to sponsor the sport. On the international scene, Cuba, and a few South American countries field teams, "but [there are] not many competitors and never any women," continued DeFrantz.

The world-class racer was originally attracted by the unusual demands of the sport.

> It's the only team sport where everyone is equal. No one can be better than anyone else, and you all have to be committed. Also, if one definition of perfection is the ability to replicate something, that's rowing. You want the perfect stroke everytime. People joke that you can give any idiot a stick and that's rowing, but it's not. It takes psychological, emotional and physical strength. You know what the pain is going to be and when it's going to start.[33]

DeFrantz sits on the U.S. Olympic Committee board, the Athletes'

Advisory Council, the President's Council on Physical Fitness, and the organizing committee for the 1984 Los Angeles Olympics. No one is a greater advocate of sports.

> You learn a great deal about other people through sports. You learn of their weaknesses as well as their strengths. But most importantly, you learn about yourself. . .We live in a society which offers little opportunity to make personal discoveries. [So] take advantage of sports. You'll learn a lot!

NOTES

[1] Signe Hammer, "My Daugher the Football Star," *Parade, Boston Sunday Globe*, 5 August 1979, p. 7.

[2] Margaret Ruth Downing, "Women's Basketball: An Historical Review of Selected Athletic Organizations Which Influenced Its Ascension Toward Advanced Competition in the U.S.," Diss. Texas Women's University 1973, p. 40.

[3] Newspaper Enterprise Association, ed., *The Good Housekeeping Woman's Almanac* (New York: Newspaper Enterprise Association, 1976), p. 412.

[4] Ellen W. Gerber, Jan Felshin, Pearl Berlin, Wareen Wyrick, *The American Woman in Sports* (Reading, Massachusetts: Addison-Wesley, 1974), pp. 71-72.

[5] Hammer, p. 7.

[6] Bill Gilbert and Nancy Williamson, "Sport is Unfair to Women," *Reader's Digest*, January 1974, p. 127.

[7] Gilbert and Williamson, p. 123.

[8] Resource Center on Sex Roles in Education, "Title IX of The Education Amendments of 1972: A Manual on Physical Education and Sports Programs" (Washington, D.C.: U.S. Office of Education and HEW, 1976), p. 1.

[9] Project on the Status and Education of Women, "Update on Title IX and Sports #2: HEW Proposed Policy Interpretation Concerning Title IX and Athletics" (Washington, D.C.: Association of American Colleges), January 1979, p. 1.

[10] Federal Register, "Title IX of the Education Amendments of 1972; A Proposed Policy Interpretation" (Washington, D.C.: GPO, 11 December 1978), p. 58070.

[11] Project on the Status and Education of Women, *What Constitutes Equality for Women in Sport? — Federal Law Puts Women in the Running* (Washington, D.C.: Association of American Colleges, 1974), n.p.

[12] Gerber, et al., pp. 66-67.

[13] *AIAW Handbook, 1979-80* (Washington, D.C.: Association of Intercollegiate Athletics for Women, 1979), n.p.

[14] "Suggestions for Title IX Changes Heard by Civil Rights Commission," *Women Today*, 6 August 1979, p. 96.

[15] "Women Can't Muscle the Men in Contact Sports," *Jet*, 9 February 1978, pp. 48-49.

[16] Project on the Status and Education of Women, "Where are the Althea Gibsons and Wilma Rudolphs of Today?" (Washington, D.C.: Association of American Colleges, Winter 1979), p. 11.

[17] Project on the Status and Education of Women, Winter 1979, pp. 11-12.

[18] Project on the Status and Education of Women, Winter 1979, pp. 11.

[19] Edwin B. Henderson, *The Negro in Sports*, rev. ed. (Washington, D.C.: Associated Publishers, Inc., 1949), p. 148.

[20] Henderson, p. 236.

[21] Henderson, p. 235.

[22] "Minority Women Target Athletics," *New Directions for Women*, Westwood, New Jersey, January 1979, p. 7.

[23] "Women Can't Muscle the Men in Contact Sports," p. 49.

[24] Tony Ferullo, "Cougarette Nessie Harris: State's Best All Around?" *Charleston News and Courier*, 21 January 1979.

[25] Gerber, et al., p. 267.

[26] Gerber. et al., p. 267.

[27] "Women in Sport: Progress Report," *Sports Illustrated*, 29 July 1974, p. 28.

[28] Peter Harris, "Support 'Pitiful' for Morgan's Women Athletes," *Baltimore Afro-American*, 22 March 1980, p. 7.

[29] "Lady Ball Player: Toni Stone First of Sex to Play With Pro Team," *Ebony*, July 1953.

[30] "Lady Ball Player."

[31] Letter received from Anita DeFrantz, 26 February 1980.

[32] Anita DeFrantz.

[33] Jane Gross, "An Olympic Rower Wants Her Chance to be No. 1," *New York Times*, January 1980, p. 8, col. 2.

CHAPTER V

SOLO PERFORMERS

Outstanding individual performances constitute any winning sports efforts. In the late nineteenth century, when it was finally admitted that women could profit from increased physical activity, individual pursuits generally gained acceptance; in contrast to team sports. Ice-skating, golf, and bowling were among the "gentler" pastimes encouraged for women at that time, and Black women have since participated in all three. Only Mabel Fairbanks is noted for having achieved distinction on the ice, however.

Foremost Pioneer: Inez Patterson

If there was ever a premier athlete whose expertise in several activities outshone many challengers, it was Inez Patterson. Born in Chester, Pennsylvania about 1911, Edwin Bancroft Henderson wrote:

> This athletic heroine typifies the ability and pluck of champion athletes. Not only has she won honores in competition with her mates, but she has successfully battered down the gates of prejudice and intolerance by her intrepid insistence on the right to meet all comers, by her ladylike sportsmanship, and undeniable athletic prowess."[1]

Not since Patterson has the race boasted so superior a woman swimmer. In 1927, she set a distance swimming record — 100 lengths of Philadelphia's 90-foot McCoach Playground pool — which remained intact as late as 1949. This feat, performed in competition, added to her wins in diving and two other swimming events, the side stroke and double-overarm (butterfly).

Patterson began setting records in junior high, where she captained the champion Philadelphia ball team; won a thirteen-mile swim contest; and took individual track honors (1925).

While at West Philadelphia High School, 1925-1928, she set a new record for the round-arm basketball throw, of 93 feet. She even was the class manager and only Black member of the girls' hockey team. Before graduation, she captained the Black champion girls' basketball team at the McCoach Playground. In July, 1928 she entered a girls' track team in a *Philadelphia Inquirer* meet, where she triumphed in the shot-put.[2]

This maverick gameswoman extended her winning streak to Temple University in 1929, where she made six all-collegiate teams: hockey, tennis, basketball, track, volleyball, and dancing. She played for the hockey team all four undergraduate years.

Apart from this outstanding champion's victories in the arena of competition, Patterson must be remembered as a Black woman who broke at least three barriers that excluded would-be Black participants: the Pennsylvania "May Day" Festival, the American Red Cross swimming proficiency examiners' course, and the Women's Athletic Association swimming meet. She was the only Black among 500 young women in a "Play Day" event at the University of Pennsylvania, and she was not content to let color alone distinguish her. She swam on the winning relay team and took honors in diving, as well.

Patterson participated in more competitions after finishing college, but later her primary contributions to women's athletics involved coaching girls in the Northern New Jersey and New York YWCAs and in organizing athletic clubs during the Thirties. In 1938 she served as national program director for the ATA. In competition, and career wise, she was truly an all-around games-woman.

The Golf Game

Black women have swung out on the fairways since the Depression-tinged Thirties, closely following the men's lead of the late Twenties when the United Golfers' Association (UGA) was organized.[3] Despite their forty-year record as tournament-level competitors, however, none have proved serious contenders in top-level national competition. Until the Fifties, segregation policies discouraged it. Since then, only Renee Powell of Canton, Ohio and former tennis champion Althea Gibson have received much notice.

The United Golfers' Association was formed much like the American Tennis Association: to provide a growing number of Black golf clubs with the tournament supervision and affiliation their growing numbers and sophistication demanded. Women auxiliaries soon staged their own contests.

The first champion among them, Marie Thompson of Chicago, took the title in 1930 and 1931 outings and the runner-up position of 1932. Lucy Williams of Indianapolis, perhaps the most outstanding player of the decade, definitely was the most persistent. She won the nationals in 1932, 1936 and 1937, and claimed runner-up laurels in 1930, 1931, 1933 and 1934.

Julia Siler of St. Louis was the 1933 champion and Ella C. Able, another Indianapolis contributor, took top honors in 1934 and 1935.

The Wake Robin Club, a women's organization, has existed since the Thirties in Washington, D.C. When Henderson first reported it, about twenty members played regularly.[4]

Melnee Moyee of Atlanta, Geneva Wilson, Cleo Ball, Aileere Davis of

Chicago, and Vivian Pitts, all won or took second in national contests between 1938 and 1942. Lucy Williams (Mitchem) reasserted her considerable powers this decade, winning the tournament in 1946. Other top-ranked women of the Forties were Geneva Wilson, Hazel Foreman, Thelma Cowans and Lorraine Sawyer.[5]

In the Fifties, "Golf. . .as Negroes expressed a desire to enjoy facilities on an equal basis with Caucasians, became a political football, and a staggering amount of time, talent, and money was expended in hearings, conferences, caucuses, and behind-the-scenes activities designed either to keep Negroes out or get them in."[6] Ann Gregory joined the forward thrust and in an historic 1956 appearance, became the first Black to play in an integrated women's amateur championship.[7] Meanwhile, dozens of anti-discrimination suits had been filed against segregated golf clubs and "public" courses in a concerted effort to bust open this lingering preserve of white sports exclusivity.

Rose Harper Elder - golfer

In more recent years, Ethel Funches, Sarah Smith, and Ethel Webb Terrell gained prominence in East Coast circles. Two wives of golf pros are also carving out reputations of their own. Rose Harper, married to Ryder Cup winner Lee Elder, and Alma Arvin, spouse of Walter "Chink" Stewart, the resident pro at the Carroll Park course in Baltimore, have turned in notable performances in the Seventies.

Renee Powell joined Althea Gibson on the Ladies' Professional Golf Association tour in 1967, but later began teaching at a men's golf club near London. Gibson preceded Powell in 1963, two years after she began her serious pursuit of the sport. By 1965, the *Indianapolis Recorder* carried the story, "Althea Gibson Hits Golf's Racial Bias," and voiced her disappointment with the situation. "I have been on the golf tour for two years and I still don't have a sponsor," she said. "Also, there are even tournaments in the South that I can't play in."[8] Some progress had been made in integrating this exclusive sports cousin of tennis, but not nearly enough it seems.

Renee Powell - professional Golfer

Black Women in Bowling

This tenpin game is one of the most popular American sports. It boasted some 26 million regular participants by the early Sixties.[9] The game grew rapidly in popularity among Blacks in the Thirties, although available lanes were hard to find outside the YMCAs or YWCAs. The National Negro Bowling Association (the "Negro" has since been dropped) was founded in 1939, partially in response to the American Bowling Congress' "Whites only" policy. Twenty years later, the Negro Bowling Association offered a $500,000 tournament purse. Meanwhile, the American Bowling Congress erased its segregated by-laws in 1951. As one response, the Negro Bowling Association today includes whites.

With integration came wider competitive — and promotional opportunities for Blacks. Two of their number have taken good advantage of them.

Sadie Dixon of Philadelphia, the Pennsylvania Individual Match Game Champion, and state and city World International Bowling Congress (WIBC) all-event titlist, was one of the first Black women to achieve distinction in this sport. One-time member of the Brunswick Advisory Staff of Champions, Dixon was one of more than a hundred stars who promoted the game in the nationwide instructional and exhibitional appearances. Rosemary Morrow of Chicago worked in a similar spot during the mid-Fifties with the AMF Company's bowling division.[10]

In another arena, Ann McNeill of Baltimore won the 1977 European Armed Forces Championship in Weisbaden, Germany.

Although nationally-ranked Black women bowlers are rare, nearly every city of consequence can claim one or two local champions.

New Age Competitors

Fencing, a sport in which competitors score points by "touching" designated areas of their opponents' bodies with the tips or sides of foils, epees, or sabres — instruments that slightly resemble swords, has been likened to chess for its great variety of moves which are similarly exacting and intricate.

Introduced in American women's college-level athletic programs as early as 1881, it has only spawned world-class Black women competitors in the past decade. It is, moreover, one of the few sports aside from basketball, track and field, and tennis in which Black women have attained that level of accomplishment.

The two outstanding competitors are Ruth White of Baltimore, and Nikki Tomlinson-Franke a Harlem native who is founder and coach of the women's fencing team at Temple University.

AT 18, White became the first Black and the youngest woman ever to win a national fencing championship. In 1969, she held four national titles: U.S. Ladies' Foil Champion; North Atlantic Sectional Ladies' Foil Champion; U.S. National Ladies' Under-19 Foil Champion; and North Atlantic Sectional Ladies' Under-19 Foil Champion. Her youthful excellence astounced most observers, since many women fencing champions are between 35 and 45 years old.

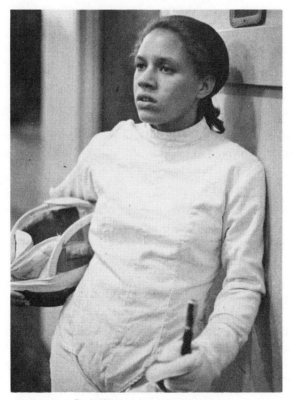

Ruth White - fencing champion
(photo courtesy of EBONY Magazine)

White first studied the sport at the YWCA and soon moved up to one of the city's club teams. Her first coach once remarked, "No coach can teach calculation of competition, distance, and timing. A fencer must feel it. For most people that takes many years. And yet Ruth White pulled off a miracle. It takes ten to fifteen years experience to do what she did in four years. I teach in Europe and the United States and I never saw such excellent woman talent."[11]

A graduate of New York University, and two-time national foil champion before being named to the U.S. team, she competed in the 1972 Munich Olympics, but lost in individual and team contests to French opponents.

Nikki Tomlinson-Franke is the third-ranked woman fencer in the country. In 1975 she won the national women's championship and a silver medal in the Pan American Games. She competed in the 1976 Montreal contests, but American fencers failed to place in either individual or team events.

Franke first learned of the sport while in high school during the late Sixties. "It was purely by chance . . . I just happened to go to a school that had a decent program. It was just a matter of being in the right place at the right time."[12]

Later, at Brooklyn College — where she now is enshrined in the college Hall of Fame — she trained under former Olympic star Denise O'Conneor and competed all four years with the varsity team.

As coach, Franke has successfully imparted the same "precision of movement, split-second timing, and deception and counter-deception" she successfully employs in her own award-winning competition. The Temple University team recently wound up their season record with 17 wins, 2 losses and a sixth-place finish among 26 teams that competed in the National tourney.

Currently working toward a doctorate in health education, Franke teaches, coaches her squad, and trains for future meets of her own. Somehow, she also makes time to prepare for her annual five-day "Black Women in Sport" workshop. The conference addresses the "unique experiences and problems of Black women involved in sports," and is directed at Black and White teachers, coaches, and administrators.

Drawing from her own experience and statistics that indicate the low participation rate of Black girls and women in all but the traditionally sought-after sports, Franke would like to see an "organized grassroots program." It would offer youngsters all the sports but allow them the freedom to participate in whatever interests them most. Once spotted, talents could be developed within these organizations. "Right now it's kind of a hit-or-miss system we have," she said.[13]

Racing: On Wheels and on the Hoof

Cheryl Glass of Seattle entered a male perserve when only 13, and has since been named Rookie of the Year in the sport. Racing quarter midget and half-midget cars, which have top speeds of 60 miles per hour, has been her specialty. As one result, for five consecutive years she placed nationally in the top ten drivers in her class.

Born in 1961, now living in Seattle, Glass is the eldest of two girls in her family and she is a college student. She recently began driving sprint cars, which are capable of 150-miles-per hour speeds.

Glass intends to be the first Black driver in the Indianapolis 500 derby. But why auto racing in the first place?

"It's mainly the competition. I've been told I can't run sprint cars competitively, and that makes me want to do it. I think I can beat [men] at their own game."[14]

Glass is already the subject of a biography: *Off to the Races*, a Prentice-Hall book.

Another young racer is Cheryl White of Rome, Ohio. Perhaps the only Black woman riding thoroughbreds, she has ridden at Thistledown, Cranwood, and Randall Park — all on the half-mile circuit.[15]

Phoebe Thomas and Rosa and Therese Gladding tried to break into the California and Arizona horse racing circuit, but gave up when mounts were denied them and the consequent inaction made keeping their weight down useless.

Women in the Ring

Last but not least of the new age sportswomen are Jackie Tonawanda and Marion "Tyger" Trimar, two of that rare breed — women boxes.

Tonawanda is called "The Female Muhammad Ali" in some circles, and as recently as the fall of 1979 announced that she expected to meet the former World Boxing Association's light-heavyweight champion, Mike Rossman. Finding competitors is always a problem, probably because most men still do not take the notion of women boxers seriously.

Trimar, born in 1953, and who weighs about 130-lbs., claims to have been interested in boxing since her childhood days when "I used to watch it on TV all the time and I remember telling myself, 'That's what I want to do'."[16]

Women in boxing confront head-on the age-old taboos against women in sports. All-out aggressiveness and strength are "musts" in the ring. Trimar, as her ring name suggests, is hardly a shrinking violet. "Women are supposed to be passive, but I'm not a passive person. I can't sit around and twiddle my thumbs," is how she accounts for her boxing drive according to a *Woman's Almanac* entry.

As for the ability of women to withstand the physical rigors of the ring, she points out that women boxers are covered by special rules, which call for bust protectors and banning of blows below the belt. As for giving and taking the punches she says, "Women have been brainwashed into thinking they aren't strong enough. With proper exercise, a woman won't get hurt."

Donna Lynn Mosley · gymnast

While Jackie Tonawanda and other Black women explore newer areas of sports and build their reputations, younger competitors train heartily for their moments of glory. Among them is Donna Lynn Mosley of Willingboro, New Jersey, the first Black to compete in the U.S. Gymnastics Federation Junior Olympic Nationals in 1977, when she was only thirteen. Specializing in vaulting and exelling in the floor exercises, she placed first "all-around" at a recent AAU Junior Olympics meet. In the Eighties, she may well lead the vanguard of future top-class athletes and become the first of the race to compete internationally in this demanding sport.

NOTES

[1] Edwin B. Henderson, *The Negro in Sports*, rev. ed. (Washington, D.C.: Associated Publishers, Inc., 1949), p. 237.

[2] Henderson, p. 239.

[3] Henderson, p. 227.

[4] Henderson, p. 227.

[5] Henderson, p. 431.

[6] A.S. "Doc" Young, *Negro Firsts in Sports* (Chicago: Johnson Publishing Co., 1963), p. 172.

[7] Young, p. 198.

[8] "Althea Gibson Hits Golf's Racial Bias," *The Indianapolis Recorder*, 10 July 1965, p. 8, col. 8.

[9] Young, p. 178.

[10] Young, p. 180.

[11] "Touche: Baltimore Girl is First Black and Youngest Woman to Ever Win a National Fencing Championship," *Ebony*, 21 January 1970, p. 53.

[12] "Nikke Franke on Fencing," *Encore*, 21 May 1979, p. 46.

[13] William S. Lewis, "The Colgate Women's Games V: And They're Off," *Encore*, 19 March 1979, p. 47.

[14] "Racing Against Odds," *Ebony*, January 1980, p. 114.

[15] Telephone interview with Dr. Leroy Walker, Olympics Track and Field Coach and Professor of Physical Education, North Carolina Central University, 3 March 1980.

[16] Newspaper Enterprise Association, ed., *The Good Housekeeping Woman's Almanac* (New York: Newspaper Enterprise Association, 1976), p. 442.

SELECTED BIBLIOGRAPHY

AIAW Handbook, 1979-80. Washington, D.C.: Association of Intercollegiate Athletics for Women, 1979.

"Althea Gibson Hits Golf's Racial Bias." *The Indianapolis Recorder,* 10 July 1965, p. 8.

Barnes, Aloma "AJ". "Renee Becomes Tennis Princess." *Black Tennis,* May-June 1979.

Barnes, M.J. *Women's Basketball.* Boston: Allyn and Bacon, Inc., 1972.

"Bazaar's Top 10 Women Athletes." *Harper's Bazaar,* May 1977, pp. 86-87.

Betts, John R. *America's Sporting Heritage: 1850-1950.* Massachusetts: Addison-Wesley Publishing Co., 1974.

"The Black Amateur and Professional Athlete." In *Reference Library of Black America, Book III.* New York: Bellwether, 1971.

"The Black Athlete, Emergence and Arrival." *International Library of Negro Life and History.* Ed. Edwin B. Henderson and the Editors of *Sport* Magazine. Miami: International Book Corporation, 1970.

"Black Women in Gola." *Sepia,* January 1970, pp. 46-49.

Bontemps, Arna. *Famous Negro Athletes.* New York: Dodd, Mead and Co., 1964.

Chalk, Ocania. *Black College Sport.* New York: Dodd, Mead and Co., 1976.

_____. *Pioneers of Black Sport.* New York: Dodd, Mead and Co., 1975.

Coffey, Margaret A. "The Modern Sportswoman." In *Sport and Society; An Anthology.* Ed. John T. Talamini and Charles H. Page. Boston: Little, Brown and Co., 1973.

Downing, Margaret Ruth. "Women's Basketball: An Historical Review of Selected Athletic Organizations Which Influenced Its Ascension Toward Advanced Competition in the U.S." Diss. Texas Women's University 1973.

Durant, John. *Highlights of the Olympics: From Ancient Times to the Present.* 4th ed. New York: Hastings House Publishers, 1973.

Edwards, Harry. *The Revolt of the Black Athlete.* New York: The Free Press, 1969.

Federal Register. "Title IX of the Education Amendments of 1972; A Proposed Policy Interpretation Concerning Title IX and Athletics." Washington, D.C.: GPO, 11 December 1978, p. 58070.

Ferullo, Tony. "Cougarette Nessie Harris: State's Best All-Around?" *Charleston News and Courier,* 21 January 1979.

Freeman, Marcus A., Jr. "Tips of the Iceberg." *Black Tennis,* September-October 1979.

Gale, Eric. "Former Olympian Benefits Tech Trac." *Lubbock Avalanche-Journal,* October 1979, p. 78.

Gerber, Ellen W., et al. *The American Woman in Sport.* Reading, Mass.: Addison-Wesley Publishing Co., 1974.

Gibson, Althea. *I Always Wanted to be Somebody.* New York: Harper, 1958.

Gilbert, Bill and Nancy Williamson. "Sport is Unfair to Women." *Sports Illustrated,* 28 May 1973, pp. 88, 92, 94, 98. Also in *Reader's Digest,* January 1974.

Greendorfer, Susan Louise. *The Nature of Female Socialization Into Sport.* Oregon: Microform Publications, 1976.

Gross, Jane. "An Olympic Rower Wants Her Chance to be No. 1." *New York Times*, January 1980, p. 8.

Gutman, Herbert G. *The Black Family Slavery and Freedom, 1750-1925.* New York: Pantheon, 1976.

Hammer, Signe. "My Daughter the Football Star." *Parade*, 5 August 1979, p. 7.

Harris, Peter. "Support 'Pitiful' for Morgan's Women Athletes." *Afro-American*, 22 March 1980, p. 7.

Henderson, Edwin B. "The Black American in Sports." In *The Black American Reference Book*. Ed. Mabel M. Symthe. Englewood Cliffs, N.J.: Prentice-Hall, Inc., 1976.

——————. *The Negro in Sports*. rev. ed. Washington, D.C.: Associated Publishers, 1949.

Henri, Florette. *Black Migration: Movement North, 1900-1920.* New York: Anchor-Doubleday, 1976.

Hodgdon, Paula Drake. *An Investigation of the Development of Interscholastic and Intercollegiate Athletes for Girls and Women From 1917-1970.* Oregon: Microform Publications, 1974.

Holmes, Dwight O.W. *The Evolution of the Negro College.* 1934; rpt. New York: AMA Press, 1970.

"The Horizon." *The Crisis*, October 1917, p. 315.

Jackson, Madeline Manning. *Running for Jesus.* Waco, Texas: Word Books, 1977.

Jackson, Nell C. *Track and Field for Girls and Women.* Minneapolis, Minn.: Burgess Publishing Co., 1968.

Jacobs, Karen Folger. "Earlene Brown: Down From Olympia." *Essence*, May 1979, p. 12.

Jones, Wally. *Black Champions Challenge American Sports.* New York: D. McKay Co., 1972.

Kahn, Roger. "Sports." *Esquire*, July 1974, p. 14.

Kaplan, Janice. *Women and Sports.* New York: Viking Press, 1979.

Killanin, Lord and John Rodda, eds. *The Olympic Games: 80 Years of People, Events and Records.* New York: Macmillan, 1976.

Klafs, Carl E. and M. Joan Lyon. *The Female Athlete; Conditioning, Compettion, and Culture.* St. Louis: Mosby, 1973.

Koehler, Gretchen M. *Agents Who Have Influenced Women to Participate in Inter-Collegiate Sport.* Oregon: Microform Publications, 1975.

"Lady Ball Player: Toni Stone First of Sex to Play With Pro Team." *Ebony*, July 1953.

Lauwick, H. *Heroines of the Sky: Women in Aviation.* Blaine, Washington: Beachcomber Books, 1973.

Lerner, Gerda. *Black Women in White America: A Documentary History.* New York: Pantheon, 1972.

Lewis, William S. "The Colgate Women's Games V: And They're Off." *Encore*, 19 March 1979.

"Mets of Cleveland Sign Black Women to Team." *Jet*, 1 May 1975, p. 50.

Miller, Kenneth Dayton. *Track and Field for Girls.* New York: Ronald Press Co., 1964.

"Minority Women Target Athletics." *New Directions for Women*. Westwood, N.J., January 1979, p. 7.

Neal, Patsy and Thomas A. Tutko. *Coaching Girls and Women: Psychological Perspectives*. Boston: Allyn and Bacon, 1975.

Newspaper Enterprise Association, eds. *The Good Housekeeping Woman's Almanac*. New York: Newspaper Enterprise Association, 1976.

"Nikke Franke on Fencing." *Encore*, 21 May 1979, p. 46.

Orr, Jack. *The Black Athlete: His Story in American History*. New York: Lion Books, 1969.

Penn, Irvine Garland. *The Afro-American Press and Its Editors*. 1891; rpt. New York: Arno Press, 1969.

Project on the Status and Education of Women. "Update on Title IX and Sports #2: HEW Proposed Policy Interpretation Concerning Title IX and Athletics." Washington, D.C.: Association of American Colleges, January 1979, p. 1.

Project on the Status and Education of Women. *What Constitutes Equality for Women in the Running*. Washington, D.C.: Association of American Colleges, 1974.

Project on the Status and Education of Women. "Where are the Althea Gibsons and Wilma Rudolphs of Today?" Washington, D.C.: Association of American Colleges, Winter 1979, p. 11.

"Racing Against Odds." *Ebony*, January 1980.

"Revolution in Women's Sports." *Women's Sports*, September 1974, pp. 33-56.

Robinson, L.D. "From Tomboys to Girl Athletes." *Essence*, September 1974, p. 16.

Rohrbaugh, Joanna Bunker. "Femininity on the Line." *Psychology Today*, August 1979, p. 42.

Rudolph, Wilma. *Wilma*. New York: National American Libraries, 1977.

Stambler, I. *Women in Sports*. Garden City, N.Y.: Doubleday and Co., Inc., 1975.

Straub, D. "Women in Athletics." *Long Beach Bar Bulletin*, November 1975, pp. 24-27.

"Suggestions for Title IX Changes Heard by Civil Rights Commission." *Women Today*, 6 August 1979, p. 96.

Thaxton, Nolan A. "A Documentary Analysis of Competitive Track and Field for Women at Tuskegee Institute and Tennessee State University." Diss. Springfield, Mass.: Springfield College 1970.

"Touche: Baltimore Girl is First Black and Youngest Woman to Ever Win a National Fencing Championship." *Ebony*, January 1970.

Twin, Stephanie. *Out of the Bleachers: Writings on Women and Sports*. Old Old Westbury, N.Y.: The Feminist Press, 1979.

Watson, Melvyn, comp. *The Encyclopedia of Athletics*. New York: St. Martin's Press, 1977.

"Weaker Sex? — My Foot." *Ebony*, November 1973, pp. 182-184.

"Welcome Back to Miss Louise Stokes." *Malden Evening News*, Malden, Mass., 10 September 1936, p. 1.

Wien, S. "The Case for Equality in Athletics." *Cleveland State Law Review*, 1973,   pp. 570-584.

Williamson, N. "The Mighty Macs." *Ms.*, April 1974, pp. 70-74.

"Wilma Rudolph Changes Gold Medals to Dollars." *Jet*, 12 January 1978, p. 52.

"Women Can't Muscle the Men in Contact Sports." *Jet*, 9 February 1978, pp. 48-49.

"Women in Sport: Progress Report." *Sports Illustrated*, 29 July 1974, p. 28.

Young, Andrew S. "Doc." *Negro Firsts in Sports*. Chicago: Johnson Publishing Co., 1963.